The PC User's Guide

Nick Anis
Craig Menefee

Osborne McGraw-Hill

Berkeley   New York   St. Louis   San Francisco
Auckland   Bogotá   Hamburg   London   Madrid
Mexico City   Milan   Montreal   New Delhi   Panama City
Paris   São Paulo   Singapore   Sydney
Tokyo   Toronto

Osborne **McGraw-Hill**
2600 Tenth Street
Berkeley, California 94710
U.S.A.

Osborne **McGraw-Hill** offers software for sale. For information on software, translations, or book distributors outside of the U.S.A., please write to Osborne **McGraw-Hill** at the above address.

The PC User's Guide

1234567890 DOC 9987654321

ISBN 0-07-881670-X

To our unofficial coauthor, Sami Menefee, who dived into this project with her customary, remarkable enthusiasm, neither asking for nor expecting any recognition.

And to our fathers, Nick Anis, Sr. and Selden Cowles Menefee, who never told us we couldn't.

CONTENTS

FOREWORD   xi
ACKNOWLEDGMENTS   xiii
INTRODUCTION   xvii

ONE   **PERSONAL COMPUTERS—**
A BASIC GUIDE **1**
WHAT IS A COMPUTER?   2
BECOMING AN EXPERT   5
TYPES OF SYSTEMS   7
THE BASIC PC   8
DATA COMMUNICATIONS   18
A WORD ABOUT SOFTWARE   18
SUMMARY   20

TWO   **SYSTEMS OVERVIEW:**
CHOOSING A COMPUTER **21**
TYPES OF IBM-COMPATIBLE COMPUTERS . .   21
COST EFFECTIVENESS   29
THE PRODUCT LIFE CYCLE   33
REACHING A DECISION   36
TRENDS   56

THREE   **UNPACKING AND SETTING UP** **57**
PRELIMINARIES   57
UNPACKING THE EQUIPMENT   68
MAKING THE SYSTEM READY   71
FINAL SETUP   74

FOUR   **SETTING IT UP AND TURNING IT ON** . .   **75**
ASSEMBLE TO TEST   75
KNOW YOUR SYSTEM   84
SMOKE TEST—THE TRIAL RUN   89
SMOKE TEST COMPLETE   100
INSTALLATION IN PLACE   103

FIVE   **OPERATING FUNDAMENTALS** 105

KNOW YOUR HARDWARE 107

STARTING YOUR COMPUTER 114

WORKING AT THE DOS PROMPT 121

INTERNAL AND EXTERNAL COMMANDS ... 123

CORRECTING COMMAND LINE MISTAKES .. 137

AUTOMATIC BOOTUP WITH

    AUTOEXEC.BAT 139

INSTALLING AND RUNNING PROGRAMS ... 142

GOOD PRACTICES: AVOIDING PROBLEMS

    THE EASY WAY 147

SUMMARY 151

SIX   **OPERATING SYSTEMS AND**

    ENVIRONMENTS 153

WHAT IS AN OPERATING SYSTEM? 154

INTERFACES AND ENVIRONMENTS 162

SUMMARY 170

SEVEN   **APPLICATIONS PROGRAMS:**

    GETTING YOUR WORK DONE 171

CHOOSING APPLICATIONS SOFTWARE 172

APPLICATIONS PROGRAM BASICS 175

A WEALTH OF APPLICATIONS 180

THE TRADITIONAL BIG FOUR

    APPLICATIONS 180

OTHER MAJOR APPLICATIONS 213

SUMMARY 232

EIGHT   **UTILITIES — COMPUTER**

    HOUSEKEEPERS 235

UTILITY PROGRAMS: WHAT ARE THEY?

    WHAT DO THEY DO? 236

DOS SHELLS 237

MENU PROGRAMS 244

COMMAND LINE EDITORS AND

    ENHANCERS 245

DESKTOP ACCESSORIES 246

HELP PROGRAMS 247

MEMORY MANAGERS 247

DISK CACHES 248

FILE RECOVERY AND DISK MEDIC

    UTILITIES 249

DISK AND DIRECTORY MAINTENANCE

    UTILITIES 250

COMPRESSION AND ARCHIVING
    UTILITIES 259
PRINTER UTILITIES 261
DATA SECURITY 262
SUMMARY 264

NINE   **WORKING WITH DOS – THE BASICS** . . . **265**
DOS BASICS 266
DOS FILES 272
SUMMARY 283

TEN   **DOS AND THE HARD DISK** **285**
ORGANIZATION: THE KEY TO THE SYSTEM . 286
DESIGNING YOUR OWN DIRECTORY TREE . 291
CREATING AND USING YOUR TREE 297
WORKING WITH DIRECTORY LISTINGS 308
SUMMARY 309

ELEVEN   **ADVANCED DOS TECHNIQUES AND**
    BATCH FILES **311**
FINE TUNING DOS TO SUIT YOUR TASTE . . . 312
PERSONALIZING YOUR COMPUTER 312
CONFIG.SYS: CONFIGURING THE SYSTEM . . 312
AUTOEXEC.BAT: SETTING UP THE
    SESSION 326
BACKING UP YOUR FILES 328
RUNNING BETTER, FASTER, MORE
    SMOOTHLY 332
USING BATCH FILES TO AUTOMATE
    COMPLEX OPERATIONS 343
OTHER ADVANCED DOS COMMANDS 367
SUMMARY 373

TWELVE   **DOS COMMAND REFERENCE** **375**
COMMONLY USED TERMS 375
DOS COMMAND LINE COMMANDS 376
BATCH FILE COMMANDS 434
CONFIG.SYS COMMANDS 435

THIRTEEN   **INTRODUCTION TO BASIC** **437**
COMPILERS, INTERPRETERS, AND BASIC . . 437
BASIC AS A COMPUTER LANGUAGE 439
EXPRESSIONS AND OPERATORS 443
LOADING BASIC 444
LOADING QUICKBASIC 446
BASIC LINES AND PROGRAMS 446
QUICKBASIC LINE FORMAT 447

THE BASIC SCREEN EDITOR 448
THE QUICKBASIC ENVIRONMENT 450

FOURTEEN   **BASIC REFERENCE** 453
BASIC COMMAND SUMMARY 453

FIFTEEN   **INSIDE YOUR COMPUTER** 485
THE SYSTEM'S ARCHITECTURE:
   THE DESIGNERS' INTENT 486
GETTING COMFORTABLE WITH YOUR
   HARDWARE 489
THE PC'S INTERNAL COMPONENTS 490
SUMMARY 508

SIXTEEN   **UNDERSTANDING YOUR HARD DISK** .. 509
HOW A HARD DISK WORKS 510
WHAT TO LOOK FOR WHEN BUYING 518
INSTALLING THE DISK 520
FORMATTING THE DISK 527
MAINTENANCE 534
SUMMARY 535

SEVENTEEN   **GETTING THE MOST FROM YOUR**
   SYSTEM 537
USING RAM EFFECTIVELY 538
IMPROVING YOUR COMMAND LINE
   TOOLBOX 552
ENHANCING HARD DISK OPERATION 558
ELIMINATING TIME STEALERS 563
CPU, SYSTEM UNIT, AND OTHER HARDWARE
   ENHANCEMENTS 565
SUMMARY 572

EIGHTEEN   **TROUBLESHOOTING, SERVICE, AND**
   REPAIR 573
AVOIDING PROBLEMS 574
OBTAINING COMPETENT SERVICE 581
TROUBLESHOOTING WITHOUT METERS ... 582
SOLVING SOFTWARE PROBLEMS 591
SOLVING HARDWARE PROBLEMS 595
SUMMARY 612

APPENDIX A   **GLOSSARY** 613

APPENDIX B   **USING THE KEYBOARD** 631
THE TYPEWRITER KEYS 633
SPECIAL KEYS 635

REPEATING KEYS VERSUS
HOLD-AND-COMBINE KEYS 637
LOCKING (OR TOGGLE) KEYS 638
FUNCTION KEYS 639
NUMERIC KEYPAD AND CURSOR-CONTROL
KEYS 639
BOXES AND OTHER SPECIAL ALT-KEY
CHARACTERS 640

APPENDIX C   **HARD DRIVES: GEOMETRIES FOR
CMOS SETTINGS** 641

APPENDIX D   **DOS ERROR MESSAGES** 655

APPENDIX E   **ASCII CODES** 691

APPENDIX F   **HOW AND WHERE TO BUY A
COMPUTER** 701
DO SOME RESEARCH 701
CHECK AT LOCAL STORES 702
THE TRADE-OFFS OF DISCOUNT PRICES . . . 704
THE USED COMPUTER MARKET 706
PICKING A COMPUTER STORE 707
LEARNING TO USE YOUR COMPUTER 709
SUMMARY 711

INDEX 713

When IBM jumped into the personal computer market in 1981, it was like the arrival of Shamu the whale in the backyard inflatable swimming pool. And although the machine may have lacked technical sophistication and design elegance, its professional package, the documentation, and the letters *IBM* on the front legitimized PC use for thousands of businesses and individuals.

Since then, hundreds of manufacturers have introduced IBM PC-compatible machines, often called clones. They run faster, often work better, and typically cost about 50 percent less than IBM's offerings. It doesn't take an industry pundit to figure out the reason why there are dozens of clones in operation for every IBM PC: the answer is affordable pricing.

With the lower prices offered by the compatibles market, however, the level of "extras" normally expected with an appliance of this complexity has declined. Chief among the missing is a good operator's manual. Thousands of fairly advanced PC-compatibles are shipped each year, with less documentation than a typical blender or toaster oven. If your clone came with a generic DOS user's manual and a BASIC reference, you're lucky.

Happily, the computer book publishing industry has grown substantially. Today you can obtain books documenting the vagaries of C and assembly language programming and the intricacies of bitmapped graphics, and there are many "how-to's" available covering the most popular applications programs—dBASE, WordPerfect, and Lotus 1-2-3—as well as for the dozens of other software packages available on today's market. These books offer the new PC owner a great opportunity for jumping in at the middle. That's not always the best place to start.

In *The PC User's Guide*, my friends Nick Anis and Craig Menefee have bridged the gap in documentation for IBM-compatible PCs. This volume furnishes a basic manual on installation, setup, and operation of the machine. Written in clear, readable language, it covers everything from selecting, unpacking, and testing a system to tapping the power of advanced DOS commands and batch files. Along the way it offers tips on how to find the right software and get the most out of the hardware; it's a comprehensive resource that belongs next to your computer. Use this book to get your PC up and running in record time, and then keep it on your desk as an invaluable reference.

John C. Dvorak
Berkeley, California

ACKNOWLEDGMENTS

A project the size and complexity of this book is never the work of only one or two people. This has been a team effort from start to finish. One of the most enjoyable parts of this endeavor was working with many of the best minds in the field. The personal mentions that follow are no doubt incomplete; we spent many hours talking on the phone and exchanging electronic messages with a host of experts. They unfailingly gave us the help we needed.

We also enjoyed support much closer to home. We'll start with our phantom coauthor—Sami Menefee, wife of coauthor Craig Menefee. Sami did research, helped with first drafts, rewrote material, proofread, and assembled artwork. In short, she did anything that needed to be done. Thank you, Sami.

Coauthor Nick Anis's wife Patty also deserves much credit, for keeping Nick in line . . . to the degree that Nick can be kept in line. She played host to visiting contributors, she coordinated a busy household while Nick obsessed on the book, and she remained calm in the face of Nick's endless hurricane of activity.

The staff at Osborne/McGraw-Hill was, as always, professional and talented. They demonstrated the ultimate mastery in managing writers, knowing when to push and when to be patient. It was a joy to work with them. In particular, we'd like to thank editor-in-chief Jeffrey Pepper, associate editor Jill Pisoni, project editor Laura Sackerman, and proofreading coordinator Kathy Krause for taking extra time and care with the manuscript. Copy editors Nancy Beckus and Carol Henry and proofreaders John Selawsky, Valerie Haynes-Perry, and Louise Sellers also deserve thanks for their hard work. A special thank-you goes to director of electronic publishing Deborah Wilson, manager of electronic publishing Judy Wohlfrom, and computer designers Marcela Hancik and Fred Lass. Thanks also to Lance Ravella, who changed our rough sketches into polished, informative figures. One sketch in particular, intended to suggest a hardware component, when viewed sideways resembled instead Burl Ives eating a hamburger. With that drawing and others, Lance pulled off miracles and created order out of chaos.

Special thanks to editorial assistant Vicki Van Ausdall who, with Jill and Laura, tracked the project to completion, coordinating changes and spending hours on the phone with us. And Ann Pharr, with steadiness and friendliness apparently built into her voice, always directed us to exactly the person we needed for any given situation.

Technical reviewer Dan Fingerman caught both technical and editorial errors; we highly appreciate his efforts. Many others, too, contributed drafts, reviews, or technical expertise simply because they were asked. Brian Dooley came through in record time with a well-assembled overview of desktop computers and their components. Both Tom Anderson and Lamont Wood helped to create an orderly, informative discussion of a computer's innards. Thanks to Bud and Alex Aaron for helping with the DOS and BASIC reference sections. James Logan spent hours on the phone with us, devising practical ways to troubleshoot a sputtering system without resorting to complicated electronic equipment.

Other much appreciated, behind-the-scenes input and support came from Mike Callahan (a.k.a. Dr. File Finder), Alfred Glossbrenner, John and Mimi Dvorak, Jack Rickard (editor and publisher of *Boardwatch Magazine*), Tom Rawson of JP Software, Chuck Guzis of Sydex, and Tanya Van Dam of Microsoft. Also, Michael Mallory of Ontrack Systems contributed his extensive knowledge and experience with hard disks and data recovery. Many thanks to all of you!

Gratitude also goes to Debra, the Federal Express driver, who went out of her way to rearrange her pick-up schedule and make the Menefee household the last stop on her route. She waited cheerfully at the door when our last-minute changes threatened to put a hitch in her own schedule.

A number of hardware manufacturers and software publishers also deserve acknowledgment here. Their equipment and programs let us test procedures and descriptions firsthand for accuracy and completeness, using a variety of systems. Thanks go to Craig Conrad and Susan Zephir of Leading Edge Products, Inc., for supplying us with their new 25 MHz D3/25 80386 computer. This fast, reliable machine with a 103MB hard disk represents the new breed of Leading Edge machines now being produced under the umbrella of giant Daewoo Corporation of South Korea.

Kudos also to Packard Bell, whose fast, small-footprint Force-SX machine provided 16 MHz, 386SX power quietly and dependably. The Force is a high-end machine with a fast VGA video controller and a SCSI hard disk controller built right into the motherboard. A lower-end version, the Legend, can be found in mass-market, value-added outlets like Office Club, with some of the standard Force features (like 1MB of memory and a multisynch video controller) made optional; the careful engineering and remarkably quiet operation remain the same. Packard Bell also provided a PB9500 laser printer, whose clean lines and TEC laser engine together complement the high quality of the Force SX computer. Like the Force, the PB9500 is a small-footprint machine that performs like a large-footprint printer.

Heartfelt thanks to Karen Novac and U.S. Robotics Corp., whose pace-setting Courier HST dual-standard modem made telecommuting practical for both coauthors. This fast modem, recently upgraded to v.42*bis* compression, as well as v.29 and v.32 speeds, cut our long-distance telephone data transfer bills to the bone. Without the HST's speed and reliability, this project would not have been possible.

Large thank-yous also to Wendy Wegner and Keith Campbell of Panasonic, who loaned us their high-speed, quiet, and versatile KX-P4450i laser printer. This machine cranked out printed pages at 11 pages a minute. The KX-P4450i is one of the most trouble-free printers ever to hit the market, and has a wide variety of optional memory cards, fonts, and automatic feeding trays.

The authors used many programs in the preparation of this manuscript. We cannot name every program here, but the primary ones include Grand-View for outlining and rough-draft preparation; PC-Write and QEdit for writing and polishing manuscript chapters in ASCII format; the Word-Finder memory-resident thesaurus for when the "right" word refused to appear on the monitor despite all coaxing; Grammatik IV and Corporate Voice for style-checking drafts; and HiJaak and InSet for the many computer screen reproductions.

Finally, to anyone who slipped by without specific mention: Thank you for your help! This book would not have been possible without you.

It's ironic ... never have personal computers been more affordable for millions of people. Yet never has it been more difficult to get started with these machines. Years ago these systems often came with copious documentation and at least some support from the vendor. You might not have understood the manuals, and the vendor's support may have been reluctant at best, but at least it was something.

Of course, the cost of such "amenities" was built into the system's price. But prices are now much lower, and since computers have become a commodity, the amenities have all but disappeared. Today's buyer, although knowing far less about computers than the pioneers who led the way, receives far less documentation and support.

As a result, to enter the Promised Land of increased productivity, computer literacy, and all things good that computers make possible, a PC user must negotiate a series of hurdles. You not only must learn how to use the equipment you've purchased, but you may also have to put it together yourself. And then you must get the machine configured and prepared to run. Without the right information, you can spend hours, days, even months on preliminaries before being able to make any real use of your investment.

NO MANUAL, NO HELP, NO KIDDING!

Too many PC clones supply ten-page pamphlets that are supposed to pass for documentation, or, worse, they supply no documentation at all. Even systems that include Microsoft's OEM version of a DOS reference manual and BASIC reference guide lack much of the essential information that you need. How can you protect your interests at the store? Should you fill out the warranty card right away? What's the most common accidental damage to a computer before you get it up and running? What's the minimum you need to know about DOS in order to be adept with your machine? What *is* DOS, for that matter? What should you do when your computer asks if you want to Fail, Abort, Retry or Ignore—how do you know which answer to give?

What kinds of programs can you get and how do you know if they'll run correctly? Where can you get the best software and hardware deals? How can you tell if the computer store with the smiling salesperson is a good place to buy a computer? How about mail-order companies and catalog warehouses—do they offer good deals? What's a batch file, and how can you make it work for you without having to learn Greek, or whatever that computer language is?

All these questions, and more, are basic to becoming reasonably computer literate. They're not complicated or highly technical questions, but answering them does require a background of computer information that you can't get from a DOS manual. And the more advanced computer books assume you already know the basics.

A Thorough PC User and Reference Guide

What's needed by millions of PC owners—current and prospective—is a comprehensive, easy-to-understand guide to fill this information void. That's why we designed *The PC User's Guide*. It gives you detailed information on

- Unpacking and assembling your system
- Understanding your system's options
- DOS basics
- BASIC basics
- Software
- How to run programs
- Hard disks
- Service and repairs
- Troubleshooting

and much more. It will solve your documentation problems.

Many hundreds of you will end up with either unbelievably skimpy documentation or none at all. Many more of you have plenty of documentation that is either incomprehensible or incomplete. Add those of you who "inherited" a PC in an office in which the documentation is around somewhere, but you don't know where to look or for what. So far, then, we've got thousands of people stuck with a box and a TV screen, and maybe some other pieces, too. What you don't have, through no fault of your own, is a way to get it all together and working.

Throughout this book you'll be provided with the information you need to set up, operate, and adjust your IBM-compatible personal computer system. In the process you'll learn about computer basics, including how to navigate the keyboard, and how to run and customize the programs you bought. You'll also find out about improvements you can make to your hardware and software that will make your system easier to use and more efficient.

ABOUT THIS BOOK

This book is organized as a reference and designed to be kept near your computer. Rather than assume you have read from start to finish, as some (not many) users do with a program or equipment manual, this book presents each chapter as an independent unit. When some prior knowledge is assumed, the chapter tells you where to find that information.

This volume proceeds from the less technical to the more technical. You don't need to be an engineer to read and understand the entire book—even the later chapters about hardware and troubleshooting. The troubleshooting procedures require no special test equipment. When the material is about to become technical, we'll let you know; those subjects are there for readers who feel comfortable working with hardware. It's not everyone's cup of tea, so we've also included hints on finding competent technical help.

In short, this is a beginner's book that guides you into the middle range of PC expertise. It is also a reference book, containing more detail than a simple "crash course" book. It is designed to be useful over the long haul, not just when you first set up your system.

How This Book Is Organized

The first four chapters focus on getting started. You'll find a basic guide to what makes a PC work. You'll take a close look at picking the right system, locating a workspace, and unpacking and testing your new equipment.

Chapter 5 takes you through everything you need to become as adept with a PC as most office-level users are. Chapters 6, 7, and 8 give you a tour of the best programs available today, from operating systems and major applications programs to the small, helpful utilities that can sometimes baffle newcomers.

In Chapter 9, you proceed into the world of the mid-level DOS user. You'll learn how to operate at the DOS command line, organize and maintain a hard disk, and tap into the power of advanced DOS commands and batch files. Chapter 12 tops off the DOS section with a complete DOS reference manual, including hints and tips absent from the generic DOS manuals.

Chapters 13 and 14 are devoted to an overview of working with BASIC, the programming language that comes with all DOS versions.

In Chapters 15 through 17, the book addresses hardware matters. These chapters describe the parts inside a computer, give the facts about hard disks (including how to install one), and show how to fine-tune or "tweak" a system to get the most out of hardware and software.

Chapter 18 rounds out the technical sections with advice on what to do when trouble crops up. It includes advice on how and when to seek help and how to save money by identifying and solving problems yourself.

Finally, the appendixes offer a detailed section on using a PC's keyboard, including the use and meaning of those odd, extra keys; CMOS settings for hard disks, to help you get up and running again if your system battery runs down; a complete set of DOS error messages, including tips on what to do about specific problems; a guide to finding money-saving sources of new computer equipment; and a table of the 256 characters recognized by all PCs.

There is also a glossary of specialized computer terms used in the text, and a complete, reference-quality index.

Here are more detailed descriptions of the book's contents.

In **Chapter 1** you'll discover what computers do, and learn a little about how they work.

In **Chapter 2** you'll explore the various system configurations and all their components. You'll get a detailed guided tour of available PC systems, giving you a complete understanding of how to pick a system that will fill your needs.

Chapter 3 covers unpacking your system, details on what to look for in your working environment, traps to avoid in the installation process, even how and why to ground a circuit if your work site has old-fashioned, two-prong outlets.

You'll step through assembling and "smoke testing" your new system in **Chapter 4**. There you'll learn the most common errors to prevent and how to get to work in record time. You'll be able to avoid frustrating trips back to the store to return components you didn't need, or to buy the ones you didn't know you did need.

Chapter 5 is a crash course in operating a personal computer. It introduces fundamentals like working with floppy disks, making backup copies of your data, and using basic DOS commands. With this information at your fingertips, you won't have to rely on the office computer guru for help with simple things like copying, renaming, or deleting files, or creating working program disks.

In **Chapter 6** you'll learn about operating systems and environments for personal computers, including graphical user interfaces like Windows.

Chapter 7 covers installing and using applications programs. Here you'll learn about word processors, electronic spreadsheets, database programs, and much more. You'll find out about what sorts of programs are available, how to select the right ones, and where to buy them. This chapter also explains user-supported shareware programs and gives tips on how to research these low-cost shareware alternatives.

Utility programs—ranging from computer housekeepers to complete working environments—are presented in **Chapter 8**. These important programs seldom receive the attention they deserve. Utilities can mean the difference between a system that usually does what you need it to do, more or less, most of the time, and a system that always does what you need— fast and well, with no bother.

Chapter 9 teaches you how to work at the DOS operating system level. It explains the DOS prompt and the DOS command line in clear, understandable terms. It will amplify your understanding of DOS and introduce you to the techniques treasured by power users. Here, the DOS commands you first read about in Chapter 5 are more thoroughly explained. Coverage also includes file naming, wildcards, and other tools that make the DOS command line a fast, powerful place to get your work done.

In **Chapter 10**, you'll read about setting up and navigating the hard disk. This is not a chapter about hardware, but rather about using your hard disk to make your work go faster, more smoothly, and with less trouble. The right techniques make a world of difference when you're working with the thousands of files that today's fast hard disks can store.

Chapter 11 takes you into the intermediate workings of DOS—the advanced commands and batch file techniques that make the difference between a competent computer user and an adept one. This section is an introduction to power techniques that will make you more than ready, should you decide to take your studies further with one of the fine power-user books available on the market.

Rounding out the DOS section is **Chapter 12**'s complete DOS command reference. It includes several rarely documented hints and tips to keep you out of trouble with the trickier commands. It also tells you when third-party utilities are best and helps you use DOS effectively.

Next, **Chapters 13 and 14** introduce you to the beginners all-purpose symbolic instruction code, or BASIC, programming language. You'll get started using BASIC and learn how the language works. Written in English-like statements, BASIC programs are often included in manuals for printers, modems, and other hardware. Our overview will remove the mystery from these programs.

The hardware section begins in **Chapter 15**, with a fast, not-too-technical overview of the components inside your system case. The philosophy here is that you don't need to know what the electrons are doing in order to understand how the highly modular parts of a computer fit together.

Chapter 16 continues in the same vein, showing you (without a lot of mumbo jumbo) how a hard disk works and how to take care of one. It advises you on what to look for when you buy a hard disk, how to install it, and how to format it—all in clear, nontechnical terms.

In **Chapter 17** you'll read about how power users tweak their hardware and software to get the greatest possible performance out of their systems. This chapter covers six important performance areas, ranging from how to make the most use of your available memory to getting rid of problems that rob your system of power. You'll also learn how to enhance the performance of your system hardware.

Finally, **Chapter 18** offers a comprehensive guide to troubleshooting. There is a surprisingly large number of things you can do to cure problems without ever having to use a voltage meter or other testing equipment. You will learn how to isolate problems so that, even if you can't fix them yourself, you'll already know what needs to be done before you take your computer to the repair shop.

A Note About the Authors

This volume taps the rich resources of the authors' combined 25 years of computer experience. Their past work with a wide variety of systems and users is reflected in the book's depth and clarity. It's an old axiom that two experts rarely agree on anything, but this project has proven to be an exception to that rule. They hope you will get as much enjoyment from using this book as they had in preparing it.

CHAPTER ONE

Personal Computers — A Basic Guide

Personal computing has changed the way people work, think, and play. Both home and workplace have been affected by the PC revolution. For many jobs, the personal computer (or PC) has become an indispensable tool. Accountants who once did all their work on columnar paper with a calculator and a pencil now use electronic spreadsheet programs; writers and secretaries use word processing programs; engineers use graphic design programs; executives use electronic planners. The list goes on, and new uses are developed constantly.

You don't need to be a computer expert to take advantage of the power a PC can give you. These days, computer companies put a lot of thought into making their products easy to use. A little familiarity with basic computer concepts is all you really need. Once you've started using your computer, you may be surprised at how little it takes to learn to use the computer programs you've selected. In no time, you'll discover all sorts of ways to turn your personal computer into a real help on the job.

In this chapter, you'll read about the basics of personal computing. You'll start with what a computer actually does, followed by an introduction to the main components—the system unit, keyboard, monitor, modem, and other basics that make up a complete PC system.

WHAT IS A COMPUTER?

A computer is just a machine that adds, subtracts, and compares numbers with blinding speed. Over the years, the things you can do with these machines have multiplied. By now you can do everything from designing spacecraft, planes, and buildings to balancing checkbooks and playing music. Computers come in various sizes, but the PCs that this book deals with are small boxes with keyboards and TV-like screens that fit on a desktop. With a PC, you can do anything you can do with a pencil on paper, and then some.

Computers didn't always fit in a small box. In the 1950s, a typical computer was a huge electronic device with glass-fronted cases containing tape reels that jerked back and forth to a rhythm no human ever devised. It did something called *data processing* in an antiseptic room. Movie directors had a wonderful time faking computers with blinking lights, buzzers, and chrome.

During this period, the computer was already indispensable to government and large industry. Computers of the time used several rooms' worth of vacuum tubes to do what we now do with hand-held calculators, but they were fast and they did not make mistakes. Later in the 1950s, an astoundingly efficient computer called a Univac was widely shown in military exhibits at state fairs. It fit inside a single semitrailer and could be moved from place to place.

Real efficiency came only with computers based on transistors. With this innovation, both size and electrical power needs plunged as computing power soared. That established a pattern that seems now to be some sort of natural law: Computers evolve by packing more power into less space for less money.

Integrated Circuits and the PC Revolution

Today, integrated circuits have given us yet a third generation of computers. With integrated circuits, a piece of silicon the size of your thumbnail does jobs that once required a room full of components. The number and complexity of circuits that can be contained on this silicon real estate is enormous and constantly increasing, even while size and costs decrease.

One result is that computers are now commonplace. We rely on them for help with our creative, administrative, clerical, and management chores.

There are still large computers around, and many of them sport a Buck Rogers look. But these days, they, too, are based on integrated circuits, and their capability dwarfs that of the early-day monster machines. The largest and fastest are called supercomputers. Some scientists believe these will someday be linked into networks that "think" independently, perhaps even becoming self-aware. These are the computers that today's Hollywood directors dress up in blinking lights and buzzers for plots that involve mad scientists, teenage hackers, and military war machines.

A step down from these are mainframes, the machines in most large company and government data processing departments. Smaller yet are computers that fall between desktop systems and mainframes in size, called minicomputers. Engineering and design companies use them to let their staff members work together on large-scale projects.

Finally, there are the subjects of this guide—the desktop, laptop, and notebook microcomputers that are the only truly personal computers. These are the machines that give us computing power on a human, not an institutional, scale.

The Bottom Line: What Can a Computer Do for You?

The range of possible uses for a personal computer is as limitless as your imagination. Things that you write can be written more easily with word processing software. Your calculations can be done more quickly and efficiently with spreadsheet software. You can maintain your records better by using database management software to store, organize, sort, and process your information. You can send messages anywhere in the world in the time it takes to make a telephone call. The list goes on and on. There is software for general purposes and for specific purposes. If you have a business problem, chances are a personal computer solution is available to help you. PCs are also useful for a variety of tasks in the home.

Computers don't care where the human operator is located, so a growing number of people have begun to *telecommute*. That means they connect their personal computer to the office computer by telephone and stay at home while they work. Telecommuting lets you avoid long rush hour drives and save hours of stress and lost productivity. It cuts down on workers' expenses and makes it possible for them to set their own hours. It lets people trade in an office desk for a front porch or a living room. Companies such as Pacific Bell have conducted studies showing that telecommuting increases a worker's productivity by as much as 20 percent. Even large companies suffering from middle management control insecurities are beginning to catch on to telecommuting.

It is important to remember that a computer will not do your thinking for you. It is a tool to make your job easier; it cannot do the job alone. A computer is particularly good at doing the boring, repetitive chores that may slow you down. It can instantly do accurate calculations, and will not tire if you need to change your figures or play "what if" with your budget. It can meticulously check the spelling of every word in a document. It can sort through hundreds of records and put them in the right order in an instant. It can store data files in the small space of a magnetic disk, give nearly instant access to information, and save cubic yards of space compared to paper file storage. But it can't think for you.

Applications Programs: Calling the Shots

A computer is a general tool. It can do a wide variety of tasks, but since it can't think for itself, someone must tell it what to do. That someone is you. And it needs very specific instructions to follow. Computer programs provide the instructions.

Specifically, the work a computer does depends entirely upon what program you load into it. Computer programs are designed to be applied to specific tasks, and so are often called *applications programs*, or, more simply, *applications*. Programs have become so well designed that you rarely have to deal directly with the computer hardware anymore; instead, you just work with programs.

The Engine in the Middle: The CPU

The PC revolution is based on a tiny piece of silicon called a *microprocessor*. This solid-state device holds millions of tiny electronic circuits integrated onto a single central processing unit (or CPU) chip. The earliest CPUs had little more power than a simple calculator, but even so required thousands of individual circuits. The newest lines of microprocessors have as much power as yesterday's mainframes, and they continue to evolve.

A computer's CPU does all of the actual data processing. It performs the comparisons, additions, and subtractions that comprise digital computing, and places the results in memory. Assorted other chips link the CPU to the keyboard, to memory, and to various storage devices and input/output ports. The CPU carries out an applications program's instructions and, in so doing, directs the entire show.

BECOMING AN EXPERT

Today, you really don't need to know too much about how a computer works from an engineering viewpoint to become adept at using one. Your main interaction with the system consists of typing on the keyboard when you see the prompts or instructions on your screen. You work with the software—the carefully laid-out instructions provided by a programmer— instead of directly with the machine. Still, there are a few fundamental concepts that it will be helpful to know about.

Binary Fundamentals

A computer is a machine designed to process binary data. This simply means that it adds, subtracts, and compares 1's and 0's. Binary numbers are another way to represent what we think of as numbers. You may remember from grade school arithmetic that in a counting system based on the number ten, you move over a column every tenth digit. That means your column positions are powers of ten: 1, 10, 100, 1000, and so on.

A computer uses a counting system based on the number 2, so it is called *binary* (as opposed to *decimal* for powers of ten). In binary counting, you add a new column to the left every time you pass a power of 2: 1, 2, 4, 8, 16, and so forth. It makes large numbers seem horribly long to eyes accustomed to decimal counting; the binary translation of the numbers 1 through 10 goes like this:

Decimal	Binary
0	0
1	1
2	10
3	11
4	100
5	101
6	110
7	111
8	1000
9	1001
10	1010

The binary 1's and 0's represent only two states: on and off. These two states, also called true and false or high and low, can represent any kind of information. For instance, binary digits can be combined to represent characters, numbers, words, and even musical notes.

Bits and Bytes

The term *binary digit* has been shortened for everyday use to the term *bit;* if you work much around computers you'll hear the term a lot. Computers generally work with groups of 8 bits at a time, known collectively as a *byte.* The eight positions in a byte are enough to represent any number from 0 (in binary, 00000000 or eight 0's) to 255 (in binary, 11111111 or eight 1's). The next number up, 256, is two raised to the ninth power, represented in binary as a 1 followed by eight 0's.

So a byte can represent any number from 0 to 255. This is enough for all the letters of the English alphabet, all required punctuation, and various special graphics and foreign characters. There's even room left over for special computer control characters. That's a lot of latitude, enough to carry out just about any required PC operation. To represent a larger number, you can link two bytes together; for example, two 8-bit bytes strung together let you count to the binary number represented by sixteen 1's in a row, or 65,535 in decimal notation.

Bytes are the basic unit processed by the computer, and are treated singly or in groups. Many personal computers today can deal with more than one byte at a time. You will hear, for example, of 16-bit computers. This quantity is often called the computer's *word*—in this case, two bytes. All you need to know about the word size is that, in general, the bigger the better because the bigger the faster. Early PCs were 8-bit systems; later, more powerful ones have a 16-bit word, and 32-bit word machines are in the planning stages.

Kilos, Megs, and Gigas

Two abbreviations that you need to know are K and M, for kilo and mega (meg). *Kilo* stands for 1000 of anything in standard usage, although in binary the closest round equivalent is 1 plus 10 zeroes, or 1024. It also happens to be the equivalent of 4 bytes' worth of data, so programmers find it handy. You will see the prefix kilo applied to bytes as *kilobytes* and to bits as *kilobits*.

 Mega, or *M,* stands loosely for a million. You'll run into the term *megabyte* meaning 1000 kilobytes, or 1,024,000 bytes. You also may run into the term *gigabyte* (or *GB*)—1000 megabytes, or 1,024,000,000 bytes. In computer representation, *K* used by itself refers to kilobytes (as in 64K). If a distinction must be made, KB means kilobytes, and Kb means kilobits. See Table 1-1 for an overview of some typical ways that binary counting applies to computers.

TYPES OF SYSTEMS

In the early days of microcomputing, before standards took root, selecting a machine from among the many available types could be difficult. Today, the overwhelming majority of systems sold are IBM-compatible. This means

---

Table 1-1

Typical Uses of Binary Quantities

Binary Quantity	Binary Representation
CD-ROM capacity	1GB and up
Hard disk capacity	10MB, 20MB, 32MB, 40MB, and up
Maximum amount represented by two linked bytes	1111111111111111 (16 binary 1's) = 64K, or 65,535 in decimal notation
Modem speed	300, 1200, 2400, or 9600 baud (roughly, bits per second)
Standard PC memory	256, 512, 640, or 1024K

that they run the same programs an IBM PC runs, and connect to the same equipment. They even use the same expansion circuit cards. IBM's recent PS/2 computer line is also compatible, although its expansion card slots have changed enough to make it a deviation from the standard. (There will be more on this subject in Chapter 2, which offers tips on picking between the various competing systems.)

Some years ago there was a great deal of difference between the IBM PC and the Apple Macintosh system, but this gap has been closing steadily. The chief PC-based competition for the Mac's easy-to-use graphical interface is available through the Microsoft Windows operating environment and OS/2's Presentation Manager. These programs are good examples of how to adapt a PC for graphics. Still, they're not the only, or even necessarily the best, way to use a PC.

To make the kinds of choices outlined in Chapter 2, "Systems Overview: Choosing a Computer," you'll need to know a little about the major components of a PC, what they do, and how they interact.

THE BASIC PC

The basic computer system components are the processor (or CPU) and system box, the external storage system, the keyboard, and the video display. A printer can be attached to the system, and there may be any number of other peripherals to fit special needs.

The system box contains the silicon microprocessor chip and the computer's basic processing and control circuits. These are mounted on a main printed circuit board called the *motherboard*. The system box also contains the file storage facilities—usually one or two floppy disk drives and/or some form of hard disk storage.

The motherboard also has special connectors into which add-on printed circuit cards can be fitted. These connectors are called *slots*. The printed circuit cards you put into the slots are called *daughter boards*. When you purchase a computer, some of these slots probably will already be occupied by necessary boards such as a disk controller, video adapter, and additional memory. Some motherboards have circuitry built in for these functions and do not need as many add-on boards.

At the rear of the system unit are connectors for peripherals. (A *peripheral* is any component not located inside the system box.) These output connector sockets are often built into daughter boards.

More detail is offered in Chapter 2, but the main components found on nearly every PC system are described briefly in the following sections.

Keyboards

With IBM PCs and compatibles, even the keyboard can be considered optional equipment. (Some special-use PCs don't bother with keyboards.) IBM has created several keyboard styles, and there are dozens of variations available from third-party manufacturers. All styles have the basic letter and number keys, special function keys, and cursor keys.

Some keyboards also have separate number key pads, extra function keys, different key locations, and other features. The appropriate keyboard depends upon the applications you intend to run. Do you need extra function keys for your word processor? Will you need a ten-key keypad for your spreadsheet program? Also consider the "feel" of the keys. Do your hands feel comfortable using the keys? There is always room for individual preference, and no need for a rigid standard.

PC Power Components

Various components determine the computer power of any given machine. These include the type of microprocessor, the amount of memory, and the type of external or disk storage.

Microprocessor (CPU)

The microprocessor is the silicon brain of the system — a tiny CPU chip containing billions of circuits. IBM systems use a line of microprocessors developed by Intel Corporation. These CPUs have distinctive numbers including, in order of increasing power:

8088, used with the PC and XT
8086, a faster chip used with the XT
80286, used with AT-class machines
80386, used with 386 (next generation AT) machines
80486, used with 486 (most recent AT) machines

The 286, 386, and 486 versions are also used with IBM's PS/2 Micro Channel Architecture machines, which are not covered in detail in this book.

Note: Some *clones,* or IBM compatibles, use other chips such as the NEC V20 instead of the Intel 8088, but Intel CPUs are the most common.

Memory (RAM)

Memory generally refers to random access memory, or RAM. This is the computer's basic "thinking space." RAM is used to load portions of the operating system and applications programs, and as a scratch pad for information processing. When you turn off the power, the information held in RAM will be cleared. This is why RAM is sometimes called temporary memory. Still, all active computing really takes place in RAM since that's where the programs run. Like the other PC circuits, RAM is contained in integrated chips and you can generally add more memory if you need it. (Memory management is covered in Chapter 17, "Getting the Most from Your System".)

Storage

Storage is where you keep your programs, your documents, and your data when you are not using them. The most common forms of storage are hard disks and floppy disks. Your computer contains units called *disk drives.* Drives can be for hard disks or floppy disks, and can be internal or external to the system unit. Internal disk drives are installed in bays provided inside the system unit. External drives have their own housing and power supplies, and are connected to the computer by data transfer cables.

Hard disks are generally located inside the system box; they store large amounts of information. Floppy disks store smaller amounts of material but are used to transfer programs and data between systems and to maintain permanent or backup files.

Floppy disks come in two basic sizes: 5 1/4-inch and 3 1/2-inch (see Figure 1-1). The 5 1/4-inch size is an older format and resembles a square of stiff but flexible plastic with a hole in its center. The 3 1/2-inch shirt-pocket sized disk has a rigid container with a spring-loaded catch. The smaller disks are harder to damage.

There are two storage capacities for each floppy disk size. The 5 1/4-inch disks come in a 360K double sided, double density format and in a 1.2MB, double sided, high density format. The 3 1/2-inch disks (sometimes called

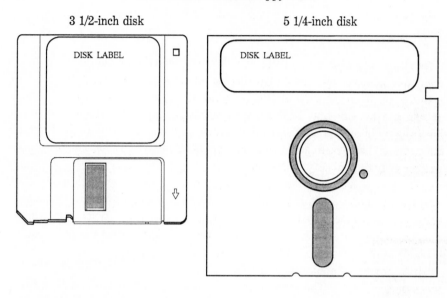

Figure 1-1

3 1/2- and 5 1/4-inch floppy disks

3 1/2-inch disk   5 1/4-inch disk

micro floppies) support 720K double sided, double density storage and 1.44MB, double sided, high density storage.

Memory Versus Storage   It is easy to confuse memory with storage. After all, both are ways to keep and manage information. They are, however, quite different. Memory is the computer's working space; it is where a computer keeps its data available for processing. All data processed by a computer must first be loaded into the computer's memory. Because of its close ties to the CPU, memory is only active when the power is turned on and the CPU is active. When you turn off the power, everything in memory disappears. If memory breaks down or power fails during processing, everything stops. Memory is strictly temporary.

Disk storage, on the other hand, is for a longer term. Storage is where you keep your electronic files—the records kept by your system. Files can be extremely large, and can be retained on magnetic disks for many years without change. Memory is generally much more limited in size than storage; it is also more expensive to purchase.

Video Display

Computing capacity and power are key considerations in deciding on a computer system, but the video display is also important. Since you will spend a lot of time gazing at the computer's display you should use care in selecting a system that best suits your needs. The video display includes both the monitor and the internal circuitry to support it. Compatibility with your other hardware and with the applications you'll be running may restrict which monitor you can use.

The choice also will depend in part on your need for high resolution graphics. Graphics have become more important in recent years as developers and users discovered the advantages of expressing ideas in pictures. Some applications such as electronic desktop publishing and computer aided design require strong graphics support.

In computer graphics, the graphics adapter card "writes" information to the monitor screen. The screen image is made up of thousands of dots of light, called *pixels,* or *pels.* The pixels act as building blocks for characters and pictures. Screen resolution depends upon how small and close together the pixels are; color possibilities are determined by the number of colors each pixel can take on.

Visual display possibilities range from simple monochrome with a green- or amber-on-black screen that can only display text, through the range of color and graphics systems. You can go from low resolution with few color choices to high resolution with many colors. The current standards, in order of screen resolution, are CGA, EGA, VGA, and SVGA. Monochrome monitors are also still in wide use.

- *Monochrome or MDA* The monochrome or MDA (monochrome display adapter) screen is usually green or amber on black. The original monochrome monitors imitated a teletype machine and lacked any graphics capabilities. They displayed text and numbers only. Because they did not handle graphics, they could work solely on text resolution, which was (and is) of high quality. You can, however, add graphics capability to these monitors with special graphics adapters.

- *CGA* The CGA (color graphics adapter) is the earliest of the graphics standards and is quite limited. In multicolor mode, it can only handle a 40-character screen width. Even in its highest resolution, the characters are granular and can be difficult to read.

- *EGA and VGA* Both EGA (enhanced graphics adapter) and VGA (video graphics array) provide high resolution graphics with clear, crisp text. VGA offers more graphics possibilities than EGA and has become the standard. Adapters for either system still support the older CGA standard, if your software does not work in the higher resolutions. VGA monitors are analog rather than digital, and so are capable of more gradual color changes requiring fewer wires than a digital system, such as the EGA, can manage.

- *Super VGA and beyond* There are many adapters that drive special VGA monitors with very high resolution. As with most add-ons, you must give up something to gain something. With the Super VGA, you sacrifice a small amount of speed for higher resolution. Special noninterlaced VGAs give very high resolution for desktop publishing and computer design work. IBM has gate-controlled and other special video display systems. As you get deeper into these high resolution, high-end monitors, there is risk of losing compatibility with software written for more general, lower resolution standards. Look around and read reviews before you buy.

It is important to match your monitor to your graphics card. Some monitors simply will not attach to certain graphics cards, while others might be damaged by a wrong selection. At the higher price levels, so-called "multisynch" monitors self-adjust to your graphics card and pretty much eliminate compatibility problems.

Printers

The printer is another standard peripheral. Printers are used to produce paper copies of computer files, sometimes called *hard copies*. Although we like to think that paper eventually will not be necessary, we still need printed paper in addition to electronic files. The printer you choose will depend on the output speed and quality you need, and on how many pages you will print. General categories include the daisy wheel (slow), dot matrix (faster), and laser printers (fastest).

Other Peripherals

You can connect all sorts of devices to your computer. There are special devices to put different types of data into the system, and other devices to export, or take data back out.

Input Devices

There are several ways to tell your computer what you want it to do besides typing in commands. Some alternatives include

- *Mice*   Mice are used to point to items on the screen and select items from menus.

- *Joysticks, trackballs, and light pens*   These devices are all used to point to specific locations on the computer screen.

- *Scanners and digitizers*   These transmit graphic images of printed documents to the computer. You can then edit or modify the images.

Output Devices

Besides the standard printers and monitors used to display the results of a computer's operations, you can add special-use devices to fill particular needs. The following are just a few of the devices now available.

- *Modems*   These devices (see Figure 1-2) translate the digital language of a computer into tones, and transmit them over phone lines to another modem. The second modem translates the tones back into digital signals and feeds them to a second computer as input. This is the basis of telephone communications between computers.

- *Plotters*   These devices transform designs and diagrams created by software into drawings, using mechanical pens of different colors.

- *Special monitors*   Monitors are available to show larger portions of a page, to project images onto a screen, and to carry out a variety of other tasks.

- *Display systems*   You can purchase ultra-high resolution display systems, complete with both special monitors and proprietary plug-in circuit cards.

Figure 1-2

Internal and external modems

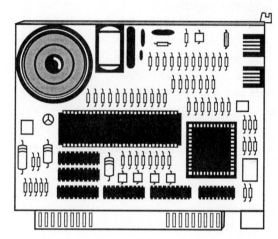

Internal modem

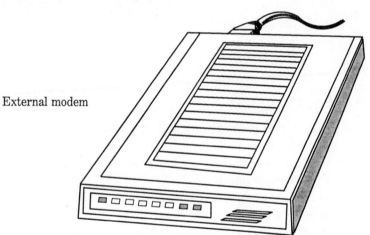

External modem

Special Storage

Sometimes the standard storage methods, such as floppy disks and even hard disks, may not meet your needs. A variety of special, often high-capacity data storage devices can keep huge amounts of data on tap, either as backup or working files. Some current alternatives are

- *Compact disk-read only memory (CD-ROM)*   A CD-ROM is an optical disk that can only be read, not recorded on. In fact, it is the same CD used in today's music systems. These disks hold enormous amounts of information, and you buy them as you would a record. Available CD-ROMs include encyclopedias, book libraries, graphic images, and huge databases. Recently these disks have started supporting digitized sound and images. For instance, you can get a CD-ROM version of the National Audubon Society's directory of birds, complete with pictures and sound recordings of their songs.

- *Digital audio tape (DAT)*   Digital audio tape is similar to the tape cassettes used in stereo systems. Special high-density recording techniques allow them to store large amounts of information; more than a gigabyte per tape.

- *Read/write optical media*   These relative newcomers allow you to both store and retrieve data using laser beams for extremely high density storage. These are not often used on desktop PC systems, but are valuable in special applications such as insurance company and government databases.

Adding Peripherals

There are several places where you can connect other equipment to your computer. The variety of attachment possibilities reflects the number of items that can be connected. Even your video output card probably has several types of cable sockets that can be used to attach different kinds of monitors. The main places where you add peripherals, however, are the external ports and the internal slots.

Parallel and Serial Ports

Most computers today come with at least one parallel and one serial port. You can identify these on the computer as the large, roughly rectangular, multipin sockets on the back of the system unit. Generally, the serial port is the one with the pins sticking out (called the male side). The parallel port is the one with the holes (the female side). Both generally use 25-pin connectors. The parallel socket, or *port*, often drives a printer, while the serial port frequently is connected to a modem, mouse, or other serial device.

The most important thing to remember is that equipment with a *parallel interface* (meaning, designed for parallel connection) can only be connected to a parallel port. Likewise, serial interface equipment must be connected to a serial port.

The technical difference between a serial and a parallel port is that the serial port sends bits out one at a time, similar to cars on a train. The parallel port sends groups of 8 bits—complete bytes—out at once. Parallel ports are slightly faster but should only be used with cables less than 18 feet long; serial ports are useful for longer distances.

Serial ports are often called RS-232C ports, that being the name of a widely accepted serial port connector. Standardized serial ports let people with different brands of computers use different brands of serial equipment. Such equipment can include printers, pointing devices, and modems. In the IBM PC world, serial ports also are called COM (communication) ports, although devices other than modems may use them. The first COM port is labeled COM1, the second is COM2, and so on.

The parallel port is often called a Centronics port, because it was first sold by the Centronics company. In the IBM PC world, it also is called an LPT (line printer) port, and the first one is called LPT1. Because so many printers now use parallel ports, the first one, LPT1, is also called the PRN device. Serial printers are still available for special purposes but are not as common as they once were.

Slots

The other main peripheral connection possibility is a system unit internal expansion slot. Here, the peripheral is actually a printed circuit board placed into an expansion slot within the computer. This is a direct connection to the computer's control lines (called its *data bus*). Once you install a circuit card, it effectively becomes a part of the computer.

SCSI Ports

An additional type of port that is coming into more frequent use is the small computer system interface port, or SCSI (pronounced "skuzzy"). This emerging standard lets many devices connect directly to the system, much like a parallel port. There is no limit to the number of attachments. A SCSI port passes more information both ways than a parallel port can. They are ideal for complex devices such as high-capacity, high-speed disk drives.

DATA COMMUNICATIONS

You can have your computer communicate with other systems in various ways. How you do this will affect the components that you select for your system. Computers can be connected directly through the serial port, but more frequently they connect to a network or over telephone lines through a modem.

The most common reasons to connect one computer to another are to transfer files, trade messages as electronic mail, or E-mail, and look up information in databases. Computer networks are complex, often needing special adapter cards and software. They are often hard-wired throughout a building, and may include the company's mainframe computers. If you are in a networked computer environment, you may need help from information systems experts to add to or change your system.

On the other hand, computers can let you communicate over normal phone lines with little extra equipment or software. All you need is a communications program and a modem. The modem attaches to your computer and to the phone line. It translates your computer's electrical signals into a form that can be transmitted without being lost or distorted. At the other end, another modem deciphers the signal and sends it to the receiving computer. Modems today generally operate at 300, 1200, 2400, 9600 or more bits per second.

With a modem, you can access all sorts of information and communications services such as CompuServe, MCI Mail, Dialog, Prodigy, and many others. There are thousands of these services; they offer everything from electronic mail to databases holding the complete texts of current magazines. You can access any other system that has an operating modem, making it possible to trade data quickly over long distances. Your software handles the details, so it is easy to get started in telephone data communications.

A WORD ABOUT SOFTWARE

Just as television would be useless without programs to watch, computers could do nothing without software. Technically, computer programs are sets of instructions that, when combined with information you supply (data), decide everything a computer does.

There are two basic levels of software: the operating system and applications. The operating system contains the most basic procedures for running the computer; it does the housekeeping chores like copying files and disks, formatting disks for use, and loading and running applications programs.

On IBM PC computers and compatibles, the usual operating system is MS-DOS (sometimes PC-DOS); Microsoft Corporation developed it for the original IBM PC. By itself, DOS provides only the most basic services, although in recent releases this is changing. More sophisticated services, similar to those the Apple Macintosh provides for its users, are available through special user interface programs. For IBM PCs and compatibles, outstanding user interfaces include Microsoft Windows and the IBM OS/2 operating system's Presentation Manager.

Applications programs are the software packages that do the basic functions for which you bought your computer. Typical general purpose applications programs include:

- Electronic spreadsheets
- Word processing software
- Data management software
- Graphics software
- Project planners
- Electronic calendars and office systems
- Communications software

Programming

Computer programs are sets of instructions in a language the machine understands called *machine code*. The instructions are just numbers—bytes—that are meaningless to non-computers (such as human beings). The instructions define parts of operations, one at a time, so it takes many separate instructions to do even the simplest things.

Creating programs in machine code is difficult, time consuming, and repetitive. At a higher level, there is assembly language, which is a way of writing machine code with some of the difficulties removed. Assembly language is still close to the basic instruction level and is mostly used for small, specialized utility programs. (A utility is a small, single-purpose program generally used as a computer housekeeping tool.) Most applications today are written in languages at the next level up.

The computer languages whose names have become familiar to many, even outside the world of computers—BASIC, Pascal, FORTRAN, COBOL, and so forth—are high level languages. (The C language you may often hear about is actually a mid-level language, just one step up from assembly language.) These languages are designed for human programmers, not for machines, and they do not much resemble machine code. The emphasis is on the capability to create complex procedures and to review them afterward. Each instruction may generate a long chain of machine code when it is finally compiled.

Compiling a program means translating the programmer's English-like commands into the machine's nonhuman code. High level languages must usually be compiled. No matter what the original language was, a compiled result has some common characteristics. On an MS-DOS computer it will be a file with the filename extension .COM or .EXE.

Some languages—notably BASIC—are *interpreted*, meaning translated line by line into machine instructions by an intermediary program. This is slower than running a compiled program, but it is much more easily controlled. On the PC, files that need interpretation often are written in BASIC and have filenames that end with the extension .BAS.

SUMMARY

This chapter has discussed the basics of what constitutes a desktop computer system and some things you can do with it. But it isn't really the computer or even the software that's the most important, it's how you decide to use the system. There are a thousand different ways to work, and none of them is wrong . . . provided it works. The PC is just a tool box filled with wonderful tools; it's up to you to apply them to your work.

In the next chapter, you'll read in more detail about the different varieties of personal computers available at this writing. In the process, you'll delve deeper into the technical differences between machines. When you finish, you'll be qualified to make an informed choice among the many varieties of competing systems.

CHAPTER TWO

Systems Overview: Choosing a Computer

This chapter takes a closer look at the sometimes bewildering maze of choices available in personal computers. What kinds are there? Which are best for what purposes? How do you decide what you need and where to get it? The following material will help guide you. The focus is on IBM-compatible (that is, MS-DOS standard) computers. This chapter assumes you've read Chapter 1 or at least know the basic parts of a desktop machine, such as the keyboard, monitor, and system unit.

TYPES OF IBM-COMPATIBLE COMPUTERS

If you've read the advertisements or have been around computers much, you've probably run into the odd mix of numbers and letters that stand for the different types of IBM-compatible machines. You've seen references to PCs, XTs, ATs, and PS/2s. There are the desktops, laptops, and notebooks. Then there are 8088, 286, 386, 386SX, and 486 machines.

It can be pretty overwhelming to a beginner, but it's important to know a little about these labels. If you know a computer's label you'll know roughly what the machine can do and where it stands in relation to the other machines.

An Array of Choices

What you're really dealing with are the basic characteristics of different machines. Here are some questions that address how well a computer will meet your needs:

- How big a program can the machine run?

- How fast can it run it?

- How much data can it process at once?

- How big, physically, is the machine?

- How many programs are available for it?

- What other machines can trade files with it?

You'll find, when considering these questions, that a rule has evolved with PCs: The faster and more powerful a machine is, the later it came along. There's nothing surprising about that. PCs have a history of requiring less and less physical space to run more and more powerful programs. Once programmers become familiar with each new machine, they learn to take full advantage of its strengths and work around its weaknesses.

Just about when a machine seems out of new possibilities, a new model comes along that's faster, less buggy, and more flexible. Programmers start writing for the new machine because their programs run faster and better. Before long, all the new and exciting programs take advantage of the new machine's capabilities. Interest and support for the older models begin to fade.

Meanwhile, the hardware engineers have stayed busy. Before long another machine is introduced, faster and more flexible than the one that came before. Programmers are pleased because they've started coming up against limits and want more power. They tell the hardware engineers, who include the requested capabilities in the next design. There has been much noise and debate about which drives the other, hardware or software. Your authors can be a help here: each drives the other.

The point is that when you ask about the machines, to some extent you're asking about PC history. When was a machine introduced, what were its characteristics, and what eventually replaced it as the newest and best model?

Older Models Still Useful

Bear in mind that the older designs are still widely used. Even the original PCs are still available as used machines, though they're no longer made by major manufacturers. The real question isn't whether a machine is old; it's whether a machine can do the job you need it to do. The following sections can give you an idea of what a particular machine can do by placing it in context: what came before and what came (or is coming) after?

Smaller Footprints

When a new machine is physically smaller, it's said to have a smaller *footprint.* That means it takes up less space on a desk. On first glance, this seems terrific—and often enough, it is. But you don't get smaller without paying a penalty. Smaller designs may mean the machine uses nonstandard or hard-to-find parts. It may be harder to repair or to change settings. It may not have enough expansion slots. Buyers need to take a good look at the trade-offs involved in giving up serviceability and expansion potential for desk space and a sleek appearance.

On the other hand, size often counts for a lot. On an executive's desk or a small writing desk, or in a plane or anyplace else with limited space, a tiny computer with the full power and capacity of a desktop machine can have much appeal. Figure 2-1 shows one elegant answer to the demand for more. The Ergo 386X-based machine (also called the Brick) is more portable and offers more power in less space with its 8-by-11-inch footprint. This 386SX can fit inside half a normal briefcase with plenty of room left over for binders containing 8 1/2-by-11-inch documents.

Since laptops are used about 85 percent of the time for commuting between two or three known locations, the Brick was designed to make the system unit itself portable. A docking system lets you snap the main unit in and out of various keyboard and monitor locations. An aluminum case doubles as a heat sink, which means that heat is easily transferred from it

Figure 2-1

Ergo 8-by-11-inch footprint 386-based machine

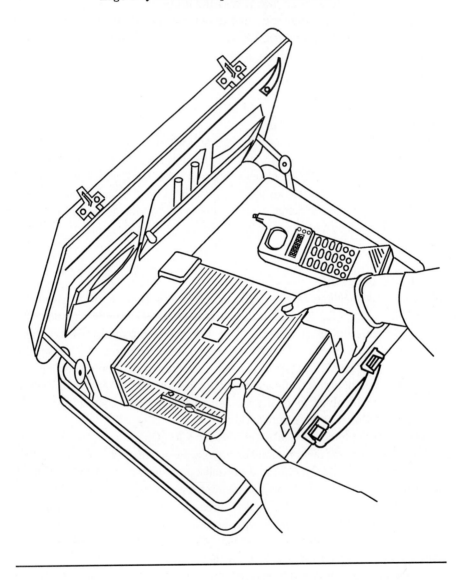

to the surrounding air and the machine does not overheat, allowing use of a super-quiet whisper fan instead of a standard noisy high-capacity fan.

Off-the-shelf technology keeps the cost of one Ergo system unit plus two VGAs and keyboards well below the cost of a 386 laptop computer.

The Brick is one of many reduced-footprint computers. Most people still opt for a more standard desktop design that offers other advantages, such as the ability to accept more add-on boards. Sleeker "executive" options are available in desktop machines if you want them.

MS-DOS Machines: A Brief History

The computers now usually called MS-DOS machines originated commercially with IBM in 1981. The original IBM PC, which gave this type of computer its name, used an Intel CPU. MS-DOS machines have pretty much stuck with Intel processors since then. As a result, people refer to these computers both by the IBM machine designator and by the number of the Intel chip they use. In the short descriptions below, the section headings will refer to both designations because that's what you'll see in ads, stores, and swap meets.

IBM PC — Intel 8088 Chip

The IBM PC (personal computer) and its clones had one or two floppy disk drives, very limited memory (or *RAM* — random access memory), and an operating system that didn't always work right. Still, the then-new Intel 8088 chip made it the first really practical desktop machine. It screamed along at 4.77 megahertz (MHz), almost 5 million cycles per second, and operated on 16 bits of data at a time. That's a lot slower than a 25 or 33 MHz 386 racing through data 32 bits at a time. But it was nearly five times as fast as the leading small computer of the time, so it blew the socks off the competition. IBM designed it from off-the-shelf parts and expected to sell around 10,000 a year, but when the PC hit the stores IBM couldn't keep up with the orders.

PC XT — Intel 8088 and 8086

The PC XT (XT for extra or maybe for extended technology, depending on who you talk to) was a 1983 upgrade that used either the 8088 or 8086 chip. The latter was an earlier chip that the original PC-DOS was written for. It could move data in and out faster than an 8088, but it had a smaller instruction set (that is, it couldn't carry out as many operations).

In practical terms, what immediately made the XT a new standard business machine was not memory, speed, or a beefed-up power supply. It was the built-in 10 megabyte (10MB) hard disk. Such a PC was bound to be a hit. It let the operator load programs and change files without fumbling through stacks of 5 1/4-inch disks. It practically eliminated one management headache—keeping track of all those migrating floppies. Now a department manager could maintain a single collection without worrying about who had which disk. (Later, IBM offered a bare-bones, floppy-only model in which the user could install a hard drive at a later date.)

The XT is still widely used. Turbo versions—fast XTs using 8088-2 chips—are popular with students, small businesses, and others. They're OK if you do not need more power or memory, or are on a tight budget. The XT is on the wane, however, as prices for low-end ATs (the next step up) drop to within about $100 of XTs. It has taken the AT longer to displace the XT than it did for the XT to displace the PC as the standard machine, but the process is nearly complete.

PC AT—Intel 80286

In 1984, Intel finished reengineering its 8088 and 8086 chips into a single fast data handler designated the 80286. This new chip's advances included higher clock speeds and the ability to handle additional memory—up to 16MB in a special protected operating mode, compared to an XT's 640K limit. The chip could not switch back and forth between normal and protected modes without restarting, or *rebooting*, the computer. This reduced the usefulness of the extra, or *extended* memory. Still, it could be used for other duties like making programs run much faster by eliminating unnecessary disk reads.

IBM designed its new PC AT (advanced technology) computer around this new CPU. Like the PC XT, it quickly became the high-end standard for business use. The AT came with 1024K or, rounding down, 1 megabyte of memory. Its hard disk stored 20MB of data, twice the capacity of the XT's hard disk. AT-class systems also introduced a 1.2 MB high density 5 1/4-inch disk drive that accepted much more data on the same size disk. This made backup file storage much less bothersome. The standard 360K disk remained the favored medium for distributing programs.

An AT is faster and more flexible than an XT. ATs did have a few problems at first, of course. The most notable snag was a flawed hard disk design. Users reported so many hard disk failures that a national computer magazine published a famous cover showing an AT being attacked with a fire ax. The hard drive design was quickly changed and the AT became the workhorse of MS-DOS computing. Many different brands and models of

286-based computers are manufactured today. As the small business computer of choice, it is only now falling under the shadow of 32-bit 80386SX and 80386 CPU machines—the next wave.

386 Machines—Intel 80386 and 80386SX

In 1986, Intel released its 80386 chip—a CPU that could process data in 32-bit, not 16-bit, chunks. It also could do two or more tasks at once without having to reboot the computer afterward. It could directly manage up to 4 *gigabytes* (4 billion bytes) of memory, compared to the AT's 16MB limit. The chip was expensive but it had significant practical advantages. IBM had another sure winner in this one, people thought.

At this time, though, a couple of significant changes happened in the PC market. First, it wasn't IBM but Compaq, an early manufacturer of IBM compatibles, that released the first 386-based computer. This remarkable machine boasted clock speeds faster than the fastest 286 AT-class machine and took full advantage of the 386-class, 32-bit processing. Second, IBM chose to abandon what had become widely regarded as the IBM standard for machines based on MS- and PC-DOS. Instead, IBM adopted a new design for the *bus* (circuitry) that carries data between different hardware components (see the next section, titled "IBM PS/2 Machines").

Now we had a Compaq standard for 386-based MS-DOS computing, not an IBM standard. The Compaq 386 took the upper end of the PC market by storm. Compaq did not keep its solitary place for long, though, as other manufacturers quickly jumped into the fray and prices dropped. At this writing, the 386 has become the business machine processor of choice because of its speed, power, and flexibility. It is not yet the workhorse of business machines, partly because it has not yet found its appropriate price level. Also, there is a huge installed base of 80286 machines. But the transition is well underway, primarily because of a less pricey version of the chip that brought 386-class computing into the 286-class price range.

This new version was dubbed the 80386SX. Introduced in 1988, the SX offers 32-bit processing on a 16-bit bus. This means that, although it can process data in 32-bit chunks like an 80386 chip, in other respects it acts more like an AT. For example, it can move data in and out of memory, storage, or other devices only in 16-bit blocks, like an AT. (16- and 32-bit bus designs are described further in Chapter 15.) The upshot is that the 386SX 16-bit bus loses some of the 386 speed advantage over a 286 chip, but it does keep other important strengths, such as 32-bit processing and doing several tasks at once (*multitasking*). The SX is also much cheaper to make. The 386SX provides a natural upgrade path for owners of 286-based machines.

IBM PS/2 Machines

In 1987, IBM stopped making PC-style (or "IBM-standard") computers. They switched to a proprietary bus interface called *Micro Channel Architecture,* or MCA, and a new operating system called *OS/2.* IBM dubbed these new computers PS/2 machines and waited for the stampede of customers. At this writing they're still waiting. For one thing, IBM wants a steep licensing fee from "clone makers," many of whom have resisted paying since it would remove their competitive advantage. So the IBM licensing fee has reduced competition in the PS/2 market.

This has not automatically made a soft bed for IBM. For one thing, there is an incredibly rich installed base of MS-DOS software and AT-style add-on boards. These do not run on MCA computers. Since converting to MCA means you've lost any existing investment in boards and software, there is no easy or natural upgrade path. In addition, a group of eight major clone makers got together and designed an upgraded bus called the *Enhanced Industry Standard Architecture,* or EISA. This 32-bit bus is available without license fees and does accept AT-style boards. Which, if either, of these new architectures will become dominant is far from settled.

AT-style boards remain the norm for stand-alone machines at this time. They're now often called *Industry Standard Architecture* or ISA boards, in a sort of backdated and reverse engineered salute to the new EISA design.

486 Machines—Intel 80486

When the first Intel 80486 computers came out late in 1989, desktop (or, more accurately, by-the-desk upright) PCs hit the big time in terms of processing power. The 486 is in a class with minicomputers in terms of speed and capacity. The new chip combines the power of the 80386 CPU, the 80387 coprocessor, and several other important enhancements that had required several complex and individually mounted chips. Pulling that off took the equivalent of nearly 1.2 million transistors on a chip less than a square inch in size.

The first 486-based machines were available in various data transfer and device interface designs. These machines are not really designed to run DOS *applications* (programs designed to carry out specific tasks); rather, they are a direct challenge to software designers to think bigger. Applications designed for the 486 can take advantage of huge physical memory space and do the same kinds of things that minicomputers and even mainframes do. Until prices drop, a 486-based machine will be a real extravagance for standard DOS applications like word processing and spreadsheets. It shows its real strength only on applications that demand high performance and massive computing capacity, such as computer aided design, multiuser networks, and advanced statistics. The main reason is that it has a math coprocessor and a memory cache built in, instead of added elsewhere on the motherboard. This saves a lot of data transfer computing time. When prices come down for this computer, it will make an ideal choice for small to medium-sized offices that could benefit from networking capabilities.

Compatibility and Value

At each level, from PC through XT, AT, 386SX, and 386, more than a dozen different manufacturers make machines that can run the same operating systems and software. The technology is still evolving at the top of the market, among the 33 MHz 80386 screamers and 80486 powerhouses. It's no surprise that some hardware and software compatibility problems have cropped up. If you're thinking about upgrading to a high-end machine, make sure it can run all your major applications before you sign the check.

Major small-computer magazines like *PC Magazine, PC World,* and others frequently run tightly controlled tests to help potential buyers compare machines. The testing often reveals any compatibility problems, and provides a basis for comparison of different machines as well. It is well worth the time to spend an afternoon at the library reading reviews before going shopping. There are some great values out there, but there are also some overpriced and overhyped dogs. Computer magazine reviews will point you toward the good values.

COST EFFECTIVENESS

If you want to use word processing, spreadsheet, database, or other standard applications, any current desktop computer will do the work. This book, of course, is geared to IBM-compatible systems, which offer many more options and features than the others. (In many respects, this power also translates into more complexity, but we'll suggest ways to simplify your operations in Chapters 6 through 11.)

It was not always the rule that what you could do on one brand of computer you could do about as well on another. In the next few sections you'll read about how things have changed through the years and how to use the patterns of the hardware and software market to your advantage.

When Software Dictated the System

Not long ago, most computer experts would have told you to pick the software you needed and then get hardware to run it. Roughly speaking, IBM specialized in words and numbers, the Apple II ran spreadsheets, and CP/M machines had thousands of general programs available. Commodore 64 computers had thousands of games and some very good small-business programs. (See Chapter 6 for more on these non-MS-DOS systems.) Specialized word processing computers had operating systems devoted solely to manipulating text—and did their job so well that many are still in use today.

Personal computer hardware and software quickly evolved to eliminate that kind of specialization. Small computers are not by nature specialized. Once a program is developed it can usually be translated without much trouble for other machines. Before long the day of specialization was over. It is no longer common for software to determine the hardware.

Letting Cost Set the Limits

With certain limited exceptions, the wealth of software developed for IBM, Apple, or Macintosh machines these days soon becomes available for other brands as well. The amount of computing power needed by a buyer is now often decided by his or her budget. The following paragraphs will suggest ways to make the most of your computing budget.

Stretching the Dollar

If you're willing to forsake the more expensive name brands, you can make a dollar go a bit further. If you're willing to buy a machine on the used

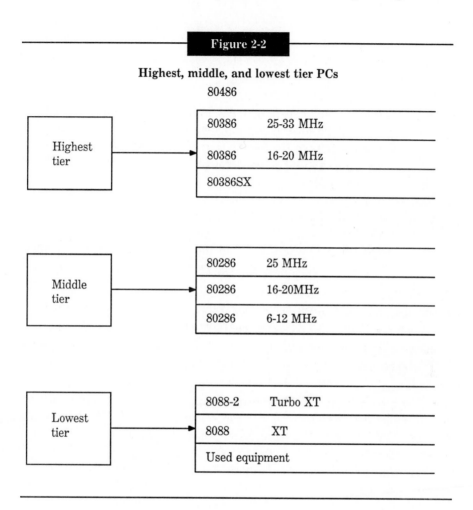

Figure 2-2

Highest, middle, and lowest tier PCs

market, you can stretch your dollar even further, although (as with anything used) you're not likely to get a warranty. (See Appendix F for a discussion of computing equipment sources.)

High, Mid, and Low Range

Among MS-DOS machines, the cost categories translate roughly into three tiers—highest, middle, and lowest. These divisions are shown in Figure 2-2. In dollar amounts, the boundaries are arbitrary but can be set roughly like this:

$2500 and higher—highest tier
$1200 to $2500—middle tier
Less than $1200—lowest tier

If you can afford it, you'll benefit by going to the low-cost end of the highest tier. The reasons will be covered in a moment. If your budget does not allow that strategy, try to stay in the middle tier. If your budget puts you in the lowest tier, consider getting a used computer; you can often find used middle tier equipment at lowest tier prices.

The reasons buying from the low-cost end of the highest tier will work in your favor include the following:

- The highest tier is where you find the currently developing computers. They will be supported by engineers and programmers for some time to come.

- High tier computers keep their value longer in the used or resale market, should you decide to upgrade someday.

- At the low end of the high range, the machines have been around for awhile. They're debugged and in their prime.

That's not to say you should be extravagant. As with anything electronic, from satellite dishes to stereos, you can spend your whole inheritance on a system . . . or you can get a basic system that barely does the job. The best course is usually somewhere between the extremes.

Buying at the low end of the high range puts you in the middle of a product's life cycle. That's the best place for most users. At this writing, the low end of the highest tier translates to an 80386- or 80386SX-based system with a clock speed of 16 to 25 MHz. Faster 33 MHz 386-based systems and the new memory-rich 486-based systems are at the pricey (and sometimes buggy) end of the highest tier. The 286 systems form the middle tier and XTs are on the lowest tier.

Used Equipment Versus New

Used equipment is not useless. Far from it. Equipment traded in by someone else may fit your needs perfectly, just as the computer you trade in may be just what someone else needs. Many users have found that used computers serve their purpose and save a lot of money. Good technology never really fades, after all. The abacus is still a best seller in Asia and pencils will be around for as long as humans need erasers. An old PC running a message center for electronic mail is as useful as ever, and buying a used machine will remain a good way to save money.

Remember, though, that engineers and programmers like to take the existing technology to its limits. They do not hang around improving old work when newer, more powerful technology comes along. For the same reason, programmers do not write new programs for old equipment. You can still run the original word processors on the original PCs, but you'll have problems running this year's graphics-oriented desktop publishing systems. There's just not enough memory. Even if there were, you could take a nap while the program reformats a single page. As for long documents, train someone to replace you in case you retire and move away before it finishes.

Older equipment can often be purchased at exceptionally low prices in the used equipment market (see Appendix F). Weigh the cost against the risks before you buy used equipment, but bear it in mind as a good way to move up a tier even with severe budget constraints.

Patterns of Change

As technology changes the old approaches evolve, even though you can find people using older products years later. Makers of automobiles and appliances discovered long ago that products based on today's technology have only a limited time at the top of the marketing heap before replacements come along. The period during which a product is considered current, or modern, is called the *product life cycle*. This cycle is described next.

THE PRODUCT LIFE CYCLE

A product's life cycle is the period from its introduction, often with much hoopla, until its retirement from the market when a newer and better (or at least different) design replaces it. With computers, this cycle can be complete long before the equipment is even paid for or amortized against taxes; the obsolete computer probably will still work perfectly well. It can rankle sometimes when that old PC in the corner, doing yeoman's service driving a printer or acting as an electronic mail center, is labeled obsolete. Well, things move fast in the world of computers. To stay even with technological advances, it's important to keep your current purchases somewhere around the middle of the life cycle.

When to Buy

Henry Ford changed from the Model T to the Model A only under protest, but these days all products have an expected marketing life cycle. The middle of this cycle is the prime of life for a computer. Buying your PC in the middle offers many advantages:

- Brand new products have bugs. When a product has been around for a year or two, the bugs have been worked out.

- Products enjoy repeated price decreases as production gears up. Eventually, at the middle of their life cycle, decreasing prices cross the curve of increasing software support and the equipment becomes cost effective. That's the time to buy.

- A mid-life product has already had several hardware enhancements, and may have several to go. As advances continue, you can often extend your machine's effective life by getting add-on products like turbo boards.

- A mid-life product has a full range of software—you won't sit around waiting, or have to invest money in software you *know* you will need to upgrade soon.

- The product made it. Sometimes poor designs are introduced with high hopes and fanfare, but they usually fall into limbo before they get to mid-life. A product that isn't going to make it usually drops out of sight within a couple of years.

Using the Life-Cycle Rule When Buying

To use the life cycle to your advantage when buying new equipment, try to stick with equipment somewhere around the middle of its cycle. That now translates to 386 and 386SX systems. The 386 has arrived, meaning 386-based computers are replacing earlier machines as the MS-DOS desktop computer of choice.

By way of contrast, the XT, though widely available at low prices, is fading fast; it is nowhere near the middle of its life cycle. The workhorse AT is current, and is available at some great prices, but it is near the end of its life cycle. As for the venerable 8088-based PC—you'll find it mostly on the used machine market. Here is the situation in more detail, as of the early 1990s.

Original PCs

The original PC systems, with their 360K disk drives, limited memory, and slow operating speeds, have joined the early CP/M machines as historical artifacts. They were terrific in their time, but their time is not now. You will find yourself constantly frustrated if you try to run today's programs on these machines; they're just not built for it. That doesn't mean they're useless if you already have one; they still can run the old programs. But if you're buying a machine, even on the used market, get a newer design.

XT Systems

For most users it no longer makes much sense to buy an XT-class system, although they are still available. With their 8-bit bus, they're too slow for current programs, even with faster clock rates. They have trouble with the computing demands of programs designed for 16 MHz and faster systems using 16- or 32-bit buses and 286 or 386 processors. Programmers write for new capabilities, so older machines may take what seems like forever chugging along at tasks that whiz by on the newer designs.

Turbo-XTs based on the 8088-2 processor chip have extended the XT's useful life. You see these fast little machines in video rental stores and other places that need only to maintain a small database or perform other routine tasks. They're used where speed and power are not terribly important. Newer XT machines sometimes have sockets to add up to a full megabyte of memory, instead of stopping at the XT's traditional upper limit of 640K. These additional memory machines can take advantage of 384K of high memory—memory above 640K—and thus can run even more like an AT. Of course, at some point you have to wonder what the advantage is in paying the extra money required to mimic an AT when you can get an AT for about the same price.

Other things being equal, try to balance the factors of price, performance, life expectancy, and resale value. With the XT cycling down and the AT available for very little more than a turbo-XT, a new XT may not be the best choice. Students and others on a tight budget may decide to get an XT and spend the extra money on additional software. But in general it makes less and less sense to stop short of an AT's capabilities. An AT now costs only $50 or $60 more than a turbo-XT. If your budget can't swing that much extra, you may want to look into the used computer market. ATs are available there at very reasonable prices.

AT Systems

The 286-based AT should still be alive and current several years from now, but it too is fading. At this writing, 286-based machines are a bargain hunter's delight, at the cheap end of the life cycle. There is a huge base of available hardware and software for this machine, and it is the workhorse of the MS-DOS world. New 286-class machines are available for not much more than a turbo-XT. And, for most stand-alone applications, an AT will do whatever you need it to do. For home and other small systems, the AT may be the most cost-effective choice until 386 systems come down more in cost.

386 and 386SX Systems

The 386 and 386SX machines are now well settled in the market. They have enjoyed several price decreases with more likely in the future, and they cost not much more than an AT. For the small extra charge, they offer enhanced computing power. In short, 386 and 386SX machines are just hitting their mid-life stride and are a safe investment for dollar-conscious buyers.

PS/2 Systems

If you're a dyed-in-the-wool IBM fan, PS/2 systems are a fine way to go. (For the rest of us, standard MS-DOS clones may be more cost effective.) Some PS/2 machines are Micro Channel Architecture, but some are not. You have a choice of using either the DOS or OS/2 operating system. This book concentrates on MS-DOS machines; for information on PS/2 and OS/2 computers, contact an authorized IBM dealer.

REACHING A DECISION

The most basic operating factors to consider are speed, capacity, and cost. Many people have trouble separating speed and capacity, and it's true they're related, but they're not quite the same thing. It's like the difference between a Boeing 747 and a jet fighter—the first has capacity, the second, speed. Only when you compare it to a Piper Cub does the 747 start to look speedy. In computing terms, a 386 has more capacity than a 286 or an 8088. An add-on turbo board may speed up an XT, but it will still not have the computing capacity of a 286.

Still, 286-based systems are less expensive and can perform tasks such as word processing—and even desktop publishing—fast enough for many users. When selecting between systems, you have considerable latitude in several areas. The following section offers some pros and cons for various types of systems. The right choice is one that balances cost against speed, capacity, and possibly resale value.

Capacity, Flexibility, and Options

It's important not to under-buy your system. Given a choice, do say "yes" to options like a hard disk, good first-run software, and a good color or graphics monochrome monitor. There are uncounted closets out there hiding computers without hard disks, or with low-resolution color or monochrome displays. Without computing capacity or the right kind and amount of software, the system's main value to you may be as a yard sale item.

Years ago, the cost of items like hard disks, tape backup units, and other add-ons was very high relative to the entire system. Expensive "extras" might have doubled the cost of your system.

It's a lot easier now because buyers get more for their money. Increasing capacity, power, and flexibility at lower prices have made decisions easier, except perhaps for starving students and habitual bargain hunters. A hard disk can cost as little as $200, and a good color monitor about the same. These are extras you'll be truly glad you have once you've been computing for awhile.

Choices

If you buy a prepackaged computer at a mass outlet, many of your choices will have been made for you. There are advantages and disadvantages to this (see Appendix F). We'll assume here that you're configuring your own system and will need to make some decisions. Remember that hardware and software together form a system, and your selections in one area will affect what options are practical in the other. For example, resource hungry applications like computer aided design, desktop publishing, and multitasking systems require adequate raw computing power, disk storage, and memory.

You and your dealer are in the best position to decide which system best fits your needs. Talk to computer-literate friends and colleagues before you go shopping; their experience and opinions will often be invaluable. Ask them to help you familiarize yourself with the various models available. Your dealer also can offer valuable guidance, but even the most helpful salesperson will have a big stake in making a final sale. You must be the final judge of your own needs.

Before going into a store or choosing your system, you may find it helpful to make a wish list to help you set priorities. Glance through Appendix F for suggestions on judging stores and other computer supply channels.

Here are some other selection guidelines.

FCC Approval

The Federal Communication Commission (FCC) issues Class A and Class B ratings and approvals for computers sold for use in the United States. Class A machines may be used in places of business, where interference with radio and television is not usually a central issue. Class B machines, which require shielded interface cables, are approved for residential as well as business use.

FCC rating notices in the front of computer manuals may seem like just more government small print, but the agency is touchy about radio noise. Ham operators who hear buzzing on a ham channel sometimes will walk around a neighborhood ringing door bells. They're trying to find unfiltered TVs or non-FCC computer systems or even vacuum cleaners making static. If the ham operator reports you to the FCC, the agency *will* investigate; the FCC does not ignore complaints, and has been known to confiscate unapproved equipment.

If the FCC has rated your computer for the use you intend (home or business environment), you also will be safer from low-level emissions. Danger from such emissions is not proved, but the evidence is mounting. It makes sense to buy equipment that complies with FCC rules.

Computer Model

In decreasing order of size, models include desktop, upright or floor models, portables or "luggables," laptops, and notebooks. In general terms, the

---

Figure 2-3

Desktop computer

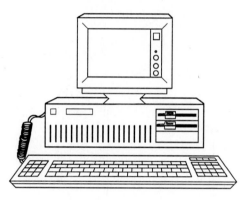

---

smaller the computer, the newer and more expensive it is and the less proven its technology.

Desktop Models   This, the oldest design, is also the most widely used. You'll often see this design sitting on a desk with a monitor on top and keyboard in front (see Figure 2-3). In many respects this is the most convenient design, although it takes up more desk space than some other designs.

Upright Models   This floor model design, introduced by NEC as the trademarked Tower, takes the computer off the desk and sets it on end beside the desk (see Figure 2-4). Upright models save the desk space for the human, and so are very popular. Some potential problems, especially with cheaper models, include:

- *Dust*   They're on the floor, close to the source.

- *Heat*   The power supply is usually at the bottom of the unit, and heat rises; this is bad for electronic components.

- *Vulnerability*   The units are out of sight and subject to being jarred accidentally by knees, chair legs, passersby, and so on.

Figure 2-1

Upright (floor model) computer

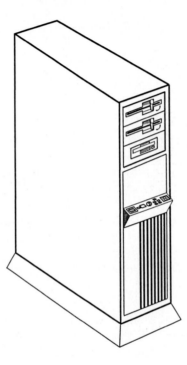

A hefty cooling fan that can provide more than normal air flow through the case will help the heat problem. Some high-end models even have two cooling fans. Dust may or may not be a factor in your environment. Picking a good location (refer to Chapter 3), out of harm's way, will minimize the risks of jarring.

Transportables   This category includes the original Compaq "luggable" computer and its look-alikes. These machines (see Figure 2-5) are about the size of a sewing machine, and just about as heavy. Luggables are still available on the used market. They are not battery powered and must be plugged into a normal power outlet. They are transportable mainly in the sense that, like the sewing machines they resemble, you can put them away

Figure 2-5

Portable ("luggable") computer

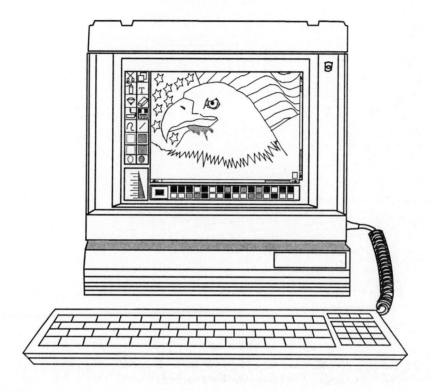

between sessions without fooling around with too many cables and connectors.

Laptops   These machines (see Figure 2-6), while not comfortable to operate on your lap, are the first truly portable computers. Like portable radios, you can pick them up by their handles, carry them around, and turn them on wherever you want. Many models can run for several hours on battery power, although some require an AC outlet. Most laptops have twisted crystal or gas plasma video displays less than an inch thick. These new displays are getting more readable as the technology improves. Newer laptops sport hard disks and full size keyboards, and many people use them like portables—they take out the laptop and turn it on when they need a

Figure 2-6

Laptop computer

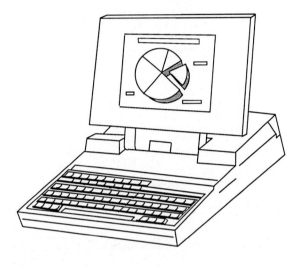

computer, then put it away again between sessions. Others use laptops to take work between home and office, or between other locations.

The technology to produce working computers this size is new and bugs are still being worked out. If you opt for a laptop, be prepared to pay a premium. Laptops are becoming increasingly popular as the screens get more readable and the miniature hard disks get more reliable, but prices haven't yet stabilized.

Notebooks   These tiny computers (see Figure 2-7) are the newest design to hit the market, and are still under development. Notebook computers may use battery-backed RAM for storage instead of actual hard disks, an approach pioneered by NEC in its UltraLite notebook. If your notebook computer doesn't have a 3 1/2-inch drive, you will need a modem or direct cable to another computer to save or share your working files. Many notebooks use battery power-saving features that blank the screen after a period of non-use or temporarily cut power to the processor without blank-

Figure 2-7

Notebook computer

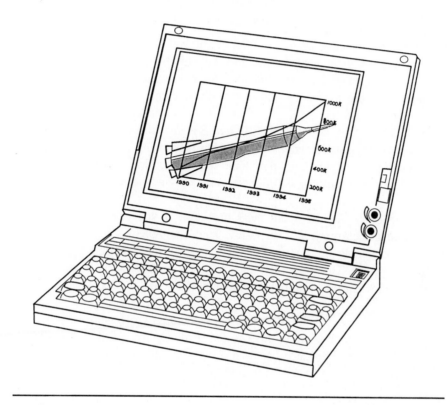

ing the memory. The aim of such schemes is to let the unit run longer between charges.

Notebook computers are very popular with reporters and others who need to take electronic notes when no wall outlets are available. Notebooks typically weigh seven pounds or less, so you can carry one around for hours without tiring. They are the first computers you can use easily on an airplane, even when the passenger in front of you leans the seat back in snooze position. (Be aware, though, that a pilot may ban the use of computers during flights, and the pilot has the last word.)

New credit-card sized hard disks may make notebooks practical, like laptops, as primary computers. Still, they are best used as secondary computers unless you do nearly all your computing on the go.

Central Processing Unit (CPU)

Once you've decided what style of computer you want, the next question is what processor to get. Original-style PCs should be out of the running; even on the used market, XTs are available for about the same price. The new 486 machines are expensive and not really designed for stand-alone, MS-DOS-type applications.

That leaves the XT, AT, 386SX, and 386 machines. These choices are listed below, roughly in order of computing power and cost. Note, however, that the newest laptop and notebook technology will eat large holes in limited budgets, especially if you insist on a full-fledged 386-based machine.

8088 or 8088-2   An XT is an 8088 machine. If you can afford one, you should think about getting a turbo-XT. That's an 8088-2—a faster machine. Both are available in the used market and at mass outlets for bargain basement prices. However, low-end AT-class machines with small hard disks and monochrome monitors are available for under $800.

80286   This seems like the next step up, but unless you have severe budget constraints, consider shelling out the extra money for a full 386 or 386SX system. The price difference between a high-end 286 and a low-end 386SX machine can be as little as $100, and the performance will be noticeably better for many tasks.

If your needs do not include any graphics, design work, or complex number crunching, a 286 machine with a graphics monochrome monitor may do fine and will save you money. Remember, though, that the 286 is on its way out and that programmers are now writing primarily for 386-class machines.

80386 or 80386SX   If you're buying a new machine, take a good look at 386 and 386SX machines. The 386SX in particular is available at prices close to those for new 286 machines, but provides much more power and computing capacity. It does all the sophisticated tricks of a full 386 CPU and is a hard value to beat. Early in the 1990s, new-machine prices for 386-based computers can be expected to fall rapidly as production gears up. They'll be well into their life cycle, debugged, reasonably priced, and worth getting.

Memory Configurations

After picking a processor, decide how much memory you need. It will depend in part on whether you think you'll need to expand any time soon. Take into account the sizes of RAM chips now available and their cost both now and for future upgrades.

Size   For all but machines dedicated to very limited uses, get a full megabyte of memory even if you have to give up something else to get it. These are the common memory configurations:

- *512K*   This was long the standard for business computers but now is just a practical minimum. Many programs won't run in less memory, although, at this writing, few programs need more. The advantage of 512K is that you won't have to throw out memory chips, wasting money, to plug in another 512 later for a full, 1MB machine.

- *640K*   The advantage in getting a 640K machine is that all current MS-DOS programs can run in this amount of memory. It is the largest amount of memory a traditional XT-style machine can directly manage. The disadvantage is that, if you upgrade to 1MB or more, you will have to throw out as many as eighteen 64K chips—and chips cost too much to waste casually. (See Chapter 15 for more on how chips are loaded onto the motherboard.)

- *1MB*   This is the way to go, if you can manage it. All current programs will run and you needn't worry about upgrading. Also, there is usually room for additional memory on ATs and 386 machines without changing any existing chips. If you're lucky (or careful) you may get a single 1MB chip. Then you can expand to the limit of the motherboard before fussing with add-on memory boards or the like. Many ATs and all 386 machines will take up to 4, 8, or even 16MB of memory on the motherboard. Memory prices fluctuate. Currently, the difference between 640K and 1MB of memory is $75 to $150. You can cut your memory cost in half by getting started with 1MB and avoiding the expense of changing over.

Data Storage: Hard Disks, Easy Choices

In all but the most basic single-application machines, a hard disk has become a practical necessity. Many applications won't run without one, or will run only in limited form. Hard disks are now considered low-end storage devices. Engineers are busy with high-density approaches that would have boggled minds in the days of the early, room-sized Univac computers some 40 years ago.

On the other hand, the basic long-term and backup data storage device remains the floppy disk. As machines evolved from 8088 to 386 and 486 processors, disks evolved too, in the direction of more storage in less space. The next couple of paragraphs describe disks and hard drives used in various classes of MS-DOS machines.

Disk Drives   Floppy disk drives, as described in Chapter 1, come in various sizes and densities. Except for the 2-inch diameter disks used for awhile in some laptop machines, disk storage has settled on two sizes, 3 1/2-inch and 5 1/4-inch. Each size comes in two densities, *double sided, double density* (40-track) and *high density* (80-track) storage. These choices are summarized in Table 2-1.

Your disk format will depend, at least in part, upon which type of machine you have. When buying new computers, many people specify both 3 1/2-inch and 5 1/4-inch drives to make it easier to transport files between machines. Here is a rundown on what's available for which machines. When choosing, try to keep files transportable between your computer and other computers.

- *Laptops and PS/2s*   Both laptop and PS/2 computers use 3 1/2-inch drives. If you need to trade files with laptop or PS/2 users you'll need a 3 1/2-inch drive for file portability. There are special programs (see

---

Table 2-1

Disk Drive Sizes and Capacities

Size (inches)	Description	Capacity (bytes)
5.25	Single-sided	160K/180K
5.25	Double-sided	320K/360K
5.25	High-capacity	1.2MB
3.5	Double-sided	720KB
3.5	High-capacity	1.44MB

Chapter 7) to allow file transfers using null modem cables or modems, but these are less convenient.

- *PCs and XTs* If you need transportability between your computer and an old style PC or XT machine, get a 40-track, 5 1/4-inch drive. High density (80-track) 5 1/4-inch drives can read and write to low density (40 track) disks, but they use a technique called *half-tracking*. That means they use only one of their two heads to create a 40-track disk; the tracks are only half as wide as those of standard 360K disks. PCs and XTs with 40-track drives usually cannot read half-tracked disks.

- *AT-class machines* As old-style PCs and XTs disappear from the marketplace, the need for a 40-track, 360K disk drive is diminishing. AT-class machines use 80-track, high density drives.

If you get a floppy-only system, get at least one high density, 80-track drive. These floppies of 1.2MB (5 1/4-inch) or 1.44MB (3 1/2-inch) capacity are large enough to run most common applications on a single disk.

Hard Disk Size If you do get a hard disk—and most systems really need one—should you get one in the 20 to 40MB range, or get one 70MB or larger? If you can afford it, get at least a 40MB model. Applications programs keep getting larger, and the 20MB disk standard is just too limited now for most users.

For general business use, larger hard disks are preferable. Business applications are likely to run the gamut from databases to desktop publishing. A 40MB hard disk probably won't hold everything at once, leaving you to make room for one application at the expense of another. There are ways to do this (for example, you can load applications onto the hard disk only when using them), but they are not convenient.

Machines used for only one or two major applications programs may be fine with a single 40MB hard disk. Bear in mind that programs get bigger as the machines for which they are written gain computing capacity. Not long ago few thought anyone would ever "really need" more than 10MB of storage on a PC. A 100MB hard disk may be more than you "really need" now, but experience shows this can change before you know it.

Monitors

After the storage devices, you need to pick a monitor. The video display you select when buying will likely be the one you keep, because otherwise you'll need to replace graphic boards and other expensive components. Pick the one you want at the start and you won't have to worry about upgrading.

Monitors come in various sizes, shapes, and capabilities, from straight monochrome to high-resolution color to black-on-white Super VGAs with full-page screens for desktop publishing. For now, the VGA is the standard color display.

Should you, then, get a VGA monitor? If you can, go for it. If the choice comes down to a monochrome monitor and another component like a printer or modem versus a VGA without the other component, take a hard look at what kind of computing you do. Color is getting more important as programmers design their screens for color instead of monochrome display. Clerks may say you don't need color if your budget is limited. They'll tell you that color is optional and doesn't add much. Here are some reasons why they're wrong.

- More and more business programs use color to guide the eye, highlight data, and in other ways make programs easier to use. Using them in monochrome is harder and can lead to mistakes.

- Almost any game or other entertainment program requires color and many won't run at all without it.

- Even desktop publishing programs increasingly use color to help the eye while arranging pages, columns, and graphics.

When buying, look at a color or high-resolution monochrome monitor the way you would a car radio—the machine runs perfectly well without it, but it won't satisfy everyone. Color adds value, takes full advantage of many programs' visual approaches, and for many users is worth getting. For those reasons, among others, conversion from monochrome to color is the most common type of system upgrade. You're better off getting a good quality color monitor (or car radio) in the first place.

Monochrome Choices   With monochrome monitors, your main choices are between amber and green. Some European studies have suggested that amber is better for the eyes, although people with astigmatism often find a green monitor more restful. Some ancient computers may still use white-on-black, alphanumeric monitors with no graphic capabilities. These were common in the early days, but they caused serious eye strain and have mostly been converted to planters, ashtrays, and boat anchors.

One other type of monochrome monitor, the black-on-white desktop publishing monitor, is actually a special purpose, high-resolution graphics monitor. This type of monitor often can display a full page at a time, including graphics and typefaces, with little or no distortion.

Resolution Whether you select color or monochrome, your next choice has to do with resolution. The resolution of a monitor is a measure of how detailed a picture it can produce. For more detail on video display technology, see Chapter 15. For most desktop machine users, the choice is between mono (MGA), CGA, EGA, VGA, and Super VGA.

Other types of monitors include liquid crystal displays and gas plasma displays used by high-end laptops and notebooks. Such displays usually come with their computers and are not specifically selectable. We'll assume here that you're going for a color monitor. Here are the commonly available choices:

- *CGA* The color graphics adaptor was the first IBM color display, and it is now out of date, although quite a few are still in use. There's no good reason to buy a new CGA—many programs now drive CGA only as an afterthought, and it shows. By EGA and VGA standards, CGA displays are very rough edged.

- *EGA* An enhanced graphics adaptor is a significant step up from CGA and provides a very readable display. The EGA's main virtue, though, is that it is easy to find on the used market and so is an inexpensive way to get high-quality graphics. If buying new, though, it is better to pay a little extra and move up to VGA.

- *VGA* The video graphics array controller works much like a TV screen controller and produces a truly readable screen. VGA monitors are now the accepted standard, so prices have fallen—a VGA monitor now costs about what an EGA cost a couple of years ago. The VGA is in the prime of its life and, at least for the next few years, will most likely be your best value.

- *Super VGA or SVGA* This controller/monitor combination gives much better resolution and better color or gray-scale sensitivity than VGA, but is an extravagance for most applications. Not many programs demand SVGA and there's no real guarantee the SVGA won't be replaced by something better. Unless you work extensively with graphics, your money may be better spent on additional memory or more storage. If you do get a Super VGA monitor, make sure you have enough memory on your VGA controller. Super VGA monitors require additional memory (512K instead of 256K, usually) on the VGA card. Without it, you might as well go for a simple VGA display.

Since VGA is the current display standard, it is the display for which programmers write. Their programs take advantage of the system's full graphics capabilities. The coming wave in word processing programs, for example, is "WYSIWYG," meaning What You See Is What You Get. Programs offering WYSIWYG screens work better and are easier to use with VGA-level graphics and color. On balance, if you get color at all and you don't get the VGA monitor, you won't get the full benefit of your programs.

Keyboards

The next important component is the keyboard. Personal tastes differ, and the only way to make an informed selection is to sit at a candidate computer and try typing on it. Most of today's keyboards are quite good and will feel familiar to touch typists. It's a standard feel established by IBM with its Selectric typewriters and, later, its standard keyboards. The "IBM feel" includes tactile feedback, which means you can feel it through your fingers when you've hit the key hard enough to send the signal on its way to the system unit. It also may have aural feedback, meaning the key clicks when you've hit it hard enough to connect.

This sort of feedback is very important to fast typists. At first, among the clone makers, keyboards often had a soft or mushy feel—your fingers would hit the key and travel down, but never reach a clear stopping point. It was possible to get used to these keyboards, but fast typists hated them. They are now, thankfully, no more than a memory.

Designs do differ. Northgate, for example, markets an Omni keyboard (see Figure 2-8) with 12 function keys, all on the left side. Other manufacturers now offer similar arrangements. If you learned to type on an older, XT-style keyboard (see Figure 2-9), with function keys on the left, Omni-type keyboards will feel very good. If you learned on an enhanced AT-style keyboard with function keys across the top (see Figure 2-10), you'll probably prefer one of those.

Printers

The monitor and keyboard are necessities. A printer is not quite, but it is close. You can share a printer with another workstation, or send files out for printing if you have to. It's next to impossible to get any work done

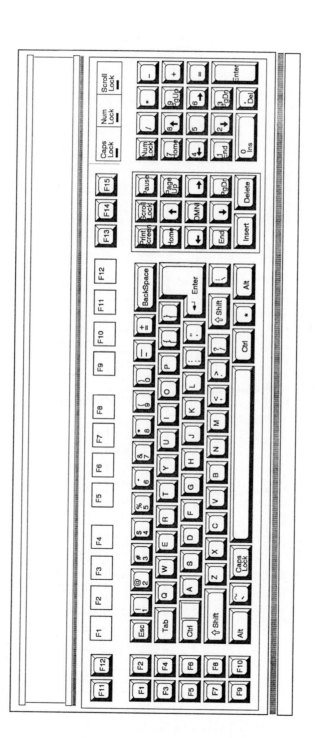

Figure 2-8

Omni keyboard (12 function keys on left)

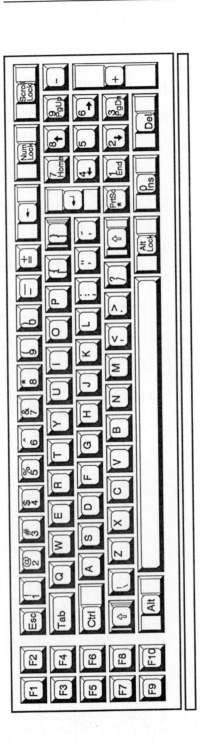

Figure 2-9

XT-style keyboard (10 function keys on left)

Figure 2-10

AT enhanced keyboard (12 function keys across top)

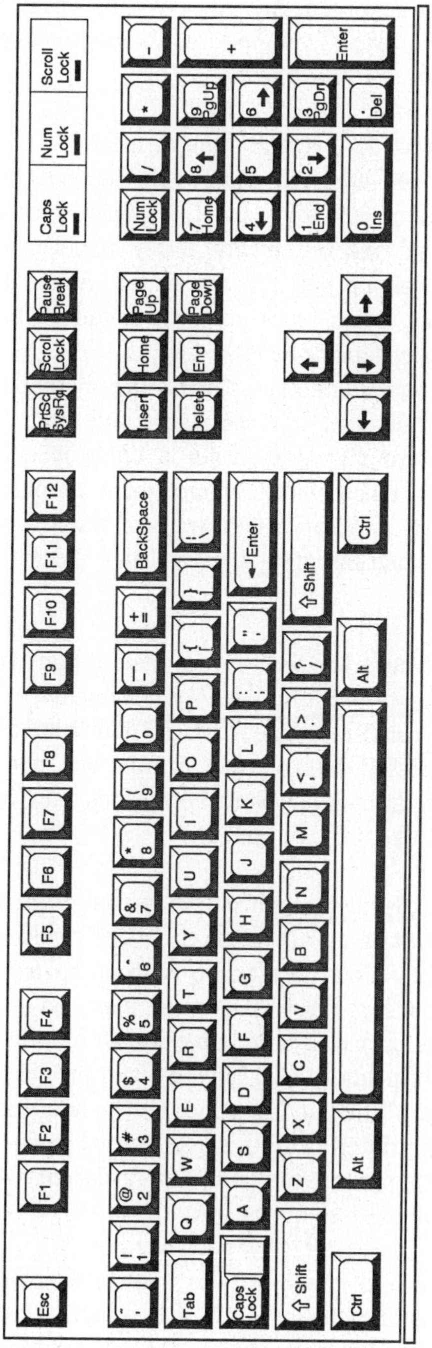

without a monitor and keyboard. Assuming you do get a printer, your next decision must be what type. Your options, in roughly increasing order of sophistication and cost, are listed here.

Daisy Wheel   This was the original style of most PC printers. Like typewriters, they strike an upraised image of the selected letter against a ribbon, which transfers it onto a sheet of paper. This resemblance to a typewriter has its good and bad points. Daisy wheel printers are terribly slow and noisy but their output is sharp edged. Also, they are useful for making multiple copies. Being more purely mechanical than other printers, they sometimes suffer reliability problems.

Daisy wheel printers were once the business standard because their output looked typed, not printed. Consultants and others who rely a great deal on personal letters may still prefer a daisy wheel printer for that reason. Unfortunately, daisy wheels cannot print graphics, a major weakness for most business applications. Nowadays, daisy wheel printers have been replaced as a business standard by laser printers and 24-pin dot matrix printers.

9-Pin Dot Matrix   These printers have a fast, rough output that is good for printing spreadsheets and draft-quality documents. A 9-pin or an inexpensive daisy wheel printer is the practical minimum choice for any but purely games-oriented PC use. A 9-pin printer will not suffice when you require high quality, although several programs can improve the 9-pin output to near letter, or business, quality.

24-Pin Dot Matrix   Because 9-pin output is rough, a 24-pin printer has about the same priority as a VGA monitor. Many would get the VGA first, but if you need to print business-quality output on a budget, the 24-pin printer is more important. It will provide *near letter quality* or NLQ printing, meaning the output is acceptable for all but the fanciest business use. The better 24-pin printers also have built-in proportional fonts, meaning letters like "i" and "l" take up less space on the line than "m" or "w." Such output resembles the printed page in books and magazines, and is easier to read than standard typed output. Some very decent 24-pin printers are available at reasonable prices.

Ink Jet   Ink jet printers spray tiny dot-matrix droplets of ink onto the paper instead of impacting pins onto a ribbon against the paper to form the characters. As a result, they are extremely quiet, lightweight power misers and are mechanically quite reliable. The earliest ink jet printers needed clay-coated paper to hold the droplets in place while drying, to keep them from bleeding like a fountain pen held against a napkin. However, newer ink jet printers use plain paper and have outputs of near-laser printer quality. These laser-like printers are still early in their life cycle, so price decreases and technical enhancements are likely in the near term.

Laser   These high-resolution printers are increasingly the standard for business use. Not many nonbusiness users can justify the expense, although this is changing as prices drop. For the time being, unless top quality printing is a high priority and you have a sizeable budget, you may want to save the laser printer for later.

Plotter   Depending upon what types of jobs you do, you may find a plotter more important than a high-quality printer. Plotters are often preferable to printers for computer aided design and other highly graphic work. Architects and engineers, for example, often rely on plotters. Like laser printers, plotters are a budget item you may want to save for later.

Color   If business or presentation graphics are your main concern, you may need a color printer to develop compelling and attractive illustrations, transparencies, charts, and other multicolor printed output. For this type of computing you also may want a more graphically oriented system than an MS-DOS machine. Many graphic artists, for example, choose an Amiga or Atari ST computer. However, this is changing as MS-DOS machines become faster and gain capacity.

Modems

A modem fulfills what used to be considered one of four basic desktop computer functions—communications. (The other basic functions were word processing, databases, and spreadsheets.) Now that fax machines are common, some feel that a modem is not really needed. But without a modem, a computer is not complete. Lack of a modem reduces the machine's capabilities drastically. Electronic messaging, or E-mail, is increasingly important for business purposes, and every serious computing system should have a modem. There is more on picking the right modem in Chapter 17.

Other Extras

See Chapter 17 for more on adding extras to your system, such as a mouse, tape backup, additional memory, scanners, and fax boards.

TRENDS

Increasingly, computers include more, faster, and better options built into the design. You can still add capabilities to your heart's content, but the days when it cost extra just to have a battery-operated clock in your machine are long past. This is great for the user, who saves a lot of trouble and expense. It does, however, have one drawback—built-in options are more rigid, so compatibility problems become harder to cope with.

At this writing, the PC market is no longer as wide open as it once was. Many people with an interest or need for a PC already have one. As a result, it is becoming a buyer's market, and all buyers reap the benefit as prices plunge. Through the next five years or so, most true innovations may be in the area of networks. Jobs that were once reserved for mainframes and minicomputers are being done by less expensive 386- and 486-based microcomputers.

This trend should continue as small businesses, medical and dental offices, retailers, and others "go digital" with low-cost computer stations that tap into continually updated databases. Meanwhile, PCs will continue to take over the boring, laborious jobs. Whenever computers bring new business methods to a company, things get shaken loose; organizations change, procedures change, requirements change.

Some observers believe that, as 386 machines with large banks of RAM become more prevalent, DOS itself will be replaced by OS/2 or some other multitasking operating system (see Chapter 6). That remains to be seen. Whatever comes about, the available hardware will play a major role.

The next chapter will take you through the first steps of putting a computer to work in your home or office—selecting a work area, unpacking the computer you selected, and installing it safely and effectively where you will be using it.

CHAPTER THREE

Unpacking and Setting Up

This chapter offers pointers on picking a good work place. You'll take the packing case there and unpack your computer where it will be installed. Before you begin, you should have read Chapters 1 and 2 so that you are familiar with the basic parts of a computer system.

PRELIMINARIES

Before you open the packing case, you need to decide where to install the computer. Take the box to that place and open it there. The reason? Packing boxes are cushioned for shipping. If something happens on the way and you drop the box, the cushioning may help your computer survive the trauma. When opening the packing case, do not damage the box so much that it can't be used again. You'll need it if you have to return the system to the manufacturer.

Where Will You Put It?

Choosing a good location for your personal computer system is important. You need to consider your physical environment, but it doesn't stop there. You also must consider how much space is available, the conditions there, the foot traffic by your work area, and the available lighting and power.

Physical Environment

A good computing environment is open, airy, well-lit, dust-free, and roomy enough for you to work comfortably. In short, it is a place where you would *like* to work. A normal, well-lit office space is fine. The simple rule is, if you'll be comfortable working there, so will your computer.

A bad environment is dusty, dark, drafty, cramped, wet, or dirty. Given a choice, don't convert a garage or closet into your computer room. The section "Make the Most of Available Space" later in this chapter tells how to use limited space to advantage. Read "A Good Place to Work" for some additional guidelines on choosing your computing environment.

Power Supply

You'll need enough electricity to power your computer and all its attached equipment. To be on the safe side, it's best to use a dedicated circuit that can supply at least 15 amps without throwing a breaker. Ideally, the circuit should be used only for your computing equipment. A full 15 amps leaves room for computer equipment power demand fluctuations.

When calculating your power requirements, be sure to include all your equipment. Here's a list of common electrical devices, in rough order of power usage:

Laser printer
Other printers
Monitor
UPS (uninterrupted power supply) system
Computer
Scanner
Desk lamp

READ.ME

A Good Place to Work

When selecting your work location, keep in mind the following:

- Avoid the damp in winter, dusty in summer spare-room type of space. If you have no choice, use air cleaners and space heaters to moderate conditions as much as possible.

- Avoid high traffic areas like office entryways where people coming and going can trip, spill coffee, shake out umbrellas, and commit other unintentional mischief.

- Don't expose the computer to direct sunlight, winter drafts, or air flow from cycling heaters and coolers. Sudden temperature changes cause problems.

- Avoid direct backlighting, as from a window directly behind you. It creates screen glare.

- By the same token, avoid facing the window directly yourself. It is hard to look at a screen surrounded by glare.

- Good ventilation (not gusty drafts) is essential. Steady air circulation will help your computer maintain an even temperature.

- Don't push your computer flush against a wall or set it up in a closed-in corner. Check to see that the cooling fan exhaust (in the rear of the main computer box) and the front ventilation ports will be clear and unobstructed.

- Choose a flat, stable work surface. Rickety furniture like card tables and surfaces that are subject to vibration can damage a computer.

- Avoid soft surfaces like beds or sofas unless you have a laptop or notebook computer. Desktop computers need to be just that—located on a solid, desk-like surface.

- Keep the system away from strong magnetic sources such as telephones, photocopiers, and motor-generators. Even a magnetized paper clip can destroy data on your disks. (Office supply stores sell plastic paper clips for just that reason.)

Grounding

Computer power cords come with three-pronged, grounded plugs. There is a good reason for this: computers are terribly vulnerable to excess electrical charges from static electricity. Static electrical sparks, the kind that build up when you walk across a rug on a cold, dry day, can pack a wallop of 50,000 volts or more. They don't carry much current; otherwise, the spark would fry your hand the first time an office doorknob zapped you. However, it doesn't take much current to fry a computer chip. Some solid state current paths are only one or two wavelengths of light wide, which doesn't allow much variation of current. An ungrounded system has no way to drain off excess static and other electrical charges. Electrical paths can short out, resulting in all kinds of havoc.

There's a small industry built around warding off the evil static electrical spark. You can buy special mats to put under your chair, special grounding wires for your keyboard, and other devices. Most of the time you won't need these unless your office rug is thick enough to require a chair mat anyway. If you need a chair mat, it won't hurt to get a grounded one.

An important step in readying your work area for your computer system is determining whether you have grounded circuits. If your work area is in a new building, your outlets will probably accept three-pronged plugs. If so, the system is grounded and you can skip over this section. In some older buildings and homes you may have old-fashioned, two-pronged wall outlets. In that case, you'll have to supply your own grounding circuit.

Start by getting a ground adapter that allows three-pronged plugs to fit into two-pronged outlets. *Make sure the system is really grounded* before you use it. An ungrounded adapter is begging for trouble. Often, attaching the adapter's ground wire to the outlet faceplate screw is all you need. This is especially true in older buildings with metal conduits in the walls. Sometimes, though, this won't do the job, and you'll need to take additional steps.

Checking for Ground   Ground adapters have a wire or small metal fitting that you attach to the outlet using the small screw that mounts the faceplate to the outlet. Use an *ohmmeter* or *multimeter*, as shown here,

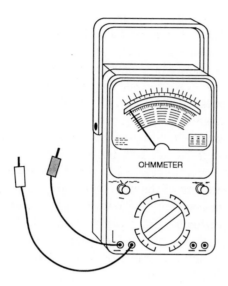

to measure resistance between the mounting screw and something that you *know* is well grounded. Any metal water pipe is a good ground. So is the soil outside your window (which is how engineers came up with the term *ground* in the first place). You should measure no resistance or, at most, one or two ohms between the adapter ground wire and the water pipe or other ground.

If water pipes or outside soil are not convenient, you could check instead between the adapter ground and something that you know *should* be grounded. For example, there should be no resistance between your adapter's ground wire and the faceplate screw of another outlet in the room.

If you don't have an ohmmeter, or don't know how to use one, call a do-it-yourselfer friend and ask for help. In the worst case, you can call a handyman or an electrician to do the checking. Such drastic steps aren't often necessary with personal computers, but for a grounded electrical system, it's worth the trouble and expense.

If you measure more than an ohm or two between your grounding point and the test point, you'll need to run a separate ground wire. It's a minor inconvenience but well worth it to protect your computer.

Running a Ground Wire   Figure 3-1 shows how to ground a two-pronged system to a nearby water pipe. You can get similar results by driving a pipe or rod a foot or more into the soil outside your window and attaching the ground wire to that. Avoid telephone or power company grounding devices, since they're designed to keep people, not equipment, safe from lightning. Utility companies install miles of wires that attract lightning. Static sparks are bad enough for your equipment—don't take chances with lightning!

When running a ground wire, there's no need to over-engineer it. Twisted lamp cord wire is inexpensive and available at any hardware store; it will do fine. Keep the wire off the floor and out of the way. Strip off about an inch of insulation at each end of the wire (hardware stores sell tools for just such a purpose). Secure one end to the water pipe using a hose clamp. Attach the other end to the adapter and faceplate using the faceplate screw, as shown in Figure 3-1. Presto—a grounded computer system. If you do the job yourself, it should cost under $5 and take maybe a half hour to run the wire.

Surge Protection

You can get inexpensive surge protectors (see Figure 3-2) at hardware stores and at Radio Shack. A surge protector is the *minimum* power supply protection you should use. Some models include noise filters; that is, they eliminate all but the basic 60 Hz (60 cycle) power needed by your equipment. Noise protection is desirable if you plan to use a modem. If your local power is not dependable, you may want to consider getting an uninterruptible power supply (discussed next) instead.

Local Power Supply

Are blackouts or brownouts common in your area? In brownouts, the lights go dim for a moment or two but the power does not fail entirely. Brownouts can damage computers more than blackouts, but both can destroy data and damage equipment. An uninterruptible power supply, or UPS, can prevent damage in areas where the power supply is undependable.

Uninterruptible Power Supply   A UPS is a battery-backup system that supplies your computer with power even when local power fails. (See Chapter 15 for more on power supplies.) UPS units are not cheap, nor do most people need them. They're for operations that handle very sensitive data or locations that frequently experience loss of power.

Figure 3-1

Adapter grounded by wire to water pipe

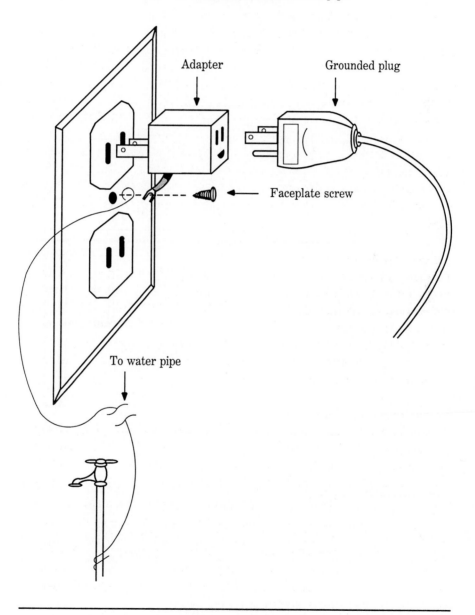

Adapter

Grounded plug

Faceplate screw

To water pipe

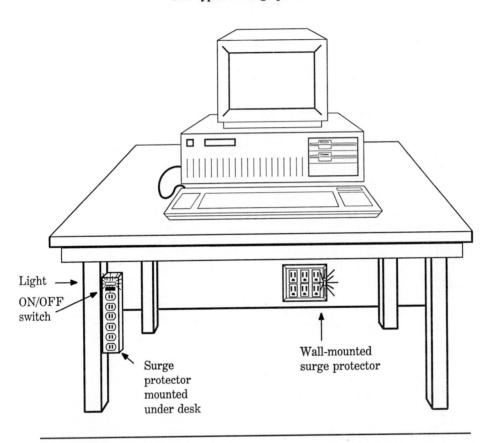

Figure 3-2

Two types of surge protectors

Light →
ON/OFF
switch →

Surge
protector
mounted
under desk

Wall-mounted
surge protector

Outlets

Computers and their attendant gear need a surprising number of outlets, but most walls only make one double outlet available. Make sure you have enough outlets for all of your equipment. Most people do fine with the six outlets on a normal surge protector of the sort described earlier. Using two surge protectors, as shown in Figure 3-2, offers extra protection.

Make the Most of Available Space

When space is limited, get furniture designed to make the most of what space you do have. Even when you have plenty of room, you'll find your working hours more productive and comfortable if you include some work-area extras in your master plan. The following sections will help familiarize you with some of these extras and some possible problems.

Computer Desk

The best computer work place includes a desk designed for computers. Many stores sell special desks with hutches that have compartments to fit the main system, as well as the monitor, books, programs, and other computer gear. Whatever setup you choose, make sure you have enough shelves, drawers, and cubbyholes to hold your supplies in a more or less organized fashion. If you will be spending long hours typing, make sure that the keyboard is at a comfortable typing level for you. Choose a chair that will support your back, maybe one with wheels so you can move freely from desk to bookcase. Comfort is a very worthwhile investment. A bare tabletop, while usable if the table is firm, will eventually get too cluttered for most people to find comfortable.

Special Furniture

Other special furniture is available. No one absolutely requires the following items, but they can make work easier, more organized, and more productive:

- Floor stand for computer (see Figure 3-3)
- Stackable trays or boxes for books and so on
- Bookcases
- Disk file boxes
- Stand-alone storage cabinet for paper, supplies, and so on

Other Considerations

Pause during the planning stages and try to think of small things that may affect how well you can work. Things that do go wrong with computers are sometimes embarrassingly obvious — *after* they happen. For example, do you have a toddler with busy hands? Think twice about putting your computer in a floor stand.

Computer in floor stand

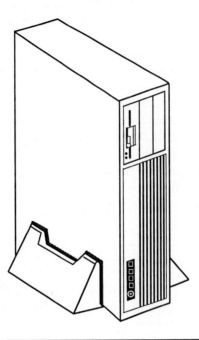

Spill Potential
Stay out of the way of spills—for example, if you're using a table, don't keep the computer right under a coffee pot. Are there pipes in the room that might flood the floor? Use cables that are long enough to keep connections off the floor. Are you a coffee drinker? Keyboards are especially apt to have coffee or soft drinks spilled on them, because that's where your hands are moving around. If you like to sip coffee or a soft drink while you work, reserve a small space for it well away from the keyboard.

Floor Stand Computer Problems
Floor stands, while popular and sometimes a good idea, can bring on problems (other than toddlers, rug scrubbers, and territorial animals) that

you'd hardly anticipate. For starters, some computers simply don't seem to run as well in a floor stand as they do when set flat on a desk. This is not true of the upright design popularized by the NEC Tower configuration, although upright designs have problems of their own (see Chapter 2).

If you have a hard disk, you'll need to format or reformat it with the computer in its upright position. Otherwise it's likely to be unreliable, since the sideways position places a new set of physical stresses on the drive.

Finally, a power supply produces a lot of heat, usually in the corner diagonally opposite the disk drives. (Chapter 15 describes these hardware components.) When you up-end the system it will be with the disk drives on top to make them easy to reach and keep them off the floor. That puts the power supply right on the bottom, where it generates heat. Heat rises. It's a bit like slow-cooking the internal boards, disk drives, and other components. The only help is to make doubly sure the unit has good air circulation around it.

Accident Potential

Keep components, cables, and power cords out of the way of children, cleaning crews, animals, and vacuum cleaner cords. Most computer owners treat their machines with kid gloves but other people don't always understand the need be careful. Sometimes all it takes to get out of harm's way is to move the desk or table so it faces in a different direction. A little forethought can go a long way—ask anyone whose child has tossed a wet raincoat onto a once healthy keyboard.

Smoke

Tobacco smoke can be extremely harmful, especially to floppy disks. Smoke is probably second only to direct sunlight as the cause of floppy disk failure. If you work with smokers, or if you are a smoker, consider making the computer space a no smoking area. (Your work time there could be a grand opportunity to cut down.)

Dust

If the area is dusty, consider installing an air filtration system. An electrostatic filter, which uses an electrical charge to remove dust particles from the air, doesn't cost a lot and can save much money over the long haul.

UNPACKING THE EQUIPMENT

Most computers these days are rugged, but you can't handle them as roughly as you can a portable radio. Always unpack your equipment in the room where you plan to use it. That way it stays in its shipping carton, packed and safe to move around, until the last possible moment. If you use the following general procedure for each piece of major equipment, you can't go wrong.

Preliminary Checks

First, make sure the equipment arrived intact, undamaged, and not missing any parts. Start by examining the packing case itself.

Place the Box on a Stable Surface
Use a solid table or any other flat, stable surface available. The floor will do in a pinch.

Check the Box
Look for outward damage to the shipping carton before you open it. If there is external damage, there is likely to be internal damage as well. If you see evidence of damage, you may want to take a snapshot in case of later questions. And don't forget to save the damaged carton.

Note: Shipping companies often require you to report damaged or missing items within 24 hours. Replace any damaged items immediately.

Keep the Packing Slip
A packing slip shows what the vendor thinks is in the box. You will usually find the packing slip in an outside envelope or plastic pocket on the shipping carton. If not, it may be inside the carton on top of the contents. Remove the packing slip first and keep it handy as you unpack the box.

Open the Shipping Carton and Remove the Contents

Don't just rip the box open; you may need to return the contents. Carefully open the box and remove the contents, setting the packing material aside in case you need to return the unit later.

Be Careful with Sharp Instruments
Most electronic equipment comes with a protective shipping cover of some

type. If you puncture it while opening the shipping carton, you're liable to scratch the equipment case or cause other physical damage.

Save the Warranty or Registration Card

Hold off filling out and sending in your warranty card until you're sure you won't need to return the system for a refund or exchange. Once you've completed and submitted your warranty card, most manufacturers will only repair your unit or offer you a reconditioned replacement. Retail dealers are more likely to permit refunds or exchanges if your unit has its original packaging, with documentation and warranty card undisturbed.

Scratching and Other Common Damage

The single most common cause of damage during unpacking is scratching by the heavy staples used to close the shipping carton. These staples are best removed by pliers, although a screwdriver works if you're careful not to damage the contents. After removing the staples, discard them someplace where passing children or pets won't be able to get them. (If you reseal the box later, you can use clear plastic tape.)

The same caution goes for the plastic foam "peanuts" used for cushioning, the metal or plastic strapping bands, and any other packing materials. Keep them out of the way of children and pets.

Keep the Packing Material

Typically, major components are cushioned by sturdy packing material. Try not to tear this material when you remove it from the shipping carton. Store the original box and molded foam at least for the period of the warranty, since you may need it to ship the equipment back for service. The original packing material is also best if you need to store or transport the equipment later.

Check the Packing Slip

Vendors rarely fail to include the large parts, but with small components like adapters, mounting bolts, and so on, mistakes do happen. Even when a vendor includes everything on the list, it's easy to lose small parts in the clutter of unpacking. The first step toward finding missing parts is to know they're missing, so *do* check the packing slip.

If a part seems missing, don't panic. The paperwork may not exactly match what you get because manufacturing specifications sometimes change in minor respects from one day to the next. The real test will come when you assemble the system and turn on the power. If something important such as a power cord or major component is missing, call the dealer to find out what happened.

When setting up a typical system, you'll unpack the computer unit, the monitor, the printer, and the modem.

Computer Unit   The main system packing crate usually contains

The system unit
The keyboard
Operating software (MS-DOS, OS/2, and so on)
Disks with GW-BASIC or an equivalent program
Other software (utilities and so on)
Accessories (usually in an envelope or plastic bag; these may include
  fasteners, adapters, and so on)
A power cord
Manuals with machine-specific information
The warranty or registration card

Monitor   The box with the monitor usually contains

The monitor unit
A monitor stand (if not integral to the monitor)
A power cord (either male, for plugging into a separate outlet, or recessed,
  for plugging into the back of the computer)
A signal cable (to connect the monitor to the computer)
A manual (typically, a pamphlet with FCC information, hardware
  specifications, and some operating instructions)
The warranty or registration card

Printer   The printer box contents usually include

The main printer unit
The printer cable
A power cord
A manual and other documents
Printer attachments (for example, sheet or tractor feeders)
The warranty or registration card

Modem If you bought an internal modem, it was probably installed for you at the store or factory. (If it was not, see Chapter 15 for board installation procedures.) If you bought an external modem, the box will probably include the following:

The main modem unit

A power cord (typically, a power adapter or transformer used to convert household [alternating current] into the DC [direct current] required by the modem)

Phone cord connectors (RJ11 jacks, which are standard, single-line phone jacks that use a modular plug and four wires)

A phone cord (with an RJ11 plug)

An RS232C computer connection cable (a standardized communications cable for use with modems, mice, printers, and other devices)

A manual detailing command sets and switch and jumper settings

The warranty or registration card

Inspect the Items Removed from the Boxes

Look for external damage caused during shipment. If you find any, notify the vendor. Anything rough enough to cause external damage to a well-packed unit is likely to cause internal problems as well. So *do not* just adopt an attitude of, "It's not serious." *Do* replace any damaged items.

MAKING THE SYSTEM READY

At this point, your equipment should be out of the carton and resting on a stable surface. The next step is to make the system ready to assemble.

Switch Settings

Check your system documentation, if it has any, for the location of user control switches. In particular, look for the following switches and controls:

Power ON/OFF Switches Set all power switches to the OFF position before you plug in the power cords. With spring-return push buttons, OFF is the *out* position (because springs last longer when they're not compressed most of the time). Other types of switches will be marked.

Power Source Selection Switches   Some computers have switches to select between 60 Hz and 50 Hz or between 115 volt and 230 volt power. If you are not sure which is used in your location, check with a local appliance or electronics store. Correct line power settings are extremely important.

Power source selection switches are usually located at the rear of the equipment (see Figure 3-4) and may require a screwdriver to change settings. This is to avoid changing settings by accident. In general, 60 Hz, 115 volt power is used in the United States, while 50 Hz, 115 volt or 230 volt power is used in some other countries.

If your computer is new, it is probably set correctly for your location. If it was not used recently in another country, it is probably set correctly. If you are not positive, call your dealer or supplier and make sure. *Do not* change these settings casually or without good reason.

Figure 3-4

Back panel power selector switch (Packard Bell 386SX)

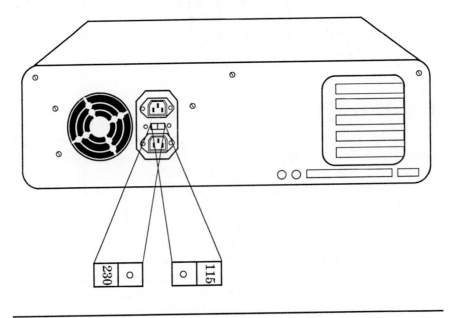

Outside DIP Switch Settings Some computers have dual in-line package (DIP) switches visible on the outside, usually at the rear of the computer, as shown here:

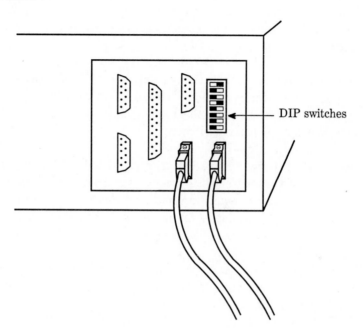

These tiny switches are usually for your video graphics adapter (the component that runs your monitor). They may also determine various technical operating characteristics of memory geometry and so on. It is best to leave the settings on DIP switches alone unless you have trouble getting your computer to run. In that case, you should consult a technician.

Battery Pack Check

Some equipment such as laptop computers, portable printers, and miniature modems comes with batteries or battery packs. Check to make sure these work and, if dated, are not too old. While a growing number of battery powered systems are shipped with fully charged batteries, many are not. Follow the directions for charging the battery that come with your system.

Battery Conditioning Pay close attention to charging periods. Some batteries require a full discharge before you can fully recharge them. Otherwise you will lose operating time, and possibly shorten the life of the

battery. Most rechargeable batteries today have circuitry designed to prevent overcharging but here, too, your best bet is to follow the directions
that come with your unit.

Manufacturers often specify rechargeable battery life in terms of usage-
hours. Look for such information on an outside nameplate and if you spot a
discrepancy, call your dealer.

Charging the Batteries   Follow the manual's instructions about charging.
Many rechargeable batteries *must* be charged for up to 24 full hours before
you use them. If you don't charge them long enough, their effective life may
be cut by as much as 50 percent or more.

Check the Battery Dates   Some batteries are dated with a specified usable or shelf life. If your battery has become over-aged, contact your dealer
for advice. Some systems require unusual and expensive batteries. These
you'll want to return immediately for newer replacements. Other systems
use common, off-the-shelf batteries that you will probably just replace
yourself and be done with it.

If the batteries are not dated, they will usually show a life in terms of
usable hours. If a battery doesn't operate for as long as it's supposed to,
return it for a newer one.

FINAL SETUP

The next step is to move the equipment to your selected work area and
hook the pieces together. Chapter 4 will cover how to connect the major
components to each other, test the system, and install it in place.

CHAPTER FOUR

Setting It Up and Turning It On

This chapter assumes you have unpacked the system's components in the area where you expect to install them. This chapter will help you connect the pieces of your system and get it operational. You can then set up the system to meet your particular requirements.

ASSEMBLE TO TEST

The first step is to set up your system so you can conduct what technicians jokingly call a "smoke test," or trial run, to make sure everything works.

Before you begin, take a look at Figure 4-1, which shows a typical PC rear panel with an assortment of connectors. The rear panel is where you will connect your external components, or peripherals. On most computers, the serial ports and parallel ports, as well as the connectors for the monitor, printer, and keyboard are labeled. The serial ports may be labeled either "serial" or "COM." Sometimes there are extra connectors for special types of monitors or other auxiliary equipment.

Figure 4-1

Rear panel

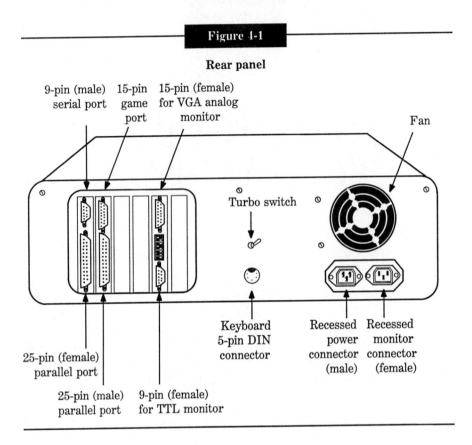

If the connectors are not clearly labeled, you're not out of luck. Cable connectors are standardized for various uses and the wrong cable simply won't fit both the rear panel connector and the associated component. Try various cable and connector combinations by trial and error. Just remember to use a gentle touch so you don't bend the pins. They are designed to "key" into the connector in a certain way; they won't fit any other.

Physical Setup

Place the system unit close to the edge of the table or desk on which you unpacked it. Position it at an angle to the table edge so you can see and work with the rear connectors.

Some PC users buy a power distribution center such as the one shown here:

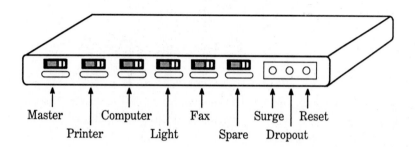

If you have one, place it near the system unit and monitor so everything can plug in easily.

Connect the Cables

Connect the keyboard and monitor to the main system, as shown in Figure 4-2. All necessary cables for the main system should have been in the carton when you unpacked it. External devices come with their own cables. The inventory you took while unpacking should have revealed any missing cables. If you did fail to notice something missing, this is another chance to find out.

Since this is just a test, do not connect the cables permanently. That is, do not tighten the mounting screws that come as part of the connector, unless the connector fits too loosely to stay on without help. Permanent connections can wait until you've moved the equipment to its final working location. For now, just push the connectors into their fittings.

To keep sparks and unintended voltage spikes from pulsing through delicate integrated circuits, hook up the signal cables first, then install the power cords. Signal cables have multi-pin connectors that fit into special fittings in the back of the computer. Power cords are thick, standard electric cords that plug into wall outlets.

Keyboard

One end of the keyboard cable usually comes attached permanently to the keyboard. The loose end usually has a round, male DIN connector that is *keyed,* as shown here:

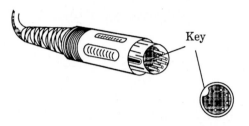

A key is a small bump or a flat area that prevents you from inserting the connector the wrong way. You may need to rotate the DIN connector slightly while applying pressure to get it started into the jack.

Figure 4-2

Cables connecting keyboard, monitor, and system unit

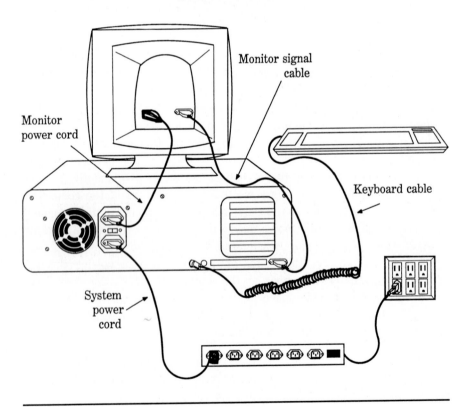

READ.ME

Saving Trouble Later

When assembling your computer system, keep the following points in mind. They'll save you trouble and frustration later.

- Loose cables and connectors cause more than half of all hardware problems. Make sure your connections are snug.

- Leave plenty of room for cooling air flow through and around the system unit. Heat is hard on electronics and death on hard disks.

- When you turn off the computer, remember to use your hard disk PARK utility, if it came with one. *Always* park your disk before moving the machine. Otherwise you can bang the read/write heads into the disk platter, which is guaranteed to cause damage.

- Make sure power is off when you connect the signal cables. Unplugging the power cord at the wall outlet is safest. Voltage spikes can play havoc with integrated circuits.

- Use a surge protector between the wall outlet and your system components.

- Observe safety rules (Chapter 5)—especially, don't plug in the computer's power cord while the system unit is open.

Most keyboards have small legs that unfold at the rear to adjust the angle and make the keyboard more comfortable to use. While setting up your keyboard, unfold the keyboard legs also.

Video Display Monitor
The monitor has two cords: a power cord and a signal cable. The signal cable is usually permanently attached to the rear of the monitor. The loose end is usually a D-type fitting, as shown here:

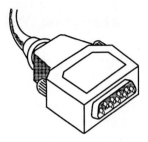

Although two other types of monitor connectors are also used, the signal cable will fit only one connector on the rear of the system unit.

Some monitors also have permanently attached power cords. If yours is not permanently attached, you'll have to plug the cord into the monitor; only one connector will fit properly. The power plug at the other end may be the familiar, three-prong grounded plug or it may be a recessed three-prong plug. These two types of plugs are shown in Figure 4-3. The normal type plugs into a surge protector. The recessed type plugs into the back of the system unit, in which case the main computer ON/OFF switch also controls the monitor. Hook up the power cords as follows:

- If it is a normal plug, connect it directly to your surge protector. The monitor will then be controlled by its own ON/OFF switch, usually located on the top or front of the monitor.

- If the plug is recessed, connect it directly to the back of your computer, near the main system power cord (see Figure 4-2). The monitor will then be controlled by the main ON/OFF switch. This arrangement is more convenient for the user, who only has to turn one switch on or off to control power to both the monitor and the system unit.

Other System Components

Other components that connect to your computer externally may include a printer, external modem, backup tape drive, scanner, and plotter. These come with separate manuals, which usually cover everything necessary to operate the equipment.

Many manuals for add-on equipment are hard to follow. If you find your system manuals confusing, see Chapter 18 for some tips on finding help. Most of all, don't be afraid to ask the vendor or manufacturer for technical support. (Look in the manual for a support telephone number.)

Figure 4-3

Normal and recessed monitor power plugs

Normal plug   Recessed plug

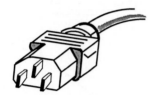

Modem   External modems connect via 25-pin RS-232C connectors (PC, XT, and PS/2 compatible models) or DB-9 connectors with 9 pins (AT-compatible models), as shown here:

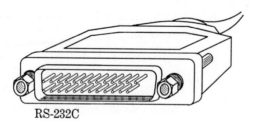

RS-232C

DB-9

Phone-line surge protectors like the one shown in Figure 4-4 are available for modems, and may be needed in locations where lightning storms are common. These special surge protectors are similar in operation to power-line surge protectors, but they protect your modem from sudden voltage changes on the phone circuit instead of on the 115 volt power line.

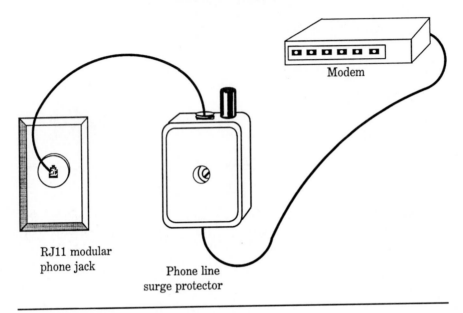

Figure 4-1

Phone line surge protector

RJ11 modular
phone jack

Modem

Phone line
surge protector

Printer   Printers use D-type, 25-pin connectors that resemble RS-232C modem connectors. You can tell a printer cable from a modem cable because, unlike a modem cable, the two ends of a printer cable will not plug into each other. Also, the printer end of the cable has a 36-contact Centronics edge connector, named for the company that first used the design. To connect it, you plug it into the printer and secure it with the two spring clips.

Pointing Devices: Mouse, Trackball, and Light Pen   The mouse, trackball, and light pen shown in Figure 4-5 are hand-operated devices that control cursor movement. They're called pointing devices because you use them to move the cursor to, or point at, a specific place on the screen—for example, a menu item. Then you click a button or take another action to make your program do something—for example, perform a menu action. Of the three devices, the mouse is by far the most widely used. See Chapter 17 for more information on using a mouse.

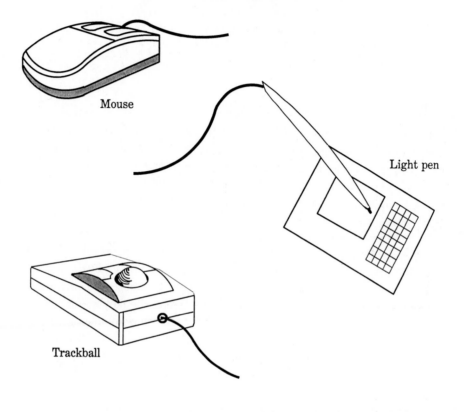

Figure 4-5

Pointing devices: mouse, trackball, and light pen

Mouse

Light pen

Trackball

A mouse or other pointing device may connect to an add-on board. More commonly, they connect to one of your computer's serial ports with a DB-9 or DIN connector. If the mouse cable does not fit correctly you may need to purchase an adapter to change from DB-9 to RS-232C or DIN. You also may need a *gender mender* to change the connector from male to female, or vice versa. A gender mender is simply an adapter that you attach to the existing connector. Computer dealers sell small gender changing adapters for very little cost.

Power-On Sequence

Wait until after the first power-on test to hook up your modem, printer, or other add-ons. Once the main system is working correctly, install the expansion (add-on) boards one at a time and repeat the test. Then install you external peripherals. That way, if you run into trouble, you'll have a pretty good idea of where the problem lies.

Assembly Complete

Your personal computer is now assembled and ready to test. If it were a radio, you could simply plug it in and turn it on. A computer system is more complex than a radio, of course. Computer users need to remember one of Murphy's better laws: "Nothing works right the first time." You should fully expect a glitch or two the first time you try out some new equipment.

If you do have a problem, it's nothing to get upset about. It just means you'll need to dig a little deeper into the technical side. Small things do go wrong and, more often than not, a bit of patient checking is all it takes to locate the problem. The solution is usually something simple. Basic remedies for startup glitches are covered in "Starting Your Computer" in Chapter 5.

Most troubleshooting can be done right from the keyboard, without removing the system unit cover. In the worst case, you may need to remove the cover and check for tight connections or something else. Troubleshooting inside the case is covered in Chapter 18.

KNOW YOUR SYSTEM

The following sections outline some of the important controls and features of your computer system components.

Check the Manuals

It is important to look through any documentation you have for your system. If the system is new, it probably came with various types of documentation including (for better brands) a system operating manual. Major components such as monitors, printers, and modems have separate manuals most of the time. Such documents won't usually mention doing a trial run, but they often will point out special interface or operating requirements. At minimum, they should tell you where to find the hardware controls and what those controls do. Look for the things suggested in the following sections.

Important Operating Controls

Most computer components have a variety of control switches, knobs, and indicator lights. It is important to have a sense of what these controls do. The best place to find out is in the documentation that came with the equipment. If documentation is missing or not adequate, look for the following standard controls before turning the system on. These controls may not all be present, but some of them certainly will be.

System Unit Controls   New designs usually place most controls on the front of the case, where users can easily reach them. Older models often had switches mounted on the side or even at the rear of the case, where the wire runs were shorter. (This is a good example of how desktop computers have evolved toward ease of use, sometimes at the expense of manufacturing or engineering convenience.) The main system unit controls are

- *ON/OFF switch*   This is the main power switch. It may be on the side of your system box but is probably in front. If it is a push button, many manufacturers will emboss a legend near it, as shown here,

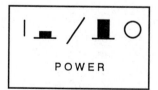

to indicate the positions: O means "OFF" and I means "ON" in standard notation. This international notation may also be used on your monitor, power distribution center, and any other components with push buttons.

- *Keyboard lock* This disables the keyboard, locking it out of the system. Some computer operations take a while to finish. You can use the keyboard lock to ensure that no one accidentally presses a key and interrupts the operation. A keyboard lock also acts as a low-level security device, discouraging snoopers in your absence.

- *Reset button* Sometimes, for no apparent reason, your keystrokes will stop getting transmitted to the computer, and the system will stop responding. This is known as a lock-up, or *crash*, and can be a major annoyance. The reset button, if your system has one, gets you out of these situations without turning off the power switch. This is a real timesaver, since anytime you turn off power you must wait until the hard disk finishes spinning down to 0 rpm before you turn power on again. Resetting turns off power only to the electronics, taking all internal chips to zero or neutral voltage but not interrupting power to the hard disk.

- *Turbo switch* This toggles your computer between fast and slow operating modes (see "Turbo Modes," later in this chapter). Newer models usually switch modes using keyboard commands, so a physical turbo switch is not needed.

Video Monitor Controls There are hundreds, if not thousands, of different monitors from which to choose, and no two brands are exactly alike. Some have special features that others lack. Most video monitors offer some or all of these controls:

- *Power ON/OFF switch* This switch may be located almost anywhere, including at the top or rear of the unit. The trend is to locate the power switch on the front, below the screen. Some monitors have it on top, others have it behind a lift-up or slide-over cosmetic panel. Some even hide it on the back of the unit.

- *Power indicator light* This light tells you if power to the unit is on or off.

- *Brightness control* This control, usually either a knob or a slide switch, controls the intensity of the screen display. There may be separate controls for background and foreground brightness. The best setting for brightness depends upon your ambient light. Generally, if there is more light (or more glare) where you are working, you will want to increase brightness.

- *Contrast control* This knob or slide switch controls the difference in intensity between the foreground and background of the screen display. If contrast is too low, the screen will be hard to read; if too high, it may strain your eyes. Adjust it to a comfortable level.

- *Horizontal/vertical holds* Many monitors have small knobs, usually at the very back, to correct for screen images that begin to scroll up or down on the screen.

- *Color controls* Color monitors often have knobs or slide switches to control the mix of onscreen colors. These are useful for controlling the appearance and brightness of intermediate colors such as brown and yellow. There also may be a switch that allows operation in a monochrome mode.

- *Size and position controls* These controls, often located in hard-to-reach places, should be set at the factory. As the monitor ages, you may find the picture changes size or "drifts" away from center. That's when you may decide to adjust these controls.

Some monitor controls may be hard to adjust. A technician servicing your monitor will use a special tool that resembles a long, slender, slotted screw driver to adjust them. Sometimes the monitor cover may have to be removed to gain access. For most users, it is best to leave such adjustments to qualified technicians.

Keyboard Controls Some keyboards have a switch at the rear or on the bottom to set them for XT or AT system units. If your keyboard came as part of a complete system, you probably will not need to change the setting—in fact, the keyboard may not even have a switch. If you bought the keyboard separately, you must set this switch correctly or your system unit will not recognize what you type. It may freeze up or even report that no keyboard is present. Some newer designs can automatically switch to the correct setting. If you notice that all your keyboard's indicator lights are on, or if nothing happens on your screen when you type something, your computer may not think there is a keyboard hooked up. Try unplugging the keyboard cable and then plugging it back in. If that doesn't help, you have good reason to suspect an incorrect switch setting. If there is no switch, your keyboard may not be compatible with the system unit, or the keyboard cable or connectors may be defective.

Turbo Modes Many computers come with selectable speeds: a slow mode and a fast, or *turbo,* mode. Computers with three speeds are also common.

Sometimes the speed must be set using a switch somewhere on the system unit. More often, at least with newer designs, the speed is selectable from the keyboard. Your manual will tell you how to select fast or slow operating speeds. For example, speed may be selected by pressing three specific keys simultaneously. The key combination will differ from brand to brand.

Keyboard selection is more convenient for the user because it doesn't require changing physical switch positions on the system unit box. Also, it probably will not require you to restart the computer to change speeds.

Most users run their machines in fast or turbo mode most of the time. Do find out how to change speeds, though, because toggling to a slower speed sometimes solves problems with certain applications programs. In particular, games often use the system clock chip to time their displays and may not work in turbo mode.

Other Equipment

Peripherals usually have independent ON/OFF switches, although some (for example, tape drives) may come on automatically when you switch on the system. If you have already connected such equipment to the system, turn off everything that you can before you turn on the power. Some peripherals, such as external disk drives, may need to be turned on before you can start the computer. The system unit usually powers these directly. If a device has a separate ON/OFF switch, the equipment's manual should be clear about whether you must turn the device on before booting. In any case, the fewer the unnecessary components you have turned on, the simpler the system is, and the easier it is to find and solve any problems.

Special Requirements

Some systems or components may have special requirements, such as battery precharges or special system setup routines. Not observing these requirements can void your warranty. Always check your owners manual for any manufacturer warnings, special requirements, and the word *void* before you turn on a new piece of equipment.

Technical Support

A growing number of manufacturers and vendors now provide a technical support phone number to call when you run into problems. That's a good

```
READ.ME
```

Technical Support: Tapping the Technology

The growing trend among manufacturers and software programmers to provide customers with free technical support has received wide (and favorable) comment. In the past, buyers often complained that they felt like buyers of used cars—once they left the lot they were on their own.

To some extent, the welcome new trend in support may be a result of the increasing importance both reviewers and the customers themselves place on support. More customers are insisting on support and many suppliers are responding. One word of caution, however: not all companies can afford heavy funding for user support. When you call a vendor's support number, be prepared to be kept on hold for a while. Some vendors make you wait for what seems like hours before a human voice comes onto the line. This is changing, but for now it still happens, and there often is no better way to get help, especially when you need specific answers to questions like: "What type of generic toner cartridge will fit my new Model X laser printer?"

Some manufacturers now use voice mail systems to help eliminate the wait on hold. For example, Packard Bell, the computer and electronics firm, takes your name and calls you back at their expense if you don't find the help you need on their detailed 800-number voice mail system. Such companies make creative use of the very technology they sell and support.

---

phone number to jot down, along with your equipment model, serial number, and purchase date. You might also want to use this information to start an automated household or office inventory system (see Chapter 7).

SMOKE TEST—THE TRIAL RUN

The trial run is called a *smoke test* because, in its purest definition, you turn on power to a new piece of equipment and look for smoke. If you see any, you turn the power off and try to figure out what went wrong.

Billows of smoke issuing from the vents are a trouble sign, for sure. Fortunately, the term is just a humorous bow to Murphy's Law: Anything that can go wrong, will. Any smoke your computer might make was made during the model's design and testing stage. By the time you buy the system, its problems or *bugs* will probably be worked out.

So, why do a smoke test? First, the equipment is new to you and it's easy to overlook something during the setup. The smoke test saves you time and trouble by letting you find and correct any problems while the system is still out on the table and easy to work with. Fixing problems is a much bigger project after you've installed everything in a hutch and hidden the connector cables behind the furniture.

Second, although manufacturers pack computers very carefully before shipping them, components do sometimes get shaken or vibrated loose. If something's not working, you may have to remove the outer case and make some simple corrections. Such fix-ups are easier when the computer is out in the open.

Treat the test run as a get-acquainted session. Turning something on for the first time makes people nervous, especially if they just assembled it themselves. Maybe it's human nature to feel a twinge of doubt just before you flip the switch. The test lets you get the system working before you commit to a permanent installation.

Before flipping the switch, take a relaxed look at your system to see if everything looks right. Have someone else look, too—sometimes another pair of eyes will spot something you missed. Are there unconnected cables or wires? Have you forgotten to plug a surge protector into the power outlet you'll be using?

A systematic approach is always best.

Remove the Shipping Inserts

Floppy disk drives are normally shipped with cardboard shipping inserts in the slots to protect the heads from damage. Remove the insert from each drive before turning on the power. Magnetic heads and their linkages are delicate, and if cardboard inserts are in the drive when power comes on, damage can result.

To remove the inserts on a 5 1/4-inch drive, rotate the latch and pull out the cardboard. On a 3 1/2-inch drive, you may have to press the release button. Keep the inserts; you'll find them handy later if you ever move or ship the unit out for service. If you're like most people, though, you'll misplace the inserts in the first five minutes. No problem—you can always use a dispensable "scratch" floppy disk instead. Just be sure to label it clearly as a scratch disk, so you won't try to store critical documents on it later.

What to Expect at Power-On

When you turn the computer on for the first time, if all goes well, the machine will flash a few cryptic messages on the screen while it self-tests its memory chips. Then, depending on how the system was set up for you before you took delivery, the command processor will ask for the time and date. Follow the directions on the screen and you'll be up and running before you know it.

The first letters you see on the screen will probably be white on a black background, even on a color monitor. If you want a more colorful screen, you'll have to change the settings. You can do this using third party screen utility programs such as Norton Utilities (see Chapter 8) or special codes known as ANSI (American National Standards Institute) escape codes, which are described in "ANSI Codes" in Chapter 11. If the machine has been set up for you by the manufacturer or by the vendor, you may next see a menu of programs or commands. Otherwise you'll see an operating system prompt similar to this:

```
C>
```

This is a signal from the computer that it is ready to accept commands. Prompts are described further in Chapters 5 and 9.

If all does not go well, the machine may flash an error message describing a specific problem, or you may simply not see anything happen at all. This is not a big deal the first time you turn on a computer. You may need to run a setup program and adjust some settings before the computer can start up normally.

What do you do if it doesn't start right up? Don't worry about it. Refer to "Running a Setup" later in this chapter. Chances are the problem will be simple to fix.

Turning the System On

We'll assume here that you have a hard disk set up to start the computer when power is turned on. If you do not have a hard disk, or if the system doesn't start when power is supplied, you'll need to use a formatted floppy disk and perhaps run a setup program. See Chapter 5 for instructions on making and using a bootable floppy disk. See "Running a Setup" later in this chapter for information on setting up an AT-class machine.

To start your computer from the hard disk, make certain that all floppy disk drives are empty, or at least that the drive latch is in the open position. (Some floppy drives have interlocks to prevent the latch from closing unless

---

READ.ME

Lost Keys and Computer Security

The problem with keyboard locks is that the keys can be lost or misplaced and the locks do not really provide much security. If you lose the key, or maybe just leave it at home, you've created an annoying problem for yourself. If you don't have a spare key, the problem grows larger; you'll probably have to call a technician to disable the keyboard lock or install a new one.

Some manufacturers ship their systems with two sets of keys, often attached to the system unit power supply vent to prevent loss during shipment or unpacking. You can use one key and store the other in a safe place to reduce the magnitude of the lost key problem.

If security is not a problem, you may decide just to keep your keyboard unlocked on the grounds that the lock is more a nuisance than a benefit. Keyboard locks only provide low-level security; no self-respecting computer thief will be put off by one for long. Security experts consider a false sense of security to be worse than no security at all. At least if you have no security measures at all, you probably will not act as if you do.

There are effective software alternatives to keyboard locks. Some programs, such as Borland's SuperKey, include commands to disable the keyboard until you enter a password that you set yourself. There are free or shareware utilities available that do the same. Any such program is good enough to prevent accidental keypresses and casual snooping when you step away from your desk. If you lose your password, you can just reboot the machine; you won't have to contend with a hardware problem.

When security is a concern, you can choose from a wide range of software and hardware solutions. Any of these will provide much better computer and data access control than a keyboard lock. See Chapter 8 for more on computer security.

a disk is present.) If the latch is closed and a disk is in the drive, the computer will try to read its MS-DOS files from the disk in the floppy drive instead of from the hard disk. If there is a nonbootable floppy disk in drive A (the top or left-hand drive in a two-drive system), the computer will not boot successfully.

Next, unlock the keyboard lock if your system has one. Then push or turn the monitor's ON/OFF switch to the ON position, and do the same for the system unit. If your monitor plugs into the back of your system unit, you can simply turn on the system unit power switch. The system unit will supply power to the monitor at the correct time during startup. Otherwise, turn power on for the monitor first—multimode (multisynch) monitors in particular may need to receive operating-mode commands when the system unit comes on. To do so, they need to be turned on before the system unit.

Initial Self-Tests

When you turn the system unit on, you may see onscreen reports of memory chip testing and other operations. These reports constitute the *power on self-test,* or POST. If the memory chips test OK, the machine will pause, beep, and begin checking what equipment is hooked up to the system. In this part of the startup, the machine will test each disk drive in turn. You'll hear the heads move in the floppy disk drives. You'll also hear your printer head travel back and forth and see your modem lights flash if a dot matrix printer and external modem are connected. During this automatic POST procedure, the machine is establishing what equipment is where, so it will know what it can and cannot do.

On original PCs, very little was reported to the screen during the POST. You just had to accept that the tests were going on. On AT-class machines and higher, both testing and error reporting may be a lot more extensive. Newer models often self-correct common problems, as shown on the screen in Figure 4-6. When testing is complete, the computer will beep, pause, and go through its startup, or boot, procedure. (See "Lifted by Its Own Bootstraps" for more on the technical side of booting up.)

Startup Problems

The first time you start your machine, make sure the indicator lights are working and watch the monitor for alarms and error messages. Listen for

Figure 1-6

Packard Bell 386SX self-correcting setup

```
Errors have been found during the power on self test in your computer.  The
errors were:


Incorrect configuration data in CMOS
Memory size in CMOS invalid








SETUP will attempt to correct these errors through auto-configuration.
Hit any key to continue:
```

beeps and, yes, look for smoke. If something does go wrong, turn off the power before deciding what to do next. Since your system is still out on the open surface where you assembled it, you won't have to crawl under a desk, unscrew cable connections, or manhandle components out of hutch compartments.

If everything seems fine, skip to "Peripherals and Add-On Boards," later in this chapter. Otherwise, turn off the power, wait at least 30 seconds for stray voltages to bleed away, and try again. Sometimes hard disks are specially prepared for shipment and need a couple of tries before they work properly.

If turning the machine off then on again doesn't help, check the following symptoms; the problem may be easy to fix. If necessary, refer to Chapter 18 for more detailed troubleshooting procedures.

READ.ME

Lifted by Its Own Bootstraps

When you turn on power to your computer, it goes through a process called *booting up* or *bootstrapping*. The term is descriptive—if turning power on were all that happened, you'd have nothing but computer chips with voltages applied. There would be no way to interpret the keyboard, disk drives, or anything else.

In the lab, technical experts make such a computer ready for input. They can set switches, connect to outside memory, transfer programs, and so forth. For the device to be useful as a desktop computer, though, it must configure itself, with no help from engineers or other outsiders. It must lift itself into "computer awareness" by its own bootstraps.

The engineers came up with a way. On an MS-DOS type machine, bootstrapping works as follows.

ROM BIOS When you turn on the power switch, power goes to, among other things, a ROM BIOS (read only memory, basic input/output system). The ROM BIOS has a permanent program that isn't lost when power is turned off. The first thing this permanent program does is check out installed hardware. Next, the ROM BIOS initializes the system, meaning it sets all working RAM (random access memory) to zero and other components to their correct startup values.

CMOS (Complimentary Metal Oxide Semiconductor) On AT-class machines, the ROM BIOS then compares what it finds in the system to values stored in a special battery-backed setup chip called the CMOS. CMOS chips might be used for everything in the computer if they weren't so expensive to manufacture because they take very little power to run. (Some high-end laptops do use CMOS to extend their running time.) If there are any discrepancies between the CMOS chip and what the ROM BIOS finds, the computer notifies you onscreen and suggests setting up the machine again (see the section called "Running a Setup" in this chapter).

First Sector Finally, the ROM BIOS tries to read into working RAM the first sector on any disk in drive A. If you don't have a disk in drive A, or if the drive door is open, the ROM BIOS looks for the first sector on a hard disk.

BASIC If the ROM BIOS doesn't find a hard disk, on IBM machines it will load BASIC from another ROM, print the word OK on the screen and stop. From the OK prompt you can manually key in and run any BASIC program.

READ.ME

Lifted by Its Own Bootstraps (*continued*)

On non-IBM brands, BASIC is not available from a ROM. If the ROM BIOS doesn't find its program in drive A or on a hard disk, it prints an error message on the screen and halts. It has reached a dead end.

Bootstrap Loader The file the ROM BIOS is looking for on the first sector of a disk is called the *bootstrap loader*. This tiny bit of programming in turn reads (loads) the operating system into memory (see Chapter 6).

Partition Loader When booting from a hard disk, the ROM BIOS looks for a partition loader, which tells it where on the hard disk to find the bootstrap loader. It then reads the bootstrap loader, which in turn loads the operating system.

Operating System Once loaded, the operating system looks for two files. The first, CONFIG.SYS, tells it how to set up or *configure* itself. If it doesn't find CONFIG.SYS, it uses default values. Then the operating system looks for a second file, AUTOEXEC.BAT, which automatically executes any instructions you've included there. If there's no AUTOEXEC.BAT, the operating system executes the DOS command processor, COMMAND.COM, which then asks for the current time and date to verify the CMOS settings. (See Chapter 11 for more information on these files.)

To sum up, when you turn on the power, the following happens.

1. ROM BIOS checks out and initializes the system.

2. ROM BIOS compares an AT setup with the system.

3. ROM BIOS reads the first sector of a floppy or hard disk into memory.

4. The bootstrap loader/partition loader loads the operating system.

5. The operating system configures itself according to instructions in the file named CONFIG.SYS, if that file is present.

6. The operating system automatically executes all instructions in the file named AUTOEXEC.BAT, if that file is present.

7. If AUTOEXEC.BAT is not available, the operating system executes COMMAND.COM, the DOS command processor.

When the sequence is finished, your machine has used a ROM chip to read a tiny program, which starts a process of loading successively larger programs until it's ready to accept your commands. It has pulled itself up by its own bootstraps.

Nothing Happens The most obvious sign of trouble is a blank monitor screen and a completely silent computer—in short, nothing happens. Check the following:

- Are the computer and its surge protector both plugged in?

- Is the monitor power cord plugged into the system unit or surge protector?

- Is the monitor turned on?

- Turn the brightness and contrast controls all the way up to see if an image appears.

If none of these simple steps solves the problem, refer to Chapter 18, "Troubleshooting, Service, and Repair," for more detailed troubleshooting procedures.

You Hear Beeps but Nothing Else Happens Some older PCs use beeps instead of messages as their entire bootup troubleshooting aid. Newer computers still use patterns of diagnostic beeps at bootup, but primarily as a supplement to the onscreen error messages. One beep may mean a memory chip failure, two a ROM BIOS failure, and so forth. A system of beeps gives you or a technician a head start on diagnosing trouble. They may work even when the problem occurs before the video monitor can be activated. If you hear what sounds like a coded series of beeps, check your manual to see what they mean. Standard beep code meanings are also listed in Chapter 18, Table 18-1. You may have to send the machine in for service, but there is a good chance you'll only need to run your computer's hardware setup program (see the section "Running a Setup," later in this chapter).

Loose Cables, Connectors, and Boards Many startup problems can be traced to just one simple problem—loose cables, connectors, chips, or boards. An erratic computer may exhibit seemingly random screen flickers, drive lights that go on and off, or lock-ups that you can cure only by turning off power. In all these cases a loose board, chip, cable, or connector may be the villian. See Chapter 18 for troubleshooting procedures at the basic hardware level.

Error Messages An *error message* is a line or two of text provided as an aid for when things don't go exactly right. Most newer computers are designed to give detailed error messages when something goes wrong at bootup.

In the case of the initial bootup, the most likely cause of problems is a hard or floppy disk that is not bootable—that is, a damaged disk or one that is not set up correctly. Figure 4-7 shows an error message that occurred when a machine was booted with a non-DOS disk.

If you see this or an equivalent error message, you'll need to get or create a bootable or *system* disk. Your dealer probably gave you one with the computer; look for a disk labeled MS-DOS, PC-DOS, or something similar. If you don't find one, call your vendor or buy a copy of DOS at your computer store.

You can use a DOS disk to get up and running until you format your hard disk. A bootable or system disk is one that contains the boot record and system files described earlier in "Lifted by Its Own Boot-straps."

Chapter 5 covers booting from your DOS disk and formatting a system disk. Chapter 16 describes formatting a bootable hard disk.

Figure 4-7

Non-bootable disk error message

```
Phoenix Advanced Video BIOS Version 1.05 00
Phoenix 80386 ROM BIOS PLUS Version 1.10 02
Copyright (C) 1985-1989 Phoenix Technologies Ltd.
All Rights Reserved

Packard Bell 386sx - V1.0x


Non-System disk or disk error
Replace and strike any key when ready
```

Setup Errors

If the smoke test shows a CMOS or setup problem, you'll need to run a setup program. All AT-class machines and higher provide for some type of setup procedure. The machine's manual should tell you how to do it.

Sometimes the error report will show a way to run the setup routine immediately, as shown here,

```
Invalid configuration information - please run SETUP program I
   Strike the F1 key to continue, F2 to run the setup utility
```

and you can follow the procedure shown on your screen to do a setup. The system may be self-correcting. If there is no immediate way to do a setup, continue the bootup if the machine allows it, or boot from a floppy disk. Then find your setup program, often named SETUP.COM or something similar, most likely on your DOS disk. To run it, type the program's name and press the ENTER key or get help from someone who is technically qualified.

Running a Setup

AT-class and higher computers save the time, date, and other important information in their CMOS chips between sessions. This information can be accessed and changed using a setup program or built-in setup procedure; see your machine's documentation for how to access your own setup screens. Figure 4-8 shows a representative setup screen from a 386SX computer. Note that it includes information about memory settings, hard and floppy disk drives, the display, the keyboard, CPU speed, and the coprocessor. A second screen allows you to set up the system to operate the ROM BIOS from memory set aside for the purpose (called *shadow ROM BIOS*), and other advanced features.

On newer designs, often the setup is resident in the hardware. You can access the setup and change clock speeds, and so on, at any time by pressing a combination of keys. On other designs, you may need to run a separate setup program from the DOS prompt. Some programs may require you to reboot the computer before the changes take effect.

—————————————— **Figure 1-8** ——————————————

CMOS setup screen

```
                    Phoenix Technologies Ltd.    Version
                    System Configuration Setup   4.03 00
Time:  14:36:11
Date:  Mon Sep 24, 1990

Diskette A:          5.25 Inch, 1.2 MB
Diskette B:          3.5 Inch, 1.44 MB    Cyl  Hd  Pre   LZ   Sec Size
Hard Disk 1:         Type 49              1024  9  512  1024  30  135
Hard Disk 2:         Not Installed
Base Memory:         640 KB
Extended Memory:     320 KB
Display:             VGA/EGA
Keyboard:            Installed
CPU Speed:           Fast

Coprocessor:         Not Installed

PgUp for options. Up/Down Arrow to select. Left/Right Arrow to change.
F1 for help. F10 to Exit. Esc to reboot.
```

SMOKE TEST COMPLETE

At this point, your computer should be up and running. If it is not, and if you have followed all the hints in this chapter, refer to the user-level troubleshooting procedures in Chapter 18. If you still cannot get the machine to boot properly, it is likely that something serious (or at least hard to find) has gone wrong.

You may now decide to call in a technician to help. You might also take the computer back to your vendor for help, or dig a little deeper into the machine's hardware.

If the machine is running, now is the time to park the disk, turn the power switch off, and decide whether you want to install any add-on expansion boards.

Parking the Hard Disk

If your computer has a hard disk, chances are good that you also received a small program that does nothing but park the disk. Or you may have a Park (or Power Off) option on an installed menu system. In either case, it is important to park the hard disk now, before you turn off the power, because you are about to move the computer. If the computer doesn't work, you'll be taking it to the shop or shipping it out for repair. If it does work, you'll be moving it to its final installation point.

Disk parking programs move the read/write heads from somewhere in the middle of the disk platters to the outside edges, where they won't hurt the disk's usability if the heads get jarred against the recording surface.

If your disk has no parking utility, you can get one; any computer store has at least one, and many will give you a free copy if you ask. Or you can try to be very gentle and careful with the machine as you move it. Getting a disk parking program is the safer course.

Self-Parking Disks   Some disks are self-parking, meaning you do not have to use a parking program when you turn off the power. If your system did not come with a disk head parking program (usually named PARK, SHUT-DOWN, HEADPARK, or something similar), your disk is probably self-parking. With self-parking disks, a parking program can cause minor problems by seating the heads too firmly. The heads may then refuse to move the next time you turn on the power, and it may take several tries to get the computer to boot correctly. You won't want to fight such a startup problem every time you turn on the power, but when you *know* you're about to move the computer, your disk's safety is worth the minor, potential extra hassle.

If you have no park program and you're not sure the disk is self-parking, check the documentation that came with the disk. If the manual doesn't say, it's worth the time and expense to call the manufacturer or a qualified disk technician and ask. Be sure to have the disk model number on hand when you call.

Peripherals and Add-On Boards

Do you have any add-on products that the vendor did not install for you? Assuming your computer is working as it should, now is a good time to install them. Such add-ons could include an internal modem, fax board, scanner driver, and similar extras. To install them, you'll have to open the system unit case.

Opening the case is nothing to be nervous about. Just take some care not to handle electronic connections directly with your fingers, since the oils and acids on your skin can cause problems later. It's also a good idea to let a computer rest with power turned off for ten minutes or so before opening it up, so capacitive charges can drain away and you won't get shocked. Always pay attention to stickers warning that "no user-serviceable components are inside," or the like.

There are slots inside the case for add-on boards. You'll see chips, cables, and connectors. If the idea of opening the case makes you nervous, don't hesitate to take the computer to a shop for service. If you decide to do it yourself, Chapter 15 has general information on the inner workings of the system unit. Chapter 17 includes general procedures for adding boards.

If you have more than one add-on board, install them one at a time and test the computer before installing the next one. In other words, each time you add some equipment, do a smoke test. This is especially important if you bought the equipment by mail order or at a mass outlet where support is not available. That way, if you have any trouble you can easily spot what caused it.

READ.ME

The "Get a Bigger Hammer" Approach

When you're working "under the hood," don't be careless or use excessive force. The "get a bigger hammer" theory of computer maintenance does not work very well.

Some components do take a surprising amount of force to operate or install. For example, inserting add-on boards for AT-class machines requires about 35 pounds of force—not a trivial amount. Also, screws can be very tight and require quite a bit of force to loosen.

Just remember that electronic contacts can be broken and ribbon cable connectors can bend, if you're careless. Often cable connectors are designed to refuse the wrong jacks. Forcing them can damage the jack, the connector, or both. So do watch what you're doing and use good judgment about applying force.

Peripherals such as scanners, plotters, printer sharing devices, and power distribution centers usually come with detailed manuals of their own. Follow the manufacturer's directions to install these devices.

INSTALLATION IN PLACE

Once your add-on boards are in place and the computer works to your satisfaction, you can move the system to its permanent location. If your desk has a hutch, the most common arrangement is with the computer on the main desk surface and the monitor in the compartment above it. If you do not have a hutch, you can stack the components. To stack them, place your system unit on the desk surface with the power distribution center, if you have one, on top. Then perch the monitor on top of the pile. Stacking works fine—but use reasonable care not to scratch the finish. A thin rubber sheet, rubber pads, or a paper mat can protect the surface from scratches.

Note: In hot environments, stacking components can reduce airflow and add to heat problems. You may want to get a hutch or a computer stand to improve airflow. Or you can aim a small fan at the stack, if there is room enough for air to circulate around the case.

Install Cables

Once the major components are in their final positions, you can run the connecting cables between them just as you did during the smoke test. Since this is a permanent installation, keep the wires and cables off the ground; hobby stores have plastic tie-downs you can use to gather wires together and get rid of the "spaghetti factory" under your desk.

When installing the connectors this time, use the mounting screws or finger nuts that come with them. Make sure all cable connections are snug before you plug in the power cords. Treat the first power-on as another smoke test—turn the machine on and check for any oversights or problems. If you were careful, you may not find any. If you were human, you'll most likely find some minor problem to fix.

When you have finished, your computer will be fully installed and ready for normal operation. The next chapter explains normal operating procedures, and offers some useful tips on how to minimize future trouble and extend the life of your machine.

Operating Fundamentals

To make the best use of your personal computer system, you'll need to know a few things about the hardware and about the software that runs it. As mentioned earlier, this guide focuses on machines designed to use the Microsoft Disk Operating System (MS-DOS) or its IBM equivalent, PC-DOS. If you did the smoke test trial run described in Chapter 4, you know how to turn the machine on and get it running. There's a bit more to using your machine than plugging it in and turning it on, but don't let it worry you. If you run into trouble, a PC often can diagnose itself and send you messages describing the problem.

When you finish this chapter you'll know how to:

Install a program
Carry out the fundamental DOS operations
Respond to simple trouble messages
Shut down the machine without losing any data

READ.ME

Hardware Safety

Personal computers are safe to use and work with. The connectors are all keyed to prevent misconnections, and the only high voltage area is inside the box's clearly labeled power supply safety enclosure. Compared to other electronic equipment, the PC has an impressive safety record. Even so, it is important to use due care when operating any delicate electronic equipment. Here are a few simple precautions that will help you avoid downtime, damaged equipment, and personal injury from electrical shock or fire.

- Read and follow all warnings and instructions that come with the system.

- Locate all power switches. Be sure to turn them on in the correct order—printer, monitor, and other peripherals first, then the computer.

- Don't flip the power switch off and on rapidly. The resulting voltage spikes are very destructive to hard disks and other components. The power supply needs 10 to 20 seconds to reset before you turn the power back on.

- Don't turn off the power every time you leave the keyboard and then turn it back on again minutes later. This common practice is very destructive to chips and hard disks. Leaving your computer turned on all day and turning it off only to shut down for the night will make it much less prone to failures caused by repeated changes in operating temperature.

- When you move the system or suspect that a switch on the back of the system might have been reset, check that the 115V/230V voltage selector switch (if your computer has one) matches your local power supply before you turn on the machine. In the United States, 115V is standard.

- Disconnect the power before you clean external parts. If your surge protector has a power switch, you can use that to disconnect power.

- Never spray a liquid directly onto any part. Never immerse any part in water, use around water, or allow liquids to spill onto the equipment.

- Use your system on a stable surface. Avoid card tables or other surfaces that vibrate or are unstable. PCs do not take kindly to vibration and falls.

READ.ME

Hardware Safety (*continued*)

- Your system unit has a powerful fan at the rear and ventilation ports at the front. Do not block or cover these openings. An overheated computer quickly becomes unreliable.

- Do not locate the computer or its components next to a heater or other heat source.

- Dust and tobacco smoke often ruin disks. Don't smoke near your system. Stay away from dusty environments and smoky fireplaces, too.

- Consider investing in a grounding pad if static electricity of the sort that zaps your fingers when you touch a doorknob is common where you use your computer.

KNOW YOUR HARDWARE

If you followed the setup and testing procedures in Chapter 4, you already know your computer pretty well. The following sections take you deeper into your computer's hardware components.

Disk Drives

You'll be storing your work files on a hard disk or floppy disks. PC disk drives are designated by letters: drive A, drive C, and so forth. DOS assigns the letters automatically. The letter designations depend on your computer's drive types:

- *Floppy drives* Most systems have either one or two floppy disk drives. The first floppy drive (on the top, as shown in Figure 5-1, or on the left), is drive A. The second, underneath or to the right, is drive B (in Figure 5-1, a 3 1/2-inch drive). If you have no second internal floppy drive, DOS still reserves the letter B as a phantom drive for use in operations that require a drive B to be available.

- *Hard drives* The first hard disk drive—the one DOS uses as a startup drive if there is no floppy disk in drive A—is always called drive C. Hard drive capacities vary from 5MB to more than 1 gigabyte (over a billion bytes). Available hard drive letters go from C through E by default.

The Most Common Setups

This chapter assumes your system has two floppy disk drives lettered A and B. In the examples, drive A will be the startup (or bootable) drive—that is, the drive with the DOS disk. Drive B will be the other floppy drive, used for a working disk. Figure 5-2 shows how to insert a floppy disk properly.

Other disk drive arrangements are also common. For example, if your computer has a hard disk, drive C will be your bootable drive. The three most common disk drive setups are described here.

- *One floppy disk drive* All PCs that can be used as stand-alone desktop machines have at least one floppy disk drive. DOS assigns this first floppy drive the name "drive A." Some commands, such as early versions of DISKCOPY (described in the section "COPY, XCOPY, and DISKCOPY: Making Duplicates" later in this chapter), switch the single drive's letter back and forth from A to B as a way of keeping track of which disk you have in the drive.

Figure 5-1

Floppy drive types (AT-style case)

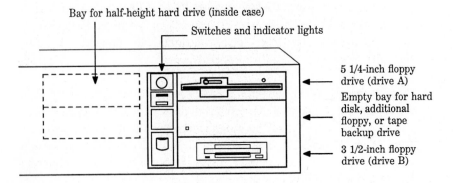

Bay for half-height hard drive (inside case)

Switches and indicator lights

5 1/4-inch floppy drive (drive A)

Empty bay for hard disk, additional floppy, or tape backup drive

3 1/2-inch floppy drive (drive B)

- *Two floppy disk drives* If your computer has two floppy disk drives, the drive at the top or left is drive A and the drive at the bottom or right is drive B. You can have disks in both drive A and drive B at the same time.

- *One floppy disk drive and a hard disk drive* If your computer has one floppy disk drive and one hard disk drive, the floppy disk drive is drive A and the hard disk drive is drive C. (Drive B is always reserved for a second internal floppy drive.)

Figure 5-2

Inserting a floppy disk

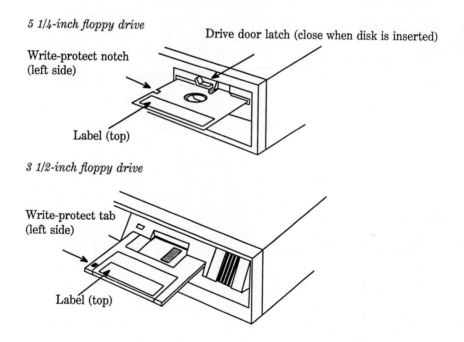

5 1/4-inch floppy drive

Drive door latch (close when disk is inserted)

Write-protect notch
(left side)

Label (top)

3 1/2-inch floppy drive

Write-protect tab
(left side)

Label (top)

If your system has a hard drive you may want to read Chapter 10 for additional information on operating with a hard disk.

Floppy Drive Sizes   Standard floppy disks (also called diskettes) have either 3 1/2-inch or 5 1/4-inch diameters, though a few odd sizes also are in use. Standard disks can be either high density or low (double) density. DOS will automatically detect your floppy drive sizes and capacities.

- *5 1/4-inch drives*   These may be high density (1.2MB) or double density (160K, 180K, 320K, or 360K). The wider range of double density capacities reflects whether the disk is one sided or two sided and the number of sectors used per track.

- *3 1/2-inch drives*   These may be high density (1.44MB) or double density (720K).

High density drives can read and write to same-size double density disks, but double density drives normally cannot read data written by high density drives. This can cause problems if you need to trade files between a machine with a high-density drive and a machine with a double-density drive.

Write-Protection

You can write-protect any floppy disk to keep from accidentally formatting it or otherwise destroying important data. You can read the data or programs on a write-protected disk, but you cannot format it or copy files to it. Figure 5-3 shows how to write-protect disks.

Note: Write-protecting a disk does not eliminate the need for backup copies. Write-protection gives floppy disks no immunity against damage, wear, or loss.

Write-protection on floppy disks is based on an internal disk drive light or mechanical rod that detects whether a notch or window is covered. To write-protect your disks, follow these guidelines:

- *5 1/4-inch floppy disks*   Look for a square, cut-out notch on the right side of a 5 1/4-inch floppy disk as you hold the disk with the label at the top. If the notch is covered with an opaque tab, the disk is write-protected. Write-protect tabs usually come with the disks, but any form of opaque tape will do the trick.

- *3 1/2-inch floppy disks*   With the disk facing you, look in the left-hand corner as you insert it. Find the small cut-out square or window. Directly below the window is a plastic tab that slides up and down to open and close the window. When the window is open, the floppy disk is write-protected.

READ.ME

Handling Floppy Disks

Floppy disks are sturdy enough to be reused many times, but they must be handled properly. Unlike a phonograph record, a disk with a few scratches will be useless. Fingerprints, liquid spills, and dust will cause poor performance, even on 3 1/2-inch disks, which have rigid cases. Flexible-case, 5 1/4-inch disks are especially subject to damage if you are careless.

Figure 5-4 shows right and wrong ways to handle floppy disks. Here are some additional do's and don'ts.

- Most disks come with adhesive labels for indicating the contents. You should definitely use them. Labeling your disks takes only a little time, and can save much frustration.

- Write on the label before you stick it on the disk. If the label is already applied to the disk, use only a felt-tip marker or other soft tipped pen.

- Keep disks in their dust jackets when not in use.

- Avoid extremes of temperature and humidity. Do not leave a floppy disk in direct sunlight or on top of a radiator or space heater.

- Don't place heavy objects on disks or jam them together in storage. Pressure can grind in particles of dirt and dust, making the data unreadable and possibly damaging a drive's read/write heads.

- Don't let anything touch the recording surface inside the plastic disk casing. Even the softest, cleanest object may leave behind scratches or dirt. Dirt, oil, and dust can make data unreliable even on rigid-cased 3 1/2-inch disks.

- Protect floppy disks from magnetic fields such as paper clip holders, metal typing stands, telephones, and anything with a motor (such as desk fans and photocopiers).

Figure 5-3

Write-protecting floppy disks

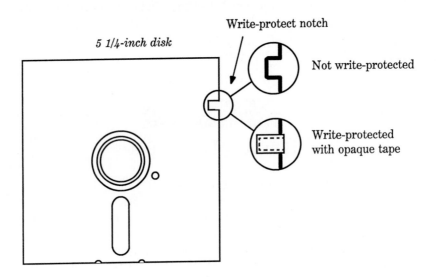

Write-protect notch

5 1/4-inch disk

Not write-protected

Write-protected
with opaque tape

3 1/2-inch disk

Turn disk over to see
write-protect tab

Not write-
protected
(closed)

Write-protected
(open)

Figure 5-1

Handling floppy disks

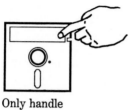

Only handle
at corner

Store and transport
in dust jacket

Use only felt-tip
marking pen

Never bend or fold

Never write on with
pencil or ballpoint pen

Never expose to
direct heat or
sunlight

Never wipe the
disk to clean

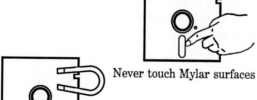

Never use near
magnetic fields

Never touch Mylar surfaces

The Write-Protect Error Message   An error message is a notice sent by DOS to the display telling you a problem has occurred. If you try to copy files or data to a write-protected floppy disk, you will get something similar to the following message and prompt:

```
Write protect error writing drive B
Abort, Retry, Ignore?
```

Type **A** to abort the operation. Then remove the write-protection or insert a different disk.

Keyboard and Monitor

A computer keyboard is used much like a typewriter, and any touch typist will quickly feel at home. Many beginning users feel a bit nervous about handling it, but you can't hurt anything by hitting the wrong key. The worst you can do is make a typing error. Inside a program you might get some unexpected results if you hit the wrong key, but you won't damage the computer.

Note: Appendix B details how to operate a typical extended (99-, 101-, or 102-key) keyboard. These are the keyboards you'll likely get with new PCs. If you're not familiar with your extended keyboard, you might want to look through Appendix B before reading on.

As you type at the keyboard you'll see the letters or numbers appear on the monitor. A *cursor* on the screen shows where the next letter will appear. A cursor usually looks like a short, blinking line, although it may appear as a solid block on some machines, such as laptops.

New keyboards usually have separate cursor control keys labeled with up, down, left, and right arrows. You use these keys to move the cursor around the screen.

STARTING YOUR COMPUTER

When you turn on the power, your computer self-starts...to a point. You should hear the fan start and a series of beeps and other sounds indicating that the computer is running system self-checks. The beeps are part of the power on self test, or POST, and they act as diagnostic tools if something goes wrong. (See Chapter 18 for more on interpreting the POST beeps.) During the POST, the monitor may display information about its ROM BIOS. When startup is complete, a prompt appears onscreen that indicates the active drive (usually A or C). DOS is now loaded into memory and the computer is waiting for further instructions.

Bootup Errors

Sometimes when you boot your computer, DOS will print an error message on the screen and will shut down until you correct whatever is wrong. This situation is hardly ever serious; you can generally just mutter "Oops!" and

READ.ME

Off to a Smooth Start

A couple of easy-to-acquire habits when starting your computer can get you off to a smooth start most of the time and alert you to problems before they become serious.

- *Use the correct sequence* First turn on your printer, then your monitor, then your computer. Computer power centers are available that will not only control voltage surges, spikes, and line noise, but will turn components on in the correct sequence with short delays in between. They also give you control over which components are turned on at startup. If you have no power center, you can use a good quality multi-outlet surge protector. (Be careful of low-quality surge protectors—they can sometimes spark if you use them to turn the system on and off. If you get your power protector in a computer store, or if it is rated for computers, it should be OK.)

- *Watch your cursor after bootup* You can use the cursor to keep track of where you are. For instance, at the DOS command line or in your word processor, the cursor tells you where the next letter you type will appear. If you're unaware or not watching, what you type can sometimes have unintended results. Some programs turn off the cursor, but they will provide highlighted menu choices in its place. The highlight will show both where you are and which selection is current.

correct the problem. Some common bootup errors on floppy-based systems include

An open drive door latch
A nonbootable disk in drive A
An incorrectly inserted disk
An unreadable disk
A bad, unconnected, or locked keyboard

On a hard disk system, common bootup errors include

Forgetting to open the floppy disk door latch
Leaving a nonbootable disk in drive A
On AT-class systems, forgetting to unlock the keyboard lock
A damaged hard disk, with unreadable or missing startup files
A bad keyboard connection

To correct such problems, simply follow the instructions that appear on the screen.

Note: On a hard disk system, if DOS fails to recognize your C drive as a bootable hard disk, the problem may run a bit deeper. See Appendix D for information on some of the thornier DOS error messages.

Date and Time Display

In a machine that has not been set up by you or the dealer, the first information on the screen after the self-test is complete will be prompts to set the current date and time. On an XT with a system clock installed and on AT-class machines, once the time and date are set you won't have to reset the clock again every time you switch on the power.

On systems without a built-in clock it may be tempting to press ENTER and bypass typing in the correct date and time. If you do this, you'll have no way to tell the most recent version of several work files. Most people find it less trouble in the long run to set the correct time and date when they boot.

Current Date Here is how DOS displays what it thinks is the current date:

```
Current date is Tue 1-01-1980
Enter new date:_
```

The date shown is the DOS default (the assumed date) for XT-class and earlier machines, which have no built-in clock. AT-class and later machines, which have a built-in clock, may or may not display the correct date the first time you start them up. Either way, DOS is asking you to enter a new date or confirm the current setting. If the date is correct, just press the ENTER key to confirm it. If the date is wrong, enter the correct date in the same format as shown on the screen: month, day, and year, separated by hyphens (*mm-dd-yy*), where

- *mm* stands for the two digits representing the month; on single digit months, you do not need a leading 0

- *dd* stands for the two digits representing the day; on single digit days, you may leave off the leading 0

- *yy* stands for the last two digits of the year; you can use all four digits, for example, 1991, if you like, but they are not required. Use hyphens, not slashes or spaces. DOS will compute the day of the week automatically

For example, if today's date is November 12, 1991, type **11-12-91** and press ENTER.

If you make a mistake, press the BACKSPACE key until the mistake is erased, and try again. When the date is correct, press ENTER and DOS will accept it.

Current Time   After you set the date, DOS displays its idea of the current time:

```
Current date is Tue 1-01-1980
Enter new date: 11-12-91
Current time is 0:00:43.55
Enter new time:_
```

If DOS' time is correct, accept it by pressing ENTER. If not, type the correct time in the same format that DOS uses. Omit seconds and fractions of a second.

For example, when you boot up, DOS shows a default time of midnight. It's really 9:30 A.M. To correct the time, enter in *hh:mm* format:

```
Current time is 0:00:43.55
Enter new time: 9:30
```

Here are some tips for setting the correct time.

- Use the digits 0 and 1, not the letters O and the lowercase L.

- Use a colon (which requires you to use the SHIFT key), not a hyphen or a semicolon, between the *hh* and the *mm*.

- Don't put a colon or a period after the minutes.

- You don't need to put in leading zeros for single digit hours.

- Use 24-hour notation for times later than 12:59 P.M.

To convert to 24-hour clock time, for 1:00 P.M., enter 12 (noon) plus 1 hour, or 13:00; for 9:30 P.M., enter 12 plus 9:30, or 21:30.

After you enter the time, DOS displays its version number, a copyright notice, and the DOS prompt.

Bootup Complete

With bootup complete, your machine waits for further input. If you have installed a menu or shell program, you see the menu or shell opening screen. If you have a shell installed, your screen may resemble the QDOS shell screen shown in Figure 5-5. If you haven't installed a menu or shell system, you see the blinking cursor to the right of the DOS prompt. Whatever you type at the DOS prompt, the computer will accept it as a command and do its best to carry it out.

Booting from a Hard Disk

To boot from a hard disk, make sure drive A is empty, or at least that the drive door latch is open. Then turn on your computer. If the computer finds a disk in drive A, DOS will try to boot from it. With the drive door latch open, DOS will boot from the hard disk (drive C) instead.

When you boot from the hard disk, drive C automatically becomes your current, or default, drive. On newly purchased hard disk systems, vendors

Figure 5-5

QDOS shell menu

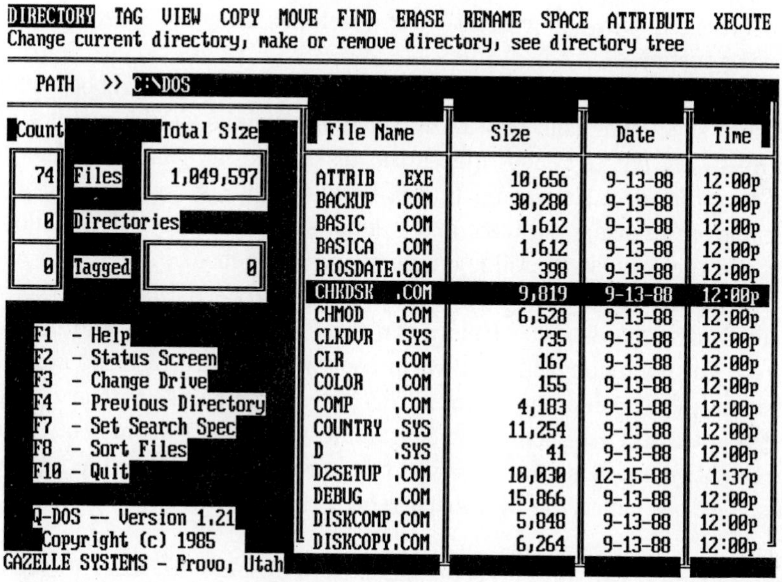

```
DIRECTORY  TAG  VIEW  COPY  MOVE  FIND  ERASE  RENAME  SPACE  ATTRIBUTE  XECUTE
Change current directory, make or remove directory, see directory tree
```

```
   PATH  >> C:\DOS

 Count         Total Size      File Name        Size       Date       Time

   74  Files    1,049,597     ATTRIB   .EXE     18,656    9-13-88    12:00p
                              BACKUP   .COM     30,280    9-13-88    12:00p
    0  Directories            BASIC    .COM      1,612    9-13-88    12:00p
                              BASICA   .COM      1,612    9-13-88    12:00p
                              BIOSDATE.COM         398    9-13-88    12:00p
    0  Tagged           0     CHKDSK   .COM      9,819    9-13-88    12:00p
                              CHMOD    .COM      6,528    9-13-88    12:00p
  F1  - Help                  CLKDVR   .SYS        735    9-13-88    12:00p
  F2  - Status Screen         CLR      .COM        167    9-13-88    12:00p
  F3  - Change Drive          COLOR    .COM        155    9-13-88    12:00p
  F4  - Previous Directory    COMP     .COM      4,183    9-13-88    12:00p
  F7  - Set Search Spec       COUNTRY  .SYS     11,254    9-13-88    12:00p
  F8  - Sort Files            D        .SYS         41    9-13-88    12:00p
  F10 - Quit                  D2SETUP  .COM     10,030   12-15-88     1:37p
                              DEBUG    .COM     15,866    9-13-88    12:00p
  Q-DOS -- Version 1.21       DISKCOMP.COM       5,848    9-13-88    12:00p
    Copyright (c) 1985        DISKCOPY.COM       6,264    9-13-88    12:00p
GAZELLE SYSTEMS - Provo, Utah
```

often will have installed DOS for you, and drive C will contain copies of all
the standard DOS command files and data files.

Non-DOS Hard Disks If your computer has a non-DOS hard disk (one
not formatted using the DOS FORMAT /s command) and you wish to boot
using MS-DOS as your operating system, you must boot from a floppy disk.
You can still get most of the convenience of booting from a hard disk by
making the hard disk your default drive after you boot. If you keep copies
of your DOS disk's files on the hard disk and use the statement SET
COMSPEC = C:\COMMAND.COM in your AUTOEXEC.BAT file, your
computer will use the DOS floppy disk only for the few functions that it
requires in order to boot.

Restarting Your Computer

When using your computer, you may run into some situations that don't
have a quick and easy solution. The keyboard may freeze up or a program

may behave erratically for no obvious reason. That's when you will need to restart the machine from scratch. Fortunately, you don't always, or even usually, have to turn off the power, wait for your disk drives to spin down to a stop, and then turn on the power again in order to restart. DOS provides three different ways to restart your machine. They're described in the following sections.

A note of caution, however: You can lose data if you reboot while a program "save" command or a DOS command such as COPY is still writing to a disk. Try not to reboot unless the disk drive light is off. If the drive light stays on for a slow count to ten, try using the program's built-in exit command or pressing the CTRL and C keys simultaneously. If that doesn't work and the drive light still is on, go ahead and reboot.

Warm Boot—CTRL-ALT-DEL   Hold down the CTRL and ALT keys and press the DEL key. The computer will do a warm boot when you release the keys. In a warm boot, your computer resets all RAM (random access memory), wiping out its contents. There is no time-consuming POST, so a warm boot is faster than the other methods. Because you trigger this reboot from the keyboard, it is sometimes called the "keyboard reboot."

Reset—Press a Button   In some cases the keyboard freezes and pressing CTRL-ALT-DEL does not work. If this happens, try using the reset button; it's located on the front of most new machines. Some older machines may have it at the rear of the case or do not have one at all. The reset button bypasses the keyboard and starts over at the POST. That should overcome whatever froze the keyboard.

This procedure takes somewhat longer than a warm boot, because of the POST. Many machines will end the POST early if you press any key after the POST process begins. This is a little riskier than waiting while the POST completes, but it saves time if you're in a hurry.

Cold Boot—Turn Off the Power and Wait   If your computer lacks a reset button, you can turn off power to the machine and wait until you hear the disk drives spin to a complete stop (give it a minute to be safe). Then turn the power back on and the machine will boot just as if it had been turned off overnight.

Most of the time you should not use this drastic measure. Turning off the power is not a recommended way to reboot, because every time you turn on your computer there are small voltage surges and temperature fluctuations. Over time, these can create tiny, almost molecular-level cracks in your solid-state circuits. Such cracks can reduce the life of your hardware.

Another tip regarding care of your machine is never to flip the power switch back and forth between the on and off positions. It may damage the circuits or break the power switch. The most common repair for a broken power switch is to replace the entire power supply, because labor is too expensive to replace only the switch. Also, the voltage spikes that result from flipping the switch back and forth can be very bad for hard disks and other components. Be sure to wait 30 to 60 seconds before you turn the power back on.

WORKING AT THE DOS PROMPT

You don't have to become a DOS expert to use the basic DOS commands, and that's all many people ever need to learn about DOS. DOS commands are not difficult or mysterious, and without some knowledge of them, you may soon run into trouble.

Once you learn the DOS fundamentals, you'll know

Which disk drive is currently active
Which files are stored on a given disk
How to copy files to another disk for safekeeping
How to create a bootable DOS disk
How to name a file

The commands for basic DOS tasks have such straightforward names as DEL for delete, REN for rename, COPY for copy, COMP for compare, DIR to get a directory listing, VOL to find out a disk volume name, and CHKDSK to check a disk's condition.

Before dealing with specific DOS commands, its a good idea to take a look at the DOS command line and how it works.

The DOS Command Line

The DOS command line consists of the prompt, the command, and the command parameters. In this guide, when you see a phrase such as, "Enter the COPY command," it means type **COPY** and then press the ENTER key. Here's a sample command line, with its parts labeled:

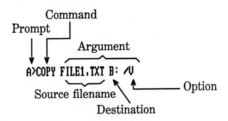

When you finish typing a command, remember to tell DOS you're finished by pressing ENTER, so it will execute whatever command you just typed.

Note: In the main text of this guide, all DOS commands are shown in CAPITAL LETTERS for visibility, but DOS doesn't care whether you use upper- or lowercase letters. Most people type commands in lowercase letters because it doesn't require using the SHIFT key. Text for you to type is shown in **boldface** type in this book.

Wildcard Commands

You can use the wildcard characters, * and ?, to save time and keystrokes. For example, say you have three files, all with similar names (FILE1.TXT, FILE2.TXT, and FILE3.TXT). You could type three separate commands to copy these files to drive B:

A> **copy file1.txt b:**   *(Type command and press ENTER)*
One file(s) copied   *(File copied successfully)*

A> **copy file2.txt b:**   *(Repeat for second file)*
One file(s) copied

A> **copy file3.txt b:**   *(Repeat for third file)*
One file(s) copied

A>_

By using a wildcard character instead, you can copy all three files with one command. Here, in brief, is how to use them. (Wildcards are discussed in more detail in Chapter 9.)

The Question Mark (?) Wildcard The question mark represents any character in the exact position of the question mark. This means you could accomplish the earlier three separate COPY commands with a single command:

```
A> copy file?.txt b:      (Type ? wildcard command)
Three file(s) copied      (DOS finds three files that fit filename)
A>_
```

The ? in this command matches the 1, 2, and 3 found in the filenames, so all three files are copied to drive B.

The Asterisk (*) Wildcard An asterisk stands for any number of characters at or after the asterisk position. That sounds confusing, but it just means that the asterisk can represent more than a single character in the filename. It's a more generalized wildcard. For example, the following lets you copy the same files as above:

```
A> copy f*.txt.b:         (Type * wildcard command)
Three file(s) copied      (DOS finds three files)
A>_
```

You should be aware that F*.TXT will also match any other file that begins with the letter *F*. If you happen to have a file named FOO.TXT on the same disk, the COPY F*.TXT command would copy FOO.TXT as well as FILE1.TXT, FILE2.TXT, and FILE3.TXT.

INTERNAL AND EXTERNAL COMMANDS

DOS commands can be internal or external. Ultimately, DOS is just a system for interpreting commands, managing files, and keeping a computer running smoothly. Much of what it needs to do this is built in to the central command processor. When you boot up, a file named COMMAND.COM loads a set of built-in commands into memory, where they stay in what is referred to as a DOS kernel. The commands in the DOS kernel are called *internal* or *resident commands*, and may be used anytime the DOS command line is available.

External DOS commands are small stand-alone programs that do specific tasks. Such commands are called utility programs if they didn't come with DOS and you add them on separately. The DOS external commands are not loaded into memory automatically. To be used, they must be on a disk where DOS can find them or DOS will report that you issued an invalid command.

The rule is: You can access internal commands from the DOS command line whenever the machine is running, without a thought to whether DOS would be able to find a program by that name on one of your drives. To use an external command, DOS must be able to find the program on your hard disk or a floppy disk.

The Basic Commands

Of all the hundred or so DOS commands, you really need only eleven to manage your files. With those eleven basic commands, you'll be able to do everything you need to keep your system going. Of the eleven, six are internal and five are external, as shown in Table 5-1.

The external commands are included in your DOS program. If DOS can't find its external command utility program, it will issue a "Bad command or filename" error message. In that case, reinsert your DOS disk and reenter the command if you are using a floppy disk system, or make sure you are logged in to the directory where your DOS files are kept, if you have a hard disk.

Table 5-1

The Eleven Basic DOS Commands

Internal	External
COPY	COMP
DEL	XCOPY
DIR	CHKDSK
REN	FORMAT
TYPE	DISKCOPY
VOL	

These eleven basic commands are discussed in detail in Chapters 9 through 11 and so will only be introduced here. (Table 5-2 has a list of these and the other most important DOS commands and what they do. See Chapter 12 for a complete DOS command reference.)

DIR: Reporting the Files at Your Disposal

The DIR command lists the contents of your default (current) floppy or hard disk directory. It tells you where you are and which files and programs are available. Listing a directory is similar to looking at the business directory in the lobby of an office building—it tells you what is located there.

To see which files are contained in a disk directory, enter **DIR** (type the letters **DIR** and press ENTER). The computer displays a directory resembling the one in Figure 5-6. The first part of the list may scroll off the top of the screen before you've reached the end of the list, but you'll learn how to prevent that in a moment.

Each line in a directory listing represents a single file; that is, an area on the disk that holds a collection of data, a program, or some other collection of information. It's similar to what you'd store in a folder inside a filing cabinet, only it's in electronic form. The directory acts as a table of contents for the electronic filing cabinet—the disk—that holds the files.

In the directory listing shown in Figure 5-6, the first two columns show the two main parts of a file's name, the filename and the extension. The third column shows the file size, in bytes; and the last two columns show the date and time (called the date stamp and time stamp) when the file was created or last changed.

If you're ever unsure about which disk you have in the current disk drive, or need to find out which programs and files are on the default disk, type **DIR** to find out.

File Naming Rules Figure 5-6 also demonstrates the DOS file naming conventions. Note, in column one, that there are exactly eight spaces available for the filename. DISKCOPY uses all eight available letters; SYS uses only three letters. The minimum filename length is one letter.

In column two, you can see that three spaces are available for the filename extension. All the illustrated files use all three spaces, but the extension is strictly optional. A filename with no extension at all is perfectly legal, as are filenames with extensions one, two, or three letters long. Many people use filename extensions to identify different types of files—.LET for

---

Table 5-2

DOS Quick Command Reference

Command	Description
ASSIGN	Reassigns drive letters to make DOS treat one drive as another.
ATTRIB	Shows or changes file attributes.
BACKUP	Backs up hard disk files.
BREAK	The command BREAK ON causes DOS to check more often for CTRL-C, making it easier to stop runaway programs or batch files.
CHDIR	Shows the current (or working) directory; changes to different directory; same as CD.
CHKDSK	Looks for common errors or faults on a disk.
CLS	Clears the screen.
COMMAND	Tells the command processor to begin.
COMP	Compares two files.
COPY	Copies a file or files to a specified destination.
DATE	Shows the date; resets it if desired.
DEL	Deletes specified files.
DIR	Displays files in current directory.
DISKCOMP	Compares two disks.
DISKCOPY	Creates duplicate disk.
ERASE	Erases specified files; same as DEL.
EXIT	Leaves the current command processor; returns to previous working area.
FASTOPEN	Makes it faster to open often-used files and directories.
FC	Compares and shows the differences between files.
FDISK	Partitions a hard disk, erasing all data; use with care.
FIND	Finds specified text or files on disk.
FORMAT	Makes a disk usable by DOS.
GRAFTABLE	Puts extended graphics characters into memory for use with a color monitor.
GRAPHICS	Lets you use SHIFT-PRINT SCREEN to print nontext (graphical) information, dot-by-dot.
LABEL	Creates specific disk volume labels (names).
MKDIR	Makes directories or subdirectories; same as MD.
MORE	Shows a command's output, one screen at a time.

Table 5-2

DOS Quick Command Reference (*continued*)

Command	Description
PATH	Sets or displays a command's search path.
PRINT	Prints files in the background while the user does other tasks.
PROMPT	Defines the command prompt.
RECOVER	Attempts to recover files from bad sectors; very dangerous program—do not use!
REN	Renames specified files; same as RENAME.
RESTORE	Restores files that were backed up using BACKUP.
RMDIR	Removes a given empty directory; same as RD.
SELECT	Sets up a DOS format on a new disk with selected country-specific information and keyboard layout.
SET	Displays or changes environment entries.
SHARE	Allows file sharing.
SORT	Sorts data.
SUBST	Exchanges a drive name (or string) for a path.
SYS	Moves the hidden operating system files to a target disk.
TIME	Sets the time; also shows it.
TREE	Shows directory structure, including filenames.
TYPE	Shows the contents of a text (ASCII) file.
VER	Shows the DOS version being used.
VERIFY	Verifies all writes to disk. Can be on or off.
VOL	Shows the volume name (label).
XCOPY	Copies files and subdirectories; extended COPY command.

---

letters, .MEM for memos, .DAT for data files and so forth. Some extensions, such as .EXE, .COM, and .BAT, are reserved by DOS for specific types of files. Others have become reserved by custom; a list is given in Chapter 9. In time you'll probably develop systems of your own.

Dealing with Large Directories: The /p and /w Options   Sometimes a directory listing may scroll off the top of the screen before the bottom of the listing appears. This makes it impossible to use DIR to see information on the first lines in a long list. DOS provides two ways to deal with this problem.

Figure 5-6

Partial DOS directory listing

Date created

Time created

```
Volume in drive A is INST V401
Directory of  A:\

AUTOEXEC BAT       39    4-07-89   12:00a
COMMAND  COM    37557    4-07-89   12:00a
CONFIG   SYS       96    4-07-89   12:00a
COUNTRY  SYS    12806    4-07-89   12:00a
DISKCOPY COM    10396    4-07-89   12:00a
DISPLAY  SYS    15692    4-07-89   12:00a
FDISK    EXE    60935    4-07-89   12:00a
FORMAT   COM    22875    4-07-89   12:00a
KEYB     COM    14727    4-07-89   12:00a
KEYBOARD SYS    23328    4-07-89   12:00a
REPLACE  EXE    19415    4-07-89   12:00a
SELECT   COM     3642    4-07-89   12:00a
SELECT   HLP    28695    4-07-89   12:00a
SELECT   PRT     1329    4-07-89   12:00a
SYS      COM    11456    4-07-89   12:00a
        15 File(s)     18432 bytes free
```

Filename   Extension

File size

- *Pause /p option*   If you enter DIR /p, DOS will halt the directory display every 25 lines. When you're done reading a section, press any key and the listing scrolls the next 25 lines of the directory onto the screen.

- *Wide directory /w option*   You may just want to see every filename on a disk, rather than a long directory that takes several screens to see and includes a lot of extra information. If you enter DIR /w, you'll get a wide directory listing (five columns wide) showing only the filename and extension of each file. A wide listing for a backup disk used while writing this guide is shown in Figure 5-7.

Adding a Target Drive Name   You can add a target drive letter to your DIR command to tell DOS that the file you're looking for isn't stored on the default drive or disk. You can also indicate which specific file you are looking for and DOS will only list the information for that file. This is called

Figure 5-7

The DIR /w command

```
A>dir /w

Volume in drive A is Users Texts
Directory of  A:\

CHAP1    PCW    CHAP2    PCW    2-ADDEN PCW    2TERMS   PCW    CHAP3    PCW
3TERMS   PCW    CHAP4    PCW    4TERMS   PCW    CHAP6    PCW    CH6-TABL PCW
CHAP7    PCW    CHAP9    PCW    CH9-TABS PCW    CHAP10   PCW    CH10HEDS PCW
CH10ILL  PCW    CHAP11   PCW    CHAP11   ASC    CH11PIX  ZIP    11TERMS  ASC
CHAP12   PCW    CHAP13   PCW    CHAP14   PCW    CHAP18   PCW    CH18PIX  ZIP
FILEINFO FI     FILENOTE
        27 File(s)    263168 bytes free

A>
```

"pointing," and is discussed further in Chapter 9. To cause DIR to display information about a file named TREE.COM on the disk in drive B, you would enter B: and the filename after the DIR command:

A>**dir b:tree.com**   *(Enter this command)*

```
 Volume in drive B is DOS-WORK      (DOS displays the information)
 Directory of  B:\

TREE     COM    3540   7-24-87  12:00a
       1 File(s)   79472 bytes free
```

The command parameter, B:TREE.COM, is a complete file specification giving the file's filename and extension, plus the drive where DOS can find it. (You would read this command as "B colon tree dot com.")

Note that no space follows the colon in the command argument. To DOS, B:TREE.COM without a space is a single section of the command. If you include a space, DOS interprets it as two separate parts of the command. That's because DOS uses spaces as *delimiters*. That is, a space is a character that marks the cutoff between two different sections of a command. If the notion of a space as a character seems a bit strange, bear in mind that when you press a key on your keyboard, it sends a signal called a *scan code* to the CPU telling it which key was pressed. The CPU interprets the spacebar's scan code as the space character, one of 256 ASCII characters (Appendix E lists all 256 of them).

Never type random spaces into a command. If you type the command DIR B:TREE.COM as DIR B: TREE.COM, DOS interprets TREE.COM as a parameter that doesn't fit the DIR B: command. DOS issues a message, "Invalid parameter," and returns you to the prompt. Some programs are more forgiving and will ignore excess spaces, but most programs require parameters to be entered in a specific way.

Changing Drives   To change to a different default drive, enter the new drive's letter followed by a colon, as in the following example:

```
A>:b             (Tell DOS to make drive B the default)
B>_              (New prompt shows drive B as default)
```

Drive B is now your default drive. If you type **DIR** you will see a listing of the files in drive B, not those in drive A. If you enter an invalid drive letter, you will get an error message and be returned to the current prompt in this way:

```
A>:z
Invalid drive specification
A>_
```

VOL: The Name of the Disk

In DOS 2.0 and later, you can display a disk's volume label any time you are at the DOS prompt by using the VOL command. When you're working with floppy disks, this command can save much confusion—especially if you forget for a moment which disk you have in the other drive. To display the volume label of the disk in drive B, enter

```
A>vol b:
Volume in drive B is WS-FILES
A>_
```

Another way to display a disk volume label is to enter the command DIR, since DOS always starts a directory listing with the name of the current volume. But DIR takes longer to run than VOL, since it displays more information. (See "Adding a Volume Label: The /v Option," later in this chapter, for how to create volume labels for your disks.)

TYPE: Taking a Quick Look at a File

The TYPE command is a fast, easy way to take a quick peek inside a file when you're not sure of its contents. You can tell DOS to display the contents of any file by using the command TYPE *filename.ext* (TYPE followed by the file's filename and extension). The file's contents display onscreen and, if it is an ASCII file, you can read it right then. If it is a program or other binary file, containing binary strings that translate only loosely into ASCII symbols, it will look like what is sometimes called Martian poetry (Figure 5-8). If this happens, you must take other steps to read the file, if it is a readable file. This may mean you need to load your word processor into memory and then open the file. There are also a number of file-listing utility programs available that make peeking inside a file even easier.

COPY, XCOPY, and DISKCOPY: Making Duplicate Files and Disks

The COPY command is internal, so it works whenever the computer is running under DOS. The XCOPY and DISKCOPY commands are external

Figure 5-8

Martian poetry: A binary file displayed onscreen

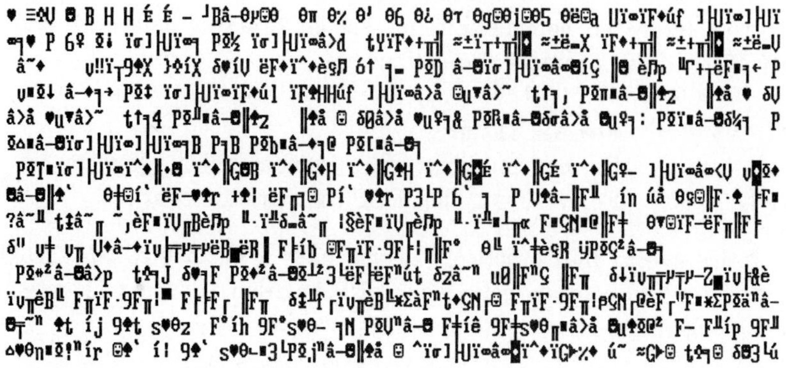

utilities. XCOPY was introduced with DOS 3.2, and supports all of the DOS COPY command options (meaning you can use any legal COPY options with XCOPY as well), plus additional options of its own. Essentially, it is a much enhanced COPY command. To use it, you must have a copy of XCOPY.EXE available in one of your drives, or DOS will return a "Bad command or file name" error message.

DISKCOPY, also an external utility, creates exact copies of floppy disks. Unlike COPY and XCOPY, it copies everything on a disk, including hidden and other special files. It is especially handy when making working copies of your programs, and is discussed in the section called "Installation Procedures," later in this chapter. DISKCOPY can be used only to copy the contents of one floppy disk to another floppy disk.

As you might expect, COPY and XCOPY are used to copy files to a specified new location, such as another disk. Unlike DISKCOPY, COPY and XCOPY allow you to transfer files from floppies to a hard disk and vice versa. As an organizational tool, XCOPY, in particular, is a quick way to move multiple files from one disk to another. The COPY and XCOPY commands are excellent ways to back up your program and your working disks. (There are more effective ways to back up a hard disk described in Chapters 8 and 11.)

Using the COPY Command   COPY is a simple command with a few optional features. To copy a file, tell the system what you want to do (COPY), what you want copied (the source file), and where you want the copy to go (the destination file or drive). The command syntax is

COPY *source file destination file* [/v] [/a *or* /b]

The italic text describes parameters that you replace with the actual values when you enter the command. The text in brackets indicates optional parameters. In this example, the options are

/a	For ASCII files
/b	For copying binary files (such as utility programs)
/v	For verifying that DOS can read the copy

To put this syntax into practice, say you have a file named SMITH.DAT that you want to copy to your work disk in drive B. You will enter the command like this:

```
A>copy smith.dat b:
```

If you want DOS to verify that the COPY operation succeeded, add the /v option to the command, in this way:

A>**copy smith.dat b: /v**   (*/v adds target disk verification*)

The /v option does not compare the copy with the original file, as you might suppose. But it does check the target disk to make sure DOS can read the copy. (If you want to compare the original with the copy, use the COMP command described in a later section.)

If you are copying to the current drive from another drive, you can leave off the target drive specification. DOS will assume you mean to copy to your default directory, as in the following:

A>**copy b:filename.ext**   (*Default directory is target*)

If you are copying from your current location to another and forget to specify the destination (the file or drive name where you want the copy to end up) you will see an error message:

A file cannot be copied onto itself

The /a and /b options are advanced switches described in Chapter 12. Most people rarely need to use them.

The XCOPY Command   XCOPY, an external utility command, is similar to but faster than COPY, especially for copying files specified with wild-cards. It reads as many source files into memory as it can hold before starting to write the copies to the destination. COPY, by contrast, can only handle one file at a time and must handle long files in multiple reads no longer than 64K. This means that with XCOPY, DOS does not have to wait for disks to spin up to speed as often as with the COPY command. The XCOPY command syntax is the same as for COPY, with some extra options for advanced users (see Chapter 12 for details). XCOPY is available in DOS versions 3.2 and higher.

COMP: Comparing Two Files

All versions of PC-DOS and most versions of MS-DOS provide the external utility command COMP. You use this command to tell if two files are identical. The command syntax is

COMP *file1 file2*

For example, to compare a file named LETTER.TXT on drive A to a file named LETTER1.TXT on drive C, you would enter

```
A> comp a:letter.txt c:letter1.txt
```

Since drive A is your default drive, you could omit the A: before the first filename.

COMP stops comparing after it finds ten differences between the two files. The program is especially useful for making sure a copied file is identical to the original. If your version of DOS lacks the COMP program, alternative file comparing programs are available commercially or through shareware (user-supported software that you get through disk vendors, electronic bulletin boards, and online information services).

REN: Renaming Files
The REN command, short for RENAME, changes a file's name. The syntax is

REN *original name new name*

You can spell out the word RENAME when you type the command if you find it easier to remember that way.

DEL: Deleting Files
Be very careful with the DEL command, which deletes files from a disk. By simply entering DEL *filename* you wipe out a file's directory entry. There is no way to get a file back without using a special utility to do it.

In DOS 4.0 and higher, you can add the /p option to have DOS prompt you before deleting any files:

```
A>del this*.ext /p          (/p requires verification)
THISFILE.EXT, Delete (Y/N)?  (DOS confirmation request)
```

At this point you can type Y or N to delete or not. Earlier versions of DOS don't ask if you're sure, but you can use various public domain utilities and

READ.ME

Getting Back What You Erased

If you read your DOS manual, you might see a warning to the effect that, once you erase a file, you'll never get it back. That's not always true. Someone who is knowledgeable in DOS can often unerase a deleted file.

The DOS DEL command doesn't really erase files in the sense of writing over the old information. Instead, it just changes the first character in the directory area of the disk to a special character that tells DOS to treat it as an erased entry. The file itself is still there—or at least it will be until DOS stores something else in the space the file occupied.

Until DOS reuses the space, you can get the file back using any of several "undelete" utilities available commercially and through shareware channels. If you're like most people, once you've deleted a file or two accidentally, you'll go out and get one of the undelete utilities.

In the meantime, if you accidentally delete a file, stop what you're doing immediately. The longer you continue operating, the more likely it is that DOS will copy something onto the erased file. That will truly make the file unrecoverable.

The three biggest of the utility program collections—Mace, Norton, and PC Tools—all have sophisticated file recovery programs.

If you want to make sure a file cannot be undeleted, use a "wipe" utility, available commercially and through shareware channels. These utilities really do erase a file, in the sense that they copy a series of characters (any character will do) over the space that an erased file occupied. Such files cannot be recovered later. Be careful with such utilities, however, since some of them have the ability to wipe out an entire disk at a time.

third-party file managers that interact with DOS and allow you to confirm or cancel. Such programs are far safer than the naked DOS DEL command in DOS versions earlier than 4.0, and are available through either commercial or shareware sources. (See Chapter 8 for more on small utility programs.)

FORMAT: Making a Disk Ready to Receive Files

You must format each new floppy disk before DOS can use it. To format a floppy disk, insert it in drive A or B and enter

```
A>format a:
```

or

```
A>format b:
```

Do not use the FORMAT command every time you want to put information on a floppy disk. Use it only on new floppy disks or on floppy disks you want to reuse, because FORMAT wipes out any data already on the disk. There are two options, /s and /v, that may be used separately or together, as described in the following sections.

Creating a Boot Disk: The /s Option   If you use the following syntax,

FORMAT *drive*: /s

DOS copies COMMAND.COM and the two hidden system files to the disk being formatted. That makes the disk a bootable DOS, or system, disk.

Adding a Volume Label: The /v Option   If you enter FORMAT *drive*: /v, once FORMAT has processed the disk you will see the following prompt:

```
Volume label (11 characters, ENTER for none)
```

At this point you can type a volume name of up to 11 characters for the disk. It is best to make your volume names correspond with whatever name you print (using a felt-tip pen) on a disk's adhesive label.

CHKDSK: Checking a Disk's Condition

As mentioned earlier, CHKDSK stands for check disk. This command checks the condition of a floppy disk or hard disk. You can tack on various options (see Chapter 12), but its simplest use is to discover problems on a disk before you stake your data's reliability on it. To see the CHKDSK report, simply enter CHKDSK, as shown here:

```
A>CHKDSK
Volume INST V401   created Apr 7, 1991 4:25p

   362496 bytes total disk space
    71680 bytes in 3 hidden files
   272384 bytes in 15 user files
    18432 bytes available on disk

   655360 bytes total memory
   380000 bytes free
A>_
```

The report shows the disk's volume name, how much space is left, and how much usable memory remains for programs. If CHKDSK encounters any bad areas on your disk, it will ask if you want to fix the problem. Answer "N" for No and look through Chapter 18, "Troubleshooting, Service, and Repair," before proceeding further. Floppy disks that start showing bad sectors often become unusable soon; it is best to copy all files onto another floppy disk immediately rather than to take chances.

With certain options, CHKDSK can list all your files and even do minor disk repair work. See Chapter 12 for information on these parameters and Chapter 18 for CHKDSK as a troubleshooting tool.

CHKDSK and Floppy Disks   If you're working with a floppy-based system, as this chapter has assumed for most purposes, it will pay to use CHKDSK regularly on your work disks. You can't use floppies without handling them, and eventually they wear out. When CHKDSK reports a problem on a floppy disk, the safest tack is to copy the contents onto a newly formatted floppy and throw the damaged one out. Some third-party utilities can extend a floppy's life (for example, the PC Tools DISKFIX program), but on the whole, it's safer to format a new one.

CORRECTING COMMAND LINE MISTAKES

If you press the wrong key while entering a DOS command, it is not serious. You have a couple of ways to correct command line typing mistakes.

The easiest is simply to erase your mistake by pressing the BACKSPACE key. Let's say you intend to type DIR to get a directory listing, but instead you type

A>**dur**

and haven't yet pressed ENTER. Press BACKSPACE twice to erase as far back as the incorrect character and then complete the command correctly.

DOS also lets you discard an entire command line anytime before you press ENTER. To discard your command line, simply press the ESC key. Then you can enter or reenter any command you choose. DOS will drop the cursor down one line and treat it as a brand new command line. Some third-party command line editors cancel the command more gracefully by removing the discarded command and putting the cursor back at the beginning of the prompt (see Chapter 8). But the DOS approach works fine, even if it looks messy.

If you enter an erroneous DOS command and press ENTER, nothing terrible will happen. DOS simply reports that you typed in a bad command. Try entering a misspelled command or a line of complete nonsense just to see how your computer responds.

Halting Your Computer in the Middle of a Command

Sometimes you may want to pause in the middle of a command's execution to examine what is on the monitor. You might do this when a DIR listing starts to scroll off the top of your screen or when you use the TYPE command to take a quick look at a file.

To make the system pause, hold down the CTRL key and type S or press the NUM LOCK key. (On an expanded keyboard, you can also press the PAUSE key.) To restart the display, press any of the basic typewriter keys.

Breaking Out of a Program

If you enter a DOS command and then change your mind, often you can break out of the command and return to the command line by holding down the CTRL key and pressing either C or the BREAK key. The CTRL-C or CTRL-BREAK combination also will sometimes break out of a runaway program. If a program starts running out of control, for example when a program is running in a loop, try CTRL-BREAK to stop it.

Editing an Old Command Line

When you type a line of text and press ENTER, DOS copies the line into a buffer for temporary storage (a buffer is an area set aside in memory for temporary storage of any kind of data, in this case, your keystrokes). The keyboard buffer is a timesaver that lets you use the command again or alter it into a new command. To recall your last command, press the F3 key. This is handy if you need to correct a typing mistake, or just need to use the same command several times in a row. To recall your last command one character at a time, press F1 or RIGHT ARROW.

Other DOS editing keys are used in fairly complex ways to edit the command line before it is recalled from the input buffer. Most people who frequently modify commands at the command line level get a command editing program such as PCED or ANARKEY. See Chapters 8 and 17 for more on the subject of command line editors.

AUTOMATIC BOOTUP WITH AUTOEXEC.BAT

Batch files are a powerful DOS enhancement. A batch file is nothing more than a list of legal DOS commands that DOS carries out one at a time as it reads the file. These lists can be as long as you want them to be. To run a batch file you only need to enter the batch file's name. DOS will then execute the entire list of commands. This saves you a lot of keystrokes. Chapter 11 covers batch files in detail, but AUTOEXEC.BAT is a special batch file you'll want to know about right away.

DOS looks for AUTOEXEC.BAT every time you turn on the power. It can be used to take care of the more tiresome chores of startup. For example, do you tire of seeing the time and date prompts every time you turn on the power? To eliminate those prompts and not give DOS any other special instructions, you could create an empty AUTOEXEC.BAT file by entering this command:

Your DOS prompt

↓

A>REM >AUTOEXEC.BAT

Type command
exactly as shown

DOS would create a filename, AUTOEXEC.BAT, in your root directory—
with absolutely nothing in the file. When you looked at the directory, DOS
would report that AUTOEXEC.BAT existed, but contained 0 bytes. You
would no longer be asked the date and time.

You can use the AUTOEXEC.BAT file in other, more powerful ways.
For example, you might want to set your XT system clock automatically and
change your prompt to one that always tells you exactly where you are in
your system.

Setting a PC or XT Clock

If your computer is an AT or similar machine, time and date are maintained
in a battery-operated clock. On an XT or PC with a clock card, you'll
probably need to run an automatic clock-setting program. That's done best
from the AUTOEXEC.BAT file. Let's say that, to set your system clock,
you must run the program CLOCK.COM. To run this program, type in the
following commands at the prompt. (Substitute the name of your own clock
setting program if you have one—if you're not sure, look in your computer
manual or call your dealer.)

```
A>copy con autoexec.bat   (Create filename in directory)
clock set                 (CLOCK program startup command)
```

The COPY CON AUTOEXEC.BAT command stands for COPY CONSOLE
to AUTOEXEC.BAT. In other words, copy whatever you type on the
following lines into a file named AUTOEXEC.BAT. The next line, CLOCK
SET, is the clock setting command. Note that it is a legal command, on a
line all by itself. When DOS reads that line in the AUTOEXEC.BAT file
during bootup, it will carry out the CLOCK SET command just as if you
had typed it at the DOS prompt.

Now press the F6 function key; you'll see "^Z" appear on the screen,
telling DOS that you've finished typing into the file. Press ENTER and you're

done. Your machine will boot up and set the time and date automatically from now on, with no need for you to type in the CLOCK SET command or to set the time and date by hand.

The Advantages of a "Pregnant Prompt"

The regular prompt, the one you see when DOS starts, only shows what drive you're on—it looks like A> on a floppy disk drive or C> on a hard disk drive. You can include instructions in the AUTOEXEC.BAT file to display instead what's sometimes called a "pregnant prompt." This special DOS prompt identifies both your current drive and your current directory— that is, it tells your current path.

To set a "pregnant prompt" and at the same time set the system clock, enter the following lines:

```
A>copy con autoexec.bat
prompt $p$g               (Set "pregnant prompt")
clock set                 (Start CLOCK program)
```

Now press the F6 function key to get the ^Z symbol, and then press ENTER. From now on, when you start your computer, your clock program will run and you'll have a DOS prompt that looks like this:

```
A:\>
```

The A: tells you that drive A is the default drive, and the backslash (\) represents the root directory (where you always begin when booting up).

To enter other startup commands in your AUTOEXEC.BAT file, such as to start an applications program, echo messages so you can see them onscreen, run CHKDSK, or carry out any other legal DOS command, just add one command per line. DOS will carry out each command in the file.

Breaking Out of a Batch File

If your AUTOEXEC.BAT file doesn't work correctly, your computer may not run. Rebooting won't do any good, because the machine will simply stop again every time AUTOEXEC.BAT makes DOS try to execute the problem command. There are two ways to solve this problem.

You can break out of any batch file operation, including AUTOEXEC
.BAT, before it is completed by pressing the CTRL-C or CTRL-BREAK key combination. DOS will ask you, "Terminate batch job (Y/N)?" Press Y and you will
find yourself at the DOS prompt. At that point you can edit your troublesome AUTOEXEC.BAT file to eliminate the problem command. The second
method is to insert a DOS disk that lacks the problem AUTOEXEC.BAT
file into drive A and simply avoid the problem.

Note: For more on using batch files, and on AUTOEXEC.BAT in particular, see Chapter 11. For a description of text editors, see Chapter 7.

INSTALLING AND RUNNING PROGRAMS

Chapters 6, 7, and 8 will give you an overview of various types of programs,
describe what they can do, and tell where to get them. You will need to
choose the programs you will use to meet your own particular needs.
However, most computers are sold with various programs already supplied.
If your dealer has not installed them on your machine, installing them
yourself is the next step.

Installation Procedures

Program installation procedures differ from one program to the next. Most
software comes with install programs or printed documentation to make the
process as painless as possible. Often installation consists of nothing more
than running the install program or copying files onto a working disk or
into a hard disk directory.

If your software comes with an install program, the printed documentation will tell you how to run it. Just follow the printed instructions and
screen prompts. As part of the installation procedure, some programs ask
you to configure them for your particular system. They ask questions about
what type of monitor you have, what printer you're using, and so forth. If
you don't know the answers to some of the questions, accept the default
values or look up the answers in your documentation. Don't worry, the
installation program will wait while you find the right answer. If you run
into trouble installing a program, here are some helpful hints.

- To avoid problems from the beginning, look in the manual for a
  section named something like "Read Me First." Such sections often
  have important information on installation procedures.

- Look on the disk for a file named READ.ME, README, README.1ST, or the like. These files hold information that didn't make it into the manual, often because the features they describe were added after the manual was printed. They may also hold warnings on hardware or other programs that have had compatibility problems with the software. To read a READ.ME file, use the DOS TYPE command followed by the filename.

- Check the manual for compatibility warnings. If a program manual has a section titled "Compatibility," "Working with Other Programs," or the like, read it and pay attention. The program author is warning you about known problems running the software with other programs or on non-IBM machines.

- Look through the program manual before you install or use a program. It's often not necessary to read an entire manual; they are designed to be references, not novels. But just by leafing through you may come across important warnings and other information.

- Many programs come in the form of compressed files. These are files whose data has been encoded to take less space on the disk; they usually have an extension of .ZIP, .ARC, .PAK, or .LZH. Follow the directions that come with the program to uncompress these files before you try to use them. (See Chapter 8 for a general discussion of compression and archiving utilities.)

Creating Working Program Disks

After you install a program, never work with the master program disks. Instead, make working copies and store the masters in a safe place. If your working disk is damaged, you will still have the master and so will be able to make a new working copy. If you've been using a master and it becomes damaged, you'll be off to the store to buy a new copy of the program. That wastes time and gets expensive.

Using DISKCOPY DISKCOPY is a DOS utility that creates an exact duplicate of your source program disks. It will even format your target (copy) disk as it copies.

To use DISKCOPY, the master and copy disks must be the same size and capacity, but otherwise DISKCOPY takes care of the details. You need not worry about running out of room or changing disks when one gets full. The program will prompt you when you need to take an action.

If you have two floppy disk drives and no hard drive, place your DOS disk in drive A and enter the following command:

```
A>diskcopy a: b:
```

Follow the screen prompts from there.

On a system with only a single floppy drive, make sure you are logged on to the floppy drive (you will see the A prompt), and enter the command DISKCOPY by itself, with no specified source and target drive. DISKCOPY will prompt you to change disks as you go, using only drive A. Be sure to wait for the disk drive light to go off each time you open the drive door latch to change floppy disks.

Checking the Results with DISKCOMP　DISKCOMP is a companion program to DISKCOPY that compares the master and the copy, reporting if there are copying errors. After you use DISKCOPY to copy a disk, it is a good practice to run the DISKCOMP comparison program to make sure the copy is exact. If DISKCOMP runs into differences between the source and target disks it will tell you and you can repeat the DISKCOPY procedure with another target disk.

Note: Bad copies are not common, but the one time it occurs will be enough to convince you that it is better to avoid the problem by running a simple DISKCOMP comparison.

Save Your Master Disk　When the working disk copy is made, label it using a felt-tip pen and an adhesive label. Put the original master disk into its jacket and store it in a safe place. You might need it someday, since working floppy disks eventually wear out or can become damaged.

Note: With your DOS disk and other critically important files, you might make two backups—keeping one of them some place separate from the master set.

Copy Protection

Some programs are *copy protected*, meaning you cannot freely make backup copies. Some copy protection designs let you make one, two, or some other specific number of copies for backup purposes. Others require you to keep the original distribution disk on hand when running a program. Such schemes are a burden on the user and occasionally lead to loss of data, especially if they limit the number of hard disk installations you can make.

Buyers who have felt burned by such systems sometimes refuse to purchase replacement copies or to buy other programs from the manufacturer. Customer reactions do have an effect, and copy protection is less common than before. It does still exist, however. If you've bought a copy-protected program, pay close attention to the requirements or you may lose the use of your program. Your program manual will tell you what to do.

Warranty and Registration

Programs are usually sealed with a notice similar to the one shown here.

> The programs on the disk are
> licensed to the user.
> By breaking the seal on the disk,
> you indicate your acceptance of
> the License Agreement.

Once you break the seal on a disk envelope, you have agreed to accept the program's restrictions, warranty agreements, fees, and any other vendor obligation.

Registration cards are included with your software. Once you're committed to using a program, send them in. Usually you must send in the cards to get technical support and product updates. Dealers will sometimes let you return or exchange programs you don't want, if you haven't filled out the registration card and still have the original package.

Registered users often get free, or lower than retail, updates when new versions of a program are released. Do be careful about letting others get ahold of copies of your registered programs. Don't be an inadvertent software pirate.

Not all users register their programs. Software is sold "as is," and the warranty covers only the physical disks. There is no guarantee that a program will be reliable or even useful to you. The real reason to register it is to become eligible for program support and upgrades.

Practice First

Practice using the different tools and commands your programs provide. See how the program interacts with your computer, your mouse, and your printer. The more you practice, the faster you'll learn a program's quirks, shortcuts, and tricks. But do your practice on unimportant files; don't use that 30-page proposal that must go out tomorrow morning.

Where to Get Help

If you're not thoroughly familiar with a program when you install it, there are some sources of help nearby. Here are some places to look for help while learning a new program.

Program Manuals

All systems, whether hardware or software, come with documentation. For simple programs it may be only an instruction sheet giving the command syntax. Documentation for more complex programs may include a command reference, a tutorial, and training books. Some manuals are easier to read than others, but all have some useful information. Take a little time with the manual before you charge blindly into action with a new program.

Is the manual easy to read and well-written? Does it make everything clear or just add to your confusion? Too many manuals are murky, garbled, and badly organized. But even if the manual is a good one, getting a second "How-To" book can often make a big difference.

Technical Support

Keep the program publisher's technical support number handy. If they don't have one, use your local dealer's number, or the number of a local support group. Most software manufacturers provide telephone technical support, and many even provide toll-free numbers for you to call. Some have 24-hour staff available for late-night questions.

If you think you may need personal support when learning programs, consider buying training from a local computer store. The staff there can often answer your questions.

Other Sources of Support

Some handy reference sources include

- *After market books*   Often, reading about a program in books by authors other than the program publisher's in-house technical writers will help clarify procedures and head off problems.

- *Tutorials*   These may be built into your program. They take you step by step through the learning process.

- *Help disks* If your software supplies a help program, load it into your system's memory.

- *Reference cards* These are printouts of commands used by a particular program.

- *Keyboard templates* Many programs supply these handy tools. They slip over your function keys to tell you what each one does.

- *Phone numbers* There's a world of support out there—the salesperson, the manufacturer's technical support staff, the software company's technical support people, friends with more skill than you, and user groups. Also, online bulletin board systems often have special interest groups (SIGs) that concentrate on a particular issue, topic, or type of system.

GOOD PRACTICES: AVOIDING PROBLEMS THE EASY WAY

Here are some easy ways to avoid trouble with your hardware and software.

Keep a Spare Boot Disk On Hand

Always keep a spare bootable floppy disk on hand, just in case the hard disk doesn't start. Include any device drivers or utility programs you'll need for full operation. After you start your system from the floppy, you may need to reenter some system settings or restore your hard disk contents from a backup copy.

Don't mix DOS versions on your spare boot disk. Make sure your backup boot disk is the same DOS version as is installed on your hard disk or program disk. Often, a program that runs well under one version of DOS is incompatible with another, and it won't cheer you up to discover such a problem while your system is suffering downtime.

Remember the Count-Three Rule

This rule will save you more grief than practically anything else, and all it takes is a couple of seconds. It goes like this:

Whenever DOS asks, "Are you sure?" pause for a count of three while you think about your answer.

Ask yourself whether this is the DOS response you expected. If it is not, do not answer "Y"; instead, answer "N" to back out of the command. Once you're back at the DOS prompt, rethink the situation. Chances are good that a command you didn't intend to enter has caused DOS to warn you that something drastic, such as deleting a whole directory, is about to happen.

It's a good idea to pause for two or three seconds before you answer any onscreen prompt from DOS, because once you start doing something it's often not possible to change your mind. Pause to figure out what's happening before you charge ahead.

Save Your Work Often

It is important to save your work frequently. Power spikes, storms, power outages, and accidental unplugging can—and do—occur. The more often you save your work, the less you'll lose when your system goes down.

This doesn't mean doing an entire backup every hour. Just save the file you're working on from time to time. In a word processor, save your work every few pages or every 15 minutes or so. Saving your file is especially important if you are about to run another program either simultaneously or in addition to the original program (such as running a grammar check on a long word-processed document).

Sometimes your program may stop everything to ask if you would like to save your work. Always answer "Yes," because there's a good chance that something is going wrong and the program senses it. Better to waste a moment or two saving your file than to realize, when the machine locks up a few moments later, that you passed up a golden chance to save many hours of hard work.

Along this line, there are several small automatic saving utilities that will save your work for you every so often, at an interval that you specify. These are available commercially and can help make your life much more trouble free.

Organize Your Floppy Disks

Use a rational system to store your floppy disks—something you find easy to remember. For example, keep like types of files grouped together. Keep

DOS masters in one group, program masters in another, backup disks in a third, and utilities and other special purpose programs in a fourth group. Word processing files should be on separate disks from database files, and so forth. Adhesive disk labels are cheap, so don't be hesitant about using them. Properly labeled disks make it easy to find quickly whatever type or group of files you need.

Use Built-In Exit Commands

Many programs have special commands for ending and returning to DOS. You should always use a program's exit command, if one exists, instead of CTRL-BREAK or just turning off the power switch (a very bad practice). This will ensure that the program ends in an orderly way and that the files are left in a usable state. Reserve CTRL-BREAK for ending DOS commands and other programs that have no exit command of their own, and for emergencies when a program's own exit command does not seem to work.

Only rarely will you cause real damage to a program or data by using CTRL-C or CTRL-BREAK instead of the program's built-in exit command. But you are likely to lose any work that you have not already saved.

Park Your Hard Disk Heads

If you have a hard disk in your system, the convenience and speed bring a few extra care requirements. A hard disk is an important system component and probably has valuable data on it; both are worth taking care of.

When you turn off the power to your system, unless your hard disk is self-parking, you need to park the heads so they don't jiggle around if the system is moved or jarred. Parking your hard disk heads is also a good habit to get into when the machine is just sitting idle at your workstation for any length of time. Parking the heads on a hard disk is covered in more detail in Chapter 4, "Setting It Up and Turning It On."

Don't Spin Down Too Often

Hard disks are tough, but they do eventually wear out. The electric motor that spins a hard disk produces heat, which causes the metal disks to warm up in the first few minutes after they start. When you turn your machine off, the disks cool down. Turning the power on and off makes the disk fail sooner. The reason is that all disks record your data magnetically using a coating of metal oxides on a platter made of a different metal. All metals expand and contract at different rates. Since a disk's platter and its metal oxide coating are bonded together, this uneven expansion creates stresses that can eventually peel the recording surface off the disk.

You can add much useful working life to your equipment by not turning the machine off every time you leave your desk for an hour or two. Leave it running until you shut down for the day. If data security is the problem, use a software menu system or security utility to limit access in your absence (see Chapter 8).

Cleaning the Machine

Occasionally, you will have to clean off your keyboard and dust your monitor. You might even need to clean inside your system's box once in a while. If you live in a wooded area, as one of the coauthors does, you may find that spiders make their homes inside, where it stays warm. The point is: housekeeping needs to be done every so often.

Never use cleaners or sprays around your system while it is running. The system's cooling fan will suck small, moist particles into the front vent openings and all sorts of potential fireworks can result.

Spray cleaners are somewhat harsh, but many people use them to clean the case and keyboard. Manufacturers generally recommend using only a damp cloth, but you may find that too weak to remove accumulated grime. To use stronger cleaners, moisten a soft cloth rather than spraying it directly onto the case or keyboard surfaces. Use a dampened cotton swab to get into cracks. Avoid strong cleaners and solvents on your monitor screen.

Some monitors have a protective coating on the glass surface, as do the plastic antiglare screens many users like. These may scratch if you are careless with them. Use a glass cleaner that has no ammonia or other harsh cleaners, and wipe the surface with a soft cloth. (You can find special video display cleaners in computer catalogs or at your local computer store, if you want to be doubly cautious.) Monitors with netting added to the glass surface to cut down glare may stain permanently if they become wet.

You probably won't need to open the system unit very often, but occasionally you may want a new component that requires installing an add-on board. Whenever the case is open, take a look inside. Is it dusty? If you are a cigarette smoker (cigars and pipes count, too) and you smoke around your unit, take off the cover after a few months and look—you may be surprised at how much tar accumulates on the internal parts. This can change electrical resistances, causing strange results.

Whenever you have the cover off, carefully dust inside. Catalogs offer small vacuum cleaners and other tools for just that purpose, or you can use "canned air," available in electronics stores, to blow away accumulated debris.

SUMMARY

This chapter covered the essentials of operating a PC. You are now as qualified as most casual PC users to do all the things needed to turn your PC into a true productivity tool. If you bought your machine for a specific purpose, or if a dealer helped you set the machine up, you can probably use it right now without too much trouble. Even if you stop reading for a while now and just practice using the computer, keep this guide handy as a reference tool.

The rest of this book will help you make even better use of your machine. In the next chapter you'll read about the most basic software in your PC—the operating system—and about various software environments that can make your working hours easier and more pleasant.

CHAPTER SIX

Operating Systems and Environments

You may recall from "Lifted by Its Own Bootstraps" in Chapter 4 that your computer's ROM BIOS holds just enough information to tell the machine where to look for more instructions when you turn on the power. The operating system determines what those further instructions will be. If your dealer didn't install an operating system, the computer will just sit there, waiting. With no operating system loaded, the machine won't be able to run the applications you plan to use, such as a word processor or a spreadsheet program.

The first part of this chapter compares different types of operating systems. Since this book focuses on IBM-compatible PCs, the primary operating systems discussed will be for those machines. MS-DOS or PC-DOS, OS/2, and UNIX are a few popular operating systems available for PCs. Other types of operating systems, for other types of machines, will be mentioned to give you an overview of some alternative approaches.

The second part of this chapter covers environments and user interfaces—what they are and how they enhance your system. Most environments act like extensions of the operating system, meaning they provide services to the user that the operating system alone cannot do. They are not substitutes; they require an operating system to be installed before they will work.

WHAT IS AN OPERATING SYSTEM?

Basically, an operating system (or OS) is a set of programs designed by a software company to supervise a computer's hardware and software operations. The OS acts as a layer of software between you, your programs, and hardware such as the CPU, memory, disk drives, keyboard, and display. It controls the lowest level, the most basic functions of your computer. It is what runs until you install a second program in memory. The second program may be an application (discussed in Chapter 7), a utility (discussed in Chapter 8), or a special user interface (discussed later in this chapter). Whatever the second program may be, it relies upon the operating system to coordinate the computer's activities.

As shown in Figure 6-1, the operating system sits in the lowest part of working RAM, where it manages all the interconnected activities of your hardware and software. It is the final, major player called into action at the end of the bootup sequence. It is the software component that gives you a prompt (refer to Chapter 5) to let you know it's awaiting your command.

When you buy your computer, unless it comes with no software at all, it will have some kind of operating system installed. On most PCs, your computer vendor probably included a version of DOS with your machine. If so, the hard disk or floppy disk you use for booting up contains the operating system, and is called the *boot disk* or *startup disk*. This disk has two hidden files (meaning they don't show up when you use the DIR command to see what files you have) and a program named COMMAND .COM. It is COMMAND.COM's job to interpret your commands and see that the machine carries them out.

In other operating systems the boot files may have different names, but they all carry out the same basic tasks.

What the OS Does

The operating system is your computer's housekeeper, general manager, and record keeper. The name "DOS" stands for disk operating system; its

Figure 6-1

Operating system and other layers of memory

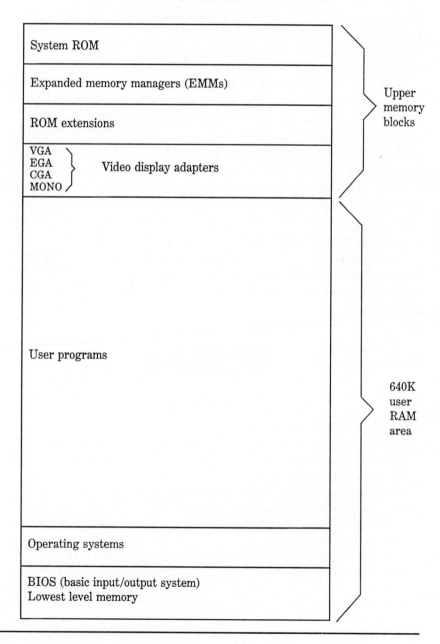

functions include the crucial job of saving (writing) data onto magnetic disks and retrieving (reading) the saved data back into memory on demand. But the OS does a lot more than read and write files. The OS maintains disk directories, allocates memory to applications programs, routes the input signals sent by the keyboard, and executes (runs) applications programs. Operating systems also link together subprograms and manage the opening, reading, writing, and closing of temporary work files.

Part of the operating system's job is to manage your hardware, such as the input/output (I/O) routines that run the printer, keyboard, monitor, COM ports, and disk drives. It routes data and operating instructions from one device to another, for instance, from keyboard to disk, or from disk to monitor. It brings your system up and running, ready to do your bidding. (See "Digging Deeper" for more on the technical part of operating systems.)

The OS also functions as a software manager, providing the necessary flexibility for handling constantly changing files. MS-DOS includes many small, external utility programs to help with these tasks, and is so dependent upon them that Microsoft refers to them as *external commands*. Many other programs offer enhanced ways of doing the same jobs, but the tools that come with DOS will accomplish 90 percent of what you need to do, and they don't take extra time and money to collect. They're the best place to start.

READ.ME

Digging Deeper

The hardware part of your computer's operating system is on a chip, or series of chips, on the main circuit board, called the motherboard. These chips make up the basic input/output system, or BIOS. When the computer starts up, the BIOS tests the other system chips, then looks for available disk drives. From the active drive (drive A on floppy-based systems) it pulls up more information by reading a series of small bootstrap programs into memory; those small programs take it from there.

Only the most basic information is programmed into your computer's BIOS chips. This information includes instructions that tell the system where to find the more complex software for bootstrapping. As the bootstrapping process continues, the OS is loaded into memory in ever more powerful stages.

Digging Deeper (*continued*)

In the final stage, the system loads a command interpreter (the COMMAND
.COM file in DOS) and sets it up to perform complicated tasks like hardware,
software, and memory management.

Once loaded, the OS acts as a command translator. It lets you type in
English-like commands (such as DIR), translates them into the binary 1's and
0's that your hardware understands, and coordinates the complex and intricate activities the computer performs to complete the task. In addition to
controlling internal functions, the OS acts as a peripheral device manager. You
can have your printer reproduce a document, tell your modem to call an
electronic message center, copy files and disks, and do all your other OS-level
chores ... all just by entering a few keystrokes.

On a more technical level, you can group the major tasks of your OS into
three separate areas.

1. The OS manages the data connections and exchanges among different
   parts of the computer system.

   • It organizes information on the disk drives and does the work of
     storage and retrieval.
   • It supervises character transfers between the CPU and the key-
     board, video screen, modem, network connection, printer, or other
     I/O devices.

2. The OS allocates resources among competing demands in high-
   powered machines such as 80386 models.

   • It assigns CPU time to different users in multiuser systems, and to
     different programs in multitasking systems.
   • It shuffles large amounts of RAM among different tasks to improve
     program efficiency.

3. The OS establishes a standard means of communication between users
   and their machines.

   • It maintains a user interface that lets it accept and understand a
     user's commands.
   • It provides system calls that advanced programmers use to gain
     direct access to other OS functions—such as to provide for timed
     automatic file saving.

Note: Utilities are small programs for managing disks, files, and system housekeeping operations. The more adept you become at the DOS prompt, the more important a good set of utility programs will be. Chapter 8 describes some third-party enhanced utilities that many have come to rely on. Chapters 9 through 12 describe the many external commands that come with the various versions of DOS.

OS Choices, Application Choices

As mentioned previously, your computer probably came equipped with an operating system when you bought it. Vendors may offer an assortment of operating systems, and will recommend an OS based on what you intend to do with the computer. Your best bet for good advice is to ask your vendor, a knowledgeable friend, or a computer hobbyist.

Why, then, bother to learn about OSs at this point? The answer is that, even though OSs do basically the same things in different ways, they are not all compatible with the same applications programs. You need to know a bit about your OS's capabilities and limitations before you go out and spend money on applications programs (described in Chapter 7).

Operating System Types

Operating systems come in various types. The OS you use may allow you to do only one task at a time, like MS-DOS and Apple ProDOS, or it may allow you to run more than one program at a time, like OS/2 and UNIX. Text-based add-on systems like DesqView can enhance DOS and give it *multitasking* capabilities, the ability to run two or more programs simultaneously. Graphics-based add-on systems like Microsoft Windows combine a graphical environment with multitasking. Carousel and Back and Forth can allow a user to switch tasks so quickly that they seem like they are multitasking—a good approach for an older, slower system. Add-on programs can enhance text-based operating systems to make them seem graphics-oriented. Such systems work well with any CPU from the 8088 on up.

Most PCs are sold with PC- or MS-DOS, so this book concentrates on that operating system. Tips for running your system under DOS are discussed in Chapters 9 through 12. DOS and other popular operating systems—ProDOS, UNIX, OS/2, and CP/M—will be described in the next sections.

CP/M   CP/M (Control Program/Microcomputers) was the first operating system written specifically for microcomputers. As a direct ancestor of MS-DOS, it uses many of the same commands. CP/M works with a wide variety of now obsolete microcomputers and runs early versions of many programs that are now popular on the IBM PC. It is becoming harder to find applications designed to run with CP/M, in part because of its built-in 64K program size limitation. Currently, CP/M is used mainly on modified Apple II computers with add-in Z80 coprocessor cards installed.

Some small businesses that don't need much speed and power still use CP/M based computers for everyday bookkeeping chores. There are also many hobbyists who admire the tight programming style that CP/M requires, and who network with each other through specialized user groups.

If CP/M based machines interest you, see Appendix F for tips on buying used equipment. Chapter 7 has some tips on finding a local user group.

Apple DOS and ProDOS   Apple DOS was the first operating system for the Apple II family of computers. It is now obsolete, but is important historically because it was the system that launched most of the original game and educational software—not to mention VisiCalc, the first spreadsheet program.

ProDOS is the current operating system for the Apple II family of computers. This system differs from CP/M, MS-DOS, and Apple DOS in being menu driven rather than command driven. This means that it presents a menu from which you choose what to do next instead of giving you a prompt and waiting for you to enter a command. Some people find the menu system limiting; others admire its ease of use.

ProDOS does not support multitasking, so only one program can run at a time. It has a text-based user interface, but does support a mouse driver. Most Apple users prefer to use a mouse with the built-in menus and the many graphics programs that ProDOS supports.

MS-DOS and PC-DOS   When IBM developed its first PC, the computer's operating system, DOS 1.0, was very similar to CP/M. Actually, DOS borrowed many of its operating features directly from CP/M in order to make the two systems alike. That was smart because it meant programmers had little trouble making existing CP/M programs DOS-compatible. The first really powerful microcomputer word processor, WordStar, and the database program dBASE II, for example, were quickly ready with a DOS version. There was no long wait for supporting software, so success for the new PC was a foregone conclusion. That was in 1981. Since then, CP/M has fallen by the wayside and MS-DOS has become the standard OS for IBM-style computers.

DOS has gone through a series of updates and improvements since 1981, as outlined in Table 6-1, but it still retains its command-driven nature. It does not, by itself, provide graphical user interfaces (described later in this chapter), but several add-ons have been produced that use graphics under DOS. Although DOS itself isn't designed for multitasking, the popular DesqView package provides a windowed, multitasking environment.

DOS has evolved into a powerful, flexible system that has opened the door to a rich variety of enhancements and add-ons. That may be one reason it is the standard OS for machines that use the Intel CPU. Eventually, MS-DOS will be replaced with a newer, more advanced operating

---

Table 6-1

The Evolution of DOS

Version	Year	Description
1.0	1981	Initial operating system
1.1	1982	Adds double-sided disk support
2.0	1983	PC XT edition. Supports 10MB hard drives, hard disk boot, hierarchical directories, and I/O redirection
2.1	1984	PCjr edition
3.0	1984	PC AT edition. Supports 20MB hard drives, introduces new keyboard design, and 80286 multitasking
3.1	1985	Provides network support
3.2	1986	PC-Convertible edition. Provides 720K, 3 1/2-inch floppy disk support
3.3	1987	PS/2 edition. Provides 1.44 MB, 3 1/2-inch floppy disk support
4.0	1988	Supports large (greater than 32MB) disks; incorporated first Microsoft shell program; not widely used

---

system, which itself will eventually be replaced. There is some belief among computer writers that the MS-DOS glory days are over and that OS/2 or some other multitasking OS will take over, but that hasn't happened yet.

Note: PC-DOS is the IBM version of MS-DOS, distributed specifically for IBM computers. Other variations exist for specific machines, such as AST and Compaq, that take advantage of those machines' particular hardware designs. MS-DOS is the generic version used on most Intel-based machines.

OS/2   OS/2 (operating system, second generation) is designed for the IBM PS/2 family of personal computers. OS/2 compensates for some of DOS' limitations by adding multitasking, plus menu and icon command selection techniques similar to those that have become so popular on the Apple Macintosh.

OS/2 is a powerful program, and it takes a lot of power to run it. You must have at least a 286 chip in your computer, and Microsoft recommends that you use a 386 if you want to realize OS/2's full power. OS/2 can handle 16MB or more of memory, for very large applications programs, and you should have at least 4MB of memory to get maximum benefit. OS/2 requires 8 to 20MB of disk space for any version; the amount of additional storage you'll need will depend on what applications you install and what drivers you use. OS/2 can multitask, allowing you to run a number of different applications at the same time.

Not all programs can run under OS/2, but that picture is rapidly changing for both OS/2 and Presentation Manager, its graphical user interface. If OS/2 eventually replaces the MS-DOS operating system, it will need many more applications than it now has. As OS/2 evolves (see Table 6-2), applications are evolving to run with it. Early reviews of Presentation Manager have been impressive. Program developers are getting the idea that OS/2 is finally a hot item, and the transition to OS/2 may be under way.

UNIX   UNIX began as an operating system designed for academic and scientific applications on minicomputers, but has been adapted for IBM-compatible machines. It is large and complex but will permit powerful minicomputer software to run on some top-of-the-line personal computers. UNIX is multitasking, letting you run as many simultaneous programs as you need, limited only by your system's memory. Several people can use a UNIX system at one time, something that may be overkill for a stand-alone

Table 6-2

The Evolution of the OS/2 Operating System

Version	Year	Description
1.0	1987	Comparable to DOS 1.0. Requires 1.5MB of RAM
1.1	1988	Introduced Presentation Manager, which worked like a combination of DOS and Windows simultaneously. This version needs at least 2 to 3MB of RAM to run
1.2	1989	Comparable to DOS 2.0. Introduced the new high performance file system, extended attributes, an improved Presentation Manager, and other enhancements
2.0	1990	This powerful program has the capability of running on multiple machines and uses DOS applications

personal computer, but is a powerful and useful feature on mainframes, minicomputers, and large microsystems using local area networks. It is also useful for multinode electronic bulletin board systems.

UNIX's advanced capabilities in areas like multitasking and multiple system operation has led to the development of DOS-under-UNIX software. This attempt to merge the strengths of both operating systems may be the answer for many users who want to upgrade to a more powerful system yet continue with the familiarity of DOS.

INTERFACES AND ENVIRONMENTS

Once you have an operating system (which, for this book, we'll assume is DOS), you can stop right there, buy your applications programs, and start work. Or you can enhance your system by changing the way you interface with your computer. The interface is where user meets machine. Changing, improving, speeding up, and otherwise affecting this interface has led to an entire special software area, sometimes called the user environment.

User Environments

Just as the area around your computer is called your working environment, the interface between user and machine is considered the *user environment*. At its simplest, the user environment consists of nothing more than the DOS prompt. More advanced user environments offer mouse support and colorful graphics. Some available interfaces are general in nature, designed as a user-friendly umbrella for all your applications. Others are highly specific—for example, engineering and program design environments that amount to special applications in their own right. Still other environments combine limited graphical features with pull-down menu systems.

Keep in mind that a user interface is useful only if your applications are compatible with it. Before you buy a user environment, talk with other people who have the types of programs you might want. You may not need the power of a full graphical user interface, for example, if you only want to type simple documents. But if your goal is to produce newsletters or brochures, you might need an environment like Microsoft Windows that supports more advanced desktop publishing programs with more visual zip. Don't just jump into a new interface; do a little homework to see if it will really solve problems and enhance your hours of computer use. Here are some things to take into account depending on your particular needs:

- *Single program users* If you usually work with only one or two programs, you might consider creating, or having a friend create, a simple batch file menu (see Chapter 11 for more on creating DOS batch files). It will run fast, require less typing to get your program started, and be simple enough that if something goes wrong, anyone who understands batch files can troubleshoot it.

- *Occasional, general users* If you are not an experienced DOS user, you may want to consider full menus or one of the more powerful shell programs (see Chapter 8). Such systems can be made fairly automatic for ease of use, but still provide all the flexibility you need to add new programs.

- *Physically disabled users* Some user environments are built around the special needs of disabled persons, offering mouse support for those with limited typing ability, large type for visually impaired persons, and so on. There is even one experimental system that lets a completely paralyzed person select menu items by focusing his or her eyes on the screen.

- *Power users*   On 286 or 386 systems you may wish to operate in a graphical or windowed environment that you configure yourself. If your machine is slower, you will probably want to work directly at the DOS prompt level because of the extra time required to process commands with graphical environments.

- *Special hardware users*   Do you have a mouse? A good, high resolution video display? A super-fast 486 system or the processor that started it all, the 8088? Make sure that the environment you select is compatible and performs well with your hardware and other software.

Types of Interfaces

Once you've identified how you'll be using your system, you'll have a good idea of what kind of interface you'll need. The object is to choose an environment that lets you take maximum advantage of your experience level without losing efficiency or getting bored and frustrated. Choose an environment that keeps you interested but does not make you spend half your time checking a book to see what you should do next.

Command-Driven Interfaces   Command-driven programs may feel complicated at first. You need to know exactly what you want to do and how to phrase the command. Then you must enter the command with no typing mistakes. Command-driven programs are not as intuitive as other types of interfaces because they don't present you with menus that guide you through your options. For example, some new users are bewildered by the stark, unexplained DOS prompt in the upper-left corner of an otherwise blank screen the first time they turn on their machine. On the other hand, DOS is a fast, simple interface once you know a few basic commands (discussed in Chapters 5, 9, 10, and 11).

The command line is the fastest way to tell a program what to do. Command-driven programs require less memory space and processing power than menus or graphical user interfaces. These are also often more powerful and flexible than more structured interfaces. For those reasons, the command line interface is preferred by many power users.

Menu-Driven Interfaces   A menu-driven system lets you see your options at a glance and choose what you want to do or where you want to go. Most menus are text based, meaning you don't get fancy pictures, but they do let you move a sliding light bar to indicate which item you want and have other point-and-shoot menu item selection methods. In addition, most menu systems offer mouse support. These systems may feel limiting to power users, but once set up by someone who knows how to do it, they can make life a lot easier. Menus help make programs more user friendly, and can be a real help to new or occasional users of a program.

Icon-Driven Interfaces   Icon-driven interfaces differ from menus in that they show you pictures or symbols that indicate the actions you can take. You might point an arrow at a file folder and click a mouse button to see the names of files in a directory, for example. Many icon-driven programs also feature pull-down submenus for more detailed choices. You move an arrow to point to the option and click a mouse button or press the ENTER key to open the submenu. Many users appreciate the ability to point and shoot at options that would otherwise require typing a complex command line.

Graphical User Interfaces (GUIs)

A graphical user interface, or GUI, is an operating environment that runs in graphics mode. That means the display is bitmapped, or "painted" one pixel at a time, bit by bit, rather than one character at a time. Every currently available OS has a GUI up and running or in the works. GUIs are powerful programs, but they can be hard to install and learn. Their ease of use is improving all the time, as several new GUI versions have demonstrated. Once installed, a well designed GUI on a fast machine can save time and make programs easier and more fun to use. A GUI can make it easier to tap a machine's full power and, by eliminating complex command lines, make it easier and faster to learn programs.

On the downside, GUIs require a lot of computing resources. If you're accustomed to the execution speed of commands entered at the DOS prompt, a GUI may make you fret at the delay on machines slower than a 20 MHz 386-based machine. Is the slowdown worth it? Many users, including power users, firmly believe that it is, because GUIs are so easy to use.

On any PC, but especially on the slower designs, you should try a graphical interface before you buy it.

In return for the reduction in speed and memory resources, GUIs let you display many programs on your screen at once. Some GUIs let you run several of the displayed programs at the same time, which is what is meant by multitasking. You can switch windows around, change their size and relative position, and move data between programs. Programmers can customize the built-in pull-down menus, dialog boxes, icons, and scroll bars for their own programs. They can use graphics modes that would be complicated and impractical to use from the command line.

This kind of capability has become critical in some programs; several major graphic interface applications like PageMaker, Microsoft Excel, Micrografx Designer, AutoCAD, and Ventura Publisher only run (or run best) under specific GUI environments. Similarly, design engineers using CADD programs (discussed in Chapter 7) to show 3-D images, sales representatives needing presentation 3-D graphics, desktop publishers who mix art with different text-font styles, and in fact anyone who wants to turn out a better-looking document for the same amount of work, quickly comes to rely on the capabilities of GUIs.

Run-Time Environments

Some major applications are designed for specific graphical environments. For example, for a long time Ventura Publisher required the GEM environment (although they're shifting over to Windows 3). Some applications give you a choice between a basic run-time version of the environment, which is included with the application, and a version that will run only when the complete environment is installed. In the latter case, you must purchase the complete environment separately.

Run-time environments are limited to the applications with which they come packaged. They cannot act as an environment for other programs. This is desirable for some users who want the environment only when running that application but who use the DOS command line, or some other environment, at other times.

Run-time versions of windowed environments are being phased out at this writing. If you're in the market for a major Windows-based application like PageMaker or Microsoft Excel, and you're not already using Windows, you may still be able to find some editions with special run-time versions. However, you will be better off getting the separate environment instead, to ensure compatibility with future program upgrades.

Hardware Requirements

To run smoothly, GUIs need high-speed processing and substantial memory resources. For example, to take full advantage of Microsoft Windows 3, you need at least 2MB of memory. That's one reason users stayed away from GUIs until 386-class speed and power became available. To many, the earlier computer systems seemed over-challenged by graphical interfaces that required too much processing power, speed, and screen resolution.

READ.ME

The Ideal GUI

No single GUI has achieved perfection, and they all involve tradeoffs among power, speed, and ease of use. Here are some qualities a perfect GUI would have:

- Icon-rich graphic interface.

- Good-looking screen; fun to work with.

- Direct, graphic handling of screen elements. Page margins or spreadsheet cells can be sized by dragging with a mouse, for example, instead of entering figures in dialog boxes.

- Bitmapped displays with true WYSIWYG screen views of printed documents.

- Support for a wide range of printers.

- Standardized control elements, such as menus and dialog boxes to make it easy to learn.

- Same feel on different computer platforms (MS-DOS and Apple, for example) as well as in different applications.

- Object-action command strategy, so you can, for example, click the mouse on a file then on a word processor to edit the selected file.

- Easy to install, configure, personalize, and use.

- Compatibility with earlier hardware and software.

- Support for data interchange between programs.

Faster CPUs, multimegabyte memory upgrades, full megabyte memory chips, and high resolution graphics adapters and monitors have made GUIs more practical.

No matter what operating system, environment, or GUI you select, make sure it can run your applications. A GUI or other modified user environment should be an enhancement, but it is no enhancement if it won't run your spreadsheet or word processing program. Be sure to ask questions and read the fine print about compatibility before you shell out hard-earned cash for an enhanced interface.

Some Popular GUIs The following is a list of some of the more popular GUIs now available.

- *Microsoft Windows* There are three current versions: Windows/286, Windows/386, and Windows 3. Windows uses sophisticated memory management techniques and fully supports expanded memory. Installation is not the easiest process, requiring a lot of screen reading and time. Once you have Windows installed, working in it can become addictive, especially on fast, 386-based machines. Windows/286 is a good GUI for medium-power PC systems. It requires a 286 machine with 512K of RAM, a graphics adapter, and DOS 3.0 or later. Many applications are available. Windows/386 will run almost all DOS applications. It requires 2MB of RAM but 4MB is recommended. It needs DOS 3.0 or later, a VGA or better graphics adapter, and a mouse. Windows 3.0 is the newest version at this writing, and has made the other two versions obsolete for newer machines. It is easier to use and has a special 386 running mode that lets you multitask non-Windows applications programs. This new Windows version has solidified the program's position as the premier GUI for MS-DOS machines.

- *GEM/Desktop* A powerful package, Digital Research's GEM/Desktop used to be required to run Ventura Publisher. (Ventura now runs under Windows 3 and has announced versions that will run under UNIX and the Apple Macintosh.) GEM also runs other DOS applications, including Windows. It replaces DOS commands with icons that allow GUI movements, such as clicking on a representation of an object (icon or button) and dragging it to another onscreen location in order to accomplish some action.

- *DeskMate*   Easy to learn and use, this Tandy Computer interface is a somewhat limited GUI. (It doesn't support multiple onscreen windows, for example.) It works with any of the 80-series Intel chips, and requires 512K of RAM, a graphics adapter, and DOS 3.2 or later. It is bundled with the Tandy 1000SL and 1000TL machines, but is available for all MS-DOS machines for under $100. DeskMate is a true graphical interface but is not multitasking. Several applications come with and are part of the basic package. It works with drop-down menus, dialog boxes, graphical push buttons, and keyboard substitutes if you don't have a mouse.

- *Presentation Manager*   IBM / Microsoft Presentation Manager is a graphics/mouse user interface program that can be used with the standard OS/2 text interface. Presentation Manager requires a large memory allocation. You'll probably want more than 1MB of memory on your machine to run this program.

- *Open Look* and *Motif*   These are two new GUIs for UNIX. They are close cousins to the Windows / Presentation Manager standard interface.

- *Finder*   This easy-to-use Apple Macintosh GUI is a point-and-click, icon-driven user interface. It is a multitasking, windowing environment that can operate several programs at once and show them onscreen. It can reduce or enlarge windows and move data from one program to another freely, as long as the window stays open.

- *Hewlett-Packard NewWave*   This environment has much impressed testers, but at this writing has not yet been released. It provides an object-oriented environment on top of Windows. You can click on an icon and immediately load a file into a word processor, directly lift graphics from unassociated spreadsheets, and do other tricks designed to make the entire file structure available to you from one central command post. This program is worth watching for.

Other Popular Interfaces

Some of the following programs seem almost to act as full-fledged operating systems. However, they do require an operating system with which to interface. They are fast, non-graphical environments that allow you to jump back and forth directly between applications. Many users prefer these environments to fully graphical ones because of their speed and convenience.

- *DesqView* This is a powerful multitasking, windowing system by Quarterdeck Office Systems that operates equally well with or without a mouse. It is quicker and easier to install than Windows (although not always as easy to use), and has somewhat limited graphics. It does not have a true graphical user interface but has long been considered one of the best and most flexible multiwindow user interfaces available. It works in monochrome, and is the only system that can multitask on 8088 and 80286 systems in "real" operating mode.

- *HyperPad* Bill Roberts' HyperPad is a development tool that lets you design your own DOS interface. It provides pop-up menus, pull-down menus, and dialog boxes. It can run on a monochrome monitor, and can use a keyboard or mouse for commands. It can use color (if available), and has special characters to simulate graphics without slow screen-bitmapping. It allows you to create onscreen buttons that you push to run batch files or DOS commands.

- *VP/ix* and *Merge 386* These DOS-under-UNIX environments allow multiple users. They take advantage of UNIX's high configurability, power, and complexity, and let you enter DOS commands and use DOS applications. They support multiple console sessions (more than one simultaneously running system using the same programs).

SUMMARY

In this chapter you have read about various operating systems and the user interface environments available within them. The various tasks done by an OS were described, in terms of how system components are kept coordinated. Graphical user interfaces, or GUIs, were described in some detail, including both their capabilities and the amount of computing power they require.

The next chapter will sample some of the many applications programs available under MS-DOS. Applications are the programs that let you word process, calculate spreadsheets, and carry out all the other tasks that make computers such powerful tools.

CHAPTER SEVEN

Applications Programs: Getting Your Work Done

An applications program is a set of computer instructions that lets you carry out a specific job. For example, a word processing program lets you create, edit, and print documents; an accounting or financial planning program helps you project your company's monthly earnings. You may use only one or two programs or you may use your computer for many applications. In a single day you might use a word processor, a database program, a drafting program, and a desktop publishing program. At some point your office management software might cause your computer to beep and put a reminder on the screen about an important meeting in five minutes. Later, you might suspend other tasks to sign on to an electronic mail service using your telecommunications program and collect messages or distribute a memo. Within each category of application—word processing, database, desktop publishing, and so on—there are many program choices available.

CHOOSING APPLICATIONS SOFTWARE

Picking the applications programs that are best for you takes a little work. A welter of products competes loudly for your attention, and each program is advertised as the best. To make an informed decision, read reviews, talk to friends, and do some research on each product's features.

For some applications, such as word processing, the choice involves many programs with similar capabilities. For other applications, such as spreadsheets and databases, there are products with more clear-cut strengths and weaknesses in certain areas. Choosing between these products requires matching your needs with a product's strong points. It's easiest of all to choose a program when one or two products absolutely stand out. Sometimes this happens with a breakthrough new release of a familiar product that incorporates many new features. Finally, there's a group that might be called Eureka! applications. You'll know them because they exactly match your needs. Let's say you've searched long and hard for a good way to keep track of your canary feathers, along with digitized images of all species of canaries. Then you stumble upon CANARY.EXE, the perfect canary feather database program. You shout "Eureka!" and look no more.

What Makes a Good Program?

Ultimately, there's only one reason to keep any program in your software collection, no matter how aggressively marketed or fancy looking it is: it must help you accomplish some task. As the user, you are the final judge of whether a program is useful to you. Buying something untried is risky, of course, but there is some safety in numbers. If everyone gives a program high ratings, you're on pretty safe ground buying it. If someone across the street or down the hall is already adept at using a certain program and is willing to help you learn it, you're a step ahead if you buy that program.

There is one good rule of thumb: an applications program runs best on machines with more capacity than the program was written for. If speed is your goal, one of the simplest ways to get it is to run programs designed for the previous hardware cycle. For example, if a program was written for a 286 machine, it will scream along on a 386. If 20 MHz was top of the line when a program was written, it'll really fly at 25 MHz.

Where to Start

There are tens of thousands of programs available. No one person is expert in all or even most of them. It is not the purpose of this book to list all those programs, their functions, and their costs. Rather, this chapter will help you get a better sense of your specific needs, and you'll find it easier to match those needs to candidate programs when you make your selection. Whatever application you start with probably will be only the first in a series of programs. If you are like most people, you will accumulate more programs quickly. That's to be expected. A computer is a very versatile tool; the more programs you have, the more you can do with it.

Chapter Overview

The rest of this chapter describes different types of applications and suggests a few good programs in each area. It can be used as the first step in your research. The programs mentioned are for MS-DOS machines, but if you have another type of machine the same kind of reasoning described will apply to your software purchase decisions.

READ.ME

Historical Marker:
Applications and the PC Revolution

When Apple II personal computers first appeared on the scene in the mid- to late 1970s, computer buffs were fascinated, but the business world mostly yawned. There had been special-purpose word processing machines for years, and most large companies used them. These machines could store documents, merge data into form letters, and even check spelling. Print quality using daisy wheel printers was excellent.

Smaller firms had the electric typewriter. If you needed real computing power, you could rent time and memory space on a time-sharing mainframe computer for reasonable fees. Why on earth would any business need a tiny (64K) computer that could only drive a crude 9-pin printer, run simple games, and do very little else?

There matters stood for a while. It would take something new to change minds, to make businesspeople think they just *had* to have the new gadget. An application was needed that would make general purpose desktop computers look like something that no well-run business could do without. Until that happened, desktop computers were only a curiosity. After all, new technology without a purpose is just new technology.

READ.ME

Historical Marker:
Applications and the PC Revolution (*continued*)

Enter Dan Bricklin and Bob Frankston in 1978. These two visionaries teamed up to create a product that turned the Apple computer into the backbone of a multibillion-dollar industry. Working together, Bricklin and Frankston created a "visible calculator" they named VisiCalc and formed a company called VisiCorp to market their product. VisiCalc was the first electronic spreadsheet program. It profoundly affected the way business would be conducted from then on. (It also bequeathed us a legion of products with odd capital letters in their names—the HiTech OddCap tradition, you might term it.)

With VisiCalc, project cost or sales estimates that formerly might have taken weeks to complete could be done in an afternoon. You could change some numbers—say, the percentage of hours budgeted for overtime—and watch the repercussions ripple down the screen, right into the bottom line.

During the period from 1978 to 1982 VisiCalc was the spreadsheet program to have. Just about every Fortune 500 (now 1000) firm had an arsenal of Apple II systems, each equipped with a fresh copy of VisiCalc.

The appearance in 1981 of IBM's PC changed the picture. A version of VisiCalc was quickly developed for IBM systems, but the program did not translate well; it was less efficient than the Apple version. Around this time, one of VisiCorp's key people, Mitch Kapor, left to form a new company called Lotus. He announced a new product, Lotus 1-2-3, with loud fanfare at the 1982 Fall COMDEX, one of the great annual computer trade shows.

Kapor was a master showman. The rollout for Lotus 1-2-3 took place in a rented airplane hanger complete with champagne, slick literature, and flashy demonstrations. Soon Kapor's catchy slogan spread through the industry:

1 for Spreadsheet
2 for Database
3 for Graphics

The impact of Kapor's marketing strengths and Lotus 1-2-3's powerful integration quickly became apparent. VisiCalc lost its position of dominance, its parent firms suffered huge financial losses, and eventually VisiCorp was purchased by its slayer—Lotus Development Corporation. It is ironic that the company formed by Bricklin and Frankston, who together created VisiCalc and launched the personal computer industry, became an early casualty of the very currents it had helped set in motion.

If you're just starting out, the simple approach is probably best. Pick an application you know you need, buy a program that will fill that need, and go from there. As you learn to use your machine, you can expand the limits—both yours and your system's.

APPLICATIONS PROGRAM BASICS

Throughout this chapter, as you become familiar with the major types of software, you'll have an opportunity to think about the kind of system you want to establish. Like the tools in your workshop, computer programs come in many sizes, with many purposes. No two expert mechanics have the same set of tools; likewise, no two computer users have exactly the same needs or programs.

Most people get a computer for both specific and general reasons. General reasons may include increasing personal productivity, staying current with technology, or qualifying for a class or job that requires familiarity with a PC.

More specific reasons tie in with specific applications. They include a need to prepare written documents, create spreadsheets, publish a newsletter, or accomplish some other well-defined task. There's your starting point when buying software—look for a program that will fulfill any *specific reasons* you had for buying the machine. For most people, that means using one or more of these applications:

Word processing
Spreadsheets
Record keeping (databases)
Telecommunications
Desktop publishing
Investment and financial management
Science and engineering
Graphics
Simulations and games

If your computer did not come with appropriate software already installed—or if you just want to get a better handle on the software you do have or still need to get—you will benefit from looking at some basic differences between programs.

Power, Simplicity, and the User Interface

Some of the differences among programs aimed at the same applications are their relative size, power, simplicity, cost, and ease of use. All design work, whether of hardware or software, involves trade-offs. In programming, a common trade-off is between power and simplicity. Generally speaking, the more a program can do, the more you must know in order to take full advantage of its capabilities.

However, the trade-off between power and simplicity is beginning to disappear. Menu-driven programs are now standard and graphical user interfaces are common, so powerful programs are becoming easier to use. The transformation to power plus ease of use is not yet complete, but among the most powerful programs, most now use menus and have mouse drivers. If you use a mouse or some other special input device with these programs, the investment is returned manyfold in ease of use.

As people become accustomed to using menus and graphics, many programs have adopted cursor-key scroll bar menus, as shown in Figure 7-1, as a sort of standard. To select an item from this type of menu, you move the scroll bar over your selection and either click a mouse button or press the

Figure 7-1

Qmodem pull-down setup menu

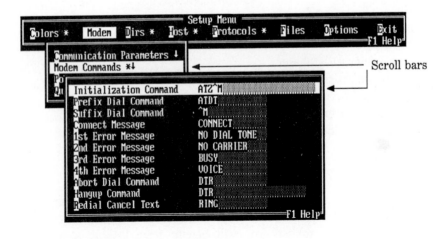

ENTER key. Pointing at a menu item in this way is much easier than trying to remember a series of commands.

Several Small Programs Versus One Large Program

Even with the best full-menu interface, you must know what the available commands mean. So it is still true that the more commands there are, the more there is to learn. It takes time to look through the manuals, check out the menu choices, and try the various commands. With large programs, it can take most of a day just to learn the basics. To become truly adept can take much longer.

Some people prefer a smaller-is-better approach. They like to use several small programs, each of which does one thing well. If you don't need the power of one large program right away, this can be a good choice. An advantage of using small programs is that they are quick to load and easy to learn. They're usually peppy in operation, and their simplicity keeps bugs to a minimum.

A disadvantage is that it may take several small programs to do what a more powerful program can do in a single pass. The small programs may not be compatible. Also, learning several sets of unrelated command systems can be more difficult than learning one large but consistent set of commands.

At some point, your tasks may become complex enough that you decide to switch from several simple programs to a single, more muscular program. You would not necessarily have been better off with more power in the first place. While you were coming up to speed with your system and learning the simple tasks first, the powerful programs were evolving. The trend in computing is toward more power in less space for less money—and that is true of software as well as hardware. By waiting until you actually need more power, you may rack up benefits in price, power, ease of use, and reliability.

A simple start also lets you grow into your system. You'll be more experienced and be able to make more informed decisions when you upgrade. Do you really need the power of advanced programs like Lucid 3D, SuperCalc 5, or Quattro, or should you go with the de facto standard, Lotus 1-2-3? Do you need an expensive word processor, or would a small, fast text editor and a desktop publishing program serve you better? A little experience will make it easier to decide.

Some Questions, Some Suggestions   One advantage of starting simple is that you don't pay for advanced features you may not need. Ask yourself if you are fairly certain about what you need your software to accomplish. If you are not, by all means consider starting simple. Your starting point might be an affordable integrated program or a collection of shareware programs. An integrated program combines several applications in one package and is designed for breadth, not for depth in any one of its applications. Shareware, with some exceptions, is designed to be fast, effective, and affordable for a single application. Some shareware programs, such as ButtonWare's PC-File and Quicksoft's PC-Write, are regularly rated higher than many of their much more expensive commercial competitors. Medium-range integrated programs like Microsoft Works and WordPerfect Executive are becoming standard for executive and professional users—and for laptop and notebook computers, where storage space is limited.

In general, it is a good idea to work your way up to the brawnier commercial packages after you've had a chance to learn whether you really need or want the extra features. You save time because simpler, less expensive programs tend to be easier to learn. And the risk is less. If a program doesn't quite fit the bill, you haven't lost an arm and a leg finding out.

Where to Get Software

Once you've decided what types of programs to get, you're ready to find a vendor. You can get programs from a dizzying number of sources.

Bundled Software

Start with the store or company that sells you your computer system: it's likely they'll bundle your machine with a variety of programs. *Bundling* means including something extra in the deal—in this case, software programs. You buy the hardware and get a bundle of software with it. Vendors have discovered that new users want to be able to get started with their system as soon as they flip on the power switch for the first time. Many vendors try to help by throwing in one or two major programs they think you may need. The bundled programs may not turn out to be exactly right for you, but they'll be a good start.

Local Sources

When you get a better feel for your particular needs, look around for good values. Search the local bulletin board systems if you have a modem. Talk to people in user groups. Browse at your local computer store; it will not only have software, but probably have a machine up and running where you can try different programs. If the program that interests you isn't installed, don't be shy. Ask the salesperson to install it (that is their job, to do what it takes to sell you software). The salesperson may stay with you to show you the program's strengths; you'll have to discover the weaknesses for yourself, unfortunately. Any such test drives are useful, since you can begin to figure out a program out in the store where you have guidance.

Many bookstores have sections devoted to computer books and programs. Some popular computer books come with bound-in software collections on disks.

Computer magazines are a good source of advertisements. Some, like *Computer Shopper*, are so packed with ads that you can spend hours browsing through the hardware, software, add-ons, and new products. When browsing in magazines, look for discount mail-order services — some mail-order houses offer discounts of 20 to 60 percent off suggested list prices. (Be sure you know what you need before you buy.)

Don't let price be your sole concern. Quality, service, and convenience count for a lot. Paying a few extra dollars for the sort of help and support a local vendor can offer is often a good investment.

Catalogs

If you subscribe to a computer magazine or two, you'll soon begin to receive catalogs in the mail. You can refuse permission to put your name on catalog mailing lists, of course, but catalogs can be fine hardware and software supermarkets. Some catalogs are of the best picks type, with software selected by the editor or publisher as best-of-class or as unsung gems. Other catalogs specialize in business, finance, games, graphics, or other applications. Some aim at high-ticket audiences while others are strictly discount oriented. One prominent catalog, *DAK*, offers can't-beat-'em bargains on current and non-current versions of popular programs; pennies on the dollar may get you, say, version 4.3 of a powerhouse program for which version 4.4 was recently released.

Shareware

Some extraordinary applications programs are available at very low cost in the form of shareware. Shareware is a marketing approach many independent software authors use to publish their work. With shareware, you can use a program and see if you like it before you pay for it. If you do like the program, you pay a low registration fee. Frequently, the program fee also entitles you to technical support, printed manuals, and sometimes, additional program capabilities. You also get the good feeling of knowing you're helping an independent spirit bring new ideas to market.

Shareware is a great way for program authors to distribute their work when they lack the $20,000 or more that a full-page ad costs in a national magazine. The author releases a new program and its documentation into established shareware channels, such as bulletin board systems, and waits for a response from users. If a sufficient number of people like the program well enough to register, the author continues to improve the program. Otherwise, well, maybe there's another project on the horizon.

Because shareware promotional costs are so low, the publishers can afford to let users license (purchase the right to use) their programs for quite modest fees. Since distribution costs are so low, authors can continually upgrade their products. Unlike the huge commercial software houses, shareware publishers don't require costly product rollouts, huge paid staffs, and expensive marketing hype for every new release. That's a significant advantage, since it means the publisher can be extremely responsive to users' demands. If a user reports a bug, the author can fix it and release a new version that afternoon. If several users request a new feature, the author can accommodate them quickly.

Shareware programs are distributed through a variety of channels, described in "The World of Low-Cost Shareware," in this chapter.

A WEALTH OF APPLICATIONS

In the rest of this chapter you will read about some of the many applications available to PC users. They range from the so-called Big Four that early users thought covered just about everything useful a PC could do, to some fields like desktop publishing that came along later.

THE TRADITIONAL BIG FOUR APPLICATIONS

By the time the Apple II and the IBM PC had finished making the desktop computer a business necessity and a household word, the software market had settled down. Revolutionary changes no longer came along every six or eight months. Important innovations still occur, but the pace is much less giddy than in the early days.

READ.ME

The World of Low-Cost Shareware

Shareware is a term originally coined by Bob Wallace, the author of a powerful shareware word processor named PC-Write. Wallace shares with two other program authors the distinction of creating an entirely new marketing approach: put a program into free distribution, let potential users try it, and trust them to register by sending in a fee if they like the program and will continue to use it.

When Wallace coined the term shareware, it was because PC-Write users who recruited other users shared some of the resulting registration fees. It is a policy that Wallace's firm, Quicksoft, still follows. However, since Wallace donated the term to the public domain, it has become the generic name for all software that is freely distributed and depends upon satisfied customers to register voluntarily after a trial run.

The other two early pioneers of the shareware concept are Jim Button, author of PC-File and founder of Buttonware, and the late Andrew Fluegelman, author of PC-Talk and publisher of *The Headlands Press*. Fluegelman used the term *Freeware*, but he trademarked the name for *The Headlands Press*. Besides, the term is misleading since users must pay to register. Everyone uses the term shareware instead.

To the surprise of some cynics, the system works well. Shareware has become a software institution. All types of programs are available as shareware, often for a fraction of the cost of similar commercial products. Extremely powerful shareware is available at prices from $10 to $150, depending upon the size and power of the program. For a direct route into the world of shareware, plug into one of the following distribution channels.

Computer User Groups

Computer user groups can be found just about anywhere. They are mutual interest groups or clubs, usually run by volunteers (although some user groups have paid directors). Since user groups attract the most dedicated and knowledgeable PC users, there's no better place to go for freely shared expertise. Many user groups maintain bulletin board systems (BBSs), send out newsletters, maintain their own software libraries, and provide help to members on request. To find a local user group, ask a salesperson (or better yet, a technician) at your local computer store; go to a computer fair or swap meet; call a local college or computer training school; and look in *Computer Shopper*, a computer tabloid that has become one of the all-time great computer resources. Once you join a user group, you'll never be more than a phone call away from competent help when you have problems. You'll also tap directly into one of the main shareware distribution channels.

READ.ME

The World of Low-Cost Shareware (*continued*)

Electronic Bulletin Board Systems

Electronic bulletin board systems (BBSs) are run by hobbyists and entrepreneurs in just about every city in the United States, and increasingly throughout the world. In the past five years or so the electronic world of BBSs has caught fire. It is fertile ground for world-wide information exchange. You can have your computer call a BBS and obtain copies of any of thousands of powerful programs. To find a local BBS, call your computer store or electronics shop; if a salesperson doesn't know where to find a BBS, one of the technicians probably will. Once you reach your first BBS, you'll be into the network. Other BBSers will help you go from there.

Commercial Disk Vendors

Commercial disk vendors maintain extensive libraries of shareware and uncopyrighted public domain programs, which they sell through catalogs at $2 to $6 a disk. Although vending companies are for-profit operations, their margin is not high and the good ones earn their keep by acting something like purchasing agents for shareware users. Vendors screen programs, store them on disks in logical groups, and stay current with new releases. A vendor-supplied disk usually contains several programs, and may include applications, utilities (refer to Chapter 8), games, and other types of programs. The established disk vendors advertise in computer magazines, offering their catalogs for free or for a small fee. You may find these catalogs better organized and more selective than the libraries maintained by user groups, since program screening is part of the service that lets a disk vendor succeed in a highly competitive business.

Note: The vendor's fee for a shareware disk covers only direct costs, not program registration fees. Shareware registration fees typically run from $10 to $150 per program, with larger and more powerful programs costing more.

Commercial Information Services

The giant electronic information services, such as CompuServe, GEnie, and Delphi, are the mainstay of many modem users. You can buy starter kits for CompuServe at many computer stores. The leading online information services have free 800 numbers you can call to sign up. CompuServe is currently the largest of the information services, with a huge number of IBM-oriented special interest groups, or SIGs. Online information services typically charge from $6 to $12.50 an hour for the time you are connected to them. They provide their subscribers with rapid-response answers to questions and, for many shareware authors, are the preferred method of distribution.

This change had already begun when the PC AT was introduced in 1985. At that time, most of the major software programs fell into one of four application categories:

Word processing
Spreadsheets
Telecommunications
Databases

This list is in descending order of *installed user base,* or number of people who own the program. Many industry watchers were surprised by this order. For one thing, the spreadsheet, not word processing, started the computer revolution. For another, record keeping (maintaining a database) had for years been the most common application for large computers, yet it didn't carry over to PCs.

Now, databases and telecommunications both have faded a bit. Other programs have usurped their positions on the list of primary applications. Categories like desktop publishing and presentation graphics have drawn the limelight while telecommunication by modem has been (perhaps temporarily) eclipsed by the fax machine. In fact, the list of major applications has expanded tremendously. Still, if a computer user mentions the Big Four, people familiar with the field still think of the four mentioned previously.

Word Processors

Word processors may not have started the PC revolution, but it wasn't long before 85 to 90 percent of all people with desktop computers had *and used* a word processor. Spreadsheet programs are as popular as ever, but word processing is the most widely used PC application. One reason is that word processing is a near universal need. Most people who use computers need to compose written reports, letters, memos, or other documents.

A Word Processing Overview

The field of word processing has come a long way since the early days. When word processing programs appeared, they did little more than mimic electronic typewriters, using a screen instead of paper. Available programs had few features. The basic functions were there, such as move up or down a line, insert or delete a letter, and move right or left. There was always a command to save a file and, usually, a command to print it, although some programs relied on the DOS PRINT command for that function.

As computer speed and capacity improved, so did features in word processing programs. Users realized that it was fastest to type along quickly and take advantage of onscreen editing features when the document was complete. They also needed *more* features, such as a way to delete whole lines instead of pressing the delete or backspace key many times in a row. They needed the ability to move or copy words, phrases, and paragraphs at a time. They needed to be able to change one string of characters to another (for example, Mr. Smith to Ms. Jones) throughout a file, all at once. And computers ought to be able to check for spelling mistakes.

Spelling Checkers   To satisfy these vocal power users, many new features appeared, including spelling checkers and electronic thesauruses. The first spelling checkers tagged as misspelled any word not in their dictionary, and you couldn't just look up the correct spelling and fix it right then. Instead, you had to go back later and enter your corrections. Checking the spelling in a short file could take five or six minutes, and the tagged words often turned out to be spelled correctly. The early 10,000 to 20,000 word spelling dictionaries were simply too small for normal business use, let alone specialty fields like law, medicine, or engineering. Many people gave up on these early spelling checkers in disgust.

The next generation of spelling checkers had larger dictionaries and gave you better options. You could press a button to correct a word or ignore the unrecognized spelling and go on to the next one. These more powerful spelling checkers were expensive options on many word processors, but users quickly came to consider them essential.

Competition has made the spelling checker a standard feature. Figure 7-2 shows a spelling checker screen from WordStar. Checkers suggest corrections that you can make in less than a second. Some spelling checkers know when to capitalize letters. Some let you check definitions. Most know about proper nouns; will let you add or delete words from your working dictionary; and can use special medical, legal, scientific, or foreign language dictionaries.

Grammar Checkers   Grammar checkers make sure you have two spaces after a period and one after a comma and ensure all parentheses and quotes are used in opening and closing pairs. They scan for sexist, cliched, or hackneyed expressions, for slang, overused words, incomplete sentences,

Figure 7-2

WordStar spelling checker

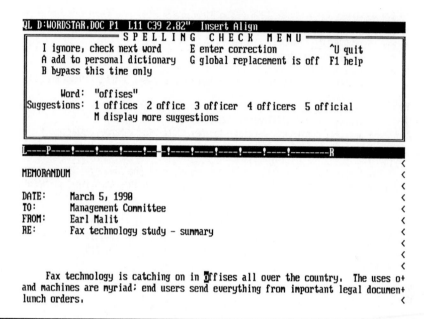

```
QL D:WORDSTAR.DOC P1  L11 C39 2.82"  Insert Align
═══════════════ S P E L L I N G   C H E C K   M E N U ═══════════
  I ignore, check next word      E enter correction           ^U quit
  A add to personal dictionary   G global replacement is off  F1 help
  B bypass this time only


       Word:  "offises"
 Suggestions:  1 offices  2 office  3 officer  4 officers  5 official
               M display more suggestions


 L----P----!----!----!----!--!-!----!----!----!----!----!-------R
                                                                  <
 MEMORANDUM                                                       <
                                                                  <
 DATE:      March 5, 1990                                         <
 TO:        Management Committee                                  <
 FROM:      Earl Malit                                            <
 RE:        Fax technology study - summary                       <
                                                                  <
                                                                  <
                                                                  <
     Fax technology is catching on in Offises all over the country.  The uses of
 and machines are myriad; end users send everything from important legal document
 lunch orders.                                                    <
```

and wordiness. The result can be stronger, better writing, although slavish obedience to a grammar checker can make your prose deadly dull. The same is true of an electronic thesaurus; overuse of any such tool can make your style seem pretentious or flat.

Advances and Advantages

Word processors represent a tremendous advance over the typewriter. Their main advantages are ease of revision and automated help you can call on when needed. Easy revision means you can rapidly shuffle paragraphs, change sentences, or replace words without retyping an entire document. Automated help may include a spelling checker, a thesaurus, and style guides. User-defined styles let you switch automatically from one paragraph style to another; for example, from outline style to flush left text. A thesaurus lets you choose the word you want from a list of words with closely related meanings (see Figure 7-3)—a blessing if you catch yourself using the same word five times on a page.

Figure 7-3

Word Finder thesaurus screen

```
════════════════ WORD FINDER from Micrologics, Inc. ══════════════════
increase:                                                    MORE: PgDn
noun •  enlargement, growth, rise, swell;
     •  addition, increment.
verb •  add, append, attach, join;
     •  amplify, bolster, encourage, enhance, enhearten, hearten, inspire,
        reassure, strengthen, support;
     •  amplify, bloat, dilate, distend, enlarge, expand, fatten, grow,
        inflate, magnify, stretch, swell, widen;
     •  amplify, construct, develop, devise, elaborate, enhance, enlarge,
        expand, expound, refine;
    ↑↓←→:point       RTN:replace       ESC:exit       Shift-F6 :look up
```

Fax technology is catching on in offices all over the country. The uses o↑
and machines are myriad; end users send everything from important legal documen↑
lunch orders.   <

The report findings suggest good news for vendors of fax technology. Expe↑
to increased productivity as the key. Paul Schrock, senior analyst at McCracke↑
ates, observes, "The potential for substantive increases in the productivity of↑
is immense with the fax technology."   <

READ.ME

The Word Processor Wars

If there is a dominant force in word processing at this writing, it is Word-
Perfect. One reason WordPerfect is in the top position is an exemplary
technical support policy. You can call WordPerfect on their 800-number support line and receive immediate answers without tiresome proof-of-purchase
questions. Another factor is WordPerfect's record of frequent interim upgrades between major releases. These upgrades are available to registered
users for shareware-like prices—on the order of $10 a disk. WordPerfect also
supports nearly every printer ever made, and if you change printers, you can
get the driver you need by calling the WordPerfect bulletin board system via
your modem. In short, WordPerfect has been judged a superior product,
which sets new standards for user support and value in its price range.

Other word processor companies have greatly enhanced their own products and are working hard to overturn the current industry standards for
price and performance. As a result, today's market is a buyer's delight. If a

READ.ME

The Word Processor Wars (*continued*)

word processing software publisher doesn't offer extensive user support, you probably should keep looking.

Methods of product support vary widely from publisher to publisher. Some publishers subtract the cost of support from their total product price by making it an optional purchase. Some vendors have started fax-back services to fax to users, at the vendor's expense, the pertinent pages of the manual, as well as update notes and tip sheets. For some word processing software, such as PC-Write, telephone support is offered for a specified period as a separate purchase. With other publishers, such as Lotus Development Corporation and ButtonWare Inc., technical support is via a 900 number and you are billed for each minute you're on the line. (Don't get put on hold!) Some vendors limit support to a total time limit, such as two hours.

WordStar, in version 6.0 at this writing, is very much back in the marketplace. Like VisiCalc among spreadsheets, WordStar was at one time so dominant that nearly every word processor and text editor on the market still recognizes the basic WordStar command set.

Many people consider WordStar as good as or superior to WordPerfect. It bills itself as the only major word processor that can be used comfortably by fast touch-typists. Although some supporters of XyWrite dispute that claim, it is certainly true that when working in WordStar you don't have to use the function keys or a mouse unless you want to. Every WordStar command can be executed with the main typing keys, using the ALT or CTRL key plus a regular alphabet or numeric key. For touch typists accustomed to standard keyboards, disrupting the typing rhythm to hunt for a particular function key can be an annoyance.

Less expensive word processors are adopting high-end extras and should also be considered. Shareware products like PC-Write are changing the game, making high-end features accessible to students, home users, and others on a tight budget. Before making a final decision on what word processor to buy, take time to read some recent magazine reviews. The relative merits of various programs are constantly changing.

Many word processors will show you your document as it will look when printed, so you can adjust short lines and awkward page breaks. Figures 7-4 and 7-5 show some print preview options from different programs. Word processors make it possible for you to move sections of text within a document and export paragraphs or pages to another document. When you type in a word processing program, the words automatically *wrap* (continue

Figure 7-4

Microsoft Works page preview

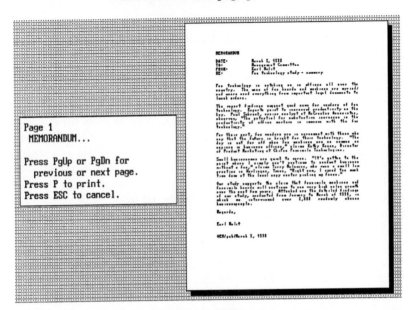

Figure 7-5

First Publisher showing a print preview of a desktop published memo

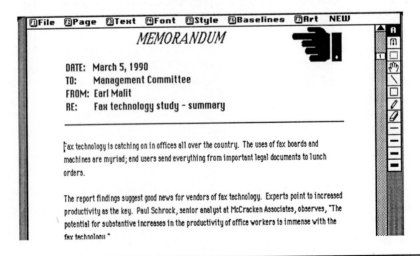

Figure 7-6

Text without automatic hyphenation

```
    Your personal taste and your pocketbook are the only
restrictions on choosing a spreadsheet program.  There are some
very powerful, very complicated and very expensive ones on the
market.  Integrated programs like MS Works include simple
spreadsheets that interact beautifully with the other program
modules, like their databases and their not-always-simple word
processors.  You can find friendly, easy to use programs
including some very good Shareware offerings.  Then there are the
spreadsheet "biggies," starting with Lotus.
```

---

onto the next line) when you reach the end of a line. Some programs even provide automatic hyphenation to keep an unjustified right margin from getting too ragged or the words in justified text from being spaced too far apart. (See Figures 7-6 and 7-7.)

A single keystroke lets you know just how many words you've typed, the exact number of characters, how many lines you have on each page, and the total number of pages in the document. When printing, the program can automatically provide page numbers and create professional-looking headings across the top of each page. You can import graphics, including charts, line drawings, and photographs, so they print as part of the document. You can save your document to a file and call it up again later to incorporate comments or borrow the parts you like best for another document. The features are almost limitless.

Figure 7-7

Text showing automatic hyphenation

```
    Your personal taste and your pocketbook are the only re-
strictions on choosing a spreadsheet program.  There are some
very powerful, very complicated and very expensive ones on the
market.  Integrated programs like MS Works include simple spread-
sheets that interact beautifully with the other program modules,
like their databases and their not-always-simple word processors.
You can find friendly, easy to use programs including some very
good Shareware offerings.  Then there are the spreadsheet "big-
gies," starting with Lotus.
```

You can also use special fonts and formats in your document. For example, you can print a section of text in italics, boldface, or underlined, in a variety of typefaces and letter sizes. Different programs show formatting onscreen in different ways.

WYSIWYG Programs   In a graphic-mode word processor like Microsoft Word, special characters and fonts like italics and underline show on the screen the way they will print out (see Figure 7-8). This is called *WYSI-WYG* (pronounced "wizzy-wig") for what you see is what you get. WYSIWYG programs require graphics capability and work best with at least VGA resolution levels.

Control Characters   PC-Write and other programs combine special characters like happy faces with onscreen effects including highlights and colors (see Figure 7-9). You have to know what these special characters and highlights mean to interpret the screen.

Special Format Characters   Some powerhouse programs like Word-Perfect and WordStar give you the option of showing or hiding spelled-out interpretations of special formats. This can make for a cluttered screen, as shown in Figure 7-10. You can unclutter the screen by hiding the special format characters when you don't need to see them, as in Figure 7-11.

Figure 7-8

Microsoft Works WYSIWYG screen

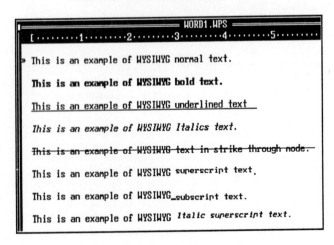

Figure 7-9

PC-Write special characters

```
L---+Q--T1----+-T--2----T----3--T-+----4T---+--T5---+-T--6----T----7--T-+--R
         What you're ‡really‡ dealing with are the basic characteristics
of different machines, the questions that address how well a
computer will meet your needs:

8-8    § How big a program can the machine run?
8-8    § How fast can it run it?
8-8    § How much data can it process at once?
8-8    § How big, physically, is the machine?
8-8    § How many programs are available for it?
8-8    § What other machines can trade files with it?
```

Figure 7-10

WordStar file showing format characters

```
E:USER3.WS    P2  L16 C12 .83"   Insert Align
      P--L-!----!----!----!----!----!----!----R
.pn2                                                                    1
<Heading 2>  {Passwords, Chan}Changing Passwords                        <
                                                                        <
<Body text>     {Passwords, rule}You can change your own Password whenever you +
changing about once a month, just to avoid possible problems.  Passwords must f+
these rules:                                                            <
                                                                        <
<Body text>    ►    <LINE PR 17 PC>■<HELV 12 N ASCII> Not less than 8 charact+
          ►   <LINE PR 17 PC>■<HELV 12 N ASCII> Not more than 64 characters long. <
          ►   <LINE PR 17 PC>■<HELV 12 N ASCII> Not all numerals.       <
          ►   <LINE PR 17 PC>■<HELV 12 N ASCII> No more than 3 identical character+
          ►   <LINE PR 17 PC>■<HELV 12 N ASCII> No character strings containing th+
          ►   <LINE PR 17 PC>■<HELV 12 N ASCII> No Password the same as the User I+
                                                                        <
<Body text>    To change your password:                                 <
                                                                        <
<Hanging indent>    (1)   {Passwords, proc}Reboot the computer by turning it o+
          DEL^Y key combination built into DOS).                        <
```

────────── **Figure 7-11** ──────────

WordStar file with format characters hidden

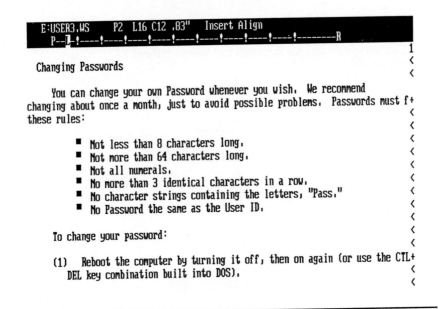

Some Popular Word Processors
The following is a partial list of well-known full-featured word processors. The brief description of each program's features should give you some idea of its strengths.

- *WordPerfect* Features of WordPerfect include a function-key orientation, a terrific help system, direct graphics import, an outliner, and an equation editor.

- *WordStar* Features of this program include keyboard orientation, which is billed as the standard for touch-typists, and a great page preview system.

- *Microsoft Word* Some features of Microsoft Word include graphical interface, mouse orientation, WYSIWYG display, outstanding formatting power, and an outliner.

- *Lotus Manuscript* The features of Lotus Manuscript include an equation editor and an outliner.

- *Nota Bene* This program features Lotus-style menus, customizable outlines, the ability to create footnotes and cross-references, and quick access to huge files.

- *XyWrite* XyWrite is command driven and is very fast. It is a favorite of writers and journalists.

- *PC-Write* This program is ASCII-oriented, very fast, and has flexible macros. It is affordable and is available as shareware.

- *Professional Write* Features of Professional Write include powerful formatting, graphics, and database capabilities. It is also very easy to learn and use.

- *Borland SPRINT* SPRINT features customizable menus and auto-indexing. It also mimics other interfaces.

- *Q&A Write* Q&A Write is Microsoft Windows- and WYSIWYG-oriented. It has flexible style sheets and size-it-yourself graphics.

- *AMI* Using the Windows environment, this program features effortless graphics and can double as a desktop publisher.

Text Editors

Text editors are more compact and limited than word processors. They provide most of a word processor's text manipulation abilities, but leave out features like fancy formatting and built-in spelling checkers. As a result, they tend to be smaller and faster than word processors.

Text editors usually store files in ASCII format; they do not use special formatting characters. Although most word processors have what WordStar calls a *nondocument mode,* in which files are saved in ASCII, many people prefer to use a small, fast-loading editor program for tasks that require ASCII files. ASCII output is necessary for creating batch files (Chapter 11) and for sending electronic messages.

Many outstanding text editors are marketed as shareware. Many people who use full-featured text editors like QEdit, New York Word, Galaxy, VDE, BlackBeard, or Edwin swear by them. Whether you will prefer a text editor to a word processor is a matter of personal taste and style, as well as what capabilities you need. If you are just starting out, a final consideration is that many text editors lack the kind of polished, detailed manuals that you get with most well-known word processors.

Some Popular Text Editing Programs

The following list of text editors does not begin to exhaust the available programs, but one or more of these will be available through just about any shareware source. Some of these editors, like QEdit and New York Word, are almost full-fledged word processors. Others, like TEdit, go for fast-and-tiny. VDE can read and write directly to both WordStar and WordPerfect files; the others handle ASCII files only.

- *QEdit*   This editor is fast, powerful, and command- and menu-driven.
- *New York Word*   This text editor is fast, powerful, and full featured.
- *Word Manager*   Word Manager is mouse-oriented, similar to Microsoft Word.
- *Galaxy*   Galaxy is also mouse-oriented and is easy to learn.
- *PC-Lite*   This is a small version of PC-Write.
- *Mind Reader*   Using AI (artificial intelligence), Mind Reader anticipates your words.
- *TEdit*   TEdit is tiny and fast—like a small QEdit.
- *VDE*   VDE is small, command- or menu-driven, and handles WordPerfect and WordStar files.
- *BlackBeard*   BlackBeard is a programmer's editor with some sophisticated word processing features. It is easy to learn and use.

Outliners

Outliners are terrific productivity tools on a PC. A combination thought organizer, information manager, and word processor, they help you organize ideas, keep to-do and other lists, and prepare articles, letters, contracts, and other documents.

Outliners allow you to restructure and rearrange your thoughts in new and productive ways. You can take a document prepared with an outliner, hide everything but the headlines, and rearrange the sections into a new and better order. You can break long sections apart and move the parts into new arrangements. When you are done, you can transfer the results to a word processor or desktop publisher for final preparation.

Because outliners are powerful thinking tools, many good word processors (and even some best-selling utility packages, such as Sidekick Plus and PC-Tools) feature some outlining capability. The outliner built into Microsoft Word is particularly good; WordPerfect includes a built-in outliner; and WordStar is bundled with a special, semi-integrated edition of PC-Outline, a dedicated outline processor. Other word processors also include limited outlining capabilities.

The original outliner, ThinkTank, now is sold only in upgraded form as a Macintosh program named More. If you have an old MS-DOS version of the program, don't throw it out. Its publisher, LVT (Living VideoTex, a division of Symantec) still supports it. The current best known MS-DOS outliners are

- *PC-Outline* Originally shareware, PC-Outline is now a commercial product. It has easy headline movement, is fast and flexible, has macros, up to nine windows, and great text control. It has a memory resident option and is menu- or command-driven.

- *GrandView* This is a powerful program with a memory-resident option that takes only 17K. It can process up to nine outlines at once, supports use of expanded memory, and can have direct interface with Harvard Graphics or Lotus Freelance for instant slide shows. Other features include calendar links, a spelling checker, the ability to assign job priorities and schedule writing tasks or other simple kinds of project management tasks, and the ability to import other outliner files.

- *MaxThink* This program allows multiple file access from within an outline. A related Houdini module creates "idea nodes" instead of text outlines. MaxThink is topic oriented and allows sorts of randomized topic sequences as prods to thought. It also features easy, powerful macros.

- *IZE* This is a high-end outlining program. It features text retrieval and can link to other applications including Lotus 1-2-3, Q&A, Quattro, and more than 20 different word processors. It can be somewhat awkward to use.

Spreadsheets

Spreadsheet programs launched personal computers as a huge industry, and their importance hasn't flagged. When introduced, they were called *electronic spreadsheets* to distinguish them from spreadsheets produced by hand. The *electronic* has been dropped now; if it's a spreadsheet, people assume it was done electronically.

Spreadsheets are important to business because they do, at lightning speed, anything with numbers that you can do with paper, a pencil, and a lot of time. With a spreadsheet program, if you change a number the program instantaneously recalculates every number that is affected by the change. That makes spreadsheets great what-if tools. What if you hire one more employee instead of scheduling more overtime? What if you move your assembly operations to another location with lower rent? What if you buy a new building and depreciate it for tax purposes over the next seven years?

Best of all, spreadsheet programs minimize errors and make it easy to create a neat final product. You'll never again have to use a ruler to split columns in two because you need twelve columns but only have eight on a page. And when you're done, it's already typed and ready for printing. It's no wonder VisiCalc took the market by storm and turned desktop computers into business necessities.

Using a Spreadsheet

Figure 7-12 shows an example of a spreadsheet. In their most basic application, spreadsheet programs keep your numbers in a straight line and allow you to edit your figures before you print them out. But spreadsheet programs really shine when you allow them to work for you. Some programs now have built-in desktop publishing capabilities. With these programs, you can generate graphics, incorporate them into reports, and make your documents both visually elegant and easy to understand.

The art of using spreadsheets lies in setting them up so that you enter the minimum amount of data and allow the program to calculate as many figures as possible.

A spreadsheet *cell* is the intersection of a horizontal row and a vertical column. The entry in a cell can be text, a number, or a formula. The only restriction is that you stay within the column and row format.

Some three-dimensional spreadsheet programs like Lotus 1-2-3, Super-Calc, and Lucid 3D let you *stack* spreadsheets. For example, let's say you keep a separate profit-and-loss statement for each of your company's outlets. You can link each statement spreadsheet to your regional summaries in another spreadsheet file, and then link the regional figures to an overall performance report in another spreadsheet. When you change figures in one spreadsheet, calculations affected by the change are adjusted in all the

Figure 7-12

Sample Excel spreadsheet

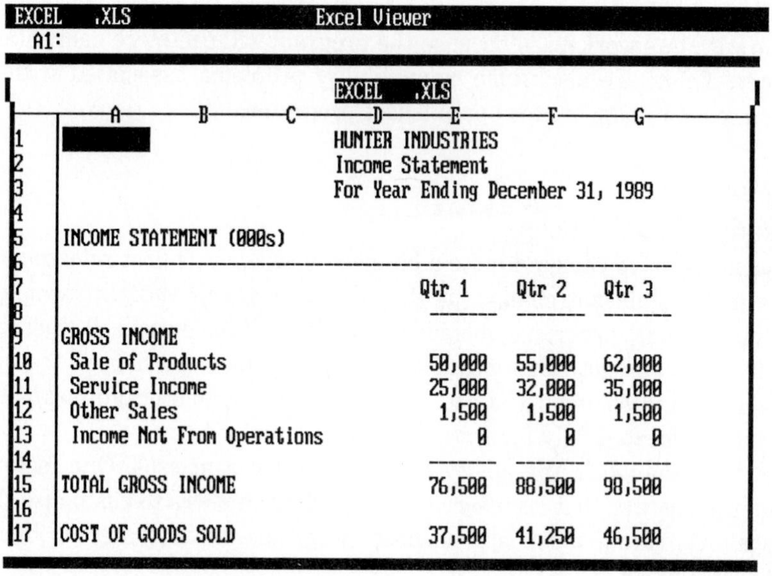

```
EXCEL    .XLS                    Excel Viewer
  A1:

                              EXCEL    .XLS
         A       B       C       D       E       F       G
1                              HUNTER INDUSTRIES
2                              Income Statement
3                              For Year Ending December 31, 1989
4
5      INCOME STATEMENT (000s)
6      ------------------------------------------------
7                                Qtr 1   Qtr 2   Qtr 3
8                                ------  ------  ------
9      GROSS INCOME
10      Sale of Products         50,000  55,000  62,000
11      Service Income           25,000  32,000  35,000
12      Other Sales               1,500   1,500   1,500
13      Income Not From Operations    0       0       0
14                               ------  ------  ------
15     TOTAL GROSS INCOME        76,500  88,500  98,500
16
17     COST OF GOODS SOLD        37,500  41,250  46,500
```

linked spreadsheets. Some programs have no limit on how many spreadsheets may be linked.

Benefits and Limitations

Spreadsheets allow you to expand your horizons. Once you have entered your formulas, you can analyze how changing a number here or there affects the larger picture. It can be amazing what an afternoon spent with a good spreadsheet program can reveal about a company. The experience has changed more than one firm's approach to conducting business.

While spreadsheets are great for "what if" analysis, your needs may make a full-featured accounting program a better choice. Accounting packages let you manage a general ledger, accounts receivable, accounts payable, inventory, payroll, and other complex financial operations with one program. A general-purpose spreadsheet can mimic these operations, but programs written for the purpose may fill your needs better.

One possible drawback to using spreadsheet programs deals with expanded memory. All commercial spreadsheet programs and some shareware programs can load spreadsheets into expanded memory. Expanded RAM support is a mixed blessing. Users who don't have expanded memory will end up with less workspace because the program will use more conventional memory. There are also some compatibility problems associated with expanded memory support for spreadsheet programs.

Spreadsheet Advances

Spreadsheets have changed quite a bit since VisiCalc was first released. One of the most significant changes is the advent of *sparse matrix storage.* In early spreadsheet programs, memory was allocated for every cell whether it contained data or not. This meant that computer memory limited the number of rows and columns you could use. Sparse matrix storage means that memory is allocated only for those cells that contain data.

Another change is the ability to create and use macros. One factor in 1-2-3's success was that its macro language allowed users to customize their spreadsheets. Now most spreadsheet programs have powerful built-in macro capabilities.

Popular Spreadsheet Programs

Your personal taste and your pocketbook are the only restrictions when choosing a spreadsheet program. There are some powerful, complicated, and expensive programs on the market. Integrated programs like Microsoft Works include simple spreadsheets that interact beautifully with the other program modules, including the database and the capable word processor. You can find friendly, easy to use spreadsheet programs, including some good, affordable shareware offerings. Then there are the spreadsheet biggies, starting with Lotus.

The route you take is up to you. The following list is by no means comprehensive, but it should give you an idea of what is available.

- *Lotus 1-2-3* Features include graphics, network support, macros, limited file linking, and DOS and OS/2 versions.

- *Quattro Pro* This is a strong new contender. It is flexible, easy to use, allows windowing, and can be run on a 640 XT.

- *Excel* Excel is an integrated, full-featured spreadsheet with database and charting capabilities, powerful macros, and excellent publishing support.

READ.ME

Historical Marker: The Lotus Empire

While competition among word processors is fierce, Lotus 1-2-3 retains a solid hold on many loyal spreadsheet users. The difference in competition shows up most dramatically in the number of users. While the top word processor may have up to 2.5 million users, estimates of the established Lotus user base run to 4 million or more.

One reason for the immediate success of Lotus 1-2-3 was that it was not just a spreadsheet. Mitch Kapor, the founder of Lotus, wanted a program that could integrate the functions of number crunching, record keeping, and word processing. He wanted to be able to calculate numbers, graph the results, and produce elegant reports.

The idea was grand. Unfortunately, it was ahead of its time; the technology just wasn't available. Still, Lotus 1-2-3 came close, and Lotus Development Corporation is still reaping the rewards. Lotus 1-2-3 could put your data into any order you chose, organized however you wanted it. Reviewers likened it to a word processor for numbers. It had its failings—it wasn't all that well integrated—but it was better than anything else then available.

The Lotus command system is an industry standard, much like the WordStar command set in word processing used to be. Lotus 1-2-3 has attracted a wealth of second-market program publishers, who offer products to enhance Lotus' performance in areas like file viewing and report printing.

Lotus has serious challengers, of course. Quattro PRO, Excel, and SuperCalc receive consistent rave reviews and are cutting themselves larger market shares. At present, Lotus must keep up with three-dimensional spreadsheets, fully integrated powerhouse environments, pop-up spreadsheets, and other innovations. Also, Lotus was late to drop its copy protection schemes, which have made it unpopular with many hard disk users. And keeping multiple releases in the marketplace at once—versions 2 and 3—has introduced a question of which Lotus, in particular, is so dominant.

Meanwhile Lotus Development Corporation is not standing still; its product is still evolving, and a large group of loyal users bears witness to its continuing power in the marketplace.

- *SuperCalc*   This is a three-dimensional spreadsheet program that is multifaceted, has good auditing features, and is flexible. It features macros but has a difficult interface for beginners.

- *PlanPerfect*   PlanPerfect features a direct WordPerfect interface and has moderate power and good printer control.

- *Lucid 3D*   Economical and easy to use, Lucid 3D can be stand-alone or memory resident, has a windows interface, is very convenient, and is moderately powerful.

Some shareware candidates you may want to investigate are

- *AsEasyAs*   This is a powerful 1-2-3 work-alike.

- *Express Calc*   This program is a business forecast specialist.

- *EZ-Spreadsheet*   As the name implies, EZ-Spreadsheet features basic operations, simplicity, and ease of use.

- *Instacalc*   This is a handy pop-up spreadsheet for "on-the-fly" use.

- *PC-Calc+*   PC-Calc+ is three-dimensional, has powerful sorting and macro capabilities, and features direct interface with PC-Type and PC-File.

- *Qubecalc*   This program features advanced spreadsheet functions and a three-dimensional interface.

Databases

Imagine that you had a file clerk who never made a mistake, never went home, could always find things for you, and never (well, hardly ever) refused to carry out instructions. Depending on your database program and related utility programs, you could have all this and more. A database program will organize your information, then sort, combine, or retrieve it for you on any basis you specify.

Consider a commercial inventory. A database program can give you accurate statistics with little effort. You could find out whether green gizmos sell better than blue ones. You could learn how long it takes to restock your gizmos, and how long it takes to sell 10 percent of your gizmo restocking order. With that information, you could schedule reordering so you never overstock and never run out of gizmos because you reordered too late.

A database program could also help you know your customers. You could find out how many use cash, checks, or credit cards. The program could help you send a special mailing to customers who buy something once a week or more or who haven't been in for the past two months.

In both these cases, a database program can make it a breeze to get your hands on just the information you need. All you have to do is keep a record of your sales and related information. Then you can tell your database program to sort through your records for the required data and create a report. You can read the report on the screen, decide if you want to refine it a bit—for example, to limit a mailing to customers who live outside your ZIP code, haven't been in recently, and have a good bill-paying record. When you're satisfied, you have the program print out the list or save it to disk. If you're preparing a mailing, you can have the program print out individually addressed letters and envelopes. (Figure 7-13 shows a sample mailing list.) All you need to do yourself is sign the letters (if you want to be really personal about it) and mail them out.

For many companies, large and small, keeping track of information makes the difference between succeeding and going under. Database programs keep tabs on information much better than unaided human beings can.

Exactly what you do with a collection of data, and how to go about it, will depend on your database management system, or DBMS. Some DBMSs are completely unstructured (they're often called personal information managers, or PIMs, described later in this chapter). Others are very structured, leaving you very little room to deviate from the prescribed format. Detailed inventory management or credit record systems are usually very structured, for example.

What DBMS Programs Have in Common

All database programs have some features in common. Data is stored in roughly the same way and all databases offer some basic data manipulation capabilities.

Fields   In a database, a *field* is a group of data treated as a single unit. It can consist of characters or numbers. For example, in a phone book database there might be one field for the last name, one for the first name, and a third for the telephone number.

Figure 7-13

Names and addresses in a dBASE file

DBASE .DBF		Data Base Viewer	1 of 23
FIRSTNAME	**LASTNAME**	**POSITION**	**COMPA**
Michael	Applegate	Manager, Information Systems	North
Pamela	Chatman	Director of R & D	Pacif
Marty	Craig	Sales Associate	Olymp
Heather	Toolson	Product Manager	Diane
Alicia	Kite	Chief Engineer	Mosai
John	Christensen	President	Micro
Phil	Preston	Director, Information Systems	Micro
Nancy	Foster	Product Manager	Decis
Livingston	Leakey	V.P., Sales	Adapt
Danny	Aldridge	V.P., Underwriting Services	Feder
Lisa	Stockton	Manager, Western Sales	Micon
Horace	Horton	Sales Associate	High
Julia	Larson	OEM Sales Manager	Penro
Oscar	Felix	Manager, R & D	Print
Hugh	Simpson	Chief Engineer	Echo
Jennifer	Menken	President	Organ
Pamela	Bay	V.P., Communications Services	DBM A
Juan	Mejia	President	Lakes

Records   A *record* is a set of fields treated as a single, related group. In the phone book example, one complete record might be

```
LAST_NAME: Michaels
FIRST_NAME: John
NUMBER: 555-5555
```

A record can contain as many fields as the database program allows. The program also limits how many records an entire database can contain. In PC-File 5.0, for example, a record can have 128 fields and a database can hold one billion records.

Searches and Sorts   The search and sort feature arranges the records in the database in alphabetical or numerical order. To sort a database, choose one field as the primary field on which to sort. In the phone book database, the primary field could be last name. You can then choose a secondary field, such as first name. When two or more records have the same primary fields, the program will sort the records again, so that in the phone book database, "Smith, Donna" will come before "Smith, Thomas." Depending on the power of the program, sorting can continue through third, fourth, and higher field levels until you run out of fields. Usually, though, two to six levels are enough to sort any database.

Reports   Database programs can generate many different types of reports. Reports vary from simple tables to complex form letters, and can include graphs as well as text in most programs.

Relational Versus Flat File Databases

Many ideas used with PCs came originally from the world of minicomputers and mainframes. Sometimes during the translation to PCs, concepts got a bit mangled. That's the case with relational databases, first introduced to PCs as the high-end DBMS programs dBASE and R:base. They only vaguely resembled what a mainframe expert might think of as relational. In fact, they really only shared one feature with mainframe relational databases: they could draw information from more than one file at a time.

Think of a database as a flat surface, where you can store one piece of information in a field, several fields in a record, and many records in the database. You could think of it as a piece of graph paper. Each field is a square, each record is a row, and the database is the entire page. That's a flat file.

Now think of several of these flat files stacked on top of each other. Your program could search all of the flat files for related information. If you asked your program to identify "Smith, John," it could find the name in your phone book file, your credit record file, and your mailing list file. That's the PC version of a relational database.

Flat file databases are generally simpler to operate, and may be faster than relational ones, especially if there are many records. Flat file programs are gradually being replaced by relational programs because the latter are more powerful. Relational database programs have more complex searching systems. For example, a well set-up relational database can be compiled into a separate executable program, to let you print mailing labels based on credit history. Deciding between flat and relational databases comes down to choosing between simplicity and power.

Some relational database programs have been simplified by omitting a programming language. For beginners, these may be preferable, because they allow you to explore data among multiple files using preset menus rather than programming your own complex search routines. PowerBase, which lets you zoom from one file to another, is a good example.

Popular Database Programs

A sampling of popular database programs includes

- *dBASE IV* This is a powerful multiuser program that has automatic record locking. It is fully relational and very fast.

- *R:base for DOS* This program is a relational DBMS, offering both a command line and prompted query system, without the need for constant professional consultation.

- *Perform* Graphical and easy to use, Perform features custom forms and reports.

- *Reflex* This flat-file mid-range program is fast and includes the following features: GUI, mail-merge, multiple windows, mouse support, graphs, efficient memory management, cross-tabbing, mailing-label capabilities, and easy report generation.

- *DataEase* This program possesses single- and multiuser support. It is easy to learn and contains powerful search features.

- *PowerBase* A relational database without a complex language, PowerBase features automatic indexing, file-relating abilities, and a zoom feature to track a field among various files. It's very easy to use.

- *Paradox 3.0* This sophisticated program is powerful and easy to use. You can add network features to it.

- *PC-File* This is a popular flat-file database. It includes the following capabilities: graphics, mail merge, and custom forms and reports. It's easy to use and has a direct interface with PC-Type and PC-Calc. PC-File is a shareware program.

Telecommunications

Telecommunications means using a modem to call up another computer so you can exchange information. It encompasses electronic mail services, electronic bulletin board systems (or BBSs), international information services, and more. To a greater extent than the other three Big Four applications, the telecommunications market has stayed open to independent programmers. In fact, some of shareware's most dramatic successes have occurred in telecommunications.

There isn't a single, dominant telecommunications program. This may be because telecommunications is *cross-fertile* with other technologies. It shares technology with telephones and radios, among others, instead of being a pure area in its own right. Because telecommunications technology changes so rapidly, many of the best new programs will show up first on your local BBS. Some users call one BBS after another, staying in touch with other BBSers and discovering new programs. As they "roam the wires," they make friends online much the way ham radio operators do on the air.

Telecommunications is also used in business. Many companies have found they can stay in close touch with outlying operations via modem. They can communicate with other businesses and people all over the world using mail services such as MCI Mail. They can distribute documents and data files rapidly by modem.

To make telecommunications work for you, you'll need a modem and a telecommunications program. The program's purpose is to act as a go-between, governing data transmission speeds and carrying out other technical tasks. The end result will be to let your computer speak to other computers by telephone. For tips on finding a local BBS, see the section titled "The World of Low-Cost Shareware," earlier in this chapter.

A Note on File Transfer Protocols

In the world of telecommunications, there are two distinct types of files— ASCII files, consisting of letters and numbers, and binary files, which do not translate directly into alphanumeric characters. Transmitting binary files can be a real headache because they contain control characters that can play havoc with the telephone connection. Worse, if there is any line noise while you're sending or receiving a binary file, the whole transfer could be wrecked.

To compensate for incidental line noise and permit sending binary files, telecommunications programs use *file transfer protocols*. These detect errors and cause the sending program to resend any damaged sections of a file. Because both sending and receiving computers must use the same protocol, most telecommunications programs supply a variety of protocols (see Figure 7-14) to make sure users can find at least one in common. Just about every telecommunications program in the world provides a protocol called Xmodem. Xmodem is one of the oldest and slowest protocols, and program writers have come up with a slew of others that go faster. Some telecommunications programs, like Relay Gold and Crosstalk, have proprietary protocols that require the other computer to use the same program.

Popular Telecommunications Programs

Power, cost, and compatibility are the main variables in telecommunications software. You can buy good commercial programs or call various bulletin board systems or information services and they will send you a program that will put you through to their system.

Most current telecommunications programs are able to *script*, meaning you can create a file with your name, password, and other information. The telecommunications program will use that script to automate signing on to information services, BBSs, and so forth. Most programs also have help-screens that sometimes double as command menus, as shown in Figure

Figure 7-11

QModem file transfer protocol window

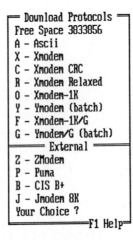

7-15. Most have program setup screens to customize operation for your own computer system, as shown in Figure 7-16. Telecommunications programs usually have a way to tell your modem to pick up the phone and call a number, and most will have a way to save an online session to a disk file.

Here is a small sampling of the programs available at this writing:

- *Crosstalk* Long referred to as Xtalk, this program features a powerful script language, background operation, dynamic data exchange (DDE) support inside Microsoft Windows, scroll bars, dialog boxes, and terminal emulation that takes advantage of an improved graphical environment. (The Windows version is sometimes called "Wind-X").

- *Relay Gold* This program is easy to use, is menu-driven, and has a manual. Features also include sophisticated scripting, a learn mode, unattended operation, and many other useful features. It supports several popular high-speed modems, offers a choice of outside file

Figure 7-15

Qmodem command menu help screen

```
════════════════════════ COMMAND MENU ═══════════════════════
─────────────── BEFORE ────────────────      ─────── TOGGLES ───────
Alt-D  Phone Directory   Alt-G  Term Emulation      Alt-0  Session Log
─────────────── DURING ────────────────             Alt-1  Backspace DEL/^H
Alt-C  Clear Screen      ^Home  Capture File         Alt-5  Host Mode
Alt-F  Execute Script    ^End   Send BREAK           Alt-8  Hi-Bit Stripping
Alt-Q  QuickLearn Mode   PgUp   Upload Files         Alt-9  Printer Echo
Alt-S  Split Screen      PgDn   Download Files       Alt-B  Beeps and Bells
Alt-T  Screen Dump       ^PgUp  PgUp (alternate)     Alt-E  Half/Full Duplex
↑      Scroll-back       ^PgDn  PgDn (alternate)     Alt-I  Order Information
─────────────── AFTER ─────────────────             Alt-M  ANSI Music Playing
Alt-H  Hang-up Modem     Alt-X  Exit Qmodem          Alt-U  Scroll-back Record
                                                     Alt-Z  Xon/Xoff Flow-ctrl.
─────────────── SETUP ─────────────────             Alt-=  DoorWay Mode
Alt-A  Translate Tables  Alt-N  Configure Qmodem     Alt--  Status Line
Alt-J  Function Keys     Alt-P  Change Baud Rate     ShTab  CR/CRLF Mode
Alt-K  Change COM Port                               Alt-2  80x25 (EGA/VGA)
                                                     Alt-4  80x43/50 (EGA/VGA)
─────────────── DOS ───────────────────      ────── COPYRIGHT ──────
Alt-L  Change Drive      Alt-V  View/Edit File       The Forbin Project, Inc.
Alt-O  Change Directory  Alt-W  List Directory       Post Office Box 702
Alt-R  DOS Shell         Alt-Y  Delete a File        Cedar Falls, IA  50613
───────── Qmodem SST Version 4.1b Production  Compiled 10/06/89 ═══F1 Help═
▓▓▓▓▓▓ Select a function,  F1 for Help  -or-  [ESC] to TERMINAL Mode ▓▓▓▓▓▓
```

Figure 7-16

ProComm Plus setup utility screen

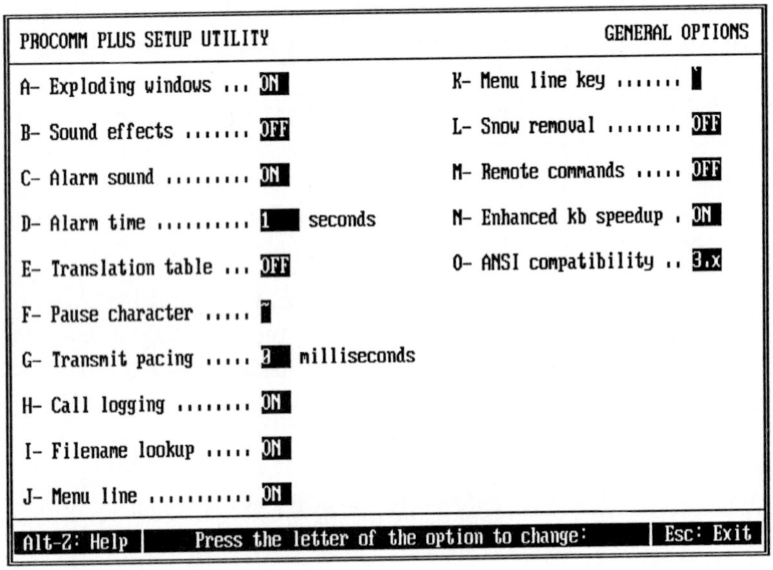

```
┌──────────────────────────────────────────────────────────────┐
│ PROCOMM PLUS SETUP UTILITY                       GENERAL OPTIONS │
│                                                                │
│  A- Exploding windows ... ON          K- Menu line key ....... ▌│
│                                                                │
│  B- Sound effects ....... OFF         L- Snow removal ........ OFF│
│                                                                │
│  C- Alarm sound ......... ON          M- Remote commands ..... OFF│
│                                                                │
│  D- Alarm time .......... 1   seconds N- Enhanced kb speedup . ON│
│                                                                │
│  E- Translation table ... OFF         O- ANSI compatibility .. 3.x│
│                                                                │
│  F- Pause character ..... ▌                                    │
│                                                                │
│  G- Transmit pacing ..... 0   milliseconds                     │
│                                                                │
│  H- Call logging ........ ON                                   │
│                                                                │
│  I- Filename lookup ..... ON                                   │
│                                                                │
│  J- Menu line ........... ON                                   │
│                                                                │
│ Alt-Z: Help │  Press the letter of the option to change: │ Esc: Exit │
└──────────────────────────────────────────────────────────────┘
```

transfer protocols, and has an internal protocol with a data compression feature to shorten file transfer times.

• *ProComm Plus* Another relatively easy-to-learn program, ProComm Plus is powerful, can auto-record for easy scripting of communications sessions, and includes hundreds of BBS numbers in ready-to-use directories. It has a complete host mode, but is not compatible with host BBS full-screen editors; it's available commercially and in a shareware version. ProComm 2.0 added various enhancements, including full-screen editing.

• *Smartcom* This program is menu-oriented, is Hayes-compatible, and supports multiple concurrent sessions. It is also compatible with several file transfer protocols, has a limited macro facility, and has a scripting language.

• *Bitcom* This is a simple program bundled with many modems. It is useful mostly for signing onto a BBS or service long enough to get a more flexible program for future sessions. Bitcom has the Xmodem protocol built in.

- *Qmodem* This program is a powerful shareware product that is menu- or command-driven and whose features include mouse support, many file transfer protocols, a powerful script language, and colorful screens. It is also flexible and easy and intuitive to use. Qmodem comes with the Doorway host utility, self-configures for most popular modems, possesses context-sensitive help, and allows you to use macros.

File Transfer (Bridge) Programs

Time was when the normal way to hook one computer directly to another was to rewire RS-232C cable connectors into null modem cables and learn how to use the potentially destructive command CTTY. The result was much faster data transfer rates between machines, but most people rarely attempted it. That was okay, since most people with a PC only had one machine. Power users and large businesses could set up a LAN (local area network) between machines if they needed extensive data exchange.

The laptop computer changed file transfer needs. Laptop and notebook computers are mostly used as second machines. Notebook computers, in particular, may not even have disk drives for transferring files to another machine. Some way was needed to hook laptops to desktop machines for fast, reliable file transfers without tying up the phone by using a modem.

The answer was the file transfer program. These programs use cables connected directly between machines and, in effect, put one machine directly into control of the other. The one in control is called the master; the one being controlled is the slave. When the master decrees, "Copy that file," the slave obediently copies it and sends it over the cable to the master. It's a great way to keep two machines in step with each other, meaning both machines have identical copies of files and data.

The direct file transfer approach was originally developed to link two computers with incompatible operating systems or different disk sizes. One of the first such programs was called Brooklyn Bridge, and it won many awards. It is still widely used and is a mainstay of many businesses, although a program named Laplink is now dominant.

The following list of bridge programs is by no means complete, but will give you an idea of what is available. Talk to your local dealer or check computer magazines for current prices and features.

- *Brooklyn Bridge* This file transfer program includes powerful features such as remote file and directory operations, peripheral sharing, macros, and automated repetitive operations. It has moderately fast transfer speeds.

- *Fastlynx*   This program is easy to install and configure and extremely easy to use. Its features include window options and fast turbo modes. It is menu-driven.

- *Laplink*   This is another program that is easy to install and run. Newer versions of Laplink self-install on remote machines and come standard on some laptops and notebooks. Laplink has turbo mode and many useful features.

- *Rapid Relay Easy*   This program is fast, menu- or command-driven, has file-scripting or automatic file transfer options, and is easy to install.

- *Fastwire*   Fast and flexible, Fastwire features three user interfaces, three ways to automate data exchange, and quick setup.

- *Paranet Turbo*   This program is an easy-to-use, simple file transfer program with no automation.

- *Commander Link*   This program features the Norton Commander shell program's built-in linking capability, two-directory links, and automatic transfers.

- *PC Shell*   This module of the popular PC Tools utility set (see Chapter 8) includes Laplink; it is configured for automatic operation with PC Shell's built-in directory management features.

The Integrated Approach

If it's likely you'll start off needing three or even all four of the Big Four applications just discussed, consider using an *integrated program*. That's a program that combines several applications into a single software system. Integrated programs are not as powerful in any one area as their equivalent separate applications programs. In return for the lack of raw power, though, they provide convenience. You only need to learn a single user interface to operate all four applications. If the function key F1 calls up a help screen in one application, it will call up help screens in all of them. If F10 exits from the word processor, it will exit from the spreadsheet. The commands in one application will make sense and feel familiar in another. If you get lost, a single manual covers all the integrated applications.

Like an Environment

At its most complex, an integrated program can resemble an entire computing environment (refer to Chapter 6). You can jump from one application to another, copy data between them, and sometimes even *link* their operations—meaning, when you change an entry in one area you change related entries in other areas.

PC Tools and Microsoft Works are examples of powerful integrated programs with intuitive user interfaces. Both programs have an arsenal of features such as a word processor, a spelling checker, and data management and mail-merge capabilities. The primary difference is one of focus. Works is application-oriented and has a spreadsheet. PC Tools is utility and file-management oriented, and offers extra utilities instead of a spreadsheet.

Microsoft Works is representative of application-oriented integrated programs. It is often called *Windows-like* because it so closely resembles working in the Microsoft Windows environment. Microsoft Works includes a word processor based on Microsoft Word, a spreadsheet, a database, and a telecommunications program. It can be mouse operated, allows free exchange of data between applications and, like Microsoft Word, gives you a choice between graphic and nongraphic operation.

Integrated applications programs often blend their modules almost seamlessly. For example, Figure 7-17 shows a screen from Microsoft Works with three files open at once: a form letter, a name and address database, and a spreadsheet. Note that Works was preparing to print a form letter at the time the screen was captured for the figure.

Like a Utility System

Other integrated programs come more from a utility program heritage. Utility programs, described in more detail in Chapter 8, concentrate on doing a single task well, and do the kinds of housekeeping chores often associated with DOS. Most utilities concentrate on file and directory management, file editing, and databases.

PC Tools is representative of utility and file-management oriented integrated programs. It includes a desktop module with a word processor and

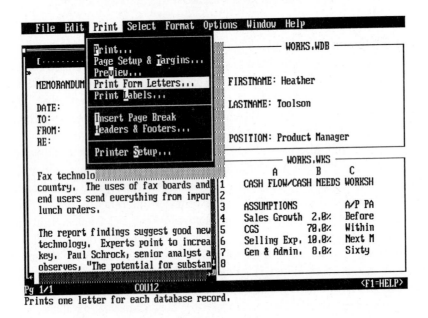

Figure 7-17

Microsoft Works printing a form letter with three windows open

Prints one letter for each database record.

spelling checker, a dBASE-compatible DBMS that can generate form letters and reports, and a complete telecommunications module to transfer files by phone. It even has a built-in Laplink bridge program.

Popular Integrated Programs
The following is a list of some currently available integrated programs:

- *AlphaWorks* This mid-range program can open up to 29 files at once. It includes a relational database and macro facilities. The word processor is relatively unsophisticated. AlphaWorks is very easy to use.

- *Better Working Eight-In-One* An economical program, this has a good WYSIWYG preview mode and a large spreadsheet. It has some powerful features but limited integration of other elements.

- *DeskMate*   This is another economical program that has many applications, including desktop tools. Tandy bundles it with its computers, but a generic DOS version is also available. Features include a graphical user interface and partial WYSIWYG display. It is moderately powerful, with limited spreadsheet capabilities and limited flexibility, but is easy to use with or without a mouse.

- *Integrated 7 Advanced*   Another mid-range program, this has a powerful spreadsheet and good windows-oriented integration, but a limited database and word processor.

- *Microsoft Works*   This general-purpose program is also in the mid-range, with good online tutorials that make the program easy to use. It features almost perfect WYSIWYG display and fully integrated modules. It is slow on some machines.

- *PFS:First Choice*   This mid-range, well-integrated program is easy to learn and has a free-form database layout.

- *PRO Staff*   This is an economical program (there is an extra charge per additional module), with a three-dimensional spreadsheet and good formatting capabilities. Equipped with a limited database and word processor, it has no graphics, desktop, or communications modules.

- *WordPerfect Executive*   Another mid-range program, this combines main features from WordPerfect, PlanPerfect, and WordPerfect Library on a 3 1/2-inch disk; it is well integrated and good for laptop use if you need limited database features.

- *Q&A*   This is a highly regarded program with a relational database, a first-class word processor, an outliner, and an advanced artificial intelligence query system. It can link to Lotus 1-2-3 for spreadsheet capabilities and is fully integrated.

- *Symphony*   Another high-end program, Symphony is somewhat difficult to install. The newest versions have an improved word processor, and the installation and other functions are more finely tuned.

OTHER MAJOR APPLICATIONS

Since the early period when the Big Four were considered the natural domain of PCs, many new applications have been designed. Some of these, like desktop publishing, have become so important that people sometimes decide what computer to buy based on whether it will run a particular publishing program.

Other new applications, like accounting packages, were anticipated earlier but took time to evolve. Some, like graphics programs, were developed after hardware (in this case, graphics adapters and printers) was manufactured that could handle them.

Desktop and Personal Publishing

The difference between word processing and desktop publishing is like the difference between a typewriter and a printing press. A typewriter is designed for getting words on paper, a printing press for putting those words into a professional-looking publication. In a similar way, a word processor puts words into a file; a desktop publisher formats the file for publication.

The two applications are closely related, and they blend into each other at the extremes. You can compose text in a desktop publisher, although it's a bit awkward to do. You can prepare attractive printed documents using a high-end word processor, although even the graphical ones don't really give you a very good picture of what will be printed. In fact, some wags have turned the acronym WYSIWYG into WYSIWYG-MOL, meaning what you see is what you get—more or less. Word processors use separate modules to create pictures on the screen of how the printed output should look. In a desktop publishing program, instead of viewing a picture of the output, you work directly in the image itself.

Some of the most powerful word processors, such as DisplayWrite Composer, Microsoft Word, and WordPerfect, are quite suitable for many desktop publishing jobs. Still, even the most powerful word processor isn't as versatile as a desktop publishing program. Desktop publishing programs use a wide variety of different fonts plus integrated graphics to get truly professional-looking results.

Some Popular Publishing Programs

Publishing programs come in two types, personal publishing and desktop publishing (DTP). Personal publishers are friendly, easy-to-use programs that allow you to have some fun while creating a document. They generally are not able to create typeset documents suitable for professional publication. The two most popular examples are Print Master and Print Shop, both of which come with hundreds of sketched graphic images.

Their more expensive desktop counterparts can generate slick, clean, professional-quality typeset documents for brochures, sales presentations, and other purposes. Desktop publishers use a personal computer and, usually, a laser printer to produce publications in a fraction of the time and at a fraction of the cost of traditional methods. You have complete control over the entire process through design, layout, and composition, until you hand the final camera-ready copy over to a print shop for reproduction.

Desktop publishing programs are complex, but they require less experience than conventional typesetters. With a desktop publisher, exact manual placement of images, drawing straight lines, using razor knives to trim edges, and taping down copy are all eliminated. You are able to compose graphics and text almost effortlessly. Many firms rely on DTP programs to create annual reports, proposals, and other documents whose appearance is important.

If you are interested in newsletters or professional-looking brochures and manuals or if you want your reports, proposals, and other documents to look professionally prepared, then you'll want to look into DTP programs. There are many very good ones available, and they get better all the time.

Low- to Mid-Range DTPs

The programs listed next all cost less than $300 at this writing:

- *PFS:First Publisher* This program is easy to use but is somewhat inflexible. It works in text mode, has rigid text flow control, good font support, plenty of available third party clip-art (Figure 7-18), and good graphics manipulation tools. A mouse is recommended. There is some difficulty with multipage documents.

- *Express Publisher* Features of this program include high-quality typefaces, a limited graphics interface, and powerful text tools. It is difficult to use on complex, image-laden documents.

- *Finesse* Here's an easy-to-use program with excellent design-intensive tools and good bitstream documentation. It has limited text-import capacity and mediocre tabs, grids, rulers, and graphics import capabilities.

Figure 7-18

Clip-art graphics for PFS:First Publisher

- *Publish It!* This program features exemplary formatting and layout, and has downloadable font support. A mouse is recommended. It suffers, however, from weak graphics importing and is difficult to use with long documents.

- *Page Builder* This package is well suited for text manipulation with limited graphics. It is difficult to learn and lacks sophistication.

- *GEM Desktop Publisher* This program offers fine control over design and typography, has advanced features for creating complex and precise formats, and excels at shorter documents (although it suffers from limited performance for long, complicated documents). A mouse is recommended.

High-End DTPs

The following DTP programs offer professional, publication-quality output, in the you-get-what-you-pay-for tradition:

- *Ventura Publisher* Fast, powerful, and graceful, this program offers GEM- or Windows-based interfaces, works well with many word processors and printers, permits graphic creativity and file combining, has many first-rate features, and is the champ for long documents.

- *PageMaker* This powerful Microsoft Windows desktop publishing application has many strong, flexible features, has good compatibility with printers and word processors, and excels at short documents.

- *The Office Publisher* This program features good graphics and unique style tag features with extensive control. It suffers from some execution limitations and a somewhat unreliable performance.

- *Legend* Legend's features include effective text-editing and table-creating tools, and fast and effective operation for long, text-only documents. Graphics performance is limited.

Personal Information Managers

Personal information managers (PIMs) let you construct electronic filing systems to keep track of those small slips of paper that pile up on your desk, get crumpled in your pocket or purse, or fall between the cracks in your busy schedule. PIMs give you a way to cross-reference, retrieve, and analyze unstructured information.

Personal information differs from corporate information because it doesn't fit into neat pigeonholes nearly as well. You need to create your own categories. You can, for example, organize your phone numbers your own way; you should be able to find the number for Mr. Jones by looking up "butcher."

Anyone who's ever searched desk drawers for a scrap of paper, only to find it days later by the kitchen phone, will understand how useful a PIM can be. Features vary, but any program can be considered a PIM if it includes some or all of the following:

- A calendar or appointment scheduler

- A text-based, unstructured database

- An outliner

- A phone directory or dialer

- A pop-up notepad for jotting down your thoughts as you work

- The ability to record personal or client information that might not fit into a standard phone book

PIMs are not necessarily for schedules, phone numbers, or any other type of information. They're for whatever you use them for.

Popular PIM Programs

Here are some popular currently available PIMs:

- *IBM Current*   This is a Microsoft Windows application. It has flexible features and good detail and structure. It's easy to use and easy to customize and it makes use of linked databases.

- *Instant Recall*   Powerful yet inexpensive, this program is relatively easy to learn, is memory resident, and has many fast and useful features.

- *Memory Mate*   A classic, Memory Mate is still one of the best. It has no defined fields (not even separate address lists); instead you create your own data entry forms. It's extremely easy to learn and has automatic reminders, multiple databases, and fast searches. It can be memory resident and can capture information directly from the screen.

- *Arriba*   This program is versatile and flexible and has first-rate search capabilities. It can handle structured and unstructured information, is easy to use, has moderate memory management, and has menu-access to note taking.

- *Agenda*   This powerful, multifeatured program categorizes and links information but is somewhat harder to learn than the other programs. It has some functional limitations.

- *askSAM*   Features of askSAM include free-form data entry, fast search capabilities, ease of use, and a dual-mode help system. It doubles as a text search utility (see Chapter 8).

Project Managers

Most large projects have hundreds of tasks to be assigned, prioritized, mapped on a timeline, and coordinated with other parts of the project. Until recently, project manager programs were not within reach of general PC users. They were costly, cumbersome, and impractical. Very few were available for under $1500. At this writing, the situation is changing. Several programs come in under $1000, and they include the kinds of scheduling and tracking features common to high-end mainframe programs.

As machines improve, the situation can only improve for the buyer. High-end, $2000-plus packages like Artemis, Open Plan, PlanTrac, Primavera, Project Planner, and ViewPoint give you thorough and complex capabilities with almost unlimited reporting. They're hard to use, but if you need them, you can probably afford an expert to run them.

The following low-end programs cost $700 or less and are representative of what is available for PC users who need less powerful project management software:

- *Microsoft Project for Windows* This program is powerful and flexible. It has good scheduling and tracking features, excellent graphics and data screens, and complete control of screen formats (font sizes, color, bar styles, and so on).

- *Time Line* Easy to use, Time Line has mouse support in its most recent version. It can use expanded memory, has improved tracking and scheduling, and has good WYSIWYG graphics (but not a GUI).

- *Syzygy* This innovative package can chart all people assigned to a given task and their roles. It has multiple task orientation, and is almost an integrated program. It is a project manager, a manager's tracking program, and a network task manager. It has no mouse support.

- *Project Scheduler 4* This is a fast, easy-to-use, interactive program. Its GUI offers good screen design and layouts. Thorough scheduling and tracking abilities are available.

- *Harvard Project Manager* Versatile but slow, this program has good use of color and a split screen. Drawbacks include limited multiple-project support, some translation quirks, and an upper limit of 280 tasks in a schedule (although you can get around this limit by specifying subprojects).

- *Super Project Expert*   Unusual features include project evaluation and review technique (PERT) charting analysis, schedule deviation analysis, and multiple levels of operation (rated by experience). Drawbacks are poor onscreen graphics, charts, and diagrams. It's also difficult to use certain functions.

Computer Aided Drafting and Design

Engineers have come to depend on computer aided drafting and design (CADD) programs much as writers and secretaries depend on word processors and desktop publishing programs. CADD programs are used for drawing designs onscreen, bypassing the need for pencil sketches and drafting boards. Drawing onscreen becomes part of the actual design process.

Fully three-dimensional drawing packages are taking over from two-dimensional packages, but the move has been rocky. Some interim programs made designs that looked three-dimensional but left the mathematics in two dimensions. Designers could use these programs to visualize their products, but still had to use third-axis math to make the design work in all three dimensions (x, y, and z).

Figure 7-19 shows a three-dimensional, PC-designed model as a collection of lines and curves in a three-axis coordinate space. This wireframe model can easily be converted into a shaded image so the designer can see what the final product will look like.

CADD programs on PCs are tricky. In addition to the software package, you need a fast 80286-based PC (some programs require a 386). A high-resolution monitor (VGA or Super VGA), a fast hard disk, and a mouse or digitizing tablet are strongly recommended. Many CADD programs won't run without a math coprocessor, and those that do suffer in performance. It helps to have a great deal of RAM, since CADD programs run best on systems with several megabytes of extended memory.

Popular CADD Programs
The following CADD programs have three-dimensional capabilities:

- *AutoCAD*   This program has strong two-dimensional capabilities and a good drafting system, but has so-so three-dimensional capabilities.

Figure 7-19

AutoCAD three-dimensional wireframe design model

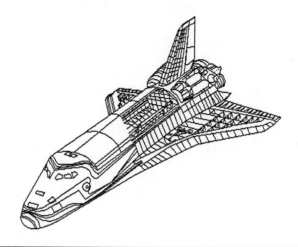

- *Cadkey* This program has two-dimensional drafting and detailing capabilities, and many three-dimensional features.

- *DesignCAD 3D* A powerful three-dimensional modeler, DesignCAD 3-D also has limited two-dimensional design capabilities.

- *MicroStation PC* This multiuser CADD program includes a good information manager.

Science and Engineering Programs

PC programs aimed at scientists and engineers run the gamut from calculators to complex mathematical modeling programs. When it comes to choosing the right scientific program, a lot depends on the task at hand. Do you need statistical analysis? Do you need to forecast future trends? Are you evaluating certain products? You have many choices beyond simple spreadsheets, including the ability to perform statistical calculations, error correction, and probability guessing. You can choose how you want to present your data, from a straight two-dimensional bar graph to a fancy three-dimensional slide show.

Good statistical analysis programs generate data for real-world uses. These might include quality control engineering, social science, biological and marketing research, and business or economic forecasting. If you need graphing, look at a program's data handling and graph-drawing capabilities. Mathematical tool boxes and equation solvers can process your numerical information, and some tool box programs can also print the results.

Take a good look at your needs before you buy, because many spreadsheet programs can do the very things you may want from a math toolbox, for example. The following program categories, which include statistical analysis, forecasting, and mathematical programs, are only some of the available types of programs.

Statistical Analysis Programs
The following programs handle sophisticated statistics:

- *Statistix* This BASIC program is good for linear modeling, but presumes some statistical knowledge on the part of the user.

- *Minitab Statistical Software* Another BASIC package, this program is easy to use, command-driven, and flexible, and it has a macro system.

- *Statgraphics* This advanced program is flexible and powerful, with an emphasis on graphics; it can be customized and extended.

Forecasting Programs
The following programs are forecasting tools for business, economics, and other uses:

- *Forecast Pro* This powerful, easy-to-use program supports 8087, 80287, and 80387 coprocessors.

- *Forecast Plus* This fairly complete program allows detailed exploratory and forecasting analysis with automatic execution of batch files.

Mathematical Toolboxes

The following are specialized math toolboxes:

- *Gauss* Programmable and speedy, this program is versatile but difficult to learn. It is a powerful number cruncher.

- *Derive* This symbolic math toolbox has a user-friendly interface and takes very little disk space. It is good for classroom use.

- *Maple* This is another symbolic math toolbox. It features powerful symbolics and a built-in programming language.

- *MathGraf* This is a programmable program with powerful language capabilities and two- and three-dimensional graphs.

- *MathCAD* This program is not programmable but has many features and a fast numerical orientation.

- *Formula/One* Nonprogrammable, Formula/One has good printer support, versatile menus, and a complex interface for advanced uses.

- *Mathematica* This highly interactive program has outstanding graphics and a powerful programming language.

Accounting Packages

A PC can streamline many general business accounting tasks, making everyone's job easier. The five basic accounting functions—general ledger, accounts receivable, accounts payable, sales invoicing/inventory control/purchasing, and payroll—are accessible with the push of a button. Computerized accounting systems not only cut the time it takes to perform these tasks, they can improve cash flow management, boost the collection rate of receivables, plan payments to take advantage of vendor discounts, and maintain inventory levels that minimize cash investment and improve customer service.

PC-specific accounting programs are especially suited for small businesses, where the owner must either be the bookkeeper or use an outside service and lose sight of the records several times a year.

The programs listed next will give you some idea of what's available. Your specific needs will influence your choice. If you have a large company, you may need a complex, powerful program. If you have a small business, you may only need a small accounting program to help you keep your bank accounts and personal budgets in order.

Before picking your program, consider the amount of work you plan to do. Look at your expected frequency of use and the software you already have. Think about whether you're willing to learn a complex new program. Consider your future plans. It may be better to buy more program than you need right now than to take the time later to convert to a more powerful program.

The following programs are listed in approximate order from the more economical to the high-end powerhouses.

Economical

- *Act 1* Features of this program include custom forms generation, good depth, invoicing capabilities, and customer statements. It can convert to UNIX and LAN operation.

- *Bedford Integrated Accounting* This package is easy to use and has useful optional features.

- *DacEasy Accounting* This program is multifeatured and easy to convert to a multiuser or LAN version.

- *Peachtree Complete III* This powerful program has a large number of add-on modules and can handle a wide range of requirements.

Mid-Range

- *Act 2* An easy upgrade from Act 1, Act 2 is a multiuser, multimode accounting package with file and record locking.

- *AccPac BPI* This easy-to-use program has report and data verification and has system modules available.

- *DacEasy's Network Accounting* This multiuser program is a smooth upgrade from the low-end program.

- *One-Write Plus Accounting System* This easy-to-use cash and accrual package can speed search, print lists, and create reports and mailing labels, and has an option to integrate with Lotus.

High-End

- *Great Plains Accounting Series* This is an easy-to-use network package with many features.

- *Macola* Fully integrated and easy to learn, Macola operates in multi-user and stand-alone environments.

- *Platinum Series* This program is fast and flexible, runs on any network, and can be used with Novell operating systems.

Graphics

It used to be that good graphics programs were limited to non-DOS computers. You needed a Macintosh, Amiga, or Commodore system to play games or run poster or paint programs. This changed as MS-DOS machines gained power and new software was written to take advantage of the enhancements. You will do best with good graphics adapters and high-resolution monitors, but good graphics are now a part of the everyday MS-DOS world.

Screen Capture Programs

Screen capture programs are designed to capture the current screen, then save it to a file in a format that a graphics program can read as an input file. With a graphics program, you can edit captured screens for illustration purposes. All the screen captures used as figures in this chapter were done using the capture functions of HiJaak and InSet.

There is a wide variety of screen capture programs available. You can get commercial programs such as those listed next, or contact any of several special interest groups on local bulletin board systems or information services to get shareware screen grabbers. Some word processors like WordPerfect come bundled with screen grabbers that produce files you can import directly into documents.

Some current popular choices are listed here:

- *Collage Plus* This is an economical program with strong file maintenance, slide shows, and the ability to view many options from the command line.

- *The Graphics Link Plus* This no-frills package is primarily a file conversion program that has added DOS and Microsoft Windows-oriented full-bodied screen capture utilities.

- *HiJaak Plus/InSet* This is a versatile screen capture program for text and graphics integration. It has view and modify options, and is fairly difficult to learn.

- *HotShot Graphics* This program handles fine-tuning at the pixel level; it also has simple cataloging features.

- *Pizazz Plus* Supporting over 300 printers, Pizazz Plus has sophisticated screen-to-printer color mapping, precise image sizing, and superior direct-to-printer screen reproduction.

Plotting Programs

For some users, the ability to plot data onscreen easily is very important. They need only a simple "quick and dirty" two-dimensional line graph. Other users need more sophisticated charts, requiring three dimensions to incorporate all pertinent information. Whether in two or three dimensions, if onscreen reproducible graphing is the goal, dedicated plotting programs may be a good answer.

Designers, architects, and engineers need to see their designs using CADD programs, and may also need to plot stress points or other data using plotting programs. Salespeople, researchers, and teachers need to plot presentation-quality graphics to ensure that their information is both appealing and informative.

The programs listed next are just a small sampling of the many plotting programs available. Plotting programs have different strengths and weaknesses, so do a little homework before making your selection. Choose one that fits your level of expertise, your pocketbook, and the task at hand. If you are new to computers, you might consider easy-to-use programs that have upgrade potential.

- *GraphiC* This program uses C procedures and functions to allow you to design and write your own programs. It has high-quality resolution capabilities.

- *Grapher* This is a flexible two-dimensional program that can preview and automate plotting.

- *Surfer* This easy-to-use, three-dimensional program is a compilation of Grid, Topo, and Surf—three useful programs.

- *SDS* This powerful program has many useful features but is difficult to install.

Presentation Graphics Programs

Computer generated graphics are a hot item right now. Slide shows, VCR presentations, and high resolution color productions can all be created using PCs. Scientists and salespeople alike find PC-generated presentations useful tools. Some of the following programs are easier to use than others:

- *Graph Plus* This program uses every Microsoft Windows tool. It features overlays, text/graphics mix, and labeling. It is good for graphics presentations but not as good for scientific data plotting.

- *GraphStation* This two-dimensional program has many flexible features and full mouse support, although it is somewhat complicated to use.

- *Harvard Graphics* Easy to use and good for word charts, Harvard Graphics has spell-checking capabilities, can create transparencies, and interfaces with the GrandView outliner.

- *Lotus Freelance Plus* This well-known program is efficient, powerful, and flexible. It is full-featured and interfaces with the GrandView outliner.

- *Microsoft Chart* This multifeatured program comes close to being the complete graphics program.

- *Perspective Junior* This program displays multiple data sets in three dimensions, has a slide show editor, is easy to use, and has strong math capabilities in a small spreadsheet section.

- *Autodesk Animator* With an icon- and menu-driven interface, Autodesk Animator is good for high-end presentations at a low cost. It can translate your edited animation to VCR format for display.

- *CorelDRAW!* This program creates outstanding transparencies, has 50 fonts and more than 43 expandable PostScript patterns, and can manipulate type. It is flexible and fun to use.

- *Image Studio*   This forgiving program allows for errors behind the camera and in the darkroom; it has airbrush effects, can remove scratches, and can do other professional photographic technical tricks.

- *Dan Bricklin's Demo II*   This program, written by one of the authors of the original VisiCalc program, produces slide shows, is screen-grab oriented, and is capable of complex screen control. It has won many awards.

- *Xerox Presents*   The Xerox package is entirely GUI based, energetic, and full-featured.

- *Arts and Letters*   A powerful graphics editor, Arts and Letters has excellent control over shades, color, image blends, and complex curves. It is a superb tool for commercial artists.

Simulations and Games

You can choose from thousands of simulation and game programs. They run the gamut from quiet, thoughtful games of chess to wild, murderous, arcade-style shoot-'em-ups. You can roam the jungles in an adventure game or fly a spaceship to a galaxy far, far away. If you like to play on a computer-versus-person level, you might go online to one of the large information services and join a special interest group specializing in games. There you can play when you feel like it, leave a game for dinner, come back, and continue to play. If "staying home" is more your style, you can buy or rent computer games at many computer and video stores. At some levels, games become serious simulations of actions, like flying an airplane, or situations, like planning a space flight.

Some popular simulators and game categories are described in the following paragraphs.

Simulators   Simulator programs let you feel you are flying an airplane, training in a jet fighter plane, sailing a boat, or driving a race car. You can even plan and execute a scientific mission aboard a NASA space station. Detailed graphics display all the necessary instrument panels and controls. Your graphics interface is the only limitation of how realistic a simulation can be. The new simulation software is fantastic.

War and Policy Games   You can play war games similar to the famous strategy games played in the Pentagon and other defense establishments. Be captain of a World War II submarine; send arms to overseas rebels, or not; support this foreign political party or another one; invade here or there or not at all. As you play, your PC calculates the results. Watch the world cave in on you or your opponent's sphere of influence shrink. Some less political variations pit your imaginary planet against other planets in interstellar trade wars. The possibilities are endless.

Arcade Games   Use a joystick, your cursor keys, or a mouse to zap aliens, race bicycles, battle the blob, search shark-infested waters for treasure, and so forth. Even if the action is not your style, these games can be worth renting for the graphics alone if you have a VGA monitor or better.

Text Adventures   In text adventures, your character interacts with the story environment in a quest-like adventure tale. You type instructions for your character, who carries on in constant danger of dying. True to the principle that an adventure is a series of dirty, dangerous events that happen to somebody else far away, sometimes your character gets eaten by the snarf, but you can always generate another character and try again. Some of these games, such as Leisure Suit Larry and Hitchhiker's Guide to the Galaxy, are quite humorous, while others are more traditional sword-and-sorcery type adventures. One fascinating game, A Mind Forever Voyaging, puts you vicariously in the position of a sentient computer just awakening to its true identity. There are many variations of text adventures.

Strategy and Board Games   Traditional games such as chess, checkers, poker, go, Monopoly, and backgammon are wonderful to play on the computer. You don't have to worry about finding a worthy opponent at odd hours of the night when you can't sleep. Since the computer can probably beat most human opponents, you can select the computer's playing skill level. These games provide great practice for when you take on a real person.

Mock Sporting Leagues   This fairly new entertainment application has taken over the computer in a lot of homes and offices. You take the positions of players, the coach, and the manager of a specific team, and compete against your computer-generated opponents. Entire seasons are played based upon variables you specify, such as who is coaching and playing on the opposing teams. Your computer generates action using real-world, historical player statistics and coaching strategies.

Game Shows and Trivia Popular television games such as Hollywood Squares, Family Feud, and Jeopardy are naturals for computer play. So is the popular living room contest Trivial Pursuit, which has inspired play-alike computer games in dozens of varieties.

Add-In Game Boards With simulations, improved sound effects, and electronic music, games have become such a hit among home-based PC owners that the hardware industry has gotten into the act. Now you can buy add-in boards to generate simulations that let you experience all the thrills of a race through the streets of San Francisco (Vette by Spectrum Holobyte), the intense action and split-second decisions an air traffic controller must make (TRACON by Wesson International), or the full experience, including your partner's comments and other sound effects, of a professional golf tournament (World Class Leader Board, by Access Software Inc.). In the music arena, PCs always had a problem because they could issue only one tone at a time. This limit led to some clever musical work-arounds like Piano-Man (which plays on the PC using SuperKey, a macro utility). Now you can get boards that make precision sounds instead of tinny ones. For example, LAPC-1 (Roland Corp.) both improves the sound quality in games and turns your PC into a music-making machine with all sorts of capabilities.

Instructional and Educational Programs

Schools have used computers for years to tailor a curriculum to the needs of individual students. Children's programs use music and vivid colors to make lessons more interesting and to hold a child's attention. If a lesson goes well, the young person is rewarded with a song or cartoon. These programs are usually part of a series, so the child can go at his or her own pace, building skills as well as confidence.

Many adults use the same technology to continue their education in the evenings, to change careers or learn new skills. Course programs (sometimes called *tutorials*) are available on just about any subject. Correspondence courses are available for people who want or need to stay at home. Seminars have been condensed and can be presented by computer. Lectures and tests can be administered, with incorrect answers flagged and the appropriate section of the lesson automatically reviewed.

You can find software to teach yourself to type, prepare taxes, cook, fix automobiles, pass construction company licensing tests—you name it. Call your local community college or adult education service for details on what's available in your area.

Home Applications

Many people operate small businesses out of their homes. Other workers *telecommute*, that is, work at home and communicate with the office via modem, telephone, and fax machine. Writers, bookkeepers, medical transcriptionists, data entry clerks, and others can receive new assignments, transmit finished work, and get information from the library or online sources—all without leaving the house. Wear and tear on cars and clothes diminishes, although phone bills are higher.

Household Inventory Programs

One useful home application is the household inventory program, designed to help keep track of valuables and household effects. These programs let you keep track of what you own, including purchase prices, replacement costs, depreciation or appreciation values, and other insurance-oriented dollar amounts. Business items can be separated from personal use items.

Insurance companies love customers who keep such lists. A word of caution: Keep the information disk in a safe place where it can't be lost, damaged, or destroyed with the very possessions it documents. The freezer might be a fine place for insurance papers, stocks, and inventory printouts, but don't keep your floppy disks there. A safe deposit box at your bank is a good choice for safe storage. This practice is inconvenient for adding and deleting information, but once you get into the habit of updating your records once a month or so, you will have a secure database should the worst happen.

Personal Finance and Budget Programs

There are some best-selling personal finance programs, but most people just use them to balance their checkbooks. When these programs originally came out, people found it was more work to enter all their checks into the program than to keep track of them manually. Now personal finance programs have many fields keyed in for you, which saves work. They can automatically repeat regular monthly payments, print checks, handle electronic payments, split paychecks out in multiple ways for tax or accounting purposes, and even enter large portions of your finances into the next year's tax preparation program automatically. Now, *that* makes it worthwhile to use such a program. Some personal finance programs are powerful enough to act as accounting programs for small businesses with moderate accounting requirements.

Following is a list of some popular personal finance programs:

- *MoneyCounts*   This is a low-cost financial manager with many high-end features such as three-dimensional graphics, a mailing list manager, and a pop-up notepad.

- *Quicken*   This handy program manages personal finances, handles moderate small business accounting, writes checks, and has some tax management features.

- *Managing Your Money*   One of the all-time best sellers, this mid-range program is powerful, provides great online help, and is easy to use.

- *Dollars & Cents*   This mid-range program offers personal finance with a cash flow orientation.

- *Check Free*   Compatible with electronic banking transfer systems, Check Free pays bills electronically and monitors personal budgets. There's a startup cost and monthly charge for service.

- *Personal Tax Preparer*   This program is economical, easy to use, and includes forms. It can import entries directly from MoneyCounts, Managing Your Money, Quicken, or Dollars & Cents.

- *Tax Cut*   This mid-range program is easy to use and includes good-looking forms. It has a friendly interviewing style.

SUMMARY

This chapter has given you an overview of the major types of programs available to PC users. Use the lists as a general guide only. When it comes time to actually purchase a program, take the time to look in some recent computer magazines, talk to your local user group, or consult with your software vendor for advice. These programs change constantly, and today's rising star may be tomorrow's historical footnote.

Chapter 8 covers utility programs—the housekeeping programs that keep your files and hard disk directories in order, handle maintenance chores, provide security, and do the other everyday tasks that keep everything running smoothly on your PC.

Utilities — Computer Housekeepers

In the last chapter, you learned about applications programs — the software programs that most users have in mind when they start using a computer. For example, you might have a word processor, database and spreadsheet programs, and perhaps an appointment or project manager. But no single application, or even a collection of major programs, can do everything you need to keep a system working smoothly.

That's where *utilities* come into play. These are the workhorses of computing. They are concise, specific programs that take care of little jobs that seem to have been swept into the corner and forgotten by other software publishers. Utility programs are the computing answer to the remark, "There oughtta be a way...."

Many of the utilities described in this chapter were invented because someone had a small job to do and couldn't find a program to do it right. Or someone saw a failing in a popular program and decided to fix it by writing a new program to take care of that specific task. You've read elsewhere in this book that there are a thousand ways to use a computer — none of them wrong if they work. That principle is never more apparent than with utilities, where dozens of different programs may exist to carry out similar or identical tasks.

This chapter is an overview of available utilities. Most of the recommendations are general because what works for one person may not be right for another. You'll need to experiment, and once you have a set of utilities that works for you, you may not want to switch.

Shareware and public domain utilities are a gold mine of useful programs. Those found in one part of the country are often different from those found elsewhere. They get passed from person to person, or from BBS to BBS, often never leaving the local calling area. Part of the fun of building a utility collection is in finding the programs, and what you find when you go looking will change over time, by geographical area, and by online system.

UTILITY PROGRAMS: WHAT ARE THEY? WHAT DO THEY DO?

Utilities, as a category, embrace a broad range of programs. Some very successful utility collections are so powerful that they hardly resemble utilities at all; they're more like full-scale applications programs. For example, PC Tools, long an outstanding set of disk utilities, has all the earmarks of a complete, fully integrated desktop manager, such as Microsoft Works or Alpha Works. Interlocking collections like the Norton Utilities, PC Tools, and Mace Utilities illustrate how an all-inclusive concept such as "utility programs" loses its meaning when you try to categorize it.

That said, it's still true that most utilities share basic characteristics that define them as a family. They tend to be small, single-purpose programs that load fast, don't take up much disk space or memory, and do one task quickly and well. A utility that wins popularity may grow in size and complexity over time, but will maintain its basic, efficient role.

How Utilities Help You

You can find a utility to make your computer do just about anything a computer *can* do, from searching a document to dialing a telephone. Utilities rearrange file directories, picking files up from a disk and laying them back down in a more organized fashion. Utilities restore files deleted by accident, and change a file's time stamp or attribute flags. They compare files in two directories and tell you the differences. Utilities keep a log of your work activities, make your keyboard run faster, check a disk for damage, and change your screen colors. DOS shell utilities cushion you from the naked DOS prompt and help you organize the files on your hard disk. Clearly, a good set of utilities will do nearly all the housekeeping tasks involved in maintaining a well-run system.

As you become more familiar with your PC, you're likely to get annoyed by repetitive keystrokes and wish you had some way to enter them automatically. You may tire of going on the hunt for files that you stored somewhere on drive C . . . or was it drive D? Wouldn't it be nice if the computer would find those files for you? Maybe you wish you had a way to do something specific in a batch file, such as accept user input for an activity log. Or you're tired of going through your hard disk directories to look for and delete obsolete backup files. Remember the day you accidentally erased that important memo to the boss, minutes before it was due? You thought there was no way to unerase that file . . . and you'll bless the day you ran across that little program called Unerase or Undelete that gets it all back for you.

You'll be happy to know there are utilities to do all the "things that DOS forgot," and more. Nearly everyone who has worked with a computer for more than a few months has at least a few favorite utilities. You may not even be aware that you're using a utility program—you just are grateful for that handy little program that gets rid of all those .BAK files, or that shows a long directory in several columns, so it fits on a single screen.

The rest of this chapter describes various types of utilities and offers some tips on what qualities to look for in a good utility program.

DOS SHELLS

DOS shell programs usually perform all the major file management functions in a way that many people find more convenient than working at the DOS prompt. DOS shells are designed to enhance your interface with DOS, not act as stand-alone programs. At their most complex, shells are becoming full-scale operating environments of the sort discussed in Chapter 6. Shells may also include bonuses like menu systems, automatic program selection based on file type, and other user interface enhancements.

READ.ME

Where to Find Utilities

Computer stores, discount software stores, and many standard outlets such as discount warehouses, large bookstores, and department stores carry computer programs, including utilities. These are fine places in which to find commercial utility collections. They also are likely to carry major single-purpose utility programs like memory managers, DOS shells, and hard-disk backup programs.

Mail-order catalogs and ads in computer magazines are also good sources of special-purpose programs. Look in the back of any computer magazine for catalog ads, and send in for two or three. Before you know it, you'll be receiving catalogs from all over the country. You can find some great discounts that way, as well as a broad selection of the best programs available.

For an even broader selection, you can tap into shareware distribution channels (see Chapter 7). User groups and local BBSs, as well as the large online services, are mother lodes of utility programs. If you're just starting out, check the disk vendor catalogs for utility collections. And if you do use shareware, please support the authors—it's only fair, and it keeps the new, low-cost programs coming.

A Word About Viruses   Both shareware and BBSs have been the target of unfavorable and inaccurate publicity about viruses. The fact is that viruses spread mainly through floppy-disk boot sectors and pirated commercial programs. If you don't pass floppy disks around or use illegal copies of commercial programs, you'll be safe from the majority of viruses. The rest are spread through networks, malicious mischief, and even returned commercial software that has been repackaged, shrink-wrapped, and reissued. Compared to other software sources, neither shareware nor BBSs are major sources of virus infection.

Shell programs can have a wide variety of bells and whistles. There are easy programs, such as DOS Partner, QDOS, and PowerPanel, that power users may find limiting. Then there are programs like PowerMenu, Direc-Tree Plus, XTree Gold, PC Shell, and others, that throw in everything but the kitchen sink and take a novice some time to learn.

To be useful, a DOS shell should handle the standard DOS functions more easily than DOS itself does and offer extended capabilities and functions as well. There would be little reason to bother with a shell otherwise. Since most DOS commands concern file, directory, or disk operations, the shell you pick should make your life easier in those areas. After that, you can consider some of the added attractions described in the following sections.

Special Shell Features

Many useful features are available in file managers and DOS shells. These added attractions are often linked to other command line utilities, especially in the case of file managers. For example, Quick Filer works in conjunction with the independent file listing program QLIST and the independent compression utilities PKZIP and ARC. Other file managers interface with Vern Buerg's popular file lister, LIST. With some time and effort, you can assemble a group of these interconnected utilities that will work together flawlessly, giving you a unique and personal computing toolbox. Some options to look for in a shell are described next.

Fast File-Finders
Hard disks can hold thousands of files in hundreds of directories, and it can take time to locate the exact file you want. Trying to find a file on a 100MB hard disk that has been partitioned into several drives is time consuming, frustrating, and often futile. Many shell and file management programs offer cross-volume and cross-directory file searching. There are also many stand-alone utilities that do fast file-searches, from Keith Ledbetter's classic WHEREIS program to full-screen, multidisk scanners like S.B. Behman's WHIZ, Norton Utilities' FILEFIND, and Jim Derr's FFF.

Text Searchers
A good file manager or shell has, or can link to, a text-searching utility that looks inside files for specific text strings. Maybe you want to search for "Diamond Supplies, Inc.", the addressee of that letter you're sure you sent out last Monday....

Searching through text, inside and outside of compressed archives (explained later in this chapter), has become an art. MAGELLAN, a recent hit, can index every word in every file on your disk, and give you almost instant access to any file you care to search for. DOS shell/file managers like XTree Gold and PC Tools also have excellent file locators that can do a file-by-file search for a specified string.

File Tagging

Most shells and managers let you tag files for subsequent operations. The QFILER screen, illustrated in Figure 8-1, shows three files tagged with a diamond for copying, moving, or deleting. This feature is not only convenient, but helps avoid mistakes by letting you see exactly which files will be affected—*before* you do anything.

Figure 8-1

The QFILER file manager (double screen report)

```
         CSM Assoc C                    CSM Assoc C
        C:\BOOT                  ↑      C:\BELFRY
QUIT     BAT      0 080189 19:16    <PARENT>    <DIR>     082290 18:14
MENU     COM   1898 080389 14:29R   BUFFER   BAT      60 080190 14:11
FILEINFO FI     904 101190  9:35a   CCOM     BAT     204 080190 14:11
1PUBLSH  FIL   1936 101490  7:35a   CHOOSE   BAT    8694 102990 15:11a
1PUBSYS  FIL    119 051090  9:14    COMPR    BAT    1208 080190 14:11
◆4DOSEXE FIL   1610 051090  9:06    CUT      BAT    2677 080190 14:11
◆4DOSSYS FIL    168 051090  9:14    DELYES   BAT     469 090390 17:21
◆BROAUTO FIL   2549 101490  7:36a   DOIT     BAT    1475 101090  9:03a
CCOMSYS  FIL    183 060190  1:47    DOIT2    BAT    3111 101090  9:52a
COMUNIC  FIL   1984 101490  7:36a   EDD      BAT    1065 082590  9:40
EXPMEM   FIL   1391 101490  7:36a   EDDSM    BAT     670 082290 15:42
EXPSYS   FIL    196 082590  9:59    EDG      BAT     248 082590  9:41
NOFMARK  FIL   2127 101490  7:36a   EDIT     BAT      27 110590 17:11a
PC-KSYS  FIL    201 082490 21:16    ERA      BAT    1330 091290 13:47
PC-KWIK  FIL   1752 101490  7:37a   FOG      BAT     111 080190 14:11
PCCACHE  FIL   1723 101490  7:37a   FORMAT   BAT     126 080190 14:11
PCCASYS  FIL    215 082990 18:54    FORMFEED BAT      13 100590 17:40a
PCTOOLS  FIL    409 101490  7:37a   FY       BAT    1089 080190 14:11
PCWF-SK  FIL   2734 101490  7:37a   GU       BAT     810 102790 16:41a
PLVANIL  FIL   1192 110290  8:47a   HIDE     BAT     669 080190 14:11
dir:  33K  tag:   4K  left: 6043K ↓ dir:  64K  tag:   0K  left: 6043K
    Clear all tagged files.  (Press "/" for menu, "H" for help)   (308565)
UnTagAll Copy Move Delete TagAll Rename Exec Pick List Volume Quit
```

File Listing

A good file or directory manager provides a way to list a file to the screen. *File listers* display a file onscreen for you to read but not edit, so they tend to be small and fast—the classic characteristics of a good utility. Many file and directory managers have a built-in file lister. Others link to Vern Buerg's LIST, a file lister which is perhaps the most popular user-supported program ever written. (The newest releases of LIST include a "plus" version that is itself nearly a full-scale file manager.) The point is, when you highlight a filename, you should be able to view its contents simply by pressing ENTER, or at most one or two other keys.

Windows and Split Screens

A *window* is an area of the screen reserved for one file or program. Multiple onscreen windows can make computer work a little easier, because you can see two files at once and compare them or transfer data between them. Some programs let you size the window, others let you zoom in on an active window, and some let you move the windows around the screen.

A *split screen* is like having two windows available. In a file manager, it lets you see what's in another directory without having to return to the DOS command, or trying to flip back and forth. That way you don't have to remember every file in every directory.

Directory Tree

An onscreen, visually appealing, and easily understood *directory tree* tells you what directories you have on your disk. In Figure 8-2, PC Shell shows a directory tree in the left window. The highlighted C:\DOS directory's contents are shown in the right window. Most programs with this feature let you change locations by moving a highlight bar, and perform other file management functions from this screen.

More Fancy Fittings

Shell programs continue to evolve. New versions add quality and quantity to already bursting packages. Fancier programs include communications options, printer spoolers, network link-ups, phone dialers, disk backup and diagnostics, memory managers, disk caches, disk optimizers and organizers, graphics and format converters, keyboard enhancers and macros, virus protection, label makers, and video blankers.

Figure 8-2

PC Shell, showing directory tree in left window

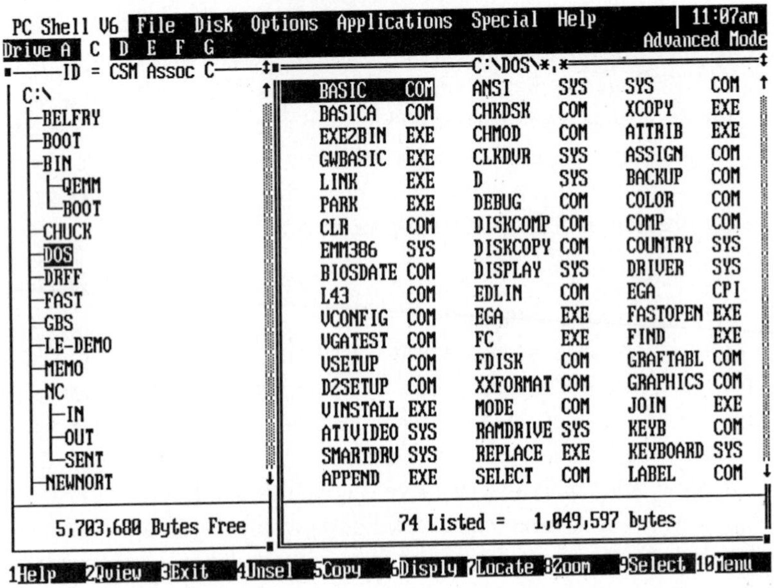

```
PC Shell V6 ▐File  Disk  Options  Applications  Special  Help    | 11:07am
Drive A▐C▐D▐E▐F▐G                                      Advanced Mode
▪─────ID = CSM Assoc C───┴▪═══════════C:\DOS\*.*═════════════┬▪
 C:\                     ↑  BASIC    COM   ANSI     SYS   SYS      COM  ↑
  ├─BELFRY                  BASICA   COM   CHKDSK   COM   XCOPY    EXE
  ├─BOOT                    EXE2BIN  EXE   CHMOD    COM   ATTRIB   EXE
  ├─BIN                     GWBASIC  EXE   CLKDVR   SYS   ASSIGN   COM
  │  ├─QEMM                 LINK     EXE   D        SYS   BACKUP   COM
  │  └─BOOT                 PARK     EXE   DEBUG    COM   COLOR    COM
  ├─CHUCK                   CLR      COM   DISKCOMP COM   COMP     COM
  ├─DOS                     EMM386   SYS   DISKCOPY COM   COUNTRY  SYS
  ├─DRFF                    BIOSDATE COM   DISPLAY  SYS   DRIVER   SYS
  ├─FAST                    L43      COM   EDLIN    COM   EGA      CPI
  ├─GBS                     VCONFIG  COM   EGA      EXE   FASTOPEN EXE
  ├─LE-DEMO                 VGATEST  COM   FC       EXE   FIND     EXE
  ├─MEMO                    VSETUP   COM   FDISK    COM   GRAFTABL COM
  ├─NC                      D2SETUP  COM   XXFORMAT COM   GRAPHICS COM
  │  ├─IN                   VINSTALL EXE   MODE     COM   JOIN     EXE
  │  ├─OUT                  ATIVIDEO SYS   RAMDRIVE SYS   KEYB     COM
  │  └─SENT                 SMARTDRV SYS   REPLACE  EXE   KEYBOARD SYS
  ├─NEWNORT              ↓  APPEND   EXE   SELECT   COM   LABEL    COM  ↓
 ├─────────────────────┤ ├──────────────────────────────────────────┤
    5,703,680 Bytes Free        74 Listed =   1,049,597 bytes
 ├─────────────────────┴─┴──────────────────────────────────────────┤
 1Help   2Uview  3Exit   4Unsel  5Copy   6Display 7Locate 8Zoom   9Select 10Menu
```

Some additions are unique to a single program. For example, the Disc Director shell creates a *virtual directory,* which is a central work area that can hold a list of filenames from several different drives or directories. You can store files wherever you want, and have one phantom (virtual) directory in which you do all your work.

Other such specialties continually arrive on the shell scene, and the ones users really like eventually join the list of standard features.

File Managers

File managers are hard to distinguish from DOS shells, since today's shells contain file management functions among their other features. File managers, in contrast to DOS shells, show their command line heritage. They act as classic utilities, in that you call them from the command line, use them for specific tasks, and then exit to the DOS prompt again. The trade-off is that they are fast and small compared to a full-featured shell. File managers may do any combination of the following:

- Show a graphic directory tree

- Copy, delete, rename, and move files and directories

- Tag files for later actions

- Sort files or display sorted directories

- Manipulate a file's archive, read-only, system, and hidden attributes

- Let you issue DOS commands directly from within the program

- "Shell out" to the DOS prompt, from which you can run any external program of your choosing.

- Search for files, or for text strings within files

A classic file manager utility of the stand-alone type is Kenn Flee's shareware program, Quick Filer, or QFILER. As illustrated earlier in Figure 8-1, it can display two subdirectories at once. Tagged files can be moved, copied, or deleted as a group. The bottom line offers the standard file manager options. A pull-down menu system is also available. The second window also can show a directory tree or a series of help screens.

A file manager such as QFILER can keep your directories organized and free of unneeded files. If you use a shell, these file management functions will probably be included in that program.

Selecting a Shell or File Manager

The best shell and file manager programs are uncomplicated enough for the novice, yet powerful and fast enough for the advanced user.

Two things will help you pick a shell or file management program. First, you can usually trust the reports of other users. For example, programs such as PC Shell, Norton Commander, XTree Gold, and QDOS are almost uniformly praised by reviewers. Any program so well liked is a safe bet. Also, you should try various shareware programs before you pay for them.

Then, if one doesn't meet your needs, you can try another candidate before picking the one you will register and keep.

Here are some areas to consider when deciding on a program.

- *Environment*   Is it compatible with your equipment? Can it work with (or on) a network? Does it need expanded or extended memory? Does it run only as a TSR? How much conventional memory does it use?

- *Interface*   What is the program's interface like? Can it automatically install itself? Does it have a center-screen menu? Does it have menus? Does it support a mouse? Is the mouse driver included? Is the output generic ASCII, or formatted? How many printer drivers are supplied? Can it print to a file instead of to a printer? All of these areas may be of concern, depending upon your level of expertise and the main uses to which you put your computer.

- *File management*   What are the program's file management capabilities? Can it display a directory tree? Does it easily copy, delete, and move files, directories, and subdirectories? Can it tag files for later actions, group or individual? Will it sort files? Which DOS commands does it use? How does it search for data—by filename, contents, exact words, patterns, or wildcards?

- *Utilities*   What are the program's other utility functions? Does it run other programs from a menu? From a command line? Does it set up file folders and directories, attach comments to files, launch applications, and create menus?

If you're just starting, don't be afraid to pick a utility that feels comfortable; you can always switch to something more complex later on.

MENU PROGRAMS

Menu programs let you select specific programs or activities, and then launch those selections automatically. Menus make life easier for beginners, and help prevent errors no matter what your level of expertise. The main drawback for experienced users is that menu programs limit your choices to what can be presented on a single screen. You cannot easily modify how a given program will run, as you can from the DOS command line. However, if exiting to the DOS command line is one of the menu options, even that objection disappears.

Most menu programs let you (or a network administrator) establish a password for some activities. For example, you may want to keep beginners away from the DOS prompt. Passwords also give you control over access to sensitive information such as payroll records.

Many menu systems are available through both commercial and shareware channels. One best-seller is the shareware classic AUTOMENU.

COMMAND LINE EDITORS AND ENHANCERS

Command line editors and enhancers let you recall previous commands to the screen and edit them to correct mistakes, change options, and so on. They may also let you create *synonyms*, or abbreviations, for commands that you use on a regular basis. Synonyms work much like word processing macros but operate at the DOS prompt instead of inside a program. For example, you may get tired of entering the /p switch with DIR when you display a long directory. With a synonym program, you can define the command DP to mean DIR /p. Then when you enter DP, you'll always get a directory listing that pauses after every screenful of files.

These programs are even more useful when you need a long, complicated command line to run a program you only use occasionally. For example, say you have a text comparison program that shows the differences between two versions of the same file. Comparison programs need a lot of command line information telling them which files to examine, how to report the differences, and so on, and require command lines like this one:

C:\> difcomp /o:e:\difcomp.fil /n:10 *file1 file2*

In a command like this, you can easily make frustrating typing mistakes, and you'll probably always have to look up the command syntax unless you have it memorized.

One solution is to create a tiny batch file as outlined in Chapter 11. Tiny files, however, waste a lot of disk space. A command line editor, on the other hand, lets you define the command DIFCOMP to mean the entire command line, so you could enter just DIFCOMP *file1 file2* (substituting the real filenames for *file1* and *file2*). This technique is much easier, much less open to error, and doesn't require a space-wasting tiny batch file.

Three of the most popular command line editors are the shareware programs ANARKEY, ALIAS, and CED. An enhanced commercial version of CED is available as PCED. Proprietary DOS substitutes, such as 4DOS and DR DOS, also offer the ability to use command synonyms.

Batch File Utilities

Like command line editors, batch files expand what you can do with a simple one- or two-word command at the DOS prompt. *Batch file utilities* play an important role in what you can accomplish with a batch file.

Batch file utilities make it possible to write small batch file programs that allow you to select what to do next. They might direct you to enter a word into a simple password system, log on to a system as a current user, and so forth. Batch file utilities generally do this by setting a DOS value called an exit code, or *errorlevel*, that a batch file uses to determine its next action. Of the DOS commands, only a handful return such exit codes, generally just reporting whether an operation was successful. Utilities such as STACKEY, BATUTIL, BATCHMAN, and the Norton Utility Batch Enhancer are designed to give DOS batch files more flexibility by making creative use of DOS errorlevels.

See Chapter 11 for more on how to tap the power and flexibility of DOS batch files.

DESKTOP ACCESSORIES

Desktop accessories are utility programs or DOS shell features that mimic a desktop and provide clipboards, calculators, ASCII tables, phone dialers, and the like. Some of these utility services were described earlier, in the section on DOS shells.

Often these desktop programs are memory resident, which means they stay in RAM and wait for you to press a designated key combination, or *hot key*, to call them into action. When the hot key is pressed, they pop up on the screen and become the active program. When you are finished, the program disappears from the screen, handing control back to the original program. It's not really gone, however, because all that's needed to reactivate the program is to press the hot key again. Such programs are often called TSR programs, for terminate-and-stay-resident.

One of the earliest TSRs was the original version of Borland's Sidekick, a program still in wide use. Many users feel that the quickness and elegance of this program has never been surpassed. It does, however, have a reputation for taking a lot of memory and causing occasional compatibility problems. A host of alternative desktop utilities include Sidekick Plus (the original's enhanced, but slower upgrade), Sidekick 2.0 (a faster upgrade), HomeBase, Memory Mate, Instant Recall, and PC Tools Desktop.

HELP PROGRAMS

If you are new to DOS, or are an occasional user of major applications like CADD programs, WordPerfect, and Lotus 1-2-3, then memory resident pop-up help screens like the Norton Guides can help you learn to use these programs. Most software dealers carry at least one or two DOS help programs and books, plus a help utility or two for the major applications. Many help programs and tutorials are available through shareware channels.

MEMORY MANAGERS

DOS-based hardware systems now offer the capabilities OS/2 users take for granted, but they need a boost in the memory management department. *Memory managers* move whatever resident software they can (such as device drivers and TSR utilities) into memory above the 640K limit. This makes more room available within the DOS 640K conventional memory area. They may also allow you to remap your system's ROM BIOS and your graphics adapter card's video BIOS into faster RAM areas.

A good memory manager can release more memory to programs and speed up machine operations. Those happy results have made programs such as QEMM, HeadRoom, and 386-MAX must-have utilities for any 386-based DOS system with more than 640K of memory. Users with 286-based systems can choose Above Disc, which offers many of the QEMM-386 and 386-MAX's TSR features.

TSR Managers   TSR programs like Sidekick and many others have become so popular that many users wouldn't be without their favorites. They do, however, sometimes conflict with one another, and you sometimes have no recourse but to reboot your machine to get things working again. TSR managers largely do away with the rebooting problem. There are many such programs available, of which the granddaddy is the TSRCOM utility set published by TurboPower Software, for which no registration or purchase fee is required. You can get TSRCOM utilities through shareware channels.

DISK CACHES

Disk cache utilities reduce wear and tear on your hard disk, and greatly decrease file access times, by holding recent disk reads and writes in memory. Many programs refer to the same data repeatedly and expect to read it fresh each time from your disk. A disk cache provides this access to data, so that your hard disk doesn't have to physically locate it each time the information is requested.

Disk caches can speed up your disk operations by several hundred percent, and are not terribly expensive. They work on both hard and floppy disks, and are included in commercial utility collections such as PC Tools, Norton, Mace, and PC-Kwik. Useful public domain and shareware disk caches also are available. One commercial product, Multisoft's PC-Kwik Power Pak utilities, combines a disk cache with some power tools (RAM disks and printer spoolers), and dynamically shares RAM. That means it can borrow from one function, such as the RAM disk, to enlarge another function, such as the printer spooler, on demand. Later versions of DOS supply a disk cache called SMARTDRV.SYS, although its speed and features are limited.

A good disk cache has become a virtual necessity for efficient operation with DOS. If you don't have one with your system, it is worth the effort and minor expense to get one. Your disk drives will thank you for it. The use of disk caches will be covered in Chapter 17.

Some Cautions About Caches

Disk caches have been used for years, and the technology is well proven. However, so many different combinations of hardware and software are in use, and DOS reads and writes are so fundamental to a computer's operation, that some caution is advised.

Be sure to use the current version and correct options with these programs. Also, be especially careful with disk caches if your disk is not a standard type. Other potential trouble spots include

- High-memory TSRs on 386-based systems
- Nonstandard floppy or hard disk controllers
- Programs (such as security managers) that write directly to a disk, bypassing the BIOS

Many makers of disk optimizers (described later in this chapter) warn against using them with incompatible disk cache programs, and it is important to heed such warnings.

Disk cache software pays for itself quickly in faster operation and reduced drive wear. When you are about to do something fundamental like reorganizing the entire disk, however, be sure to first disable or remove your disk cache and back up your files.

FILE RECOVERY AND DISK MEDIC UTILITIES

When you are constantly adding and deleting files, moving them from directory to directory, and reorganizing your disk, you will inevitably delete or reformat a file by accident. That's when you will need a *file recovery utility* of the sort that made both Paul Mace and Peter Norton famous. Many such file recovery utilities are now available; some of the best are in the Mace, Norton, and PC Tools collections. You also can find some good shareware unerase utilities.

Unintentional deletions aren't the only accidents that can happen— especially to a disk that's been allowed to become badly disorganized. If you suddenly can't get DOS to read a file, you can often solve the problem simply by rebooting the machine. When that doesn't work, the *disk medic* type of utilities can often help. You should consider buying at least one of the major utility collections, just to have the disk medics available when needed. Candidate disk medics for your collection include DISKFIX (PC Tools), Power Disk (PC-Kwik), Emergency Room (Mace Utilities), and Norton Disk Doctor (Norton Utilities).

Let's look at some typical problems that any of these major collections may deal with better than their DOS equivalent, CHKDSK.

Lost Clusters

Clusters get lost when DOS allocates space to a file but doesn't properly tie the data to a filename. It is a common problem, usually harmless. It can happen when you must exit a program inappropriately, for example, if your keyboard locks up and you must reboot while an application is still running. As a result, data clusters are marked as if in use by a file, but are not linked to any filename—they get lost; stranded on the disk without a known home.

The DOS CHKDSK command tells you if it finds lost clusters. If you add the /f option to CHKDSK, it also retrieves those lost clusters as best it can. But any of the third-party utilities mentioned above can probably do a better job for you, with more complete reports and higher likelihood of successful recovery.

Cross-Linked Files

Cross-linked files happen when two different files claim ownership of the same data, or when a single file, instead of ending, points back to the middle of itself in a circular fashion. This can happen if a defragmenter goes awry (see "Disk Defragmenters and Optimizers" in this chapter), or a disk cache is incompatible with a program, or an application loses track of file data, or because of other software conflicts. Hardware problems that lead to cross-linking are less common, but do occur. The system might have received a small power spike, for example.

Whatever the cause, a disk medic will try to figure out which file owns the data, or where a file should properly end. If you haven't rebooted more than once since the cross-linking occurred, the disk medics have a fair chance of success. *Just remember to stop as soon as you discover a problem!* Otherwise, the damage may be irreversible. After you use a disk medic, always reboot your system.

DISK AND DIRECTORY MAINTENANCE UTILITIES

Organization and simplification are two goals for which people turn to computers. With proper attention, your system can be an extremely useful tool, one that brings order to your working universe. But neglect can render your files disorganized, useless, or even lost in a clutter of random files and subdirectories. About the time you realize your file structure has slipped into chaos, the honeymoon will be over.

Your disks and directories are your data storage areas, and a bit of planning and order goes a long way. As with a file cabinet, you need to stop occasionally and sort through the files, clean out the clutter, and put the "keepers" where you can find them later.

Regular maintenance also will help your equipment last. Moving parts won't have to work so hard to find files scattered all over your disks. Your chances of losing files are reduced. When you know which directories and disks contain which files, you are less likely to accidentally erase or copy over important data. And, if you do accidentally erase something, a regularly maintained system will help you notice the mistake sooner; this helps you recover the files before they are irretrievably lost.

The following paragraphs describe some areas where utility programs may be particularly helpful in lending order to your directories.

Directory Programs

When DOS searches for a file, it reads a directory's filenames in the order found, just as it does when you enter the DIR command. After you've worked inside a directory for any length of time, the files can lose all rational order (see Figure 8-3). This makes the directory hard to work with. You can solve this problem in several ways.

You may find it helpful to get a multicolumn directory program that lets you specify how to display the directory listing. There are many available. Figure 8-4 shows the same directory listed in two columns, sorted alphabetically by name, produced by an early version of the popular utility SDIR (for sorted directory). Later versions of SDIR finally evolved into a small, flexible shell program. (Many users still keep an early version on hand because it is simple and quick.)

A second approach is to get a program that changes the order of the file listings within the directory, so that the DOS DIR command can produce a sorted listing, as shown (sorted by size) in Figure 8-5. The Norton 4.5 utility DIRSORT (Figure 8-6) can sort a directory one file at a time, or by name, extension, size, date, or time. The shareware program DIREDIT (Figure 8-7) also physically edits a directory one file name at a time. The primary use for such file-by-file editing is to group files that would be separated if sorted by name, extension, size, or date. For example, you may find it convenient to keep a program and its associated program files together in a directory that also contains other programs.

The secret to sorting for speed is to put most-used files at the top, where DOS will find them first. The secret to sorting for convenience, at least with

Figure 8-3

An unsorted directory listing

```
Volume in drive A is CSM Assoc
Directory of  A:\UTIL

.              <DIR>       4-01-91   6:56p
..             <DIR>       4-01-91   6:56p
GET      EXE     4095      1-12-90   4:26p
DSPACE   EXE    14124      7-10-88   9:53p
POP      COM      628     12-01-86   1:43p
COPYIT   EXE    61920      1-12-90   5:24p
PCOPY    EXE   107706      8-01-90  12:00a
BCOPY    COM     2294      3-17-89   2:54p
DIRMAGIC COM     8564      6-07-90   7:28p
ADDPATH  COM     4498      2-13-89   8:17p
FFF      EXE    43964      1-30-91   2:07p
PUSH     COM      717     12-01-86   1:43p
LCD      EXE    11614     10-15-90   7:06p
SDIR     COM     3328      3-12-87   9:06p
DD       COM      796      9-05-85   3:39p
WHEREIS  EXE    18960      4-02-90   8:33a
PRUNE    COM     7488     12-09-90  11:58a
QF       EXE   119632      8-24-89   3:01a
DISKMEM  EXE    18040     10-27-90   9:13a
         19 File(s)   6260736 bytes free

A:\UTIL *
```

Figure 8-4

The directory from Figure 8-3 sorted by name

```
A:\UTIL *sdir /2
SDIR  Sorted DIRectory Listing, Version 2.6  Volume CSM Assoc    04/01/91 19:23
!OPTIONS: /Cls /WrIte /Pause /All !COLUMN: /2 /6 !SORT: /No /Size /Date /eXt
                    Directory of A:\UTIL
```

Filespec.ext	Bytes	Atr	-Last Change-	Filespec.ext	Bytes	Atr	-Last Change-
ADDPATH .COM	4498	A	02/13/89 20:17	LCD .EXE	11614	A	10/15/90 19:06
BCOPY .COM	2294	A	03/17/89 14:54	PCOPY .EXE	107706	A	08/01/90 00:00
COPYIT .EXE	61920	A	01/12/90 17:24	POP .COM	628	A	12/01/86 13:43
DD .COM	796	A	09/05/85 15:39	PRUNE .COM	7488	A	12/09/90 11:58
DIRMAGIC.COM	8564	A	06/07/90 19:28	PUSH .COM	717	A	12/01/86 13:43
DISKMEM .EXE	18040	A	10/27/90 09:13	QF .EXE	119632	A	08/24/89 03:01
DSPACE .EXE	14124	A	07/10/88 21:53	SDIR .COM	3328	A	03/12/87 21:06
FFF .EXE	43964	A	01/30/91 14:07	WHEREIS .EXE	18960	A	04/02/90 08:33
GET .EXE	4095	A	01/12/90 16:26				

```
  428368 Bytes in       17 File(s);  6193152 bytes free...
A:\UTIL *
```

Figure 8-5

The same directory after an on-disk sort by size

```
Volume in drive A is CSM Assoc
Directory of  A:\UTIL

.                  <DIR>      4-01-91   6:56p
..                 <DIR>      4-01-91   6:56p
POP       COM        628     12-01-86   1:43p
PUSH      COM        717     12-01-86   1:43p
DD        COM        796      9-05-85   3:39p
BCOPY     COM       2294      3-17-89   2:54p
SDIR      COM       3328      3-12-87   9:06p
GET       EXE       4095      1-12-90   4:26p
ADDPATH   COM       4498      2-13-89   8:17p
PRUNE     COM       7400     12-09-90  11:58a
DIRMAGIC  COM       8564      6-07-90   7:28p
LCD       EXE      11614     10-15-90   7:06p
DSPACE    EXE      14124      7-10-88   9:53p
DISKMEM   EXE      18040     10-27-90   9:13a
WHEREIS   EXE      18960      4-02-90   8:33a
FFF       EXE      43964      1-30-91   2:07p
COPYIT    EXE      61920      1-12-90   5:24p
PCOPY     EXE     107706      8-01-90  12:00a
QF        EXE     119632      8-24-89   3:01a
        19 File(s)   6182912 bytes free


A:\UTIL ➤
```

Figure 8-6

DIRSORT, showing highlighted files being moved

```
┌──────────────────── Directory Sort ────────────────────┐
│ ┌─────── E:\GUIDE\8UTILS ──────┐                         │
│ │  Name      Size     Date       Time   │  Sort by    Order│
│ │ 8cascade     420   Oct 30 90  10:53 am │              │
│ │ 8intro       305   Aug 13 90   9:14 pm │              │
│ │ 8secur       604   Oct 30 90  10:53 am │  Name       + │
│ │ common    46,004   Jul 23 90   8:56 pm │  Extension  + │
│ │ util-1       556   Aug  8 90   8:55 am │              │
│ │ chap8    4pr 43,594 Oct 30 90  6:13 pm │              │
│ │ mark     doc  2,103 Nov  5 90  6:06 am │              │
│ │ diskmap  fst 75,761 Nov  5 90  2:34 pm │              │
│ │ 8ref     gv   5,968 Oct 30 90  7:03 pm │              │
│ │ chap8    bak 46,240 Oct 30 90  9:26 pm │  Name        │
│ │ chap8out gv 47,632 Nov  1 90  10:12 am │  Extension   │
│ │ chap8    pco 11,952 Jul 28 90  8:22 pm │  Date        │
│ │ chap8    pcw 62,253 Nov  6 90  11:03 am │  Time        │
│ │ diredit  pix  2,559 Nov  6 90  11:05 am │  Size        │
│ │ diskmap  pix  2,592 Nov  5 90  2:32 pm │              │
│ │ sdir     pix  2,506 Nov  4 90  2:27 pm │              │
│ │ sorted   pix  2,032 Nov  4 90  1:59 pm │  Clear sort order│
│ └───────────────────────────────┘  Move sort entry│
│   Press <CR> when OK; <ESC> to cancel changes           │
│                                                          │
│ Re-sort    Move file(s)    Change sort order    Write changes to disk│
└──────────────── Press F1 for Help ──────────────────────┘
```

Figure 8-7

The DIREDIT shareware directory editor

```
 1:DL              ! 21:XMSDISK0.ZIP  ! 41:DX-211.ZIP     !
 2:TEMP            ! 22:ABOUTEMS.ZIP  ! 42:TYPED.EXE      !
 3:PDAILY.DAT      ! 23:TELEPORT.ARC  ! 43:SCANV67.ZIP    !
 4:PCFN            ! 24:FIND213.ZIP   ! 44:MYSTIC.ZIP     !
 5:MIRORSAV.FIL    ! 25:VALIDATE.EXE  ! 45:96BB1090.ZIP   !
 6:TREEINFO.NCD    ! 26:SNIP22.ZIP    ! 46:DIREDIT.TXT    !
 7:FLAG2.BAT       ! 27:CP3.ARC       ! 47:DIREDIT.DOC    !
 8:README.1ST      ! 28:DIFFX.ZIP     ! 48:DIREDIT.EXE    !
 9:USSR-BBS.ZIP    ! 29:WPTROUBL.ZIP  ! 49:DX-D20.ZIP     !
10:EZMENU36.ZIP    ! 30:PASTE22.ZIP   ! 50:CRYP-MPJ.ZIP   !
11:DPATH.ZIP       ! 31:FSTHST21.ZIP  ! 51:PRINTE.ZIP     !
12:DIREDIT.OVV     ! 32:QDISK.ZIP     ! 52:DIRED305.ZIP   !
13:NEWFILES.ARC    ! 33:SPHERES.ZIP   ! 53:ASP3201.ZIP    !
14:MSOFTFIX.ZIP    ! 34:EEMRAM22.ZIP  ! 54:GEOCLK40.ZIP   !
15:DPATH.DOC       ! 35:EEMRAM21.ZIP  ! 55:VM386.ZIP      !
16:PLUCK20.ZIP     ! 36:KUTSGLU1.ZIP  !
17:KEYCODES.ZIP    ! 37:MIRROR.BAK    !
18:DIREDIT.HLP     ! 38:MIRROR.FIL    !
19:HIMEMBUG.ZIP    ! 39:CUTOUT.ZIP    !
20:MAKETXT.EXE     ! 40:WAS050.ZIP    !
Cursor-> DIREDIT.OVV   May 27, 1990   20:58:28    4262 Bytes
Moving->
PgUp : window up ! PgDn : window down ! Home : Dir top ! End
                 ! M : next menu line - Windows are locked
Editing directory: F:\
```

---

long directories, is to put your most-used filenames at the bottom of the directory, where they don't scroll off the screen in a directory listing.

A Note About Norton 5.0 DIRSORT was left out of Norton 5.0. If you have Norton 5.0 and would like DIRSORT at no cost, call Norton's technical support (check your documentation for the current number) and ask for it. They'll send a floppy disk with the missing program. While you're at it, ask for the Norton 4.5 program FILEINFO, which lets you attach brief file descriptions to directory listings. Both programs may be restored to the Utilities in later releases. The Norton 5.0 program Speed Disk does allow file sorting, but not on a file-by-file basis.

Backup Programs

Backing up a hard disk has been important ever since the original IBM PC XT appeared, with its 10MB hard disk, in 1983. DOS itself provided the first backup utility, with BACKUP and RESTORE. The early versions had problems, but with DOS 3.2, BACKUP and RESTORE had become reasonably fast and reliable programs. Because of the buggy early versions, however, third parties started coming up with better approaches.

Saving your data in case the hard disk fails is the primary purpose of backup programs, and their manuals explain for you the types of backups performed. Today's backup programs can help you in many other ways. They can "clone" disks—that is, re-create a hard disk's contents on a second machine, or on a new hard disk. Backup software can transfer specific programs or files between machines on what's been called the "sneaker net"—(that's where you copy files onto a floppy and walk with it to a second machine). If a file is too long to store on a single floppy, backup programs offer a good solution: they can break a file into several pieces, one per disk, without losing anything. And most backup programs also offer file compression, which reduces the number of disks needed for a backup.

Many excellent backup programs are available. Some widely used programs are PC Backup (PC Tools), Fastback Plus (Fifth Generation Systems), DMS/IB Intelligent Backup (Sterling Software), BackEZ (EZ-Logic), Back-It (Gazelle Systems), and PC-Fullbak (Westlake Data). Other good systems are offered by Norton Computing and by the Mace Utilities. There are shareware backup utilities, too, but the commercial backup programs are faster, more polished, and use fewer disks.

Disk Defragmenters and Optimizers

On a hard disk, the physical location of your subdirectories affects the speed with which DOS loads programs and finds files. For the fastest access time, you need to locate your subdirectory entries close to the outer rim of the disk.

There are two ways to accomplish this. One approach is to create the subdirectory tree structure on a freshly formatted hard disk—*before* you copy any files to the disk. Then stick with that structure, and never create any new subdirectories. This approach is not practical for most users, since directory structures tend to change over time.

A better method is to use a *disk defragmenter,* or *optimizer.* These programs physically reorganize files and subdirectory entries on the hard disk, rather than changing how they are indexed in the directory area. All major utility collections can reorganize a disk, as can many excellent single-purpose utilities. Available disk optimizing programs include Compress (PC

Tools), Speed Disk (Norton), Unfrag (Mace), Power Disk (PC-Kwik), VOPT (Golden Bow Systems), OPTune (Gazelle Systems), Disk OrGanizer (DOG, a dedicated utility program), and Disk Optimizer (another dedicated utility).

How Fragmentation Happens

On an unused disk, files are stored contiguously as you add them; that is, they are laid down in consecutive magnetic sectors rather than scattered all about. As you erase files, though, DOS frees the space they occupied, to be used again for storage. On a map of the disk, the newly empty space appears as gaps (see Figure 8-8). As more files get saved, DOS reuses this space. If a file is too long for the space available, DOS fills that space, finds another empty space, and puts more of the file there. This process continues

Figure 8-8

Map of disk shows empty space left by deleted files

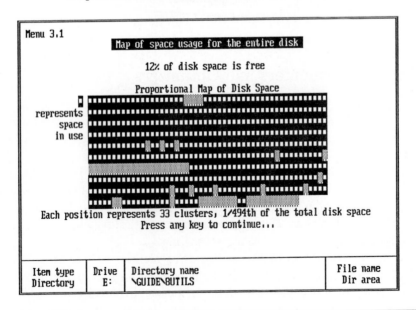

until the entire file has been written to disk, in however many fragments are necessary to hold it. Over time, file fragments will be written all over the physical surface of the recording medium—this is called *fragmentation.*

Fragmentation affects access speed. When a file is continuous, DOS can read it as a series of sectors, say from sector 5 through sector 15. When the same file is fragmented, DOS may have to jump from sector 5 across to sector 215, then back to sector 106, and so forth. The result is slower disk access and more wear on mechanical parts.

How Defragmenting Works

When you run a disk optimizer, the program relocates all fragmented files so they are contiguous. Most defragmenters also close up the gaps on the disk, so files saved later have a better chance of being written to contiguous sectors. On a badly fragmented hard disk this reorganization can take time, but the results are worth it. This process is not the same as sorting a directory where you arrange which filenames come up first in a listing. When you defragment a disk, you change the actual physical location of a file's contents, moving the binary ones and zeros from one place to another on the surface of the disk.

Some disk optimizing programs let you dictate the order of the files on the disk; others just defragment your files and close the open areas. Defragmenters do run faster, but programs that also change the physical storage arrangement can put the most frequently used files closer to the file allocaton table (FAT). When loading a file, DOS first reads the FAT to find out where to locate the file; the FAT knows the physical location of each sector of the file. Moving the read/write heads back and forth between the file and the FAT takes time, so storing a file closer to the FAT reduces both seek time and mechanical wear.

Caution: Reorganizing an entire disk involves intensive read/write activity. It is important to always back up your files before you start, and follow the program's instructions carefully.

Many users run a fast defragmenter, such as Golden Bow Systems' VOPT, daily or weekly, and then a more complete disk organizer, such as PC Tools' COMPRESS, monthly. COMPRESS and other disk organizers also offer faster, less comprehensive operating modes, so you can switch back and forth if you prefer.

When you have the option of specifying a file order, place the more stable files—.COM, .EXE, .SYS, .OVL, and .OVR files—closest to the FAT. Data files, which are most likely to get fragmented as you work, should be furthest away, where they take less time to defragment. PC Tools, Mace, Norton, DOG, and OPTune all can relocate files and directories in any order you specify. If you wish to go all the way—to specify the relative positions of files and directories on your disk—DOG and Norton will do it. Remember, although simple defragmenting is faster than complete reorganization, cleaning away the debris from your disk always takes a bit of time—no matter what program you choose.

Directory Squeezing

When you delete a file or a subdirectory, DOS does not actually delete anything. Rather, it changes the first letter of the filename in the file index to the lowercase Greek letter sigma and marks the data area as erased. Figure 8-9 illustrates the display of erased entries produced by the Norton Utilities DISKEDIT program. Notice the sigma character at the beginning of certain filenames.

Figure 8-9

DISKEDIT's screen, with the first erased filename highlighted

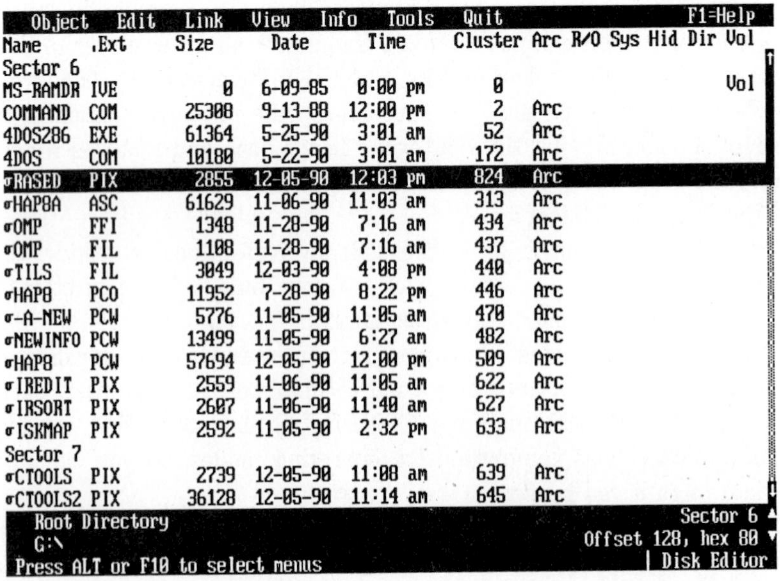

```
  Object   Edit   Link   View   Info   Tools   Quit                    F1=Help
 Name       .Ext   Size     Date        Time    Cluster Arc R/O Sys Hid Dir Vol
 Sector 6
 MS-RAMDR IVE         0   6-09-85   0:00 pm         0                          Vol
 COMMAND  COM     25300   9-13-88  12:00 pm         2    Arc
 4DOS286  EXE     61364   5-25-90   3:01 am        52    Arc
 4DOS     COM     10100   5-22-90   3:01 am       172    Arc
 σRASED   PIX      2855  12-05-90  12:03 pm       824    Arc
 σHAP8A   ASC     61629  11-06-90  11:03 am       313    Arc
 σOMP     FFI      1340  11-20-90   7:16 am       434    Arc
 σOMP     FIL      1100  11-20-90   7:16 am       437    Arc
 σTILS    FIL      3049  12-03-90   4:08 pm       440    Arc
 σHAP8    PCO     11952   7-20-90   8:22 am       446    Arc
 σ-A-NEW  PCW      5776  11-05-90  11:05 am       470    Arc
 σNEWINFO PCW     13499  11-05-90   6:27 am       482    Arc
 σHAP8    PCW     57694  12-05-90  12:00 pm       509    Arc
 σIREDIT  PIX      2559  11-06-90  11:05 am       622    Arc
 σIRSORT  PIX      2607  11-06-90  11:40 am       627    Arc
 σISKMAP  PIX      2592  11-05-90   2:32 pm       633    Arc
 Sector 7
 σCTOOLS  PIX      2739  12-05-90  11:00 am       639    Arc
 σCTOOLS2 PIX     36128  12-05-90  11:14 am       645    Arc
     Root Directory                                            Sector 6  ▲
     G:\                                                  Offset 128, hex 80  ▼
     Press ALT or F10 to select menus                          | Disk Editor
```

Because erased files remain on the disk, access speed is affected. When you delete a directory entry, DOS still must search through all directory entries, including deleted files and subdirectories, to find what it needs. It's a time waster for DOS, but sorting your directories with a program like DIREDIT or DIRSORT can help a little, since they move erased filename entries to the end of the directory list. That way DOS can find a "live" file without having to read through all the erased entries—of significant help on floppy disks. On hard disks, DOS searches along a path (discussed in Chapter 10), so moving erased entries to the end of a directory doesn't help as much.

To free your system entirely of erased subdirectory and file entries, use a *directory squeezer*. These programs explicitly remove deleted subdirectory and file entries, marking them *unused* rather than *erased*. This frees directory space and accelerates your directory searches and program loads. Most disk organizers also squeeze the directories.

COMPRESSION AND ARCHIVING UTILITIES

If you have some files that you need to keep but don't expect to use very often, you can put them in long-term storage as *compressed archives*. Archiving also works for backing up your working files so long as you remember to update your archives regularly. For daily backups you're better off using a program designed specifically to make backups. Backup programs are more automatic and, therefore, less trouble.

Both backup programs and archivers are valuable utilities, and what they do is similar.

- *Backup programs* make copies of your files on other media, so you can get the files back later if something destroys the originals.

- *Archive programs* compress files into a smaller space, so you need less disk real estate to store them.

There are dozens of ways to back up or archive files, from copying them directly onto floppy disks to duplicating entire hard disks on high-density audio tape or laser disks.

If your system is equipped with special backup hardware, you may want to read the documentation about its use, and skip to "Printer Utilities." If you have no backup system, utilities can do your archiving and backup to floppies. There are some excellent programs available, including file compression programs that can reduce by up to 50 percent the number of floppies needed to store a given amount of data.

File Compression

Inevitably, file storage uses disk space. And inefficient file storage *wastes* disk space, for several reasons. First, disks allow a minimum amount of space for each file, whether or not the file uses it. This minimum is called a *cluster*, usually 512 bytes on a floppy and 2K to 8K on a hard disk. If you have dozens of 100-byte files, each taking five times their size in disk space, you're losing a lot of useful storage space.

Another file storage problem is that files—especially ASCII and other data files—contain a lot of blank space and repeat characters. The extra space contributes to your ability to read and understand the file's contents, but it also takes up more space on disk. If you could trim that unused space from the file for storage purposes, and then restore it when you call the file back into use, you could gain storage space.

File compression utilities address precisely these two major causes of wasted space. These programs combine multiple files into a single archive file, and then compress the archive file by eliminating blank space and repeated character strings. The mathematical details get very complex, but the end result is a savings of 60 to 80 percent, or even more, on data file storage space. Binary files, which are inherently more compact, can experience a 30 to 50 percent size reduction.

Where to Find File Compressors   File compressors got their start in the world of online services and BBSs. (The more you can compress a file, the less time it takes to transmit the file by modem.) One result of this BBS heritage is that the strongest stand-alone file compression utilities are shareware or public domain programs. Some commercial TSR products are available that compress disk writes and decompress disk reads as they occur. Backup programs often compress files as they copy. These utilities effectively increase the amount of storage available on your disk, but they exact a penalty in file access time because of the forced extra processing.

A new category of compression utility works only on .COM and .EXE files. When you call the compressed program into use, it uncompresses itself directly into memory where it operates just as if it had never been compressed. Self-uncompressing programs of this sort take some extra processing time, but it is not noticeable because it occurs during the expected program loading period. Current executable program compressors are shareware programs, but commercial versions may be forthcoming. Self-uncompressing programs are useful where storage space is at a premium, such as on RAM disks or on notebook and laptop computers.

Current leading compression utilities are PKZIP (PKWare, Inc.), ARC (System Enhancement Associates), PAK (NoGate Consulting), and LHARC (public domain). Several other compression utilities are available, some fairly specialized, but they are less widely used.

Library or Cataloging Utilities

Working in tandem with archiving utilities are the many catalog, database, and library programs that remember where you've stored a particular file. If you have a large collection of programs or files, a catalog program helps when you can't quite recall where you stored your copy of that report to the general manager, or your last letter to the IRS.

Tip: On smaller systems, you might be able to use the DOS LABEL command to keep track of how your files are stored. For example, the label TAX91 might indicate your 1991 tax return files. If you're fairly well organized from the start, and don't accumulate too many files, this LABEL technique may be all you need.

PRINTER UTILITIES

Printing is one of the tightest bottlenecks in computing, because the printers simply cannot print files as fast as the computer can send them. Moreover, printers become obsolete at a brisk pace, as new printers with more elaborate features come along. The history of PC-compatible printers is much like that of the computers that drive them, with rapid advances and dropping prices. One result is a lot of printing hardware that is still in good shape, but needs some help to come up to current standards.

Thus, printer programs have become a major utilities category. Updated *printer drivers* and other utilities enhance what you can do with older printers. These programs set printing modes, switch between printer brands, and supply additional fonts for laser printers. Some utilities let you print on both sides of the paper, or even two pages per side, in tiny print. And printer *spoolers* intercept printer signals and store them in the computer's memory or on a disk file, letting you get on with your work while the spooler runs the print job in the background.

Some available printer utilities and their uses are listed here.

- *Spoolers* let you continue working while the printer prints.

- *Printer redirection programs* direct output that is going to the printer back to a disk file.

- *Text formatters* tell the system how many lines per page to print, if a footer or header is needed, and so on—all from a plain ASCII file.

- *Print packers* let you fit more characters onto a single page.

- *Print enhancers and custom fonts* improve the output capabilities of your printer unit. For example, they can let 9-pin printer output look like 24-pin. They also let you design your own characters, logos, monograms, and the like.

- *Additional software fonts* can be installed on many 24-pin printers and most laser printers on a temporary basis. Numerous download-able font systems are also available.

DATA SECURITY

Data security utilities range from password programs to full-scale data encryption. One efficient approach, if unauthorized access to files is a concern, is to use a menu system or shell that requires a password for access to certain programs or areas of the disk. When using such a program, make sure you keep a master password in a safe, preferably separate, location.

The most secure data security system, short of keeping everything under armed guard in a fireproof safe, is data *encryption*. Encryption, sometimes misnamed "coding," involves scrambling files using a secret key word or series of keystrokes so people without that key cannot access them. Unfortunately, legitimate users forget their keys and unauthorized hackers steal them, so careful key management is an absolute must with such systems. Most users are justifiably shy of encryption systems.

Still, when you need tight security (for example, for financial management or engineering development), encryption may be the best answer. Consult your dealer. And remember: *back up your files* before using any encryption system the first time.

Antivirus and Antirogue Programs

A rogue program is any program that does something malicious, causing damage or disruption to the normal flow of work. The most famous type of rogue program is the computer virus. Viruses are tiny, independent pieces of programming code that attach themselves to legitimate programs and wait for a trigger event. The trigger may be a future date, a specific usage of the infected program, or any other event the virus writer was able to specify without making the virus easily detectable. Until triggered, the virus merrily replicates itself into other programs. Some viruses are harmless, some harmful, some humorous, but all of them can increase local aspirin sales. Figure 8-10 shows one of the first IBM viruses, the Cascade Virus, which caused letters on the screen to fall, or cascade, to the bottom. It first appeared in Germany several years ago.

New antivirus programs, even antivirus hardware, arrive on the market all the time. Because viruses mutate so quickly, the successful antivirus system must be able to adapt just as quickly. As a result, many of the best antivirus programs are distributed through shareware channels. The most widely used programs utilize the following three basic approaches to countering the virus threat:

- *Catch it in action* Flu-Shot Plus (Ross Greenberg), Vaccine (Mace Utilities), and Shield (McAfee Associates) are TSRs that remain in memory, waiting for a virus to attempt to reproduce itself in a protected file.

- *Detect file changes* CheckUp (Rich Levin) writes a mathematical signature of specified files into a table. When you boot up, or at any other designated time, you can compare the previously recorded signatures against the files currently stored on disk. Any changes, such as virus modifications, are reported.

- *Detect virus signatures* SCAN (McAfee Associates) searches binary files for characteristic sequences of 1's and 0's associated with known viruses, reporting any signatures it finds.

Figure 8-10

The Cascade Virus at work

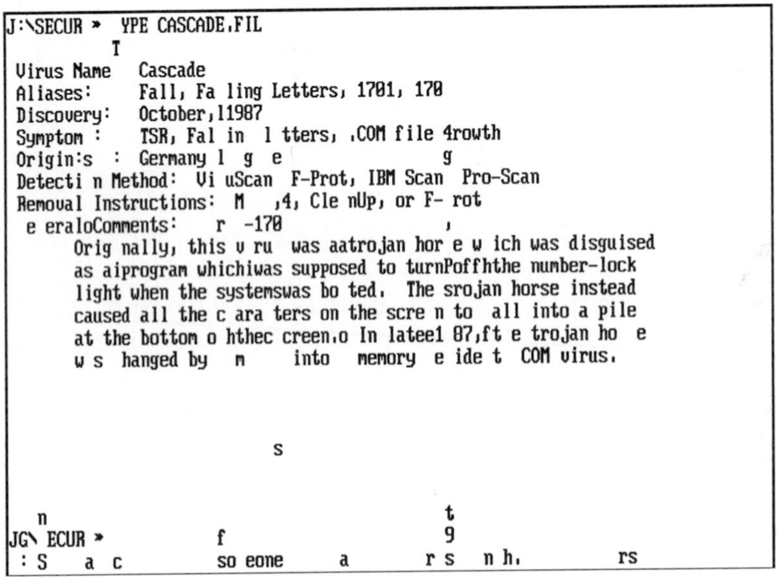

```
J:\SECUR > YPE CASCADE.FIL
          T
Virus Name    Cascade
Aliases:      Fall, Fa ling Letters, 1701, 170
Discovery:    October,11987
Symptom :     TSR, Fal in  l tters, .COM file 4rowth
Origin:s  :   Germany l  g  e                    g
Detecti n Method: Vi uScan  F-Prot, IBM Scan  Pro-Scan
Removal Instructions:  M   ,4, Cle nUp, or F- rot
  e eraloComments:    r  -170            ,
        Orig nally, this v ru  was aatrojan hor e w ich was disguised
        as a iprogram whichiwas supposed to turnPoffhthe number-lock
        light when the systemsvas bo ted.  The srojan horse instead
        caused all the c ara ters on the scre n to  all into a pile
        at the bottom o hthec creen,o In latee1 87,ft e trojan ho e
        w s hanged by  n    into   memory e ide t COM virus.



                        s


    n                                     t
JG\ ECUR >           f                    9
 : S    a c      so eone       a     r s   n h,           rs
```

All of these approaches have drawbacks, but will catch the majority of virus infections when they happen. The best ways to counter the virus threat, however, are to avoid pirated programs, and to avoid casually passing floppy disks around. These two rules, faithfully followed, will protect you from as many viruses as any antivirus program can catch during or after the infection.

SUMMARY

This chapter has discussed only a sampling of the vast array of PC utility programs. Exploring all the available utilities is beyond the scope of this guide, but if you want one for a specific purpose, just keep your eyes and ears open, and ask other users—you'll probably find the one you need.

In the coming chapters, you will read about working at the DOS command level, where many of these utilities are primarily designed to operate.

CHAPTER NINE

Working with DOS – The Basics

The last chapter described some of the utility programs designed to make life easier for MS-DOS users. These shells, menu systems, and small, quick DOS extenders all seek to improve on DOS by being faster, more powerful, easier to use, or more effective than their DOS counterparts. Few power users would be without a collection of such third-party utilities.

But the fact is that DOS can do most of what the third-party programs do. Since DOS is built entirely around the Intel 80 series chips used in most MS-DOS computers, it is indeed the operating system for the whole machine. It is the layer between the hardware and your utility or applications programs. Few people who have learned to operate at the DOS prompt want to give up DOS-level command power entirely for a shell or menu system.

You may find that you have all you need using the command power that Microsoft built into DOS augmented by two or three third-party utility programs. DOS lets you create your own batch file menus, record users' names, and do other tasks people associate with shells and menus. If you build a command system yourself, it is tailored to your own taste and needs.

It's really not hard to fashion a customized environment if you take the time to learn the basic DOS commands.

Chapter 5 introduced the most basic DOS commands. They will be covered here and in the next three chapters in more detail.

DOS BASICS

One of the most fundamental tasks DOS performs is to read and write data to magnetic storage media and let you retrieve it when needed. DOS carries out many other functions and stores data in other ways, but it was the need to store data in files and retrieve it later that led programmers to create DOS. (For a discussion of other operating system tasks, see Chapter 6.)

To keep it simple, the first part of this chapter assumes you have a system equipped with two floppy disk drives, drive A and drive B. If you have only one floppy drive, see the section titled "Sometimes It's OK to Fool MS-DOS" for tips on how to fool your machine into thinking it has two floppy drives. If you have a hard disk, anything done from a floppy drive can also be done from your hard disk, which is usually designated as drive C.

READ.ME

Sometimes It's OK to Fool MS-DOS

Systems with no hard disk and only a single floppy disk drive are not as common as they used to be, but they are still around. If you have a single floppy drive and are using DOS version 3.1 or later, you can fool DOS into thinking you have a drive B in your system. To do so, place a disk that contains a copy of the DOS utility SUBST.EXE into drive A and enter the following commands:

```
A>md \fooldos            (Type command and press ENTER)
A>subst b: a:\fooldos    (Type command and press ENTER)
```

Now any procedure requiring a drive B will work on your single-disk system. You just created a subdirectory named A:\FOOLDOS on your drive A

Sometimes It's OK to Fool MS-DOS (*continued*)

disk. You could have used any word of eight characters or less to name this subdirectory. Then you told DOS to treat A:\FOOLDOS as an actual, separate drive B installed in your system.

Note that you haven't added any space to your disk. If you were short of room before, you still will be short of room. Later in the chapter are some suggested ways to get maximum disk working space in a floppy-based system. For more on subdirectories, see Chapter 10, "DOS and the Hard Disk."

Hardware Control

When implemented as PC-DOS 1.0, the IBM-specific version, DOS already did considerably more than read and write data to disk. It became the controlling program for all the computer's hardware. DOS can store, print, communicate, and move files and data in and out of memory. The devices DOS controls can include disk drives, tape drives, modems, scanners, printers, and any other peripheral device.

To carry out its hardware control mission, DOS must perform many tasks. It must be able to read (retrieve), write (store), and successfully manage (locate, copy, display, move, update, or delete) files on a disk. It must coordinate the movement of data in and out of the system through printer or communications ports. It must manage the video display and other peripherals. It must accept commands in an English-like or other "natural" language. And while it does all this, it must be both fast and reliable.

The Command Line Interface

To fill these complex needs, DOS has a flexible and powerful command line interface that you use to communicate and interact with your computer. You read in Chapter 8 about menus and shells that handle this communication for you; in a command line interface, you communicate directly using commands that you type in at the DOS prompt.

The DOS command line interface is surprisingly easy to use, once you understand some of the basic commands. As noted before, there aren't many commands to learn, and the rules are basically the same for both floppy and hard disk users. With these rules and a reference guide, such as the DOS command reference in Chapter 12, you'll have all you need to make full use of the DOS command line interface.

The DOS Prompt

The first thing you see when your computer finishes booting up, if your setup doesn't take you directly to a menu, shell, or applications program, is the DOS prompt. Look in the upper-left corner of your screen; you'll see a symbol like this:

```
A>
```

That's the prompt. The letter represents your startup disk drive, known as the current or default drive. The greater-than symbol (>) is DOS's way of saying that it is ready and waiting for you to enter a line of input from your keyboard.

If you use the "pregnant prompt" (PROMPT PG), as described in Chapter 5, your prompt will look like this:

```
A:\>
```

The prompt now conveys additional information. It tells you you're on drive A, in the startup or root directory (signified by the backslash), and that DOS is waiting for you to type some input. (On a hard disk system, you will see C> or C:\> after bootup, instead of A> or A:\>.)

What you type next will cause DOS to perform a specific action, so it's called a command. That's why, when you see the cursor blinking after the prompt, you're said to be "at the command line."

There are ways to tweak your prompt into giving more information than the default drive and path, but you'll get to that in Chapter 11. For now, just remember that the DOS prompt is your cue to enter a command.

DOS Commands

When you type a DOS command, you must tell DOS where it can find the programs and files you want to work with. Unless you say otherwise, DOS assumes it should carry out its commands in the current directory. If that's not the case, you must specify the correct path in your command. Some examples follow.

Using Default Values Let's say you load your file editor by using the command EDIT. To edit a file named PROPOSAL.DOC, your simplest command line would include the command EDIT and the parameter PRO-POSAL.DOC. A *parameter* is the specific information that indicates how DOS should carry out the command. Typical parameters are the files on which DOS will take action and any command options you want to be carried out. Your command line calling the editor program might look like this:

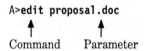

A>**edit proposal.doc**

Command   Parameter

You may recognize the command structure from Chapter 5. This type of command contains several assumptions. Stated more precisely, it relies on default values—that is, values DOS assumes to be true because you didn't say otherwise. Here is how the command would look if you were on drive A and specifically included the default values:

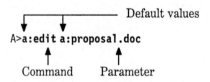

Default values

A>**a:edit a:proposal.doc**

Command   Parameter

The first A: is the default value for the drive containing the EDIT program. The second A: is the default value for the drive containing the file named PROPOSAL.DOC. If you were on drive C, the default value for the drive would be C.

Pointing to a Different Drive You can include the drive designations in your command parameters to tell DOS that any named files reside on a different disk drive. Let's say you are currently on drive A but you want to use DIR to display the file list for drive B. To do so, point to drive B like this:

```
A>dir b:
```
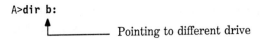

Pointing to different drive

The result is a full directory listing for drive B. Drive A remains your current drive.

You can use the same pointing technique to edit a file on a different drive:

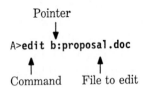

Pointer

```
A>edit b:proposal.doc
```

Command   File to edit

This tells DOS to look on drive B for the target file and process it using a program named EDIT that it can find in the current drive and directory. Note that there is no space between the drive name (B:) and the target file (PROPOSAL.DOC). Never put a space between the drive name and the filename, or DOS will assume you're entering two separate parameters, won't be able to find the file, and will issue an error message. (See "DOS and Punctuation," later in this chapter, for more on the subject of spaces in commands.)

You can also point to a different drive to get information about a specific file. Let's say you want to find out if drive B contains a DOS utility called TREE.COM, but you want to keep drive A as your current drive. To do this, you enter

```
A>dir b:tree.com
```

The command parameter (B:TREE.COM) gives both the filename and the location in which to look. The DOS response might look like this:

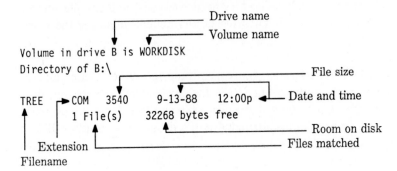

The directory listing includes the filename, extension, size in bytes, and the date and time it was created or last changed. It also shows the number of files that match the parameter, and how much room is left on the target disk (bytes free).

Changing Drives   Another way to use commands that affect another drive is simply to go there—that is, to make the second drive your default. If your data files are on drive B and you are on drive A, for example, you can tell DOS to make drive B the current drive by typing **B:** and pressing ENTER. DOS checks to make sure the requested drive exists and, if it does, makes it the current drive. The drive letter in your new prompt reflects the new drive status:

```
A>          (The original default drive prompt)
A>b:        (Type b: then press ENTER to change drives)
B>          (The prompt shows the new current drive)
```

Once on drive B, if you have DOS version 2.1 or higher, you can still use programs located on drive A by pointing to the drive containing the program, as shown here:

```
B>a:edit proposal.doc
```

In this case, DOS looks for the EDIT program on drive A. Then DOS looks for the target file (PROPOSAL.DOC) on the default drive B.

Internal and External Commands

As discussed in Chapter 5, there are two types of DOS commands: internal and external. It is important to know how to point to drives and directories if you are going to use external DOS commands. Internal commands are built into the DOS command interpreter, which is a program named COMMAND.COM. COMMAND.COM is loaded into memory every time you boot up your computer. When you enter an internal command at the prompt, DOS responds immediately because a COMMAND.COM table of internal commands is always in memory. There is no need for DOS to look for a program with the name of the command and then read it from the disk.

External commands, on the other hand, are small, independent utility programs, and do not stay in memory when they're not being used. DOS does have a few memory resident utilities of the sort described in Chapter 8, but they are the exception. Most external commands are reloaded each time you run them. That means you must have the utility programs available to DOS in order to use them. They must be stored on a disk that is either in your current drive, in a drive you can make the current drive, or in a drive you can point to in your command line.

Table 9-1 shows DOS internal and external commands. For a complete reference of these commands, see Chapter 12.

DOS FILES

You've learned about the DOS prompt, the command line, how to move from one disk drive to another, and how to point to another drive in your

---

Table 9-1

DOS Internal and External Commands

Internal		External	
BREAK	MKDIR or MD	APPEND	GRAPHICS
CHCP	PATH	ASSIGN	JOIN
CHDIR or CD	PROMPT	ATTRIB	KEYB
CLS	RENAME or REN	BACKUP	LABEL
COPY	RMDIR or RD	CHKDSK	MODE
CTTY	SET	COMMAND	MORE
DATE	TIME	COMP	NLSFUNC
DEL	TYPE	DEBUG	PRINT
DIR	VER	DISKCOMP	RECOVER
ERASE	VERIFY	DISKCOPY	REPLACE
EXIT	VOL	EDLIN	RESTORE
		EXE2BIN	SELECT
		FASTOPEN	SHARE
		FC	SORT
		FDISK	SUBST
		FIND	SYS
		FORMAT	TREE
		GRAFTABL	XCOPY

command line without actually moving there. The next step is to learn how to use DOS files and file specifications. A file may be text, a letter, a program, a spreadsheet, or any other collection of information. A disk can hold many files, limited only by available space and maximum directory size.

The DOS Directory

When you format a disk, DOS creates a directory space and a file allocation table (FAT) on that disk to help it keep track of the disk's contents. Because the directory is so important both to DOS and to the user, there are rules about how files must be named. There are also limits to how many files can fit into a directory.

The number of files you can store in a directory depends upon what type of hard or floppy disk you have. You may reach the limit if you're storing many tiny files on a single disk. (See Chapter 10 for more on how files are physically stored on hard and floppy disks.)

Table 9-2 shows the maximum number of directory entries, format type, size, and storage capacity for different types of floppy disks. Table 9-3 shows what disks each type of floppy drive can work with.

The Problem of Overloaded Disks   A good way to solve the problem of overcrowded program disks, if you can't purchase a hard disk, is to keep your programs on one disk and your data on another. This works best if your computer has two floppy disk drives. You can boot from drive A and work on data files on a disk in drive B. You can change data disks whenever you need to, because DOS continues to refer to drive A for its running instructions.

How DOS Files Are Named

Each DOS filename must be unique, or DOS won't know which file you want to work with. In fact, DOS has a built-in naming system to prevent you from creating two files with the same name. DOS also gives some automatic help; for example, it changes all directory characters to uppercase, so you can't accidentally create two files named, say, crucial.fil and CRUCIAL.FIL.

Table 9-2

Storage and Directory Capacities by Disk Type

Disk Format Type	Disk Diameter (Inches)	Storage Capacity (Bytes)[*]	Maximum Root Directory Entries[**]
SSDD/8[1]	5 1/4	163,840 (160K)	64
SSDD/9	5 1/4	184,320 (180K)	64
DSDD/8[2]	5 1/4	327,680 (320K)	112
DSDD/9	5 1/4	368,640 (360K)	112
DSHD/15[3]	5 1/4	1,228,800 (1.2 MB)	224
DSHD/9[4]	3 1/2	737,280 (720K)	112
DSHD/18	3 1/2	1,474,560 (1.44MB)	224

1. Single-sided, double-density disks with 8 or 9 sectors per track
2. Double-sided, double-density disks with 8 or 9 sectors per track
3. Double-sided, high density disks with 15 sectors per track
4. Double-sided, high density 3 1/2-inch disks with 9 or 18 sectors per track

[*]   Figure in bytes = (rated K) × (1024 bytes/K)

[**] Subdirectories have no limit on entries but normally are used only on hard disks; see Chapter 10, "DOS and the Hard Disk."

The best way to see what DOS filenames look like is to look at a directory listing using the DOS DIR command introduced in Chapter 5. With your DOS disk in drive A, enter the following command:

`A>dir`   *(Type* **dir** *and press* ENTER *to get a listing)*

Figure 9-1 shows part of the directory information you might see as a result of the DIR command. Each line in the output describes one file. Now consider just one line of that DIR list:

`ATTRIB   EXE    10656   7-24-87  12:00a`

The first word, ATTRIB, is the filename. It serves as the file's primary name and can be up to eight characters long. The second word, EXE, is the filename extension (or just extension). It can be up to three characters long

Table 9-3

Disk Drive Compatibility

Drive	Can Read and Write to
160/180K single-sided (5 1/4-inch)	160/180K single-sided, double-density disks
320/360K double-sided (5 1/4-inch)	160/180K single-sided, double-density disks 320/360K double-sided, double-density disks
1.2MB high-capacity (5 1/4 inch)	160/180K single-sided, double-density disks* 320/360K double-sided, double-density disks* 1.2MB high-capacity, double-density disks
720K double-sided (3 1/2-inch)	720K double-sided, double-density disks
1.44MB double-sided (3 1/2-inch)	720K double-sided double-density disks 1.44MB double-sided, double-density disks

*When low density disks are formatted in high density drives, the tracks are only half as wide as when formatted by a low density drive. This is called halftracking. The result is that low density drives may not be able to read disks written by high density drives even though they are written in low density format.

and identifies what type of file it is. The filename and extension combination is the file specification, or just filespec for short.

The first 8 plus the second 3 add up to just 11 characters with which to identify a file and its type. That's not a lot, but it's enough to convey a surprisingly large amount of information. (See the following section, "Helpful Filenames and Extensions.")

If 11 characters seems too restricted for you, many of the file management utilities mentioned in Chapter 8 as well as many applications programs let you tack file descriptions onto filenames. They won't affect the actual DOS directory, but the descriptions will be available to help you remember what a file contains. Figure 9-2 shows part of a utility directory with the programs annotated by a utility program called PC File Notes.

Helpful Filenames and Extensions

A good filename will help you recognize or remember the contents of the file. For example, you might use the filename PAYR0591 for a file containing

Figure 9-1

Partial directory listing

```
Volume in drive A is DOS
Directory of  A:\

APPEND   EXE     5794   7-24-87  12:00a
ATTRIB   EXE    10656   7-24-87  12:00a
EXE2BIN  EXE     3050   7-24-87  12:00a
FASTOPEN EXE     3888   7-24-87  12:00a
FC       EXE    15974   7-24-87  12:00a
FIND     EXE     6403   7-24-87  12:00a
GWBASIC  EXE    80592   7-24-87  12:00a
HELPDOS  EXE    32999  10-22-88  10:41p
JOIN     EXE     9612   7-24-87  12:00a
LINK     EXE    43988   2-09-88  12:00a
MASM     EXE    85566   7-24-87  12:00a
NLSFUNC  EXE     3029   7-24-87  12:00a
PARK     EXE     1135  11-27-86  10:38a
PATCHER  EXE    12423   7-13-89   7:50a
REPLACE  EXE    13234   7-24-87  12:00a
SHARE    EXE     8608   7-24-87  12:00a
SORT     EXE     1946   3-22-88   1:25p
SUBST    EXE    10552   7-24-87  12:00a
XCOPY    EXE    11216   7-24-87  12:00a
     19 File(s)    7733248 bytes free
```

Figure 9-2

File described using PC File Notes program

```
F:\                                    35 files  3616768 bytes free

DL         dir    0   9-02-90  3:57p │ PCFN14   EXE  30214  9-07-90  7:02
PCFN       dir    0   9-07-90  7:19  │ PDAILY   DAT      0  9-16-90 10:59p
TEMP       dir    0   8-31-90  5:02  │ PROGRAMS       8883  9-03-90 11:10
ARCE   COM      6690  5-14-90  4:06  │ QDISK    ZIP  17262  8-26-88  3:03p
COLOR  PAT       236  2-03-90  7:30  │ README   NOW   3226  7-25-90  3:54p
CRYP-MPJ ZIP   67763  1-07-89  7:59p │ RUSHHR   ZIP  34152  9-09-87  9:28p
DIALER PAT       201  2-03-90  7:30  │
DIFFX  ZIP     15653  7-24-90  4:35p │ ┌──────────────────────────────┐
DIRR   COM      8875  9-06-90 12:04p │ │ Non-resident version of PC File│
FILENOTE         158  9-17-90  8:22  │ │ Note's commented directory listing│
FV     DOC      6708  9-03-90  1:33  │ │                                │
LICENSE         9290  8-06-90  7:40  │ │                                │
LIST   DOC    102976  8-30-90  7:50  │ │                                │
LIST   HST      6758  9-03-90  7:51  │ │                                │
LIST75B ZIP    92309  9-10-90  4:57  │ ZILCH    ARC    586  9-07-90  7:11
MAILER          1357  9-03-90  7:51  │
MIRORSAV FIL sys  41  9-16-90 10:59p │
MIRROR BAK rdo19968  9-16-90 10:53p  │
MIRROR FIL rdo19968  9-16-90 10:59p  │
MYSTIC ZIP     40230  8-28-90  1:23p │

Delete Sort View Tag Copy Quit       PC-FileNotes (c)1990 RSE   8:22   9-17-90
Rename DriveChg Insert file note     $25 to PC-FN, POBox 1408, Auburn WA 98071
```

payroll record data from May 1991. Filename extensions should help classify a file—for example, PAYR0591.DAT might contain raw data, while PAYR0591.RPT holds the formatted report. Similarly, you might use extensions like .LTR or .LET for letters, .RPT for reports, .MSG for electronic messages, .NOT for pop-up notepad files, and so forth. After a while you'll develop a personal shorthand for naming files.

Reserved Filenames

When choosing a filename, bear in mind that some *strings*—sequences of letters—are reserved for the use of the operating system. The names listed here are reserved by DOS for specific hardware devices. Do not use them as filenames.

Name	Meaning
AUX	First serial port
CLOCK$	System clock device
COM1 through COM4	Serial ports (COM1 is the same as AUX)
CON	Console (keyboard and monitor)
LPT1 through LPT3	Parallel ports (LPT1 is the same as PRN)
NUL	Dummy device (to cancel screen reports or other output)
PRN	First parallel port (usually a printer)

Extensions Reserved by DOS

Some extensions are also for the exclusive use of DOS. Use the following reserved extensions only for the appropriate type of file. If you misuse them, you can freeze up your machine, lose any unsaved data, or encounter other unexpected mishaps.

Extension	Meaning
.BAT	A *batch* file contains DOS commands that can be executed as though they were typed at the keyboard.
.COM	A *command* file contains a program that will be run when the filename is entered as a DOS command.

.EXE   An *executable* file is similar to a COM file.

.SYS   A *system* file contains information used by DOS to control some aspect of DOS's operation.

The danger of unpredictable results prevents most users from trying to misuse reserved extensions. In other words, do not use the extension .BAT for a file that contains a letter to a company that sells batteries. If you accidentally enter a filename with the .BAT extension on a command line, DOS will think you are trying to execute a batch file. In this case, DOS would read the letter one line at a time and try to execute each line as if it were a legal DOS command.

Other Reserved Extensions

Other extensions have meanings fixed by custom. For example, .BAS normally represents a computer program written in the programming language BASIC (refer to Chapters 13 and 14). Avoid using these extensions except in their intended ways; otherwise you may confuse anyone who later tries to interpret your filenames—including yourself. For example, there's nothing to stop an athletic coach from creating a file named PROSPECT.BAS to list the names of promising basketball players. It's just not standard practice and may confuse someone working on the system later.

The filename extensions listed here have meanings set by common usage. It is best to avoid using them except for the appropriate type of file.

Extension	Meaning
.$$$	A *temporary* file, used by a program and then discarded
.ASC	A file containing only regular *ASCII* text
.ASM	*Assembly language* program source code
.BAK	*Backup,* the previous copy of a modified file
.BAS	A *BASIC* program
.BIN	A *binary* file

.BLD	*BLOAD*, a BASIC loadable binary program file
.COB	*COBOL* source code
.COD	An object *code* file for some compilers
.CBL	*COBOL* source code
.DAT	A *data* file
.DIF	A *data interchange file* used for sharing data between programs
.DOC	A *document* file, often containing word processor formatting characters
.FOR	*FORTRAN* source code
.LIB	A *library* file for a compiler
.LST	*List*, a printable file of a compiled or assembly language program
.MAP	*Map*, a memory map for a linker
.OBJ	*Object* code, compiled programs prior to linking
.OVL	*Overlay* module for a program
.OVR	Same as OVL
.PAS	*Pascal* source code
.PGM	*Program* file—like an overlay file; loadable binary program code
.PIF	A *program information file* used by Microsoft Windows and other programs
.PRN	A *print* file that can be copied to a printer, retaining format codes
.TMP	A *temporary* file, used by a program and then discarded
.TXT	A *text* file used by some word processors

Reserved Keyboard Characters

Another important filenaming rule has to do with forbidden characters. Your keyboard has some characters that you can't use in a filename because they have special meaning when used in a filename.

Note: If you are running DOS 1.1, you will find that you can use some of the characters that are listed as not permitted. DOS 1.1 programs are so limited that you should consider updating to DOS 3.3 as soon as possible. In the meantime, you may avoid problems later if you do not use the characters forbidden in filenames by DOS version 2.0 and higher.

These characters, as well as spaces, may not be used in a filespec:

ˆ * ? + = [ ] ; : \ / " , . < >

These characters are permitted in a filespec:

Any alphabetic character, A through Z
Any numeral, 0 through 9
The symbols ! @ # $ % & ( ) - _ { } ´ ` ~

All rules have exceptions. For example, of the forbidden symbols, the dot (.) separates a filename from an extension, so in that sense it is permitted in a filespec.

Conversely, some of the permitted symbols are used by applications programs to label temporary or special files. Also, some cleanup utility programs (see Chapter 8) look for and delete files using these symbols. So using haphazard symbols in filenames can lead to problems on a PC. To avoid these problems, use only letters, numbers, and the hyphen or underline in filenames. (The hyphen is more convenient than the underline character because it doesn't require the shift key; but the underline visually separates terms.)

Filespecs as Command Parameters

Many DOS commands require you to use a filename as a parameter; in fact, filenames are the most common command parameters. You saw an example earlier in this chapter, when the DIR command with the parameter B:TREE.COM produced a listing with information on the file TREE.COM only, instead of on the entire directory. Similarly, the command

```
A>type memo.msg
```

would cause a message file named MEMO.MSG to appear on the screen.

READ.ME

DOS and Punctuation

In normal English, when you type you put two spaces after a colon or a period. In DOS commands, however, you rarely follow a colon or a dot (not called a period) with a space. In DOS commands, certain characters, such as colons, spaces, dots, and so on, must be used in specific ways; no extra spaces are permitted. New DOS users often add these forbidden spaces out of old typing habits. The results are never as expected, because DOS is just as insistent in its own way as your high school English teacher.

When using both a filename and its extension on the command line, separate the two with a dot as shown here:

A>**type memo.msg** *(Correct command sequence)*

The dot tells DOS to treat the second part as an extension instead of as a separate parameter, so don't leave it out or try to replace it with a space. If you type this command with a space but no dot, as shown here, you'll get a "File not found" error message, and your command will not work.

A>**type memo msg**   *(Space instead of dot before extension)*

If you use spaces after the colon or dot in filenames, as shown here, these commands won't work either.

A>**type memo. msg**   *(Space after dot)*
A>**type b: memo. msg** *(Spaces after both the colon and the dot)*

Wildcards

Two DOS wildcard characters—the question mark (?) and the asterisk (*)—give you greater flexibility when working with directory filenames by letting you group similar filenames together when entering a command. Wildcards stand for any legal character.

The Question Mark (?)

The question mark, when used in a filename, stands for any character in that exact position in the filename. For example, if you have five chapters in a book you're writing, you might name them

```
CHAP1.TXT
CHAP2.TXT
CHAP3.TXT
CHAP4.TXT
CHAP5.TXT
```

The only difference between these names is the number that comes after the abbreviation CHAP. For a directory listing of all these files, you can enter the command

```
A>dir chap?.txt
```

and all five files will be listed onscreen. You can use several question marks if one isn't enough. For example, you could issue the command

```
A>dir cha??.txt
```

if you wanted to see the complete list of chapters as well as files named CHATS.TXT and CHARM.TXT.

The Asterisk (*)

The asterisk wildcard (*) is a general version of the question mark wildcard. While the question mark is restricted to a single character in the same position as the wildcard, an asterisk stands for any number of characters at or after the position of the wildcard.

To see how this works, consider the DIR CHA??.TXT command used before. If you replace the two question marks with an asterisk, DOS will display any filename up to eight characters long that begins with the letters *cha*. So if you enter

```
A>dir cha*.txt
```

your directory listing might appear as shown here, including the chapters, the two additional files shown with the DIR CHA??.TXT command, and several others.

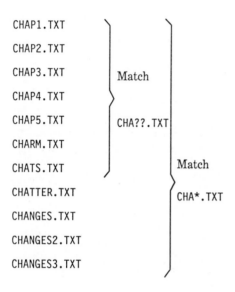

SUMMARY

This chapter examined the DOS command line interface and legal DOS command structures. You read about names and file extensions reserved by DOS (or by custom) for specific uses. The chapter described the use of filespecs and wildcards in commands.

The next three chapters will tell you more about using DOS to organize files. You will read about hard disks and other advanced topics, including the basics of batch file operations. Chapter 12 will provide a complete DOS command guide for your continuing reference when working at the DOS command level.

CHAPTER TEN

DOS and the Hard Disk

Hard disk drives are the rule on PCs these days, not the exception. IBM calls them fixed disks, but both names refer to the same thing. Working with hard disks has many advantages over working with floppies, which can be slow and tedious. To work on a file, for example, you may have to take a floppy disk out of the drive, put it in its jacket, update the label, file it away, find another disk with the data you need, put it into the drive, check the directory to make sure you have the right disk, and only then get on with your work. Some people call this the "floppy shuffle."

Hard disks, on the other hand, are much faster. They have much higher capacities so all your working files are in one place. Not only can you get a lot more done in less time, but you are also less likely to lose data.

This chapter assumes that you have a hard disk drive in your system. On most systems, drive C is a hard disk, so that's the hard disk drive letter used throughout this chapter. This chapter also assumes your disk is already partitioned, formatted, and ready to use. That's how most people get them from the dealer these days. If your hard disk is brand new and unformatted, you have some far-reaching decisions to make, such as how many logical drives and partitions to use. Chapter 16 has information on how to prepare your hard disk for use.

Finally, this chapter assumes you are familiar with the material covered in Chapter 5, "Operating Fundamentals" and Chapter 9, "Working with DOS—The Basics."

The first part of this chapter concentrates on how to effectively organize and use a hard disk. It will be useful even if you use a DOS shell or menu system, since you will still need to organize your files in order to work effectively. If you work in a shell program, you will use different commands to carry out the MKDIR, CHDIR, and RMDIR DOS functions described later in this chapter. But the principles of designing and maintaining an effective hard disk structure are the same.

ORGANIZATION: THE KEY TO THE SYSTEM

Whether your information is stored on a computer or in a paper filing system, you must be able to find what you need without wasting a lot of time looking for it. The solution, in either case, is to create a system that works for you and stick with it. The analogy between computer storage and a paper filing system goes further: if your collection of data grows larger than your existing system can easily handle, you'll need to enhance or change your system.

The Basic Disk Storage Tasks

Sometimes people using a hard disk for the first time are put off by the need for directories, subdirectories, and backups. It may help to realize that, when it comes to storing and accessing files on a computer, how you use a hard disk is not much different than how you use a floppy. So if you're accustomed to working with floppy disks, you're already familiar with the basics of hard disk management.

The material that follows—from planning your hard disk structure to moving around the directory tree—is designed to help you do five tasks as efficiently as possible:

- Organize your files into a logical directory structure before you start, so you can always find the files you need.

- Discover where you are in the directory structure and what your current directory contains.

- Move from your current directory to another one farther up, down, or across the branches of your directory tree.

- Modify the directory tree as needed, so you can add new applications and remove old ones.

- Type commands with as few keystrokes as possible, to minimize frustration due to simple typing errors.

Organizing Files on Floppies

Keeping files organized on a floppy-based system is no problem, as long as you don't accumulate too many files. You simply use a separate disk for each related set of files. You format the disk, copy the set of files onto it, and make sure your disk label tells you what type of files are stored there. If your collection of floppies grows too large to store in desktop bins, you can catalog them with a disk cataloging program like those mentioned in Chapter 8. Then you can store them away.

The advantages of using floppy disks are that they are cheap and you can easily label them with general information about their contents. You can store similar disks together, grouped by application, type of data, date recorded, or any other system that applies. The disadvantage of using floppies becomes apparent when your collection of information grows large.

When you start to spend more time looking for documents than you do actually working on them, it's time to rethink your system. With a paper filing system, you might store away older, less frequently needed documents in a closet to reduce the clutter. In a computer system, as the number of disks increases, you will probably decide to get a hard disk.

Organizing Your Hard Disk

Installing a hard disk can eliminate your problems with the floppy shuffle. It can release you from the tedious search for files and free you to do useful work. It can be like buying a large filing cabinet, with plenty of room for all of your documents; it puts any file you need right at your fingertips.

But a hard disk by itself is more like a large box than a filing cabinet. True, you can copy all your floppy disk files onto it and keep everything in one place. But you will lose the major advantage of the floppy system, its ability to keep related files together. You'll be left with no organization at all, just a large collection of unrelated documents.

Fortunately, DOS provides the tools to turn your hard disk into a hard disk "filing cabinet." These file management tools became available with DOS version 2.0, when IBM released the PC XT computer with a 10MB hard disk. The DOS hard disk file management tools consist of three commands, MKDIR or MD (make directory), CHDIR or CD (change directory), and RMDIR or RD (remove directory), that create and maintain small, independent file areas called *directories* on a hard disk. Directories allow you to group related files together.

The Directory Tree

The directory that DOS creates when it formats a disk is called the *root directory*. On floppies, that's the only directory most people ever need, but on hard disks the structure becomes more complex.

The root directory on a hard disk is the foundation for the directory structure. There is a technical limit to how many files and subdirectories you can add to a root directory—up to 509 altogether. (Once inside a subdirectory, on the other hand, your disk storage capacity sets the only limit, because DOS creates more directory space as you need it, in blocks of 64 files or directory names.)

A directory tree can be visualized as a family tree (refer to Figure 10-1). The progenitor, or original ancestor, is at the top of the chart; from there, the chart branches down through children and grandchildren. In a directory tree, the progenitor is your root directory; all the other directories branch down from there.

The directory tree structure introduces a few new concepts, which are discussed in the following sections.

Current or Default Directory   The *current directory* is the one whose files are listed on the screen when you enter a DIR command by itself, with no parameters. If you use the pregnant prompt (PROMPT PG) as shown in Chapters 5 and 9, the name of your current directory will appear in your DOS prompt.

The current directory is also known as the *default directory*, since this is where any command you enter is executed, by default, unless you specify another location.

Figure 10-1

Family tree model for a directory tree

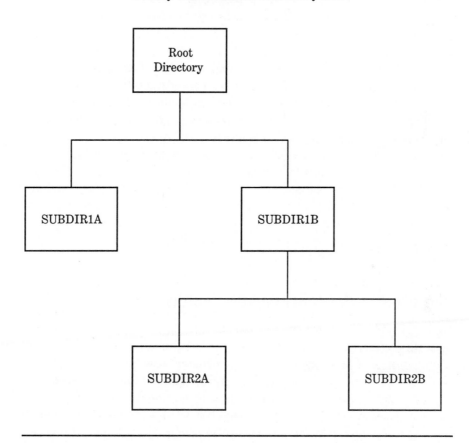

Note: A "pregnant prompt" for a subdirectory has a backslash for each subdirectory level down, ending with the current subdirectory name and no trailing backslash. You can count the backslashes to tell what directory level is your current default. For example, a prompt like this

```
C:\SUBDIR1B\SUBDIR2B>
```

has two backslashes. You are therefore two subdirectories down from your root directory.

Current Path   The *current path* is the route you would take, starting from the root directory, to get to the current directory. In Figure 10-1, for example, if you were in the box labeled SUBDIR2B, your current path would be \SUBDIR1B\SUBDIR2B. Paths will be discussed more fully later in this chapter.

You Are Here: Directories Versus Subdirectories   Sometimes you'll see the terms *subdirectory* and *directory* used interchangeably. Actually, there is one difference—the user's point of view. A subdirectory is any directory lower on the tree than your current directory. If you're in the root directory, every other directory is a subdirectory. If you're in the SUBDIR1B directory in Figure 10-1, the root directory is immediately above you and SUBDIR1B is the current directory. Below you, the box labeled SUBDIR2B would be one subdirectory or *child* of your current directory. This top-down relationship is sometimes called a *parent-child* directory structure. To put it simply, a parent directory is the directory right above you, and a child directory is any subdirectory right below you.

The DOS Disk Management Commands

To create your electronic "filing cabinet," you must divide your disk into separate directories. These act much like floppy disks, and serve to store related groups of files together. Since you control how many and what type of directories a disk contains, keeping track of files is relatively simple.

You could use any DOS shell or file management utility program to create a good hard disk filing system, but DOS is perfectly capable of creating a usable system on its own. Even if you do use a shell program, you'll find it useful to know how to use DOS. Sometimes you'll need DOS-level commands to install new programs, find where you are on your disk, and perform other fundamental computing tasks.

That means you need to learn how to make and use subdirectories. In a section on directory trees later in this chapter, you'll read more about designing efficient systems. First, though, here's a brief introduction to DOS directory management commands and how they can help organize your hard disk space.

Note: DOS directory management commands work on floppy disks as well as on hard disks, but most floppy-based system users do not bother with subdirectories. A floppy's limited capacity does not encourage over-sized root directory listings, so additional directories are rarely needed.

Also, subdirectories make a floppy disk awkward to catalog and can slow file access times. It's easier and faster in such a system to sort by disk and rely on your labels.

MKDIR or MD — Make a Directory

Just as you must name a file before you can store any data in it, you must name a directory before you can store files in it. MKDIR is the DOS command used to create a hard disk directory. (The command's short form, MD, operates exactly the same way, but this chapter will use the long form.) In technical terms, MKDIR creates a new directory one level down from the current directory; in other words, it creates a subdirectory. A root-level directory can have subdirectories down to as many levels as DOS can handle, about 32 directories deep. The actual maximum number depends on the length of your directory names. No directory path name can be more than 64 characters long, and the minimum directory path name is two characters long, the backslash plus one other character.

CHDIR or CD — Change Directories

As with MKDIR and MD, the commands CHDIR and CD are equivalent. CHDIR moves you from one directory to another. It can also be used to display the name of the current directory when you enter it by itself.

RMDIR or RD — Remove a Directory

The RMDIR or RD command removes a specified empty subdirectory from the disk. This simplifies your directories much the same way that deleting unnecessary files would simplify a floppy disk directory. The command will not work on the root directory or on the current directory.

DESIGNING YOUR OWN DIRECTORY TREE

A PC is a personal tool, and no two people will set up a directory structure exactly the same way. Your subdirectory names and file categories will be your own, and your choices will depend as much on your personal preferences as on the type of work you will be doing. But all experienced hard disk users agree on one thing: if you take the time to design your directory structure before you actually create it, you are more likely to end up with a fast, efficient, and accurate file management system.

The best way to plan your directory tree is to sketch out your ideas on a sheet of paper. The following sections describe in more detail the design of a directory tree, using the "family tree" structure discussed earlier. You'll want to start your design with the root directory at the top and add on your subdirectories from there.

Keep the Structure Simple

Although you can technically create subdirectories up to 32 levels deep, it's not a good idea to go much deeper than three or four levels. Deep directories can get pretty confusing, and you're likely to lose track of some files at that level of complexity.

Use this rule of thumb: Keep the structure broad and shallow, rather than narrow and deep, and your system will be much easier to use. Design your tree with your programs no more than one or two levels down and your working files three or four levels deep.

If you have trouble stopping at three or four levels deep, step back and take another look. There's a pretty good chance you need to branch a new subdirectory from the root directory level, instead of from a deeper level. It's usually possible to find a way to broaden, instead of deepen, your tree structure.

Keep Like Files Together

Before you can decide how to set up your directory tree, you must ask yourself two questions:

1. What programs and files do I have?
2. Where do I want to put them on my hard disk?

Most files naturally fall into logical categories—word processing, spreadsheets, graphics, DOS utilities, batch files, and so forth. These natural categories will help you to determine your subdirectories.

For example, you could put all your utility programs into a directory called \UTIL, your word processing files into a \WP directory, spreadsheet files in \SS, database files in \DB, and so forth. Similarly, your data files may group themselves naturally by customer, transaction, book chapter, revenue period, and so forth. It all depends upon what files you have and how you use your PC.

Start at the Root

With the root directory as your starting point, you are ready to design your own hard disk directory structure. Your sketch should start out resembling the following "family tree," with the root directory labeled C:\ (that is, the directory is on drive C and the single backslash indicates that it is the root directory). The lines leading down will be the paths to the various subdirectories.

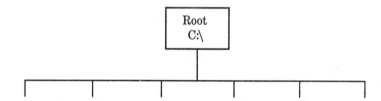

Note: The design used here is only an example. Its directory names and relationships may or may not be relevant to you. If you want to follow along, use this structure as a model and then set up your own subdirectories to meet your particular file storage needs.

First Level Subdirectories

Now you can start adding the first level of subdirectories, branching off from the root directory as shown in Figure 10-2. Your map can include as many subdirectories as you think you'll need, although it's better to err on the side of simplicity. You can always fine-tune the design later. The sample map includes the following directories:

BATCH	Batch files (see Chapter 11)
DB	Database program
DOS	DOS utility programs
SS	Spreadsheet program
UTIL	Utility programs
WP	Word processing program

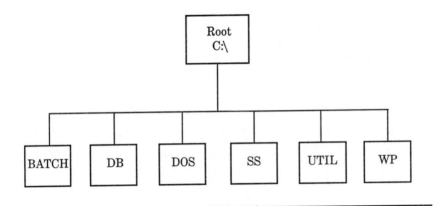

Figure 10-2

Directory tree (first level subdirectories)

READ.ME

On Short, Sweet Directory Names

The rules for naming a directory are the same as those for naming a file: The name may be one to eight characters long, and may be followed by an optional dot and an extension of one to three characters. That's a total of 11 characters available for the name, although most people do not use the three-letter extension for subdirectories, because it invites confusion with filenames.

It's advisable to keep your directory names as short as you can, thus reducing the possibility of typing errors. For instance, if you name your word processing directory \WORDPROC, you'll have to type in eight letters every time you want to call up the directory, and there will be eight opportunities for you to type the wrong letter. If you simply name it \WP, on the other hand, chances are much greater that you'll get it right the first time.

Don't overdo the brevity, however; include enough information so that you'll recognize what a directory name means. If you have a directory that contains utility programs, \UTIL or \UTILS is more recognizable than, say, \U or \BIN (for binary). Use a name that will help you recognize the contents.

Each of these categories contains an important classification of files. Each has a short name that tells you immediately what kind of files it contains; each is unique in the sense that a file that fits there would be out of place anywhere else.

Second Level Subdirectories

Now we branch down to second level subdirectories, as shown in Figure 10-3. There's no rule that each first level directory must have a second level subdirectory; in the example, only two—\DB and \UTIL—branch down further. When you do branch down, each lower level category should be more specific than its parent and each should flow naturally from the first level. The figure now includes:

\DB\INVENTRY	Inventory records
\DB\RECVABLE	Customers to be invoiced in next billing
\DB\OVERDUE	Customers who have not paid by the due date
\UTIL\MOUSE	Mouse drivers, speed setting utilities, and so on

Figure 10-3

Directory tree (second level subdirectories)

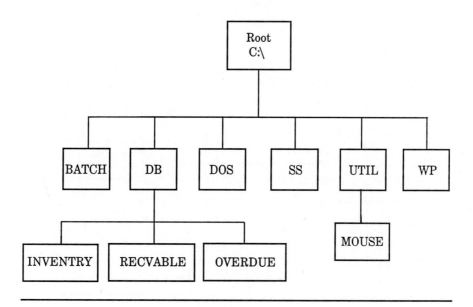

Third Level Subdirectories

Finally, we branch down to third level subdirectories, as shown in Figure 10-4. Once again, each lower level category is more specific than its parent and flows naturally from it. The figure includes

\DB\INVENTRY\ORDERED	Supplies ordered
\DB\INVENTRY\RECVD	Supplies received but not yet inventoried
\DB\OVERDUE\NOTICE1	First overdue notice sent
\DB\OVERDUE\NOTICE2	Second overdue notice sent
\DB\OVERDUE\NOTICE3	Third overdue notice sent

Figure 10-4

Directory tree (third level subdirectories)

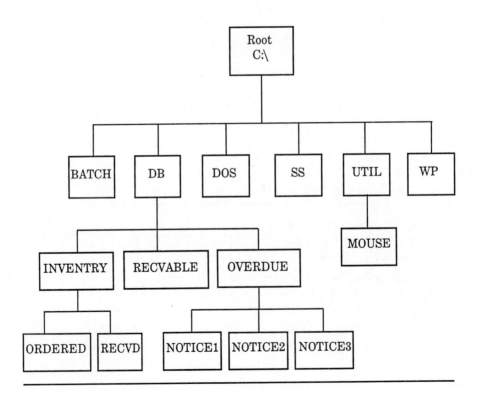

CREATING AND USING YOUR TREE

In the next section you'll read about how to actually create the directory system you just designed. For clarity, this chapter uses the long form of all directory commands. The short form is easier to use once you get used to it, and involves less typing. To restate, the three long and short form equivalent commands are:

MKDIR   Same as MD
CHDIR   Same as CD
RMDIR   Same as RD

Just as you must create a file before you can tell a program to read it, you must create a subdirectory before you can tell DOS to put a file there. You can create subdirectories as you need them, using the MKDIR command. If you already have a good idea what your directory structure will look like, the easiest and least error-prone procedure is to create all of a given level's subdirectories before moving to the next level down and repeating the process. This helps you keep track of where you are.

Follow the procedure described in the following section.

Creating Subdirectories

To create the sample directory structure designed earlier, make sure you are in the root directory of drive C. Remember, you have installed a "pregnant prompt" to tell you at a glance where you are in the directory structure. If you are on another drive, use the command line to point to drive C. (The part of the command that you type is in boldface in the following examples.)

A:\>**c:**

If you are already on drive C but are not in the root directory, you can move to the root directory by entering the following command:

C:\DOS>**chdir **

The solitary backslash (\) always stands for the root directory.

Your prompt should now be C:\>. Next, enter these commands to make six new subdirectories:

```
C:\>mkdir \batch
C:\>mkdir \db
C:\>mkdir \dos
C:\>mkdir \ss
C:\>mkdir \util
C:\>mkdir \wp
```

A schematic of your directory would now look like this:

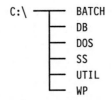

```
C:\ ──────── BATCH
        ──── DB
        ──── DOS
        ──── SS
        ──── UTIL
        ──── WP
```

Note: If your computer has a graphical directory tool like those described in Chapter 8, you can see this directory graph for yourself.

Creating Deeper Level Directories

Next, without leaving the root directory, create a deeper level of subdirectories under the \DB subdirectory:

```
C:\>mkdir \db\inventry
C:\>mkdir \db\overdue
C:\>mkdir \db\recvable
```

This is an acceptable method, but look out for typing errors. If you typed all those backslashes correctly, your directory tree now looks like the one shown here:

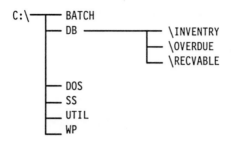

Using CHDIR to Move Around and Complete Your Tree

A better way to create deeper level subdirectories is to move to the next level down and create the second level subdirectories from there. It saves keystrokes and, therefore, reduces typing errors. You can change to the next directory level down using the CHDIR command.

Note: You could also use a shell or automatic directory changing program like those described in Chapter 8 when moving to the new parent directory. Whichever method you choose, the result will be the same.

Since you've already used the MKDIR backslash method to add subdirectories to the \DB directory, we'll use the child method next to add a MOUSE subdirectory to the \UTIL parent directory. To change to the UTIL directory—that is, to make it the current directory—enter the following command:

```
C:\>chdir \util       (Change to UTIL subdirectory)
C:\UTIL>              (UTIL becomes your new default directory)
```

Note how the "pregnant prompt" reflects your new location. Next, from \UTIL, type in the following command:

```
C:\UTIL>mkdir mouse (New subdirectory is child of current (UTIL)
                    directory)
```

Note that when you create a new subdirectory after changing to the parent directory, you do not precede the child subdirectory's name with a backslash (\). By not typing the backslash, you tell DOS it does not need to go back up to the root directory before it creates the new subdirectory. DOS assumes you mean to branch the new directory from your current directory instead.

Your subdirectory tree now looks like this:

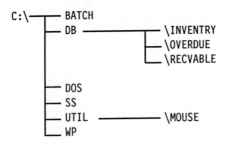

Finishing the Tree

Using the parent/child technique just described, you can complete your subdirectory structure using the following commands:

```
C:\UTIL>chdir \db\inventry        (Change directories)
C:\DB\INVENTRY>mkdir ordered      (Make subdirectory)
C:\DB\INVENTRY>mkdir recvd        (Make another subdirectory)
```

Your directory structure now has a third subdirectory level and looks like this:

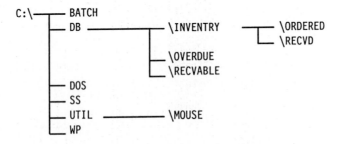

Next, make \DB\OVERDUE your default directory and complete your directory structure:

```
C:\DB\INVENTRY>chdir \db\overdue  (Change to OVERDUE directory)
C:\DB\OVERDUE>mkdir notice1       (Make a new subdirectory)
C:\DB\OVERDUE>mkdir notice2       (Make another new subdirectory)
C:\DB\OVERDUE>mkdir notice3       (Make a third new subdirectory)
```

Your directory tree now looks like the following:

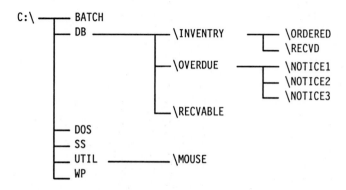

If you compare the directory tree to the original design in Figure 10-4, you'll see you've created the same structure.

Using Path Names and the PATH Command

There are two tools that make moving around in directory trees easier: the path name and the PATH command. The two are closely related but are not quite the same. Both path names and the PATH command are indispensable time-savers when working with subdirectories, and they're not hard to learn.

Path Name = Path + Name

A file's *path name* consists of its drive, path, filename, and file extension. The drive portion consists of a drive letter plus a colon. The path portion starts with the the root directory backslash (\). In the directory structure shown in Figure 10-4, you might store a copy of a Mr. Smith's first overdue notice in the NOTICE1 subdirectory. The full path name would look like this:

```
C:\DB\OVERDUE\NOTICE1\SMITH.LET
```

Note how the path name lets DOS go right down the chart three directory levels, from the root to the file named SMITH.LET.

Pointing with Path Names   You may recall from Chapter 9 that you can point to files using drive letters, for example:

`A:\>edit b:smith.let`

In this example, you tell DOS to use an editing program located on drive A to edit a target file located on drive B.

On a hard disk, separate directories are like independent floppy disks, and you use the same technique to point. The difference is that you use a file's whole path name instead of just a drive designator.

Here's an example, using the directory tree just created. Let's say you need to use your word processor (C:\WP\EDIT.EXE) to write a dunning notice to Mr. Smith. In DOS 3.0 and higher, you can use full path names from anywhere in the system to point at files. The following command will work no matter what your default drive and directory may be when you type it.

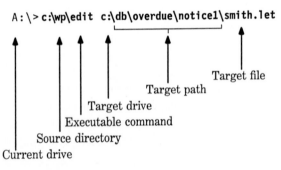

Translated, the command means: "Even though I'm in drive A right now, use the EDIT program in the drive C subdirectory named \WP to process SMITH.LET, which is located in the drive C subdirectory named \DB\OVERDUE\NOTICE1."

Note: Pointing with path name source directories works only in DOS version 3.0 or higher. DOS version 2.*x* only supports pointing to target directories. If you're using DOS 2.*x*, the PATH command (described later in "Using the PATH Command") will let DOS find your program files even when they are not in your current working directory.

Condensing the Command Line

As the last example shows, full path names can get pretty long. They're helpful for occasionally running a remote program against a remote file, but most people hate to stack up the backslashes like that. It involves too many keystrokes, the backslash feels strange to type, and long, complex commands invite errors. Ideally, you should be able to type **EDIT SMITH.LET** and be done with it.

Fortunately, DOS provides the PATH command and the convention of the default drive and directory. With them you can omit the default values from your command line—the defaults go without saying, in other words.

To see what "goes without saying" on a command line, you need only know which parts of a full path name describe your current drive, path, or directory. Let's start with the long, complete path name command used earlier:

```
A:\>c:\wp\edit c:\db\overdue\notice1\smith.let
```

Your current directory is the root directory on drive A, so you do need everything in the path name above. But let's see if we can whittle it down to a simpler, more understandable and less error-prone form:

```
edit smith.let
```

We'll start by changing the default directory.

Setting a Default Directory You know about the default directory; that's the one whose files scroll down the screen when you enter a DIR command all by itself. It's called a *default* because DOS will execute any commands by default in the current directory unless you specify otherwise.

You can use the CHDIR command to make C:\DB\OVERDUE \NOTICE1 your current directory. Your PG prompt will get longer, reflecting your new default directory:

```
A:\>c:                      (Change default drive to C)
C:\>chdir \db\overdue\notice1 (Change to NOTICE1 subdirectory)
C:\DB\OVERDUE\NOTICE1>       ($P$G prompt shows new location)
```

Your prompt now reflects the entire path down to the target file's subdirectory. That means you no longer need to type the entire target path name to point to the file. DOS assumes you mean the current subdirectory, so you can use a much simpler command line:

```
C:\DB\OVERDUE\NOTICE1>c:\wp\edit smith.let
```

DOS reads the EDIT program into memory from the C:\WP directory, looks for a file named SMITH.LET in the default directory, finds it, feeds it to the EDIT program, and you're in business.

Setting the Default Drive   Since you're now operating on drive C, there is another piece of information you can drop from your command line. You can drop the drive designator C: and simply start the command from the backslash that represents the root directory:

```
C:\DB\OVERDUE\NOTICE1>\wp\edit smith.let
```

Using the PATH Command   It would be nice to get rid of the \WP\ part of EDIT's path name, but DOS can't handle two default directories at once. That's why, with NOTICE1 as your default subdirectory, you need the first backslash in the command line to load your word processor. The first backslash tells DOS to go back to the root directory to look for the WP directory; otherwise DOS would look for it in your current directory and would not find it.

The PATH command offers a way around the command backslash. It lets you specify a list of directories for DOS to check for executable programs that it can't find in the default directory. In the example directory tree, to put all of your first-level program directories into the DOS search path, enter this command at any prompt:

```
set path=c:\batch;c:\dos;c:\util;c:\db;c:\wp;c:\ss
```

DOS will now look in all of the specified directories in the order you list them. Since DOS stops looking when it finds an executable program with a specified name, you can speed things up a bit by putting the directories you use most heavily at the front of the list. For most people, that includes their batch files and DOS utilities. You might also want to add the drive C root directory (C:\).

Note: If you have two executable programs with the same name in different subdirectories, DOS will only execute the first of these it finds as it looks along the path; the program DOS finds may not be the program you were expecting. To eliminate such problems, rename one of the programs.

If your editing program is located in the path, you can now access it from anywhere in the system, including a floppy disk drive, without specifying the editor's entire path name. In the case of our letter to Mr. Smith, if you have included C:\WP in your PATH command, your command to edit the letter to Mr. Smith can now be typed in its simplest form:

```
C:\DB\OVERDUE\NOTICE1>edit smith.let
```

Since PATH is an internal command, you need not enter it using a path name, nor do you need DOS in the current directory. If you want to change the current path, you simply type in the PATH command again with different values.

　　To display the current search path, enter the PATH command by itself. DOS will reply by echoing your PATH:

```
C:\>path
PATH=C:\BATCH;C:\DOS;C:\UTIL;C:\DB;C:\WP;C:\SS
C:\>
```

To cancel the current search path without defining a new one, type

```
C:\>path ;
```

The semicolon tells DOS to cancel the path rather than displaying the current path on the screen.

　　In some versions of DOS, you may need to use a comma instead of a semicolon, or you may need to hold down the ALT key while typing 255 on the numeric keypad. Keep trying until you find the character that works in your version of DOS.

Dot, Double-Dot, and Pointing

The dot (.) and double-dot (..) entries that you see at the top of every DIR listing except the root directory stand for the current and parent directories, respectively. Feel free to ignore them if you wish; many users do. However, if you want to learn about them, here are some ways they can help you save keystrokes.

Single Dot　The single dot is useful with some non-DOS utility programs that need both source and target parameters. Michael J. Mefford's popular directory program DIRMATCH is one example. First published in *PC*

Magazine, DIRMATCH compares two directories and copies or moves files from the source to the target directory (you need to specify both directories). For example, if you are in C:\UTIL\MOUSE and want to update a backup for that directory on a disk in drive A, you could laboriously type out the whole directory like this:

```
C:\UTIL\MOUSE>dirmatch c:\util\mouse a:
```

but you would save much typing (and possibly some frustrating mistakes) by typing simply:

```
C:\UTIL\MOUSE>dirmatch . a:
```

DOS would interpret the dot as the entire default directory path, and DIRMATCH would copy or move selected files from C:\UTIL\MOUSE to drive A at your command.

Double Dot   The double dot (..) in your directory represents the parent of the current directory. For example, in C:\UTIL\MOUSE, the .. entry represents the parent, C:\UTIL. You could move to C:\UTIL with this command:

```
C:\UTIL\MOUSE>chdir ..        (Change to parent directory)
C:\UTIL>                      (New default directory)
```

The simple CHDIR .. command will move you back up the directory tree, one parent directory at a time, until you get all the way back to the root directory.

Pointing   Pointing works well using the dot and double-dot directory symbols. For example, from C:\UTIL\MOUSE, you could view a file named READ.ME in C:\UTIL with the command

```
C:\>type ..\read.me          (Shows the parent directory's
                              READ.ME file)
```

Loading Files in Subdirectories

Now it's time to put your organizational structure into practice. You have your directory tree, so all you need to do is copy the appropriate files from your floppy disks into the appropriate directories. For example, to copy all your .DAT files from drive A into your DB directory, enter the following commands:

```
C:\>chdir db              (Changes to DB directory)
C:\DB>copy a:*.dat c:     (Copies .DAT files from drive A)
```

To keep things orderly, it is best to start at the root directory and go through each subdirectory level, one at a time. When you're done, you're in business on your hard disk.

Removing a Subdirectory with RMDIR

You know about creating and loading subdirectories. Sometimes, though, you will need to remove a directory. This could happen if you change to a new application, for instance, or make a typing mistake when creating a subdirectory.

To remove a subdirectory, first make sure that it is empty of all files and lower level subdirectories, and that it is not your current directory. Then you can use the RMDIR command to prune the subdirectory branch from the tree.

When invoking RMDIR, DOS expects only one parameter—the path to the directory to be removed. For example, to remove the subdirectory NOTICE3 from drive C, you could enter:

```
C:\>rmdir \db\overdue\notice3     (Removes NOTICE3 subdirectory)
```

or

```
C:\>chdir \db\overdue             (Goes to OVERDUE subdirectory)
C:\DB\OVERDUE>rmdir notice3       (Removes child subdirectory)
```

If the subdirectory you wish to remove contains any files or lower-level subdirectories, first erase or move all the files. If the subdirectory you wish to remove is your current directory, first change to the parent directory with the CHDIR .. command.

Do not try to remove a subdirectory using the ERASE or DEL commands. If you do, DOS will ask

```
Are you sure? (Y/N)
```

If you answer "Y," it will delete every file in the subdirectory—but leave the subdirectory itself intact. This may not be what you intended. Always exercise caution when you use the ERASE, DEL, or RMDIR commands.

WORKING WITH DIRECTORY LISTINGS

Now that you have subdirectories and working files, from time to time you'll need to display information about your current subdirectory and its contents. When you change to a different directory, for example, it's a good idea to use the DIR command to list the contents. That way, if you start copying or deleting files, you will know exactly what you have in the directory and what, if anything, should be spared.

You can use the CHDIR command to display the name of the current directory and the DIR command to examine its contents. You can also use the DOS TREE command (described in Chapter 12) to examine your directory structure, although few experienced users resort to that particular program. Most people prefer shell or file management programs of the sort discussed in Chapter 8.

In DOS version 4.0 and later, a shell program is included. With earlier versions of DOS, you'll have to look elsewhere for an alternative to TREE.

Using the TREE Command Whereas DIR lists the contents of one directory at a time, TREE scans all the directories and subdirectories on a disk and sends a complete listing to the screen. It is not a very flexible command, and is included here only because it is included with every version of DOS.

TREE is best used with a printer. The /f option adds a list of all files. You can also specify which drive to list or let it use the default drive. Chapter 11 talks about advanced commands that will redirect the output through the MORE filter utility. This makes the listing stop and wait for a key press each time the screen fills with new information, so you have a chance to see what's scrolling by.

To print out your TREE listing, make sure your printer is on and enter this command:

```
C:\>tree /f >prn
```

The /f option displays the names and specifications of all files. The "> prn" redirects output to the printer.

SUMMARY

This chapter discussed hard disk organization, the design and creation of directories and subdirectories, and techniques for working within the directory tree structure.

The next chapter will cover some advanced DOS commands, including DOS backups, the ANSI console driver, batch files, and other advanced DOS subjects.

CHAPTER ELEVEN

Advanced DOS Techniques and Batch Files

There are many intermediate-level and power-user features in DOS to help you create a truly personal computing setup. Whether you have a floppy or a hard drive system, the DOS command structure works the same way.

The first parts of this chapter address some advanced commands and some methods of enhancing a DOS-based system. You'll then read about how to put this information to work via one of DOS' most powerful tools—the batch file. Batch files let you issue long strings of complex commands with the touch of just a few keys. You can use branching logic, long strings of command-line options that execute each time you use a program, and other power-user tricks. By combining batch files with DOS' capable ANSI .SYS console driver, you can reassign your keyboard's keys, make a single keystroke do the work of a long series, create colorful menus, and control the entire screen's appearance. You'll find this chapter's batch file tips and examples useful for performing a variety of tasks. You can use these batch files as they are or, even better, as models for creating your own.

FINE TUNING DOS TO SUIT YOUR TASTE

There is usually more than one way to do a given task under DOS. DOS has the flexibility that lets you perform tasks in whatever way feels comfortable and efficient to you, and most users quickly develop their own ways of doing things. That's an important part of what makes an IBM-compatible PC a *personal* computer.

DOS doesn't care whether you have a hard disk or a floppy disk system, although a hard disk is faster and easier to use. This chapter assumes you have a hard disk and have read Chapter 5, on using a computer; Chapter 9, on operating under DOS; and Chapter 10, on navigating a hard disk. If you have a floppy-based system, most techniques discussed in this chapter apply to your bootup (system) disk in drive A.

PERSONALIZING YOUR COMPUTER

In the next section you'll be working with two special files that DOS seeks during bootup: CONFIG.SYS and AUTOEXEC.BAT. You can configure these two files to tell DOS how to allocate memory and resources, which drive designations to consider legal, and whether to use any particular programs during the startup process. Smart use of CONFIG.SYS and AUTOEXEC.BAT will help you take full advantage of your system's resources.

CONFIG.SYS: CONFIGURING THE SYSTEM

DOS reads the special file CONFIG.SYS, if it is present in your startup disk's root directory, before it reads COMMAND.COM. CONFIG.SYS holds special commands that set up your operating system and user devices. It can also allocate memory, speed up disk access, and make programs run faster, more smoothly, and more effectively.

A new computer may already have a CONFIG.SYS file created by the manufacturer or vendor. It's even more likely that a used machine will already be configured. PC dealers and applications installation programs often add to or change CONFIG.SYS. (Newer, more advanced installation programs ask your permission first, or save the original file as a backup.) The procedures for installing any major program almost always include instructions to create or change your CONFIG.SYS file.

To find out if you have a CONFIG.SYS file, type this command from any subdirectory on a hard disk:

```
dir c:\config.sys
```

If the file is present, DOS will display something similar to the following directory listing:

```
Volume in drive C is Drive C
Directory of  C:\

CONFIG    SYS      251  10-08-91   6:36p
        1 File(s)    5898240 bytes free
```

On a floppy-based system, change the drive C designation to drive A.

```
dir a:\config.sys
```

If your system doesn't have a CONFIG.SYS file, you can create one using any standard ASCII text editor, the DOS EDLIN editor, or even the following COPY CON technique. To build a minimal or generic CONFIG .SYS file using COPY CON, change to the root directory on your startup disk and then type

```
C:\>copy con config.sys
files=20
buffers=15
device=ansi.sys
```

Now press F6 (^Z will appear onscreen), and then ENTER. You now have a working CONFIG.SYS file in your root directory.

The values given above for FILES and BUFFERS will be fine for most systems, but you may need to change them for some programs. The program documentation will recommend other values when needed.

If you have a monochrome display and don't use graphics programs, you might be able to drop the DEVICE=ANSI.SYS line from your CONFIG.SYS file. Be aware, however, that some programs—not always graphics programs—do need the ANSI console driver; so it is best to include the line unless you have a good reason not to. If the file ANSI.SYS isn't stored in your root directory, you'll need to specify where you do keep it. For example, if you keep ANSI.SYS in your C:\DOS directory, the line in CONFIG.SYS might read

```
device=c:\dos\ansi.sys
```

The FILES, BUFFERS, DEVICE, and other entries in CONFIG.SYS are influenced by your specific machine and your applications programs. If you don't use a CONFIG.SYS at all, DOS will provide FILES and BUFFERS default values that will probably be too low (although the default values have improved with each new release of DOS).

Creating a CONFIG.SYS file especially for your system can improve performance dramatically. Check the elements described in the following section to see which CONFIG.SYS entries you need. Type each command you select on its own line in CONFIG.SYS. Many of these CONFIG.SYS commands are also summarized in Table 11-1.

Note: DOS only executes CONFIG.SYS during bootup, so you'll have to reboot your computer before any changes you make to the file can take effect.

BREAK

BREAK defaults to OFF. With BREAK=ON, you can use CTRL-C to break out of a running program during certain functions that you couldn't normally interrupt, such as disk reads. When BREAK is turned off, CTRL-C works only when DOS is looking for keyboard input. You can turn BREAK on or off at any time by typing **BREAK ON** or **BREAK OFF** at the DOS prompt. To turn BREAK on in the CONFIG.SYS file, use this command line:

```
break=on
```

Table 11-1

CONFIG.SYS Command Summary

Command	Purpose
BREAK	Causes DOS to check CTRL-C more frequently
BUFFERS	Sets number of buffers for disk reads
COUNTRY	Sets certain international system values
DEVICE	Installs device drivers
DRIVPARM	Sets new parameters for storage devices
FCBS	Allows file control blocks (pre-DOS 2.0)
FILES	Sets number of files DOS can open at once
INSTALL	Executes special DOS commands, such as FILEOPEN
LASTDRIVE	Sets maximum accessible drive (F-Z)
REM	Lets you add comments to CONFIG.SYS (DOS 4.0)
SHELL	Starts new command processor; expands environment
STACKS	Lets you adjust data stacks available

Buffers and Files

The following two lines in your CONFIG.SYS file will enhance file access speeds. Some applications may require even higher values, but good minimum values (unless you have a disk cache) are

```
buffers=15
files=20
```

BUFFERS

The BUFFERS command tells DOS how many blocks of memory to set aside for storing recently used data. A higher BUFFERS setting lets programs that frequently read data from disks—such as accounting systems and databases—run faster. The most recently accessed data is held in memory where a program can get to it much more quickly.

Without a BUFFERS statement, DOS defaults to a number between 2 and 15, depending upon your DOS version and your hardware. Each buffer is the size of one disk sector—usually 512 bytes. If you have a special drive with a large sector size, it makes sense to use a low value for your buffers and install a disk cache program.

You can use a lower BUFFERS value when you use a disk cache. The advantages of a disk cache include the ability to use upper memory instead of the cramped 640K working memory space. Having 20 buffers duplicate the work of a disk cache wastes memory and may even slow down your system. Since 20 buffers take about 10K of standard operating memory—a hefty chunk—you're better off sticking with a disk cache.

If you are still dissatisfied with your disk access speed and/or memory availability, it may finally come down to experimentation. If you have no disk cache, the DOS default BUFFERS setting can create data bottlenecks. With a disk cache, try setting fewer buffers. If you're short of memory and have no disk cache, successively lower the number of buffers down to 12 or even 10, until it slows your system too much. As you do away with buffers, you increase available memory for programs.

FILES

The FILES statement in CONFIG.SYS tells DOS the maximum number of file handles (including both files and devices) to keep open at once. The default value is eight files, but DOS employs at least five just by booting up. If you have device drivers (discussed in a moment), DOS can use up even more. Add the files your applications program requires for the main program and overlay files, and the default of eight becomes insufficient. You can allow up to 256 files open at a time, but that's excessive and costs operating memory. The suggested value of FILES=20 is usually enough; programs that require more (such as network systems) will usually tell you so in the manual or during installation.

COUNTRY

The CONFIG.SYS COUNTRY= statement lets DOS use different international time, date, currency, case conversion, and decimal separator formats. If no COUNTRY= statement is used, DOS defaults to the U.S. settings.

Device Drivers

Device driver files usually end with a .SYS filename extension, although some drivers use other extensions—including .DEV, .COM, and .EXE. The standard DOS device drivers are listed alphabetically and described in the following paragraphs. It is simplest to install device driver files in your root directory and enter the following line into your CONFIG.SYS file:

device = [*driver name*] [*parameters*]

Of the device drivers included with DOS, the ANSI.SYS and RAMDRIVE .SYS drivers (or VDISK.SYS in PC-DOS) are the most widely used. DRIVER.SYS also is frequently used, especially for machines with mismatched internal floppy drives or add-on 3 1/2-inch external drives.

ANSI.SYS

The device driver ANSI.SYS lets you use codes developed by the American National Standards Institute (ANSI) to control your screen appearance and cursor location. (See "ANSI Codes" later in this chapter for more details.) Many alternative ANSI drivers accept the same standard codes but offer more speed or flexibility than the standard DOS driver. Alternatives include Mark Hersey's FANSI-CONSOLE, Michael J. Mefford's ANSI.COM, and the free (shareware) ANSI drivers called NANSI.SYS and ZANSI.SYS.

DISPLAY.SYS

Containing advanced screen code-paging functions, DISPLAY.SYS displays special national characters during normal operation (the default is U.S.). It supports different video displays.

DRIVER.SYS

Featured in DOS 3.2 and higher, the main use of DRIVER.SYS is to assign a logical drive letter (for example, drive E) to an external device. Usually, this is an external 3 1/2-inch, 720K floppy disk drive (the default). DRIVER .SYS can also be used for external backup tape drives and other add-ons.

This device driver is useful for systems with high-density 1.44MB or 1.2MB floppy disk drives, because you can change how you address an existing disk drive. For example, if drive A is a 1.44MB, 3 1/2-inch floppy, DRIVER.SYS can tell DOS to treat the same physical drive as a 720K drive when referred to by a different drive letter.

DOS supplies the extra logical drive letter based on the next available drive, checking first for existing drives. Drives A and B are reserved for internal floppy drives; if your system only has one internal floppy, DOS treats it as both A and B. Drive C is the first hard drive, continuing through D, E, and so forth until you run out of hard drive partitions. After assigning hard drives, DOS looks in CONFIG.SYS and assigns letters to any device driver logical drives. The order of the CONFIG.SYS command lines determines the order of your logical drive letters. So if you want your external drive letter to come last, place the DRIVER.SYS lines last in your CONFIG.SYS file.

Here are the DRIVER.SYS usage and parameters, and definitions of the switches and options. Square brackets indicate an optional switch or option. You do not type the square brackets. Italics indicate a variable. You replace the variable with an actual value.

device = drive.sys [/d:n] [/c] [/f:n] [/h:n] [/s:n] [/t:n]

Switch/Option	Function
/c	Checks for an open drive door. Use this when telling DOS to treat the same physical drive as two different logical drives.
/d:n	The number (n) of the real drive designator; default is 2, for external drive (see Table 11-2 for other values).
/f:n	The number (n) of the form factor; default is 2, for 720K 3 1/2-inch drive (see Table 11-3 for other values).
/h:n	The number (n) of drive heads, from 1 to 99; default is 2, for double-sided disks.
/n	A nonremovable device, for example, a hard drive (DOS 3.2 and 3.3 only).
/s:n	The number (n) of sectors per track, from 1 to 99; default is 9, for a standard 3 1/2-inch, 720K external floppy drive; high-density formats would be /s:18.
/t:n	The number (n) of tracks per side, from 1 to 99; the default value is 80.

Notes

• On standard 1.2MB and 1.44MB floppy drives, only the /d: and /f: designators are required.

- If you already have a drive E, be sure to add a CONFIG.SYS line LASTDRIVE = (*letter*), where (*letter*) is high enough to allow the required additional logical drive letters. Some people simply set LASTDRIVE = Z when using DRIVER.SYS. This uses a few more bytes of memory but ensures that you have enough disk drive letters available.

Examples of DRIVER.SYS

Add external 3 1/2-inch drive: Insert this line in CONFIG.SYS:

```
device=driver.sys
```

This tells DOS to assign a drive letter, higher than your highest hard drive letter, for the external drive; typically it will be D or E.

Same drive, two sizes: You have a 1.44MB drive A but sometimes need to format 720K disks. Your highest logical drive letter is D. You can tell DOS to treat your 1.44MB drive A also as a 720K drive E, with this line in CONFIG.SYS:

```
device=driver.sys /d:0 /f:2
```

In this example, /d:0 indicates drive A, and /f:2 tells DOS the new drive is a 3 1/2-inch, 720K floppy drive. A and E are the same physical floppy drive, but DOS considers A a 1.44MB drive and E a 720K drive. You can now

---

Table 11-2

DRIVER.SYS /D:*n* Drive Designators (DOS 3.2 +)

/D:*n* Designator	Description
0	Drive A: First internal floppy drive
1	Drive B: Second internal floppy drive
2	Third (always external) floppy drive
3	Fourth (external) drive, and so on
128	First hard disk drive (always C)
129	Second hard drive, and so on
255	Highest allowed drive designator

Table 11-3

DRIVER.SYS /F:*n* Form Factors

/F:*n* Form Factor	Description
0	DSDD (360K, 5 1/4-inch) floppy
1	1.2MB, 5 1/4-inch floppy
2	720K, 3 1/2-inch microfloppy
*3	8-inch single-density disk (*obsolete*)
*4	8-inch double-density disk (*obsolete*)
*5	Hard disk (*don't use unless external*)
*6	Tape drive
7	1.44MB, 3 1/2-inch microfloppy, or other

* Valid for MS-DOS but not for PC-DOS systems

format 720K disks in your 1.44MB drive by entering the simple command **FORMAT E:**, instead of a series of complex parameters like FORMAT A: /t:80 /s:9.

Same drive, same size, extra drive letter: You have a 1.2MB drive A and a 1.44MB drive B; your highest logical drive is B. You need DOS to copy files from a 1.2MB disk in A to another 1.2MB disk in A. The logical drive letter B is taken, and the DOS COPY command won't pause to let you change disks in drive A before copying. You can tell DOS to create a 1.2MB logical drive C from the physical drive A, with this line in CONFIG.SYS:

```
device=driver.sys /d:0 /f:1 /c
```

In this example, /d:0 is drive A, and /f:1 tells DOS to create a logical 1.2MB drive C using the internal 1.2MB 5 1/4-inch floppy drive A. The /c tells DOS to check for a disk in the fictitious drive C. You now can use commands such as DISKCOPY A: C:, and DOS will tell you when to change disks in your single 1.2MB drive.

Same external drive, multiple logical drive letters: Suppose you add a single, 3 1/2-inch 1.44MB external drive to your system. You need to tell

DOS to recognize it as a legitimate drive, and you need to be able to copy files from one 3 1/2-inch disk to another. Your highest logical drive is D. To get DOS to treat your external 3 1/2-inch drive as both E and F, enter these lines in your CONFIG.SYS file:

```
device=driver.sys /d:3 /f:7 /c
device=driver.sys /d:3 /f:7 /c
```

In this example, /d:3 indicates an external floppy drive, /f:7 sets it as a 1.44MB 3 1/2-inch drive, and /c tells DOS to check for an open drive door. These two DRIVER.SYS entries set up the external drive twice, once as E and once as F. You can copy files from E to F, and DOS will tell you when to switch disks. To add yet a third drive designator, which will allow you to treat the external drive as a 720K drive instead of as 1.44MB, simply add a third CONFIG.SYS line:

```
device=driver.sys /d:3 /f:7 /c
device=driver.sys /d:3 /f:7 /c
device=driver.sys /d:3 /f:2 /c
```

This time the /f:2 sets up a 720K logical drive G.

Table 11-2 lists the /d: drive designators to use with DRIVER.SYS. Table 11-3 lists the /f: form factor values to use for various drives.

PRINTER.SYS

PRINTER.SYS is a specialty driver file that provides international code-paging on specific IBM printers. See your printer manual for instructions.

RAMDRIVE.SYS

RAMDRIVE.SYS lets you set aside a part of your computer's memory to be used as a RAM disk (sometimes called a virtual disk). In PC-DOS, the equivalent driver is VDISK.SYS and has slightly different default values. A RAM disk is many times faster than a hard or floppy disk, because the data on it is always in memory. DOS doesn't have to sit and wait while a read/write head moves back and forth across a disk surface, looking for the right location to read or write data. This arrangement is ideal for storing temporary files and program overlay files. RAMDRIVE.SYS lets you use normal, extended, or expanded memory for your RAM drive.

Here is the RAMDRIVE.SYS syntax, with explanations of the parameters.

device = ramdrive.sys [*disk size*] [*sector size*] [*# entries*] [/e ¦ /a]

Parameter	Description
disk size	Specifies the RAM disk size in kilobytes. Default is 64K. Minimum 16K (1K with VDISK.SYS); maximum determined by available memory.
sector size	Size, in bytes, of each RAM disk sector. Default is 512 bytes; allowable values are 128, 256, 512, and 1024.
# entries	Determines how many entries the RAM disk root directory can hold. Default is 64. Minimum 2 (4 with VDISK.SYS); maximum 1024 (512 with VDISK.SYS).
/e	Puts the disk into an AT's extended memory region (between 640 and 1024K). Cannot be used with /a.
/a	Puts the disk into extended memory (above an AT's 1024K main memory region). Cannot be used with /e. Not available with VDISK.SYS.

Note: The default values work best for most users. RAM drives are especially useful with large program overlay files, such as the ones used by Microsoft Windows. Even when you have a hard disk, using a RAM drive for overlays may noticeably accelerate program operation.

SMARTDRV.SYS

Available with DOS 4.0, SMARTDRV.SYS stands for SmartDrive. This relatively slow disk-cache program reduces the time spent waiting for a hard disk to read stored data. Early versions of SMARTDRV.SYS had compatibility problems with Windows 3. There are excellent, low-cost, third-party disk caches available, and many people prefer them. The DOS version comes free with DOS, and you may decide to use it. Usage is as follows:

device = smartdrv.sys [*size*] [/a]

The *size* parameter specifies how much memory to use for the disk cache. The default is 256K of extended memory and all of the available expanded memory (above 1024K). Specify a size that leaves enough memory for your applications programs that also look for and use extended or expanded memory.

The /a switch sets the cache to use expanded memory.

Non-DOS Drivers

Many third-party programs and hardware devices require you to install their own device drivers. Examples include pointing devices (mice and trackballs), non-DOS console drivers such as FANSI-CONSOLE, and enhanced disk format programs such as SpeedStor and Disk Manager.

DRIVPARM

In DOS 4.0, the DRIVPARM command lets you define parameters for block devices, and modify parameters for an existing physical drive.

FCBS

The FCBS command specifies file control blocks that can be held open. It was replaced in DOS 2.0 with the FILES= statement. FCBS is seldom used because most programs rely on the FILES= statement.

INSTALL

In DOS 4.0, INSTALL executes the FASTOPEN, KEYB, NLSFUNC, and SHARE commands during bootup. It is useful if you run various versions of AUTOEXEC.BAT during a single session and want to issue these commands only once.

LASTDRIVE

DOS has a standard of five disk drives, A through E. Of these, A and B are set aside for floppy drives, and C, D, and E are for hard disks, RAM disks, and other storage devices.

This arrangement may suffice, if your hard disk is split into (at most) drives C and D, leaving drive E open for a RAM disk. However, if you have a large hard drive split into four or five logical drives, or if you frequently use the SUBST command, you'll need more drive letters. You can add drive letters, up to Z, with the following line in your CONFIG.SYS file:

lastdrive = *letter*

The *letter* parameter is any drive letter from F through Z. Each permitted drive letter costs a small amount of main memory, so if memory is tight, add only as many drive letters as you need.

REM

Starting with DOS 4.0, the batch file command REM, when used at the beginning of a line in CONFIG.SYS, tells DOS to ignore that line and go on to the next one. Use it to insert comments explaining the contents of a file or the meaning of a line, for example:

```
REM Use Norwegian currency, time, date, and case
country=047
```

In DOS 3.*x* and 2.*x*, REM lines in the CONFIG.SYS file produce error messages but do no harm and don't interfere with the boot process.

SHELL

If you've been experimenting with fancy prompts or long PATH statements and getting messages announcing that you're "Out of environment space," the SHELL statement can solve the problem. DOS gives you a default 160 bytes to store data for the use of DOS commands, applications, and batch files. These bits of information are called *environment variables*, and 160 bytes is often not enough. You can run short after specifying just these three variables, which are always stored in the DOS environment:

COMSPEC, which indicates the location of COMMAND.COM

PATH, if one is set

PROMPT, if it is not the built-in default

If you need to add additional environment variables for use by batch files and applications, you're definitely out of space.

In DOS 3.0 and above, you can enlarge the environment to accommodate other data by putting a SHELL= statement into CONFIG.SYS.

Environment for DOS 3.0 and 3.1

To change from the 160-byte default environment size, enter the following line in your CONFIG.SYS file:

shell=c:\command.com /e:*xx* /p

In this example, the *xx* variable is the number of 16-byte segments to use for the environment. The number must be between 10 and 62—that is, from the default 160 bytes to a maximum of 992 bytes. A value of 20 doubles your environment to 320 bytes, and is a good value to try first.

The parameters for SHELL are actually COMMAND.COM options; SHELL doesn't accept any direct options. The /e: parameter tells the new copy of COMMAND.COM how much space to reserve for the environment. The /p parameter tells COMMAND.COM to make the change permanent during the current session, and tells DOS to look for AUTOEXEC.BAT during bootup. DOS won't look for AUTOEXEC.BAT if a shell is installed without /p.

Environment for DOS 3.2 and Above

SHELL in later DOS versions works much like SHELL in 3.0 and 3.1, but the environment can be larger and you don't have to calculate in 16-byte increments. Instead, enter your CONFIG.SYS line along this model:

shell=c:\command.com /e:*xxxxx* /p

In this example, *xxxxx* is the true size of the larger environment. This value can run from 160 to 32,768 bytes—which amounts to a full 32K environment. That's much more than any normal application uses. A figure of 320 or, if you still run out of environment space, 512 (half a kilobyte), is large enough for most users.

STACKS

You can change the number and the size of stacks available for hardware interrupts with STACKS. Although most users rarely change the DOS default setting, some applications programs will suggest a new STACKS setting if the program freezes or runs erratically.

AUTOEXEC.BAT: SETTING UP THE SESSION

You'll recall that CONFIG.SYS is the first file DOS looks for during startup, after reading the two hidden system files. CONFIG.SYS tells DOS how to configure its memory, ports, and so on. Next, DOS reads COMMAND.COM, and then looks for AUTOEXEC.BAT. This is the final step before DOS shows you the DOS prompt (or menu, or shell, or applications program you specify in your AUTOEXEC.BAT file).

You may already have an AUTOEXEC.BAT file on your startup disk, put there by your vendor. Or, if you used SELECT to set up the system, DOS itself will have created one. To check, you can go to your root directory and enter the command DIR AUTOEXEC.BAT. The directory listing will show the file if you have it. If you do not, you will probably want to create one.

You can create AUTOEXEC.BAT the same way as CONFIG.SYS—with any ASCII text editor. For a short, simple file, you can also use DOS EDLIN, or the COPY CON AUTOEXEC.BAT technique described earlier in "CONFIG.SYS: Configuring the System." More complex AUTOEXEC .BAT files are also possible, using the batch file techniques discussed later in this chapter.

Some power techniques to speed the bootup process are described in Chapter 17. The following example of an AUTOEXEC.BAT file will get your machine started for everyday use. It assumes you want the default country values for your computer—probably U.S. (If you do not want U.S. characters, use the SELECT command to specify the country of your choice, and then modify the AUTOEXEC.BAT file created by SELECT.) The PATH command shown is based on the directory tree used in Chapter 10.

A Sample AUTOEXEC.BAT File

The sample file created in Chapter 5 contained only two commands, setting the pregnant prompt and starting the CLOCK program. The following sequence of commands cleans up the screen and sets a prompt. It then sets the system time and date, using an automatic clock card. It sets the PATH, installs a disk cache program, goes to a working directory, and starts a database program.

```
echo off                (Turns off screen clutter)
cls                     (Clears the screen)
echo Booting...         (Reassures you something is happening)
prompt $p$g             (Sets pregnant prompt)
timedate autoclk        (Sets time and date by clock board)
path c:\batch;c:\util;c:\dos;c:\db;c:\wp   (Sets path)
cd \db\overdue          (Goes to working directory)
\db\pcfile              (Starts database program)
```

The batch file ECHO command is discussed in detail under "ECHO (DOS 2.0 and Higher)" later in this chapter. The other commands shown are standard DOS commands or the names of programs. Instead of calling a database program, you may wish to start a word processor, a DOS shell program, or a user menu. Or, instead of the last two lines in the foregoing example, you might wish to end the file with

```
cls
echo Bootup completed successfully.
```

and let the user decide what to do next, right from the DOS prompt. Also, if your machine does not have a built-in clock or clock board, you may wish to add the following commands:

```
time
date
```

This will make your time stamps accurate whenever you reboot. (An accurate time stamp is important for keeping track of the most current working files.)

As you work with your computer, you'll find yourself adjusting your AUTOEXEC.BAT file to fit your own machine and your own preferences. The important thing to remember is that each line in an AUTOEXEC.BAT file must consist of a legal command. The computer reads the batch file one line at a time and executes each line as if you had entered it at the prompt. (There's more on batch files later in this chapter.)

BACKING UP YOUR FILES

DOS provides a BACKUP program for hard disks, but easier-to-use and more widely accepted programs are available from other manufacturers. The DOS BACKUP and RESTORE commands provide options explained in the DOS command reference (Chapter 12).

Backing Up Floppies

Backing up a floppy disk, even one that has subdirectories, is simple. The DISKCOPY command copies the entire disk, subdirectories and all, as described in Chapter 5. When there are no subdirectories or hidden files, the XCOPY or COPY *.* *target drive* technique works better, because COPY and XCOPY do not duplicate bad sectors and file fragmentation as DISKCOPY does.

Note that COPY and XCOPY cannot copy hidden files. In the past, when many programs used hidden files as part of copy protection schemes, this was a serious disadvantage. Copy protection schemes are no longer as widely used, so you can use the DOS COPY command with more confidence to create backup copies. Sometimes, however, important files are hidden by applications programs to prevent them from being damaged or deleted. When in doubt, use the DOS DISKCOPY or BACKUP command.

The Hard Disk BACKUP Command

Backing up a hard disk is more complex than backing up a floppy. Hard disks are much larger, and hold more files. You must take into account a hard disk's subdirectories. The DOS BACKUP utility backs up only the current directory unless you specify otherwise. So make a habit of using the /s (subdirectory) option to make BACKUP copy all the files in the specified directory, and in subdirectories below it in the directory tree.

For example, to back up the subdirectory OVERDUE and all subdirectories whose paths go through OVERDUE, enter

```
A:\>backup c:\overdue a: /s
```

To back up an entire hard disk, start your /s command at the root directory, as follows:

```
A:\>backup c: a: /s
```

DOS will tell you when to change disks. Always prepare disk labels that show the backup disk sequence.

The Hard Disk RESTORE Command

This command restores lost files to your hard disk, provided they were previously backed up using the DOS BACKUP utility.

When you run RESTORE without options, it will not create missing subdirectories. If you want to restore files to a particular subdirectory and it does not already exist on the target drive, you must first create that subdirectory with MKDIR.

Using the /s Option   RESTORE normally copies (restores) files only from the directory you specify, but you can use the /s option to restore files from a specific directory *and* any of its subdirectories. If DOS doesn't see a subdirectory with the specified name, it creates one. That's a nice convenience, because it means the specified directory structure doesn't have to exist on the target drive in order to restore files to their original directories. RESTORE will re-create the original structure for you.

If you enter this RESTORE command:

```
C:\>restore a: c:\db /s
```

it will restore everything in and below the DB directory in the directory tree.

To restore everything in the backup set, specify the root directory and use /s, like this:

```
C:\>restore a: c:\ /s
```

A Common RESTORE Problem

Version 3.3 and later: In DOS 3.3 and later, if you specify a path with BACKUP, your backup files can only be restored to their original directory. If RESTORE doesn't find that directory, it tries to create it—but will succeed only if the path to the current (default) target directory is the same as the path to the original (backed-up) source directory. The trap is that, if the target disk is not set either to the root directory or the correct target directory, you'll get a somewhat misleading warning:

```
Warning! No files were found to restore
```

The remedy is to *run RESTORE only from the root directory* of the target drive. That way, RESTORE can always find the needed directory structure or create it if it does not already exist.

Earlier versions: In earlier versions of DOS, the problem is more difficult to control: RESTORE doesn't check the entire path, so you *must* start out in the correct directory. Otherwise, RESTORE may generate many scattered duplicated files on your hard drive. This will waste space and leave you with a confusing, disorganized directory structure.

Here's an example of what can happen: Consider this subdirectory structure, similar to that created in Chapter 10:

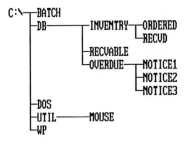

If C:\DOS is your current directory, and you realize you've lost some files from C:\DB, you might tell RESTORE to restore all the backed up files from the DB subdirectory, like this:

```
C:\dos>restore a: c:\db
```

In response to this command, RESTORE looks for a subdirectory named DB at your *default* location, but won't find it—so it creates one. All of your C:\ DB files will thus be restored to a new subdirectory, C:\ DOS\ DB, which is not at all what you intended. Here is your directory tree now:

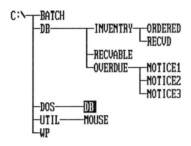

If you had used the /s command to restore the *entire* subdirectory structure, your problem gets even worse. This command:

```
C:\dos>restore a: c:\db /s
```

would result in duplicated, unattached subdirectories everywhere on your disk, as in this illustration:

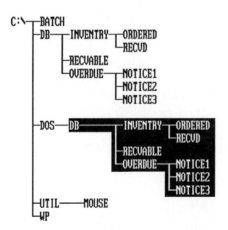

To prevent this confusion, it's important to *only use RESTORE from the root directory.* Here is the recommended sequence of commands to restore the \ DB directory:

```
A:\>c:
C:\dos>cd \
C:\>restore a: c:\db
```

Now only the files and subdirectories in C:\DB will be restored, and the original directory structure shown earlier will remain intact.

RUNNING BETTER, FASTER, MORE SMOOTHLY

The next paragraphs contain tips on how to spruce up your system—how to change from "plain vanilla" to something more customized. Although special hardware and software to do this job are readily available, a customized "feel" is more than appearance. It involves changing the way the system responds to your commands. For customizing the way your system works, nothing beats creative use of some of DOS' own file and screen control commands.

Third-Party Customization Programs and Hardware

One fast way to customize a system to your liking is to use programs, hardware, and device drivers designed to enhance DOS. For example, a mouse (hardware) coupled with a good shell or menu system (software) can make your computer seem like a new machine. Later versions of DOS offer some good DOS extenders, like the DOSSHELL utility. Other ways to customize a system using special software are covered in Chapters 6 through 8.

Tapping DOS Environment Variables

The DOS *environment* is an area of memory set aside to store system parameters. Batch files and applications use the DOS environment to store strings—combinations of characters—that hold critical operating information. *Environment variables* tell DOS where to find overlay files, which options to use, where to create temporary files, and the like.

This works fine—until you start seeing messages telling you that you have run out of environment space. If that happens, the solution is to set a larger environment at boot time, using the SHELL command described earlier.

To view your DOS environment from the DOS prompt, enter the SET command with no parameters. A typical, simple DOS environment might report

```
COMSPEC=C:\COMMAND.COM
PATH=C:\;C:\DOS;A:\
PROMPT=$p$g
```

In this example,

- COMSPEC= tells DOS to use C:\COMMAND.COM to interpret all commands.

- PATH= is a list of directories where DOS will look for executable files.

- PROMPT= defines a string of metacharacters (characters preceded by $) and regular ASCII characters that make up your DOS prompt.

The following shows a more complex environment that holds basic information on COMSPEC, PROMPT, and PATH, along with several applications programs:

```
G:\>set
COMSPEC=c:\command.com
PATH=G:\;C:\BELFRY;C:\UTIL;C:\UTIL\DIRS;C:\NEWNORT;C:\NC;D:\ARCH;C:\PCTOOLS;D:\P
CW;C:\DOS
DR=E
HOME=E:\GUIDE\11ADV
MEMO_DIR=c:\memo
MEMO_FILE=MEMO
LIST=G:\
ED=%C [!D:\PCW\ED.DEF
PROMPT=$p$g

G:\>
```

As you get more adept with managing DOS, your environment will probably become more complex; it's all part of making your system run better, requiring less work on your part.

The SET Command

The SET command is one good reason to enlarge your DOS environment, because it makes environment variables usable by batch files. The SET command syntax is

SET *variable* = *value*

where *variable* is the environment variable and *value* is the string assigned to it. For example, look at the following command:

```
SET XTGOLD=c:\xtgold
```

The environment variable is XTGOLD (DOS always translates lowercase to uppercase on the left side of the equal sign). The value of the variable is c:\xtgold (DOS retains lowercase letters to the right of the equal sign). If you now use the popular shell program XTREE GOLD, it will be able to find its overlay files by looking in the environment for the XTGOLD variable. Similarly, a batch file can check to see if XTREE GOLD is available on your system.

When using SET, remember that entries are case sensitive to the right of the equal sign and that you must not include any spaces around the equal sign.

Redirection, Piping, and Filters

Beginning with DOS 2.0, users were given some control over data input and output channels, using *redirection, piping,* and *filters.*

Redirection

Redirection lets you change the normal way that DOS uses data from its standard input and standard output devices. Here is how it works.

When you type something on the keyboard, it shows up on the screen. The keyboard is a *standard input device* (it inputs the data), and the monitor is a *standard output device* (the data's destination). There can be other input devices, such as a mouse, trackball, light pen, or even a DOS file—anything that provides data that can be displayed on the screen, or otherwise output. And there can be other output devices, such as a printer, modem, scanner, digitizer, or DOS file.

The various redirection operations and their symbols are described in the following paragraphs.

Redirecting Output   Using the output redirection (>) symbol, you can tell DOS to send information to a specific destination, such as a printer or a file, instead of to the monitor. For example, the command

```
type filename.ext >prn
```

reads the file FILENAME.EXT as usual, but sends its output to the printer (>PRN) instead of to the screen. Similarly,

```
dir >dirfile
```

sends the results of a DIR directory listing into a file named DIRFILE instead of to the screen. If you then tell DOS to

```
type dirfile
```

you will see the same information you would have seen without the redirection. Now, however, you can sort, format, edit, or otherwise manipulate the information in the listing.

When sending output to a file, you can use one > symbol to copy over old data, or two > symbols (>>) to append new data. Here are some tips for redirecting output to a file.

- The > symbol by itself *creates* a new file or *writes over* any existing files of the same name, destroying the older contents. It's a good idea to check your directory contents before using > redirection.

- A double > symbol (>>) *appends to* any existing file of the specified name. It tacks the new data onto the end of an existing file, preserving the older data; if no file exists, DOS creates one.

- Putting a space *after* the > symbol (as in DIR > DIRFILE) won't affect how redirection works.

- Omitting the space *before* the redirection symbol (as in DIR>DIRFILE) will confuse DOS and cause unpredictable results. In some versions of DOS, it may even freeze the computer.

Caution: Sometimes a command requires an answer from you—the most famous example is the "Are you sure? (Y/N)" message you see when you tell DOS to delete all files. With output redirected, you can't see the answer that you type in, and the computer will freeze. Make sure you know what to expect from DOS when you redirect output. If you know DOS will require user input, you can supply it from redirected input, as described next.

Redirecting Input   The < symbol tells DOS to use the contents of a named file instead of the keyboard as input. This technique is often used with DEBUG and other advanced commands. Files prepared for this purpose are often called *scripts*. A prepared script allows proofreading ahead of time, and so prevents typing errors during execution. When using redirected input, make sure the script is complete. If the script is incomplete (for example, if it does not end a prodedure properly and leaves the program waiting for more input), your computer can freeze, requiring you to reboot.

As an example of redirecting input, say you want to create a file named YES.FIL, containing the single letter *Y*, to allow a command like DEL*.*<YES.FIL to proceed automatically. When DOS asks if you are sure, the redirected input provides a *Y* from YES.FIL and DOS completes the operation.

Piping and Filters
Pipes and filters let you change, select, or otherwise affect data before feeding it to the standard output. This way you can search files for specific words, sort directory listings, and eliminate unwanted extra characters from text files. DOS includes three special external filter utilities that can read standard input, perform data manipulations, and write the results to standard output. They are used in conjunction with the piping symbol (¦), as described next.

Note: Piping data through DOS filters results in the creation of temporary files in the default directory. These are normally erased by DOS when the operation is finished, but if something interrupts the piping process they may be left behind. You can spot them because DOS gives them hexadecimal filenames that resemble 0939246E. If you find these files in a normal directory listing, you can safely erase them.

MORE   This useful and easy-to-understand filter lets you view your text one screen at a time, pausing while you read the contents. After 24 lines of text, MORE tells you to "Press any key" or prompts you with "-- MORE --" and waits for you to press a key to continue. It is used with redirection or piping (see "Using the Pipe (|) Symbol").

SORT   The SORT filter organizes and displays output in either ascending or descending order. By default it sorts lines alphabetically on the first column of data, but you can choose any column. SORT is most useful with files that contain a series of fixed-length records. It moves one line at a time to a new position within the file, treating upper- and lowercase letters the same. Unless you use the /r (reverse) option, it arranges all lines in ascending alphabetical order.

FIND   The FIND filter lets you search through a list of files for occurrences of a specific word or phrase, and then displays the entire line where each match occurs. Upper- and lowercase letters are considered separately. FIND can also search through a stream of standard output data for specific characters; this is useful in conjunction with the DIR command.

Using the Pipe (|) Symbol   Piping lets you turn the output of one command directly into input for another command, with no writing to screen or disk in between. The pipe (represented by the broken vertical bar, |) sends any output from the command to the left of the bar, directly to the command on the right side of the bar for processing. For example, the command

```
dir | more
```

causes a DIR directory listing to pause at every screenful of data and wait for you to press a key. You can use several | symbols in a row if you want, like this:

```
dir | sort | more
```

This command first sorts the directory listing, then sends the sorted list through the MORE filter to the screen, pausing each time the screen fills up.

Extended Characters

A computer's normal set of characters consist of the printable punctuation, letters, and numbers in the lower half (0 through 127) of the ASCII (or other specific country) code page. (See Appendix E for the entire ASCII table.) Any monitor with the appropriate code page can display these text characters, and most printers can handle them all.

Extended characters are those in the upper half of the ASCII table— codes 128 through 255. These codes produce math symbols, box lines, and other language characters, such as ñ and Ç. In most word processors (and at the command line), it's easy to create the extended characters. To do so, hold down the ALT key and press the character's decimal ASCII number. Use the numeric keypad on the right side of the keyboard for this; the top row of keys in the typewriter section won't work.

For example, if you want a small, square bullet (■), hold down the ALT key and type the number 254 on the numeric keypad.

ANSI Codes

DOS by itself treats the keyboard and monitor together as an ordinary teletype device, printing only one line at a time and keeping the cursor always on the line currently being typed. To allow the use of colors and to provide better screen and keyboard control, you can install the ANSI.SYS (or equivalent) code interpreter in your CONFIG.SYS file.

ANSI codes were created by the American National Standards Institute to control the appearance of computer displays. The ANSI system uses a series of escape codes to set color, cursor location, and other screen variables. To use ANSI codes, you must first embed them in a file you create, using any text editor that can record the ASCII escape character (027 — see Appendix E).

Since every ANSI code is preceded by ASCII code 027 (the escape character), you can't enter the ANSI codes at the DOS prompt. Here's how to create them in a text editor:

1. Hold down your ALT key and type **27** on the numeric keypad at the right-hand side of the keyboard. In most programs, the result on the screen will look like a left-pointing arrow (←). Or it may appear as

a square left bracket with a caret in front (^[). In some programs, it may look like a backslash (\ ).

2. Type a left square bracket, so what you see on screen looks like ←[. Or it may look like ^[[. This starts your escape code sequence.

3. Type in the ANSI codes (see Table 11-4) for the screen effect you want. The ending letters must be entered in the case shown, and are required. The semicolon is required only if two decimal values are specified.

The resulting one-line file can be displayed on the screen, by typing the command

```
C:\>type filename.ext
```

When ANSI codes are embedded in a batch file, the results can be striking. Some examples are shown later in this chapter in "Using Batch Files to Automate Complex Operations."

Table 11-4

ANSI Screen Control Functions

Escape Code	Explanation
Cursor Positioning:	
Esc[*row;col*H	Cursor moves to #;# row and column numbers. If no numbers are specified, cursor moves to home positon 1;1 (upper-left corner).
Esc[*#rows*A	Cursor up # rows; if # will go past top of screen, DOS stops at top.
Esc[*#rows*B	Cursor down # rows; if # will go past bottom of screen, DOS stops at bottom.
Esc[*#cols*C	Cursor right # columns; stops at far right of screen.
Esc[*#cols*D	Cursor left # columns; stops at far left of screen.
Esc[6n	Device status report (DSR) request; used by some programs.
Esc[s	Saves current position so it can be restored later using Esc[u.
Esc[u	Restores cursor position saved earlier by Esc[s.
Screen Erasing Codes:	
Esc[2J	Returns cursor home (1;1) and erases screen; in some versions of DOS, erases below current position without returning home.
Esc[K	Erases to end of current line, including current cursor position.

Table 11-1

ANSI Screen Control Functions (*continued*)

Escape Code	Explanation

Screen Color Codes:

Esc[*fg;bg*m   Sets foreground (*fg*) and background (*bg*) colors, where

Color	fg	bg
Black	30	40
Red	31	41
Green	32	42
Yellow	33	43
Blue	34	44
Magenta	35	45
Cyan	36	46
White	37	47

Screen Attribute (Noncolor) Codes:

Esc[*n*m   Sets screen attributes not associated with color selection, where

0 = Primary rendition (turns off bold, underscore, blinking, reverse video, and conceal modes)

1 = High-intensity foreground color

4 = Underscore (monochrome only)

5 = Blinking

7 = Reverse video

8 = Hidden characters (foreground same color as background)

NOTES

1. Escape character (decimal 027) is represented by Esc.

2. All numbers following the ANSI Esc[escape code beginning symbol are decimal numbers.

3. Optional numbers are noted in the explanation.

4. All codes are ended by a case-sensitive letter that defines the meaning for ANSI.SYS and cannot be omitted.

5. Codes are based on MS-DOS 4.0; earlier versions have minor differences.

Note: BASIC also offers methods of setting screen colors and other video attributes. However, attributes that you set using an ANSI device driver will override any set using BASIC.

The Fancy DOS Prompt

You know that the DOS prompt tells you that you can enter a line of input telling DOS to do something. You learned in Chapter 5 about the "pregnant prompt," which also tells you exactly what directory or subdirectory you are in.

With the help of some special DOS command characters called *metacharacters,* shown in Table 11-5, you can include even more information in your command line prompt than simply the current directory. By using metacharacters with the ANSI characters described in the foregoing section, you can use the prompt to control screen appearance as well as to convey important information. The only real limitation is the environment

---

Table 11-5

PROMPT Command Metacharacters

Metacharacter	Effect
$t	Shows current time
$d	Shows current date
$p	Shows current directory path
$v	Shows DOS version number
$n	Shows current drive specifier (letter)
$h	Backspaces one character
$e	Inserts an escape character, to be followed by any ANSI escape sequence you provide
$_	Inserts a carriage return/line feed pair
$g	Creates > character
$l	Creates < character
$b	Creates ¦ character
$q	Creates = (equal sign: ASCII 61, not 205)
$$	Creates dollar sign

---

size—every character in the prompt takes up environment space, so a very complex prompt may cost more than it is worth. You are the sole judge of how fancy to make your own prompt.

Tip: In a DOS prompt, you can start the ANSI escape sequence using the characters $e[rather than pressing ALT and typing 27 as described earlier. This allows you to type the prompt or echo it to the command line without canceling the entire resulting command, which is what the ALT-27 escape character does. The $e metacharacter stands for the ALT-27 escape character, so $e[can then be followed by any legal ANSI escape code. Using this technique, your prompt can range from the simple to the intricate, including vivid colors, boxes, bells, and whistles.

Here are some sample prompts. Display the time and date, with a modified pregnant prompt, by entering:

```
C:\>prompt Current time is $t $d $p -$g
```

You'll get a prompt like this:

```
Current time is 12:03:54.03 Sat 10-05-1991 C:\GUIDE\11ADV ->_
```

This prompt would look less cluttered if it were displayed in three lines. To accomplish this, use the $_ line return metacharacter. Change the PROMPT command to

```
C:\>prompt Current time is $t$_$d$_$p -$g
```

and you'll see

```
Current time is 12:04:33.12
Sat 10-05-1991
C:\GUIDE\11ADV ->_
```

Do you find the display of seconds and tenths of seconds annoying? To get rid of that part of the $t string, use the backspace metacharacter, $h, as shown here:

```
C:\>prompt Current time is $t$h$h$h$h$h$h$_$d$_$p -$g
```

The prompt now shows only the hour and minutes.

```
Current time is 12:05
Sat 10-05-1991
C:\GUIDE\11ADV ->_
```

USING BATCH FILES TO AUTOMATE COMPLEX OPERATIONS

A *batch file* consists of a series of DOS commands, one per line. You've already studied one batch file found on most MS-DOS machines— AUTOEXEC.BAT, explained earlier in this chapter. Other batch files are constructed in the same fashion, but you have to run them from the command line yourself.

A batch file can be any length, and can contain commands that let it branch to additional commands, or cause it to exit based on a condition. You start a batch file the same way you start a program, by entering the filename. DOS then looks for a .COM, .EXE, or .BAT file (in that order). When it finds a .BAT file, it reads the file one line at a time, executing each command in sequence until it reaches the end of the batch file.

What this means to you is that you have a tool for performing a long series of perhaps complicated commands, the same way every time. Batch files can remember long strings of command options and enter complicated key strokes for you, without any further intervention on your part. Using batch files, you can

- Enter a sequence of several commands that must be run the same way many times.

- Enter one or more applications program commands that contain long, complex parameters. No more having to memorize them or look them up in a manual.

- Enter a sequence of commands for operations that take a long time to run, such as printing documents, while you attend to other tasks.

- "Package" a sequence of commands so that an inexperienced person can run them by typing a single command line.

- Using simple third-party utility programs, build menus that allow inexperienced users to select and run complex programs, without needing help from the "office expert."

- Guide another user through a series of complex decisions; for example, installing a printer driver for a given applications program.

Creating and Using a Batch File

You create batch files using any word processor or text editor that can create ASCII files. The batch file may have any name that is not the same as the name of a .COM or .EXE command in the same directory, the name of an internal command such as COPY, or the name of a program DOS finds earlier in the PATH statement. If a batch file and a .COM or an .EXE program have the same filename, DOS will ignore the batch file when you enter the name, and run the program instead.

You can create a simple, two-line batch file by entering these two lines in a file, using your word processor or text editor:

```
chkdsk
chkdsk >prn
```

Save the file, and name it EXAMPLE.BAT. Then, at the DOS command prompt, enter the filename as a command:

```
C:\>example
```

DOS displays and runs each of the commands in your batch file, in order, just as if you had entered the commands from the keyboard. This tiny batch file is of limited use; it gives you only a screen display and a printed report of what CHKDSK finds on the default drive. But it illustrates the principle of a batch file. Substitute any series of DOS commands that would be useful to you, and you'll have a working batch file.

For example, suppose you routinely work in your \DB directory, and frequently need to see what data files are stored in a subdirectory named OVERDUE. Instead of having to enter

```
dir \db\overdue\*.dat
```

at the command line every time you need the directory, you can create the
following simple batch file, named ODUE.BAT:

```
dir c:\db\overdue\*.dat
```

Now, whenever you enter the simple command ODUE, you'll see a list of all
files in the OVERDUE subdirectory that end with the database filename
extension .DAT.

Batch Files on Other Drives or Directories

When you want to run a batch file that is not on the default drive, you can
point to it by entering its filename with a drive name or a full path, as with
any other executable file:

```
A:\>c:\batch\example
```

Aborting a Batch File

Pressing CTRL-C (or CTRL-BREAK on an enhanced keyboard) will interrupt batch
file execution. When you press CTRL-C, DOS displays the following message:

```
Terminate batch job (Y/N)  ?
```

Type **Y**, and DOS abandons the batch file and returns to the command line.
Type **N**, and DOS executes the next command in the batch file.

Fundamental Batch File Operations

Several batch file commands control screen appearance or convey information directly to the user. These commands are ECHO, REM, PAUSE, and
CLS.

ECHO (DOS 2.0 and Higher)

The ECHO command has two functions. First, it controls whether DOS
displays the batch file command lines as they are executed. Second, it can

display any message of your choice on the screen during batch file execution, so you can communicate with the user.

DOS normally displays each command line in the batch file at the prompt, as it runs the command. This is fine for short batch files, but during longer batch files it can be distracting. You can discontinue the display of command lines by starting your batch file with

```
echo off
```

ECHO OFF does not affect information displayed by commands, such as error messages or directory listings; it only stops the display of the command lines themselves. ECHO OFF also cancels the command line prompt.

To resume DOS' display of command lines and prompts, include the following command:

```
echo on
```

In DOS 3.3 and higher, you can make the ECHO OFF command itself invisible, by starting the command line with the @ sign, as in the following example:

```
@echo off
```

The @ symbol might be used at the beginning of every line in a batch file to make the ECHO OFF command unnecessary, but the single line @ECHO OFF has the same effect and saves keystrokes.

To display a specific message, the syntax is

echo *message*

This use of ECHO lets you display a message from a batch file while ECHO OFF is in effect. Entered by itself, the ECHO command will simply report whether it was last turned on or off.

REM

A batch file line beginning with REM is a remark, or comment, line. DOS does not treat the line as an executable command. Batch file writers use REM lines to explain what the next line or lines will accomplish. They are shorthand to understanding a batch file's purpose or internal logic. When ECHO is turned off, REM lines are not displayed on the screen.

PAUSE

The PAUSE command halts your computer's operation and displays the following prompt:

```
Strike a key when ready ...
```

At this point nothing else will happen until you press a typing key. Use PAUSE after an ECHO message to tell the user what to do during the pause. The following lines would prompt a user to change disks in drive B:

```
echo Insert the data floppy disk in drive B;
pause
```

When DOS gets to the PAUSE command in the course of executing the batch file, you will see this on your screen:

```
Insert the data floppy disk in drive B;
Strike a key when ready ...
```

CLS

The CLS command erases your computer's screen and moves the cursor to the upper-left corner. You can use it at the beginning of a batch file to erase leftover data from before the batch file began.

An Example Batch File

The following batch file, called SYS-A.BAT, illustrates the four commands just discussed: PAUSE, REM, ECHO, and CLS. This file must be run from the startup disk, or the DOS program SYS.COM, which makes floppy disks bootable, won't work. SYS-A.BAT places the SYS files on four disks, prompting the user as it goes. It also will echo a complete progress report to the screen. Here is the listing:

```
echo off
cls
rem SYS-A.BAT places system files on disks in drive A

echo           Placing hidden SYStem files on four diskettes.
echo      ----------------------------------------------------------

echo Insert 1st diskette in drive A and
pause
c:
cd \dos
sys a:
echo      ----------------------------------------------------------

echo Insert 2nd diskette and
pause
sys a:
echo      ----------------------------------------------------------

echo Insert 3rd diskette and
pause
sys a:
echo      ----------------------------------------------------------

echo Insert 4th diskette and
pause
sys a:
echo      ----------------------------------------------------------
echo                     End of Session.
```

The SYS-A.BAT batch file displays the screen output shown in Figure 11-1. Notice the following about the execution of this batch file:

- DOS ignores blank lines; use them to help visually if you need to read and understand the batch file weeks later

- ECHO is turned off at the top of the file. (In DOS 3.3 and higher, this line could be @ECHO OFF.) With ECHO turned off, nothing shows onscreen unless it is a specific ECHO command. This controls screen clutter and lets the batch file tell the user what is going on.

- Dashed lines help the user follow the program's progress.

Figure 11-1

SYS-A.BAT screen output

```
              Placing hidden SYStem files on four diskettes.
         ------------------------------------------------------------
         Insert 1st diskette in drive A and
         Strike a key when ready . . .
         System transferred
         ------------------------------------------------------------
         Insert 2nd diskette and
         Strike a key when ready . . .
         System transferred
         ------------------------------------------------------------
         Insert 3rd diskette and
         Strike a key when ready . . .
         System transferred
         ------------------------------------------------------------
         Insert 4th diskette and
         Strike a key when ready . . .
         System transferred
         ------------------------------------------------------------
                          End of Session.
         G:\>
```

Using Dummy (Replaceable) Parameters

A batch file executes the same sequence of commands each time you run it. You can also write a batch file that does different things based on values you supply at the DOS prompt when you run the file. For example, you can rewrite the EXAMPLE.BAT batch file (from the preceding section) so that it accepts a drive letter as a parameter and runs its CHKDSK commands for that drive.

To do this, you need to specify *dummy* or *replaceable parameters*, which are symbolized by the expressions %1 through %9. When you run the batch file, DOS replaces these expressions with the parameters you specify at the command line. DOS then behaves as though the lines in the batch file contained the specified parameters from the start.

To see how this works, edit your EXAMPLE.BAT batch file in the following way:

```
chkdsk %1
chkdsk %1 >prn
```

The expression %1 is your dummy parameter. Now put a formatted floppy disk in drive B and, from drive C, enter

```
C:\>example b:
```

As DOS processes the batch file, whenever it encounters a line that contains the dummy parameter %1, DOS substitutes your specified command parameter value of B:. The result is just as if you had entered

```
C:\>chkdsk b:
C:\>chkdsk b: >prn
```

Now run the same batch file without entering a parameter.

```
C:\>example
```

The batch file this time produces exactly the same result as before you modified it. Without a supplied parameter value, DOS does not evaluate the %1 dummy parameter, and assumes intended values are for the default drive. In effect, the dummy parameter disappeared from the file.

Multiple Dummy Parameters   A batch file may have up to nine dummy parameters, %1 through %9, and you can specify any one of them several times in the batch file. When you run the batch file, DOS replaces each %1 it finds with the first command line parameter, each %2 with the second parameter, and so forth. There's also a %0 (zero) parameter, which DOS uses to keep track of the name of the batch file itself.

For example, suppose you create a batch file named COPYDIR.BAT, containing

```
echo off          (Eliminates echo to reduce screen clutter)
copy %1 %2        (Copies %1 parameter to %2 parameter)
dir %2%1          (Lists directory of the result)
```

Now run the batch file with this command entered on drive A:

```
A>copydir *.com b:
```

You have just defined %1 as *.COM, and %2 as B:. DOS replaces the dummy parameters with your specified values, and processes the batch file as if you had entered the following:

```
C:\>copy *.com b:
C:\>dir b:*.com
```

DOS copies all the .COM files from drive A to drive B, and then displays the directory of .COM files on drive B. This simple batch file lets you copy specified files to a specified destination, and then see the results of the operation. (By the way, if the target disk, B, ran out of space, the batch file would show you which files got copied and, by elimination, which ones did not.)

Parameter substitution does not guarantee a valid result. For example, suppose you run COPYDIR.BAT with this command line:

```
A>copydir disk
```

DOS processes this command line as follows:

```
echo off
copy disk        (Replaces %1 with value DISK)
dir disk
```

Because you didn't specify a second parameter, DOS discards the %2 dummy parameter. If you have a file named DISK in your current directory, DOS thinks you're trying to copy a file named DISK on top of itself—an illegal operation. So your screen displays something like this:

```
C:\> copydir disk
File cannot be copied onto itself
        0 File(s) copied

Volume in drive C is MS-RAMDRIVE
Directory of  C:\

DISK             8   10-13-91    3:07p
       1 File(s)     780288 bytes free
C:\>_
```

Notice that the DIR command does produce the expected results, but it is preceded by a DOS error message disallowing the attempted COPY operation.

When a parameter value is not a filename, its length is limited only by the number of characters that will fit on a command line—up to 128.

Parameter Rules
Here are DOS' rules for dummy parameters in batch files.

- There are nine dummy parameters, %1 through %9.

- The n parameter in a batch file command corresponds to the dummy parameter %n.

- As DOS executes a batch file, it replaces each dummy parameter with the corresponding parameter value, but only in memory and only for this execution. The contents of the batch file itself remain unchanged and can be reused with different parameters.

- If you want to use % as a character in a batch file command line, type %% instead of %. This tells DOS you want a literal % in your command line.

- If the batch file allows more dummy parameters than the user enters on the command line, DOS disregards the empty ones.

- The parameter %0 has a special meaning in DOS. It stands for the name of the batch file or program currently being executed; DOS uses it to help keep track of what it's doing. For instance, the following line displays the name of the batch file being executed:

```
echo Now executing %0
```

- Environment variables can be used within a batch file by enclosing the variable name within % signs. The following line displays the value of the environment variable COMSPEC on the screen:

```
echo %comspec%
```

Batch File Decision Commands

DOS uses a group of *decision commands*—FOR, IF, GOTO, and SHIFT—that cause batch files to automatically make decisions like "Run this command only if that file exists," or "Run this command once for each batch file parameter." These commands let you write batch files so powerful that, in many cases, they can take the place of BASIC programs or programs written in more sophisticated programming languages.

FOR

The FOR command is one of the most powerful and underused commands in DOS. FOR is perceived as a complicated command, but learning to use it is easier once you get used to the concept of *sets* of files and operations.

The principle of the FOR command is that anything you do to more than one file, or that you do more than once, you can do to a set of files, or as a set of operations. FOR lets you execute a specified command for a whole set (or list) of files. It also lets you treat upper- and lowercase letters as equivalent when using the IF command (discussed a little later in this chapter).

Here is one example of how to use the FOR command.

```
for %%v in (jan feb mar) do dir .%%v
```

When this command is run, DOS executes these three commands in sequence:

```
dir .jan
dir .feb
dir .mar
```

The result is a directory listing of all your files that have filename extensions indicating these month names. Here's how the command works:

- After FOR, %%V represents each variable in the set. IN (JAN FEB MAR) defines the (...) set—in this case, a set of filenames with extensions defined as JAN, FEB, and MAR. (Remember, for the DIR command, DIR .JAN is equivalent to DIR *.JAN.) You can define your set using as many variables inside the parentheses as you want—all the way to DEC in this case.

- DO DIR .%%V tells DOS to run DIR once for each file extension in the specified set. Each time DIR .%%V is run, DOS substitutes one of the values named in the (. . .) set definition.

Remember: As described in "Parameter Rules" earlier in this chapter, the %% tells DOS you're not opening a place for a dummy parameter, such as %1, %2, and so on. Without the %% in a batch file, the FOR command will just generate error messages. (At the command line, use a single %, as described later in "Using FOR at the Command Line.")

Choosing a %% Letter Symbol   The symbol after %% doesn't have to be *V* for *Variable;* you can use any letter you want. Many users like %%X because X is what you solve for in algebra. Others like %%F for File.

Note: In later versions of DOS, you can even use more than one letter, to write commands such as FOR %%FILES IN (JAN FEB MAR) DO DIR %%FILES. (Be aware that such commands are not compatible with earlier versions and can cause confusion.)

The %% letter symbol can be either upper- or lowercase. Just be consistent: If you use a lowercase letter after FOR %%, you should also use a lowercase letter after DO %%.

Using FOR with Wildcards

The preceding sample FOR command does not use any wildcards. It works the way it does because, as mentioned earlier, DIR .* is the same as DIR *.* when you're requesting a directory listing.

However, these two forms of the DIR command are *not* equivalent in the FOR command. When you use wildcards with FOR, it will issue a separate command for each file that matches. For example, if you define the above set as (*.JAN *.FEB *.MAR), you'll get a separate DIR command for each matching *file,* not for each specified *extension.* Thus, in the *.JAN set, instead of DIR .JAN, you might get this series:

```
C:\>DIR WEEK1.JAN
C:\>DIR WEEK2.JAN
C:\>DIR WEEK3.JAN
C:\>DIR WEEK4.JAN
```

That's a bit messy. Still, a separate command for each file often is exactly what you do want. For example, consider this next batch file:

```
echo off
rem COMP-A.BAT Compare files to backup copies in drive A
for %%x in (*.jan *.feb *.mar) do comp %%x a:
```

This compares each first-quarter record with its backup copy on drive A, which is handy if you've changed some but not all of the records.

If your wildcard set does not match any filenames, DOS runs a command line with nothing on it, as though you had simply pressed ENTER at the keyboard. You'll see a line feed, but nothing else will happen.

To sum up, using wildcards to define a set makes FOR issue a separate command for each time the wildcard matches the file. If you leave out the wildcard, FOR issues only a single command for each variable in the set. This helps with DIR but may not be what you want with other commands. Use wildcards only when you want to operate separately on each matching file.

Using FOR to Imitate Wildcards

Not all commands accept wildcards; the TYPE command, for instance, refuses them. FOR can get around that limitation. Let's say you want to review a set of files quickly, using the TYPE command. The following READ.BAT file will accomplish this:

```
echo off
rem READ.BAT types wildcard file groups to screen
for %%t in (%1) do type %%t
```

In this FOR command, DOS substitutes the characters you specify for the %1 dummy parameter. Now enter

```
read *.txt
```

and DOS will issue a separate TYPE command for each file that has a .TXT extension. All matching files will scroll up the screen, one file at a time.

Using FOR at the Command Line

With only a slight change in command syntax, you can use FOR directly from the DOS prompt. Instead of a %% symbol, you type a single % symbol with your variable (for example, %V). DOS never uses dummy parameters from the prompt, so you don't need a %% to clarify.

FOR can be handy at the DOS prompt for on-the-fly operations. In the following command, you compare files in the current directory with files of the same name on drive B, and avoid a "File not found" error for files not present in drive B:

```
C:\>for %f in (b:*.*) do comp %f b:
```

The FOR command can be used together with the IF command (described next), to create some very flexible batch files.

IF

The IF command lets you execute a command *if* a specified condition is true. If the condition evaluates as false, DOS skips that command in the batch file and goes on to the next line.

IF tests for three types of conditions:

IF EQUAL: Are two strings of characters equal?
IF EXIST: Does a specific file (or wildcard group of files) exist?
IF ERRORLEVEL: Is the DOS errorlevel set for a specific value?

A special form, *IF NOT,* tests for a specified condition being *not* true. If the condition is not true, DOS executes the command. This makes a total of six basic IF tests.

Because IF won't execute a command unless the condition evaluates as required, you can have DOS do one thing for one result, or something else for the other result. This so-called *branching* ability gives you surprising flexibility. Let's look more closely at how IF works.

General Use of IF

Like the FOR command, IF is a powerful batch file tool that also can be used from the command line. The trick to using IF lies in setting the conditions correctly.

The IF condition evaluation translates roughly along these lines: "The user specified %1 (dummy parameter number 1) as **b:index.txt**; true or false?" Or, "There exists a file in the current directory named WEEK1.JAN; true or false?" If the condition, or answer, turns out to be true, DOS executes the specified command. If not, DOS ignores the command and goes on to the next line of the batch file.

The Equal (==) Condition for IF

In this use of IF, DOS evaluates to see if a variable *equals* a specified value. The tested variable might be a dummy parameter (%1, %2, and so on) set by the user, or a DOS environment variable.

Here's an example of how to use IF to test user input; you could use it to test whether a user is logging on as TOM.

```
echo off                              (Turns off echo clutter)
rem Sample TEST-IF.BAT batch file line
if %1 == tom echo End test User tested for TOM. (Tests %1 dummy parameter)
```

Here is a loose translation for this IF command: "If the first specified parameter (%1) is equal (==) to TOM, echo 'End test User tested for TOM.' on the screen. Otherwise, do not echo anything."

If the user enters the command **TEST-IF TOM**, the screen will report

```
End test
User tested for TOM
```

Empty Parameters If the user enters TEST-IF with no parameters, DOS runs into a problem. It can't compare something that doesn't exist (%1) with anything, so it reports a syntax error and keeps going. To avoid that problem, add any legal character to the %1 and to the comparison string on the other side of the double equal sign. For example:

```
IF [%1]==[TOM] echo User tested for TOM
```

Now if the user fails to specify a parameter, DOS sees this test:

```
IF []==[TOM] echo User tested for TOM
```

and since [ ] does not equal [TOM], DOS reports that the test failed and does not carry out the command. Here are some common character variations:

IF "%1"=="string"
IF [%1]==[string]
IF %1!==string!
IF %1empty==empty

Note: The last example tests true only if the user specifies no %1 parameter.

Other Noteworthy tips for IF   Keep in mind the following when using IF...==

- The double equal sign (==) means "is equal to." A single equal sign (=) won't work; DOS will report a syntax error.

- In the IF...== test, DOS considers upper- and lowercase characters to be *different*. (In our example, therefore, *tom* would fail the test.)

The NOT EQUAL Condition for IF

The foregoing TEST-IF batch file would be more informative if it could report on the user's entry, if that entry wasn't TOM. An IF NOT command would be executed if the user's parameter does *not* equal TOM. This form of IF can be used to improve the screen report. Here is an example:

```
echo off
rem Sample TEST-IF.BAT batch file IF and IF NOT test lines

if %1 == tom echo User tested for TOM.
if not %1 == tom echo User tested for "%1" instead of TOM.

echo End test
```

Now, if the user enters **TEST-IF TOM**, the TEST-IF batch file will report

```
User tested for "tom" instead of TOM.
End test
```

The EXIST Condition for IF

The IF EXIST command evaluates to see if a specified file exists. Wildcards are acceptable. You can use the IF EXIST test to have DOS determine whether to copy files, or carry out any other DOS command.

In the section about the FOR command, you read about using

```
for %%f in (b:*.*) do comp %%f b:
```

to compare only files that also exist on drive B. The IF EXIST test can do similar tricks. The following batch file, named UPDATEB.BAT, will copy a named file to drive B only if a file with the same name already exists there:

```
echo off
rem UPDATEB.BAT tests for B:%1 before copying
if exist b:%1 copy %1 b:
```

By using IF EXIST and IF NOT EXIST together, you can update drive B only if a file already exists there, and keep the user informed about what is going on.

```
echo off
rem UPDATEB2.BAT tests for B:%1 before copying
  if exist b:%1 echo %1 exists on drive B; updating
  if exist b:%1 copy %1 b:
  if not exist b:%1 echo "%1" does not exist on drive B; aborting
```

You could also turn UPDATEB.BAT into COPYB.BAT and avoid accidentally copying over an existing file:

```
echo off
rem COPYB.BAT Copies files only if not already present on drive B
  if exist b:%1 echo File already exists -- aborting!
if not exist b:%1 echo File not present on drive B; copying
if not exist b:%1 copy %1 b:
```

With this IF EXIST line if you enter a command such as COPYB THIS .TXT, and if THIS.TXT already exists on drive B, DOS detects it, tells the user, and stops.

The ERRORLEVEL Condition for IF

The IF ERRORLEVEL test takes action depending upon the value of a DOS variable called the *errorlevel*, which is set by programs that set an exit code when they are finished. That makes the powerful IF ERRORLEVEL test useful primarily with non-DOS utilities that are designed to enhance the power of batch files. Most DOS users have a collection of these labor-saving utilities and make frequent use of them.

Of DOS' utilities through DOS 4.0, only BACKUP and RESTORE set a useful exit code. How to use BACKUP's exit code to check for a successful backup is demonstrated in an example batch file, BACKIT.BAT, later in this chapter.

Errorlevels may be in the range 0 to 255. Most utilities and applications that set the errorlevel will set it to 0 if all operations have been successful. The meanings of exit codes depend on the program. For example, many batch file utilities use ERRORLEVEL 255 to indicate that the user pressed ESC. The shareware utility called IFF sets ERRORLEVEL 99 if a drive door is open, and ERRORLEVEL 89 if a floppy disk in the target drive has not been formatted.

To use errorlevels, remember to test for the *highest* exit code first. This is because the highest exit code includes all lower exit codes. IF ERROR-LEVEL tests are usually used with the GOTO command, described later in this chapter, for that reason.

Some applications programs also set the errorlevel to meaningful values. Consult each program's documentation to see if that program sets an exit code that you can test usefully with IF ERRORLEVEL.

Nesting IF Tests

IF tests can be *nested* in batch files; that is, you can use as many as you like on a single command line. Be careful when nesting IFs, because files that contain many of these condition statements can be hard to debug. Nested IF tests are useful for setting up "if this, but not that" conditions. For example, the following batch file line would copy a file only if the file exists in drive A, but not in drive B:

```
if exist a:thisfile if not exist b:thisfile copy a:thisfile b:
```

Using GOTO with Labels

The GOTO command tells DOS to look for a specific label in the batch file, go there, and start operations at the next line after the label. A *label* is a batch file placemarker. It is set off from normal command lines because it starts with a colon, as in this next example:

```
rem This is a remark line
:THIS IS A LABEL            (DOS looks at the first 8 characters only)
rem This is another remark line
```

DOS finds a specified label by going to the beginning of the batch file and checking the first eight characters of each line that starts with a colon.

Using GOTO has two important considerations. First, that GOTO goes to the top of the file before starting to look for the label means you can jump around within the file. If a procedure calls for you to repeat a set of steps, for example, you don't have to include them twice in the same batch file; you can just use GOTO to go to the top of the repeated sequence. Second, because GOTO looks only at the first eight characters, it cuts down considerably on the time DOS needs to find a label.

Tips on Using Labels in Batch Files

- *Use uppercase for labels* It's wise to use all capital letters for labels. This makes the labels easy to find in the lines when you add to them later. (DOS does not distinguish uppercase and lowercase in labels.)

- *Concentrate on the first eight letters* You could define one label named :DOCUMENTS and another one named :DOCUMENTA-TION, but the GOTO command would never get to the second label because DOS reads only the first eight letters of a label.

- *Use labels to speed batch operations* By preceding your REM lines with a colon, you turn them into labels, like this:

```
: rem This is a REM line turned into a label
```

```
: This is the REM line turned into a label, without the REM
```

This technique can speed up batch files that are heavily commented, because DOS reads all of a REM line, but only the first eight characters of a label. The initial colon identifies the line to DOS as a label, not a REM line, no matter what it contains. But be sure not to duplicate the first eight letters of any labels that are attached to a GOTO command.

The SHIFT Command

The SHIFT command shifts each parameter in a batch file down one number. Thus, the first time SHIFT is executed in a batch file, it makes %0 refer to the old %1, %1 refer to the old second parameter, %2 refer to the third, and so forth. The second time SHIFT is executed, it makes %1 refer to the third parameter, %2 refer to the fourth, and so on. The SHIFT command itself has no parameters.

Here is a simple READ.BAT example that uses SHIFT.

```
rem READ.BAT reads multiple files
type %1
shift
type %1
shift
type %1
```

Suppose you ran this batch file with

```
C:\>read x.txt y.txt z.txt
```

The first TYPE command types file X.TXT. The first SHIFT command makes %1 refer to the second parameter, so the second TYPE command types file Y.TXT. The second SHIFT command makes Z.TXT into %1, making the third TYPE command type file Z.TXT.

Here is a more practical example of a batch file using SHIFT. This program can erase any number of files with a single command. It uses replaceable parameters, plus the GOTO, SHIFT, ECHO, IF EQUAL, and IF NOT EQUAL commands.

```
echo off
: rem ERA.BAT erases any number of specified files (wildcards ok)
  if %1! == ! goto SYNTAX          (Show syntax if no parameters)
  goto LOOP                        (Else go to LOOP label)
```

```
:SYNTAX
  cls
  echo Correct Usage:  ERA filename-1 [filename-2] ... [filename-N]
  goto END

:LOOP
  if not exist %1 echo File %1 not found    (Report if can't find file)
  if exist %1 echo Erasing %1               (If file exists, report action)
  if exist %1 del %1                        (If file exists, delete it)
  shift                                     (Shift all parameters down 1)
  if not %1! == ! goto LOOP                 (Only if more files, repeat loop)
                                            (Else end operation)

:END
```

Run ERA.BAT to erase three files named A.TXT, B.TXT, and C.TXT with this command:

```
C:\>era a.txt b.txt c.txt
```

The first IF statement tests the value of the first parameter. If the parameter is not null, DEL is executed on it. Then SHIFT makes B.TXT the new replaceable %1 parameter. The GOTO LOOP repeats the DEL command, now on B.TXT. After the last parameter, C.TXT has been deleted. The result of the SHIFT command is to make %1 into an empty parameter. There are no more files to delete, so %1! equals ! and instead of returning to the loop the batch file ends.

Sample Batch Files

Here are three useful batch files, using the batch commands discussed above. They include branching, testing, and looping; use them as examples when creating your own batch files.

BACKIT: Backing Up a Hard Disk

The following batch file, BACKIT.BAT, makes sure you get a successful backup. It uses these batch file tools:

Dummy parameters
Test for no-parameter error
Use of colon on REM lines
IF ERRORLEVEL
IF EQUAL
IF NOT EXIST
ECHO
GOTO
Labels

BACKIT.BAT depends on the fact that BACKUP sets the DOS errorlevel
to 1 if it encounters a problem, or to 0 if backup succeeds. Notice how the
program tests for correct syntax; if the test is unsuccessful, the file displays
the correct syntax and quits. The blank lines and leading spaces are for
clarity; DOS ignores them in batch files.

```
echo off
: rem BACKIT.BAT tests for successful DOS backup
: rem based on errorlevel returned by BACKUP.EXE
    if %1x == x goto SYNTAX          (Test for no-parameter error)
    if exist %1\*.* goto START      (File not specified, just directory)
    if exist %1 goto START          (Filename specified)
    if not exist %1*.* goto SYNTAX  (Test for incorrect parameter error)

:START
    backup %1 /m (Back up only m option files that have been changed)

    if not errorlevel 1 goto OK          (Test for failed backup)
    echo *************************************
    echo Error in backup of %1 -- Redo !!!! (If no success)
    echo *************************************
    goto END

:SYNTAX
:rem show correct usage
    cls
    echo ***************************************************
    echo               Correct syntax is:
    echo     BACKIT Drive:[\path][\filename] [Target:]
    echo ***************************************************
    goto END
```

```
:OK
    echo Backup complete.
:END
```

FORMAT.BAT: Removing FORMAT's Fangs

This batch file guards against one of the most common destructive mistakes—formatting the hard disk by accident. To use this program, first rename your DOS FORMAT.COM utility program to !FORMAT.COM; this keeps you from using the file by accident. (You can still use it when needed by entering its new !FORMAT name.) Then place the following batch file in your path, preferably in your C:\BATCH or equivalent directory.

The FORMAT.BAT file uses FOR %%V in the same line as the IF EQUAL command. The FOR command lets you specify drive A or B in either upper- or lowercase. If you forget to enter a drive letter—which is usually how the hard disk gets accidentally formatted—the IF test fails. FORMAT.BAT then shows the proper command syntax on screen, and quits without formatting anything, leaving your disk unharmed.

```
echo off
: rem FORMAT.BAT requires existence of !FORMAT.COM in path
: rem If drive not specified, show usage syntax
    if %1x == x goto SYNTAX

: rem Do A or B whether capitalized or not, whether : included or not
    for %%v in (a b A B) do if %1 == %%v: goto %%v
    for %%v in (a: b: A: B:) do if %1 == %%v goto %%v

:SYNTAX
: rem If target not specified as
: rem a:, b:, A:, or B: -- show required syntax and exit
    echo Usage: FORMAT A: or FORMAT B:
    echo Aborting batch file. Try again.
    goto END

:A
: rem If drive A is specified
    echo Entering command: "!FORMAT A:" (Ctrl-C cancels)
    pause
    !format a:
    goto END
```

```
:B
: rem If drive B is specified
   echo Entering command: "!FORMAT B:" (Ctrl-C cancels)
   pause
   !format b:
:END
```

TO.BAT: Getting There from Here

One very tiresome chore on a hard disk is getting from one directory to another. With all those backslashes, and so many directory names, a simple typing error can create much frustration. While the SUBST command (described later) offers one way out of the dilemma by letting you substitute a mock drive letter for a full CHDIR statement, a batch file like the following one is also a good solution. It lets you get to, say, your C:\BATCH directory by simply entering the command TO BATCH. Where you'll really appreciate this batch file is in second-level directories, such as C:\UTIL\MOUSE. Typing TO MOUSE is much easier than typing CD C:\UTIL\MOUSE.

Use the following listing as an example. This version assumes you have only four hard disk directories, but the file structure is easy to tweak to make it fit your own hard disk setup; just add your own directory names.

```
rem -- "TO.BAT" Navigates to Any Named Directory
@echo off
if %1x == x goto USAGE
for %%v in (a a: A A:) do if %1 == %%v goto DRIVE_A
for %%v in (b b: B B:) do if %1 == %%v goto DRIVE_B
for %%v in (c c: C C: root ROOT) do if %1 == %%v goto ROOT_C
for %%v in (batch util comm BATCH UTIL COMM) do if %1 == %%v goto %%v
:USAGE
Echo USAGE: TO [A ¦ B ¦ C ¦ COMM ¦ UTIL ¦ BATCH]
goto END

:DRIVE_A
a:
goto END

:DRIVE_B
b:
goto END
```

```
:ROOT_C
c:
cd \
goto END

:BATCH
set c:
cd \belfry
goto END

:UTIL
c:
cd \util
goto END

:COMM
c:
cd \comm
goto END

:END
```

OTHER ADVANCED DOS COMMANDS

The following two sections explain how to use the advanced user commands ASSIGN, SUBST, and JOIN, and how to use the ANSI.SYS device driver to assign new functions (macros) to your keyboard keys.

Disks: Getting More Out of Less

Sometimes a program is written to operate only on a specific logical drive, but you need to run it elsewhere. DOS 2.0 added the ASSIGN command, and DOS 3.*x* augmented it with SUBST and JOIN, to solve this sort of problem.

ASSIGN and SUBST make DOS think it's writing to one logical drive when, in fact, it's writing to another. Note that Microsoft recommends against using ASSIGN if you have SUBST available, because ASSIGN is not as safe. It is covered here for users who still have DOS 2.*x* on their systems.

JOIN makes DOS think that one drive is part of another drive. This lets floppy-based systems copy files that are too long for a single disk to hold.

Caution: Not only can you fool DOS by using ASSIGN, SUBST, and JOIN, but you can even fool yourself. These three commands can create major havoc if you forget to release them when you are finished.

ASSIGN

A program may require that its program disk be in drive A and the data disk in drive B. You can use ASSIGN to make DOS treat your hard disk drive C as if it were drive A. ASSIGN does this by renaming the drive, effectively hiding its true identity from DOS. This is not very safe, as you could easily format or otherwise damage the disk drive by accident. AS-SIGN does, however, serve its limited purpose well. (See Chapter 12 for ASSIGN command syntax.)

SUBST

The SUBST command lets you treat a *directory* (not a drive) as if it were a separate *disk.* It is best to use a drive letter that is not already in use. Use the LASTDRIVE= command in your CONFIG.SYS file to make additional logical drive letters, if necessary.

The SUBST syntax is SUBST *newdrive sourcedir.* Consider this example, which substitutes the logical drive H for the working directory:

```
C:\>subst h: c:\db\overdue\notice2
```

When you are finished with this SUBST command, you can type **SUBST H:** **/d** to cancel the substitution.

Note: You cannot cancel the SUBST command when the substituted drive is your default directory. Also, if the directory has its own subdirectories, they're still subdirectories on the newly designated logical drive. In our example, if you substitute C:\DB\OVERDUE (in the directory tree developed in Chapter 10) for drive H, the new drive H will have subdirectories named H:\NOTICE1, H:\NOTICE2, and H:\NOTICE3.

JOIN

The JOIN command works as the opposite of SUBST. JOIN is especially useful in floppy-based systems, since it lets you fool DOS into thinking that a second disk is part of your current drive setup. It lets you create a larger database file, or download a larger file by modem, than can be held by a single floppy disk. Be cautious with this power-user technique; if the disks become separated, you will lose everything.

To pull off this trick, put your JOIN.EXE program into drive A. Go to drive B, and create a new empty directory. Then you can use the command syntax JOIN *drive \path* to join the drives. This entire process is illustrated here:

```
A:\>b:
B:\>mkdir \join-ab
B:\>join a: b:\join-ab
B:\>chdir \join-ab
```

From now on, DOS considers anything in drive A to be the starting point for the B:\ JOIN-AB directory, and will not recognize that a separate drive A exists. If you create a large file in your \JOIN-AB directory, DOS will start writing to the disk in drive A and, when it runs out of space, bridge smoothly to drive B. To cancel the JOIN command, enter **JOIN A: \d**.

Macros: New Meanings for Keys

One of the handiest and most basic power-user techniques is reassigning a series of characters or keystrokes, called a *macro,* to any key on your keyboard. The easiest way to do this is to create a batch file that echoes the desired ANSI key reassignment codes. To reassign a key, use one of the following formats in an ECHO statement:

ESC[*key-code;key-code*p
ESC[*"char ";"string"*p

or

ESC[*key-code;"string"*p

The elements of these format statements are as follows:

- ESC is ASCII character 27, obtained by holding down the ALT key, typing 27 on the numeric keypad, and releasing the ALT key.

- *Key-code* is a code sent to the BIOS when you press a key, telling the computer which key you pressed. Special *key-code* values for control characters and other special keys are shown in Table 11-6. For the "typewriter" keys (A through Z, 0 through 9, and normal punctuation), just use the ASCII values shown in Appendix E.

Table 11-6

Special Key Return Codes

Key	ASCII Code			
	Alone	ALT	SHIFT	CTRL
F1	0;59	0;104	0;84	0;94
F2	0;60	0;105	0;85	0;95
F3	0;61	0;106	0;86	0;96
F4	0;62	0;107	0;87	0;97
F5	0;63	0;108	0;88	0;98
F6	0;64	0;109	0;89	0;99
F7	0;65	0;110	0;90	0;100
F8	0;66	0;111	0;91	0;101
F9	0;67	0;112	0;92	0;102
F10	0;68	0;113	0;93	0;103
F11	0;133	0;139	0;135	0;137
F12	0;134	0;140	0;136	0;138
HOME	0;71	—	55	0;119
UP ARROW	0;72	—	56	—
PG UP	0;73	—	57	0;132
LEFT ARROW	0;75	—	52	0;115
DOWN ARROW	0;77	—	54	0;116
END	0;79	—	49	0;117
PG DN	0;81	—	51	0;118
INS	0;82	—	48	—
DEL	0;83	—	46	—
PRINT SCREEN	—	—	—	0;114

- *"String"* is any sequence of numbers or characters, always surrounded by double quotation marks.

- *"Char"* is any keyboard character.

- p designates the end of a key substitution code.

Let's look at an example batch file that trades the slash (/) and the question mark (?), so that the unshifted key produces a question mark and the shifted key gives the slash. We'll call the file QMARK.BAT. Since you'll probably want to reassign the keys to their original roles without rebooting, QMARK.BAT resets them if you enter the command QMARK RESET. Note that ASCII character 27, the escape character, is represented as ESC. To make the batch file work, use the actual ASCII 27 character.

```
echo off
: rem QMARK.BAT trades "?" and "/"

: rem Reset to original key layout only if %1 == reset
    for %%v in (reset RESET)  do if %1! == %%v! goto RESET

: rem User didn't ask for key reset
    echo ESC[63;47p      (Make ? key return the / character)
    echo ESC[47;63p      (Make / key return the ? character)
    goto END

:RESET
: rem user asked for key reset
    echo ESC[63;63p      (Return both keys to original state)
    echo ESC[47;47p
:END
```

Notice in the first section how a FOR-IF command is used to accept either uppercase or lowercase letters in the %1 parameter. If there is no parameter, the batch file simply sets the new key values and exits.

The RESET sequence uses ASCII values to specify the new key definitions, because this makes it obvious what is happening. When setting the macro, QMARK.BAT told key code 63 (?) to act as key code 47 (/). To reset, the keys are told to resume their original roles. Notice also that, for the typewriter keys, ANSI code numbers are the same as the ASCII values.

If you'd like to actually see what the new key definitions do, here is another set of commands that are exactly equivalent to the first batch file:

```
echo off
: rem QMARK.BAT trades "?" and "/", or resets if %1==reset
     for %%v in (reset RESET)  do if %1! == %%v! goto RESET

: rem User didn't ask for key reset
     echo ESC["?";"/"p              (Make ? key return the / character)
     echo ESC["/";"?"p              (Make / key return the ? character)
     goto END

:RESET
: rem user asked for key reset
     echo ESC["?";"?"p              (Return both keys to original state)
     echo ESC["/";"/"p
:END
```

If there is a word or phrase you type frequently, you can assign it to a shifted function key using the extended ANSI keyboard codes shown in Table 11-4. Here is an example, called PHRASE.BAT.

```
: rem PHRASE.BAT assigns phrase to CTRL-F10
     for %%v in (reset RESET)  do if %1! == %%v! goto RESET

: rem User didn't ask for key reset
: rem Shift-F10 uses double key-code "0;93"
     echo ESC[0;93;"%1 %2 %3 %4 %5 %6 %7 %8 %9"p
     goto END

:RESET
: rem user asked for key reset
     echo ESC[0;93;0;93p
:END
```

The phrase you specify (up to nine words) in your ECHO statement will now be attached to SHIFT-F10. For example, the command

```
phrase We hope to see you at the Mardi Gras!
```

will cause that phrase to be displayed whenever you press SHIFT-F10. To reset SHIFT-F10 to its original role, enter

```
phrase reset
```

Note: ANSI macros work only with applications programs that do not interfere with standard keyboard input. Many programs, including text editors, intercept function key and other keyboard codes and attach their own meanings; in that case, your macro will "disappear" until you get back to the DOS prompt.

SUMMARY

In this chapter you have learned some new ways to use some powerful DOS commands and batch file techniques.

Chapter 12 gives an alphabetical reference of DOS commands. Keep the command guide available for reference, and practice using the batch and other advanced commands discussed in this chapter, and you'll soon develop your own personal PC command approach.

DOS Command Reference

This chapter contains descriptions of DOS commands. Each entry includes the command's full form, its syntax, a description, an example, and appropriate comments.

This chapter's command references are for all DOS versions released at the time of this writing. Not all options are supported by all versions. Where appropriate, version numbers are mentioned.

COMMONLY USED TERMS

This chapter frequently uses symbols or notations for the following terms: drive, filename, path, path name, and options (or switches). Following are definitions of these terms.

Drive A disk drive, represented by a letter followed by a colon; for example, C:. (The colon is required in DOS commands.)

Filename The name of a file, usually followed by a three-letter extension. The filename and its extension are separated by a period; for example, COMMAND.COM, where COMMAND is the filename and COM is the extension.

Path One or more directory names, separated by backslash (\) characters; for example, \accting\ytd.

Path name One or more directory names followed by a filename, each name separated by a backslash (\) character; for example,

\accting\ytd\budget.ytd

Switches or Options These set the parameters for commands, each beginning with a forward slash (/) character. This book uses the term *options*. Note that it makes no difference whether you use upper- or lowercase when typing an option.

/h Help Option Some versions of DOS such as DR DOS and 4DOS have a /h option that brings up a Help screen telling how to use a given command. The /h option is not used in this guide.

DOS COMMAND LINE COMMANDS

All versions of DOS allow users to enter commands from the command line. The following is an alphabetical reference to these commands. Unless otherwise specified, references to DOS versions are to a command's first appearance and include all later versions as well. Commands noted as external require that the executable program be present in the current path. Internal commands are resident in memory whenever you see the DOS prompt.

APPEND

(External) MS/PC DOS 3.2

Description APPEND sets a path to search for nonexecutable data files and overlays.

Syntax

append *drive:path* [*;drive:path.* ..]
append [/x] or [/x:on]   (DOS 3.3 and later)
append [/x:off]   (DOS 4.0)
append [;]
append [/e]   (DOS 3.3 and later)

Examples

```
append c:\letters;d:\memos
```

Tells DOS to look for data files in the C:\LETTERS and D:\MEMOS directories.

```
append /e
```

Places an APPEND= statement in the DOS environment allowing manipulation by the SET command. Can be specified only the first time you invoke the command. Useful for applications that support append searches.

```
append /x
```

Tells DOS to use an application's SEARCH FIRST, FIND FIRST, and EXEC functions. This increases the number of programs that can use the APPEND path, but can cause problems with some programs. Can be specified only the first time you invoke APPEND. The /x:off option cancels /x in DOS 4.0.

```
append ;
```

Cancels the current APPEND search path.

Comments   Use special care with the /x option. It can cause problems with certain programs. APPEND must be used before ASSIGN, if you use ASSIGN. Entering APPEND with no parameters displays the current data file search path.

ASSIGN

(External) MS/PC DOS 3.

Description   ASSIGN lets you change the drive letter for a specified drive, typically to let you use a hard drive with programs that require you to use only drives A and B. Microsoft recommends using ASSIGN with DOS version 3.1 or higher.

Syntax

assign [*drive1*] [*drive2*] [...]

Examples

```
assign a c
assign a=c
```

The equal sign is optional. Both commands tell the program to access drive C as if it were drive A.

```
assign
```

Resets the original drive letters.

Comments   Use SUBST instead of ASSIGN if you have version 3.1 or later. The command ASSIGN A=C is similar to the command SUBST A: C:\. Use ASSIGN with caution, as it hides actual drive information (such as the device type) from commands and programs that require such drive information. The DISKCOMP and DISKCOPY commands ignore drive assignments, and will work with ASSIGN. *Never* use ASSIGN with commands that need drive information, such as BACKUP, JOIN, LABEL, PRINT, RESTORE, SUBST, and FORMAT.

To cancel ASSIGN, type **ASSIGN** with no parameters.

ATTRIB

(External) MS/PC DOS 3.0

Description   ATTRIB sets the file attributes, or flags, that tell DOS to give a file special treatment. You can use this command to prevent accidental erasure of files or to flag a file for later backup.

Syntax

attrib [+ ¦ −a] [+ ¦ −r] *path name* [/s]

Options

+a	Sets the archive flag (file needs to be backed up or archived)
−a	Clears the archive flag (file has been backed up)
+r	Makes the file read-only (cannot be changed or erased)
−r	Disables read-only (file can be written to or erased)
/s	Processes the chosen attributes for all subdirectories of the target directory

Example

```
attrib +r needed.txt
```

Sets the needed.txt file to read-only.

Comments   Non-DOS (third party) attribute-setting utilities generally allow enabling/disabling of all four attributes (archive, hidden, read-only, and system), not just two or three of them.

BACKUP

(External) MS/PC DOS 2.0

Description   BACKUP is used to make backup copies of files, usually from a hard disk to floppies or streaming tape.

Syntax

backup *source[path name] destination [options]*

Options

/s	Backs up all subdirectories beginning at the specified path name
/m	Backs up only those files modified since last backup
/a	Adds files to destination disk (does not erase files already present)
/d:*date*	Backs up only those files modified after specified date
/l:*filename*	Creates or appends to a *log file* (a list of all files backed up during the session) named *filename* in the root directory
/t:*time*	Backs up only those files modified after specified *time*
/f	Formats target disk, if not already formatted
/f:*size*	Formats to specified capacity of 160, 180, 320, 360, 720, 1200, or 1400K (DOS 4.0)

Example

```
backup c: a: /s
```

Backs up all files on drive C (including all its subdirectories) to drive A.

Comments Make sure you have enough floppy disks available. In versions before DOS 4.0, make sure they are already formatted. DOS prompts you to insert each floppy disk in numerical sequence, so be sure to mark each completed floppy disk (with a felt-tip marking pen) as soon as you replace it with the next disk to receive backup. Numbering your backup disks makes it easy to use the RESTORE command correctly.

BREAK

(Internal) MS/PC DOS 2.0

Description BREAK tells DOS how often to check for CTRL-C or CTRL-BREAK keypresses. The default is BREAK OFF. Some programs do not tolerate BREAK ON.

Syntax

break [on ¦ off]

Examples

```
break on
```

Break checking is on. DOS checks for CTRL-C or CTRL-BREAK more frequently.

```
break off
```

Break checking is off. DOS will detect CTRL-C or CTRL-BREAK only when looking for keyboard input.

Comments   To see the current BREAK setting, enter **BREAK** without ON or OFF.

CHCP

(Internal) MS/PC DOS 2.0

Description CHCP allows you to display and change the current code page.

Syntax

chcp [*nnn*]

Options   Enter the number of the code page as the *nnn* option:

Number	Code Page
437	United States English
850	Multilingual
860	Portuguese
863	Canadian French
865	Norwegian

Example

chcp 850

Selects the Multilingual code page.

Comments   DOS allows you to select different character sets for international use. For example, different code pages may use different currency symbols or vary in the way the time and date are displayed. You must issue the NLSFUNC command to select alternative code pages. To display the current code page, enter **CHCP** without any code page number.

CHDIR or CD

(Internal) MS/PC DOS 2.0

Description   CHDIR or CD allows you to switch between directories on a drive. Practice with this command. When used properly, it allows you to move through directories smoothly.

Syntax

chdir [*drive:*][*path*]
cd [*drive:*][*path*]

Examples

cd

Tells you the current directory.

cd \

Takes you to the root directory.

cd newdir

Takes you to the directory named NEWDIR directly below the current directory.

```
cd \newdir
```

The backslash tells DOS to expect to find the new directory not below the current directory but, instead, below the root directory. An initial backslash always stands for the root directory.

```
cd ..
```

The two dots tell DOS to move from a subdirectory up one level, to the parent directory.

CHKDSK

(External) MS/PC DOS 1.0

Description   The CHKDSK command checks a disk for specific problems, and reports the amount of space used and available.

Syntax

chkdsk [*drive:*] [*options*]

Options

/f	Fixes lost clusters and other disk errors
/v	Displays files and directories as checked

Example

```
chkdsk /f
```

Checks the current drive for bad sectors and logical consistency. Also fixes any file allocation errors, if you respond "Y" to the message "Convert lost clusters to files?"

Comments   It is best to reboot before answering the "Convert lost clusters?" message with yes. Sometimes the whole problem is just a minor glitch in the BIOS, and a yes answer creates unnecessary trouble. If rebooting does not fix the problem, and you don't have a third-party *disk doctor* type of utility (discussed in Chapter 8), answer "Y" to keep the problem from getting worse. When finished you will find one or more files (if there were lost clusters) with the name *filennnn.chk* (FILE0000.CHK, FILE0001.CHK, and so on). You can try the command TYPE to see what these files contain, then erase them (if the data in them is useless) to free up disk space.

CLS

(Internal) MS/PC DOS 2.0

Description   CLS clears the screen and places the prompt and cursor in the upper-left corner of the screen (the home position).

Syntax

cls

COMMAND

(External) MS/PC DOS 1.0

Description   COMMAND starts a new (secondary) command processor.

Syntax

command [*drive:*][*path*] [ctty=*device*] [/e:*nnnnn*] [/p] [/c *string*]

Options

drive:	Indicates drive containing new processor (defaults to current drive)
ctty=*device*	Lets you specify where input and output go
/e:*nnnnn*	Specifies the amount of environment space to allocate
/p	Keeps the second command processor in memory

/c string	Tells the command processor to perform the commands in the string, and return to the first command processor

Examples

```
command c:\dos ctty=com2 /e:1024
```

From a batch file, DOS looks in the C:\DOS directory for the COMMAND .COM file and installs it as the active command processor with an environment of 1024 bytes. Using that copy of COMMAND.COM, DOS then passes control of the computer to the COM2 serial port.

```
command c:\dos /c myprogrm
```

DOS installs the copy of COMMAND.COM in C:\DOS temporarily, just long enough to carry out the /c MYPROGRM command. Then it returns control to the original command processor. In a pre-DOS 3.3 batch file, COMMAND /c [*command*] is equivalent to a DOS 3.3 batch file CALL command.

```
command c:\dos\4dos.com /e:1024 /p
```

DOS installs the proprietary command processor, C:\DOS\4DOS.COM, as the permanent secondary command processor for this session with an environment size of 1024 bytes.

Comments A secondary command processor interprets your command input until you return to the primary command processor by using the EXIT command.

COMP

(External) PC DOS 1.0

Description COMP compares two files and reports whether they are alike. If it finds differences, it explains where the differences occur. It stops comparing after ten mismatches.

Syntax

comp [*drive:*][*path name1*] [*drive:*][*path name2*]

Example

```
comp new.doc c:\bak\old.doc
```

Compares file NEW.DOC in the current directory with file OLD.DOC in the
C:\BAK directory. FC is the MS-DOS command for comparing files.

COPY

(Internal) MS/PC DOS 1.0

Description   The COPY command copies one or more source files into a
specified destination. COPY can also concatenate two or more source files
into a single file, if the specified filenames are connected by a plus sign (+).
If a target filename is not specified, the concatenated files are combined into
a single file under the name of the source file.

Syntax

copy [*drive:*][*path*]source [*/option*] [*drive:*][*path*]target [*/option*]
copy *filename1* + *filename2* + . . . *filenamen* [*target filename*]

Options

/a	ASCII files
/b	Binary files
/v	Read-after-write verify. This option does not compare copies to make sure they are identical. It simply verifies whether the copy, accurate or not, is readable by DOS. To guard against copying errors, use the COMP or FC command.

Examples

```
copy my.txt a:
```

Copies the MY.TXT file to drive A. This example, with no options, illustrates the most commonly used form of the COPY command.

```
copy *.doc + finished.doc
```

Copies all .DOC files to one file called FINISHED.DOC.

```
copy my.txt prn
```

Copies the MY.TXT file to the printer.

```
copy con prn
```

Copies from the console (keyboard) to the printer, so your keyboard acts like a typewriter.

```
copy con my.txt
```

Copies console (keyboard) input directly to MY.TXT file.

Comments The last two examples shown copy your keypresses to the printer, like a typewriter, or to a file. In both cases, end the copying process by pressing F6 or ^Z. This inserts an end-of-file marker and returns you to the DOS prompt.

Get to know the /b option when copying files. Some files contain graphics or special formatting instructions that DOS may misinterpret as marking the end of a file. If you use /b, DOS will not mistakenly cut off the end of such a file.

CTTY

(Internal) MS/PC DOS 2.0

Description CTTY makes the PC behave like an old-fashioned TTY terminal, by transferring control from the console (keyboard) to another device, such as a serial port. Technically, CTTY changes the place where DOS looks for input and to which it sends output.

Syntax

ctty *device*

Examples

ctty com2

Transfers control of the computer to the COM2 serial port.

ctty aux

Gives control to an AUX (auxiliary) port, typically COM1.

ctty nul
[*any batch file command*]
ctty con

This CTTY command series is used only as part of a batch file. It clears all screen output while DOS carries out a series of commands. The CTTY CON command at the end of the series then restores screen output and keyboard control.

Comments   CTTY is useful for giving control to a second computer, such as a laptop, so you can copy files back and forth or operate by remote control. The CTTY NUL and CTTY CON series can be used as part of batch files to keep messages off the screen that cannot otherwise be kept quiet, for example "File not found." Be careful—if your batch file hangs, you'll have to reset the computer using either a reset button or the power switch—CTL-ALT-DEL won't work.

DATE

(Internal) MS/PC DOS 1.0

Description   Displays date, with option to change.

Syntax

date [*mm/dd/yy*]

Comments The format shown assumes you are using the default United States English code page. Whenever DOS asks for a new date, it will show you the default values currently in effect. Enter your new values using the same format that DOS shows. To retain the current setting, press ENTER.

DEBUG

(External) MS/PC DOS 1.0

Description DEBUG provides a controlled testing environment for working with .EXE and .COM files. You can directly change CPU register and executable file contents and test the results immediately.

Syntax

debug [*path name*] [*path name options*]

Examples

debug

DEBUG replies with a hyphen prompt (-), telling you it is ready to accept your commands.

debug myprog.exe [/*myprog options*]

Loads MYPROG.EXE into memory starting at the lowest available memory segment. /*myprog options* is any option or argument list you wish to pass to MYPROG.EXE to control its behavior.

Comments DEBUG is often used with redirected input from script files. It is a powerful program that takes some study and practice to master.

DEL

(Internal) MS/PC DOS 1.0

Description   Erases files or the entire contents of directories. DEL is the same as ERASE.

Syntax

del [*drive:*]*path name*

Examples

del myfile.txt

Deletes the MYFILE.TXT file.

del myfile.*

Deletes all files named MYFILE, no matter what their extensions are.

Comments   Be careful when using wildcards with DEL. This command tells the program to delete everything that matches, and unless you have specified DEL *.* to delete everything, DOS won't ask you for a confirmation before proceeding. Mistakes can be disastrous. For example, if you have a directory named MYTXT, and you are trying to delete a file named MY.TXT, leaving out the dot (.) in the filespec will result in an "Are you sure?" message. If you answer "Y" without thinking, you will erase the entire contents of your MYTXT subdirectory.

DIR

(Internal) MS/PC DOS 1.0

Description   DIR displays the contents of the current or specified directory.

Syntax

dir [*drive:*][*path*][*filename*] [*options*]

Options

/p	Displays one page at a time
/w	Wide directory listing (five filenames across; filenames only)

Examples

```
dir a:
```

Lists everything on drive A.

```
dir *.fil /p
```

Displays a single-column directory of all files with a .FIL extension, pausing when the screen becomes full until you press a key to continue the list.

DISKCOMP

(External) MS/PC DOS 1.0

Description   DISKCOMP compares two floppy disks of the same format and reports if differences exist.

Syntax

diskcomp [*drive1*: [*drive2*:]] [/1] [/8]

Options

/1	Compares only the first side of the disks, even if the floppy disks are double-sided
/8	Compares only 8 sectors per track, even if the first disk contains more sectors per track

Example

```
diskcomp a: b:
```

Compares the disk in drive A with the disk in drive B.

Comments   DISCOMP entered by itself will prompt you to place the source and target disks in the appropriate drives. If you have only one drive, DISKCOMP will first read the source disk, then prompt you to insert the target disk and read the target disk for comparison. Disks to be compared must be of the same size and capacity.

DISKCOPY

(External) MS/PC DOS 1.0

Description   DISKCOPY copies a disk of one format to another disk of the same format. DOS formats the disk as it copies.

Syntax

diskcopy [*drive1*: [*drive2*:]] [/1]

Options

/1   Causes DISKCOPY to copy only side 1

Example

```
diskcopy a: b:
```

Copies the contents of the disk in drive A to the disk in drive B.

Comments   If you enter DISKCOPY by itself, DOS prompts you to put the source disk into the current drive, copies as much of it as memory permits, and then prompts you to remove the source disk and insert the target disk. If the target disk is not formatted, DOS formats it automatically before copying. If the target disk already has files on it, DOS overwrites them. Always run DISKCOMP after using DISKCOPY.

DOSSHELL

(External) MS-DOS 4.0

Description   DOSSHELL is a separate DOS shell utility program (Chapter 8). This is *not* the SHELL= command used in the CONFIG.SYS file, which is described in Chapter 11. Released as a graphics extension of the DOS 4.0 operating system, DOSSHELL is a full-featured shell/utility program. It allows text or graphics mode, and has a customizable menu system, but it requires a graphics adapter to use the icon option.

Syntax

dosshell

Comments   The DOS shell is invoked from the command prompt by use of a batch file titled DOSSHELL.BAT, or as the final line in AUTOEXEC-.BAT. The DOSSHELL batch file is created during the MS-DOS 4.0 installation procedure. Options can be changed while inside the shell. Details about the various options are in the manual for running the DOS shell program.

EDLIN

(External) MS/PC DOS 1.0

Description   This is the difficult and unfriendly editing program packaged with early versions. Many third-party text editors have been created to provide a usable alternative.

Syntax

edlin *filename* [/b]

Options

/b   Loads entire file according to the size indicated in the file allocation table, even if the file contains the end-of-file mark (ASCII code 26)

Example

```
edlin myfile.txt
```

Loads MYFILE.TXT file into the editor.

Comments   The /b option works with EDLIN the same as it does with the COPY command.

ERASE

(Internal) MS/PC DOS 1.0

Description   This command erases files or the entire contents of directories. It is the same as the DEL command.

Syntax

erase [*drive:*]*path name*

Example

erase my.txt

Erases the MY.TXT file.

Comments   Be careful when using ERASE commands. See DEL for specific cautions.

EXE2BIN

(External) MS/PC DOS 2.0

Description   EXE2BIN converts an .EXE file into a binary format .COM file.

Syntax

exe2bin *filename1 filename2*

Example

exe2bin oldfile.exe newfile.com

Converts a file named OLDFILE.EXE into NEWFILE.COM.

EXIT

(Internal) MS/PC DOS 2.0

Description   EXIT returns you to a running program from a DOS shell, or cancels a running secondary processor (see COMMAND).

Syntax

exit

Comments   Typed at the DOS prompt from inside a secondary command processor, this command returns you to your original command processor. If the second processor was invoked as a shell from an applications program, typing **EXIT** returns you to your original working screen.

FASTOPEN

(External) MS/PC DOS 3.3. Cannot be used on a network.

Description   FASTOPEN speeds up access to files and directories by remembering both logical and physical file locations. This command works only on hard disks, and can work with up to four hard disks at once. Each stored directory entry takes 35 bytes of memory. The command can be invoked only once per session. Most people prefer to use a disk cache program.

Syntax

fastopen *drive:*[= *numfile*[*fileext*]] [/x]

Options

numfile	Number of files FASTOPEN will work with, from 10 to 999 (default is 10)
fileext	Number of file extent entries, from 1 to 999
/x	FASTOPEN cache of file extensions will be stored in LIM 4.0 expanded memory. (DOS 4.0)

Examples

```
fastopen c:=100
```

Lets DOS track the location of up to 100 files on drive C.

```
fastopen c:=50,10
```

DOS will track up to 50 working files on drive C, with up to 10 contiguous files open.

```
fastopen c:=100 /x
```

DOS will work with up to 100 files in expanded (LIM 4.0) memory.

Comments   Use FASTOPEN with caution, because it is not compatible with all third-party disk utilities, such as caches and disk optimizers. FAST-OPEN can be used only once per session. Don't use it with SUBST, ASSIGN, or JOIN.

FC

(External) MS-DOS 2.0

Description   This command compares two files, or sets of files, and reports differences. Its options make it more flexible than the COMP command, especially when comparing ASCII text files.

Syntax

fc [/options] [drive:]path name1 [drive:]path name2

Options

/a	Shortens the output of the ASCII comparison to the first and last line of any set of differences.
/b	Forces a binary comparison.

/c	Ignores the case of the letters.
/l	Compares files line by line (used automatically for text files).
/lb *n*	Sets the internal line buffer to the number of lines specified in *n* (default is 100). If FC finds more than *n* consecutive different lines in a file, it reports only that resync failed and stops comparing.
/n	Displays line numbers.
/t	Will not expand tabs to spaces.
/w	Compresses white space.
/*nnnnn*	Specifies the number of lines that must match after a difference (default is 2).

Example

```
fc /a myfile.txt yourfile.txt
```

Compares the two files, MYFILE.TXT and YOURFILE.TXT. The /a option abbreviates the report to be only the beginning and ending lines of the sections that are different.

Comments   Setting /lb 1 or /lb 2 will speed operation, but in most cases it will not detail the differences. Use /w to ignore extra blank lines and spaces.

FDISK

(External) MS/PC DOS 3.2. Cannot be used on a network.

Description   This is a menu-driven hard disk partitioning program. *Warning*: Improper use can cause an irrevocable loss of your hard disk files.

Syntax

fdisk

Example

```
fdisk
```

Invokes FDISK and displays the first menu.

Comments Use this command with extreme caution. It will permanently delete all current information stored on your hard disk. It is recommended for use only on hard disks that have not been used before.

FIND

(External) MS/PC DOS. Cannot be used on a network.

Description FIND searches for a string in a file or group of files and displays the lines containing the text string. The string must be inside quotation marks.

Syntax

find [/v] [/c] [/n] *"string"* [*path name...*]

Options

/v	Displays only the lines not containing *"string"*
/c	Shows how many lines contain *"string"*
/n	Displays line numbers of lines containing *"string"*

Examples

```
find "invoice" billing.doc
```

Displays all lines in BILLING.DOC that contain the word *invoice*.

```
dir | find "TXT"
```

The DIR listing is piped (using the | symbol) into the FIND program, which displays onscreen every line in the listing that includes the extension .TXT.

Comments FIND does not allow wildcards, so you have to be specific. Searches are case-sensitive. When searching files for text, FIND will not look past the first end-of-file marker that it encounters.

FIND is normally used as a filter; that is, it reads an entire file (up to the first EOF marker), looking for instances of the named string of characters. FIND's output, determined by the various options, is often used with pipes and redirection, as shown in the second example.

FORMAT

(External) MS/PC DOS 1.0. Cannot be used on a network.

Description The FORMAT command formats floppy disks according to the options selected, or to the default format for the drive.

Syntax

format [*drive:*] [*options*]

Options

/s	Copies the system files to the formatted floppy disk
/v	Allows setting of the volume name
/1	Forces single-sided format
/4	Forces 360K format on a 1.2MB drive
/8	Formats 9 sectors but uses only 8
/t:80	Sets number of tracks to 80
/t:40	Sets number of tracks to 40
/n:9	Sets number of sectors to 9
/n:8	Sets number of sectors to 8
/b	Formats 9 sectors but uses only 8; reserves space for system files
/f	In DOS 4, specifies disk capacity in K as 160, 180, 320, 360, 720, 1200, or 1440

Example

```
format a:
```

This straightforward command tells DOS to format the disk in drive A.

Comments FORMAT destroys any previous disk formatting, but sector-by-sector editors may be able to recover data. Some third-party formatting programs, such as Norton's Safe Format, save a table of old data locations to make later recovery easier. In DOS 4, if you use the /f option, you can add K, KB, M, or MB to the size designator and use 1.2 or 1.44 instead of 1200 or 1440.

GRAFTABL

(External) MS/PC DOS 3.0

Description GRAFTABL enables DOS to display different language characters for use with a color graphics adaptor (CGA). United States English is the default setting. This command set is not required on EGA and newer cards, because later standards have these characters built in. It is not required for monochrome monitors.

Syntax

graftabl [*nnn* ¦ /sta[tus] ¦ ?]

Options Enter the number of the character set as the *nnn* option:

437	United States English
850	Multilingual
865	Norwegian
860	Portuguese
863	Canadian French

The /status switch displays the currently selected country code page. Typing ? displays a Help screen.

Example

graftabl 865

Loads the Norwegian character set.

Comments   Entered with no options, GRAFTABL will load the United States English character set by default. GRAFTABL is used only with CGA monitors. You can change the active character set at any time.

GRAPHICS

(External) MS/PC DOS 2.0

Description   This command enables DOS to print onscreen graphics using IBM printers by pressing the SHIFT-PRINT SCREEN key combination. The correct syntax depends on which IBM printer you are using. See your printer manual for more information.

JOIN

(External) MS/PC DOS 3.1. Cannot be used on a network.

Description   This command lets you join a disk drive to a directory on another drive. You can thus use another drive as if it were a directory on your current drive.

Syntax

join [*drive1*: [*drive2*:*path*]] [/d]

Options

/d	Turns off (disconnects) a JOIN command
drive1:	Disk drive being joined to a subdirectory on another disk
drive2:*path*	Path name to be used for the joined disk drive (must be joined to an empty root-level subdirectory only)

Examples

```
join
```

Displays all current joins.

```
join a: c:\join
```

Makes DOS treat drive A as part of the C:\JOIN subdirectory.

```
join a: c:\work\join
```

This example will *not* work, because C:\WORK\JOIN is not a root-level subdirectory.

```
join a: /d
```

Drive A is now disconnected from a previously defined join.

Comments   JOIN fools DOS into believing that a drive is actually part of another drive. Be careful when using disk-oriented commands like SUBST or ASSIGN with JOIN. Don't use the following commands at all when JOIN is active: BACKUP, CHKDSK, DISKCOMP, DISKCOPY, FDISK, FORMAT, LABEL, RECOVER, RESTORE, and SYS.

KEYB

(External) MS/PC DOS 3.3

Description   KEYB allows the keyboard to produce characters in other languages and to use alternative keyboard layouts.

Syntax

DOS 3.3: keyb [*xx*[,[*code page*],[*filespec*]]]
DOS 4.0: keyb [*xx*[,[*code page*],[*filespec*]]][/ID:*nnn*]

Options   *xx* is a two-letter keyboard code; *code page* usually uses a three-number code page defining the set (see CHCP), *filespec* is a keyboard definition file with a default of KEYBOARD.SYS; and *nnn* is a (DOS 4.0) three-digit number specifying the keyboard in use. Table 12-1 identifies the two-letter *xx* options, code page numbers, and keyboard ID numbers to install the indicated character sets.

Table 12-1

Keyboard Codes and International Character Sets

KEYB Code	International Character Set	Code Page	KEYB ID (4.0)
US	United States English (default)	437	103
DV	Dvorak keyboard layout (MS-DOS only)	---	---
BE	Belgian	437	120
CF	Canadian French (DOS 4.0)	863	058
DF	Danish (DOS 4.0)	865	159
DK	Danish (DOS 3.3)	865	---
FR	French	437	189/120
GR	German	437	129
IT	Italian	437	141/142
LA	Latin American	437	171
NL	Dutch (Netherlands)	437	143
NO	Norwegian	865	155
PO	Portuguese	860	163
SF	Swiss French	437	150
SG	Swiss German	437	000
SP	Spanish	437	172
SU	Finnish	437	153
SV	Swedish	437	153
UK	United Kingdom English	437	166/168

Comments   KEYB entered with no options will report the current keyboard code and its related code page. After KEYB is loaded, press CTRL-ALT-F1 to select the default (United States English) keyboard or CTRL-ALT-F2 to select the alternative keyboard.

Examples

```
keyb it
```

Loads the Italian character set into a standard keyboard.

```
keyb po,,c:\dos\keyboard.sys
```

Loads the Portuguese keyboard layout and tells DOS to look for the KEYBOARD.SYS file on drive C in the \DOS subdirectory. The double commas identify for DOS which option you are specifying.

KEYB*xx*

(External) MS/PC DOS 3.0 through 3.2

Description   KEYB*xx* allows the keyboard to produce characters used in other languages.

Syntax

keyb*xx*

Options   Replace *xx* with the last two letters of the program name. The following *xx* combinations are standard:

KEYBDK	Danish
KEYBFR	French
KEYBGR	German
KEYBIT	Italian
KEYBSP	Spanish
KEYBDV	Dvorak keyboard (MS-DOS only)

Comments   The *xx* value determines which symbols will be installed. After installing one of the keyboard programs, press CTRL-ALT-F1 to select the default (United States English) keyboard, and CTRL-ALT-F2 to select the installed (non-United States English) keyboard.

Example

keybit

Loads the Italian character set.

LABEL

(External) MS/PC DOS 3.1. Cannot be used on a network.

Description   LABEL allows you to assign, change, or delete volume labels of up to 11 characters on floppies and hard disks.

Syntax

label [*drive*:][*label*]

Disallowed Characters   Do not use any of these characters in the label string:

* ? / \ | . , ; : + = < > [ ] ( ) & ^

Examples

```
label
```

Displays the current volume label, if there is one. DOS asks if you want to change or create a new label. Follow the prompts to change, keep, or delete the current label.

```
label a:save disk
```

Labels the disk in drive A as SAVE DISK.

Comments   The LABEL command allows spaces, but prints all characters as uppercase. LABEL will not work on drives currently using either SUBST or JOIN.

MEM

(External) MS/PC DOS 4.0

Description   MEM displays how much memory is used and how much is left free. MEM lists what programs are active in memory by name and memory address.

Syntax

mem [/*options*]

Options

/program   Displays programs loaded into memory
/debug   Displays programming information

Examples

mem /program

Displays location and size of programs currently in memory.

mem /debug

Displays information on programs, internal drivers, and other programming and memory information.

Comments   On systems with more than 1MB memory, MEM will show usage statistics on extended memory already in use and extended memory still available. If a LIM 4.0 driver is installed, MEM will show usage statistics for expanded memory. If the /debug option is used and a LIM 4.0 driver is installed, MEM will identify what drivers (for example, BUFFERS) and programs (for example, FASTOPEN) are currently using the expanded memory.

MKDIR or MD

(Internal) MS/PC DOS 2.0

Description   This command creates new directories.

Syntax

mkdir [*drive:*][*path*]*name*
md [*drive:*][*path*]*name*

Examples

```
md newdir
```

Creates a directory called NEWDIR, one level beneath and branching from the current directory.

```
md \newdir
```

Creates a directory called NEWDIR directly off the root directory of the current drive. An initial backslash always tells DOS to start at the root directory rather than at the current directory.

Comments   The total path name can be up to 63 characters long. DOS will permit two subdirectories with the same name on different paths; for example, \NEWDIR at the root level and \OLDDIR\NEWDIR one level down from the root. But such confusing practices are best avoided.

MODE

(External) MS/PC DOS 1.0

Description   MODE lets you configure communication parameters for external devices, such as serial printers, serial ports, and video displays. The commands and devices handled depend on the version of DOS. MODE also lets you redirect printer output. Because the syntax for each of these actions is different, they are discussed separately. All MODE commands may be reset by entering another MODE command of the same type.

Before DOS 3.0, the colon following a device name was required, not optional. In DOS 3.0 and higher, typing the optional colon as part of the command line has no effect on how MODE carries out the command. Many of the changes made for DOS 4.0 were designed to enhance local area network systems.

MODE has changed many times through the years. DOS version numbers given in the following discussions reflect the earliest version in which a particular MODE command became available. Since DOS 1.0 is no longer used, descriptions are for DOS 2.0 and above except where otherwise noted.

Syntax for MODE to Configure Printer   Sets the characteristics for IBM-compatible printers connected to a parallel printer port (LPT1, LPT2, or LPT3).

mode LPT*n*[:][*chars*][,[*lines*][,p]]   (prior to DOS 4.0)
mode LPT*n*[:][*chars*][,[*lines*][,retry=*x*]]   (DOS 4.0)

Options for MODE to Configure Printer   In DOS 4.0, *x* may equal

e	Returns error from busy port; default
b	Returns busy; same as p in earlier DOS versions
r	Forces "Ready" report even if port is busy
none	Takes no retry action

Examples of MODE to Configure Printer

mode lpt2:80,8,p

This example is for versions of DOS prior to 4.0. It sets output to LPT2, 80 characters wide, and 8 lines per inch, with continuous printer retry. Press CTRL-BREAK to stop.

mode lpt2:132,8,b

For DOS 4.0, this example sets printer output to LPT2, 132 columns (12-pitch), 8 lines per inch, continuous retry if port is busy. Press CTRL-BREAK to stop.

Comments for MODE to Configure Printer   In all DOS versions, printer output (PRN) defaults to LPT1:80,6 if not changed by MODE. Check your printer documentation for the best settings if default settings fail to work correctly.

Syntax for MODE to Configure Serial Port   This command controls configuration of the serial communications adapter.

mode COM*n*[:]*baud*[,*parity*[,*databits*[,*stopbits*[,p]]]]   (prior to DOS 4.0)
mode COM*n*[:]*baud*[,*parity*[,*databits*[,*stopbits*[,retry=*x*]]]]   (DOS 4.0)

Options for MODE to Configure Serial Port

DOS 2.0

COM*n*	COM1, COM2
baud	110, 300, 600, 1200, 2300, 4800, 9600, or 19,200 (use first 2 digits of number)
parity	n = none; o = odd; e = even
databits	7 or 8
stopbits	1 or 2 (default=1, except if baud=110, default=2)
p	Serial printer continuous retry; CTRL-BREAK stops
parity	n = none; o = odd; e = even

DOS 3.0

COM*n*	COM1, COM2, COM3, COM4

DOS 4.0

COM*n*	COM1, COM2, COM3, COM4
baud	110, 300, 600, 1200, 2300, 4800, 9600, or 19,200 (use first 2 digits of number)
parity	n = none; o = odd; e = even; m = mark; s = space
databits	5, 6, 7, or 8
stopbits	1, 1.5, or 2 (default=1, except if baud=110, default=2)
retry=*x*	*x* may be e (reports error if port busy—the default); b (reports busy if port busy—same as p in earlier DOS versions); r (forces "Ready" report); or none (no retries)

Examples for MODE to Configure Serial Port

```
mode com2:48,e,7,1,p
```

For versions of DOS prior to 4.0, this example sets COM2 for a serial printer at 4800 baud, even parity, 7 databits and 1 stopbit, with continuous retry if the printer is not ready.

```
mode com4,19,n,8
```

For DOS 4.0, this sets COM4 for serial communication at 19,200 baud, no parity, and 8 databits (it accepts a default value of 1 stopbit).

Syntax for MODE to Redirect Printer   Redirects output from a parallel port to a serial port, for serial printers.

mode lpt*n*[:] = com*n*[:]

Options for MODE to Redirect Printer

lpt*n*	Printer port number (1, 2, or 3)
com*n*	COM port number

Examples for MODE to Redirect Printer

```
mode lpt1:=com2:
```

This command redirects PRN printer output to a serial printer connected to the COM2 serial port.

Comments for MODE to Redirect Printer   For this MODE command to be effective, first configure the COM port. For example, if your serial printer operates at 4800 baud with even parity, you would first type **MODE COM2:48,e,,,p** then redirect printer output to COM2 with **MODE LPT1: = COM2**. To cancel the printer port redirection, type **MODE LPT1:**.

Syntax for MODE to Select Display   This MODE command selects the active video adapter and the display settings for a color graphics monitor. It also reconfigures the current display.

mode *display type*   (prior to DOS 4.0)
mode *display type* [cols = *c*][lines = *l*]   (DOS 4.0)
mode con[:][cols = *c*][lines = *l*]   (DOS 4.0)

Options for MODE to Select Display Specify the *display type* as one of the following:

40	Any color display, 40 columns
80	Any color display, 80 columns
bw40	Color display, 40 columns, color disabled
bw80	Color display, 80 columns, color disabled
co40	Color, 40 columns
co80	Color, 80 columns
mono	Monochrome display, 80 columns

Additional DOS 4.0 options:

cols$=c$	c may be 40 or 80
lines$=l$	l may be 25, 43, or 50 (43 is for EGA, 50 is for VGA)

Examples for MODE to Select Display

```
mode co80
```

This command sets the color display to 80 columns with color enabled.

```
mode con:lines=50
```

In DOS 4.0, this command sets a VGA monitor to 50 lines per screen.

Comments for MODE to Select Display Sometimes a display will lose the cursor on exiting from an applications program. Often, using a MODE *display type* command will return the cursor to the screen.

Syntax for MODE to Align CGA Display This MODE command shifts a CGA video display to the left or right to correct images that bleed off the screen.

mode *display* [,*shift*] [t]

Options for MODE to Align CGA Display

display	(required) 40, 80, bw40, bw80, co40, co80, mono
shift	l = left; r = right (shifts one character if set to 40 columns, two characters if 80 columns)
t	Displays test pattern after shifting, and prompts you to indicate if new alignment is correct

Example for MODE to Align CGA Display

```
mode CO80,r,t
```

This command shifts an 80-column color display to the right and shows a test pattern. It prompts you to indicate whether or not the screen is properly aligned.

Syntax for MODE to Set Keyboard Rate   In DOS 4.0, this MODE command sets the keyboard typematic (repeat) rate.

```
mode con[:] rate=r delay=d
```

Options for MODE to Set Keyboard Rate

rate=*r*	*r* is a number from 1 to 32 that sets the repeat rate
delay=*d*	*d* is a number from 1 to 4, representing intervals of one fourth of a second, setting the delay before keys start repeating

Example for MODE to Set Keyboard Rate

```
mode con rate=16 delay=1
```

This command sets the keyboard to a mid-range repeat rate, with keys to start repeating after being held down one fourth of a second.

Syntax for MODE to Prepare, Select, or Refresh Code Pages (Non-United States Fonts)   In DOS 3.3, this prepares, then selects or refreshes, code pages for parallel printer or video display. This MODE command works in conjunction with the NLSFUNC and CHCP commands.

mode *device* codepage prepare = (*code page*[,*code page*] ...) *filename*
mode *device* codepage select = *code page*
mode *device* codepage refresh
mode *device* codepage [/sta[tus]]

Options for MODE to Prepare, Select, or Refresh Code Pages

device	(required) CON, PRN, LPT1, LPT2, or LPT3
code page	437, 850, 860, 863, or 865
filename	Full path name of file containing code pages

Examples for MODE to Prepare, Select, or Refresh Code Pages

```
mode con codepage prepare=((850) c:\dos\ega.cpi)
```

This command sets the console to show code page 850 (international fonts), using the code page information (.CPI) file for EGA display.

```
mode lpt1 codepage select=850
```

This command sets the international font, code page 850, for the PRN device connected to LPT1.

```
mode con codepage refresh
```

If the code page is lost, the REFRESH option will reinstate it.

```
mode con codepage
```

This command reports the current code page status for the console device. It acts the same as entering MODE CON CODEPAGE /STA.

Comments for MODE to Prepare, Select, or Refresh Code Pages
MODE will recognize the following abbreviations:

cp	codepage
prep	prepare
sel	select
ref	refresh
/sta	/status

MORE

(External) MS/PC DOS 2.0

Description   MORE takes input from a standard device and outputs it, one screen at a time, on the display. Displays "-- More --" prompt; goes on to the next full screen when any key is pressed.

Syntax

more < [*source*]
[*source*] ¦ more

Examples

```
type my.txt ¦ more
```

Displays MY.TXT file 23 lines at a time.

```
dir ¦ more
```

Displays the directory listing 23 lines at a time.

Comments   Similar to FIND, the MORE command acts as a filter for other programs or files. MORE does not adjust to 43- or 50-line displays. If you enter MORE by itself, it will sit and wait; to return to the DOS prompt, press F6 and then ENTER.

NLSFUNC

(External) MS/PC DOS 2.0

Description   NLSFUNC loads information specific to various countries.

Syntax

nlsfunc [*drive:*][*path name*]

Options

path name	Names the file that contains the extended country information

Example

```
nlsfunc
```

Tells DOS to use the default country-specific information found in COUNTRY.SYS (must be in default directory).

Comments   DOS issues an error message if NLSFUNC is already loaded. NLSFUNC checks for the correct DOS version before loading itself. Your CONFIG.SYS file determines the default path name. You can use the DOS 4.0 INSTALL command in your CONFIG.SYS file to install NLSFUNC.EXE.

PATH

(Internal) MS/PC DOS 2.0

Description   PATH establishes a search path for executable program files. PATH is usually set in your AUTOEXEC.BAT file and is an efficient way to access your most commonly used applications and directories.

Syntax

path [*drive:path*[;*drive:path*. . .]]

Examples

`path`

Displays the search path currently in effect.

`path c:\mywork;d:\yourwork\wstar`

Sets the path through two directories—C:\MYWORK and D:\YOUR-WORK\WSTAR.

Comments   Note the semicolons (;) between directories in the second example. When you enter a command that is not internal to the COM-MAND.COM command interpreter, DOS looks for an executable file in the current (default) directory. If the program is not there, it looks next in C:\MYWORK for the executable file, and then in the D:\YOURWORK \WSTAR directory. If DOS still does not find the executable file, it tells you it cannot find the file. The maximum length for a search path is 127 characters. You can change the path at any time. The command PATH ; cancels the path entirely.

PRINT

(External) MS/PC DOS 2.0

Description   This command sets up a printer queue and prints files in the background while you continue your work in another program.

Syntax

print [*path name*] [*options*]

Options

/d:*device*   Names the output device. DOS assumes PRN
                                     (printer) if not otherwise specified. Other valid
                                     devices are LPT1, LPT2, LPT3, AUX, COM1,
                                     and COM2.

/b:*bufsize*	Buffer size, from 1 to 32767 bytes; 512 is the default.
/u:*busytick*	Number of time-ticks PRINT will wait per timeslice for the printer to become available to receive characters. A timeslice is the period during which PRINT has charge of the CPU before returning control to DOS. There are 18.2 time-ticks per second; valid range is 1 to 255; 1 is the default.
/m:*maxtick*	Maximum number of time-ticks PRINT can control the CPU during each timeslice. Range is 1 to 255; default is 2. Larger values improve printer performance by "stealing" time from foreground programs, which may perform more slowly as a result.
/s:*timeslice*	Sets number of timeslices per second during which printer will be given control of the system. Range is 1 to 255; 8 is the default.
/q:*size*	Tells DOS the number of files it can queue; range is 4 to 32; 10 is the default.
/t	Stops all printing.
/c	Removes a file from print queue.
/p	Prints preceding file and adds new files to print queue.

Examples

```
print mytext.txt
```

Adds the MYTEXT.TXT file in the current directory to the print queue. PRINT then feeds the file to the printer while you continue with other work.

```
print mytext.txt /c mytext2.txt /p
```

Cancels printing of MYTEXT.TXT (halts printing, if in progress) and adds the file MYTEXT2.TXT to the print queue.

Comments The PRINT command is equivalent to a primitive printer spooler. PRINT cannot perform any sophisticated formatting; however, if your word processor has a print-to-disk option, you can use that to create a file with printer codes already incorporated. Then you can use PRINT to get the formatted output while you continue with other work.

PROMPT

(Internal) MS/PC DOS 2.0

Description PROMPT lets you set the DOS prompt to anything you like. It uses *metacharacters* (see "Options") for information such as current path, time, date, DOS version, and so on.

Syntax

prompt [*string*]

Examples

```
prompt $p$g
```

This example produces the so-called "pregnant prompt." It displays your current directory followed by a greater-than sign. Thus, C:\UTIL> indicates you are in the UTIL directory of drive C.

```
prompt
```

Returns the prompt to its default.

```
prompt The Time Is $t$_Your Wish $_Is My Command $g
```

Creates a prompt reporting the time, followed by a string, like this:

```
The Time Is 12:23:15.32
Your Wish
Is My Command >
```

You can use six $h backspace metacharacters (see "Options") to get rid of the seconds value in the time display, leaving an *hh:mm* time report.

Options   The following are called *metacharacters*; they tell DOS to report some system value, such as the time, or take some action on the display, such as backspacing. Some produce the DOS piping and redirection characters, which you cannot type into a PROMPT string without confusing DOS.

$$	$ character
$t	Time
$d	Date
$p	Current drive and directory
$v	DOS version number
$n	Current drive
$g	> character
$l	< character
$b	¦ character
$q	= character
$h	Backspace; erases the previous character (use with $t or $d)
$e	Escape character, used to insert ANSI codes for color, and so on
$_	Begins a new line on the display

RECOVER

(External) MS/PC DOS 2.0. Cannot be used on a network.

Description   RECOVER lets you recover files from a disk if one or more sectors have gone bad.

Syntax

recover [*drive*:][*path name*]
recover *drive*:

Examples

```
recover c:\letters\myletter.txt
```

Recovers the MYLETTER.TXT file in the LETTERS directory on drive C.

```
recover a:
```

Recovers all files on drive A.

Comments   RECOVER is a dangerous command. If you specify an entire
hard disk, RECOVER will try to recover every file into the root directory—
and there's a limit to the number of files the root directory can hold at one
time. You can easily lose files instead of saving them.

   RECOVER reads the specified file sector by sector, skipping bad sectors, so it probably won't work on binary files. The files it recovers are
placed in the root directory, named FILE*nnnn*.REC, where *nnnn* is a
four-digit number beginning with 0001.

   If you recover more than one file at a time, it's easy to lose track of the
recovered files' original names. You are better off trying to recover specific
files one at a time, as in the first example. Better yet, use a third-party
utility program such as the Norton Utilities (Chapter 8) to recover lost files.

RENAME or REN

(Internal) MS/PC DOS 1.0

Description   This command renames files.

Syntax

rename [*drive:*]*path name filename*
ren [*drive:*]*path name filename*

Examples

```
ren *.doc *.wp
```

Renames all files with .DOC extension to the same filenames with a .WP
extension.

```
ren a:my.txt your.txt
```

Renames the file MY.TXT on drive A to YOUR.TXT on the same drive.
Note that the drive designation is not required for the new name.

REPLACE

(External) MS/PC DOS 3.2

Description   REPLACE selectively updates, adds, or replaces files on a destination path name with files from a source path name.

Syntax

replace [*drive:*]*source* [*destination*] [*options*]

Options

/a	Adds only files that do not already exist on the destination drive and path
/r	Allows destination files marked read-only to be overwritten
/p	Prompts you before copying files
/s	Searches all subdirectories of destination directory; cannot be used with /a option
/u	Replaces only files in the destination that are older than the same files in the source directory; goes by time and date stamps
/w	Waits for keypress so you can change source disks

Example

```
replace a:\sched.dta c:\ /s
```

Searches for files named SCHED.DTA in all directories of drive C, and replaces them with the SCHED.DTA file from the drive A root directory.

Comments   Wildcards are acceptable in the source filenames. As files are replaced or added, their filenames appear on the screen. The /p option (pause for permission) makes copying with this utility a much safer operation.

RESTORE

(External) MS/PC DOS 2.0

Description   This command restores files previously saved with BACKUP

Syntax

restore *source destination* [*path name*] [*options*]

Options (DOS 3.0 and 4.0)

/s	Restores subdirectories
/p	Prompts before restoring files that have been modified or made read-only since the last backup
/a:*mm-dd-yy*	Restores all backed-up files that have been altered *on or after* the specified date
/b:*mm-dd-yy*	Restores all backed-up files that have been altered *on or before* the specified date
/e:*hh:mm:ss*	Restores all backed-up files that have been altered *on or earlier than* the specified time (DOS 3.3)
/l:*hh:mm:ss*	Restores all backed-up files that have been altered *on or later than* the specified time (DOS 3.3)
/m	Restores all files that have been altered or deleted on the destination disk, since the last backup
/n	Restores files not on the destination disk

Examples

```
restore a: c:\ /s
```

Restores all files on the backup disk in drive A to the root directory and subdirectories of drive C—the basic full-restore operation from drive A backup disks.

```
restore a: c:\work\letters\*.doc
```

Restores all files with an extension of .DOC from the backup disk in drive A to the \WORK\LETTERS subdirectory on drive C.

Exit Codes For use with batch file IF ERRORLEVEL commands, RE-STORE issues one of the following exit codes on finishing:

0	Restore completed normally
1	No files found on source to restore on target
3	User terminated program
4	Error condition terminated program

Comments With DOS versions earlier than 3.3, be careful not to wipe out later-version system files (3.3 and later versions do not allow this mistake). Do not use /b, /a, and /n at the same time. Cancel any directory alias commands such as SUBST, ASSIGN, and JOIN before using RESTORE.

RMDIR or RD

(Internal) MS/PC DOS 2.0

Description RMDIR removes a directory. The specified directory must be empty of files and subdirectories and cannot be the default directory.

Syntax

rmdir [*drive:*]*path name*
rd [*drive:*]*path name*

Examples

```
rmdir work
```

Removes the WORK subdirectory of the current directory.

```
rd work\letters
```

Removes the LETTERS subdirectory of the WORK directory.

```
rd \letters
```

Removes the LETTERS subdirectory from the current drive's root directory.

Comments   If DOS refuses to remove an apparently empty directory, it may contain hidden files. These are sometimes created by applications programs, and may be required. Some third-party utility programs can change the hidden attribute or delete such files, but take such actions with caution.

SELECT

(External) MS/PC DOS 4.0

Description   SELECT installs DOS on a hard or floppy disk using a specified country keyboard layout and character set.

Syntax

select [[a:][b:] *destination drive* [*path*]] [*xxx* [*yy*]]

Options

a: or b:	Source drive (default is a:)
destination drive	Can be any drive (default is b:); this is the disk to be formatted
xxx	Three-digit country code
yy	Keyboard code

For *xxx* and *yy*, select from these codes:

Country	Keyboard	Country Name
001	us	United States
002	cf	French Canadian
003	la	Latin America
031	nl	Netherlands
032	be	Belgium
033	fr	France
034	sp	Spain
039	it	Italy
041		Switzerland
	sg	Swiss-German

	sf	Swiss-French
044	uk	United Kingdom
045	dk	Denmark
046	sv	Sweden
047	no	Norway
049	gr	Germany
061	us *or* uk	English (generic)
351	po	Portugal
358	su	Finland

Example

```
select b: a: 041 sf
```

This example uses a source disk in drive B to create a DOS system disk in drive A that will use Swiss time and date formats, and a Swiss-French keyboard layout.

Comments   Be careful when using this command, as it runs the FORMAT command as part of its normal operation. In DOS 4.0 and later, SELECT uses a menu and highlight bar, with the default settings highlighted. The DOS 4.0 SELECT command is more complex, requiring you to specify the amount of memory available on a system, how much memory is available, the type of printer (serial or parallel), and whether you have an expanded memory card.

SET

(Internal) MS/PC DOS 2.0

Description   This command sets environment variables.

Syntax

set [*envname* = [*param*]]

Examples

```
set
```

Displays the current environment variables.

```
set temp=c:\temp
```

Sets an environment variable named TEMP equal to C:\TEMP.

Comments Environment variables can be any string you specify, and can be used by DOS commands and applications programs. In the TEMP = C:\TEMP example, a program might find a location for its temporary files by reading an environment variable named TEMP. Batch files can also use environment variables but, before DOS 3.3, batch file use was full of bugs and not reliable.

SHARE

(External) MS/PC DOS 3.0

Description SHARE sets up file sharing and locking. It is normally used in a network environment where files are shared.

Syntax

share [*options*]

Options

/f:*n*	Allocates space for information on shared files (default value of *n* is 2048 bytes)
/l:*n*	Sets number of available locks (default is 20)

Comments With SHARE installed, all read/write activities are validated against the original opening file code. For systems smaller than 32MB, you can load SHARE by using the INSTALL command. With SHARE in place, read and write commands can be successfully completed only to the same disk that was originally in the drive. SHARE is included as a "callable" external DOS utility, because some applications packages require SHARE to be present.

SORT

(External) MS/PC DOS 2.0 and later

Description   SORT takes data from the standard input device (for example, a file or a DOS command), sorts it in ascending or descending order, and then sends it to the standard output device (a file, printer, or screen).

Syntax

sort [*options*] < *source*
source ¦ sort [*options*]

Options

/r	Sorts in reverse order
/+*n*	Starts sorting with column *n*

Examples

```
dir ¦ sort /+14
```

Displays a single-column directory listing sorted by file size starting in column 14 of the directory listing.

```
dir ¦ sort /r >revsort.txt
```

Creates file REVSORT.TXT containing the current directory's DIR listing, sorted in reverse order.

```
sort /r <address.fil >prn
```

Sorts file ADDRESS.FIL in reverse order and sends output to printer.

Comments   This filter program (see MORE and FIND) lets you alphabet-ize a file or command output, starting at a certain character position. SORT does not distinguish between upper- and lowercase letters. Before DOS 3.0, SORT placed capital letters before lowercase letters, causing "ADE" to come before "abc."

SUBST

(External) MS/PC DOS 3.1. Cannot be used on a network.

Description   SUBST lets you substitute a drive letter for a drive/path combination.

Syntax

subst [*drive*: *path*]
subst *drive*: /d

Options

/d   Removes SUBST drive assignment from drive
                            specified

Examples

subst g: c:\work\letters\may

Creates virtual drive G for the path name C:\WORK\LETTERS\MAY. You can get to the MAY directory by typing **G:**.

subst g: /d

Cancels the virtual drive G.

Comments   SUBST lets you avoid entering long path names full of \ characters. It also saves space in the PATH statement. You cannot create a virtual drive with a letter higher than the letter designated in the LASTDRIVE= statement in CONFIG.SYS (default is E). When SUBST is in effect, these commands will not work correctly: BACKUP, CHKDSK, DISKCOMP, DISCOPY, FDISK, FORMAT, LABEL, RECOVER, RE-STORE, and SYS.

SYS

(External) MS/PC DOS 1.0. Cannot be used on a network.

Description   SYS transfers DOS system files to a blank, formatted disk.

Syntax

sys *drive*:

Example

sys a:

Transfers system files to drive A.

Comments   On DOS versions earlier than 4.0, system files must reside in a specific contiguous physical area of a disk. If that area is taken by another file, SYS will report that there is no room for system files. Some utility programs, such as Norton's Disk Doctor, will relocate the "intruding" files to make room for the system files. System files are copied in this order: IO.SYS, then MSDOS.SYS. The command processor COMMAND.COM is not transferred by the SYS command. SYS will not work when JOIN or SUBST is in effect.

TIME

(Internal) MS/PC DOS 1.0

Description   TIME sets and displays the system's internal clock. You can also use this command to change the time.

Syntax

time [*hh:mm*[*:ss*[*.cc*]]]

Examples

time

Displays the time and gives the option to set a new time.

time 10:30

Sets the time to 10:30 A.M.

Comments   It is not necessary to provide DOS with the seconds (*ss*) or tenths and hundredths of seconds (*cc*). Some programs, for example utilities designed to synchronize the clocks in two machines, will provide DOS with those values if needed.

TREE

(External) MS/PC DOS 2.0

Description   TREE displays a directory tree listing of directories and files.

Syntax

tree [*drive:*] [/f] [/a]

Options

/f	Displays all the files in the subdirectories
/a	Uses the graphic characters available in code pages for printing (DOS 4.0 only)

Examples

```
tree
```

Displays the names of all directories and subdirectories on the default drive.

```
tree c: /f
```

Displays all directories, subdirectories, and files on drive C.

Comments   To pause between screens, use TREE [*options*] ¦ MORE.

TYPE

(Internal) MS/PC DOS 1.0

Description   TYPE lets you display the contents of a text file on the screen.

Syntax

type [*drive:*]*path name*

Example

```
type myletter.txt
```

Comments   To pause between pages, use the TYPE [*filename*] ¦ MORE command form. When you use the TYPE command on a binary (nontext) file, you get beeps and "Martian poetry"; it's a good way to find out whether a file is a text file. (Type ^C to exit the garbage screen.) TYPE does not accept wildcard specifications.

VER

(Internal) MS/PC DOS 2.0

Description   VER displays the DOS version number.

Syntax

ver

VERIFY

(Internal) MS/PC DOS 2.0

Description   VERIFY turns the disk write verification on or off.

Syntax

verify [on ¦ off]

Example

```
verify on
```

Comments   By itself, VERIFY tells you if it is on or off. When on, it verifies that disk writes were successful, but does not verify that a copied file is identical to the original; use COMP or FC for that purpose. VERIFY takes longer to copy, but detects and notifies you if a disk write fails.

VOL

(Internal) MS/PC DOS 2.0

Description   VOL displays the volume name (label) if one exists.

Syntax

vol [*drive:*]

Example

```
vol a:
```

XCOPY

(External) MS/PC DOS 3.2

Description   XCOPY stands for extended copy. This command allows you to specify additional parameters for a COPY operation and copies multiple files more efficiently than the internal COPY command.

Syntax

xcopy [*path name1*] [*path name2*] [*options*]

Options

/a	Copies only files with the archive bit set; leaves archive bit unchanged on source file after copying
/d:*date*	Copies only those files with a date the same as or later than the date specified
/e	Creates subdirectories on the destination disk, even if subdirectories are empty (must be used with /s)
/m	Copies files that have the archive bit set (modified files), and resets the archive bit on the source file
/p or /c	Prompts you before each file is copied
/s	Copies subdirectories
/v	Verifies data written (not a compare function)
/w	Prompts for and waits for keypress before proceeding

Examples

```
xcopy *.doc a: /s
```

Copies all .DOC files, including those in subdirectories of current directory, to drive A.

```
xcopy a:*.com /a
```

From drive A, copies only .COM files that have the archive bit set (have been changed since they were last backed up).

Exit Codes For use with batch file IF ERRORLEVEL commands, XCOPY issues one of the following exit codes on finishing:

0	Copy completed without error
1	No files found on source fitting specification
2	User terminated copy using CTRL-C
4	Error: Insufficient memory, invalid drive, bad command line syntax, file not found, or path not found
5	Int 24 error reading or writing disk: user aborted

Comments XCOPY reads all specified files at once, up to the limit of memory, before copying to the target disk; this makes it faster than the COPY command and reduces wear on drives. *Path name1* is the source disk or directory; *path name2* is the target. If you omit the target, DOS assumes you want to copy from the source to the current directory. If you omit either file specification, DOS assumes you mean to copy *.* (all files).

BATCH FILE COMMANDS

Batch files (Chapter 11) use only a limited number of commands to work their magic. Here are the built-in commands that enable batch file branching, looping, and other linear programming tricks.

Batch File Command	Description
CALL	Loads and runs a second batch file, then returns to the first batch file at the next line following the CALL command (DOS 3.3)
ECHO	Allows or inhibits the screen display of commands; displays the current settings
FOR	Sets up a loop to carry out a command multiple times
GOTO	Goes to the specified label
IF	Checks to see if a condition is true or false
PAUSE	Pauses the execution of a batch file

REM	Labels a line as a remark or comment rather than as a command to be carried out
SHIFT	Increases the number of control line variables you can have in a batch file by decrementing them one number at a time; useful for looped operations

CONFIG.SYS COMMANDS

The CONFIG.SYS file described in Chapter 11 is used primarily to install special device drivers that modify the way DOS handles disks, memory, file buffers and handles, and other basic operating elements. It also has some special commands for configuring operating startup values early in the bootstrap process.

CONFIG.SYS Commands	Description
BREAK	Determines whether to check for break sequence during command execution
BUFFERS	Sets up a number of disk sectors to buffer, or hold in memory, between disk reads (see Chapter 17)
COUNTRY	Identifies which country's time, date, currency, and case conversions you will use; most easily set using the SELECT command
DEVICE	Loads a device driver, including ANSI .SYS, DISPLAY.SYS, EMM386.SYS, DRIVER.SYS, PRINTER.SYS, RAM-DRIVE.SYS, and VDISK.SYS
DRIVPARM	Sets the parameters for a drive
FILES	Sets the number of files that can be open at the same time
LASTDRIVE	Sets the last drive (default is E; maximum is Z)
REM	Creates a remark line in a batch file (DOS 4.0)

CHAPTER THIRTEEN

Introduction to BASIC

BASIC (beginners' all-purpose symbolic instruction code) is one of the world's most popular programming languages. It is easy to learn, yet powerful enough for most personal and business applications.

The language was developed in 1964 by two educators at Dartmouth College as an introductory language for programmers who had to share a single, very large computer. Since then, BASIC has expanded dramatically, becoming the subject of a full ANSI standard in 1988. New and improved implementations like QuickBASIC can handle keyboards, display screens, printers, disk drives, and modems. In fact, there are literally hundreds of BASIC interpreters and compilers available today. This chapter will cover the most common ones in the PC and DOS world.

COMPILERS, INTERPRETERS, AND BASIC

One step up from assembly language are compiled languages, such as COBOL, Pascal, C, and FORTRAN. A COBOL compiler, for example, must be written for the CPU on which it will be run, but the same program code can be compiled to run on a variety of machines, as long as you have the COBOL compiler for that machine. On IBM-compatible systems, after compiling (and sometimes linking), a program can be directly invoked as a named machine language file, such as a .COM or .EXE file under DOS. BASIC actually began as a compiler, written strictly for use with mainframe computers.

A compiler requires a lot of memory. There is an alternative, however. A program called an *interpreter* can translate an applications program's complex code, or instructions, into simple machine language code. Interpreters can be stored in the computer's ROM (or loaded into memory). Each line of code is translated, one at a time, and executed by the computer's own internal language routines before the next statement is interpreted. It is the same whether the program is large or small; each line must be run one at a time, as in a DOS batch file. Programs run by an interpreter have extensions such as .BAS, .PAS, or .C, not .COM or .EXE.

The trend in BASIC is now back to compilers. *Incremental compilers* now exist that take each line of code and do a "partial" compilation; that is, each line is rendered into machine language separately, as you press the ENTER key. Your computer doesn't need a separate interpreter program to run the program. You can just execute the compiled code from your working environment, so you have the convenience of an interpreter with the speed and power of a compiler. You also have the option of generating a .COM or .EXE file.

Versions of BASIC

When you purchase your computer, you are likely to get BASIC, BASICA, GW-BASIC, or a version of QuickBASIC as part of your system package.

BASICA comes with IBM PCs. It cannot run on IBM-compatibles. GW-BASIC comes as part of MS-DOS (versions through 4.01), and runs on true IBM PCs, XTs, and ATs, as well as compatibles. Microsoft developed QuickBASIC as a low-cost, stand-alone modern version of BASIC.

This chapter provides a brief overview of the various BASICs. Chapter 14 is a complete guide to BASIC statements and functions. Each definition in that chapter includes the BASIC version in which the statement/function is used, and usage examples.

BASIC AS A COMPUTER LANGUAGE

Every procedural computer language, whether interpreter or compiler, has certain elemental building blocks. These elements, and any constraints that apply to them, are dictated to some extent by the fact that every line of source code must be *parsed* (broken into its component parts) by the interpreter or compiler in order to translate the code. For this reason, virtually all programming languages have a list of *keywords* (also called *reserved* words), such as PRINT, that the programmer must always use in a specific way. Misuse of these special words will confuse the compiler and usually generate a syntax error. As in English, a *syntax error* is something the compiler sees as a misinterpretation of the rules. The syntax rules are applied to a word preceded and followed by *white space* (blank spaces or tabs).

The following paragraphs explain BASIC keywords, commands, statements, functions, and variables.

Keywords

PRINT, GOTO, GOSUB, and LET are examples of the 200 or so keywords in BASIC. These words cannot be used as variable names or line labels, but they can be used in a command combination such as PRINT.LINE.FIVE or GOTO.NEXT.

Commands

All commands are keywords. Commands are used to load and save programs, to edit programs, and to perform other program maintenance operations. Commands are generally executed in *direct mode*—in other words, at the interpreter's command level. When you start BASIC, the BASIC prompt, OK, indicates that your system is at the command level.

Note: In QuickBASIC, most of the commands appear in the menu bar at the top of the screen.

Statements

Statements, such as FOR, SAVE, CLOSE, and others, are used in BASIC program lines. Running the program executes these statements as they occur. Essentially, a statement tells the program what to do next. All statements are keywords.

Functions

Functions are used in BASIC to return values. Functions are either numeric, string, or user-defined. All built-in functions, and the user-defined functions built with the BASIC DEF FN statement, are keywords.

Numeric Functions

BASIC can perform arithmetic or algebraic calculations. Examples of numeric functions are returning the sine (SIN), cosine (COS), or tangent (TAN) of an angle. Integer or single precision results are normally returned by numeric functions, but the programmer can request other results.

String Functions

TIME$ and DATE$ are examples of string functions. They return a *string* (a sequence of characters) representing the time and date. If the current time and date are entered during system startup or were in CMOS RAM at startup, the values returned by those string functions will be the time and date from the system's internal clock.

User-Defined Functions

The DEF FN statement can be used to write string or numeric functions of the programmer's choice.

Constants and Variables

The values used during the operation of a program take three forms. A value may be one that you use only once; it may be a named constant (a value that is assigned and never changes); or it may be a named variable, which is assigned new values during the execution of the program.

String and Numeric Constants or Variables

A *constant* is defined by alphanumeric characters (0 to 255) enclosed in double quotation marks. "Hello World", "$2,345.00", and "John Jones" are examples of string constants.

There are five types of numeric constants—integer, fixed point, floating point, hexadecimal, and octal. Numeric constants should be entered without commas; for example, enter 10,000 as 10000.

- *Integer values* are numbers between −32768 and +32767. An integer may not contain a decimal point.

- *Fixed point values* are positive or negative real numbers that contain decimal points.

- *Floating point values* are positive or negative numbers represented in exponential form. A floating point value consists of an integer or fixed point number (the *mantissa*), followed by the letter E and an integer (the *exponent*). Both the mantissa and the exponent may be signed.

- *Hexadecimal numbers* are prefixed with the characters &H, for example, &H76 and &H32F.

- *Octal numbers* are prefixed with the characters &O or &, for example, &O347 and &1234.

Numeric values may be integer, single precision, or double precision numbers. Integers are stored as whole numbers only. Single precision numeric values are stored as 7 digits (although only 6 may be accurate). Double precision numeric values are stored as 17 digits.

- A single precision value is any numeric value with either

    7 or fewer digits
    an exponential form using E
    a trailing exclamation point (!)

- A double precision value is any numeric value with either

    8 or more digits
    an exponential form using D
    a trailing number sign (#)

Variable Names and Declarations

Variables represent either numeric values or strings. Variable names in BASIC and QuickBASIC can be any length up to 40 characters. Letters, numbers, and the decimal point are allowed in a variable name. The first character of the variable name must be a letter. Keywords cannot be used as variable names, but a keyword can be embedded within the variable name.

Type Declaration Characters

BASIC recognizes the following type declaration characters, which indicate the type of variable being named:

Character	Type of Variable
$	String
%	Integer
!	Single precision
#	Double precision

Here are sample variable names using each type:

Variable Type	Sample Name
String	BA$
Integer	UPPER.LIM%
Single precision	MIN!
Double precision	P1#

Numeric variables default to single precision. Double precision variables, although more accurate, use more memory and calculation time. Single precision is sufficiently accurate for most applications. Variable names beginning with FN are assumed to be calls to a user-defined function.

The BASIC and QuickBASIC statements DEFINT (define integer), DEFSTR (define string), DEFSNG (define single), and DEFDBL (define double), when included in a program, declare the types of values for certain variable names.

Array Variables

Array (matrix) variables are assigned a name followed by the array dimensions enclosed in parentheses. The dimensions are separated by commas. An array variable name has as many subscripts as there are dimensions in the array.

For example, the array variable aa(9) references a value in a one-dimensional array, and aa(1,4) references a value in a two-dimensional array. You can use up to 255 dimensions in BASIC, with up to 32768 elements per dimension. The maximum number of dimensions is 8 in Quick-BASIC, with 32767 elements per dimension.

EXPRESSIONS AND OPERATORS

An expression contains operators and operands that perform certain operations when an expression is evaluated. An expression can include a string or numeric constant, a variable, or a combination of both constants and variables with operators to produce a single value.

Operators perform mathematical or logical operations on values. The operators provided by BASIC and QuickBASIC are divided into four categories:

Arithmetic
Relational
Logical
Functional

Arithmetic Operators

The following arithmetic operators are recognized by BASIC and Quick-BASIC. They are listed in the order of precedence.

Operator	Operation
^	Exponentiation
−	Negation
*	Multiplication
/	Floating point division
+	Addition
−	Subtraction

BASIC performs the operations within parentheses first. Inside the parentheses, the normal order of precedence is maintained.

Relational Operators

You can use relational operators to compare the values of two strings or two numbers (you cannot compare a string and a number). This comparison will return a true or false evaluation that can then be used to determine the program flow. Here are the relational operators recognized by BASIC and QuickBASIC:

Operator	Operation	Example
=	Equality	x=y
< >	Inequality	x< >y
<	Less than	x<y
>	Greater than	x>y
< =	Less than or equal to	x < = y
> =	Greater than or equal to	x > = y

Logical and Functional Operators

Logical operators perform logical operations on integers. In expressions, these operations are performed after the arithmetic and relational operations. Conversely, functional operators such as SQR (square root) and SIN (sine) are processed after any operations in their arguments are performed.

LOADING BASIC

Both GW-BASIC and BASICA are interpretive BASICs and must be loaded to use the language.

Loading BASIC on a Floppy Disk System

1. If you do not have DOS on your hard disk, insert your working copy of the MS-DOS disk into drive A and press ENTER.

2. After the A prompt, type the following command:

```
gwbasic
```

or

```
basica
```

3. Press ENTER.

Loading BASIC on a Hard Disk System

1. If you have not copied BASIC to your hard drive, do so now.
2. After the C prompt, type the following command:

```
gwbasic
```

or

```
basica
```

3. Press ENTER.

The BASIC prompt, OK, will appear below the line *"XXXXX* Bytes Free"* that indicates how many bytes of memory are available to BASIC. Function key assignments (F1 through F10) appear at the bottom of the screen.

Modes of Operation in BASIC

The OK prompt means BASIC is at command level, ready to accept commands, and may be used in either of two modes: direct or indirect.

Direct Mode

In direct mode, BASIC statements and commands are executed as they are entered. The results of arithmetic and logical operations can be displayed immediately or stored for later use, but the instructions themselves are lost after execution. This mode is useful for debugging BASIC programs, and for using BASIC as a calculator for quick computations that do not require a complete program. Commands, statements, and other executables entered at this level must not be preceded by a line number or label.

Indirect Mode

The indirect mode is used to enter programs. Each line in a BASICA or GW-BASIC program is preceded by a line number. You can execute a program by entering the RUN command.

LOADING QUICKBASIC

To use QuickBASIC, it must be installed on your hard disk. After the C prompt, type **qb** and press ENTER.

BASIC LINES AND PROGRAMS

A BASIC program consists of lines of code containing commands, statements, functions, and variables. In BASIC, BASICA, and GW-BASIC, each line must be preceded by a line number to indicate the program's operation sequence.

BASIC Line Format

BASIC program lines have the following format:

nnnnn statement[statement]

where *nnnnn* is a line number and *statement* is a BASIC statement.

Note: You can have multiple statements per line, but each statement after the first must be preceded by a colon (:).

A BASIC program line always begins with a line number (except for QuickBASIC's), and must contain at least one character but no more than 255 characters. Line numbers indicate the order of execution, and are also used as references. The line number that precedes a program line may be any whole integer from 1 to 65529. It is customary to use line numbers such as 10, 20, 30, and 40, in order to leave room for additional lines that you may wish to include later.

The computer runs the statements in numerical order, no matter how you enter them in the program. For example, if you enter line 35 after line 60, the computer will run line 35 after line 30 and before line 40. You can always use the RENUM (renumber) command to make room for new program lines; you need not reenter the entire program.

When a statement exceeds the width of your screen, the cursor wraps to the next screen line automatically. Use the ENTER key only to indicate the end of the line; resist the temptation to press ENTER as you approach the edge of the screen. You can also press CTRL-ENTER to move the cursor to the beginning of the next screen line without actually entering the line. Then when you press ENTER, the entire logical line is passed to BASIC for storage in the program.

In BASIC, any line of text that begins with a numeric character is considered a program line, and is processed in one of the following three ways when you press ENTER:

- If the line number is legal and if at least one alpha or special character follows the line number in the line, a new line is added to the program.

- If the line number matches an existing line number in the program, the existing line is modified or edited. *Note that reuse of an existing line number causes all of the information in the original line to be lost.* The existing line is replaced with the text of the newly entered line.

- If the line number matches the line number of an existing line and the entered line contains only a line number, the existing line is deleted.

QUICKBASIC LINE FORMAT

In a QuickBASIC program, lines have the following format:

linelabel statement[statement]

where *linelabel* is a line label and *statement* is a QuickBASIC statement.

A QuickBASIC program line can contain up to 255 characters. It may begin with a line label. Line labels are used in flow control statements to indicate the flow of the program. Since BASICA and GW-BASIC programs with line numbers will run under QuickBASIC, you may precede Quick-BASIC lines, also, with a line number. A line number or line label is required only if the line will be referenced elsewhere in the program by a GOTO, GOSUB, or similar statement.

Line labels are alphanumeric and may be up to 40 characters long. They always end with a colon (:). Line numbers can be any combination of digits from 1 to 65529. Line 0 is reserved for error and event trapping statements and should not be used. Some examples of valid line labels are scrn0lupdate:, STRTHERE:, CalculatePayroll:, and calcTAX:. Line labels are not case sensitive, so STRTHERE: and strthere: are the same.

Note: You can have multiple statements per line. Multiple statements on a line are separated by a colon (:) before each statement, after the first statement on the line.

The QuickBASIC program runs from top to bottom and may branch at flow control statements. A program line ends when you press ENTER. The computer will automatically wrap the line for you, or you can press CTRL-ENTER to continue on the next screen line without actually entering the line, as described previously for BASIC programs.

THE BASIC SCREEN EDITOR

You can edit BASIC program lines as you enter them, or after they have been saved in a file.

Editing Lines in New Files

If you type an incorrect character, simply delete it with the BACKSPACE or DEL keys, or with CTRL-H. After the character is deleted, you can continue to type on the line.

If you have not yet pressed the ENTER key to end the line, and you wish to delete the entire current line, press ESC.

To delete the entire program currently in memory, enter the NEW command. NEW lets you clear memory prior to entering a new program.

Editing Lines in Saved Files

Once you have entered your BASIC program and saved it, you may discover that you need to make some changes. To do this, first use the LIST statement to display the program lines that need modification.

1. Reload the program.

2. Type **LIST** or press F1.

3. Type the line number, or range of line numbers, to be edited.

The lines will appear on your screen, where you can edit them as needed. Just position the cursor where a change is to be made, and use any of the following techniques:

- Type over existing characters.

- Delete characters to the left of the cursor, using the BACKSPACE key.

- Delete characters at the cursor position, using the DEL key on the numeric keypad.

- Insert characters at the cursor position by pressing the INS key on the numeric keypad. Characters to the right of the cursor position will move to the right, making room for the new information you type.

- Add or delete characters at the end of the program line.

If you change more than one line, be sure to press ENTER on each modified line. You do not have to move the cursor to the end of the line before pressing the ENTER key. The GW-BASIC interpreter remembers where each line ends and records the entire edited line, even if you press ENTER when the cursor is located in the middle or at the beginning of the edited line. Also, the modified lines will be stored in the proper numerical sequence, even if you don't edit them in numerical order.

Note: Edits to an existing program line are not actually recorded in the BASIC program until the ENTER key is pressed with the cursor positioned somewhere on the edited line.

To truncate a line at the current cursor position (delete to the end of the line), press CTRL-END or press CTRL-E, and then press ENTER. If you have originally saved your program to a program file, make sure that you have also saved the edited version of your program. If you forget this step, your modifications will not be recorded.

THE QUICKBASIC ENVIRONMENT

QuickBASIC, which is far more versatile than GW-BASIC or BASICA, is run and executed from an environment. When you start QuickBASIC, a full screen editor is activated, with pull-down menus that let you enter and run programs from a windowed environment. The screen is initially divided into a menu bar, two windows—the View window and the Immediate window—and a reference bar (see Figure 13-1).

Figure 13-1

A QuickBASIC screen

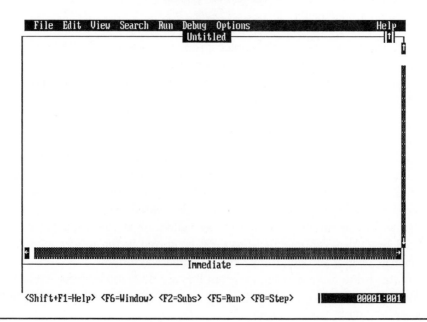

The View window is where you display and edit an existing program, or type lines for a new program. The title at the top of the window shows you which program is currently in the View window. If you start QuickBASIC without including a program name on the command line, the View window will read "Untitled." The View window is just below the menu bar (described in a moment).

The Immediate window lets you work as you would in BASIC's direct mode. In the Immediate window you can type statements to see how they work (for debugging) and do calculations. The Immediate window is just below the View window, but you can size the Immediate window to full screen.

The reference bar below the Immediate window contains information such as your location in the file, the action of the highlighted menu selection, CAPS and NUM LOCK indicators, and the help key (SHIFT-F1 = Help).

Most of your actions will take place in the menu bar area. When you pull down a menu, following some of the menu items that will appear there is a set of three dots (. . .). This means that there is a dialog box associated with that menu selection. The menu bar has the following command-related selections: File, Edit, View, Search, Run, Debug, Options, and Help. Each of these has its own menu with many selections.

CHAPTER FOURTEEN

BASIC Reference

This chapter will provide you with a guide to the commands available in recent versions of BASIC and GWBASIC. For tips on working with these commands, see Chapter 13, "Introduction to BASIC." The following sections describe the commands and give syntax. Some simple examples have been included that may help you to interpret the commands. These are intended for reference use; if you are just learning to program, you might try *GW-BASIC Made Easy* (Albrecht and Inman, Osborne/McGraw-Hill, 1989).

BASIC COMMAND SUMMARY

ABS Function

Syntax   abs(*x*)

Description   Returns the absolute value of *x*.

ASC Function

Syntax   asc(*x$*)

Description   Returns the ASCII code for the first character of the string.

ATN Function

Syntax   atn(*x*)

Description   Returns the arctangent of *x*, where *x* is in radians.

AUTO Command

Syntax   auto *line,increment*

Description   Enables auto line numbering as you enter a program.

BEEP Statement

Syntax   beep

Description   Sounds the speaker; same as PRINT CHR$(07).

BLOAD Command

Syntax   bload *filename,offset*

Description   Loads a memory image from disk into memory.

BSAVE Command

Syntax   bsave *filename,offset,length*

Description   Saves a specified portion of memory to a specified device.

CALL Statement

Syntax   call *subroutine,args*

Description   Calls machine language code.

CDBL Function

Syntax   cdbl(*x*)

Description   Converts an expression to a double-precision number.

CHAIN Statement

Syntax   chain merge *filename,line*,all,delete,*range*

Description   Runs a new program and passes the variables to it.

CHDIR Command

Syntax   chdir *path*

Description   Changes the current directory.

CHR$ Function

Syntax   chr$(*x*)

Description   Converts a number into the ASCII character of the value *x*.

CINT Function

Syntax   cint(*x*)

Description   Converts an expression to an integer.

CIRCLE Statement

Syntax   circle (*x,y*),*radius,color,start,end,aspect*

Description   Draws a circle on a graphics screen.

CLEAR Command

Syntax   clear ,*x,y*

Description   Clears all variables; the second parameter is stack space.

CLOSE Statement

Syntax   close #*x*,#*y*

Description   Closes disk files; parameters are file numbers under which files were opened; CLOSE by itself will close all disk files.

CLS Statement

Syntax   cls

Description   Clears the screen.

COLOR Statement

Syntax   color x,y,z

Description   Allows the selection of foreground, background, and border colors.

COM Statement

Syntax   com(n) on
           com(n) off
           com(n) stop

Description   Allows monitoring of communication activity.

COMMON Statement

Syntax   common x,y

Description   Allows the passing of variables between programs.

CONT Command

Syntax   cont

Description   Continues program execution after a break.

COS Function

Syntax   cos(x)

Description   Returns the cosine of x, where x is in radians.

CSNG Function

Syntax   csng(x)

Description   Converts an expression to a single-precision number.

CSRLIN Variable

Syntax x = csrlin

Description   Returns the current line position of the cursor.

CVD, CVI, CVS Function

Syntax $y\#$ = cvd($x\$$)
$y\%$ = cvi($x\$$)
$y!$ = cvs($x\$$)

Description   Converts the strings to numbers for random-access file handling.

DATA Statement

Syntax   data x,y,z ...

Description   Acts as data-storage line for the READ statement.

DATE$ Statement and Variable

Syntax date$ = *x*$
        x$ = date$

Description Allows retrieval and changing of the system dates.

DEF FN Statement

Syntax def fn *name paramlist = funcdef*

Description Defines a user-written function.

DEF SEG Statement

Syntax def seg = *address*

Description Sets the current segment address for a CALL statement.

DEF*type* Statement

Syntax defdbl
       defint
       defsng
       defstr

Description Defines the variables as double, integer, single, or string.

DEF USR Statement

Syntax def usr*x* = *intexp*

Description Sets the starting address of an assembly language subroutine.

DELETE Command

Syntax delete *line1-line2*

Description Deletes lines in a program.

DIM Statement

Syntax dim *var(sub),var(sub)*

Description Dimensions of subscripted variables.

DRAW Statement

Syntax draw *x$*

Description Allows drawing of objects.

EDIT Command

Syntax edit *line*
      edit .

Description Allows editing of program lines; the period (dot) means the current line.

END Statement

Syntax end

Description Ends the execution of a program.

ENVIRON Statement

Syntax   environ *x*$

Description   Allows changing of the system environment string.

ENVIRON$ Function

Syntax   environ$(*x*)
environ$(*x*$)

Description   Reads the system environment string.

EOF Function

Syntax   eof (*filenum*)

Description   Returns −1 (true) if the end of the file is reached, 0 if not.

ERASE Statement

Syntax   erase *arraylist*

Description   Allows the undimensioning of variables.

ERDEV$ and ERDEV Functions

Syntax   erdev$
erdev

Description   Returns the error code and identifies the device that had the error.

ERL and ERR Variables

Syntax   erl
            err

Description   ERR returns the error code; ERL indicates on what line the error occurred. Used in IF ... THEN statements.

ERROR Statement

Syntax   error *x*

Description   Simulates error conditions.

EXP Function

Syntax   exp(*x*)

Description   Returns the exponent of the expression.

FIELD Statement

Syntax   field *filenum,width* as *x$,y$*...
            field# *filenum,width* as *x$,y$*...

Description   Allocates space in the random-file buffer for variables.

FILES Statement

Syntax   files *filename*

Description   Prints the directory of the drive; works like the DOS DIR command.

FIX Function

Syntax   fix(x)

Description   Returns the absolute integer portion of an expression.

FOR-NEXT Statement

Syntax   for *var* = *x* to *y* next *var* for *var* = *x* to *y* step *z* next *var*

Description   Allows a program to loop a specific number of times.

FRE Function

Syntax   fre(x) fre($x\$$)

Description   Returns the amount of memory not used by BASIC.

GET Statements

Syntax   get #*filenum,recordnum*
get #*filenum,numbytes*
get *x1,y1 − x2,y2,arrayname*

Description   Reads a record into the random-access buffer from a random-access file; allows fixed-length I/O for COM; reads pixels from an area on the screen.

GOSUB-RETURN Statement

Syntax   gosub *line* return

Description   Branches to a user-defined subroutine; RETURN returns control to the main program.

GOTO Statement

Syntax   goto *line*

Description   Branches unconditionally to a specified line number.

HEX$ Function

Syntax   hex$(*x*)

Description   Returns the hexadecimal equivalent of the expression.

IF-THEN-ELSE Statements

Syntax   if *exp* then *line #* else *line #*
         if *exp* goto *line* else *stmt line*

Description   Makes a decision regarding program flow based on the result of an expression.

INKEY$ Variable

Syntax   inkey$

Description   Returns either a one-character string containing a character read from the computer or a null string.

INP Function

Syntax   inp(x)

Description   Returns the byte read from port x; valid machine ports are 1 to 65535.

INPUT Statements

Syntax   input ; *"string"* ;, x,y,z...
          input# *filenum, varlist*
          input$($x,\#y$)

Description   Allows keyboard input during program execution; reads data from a sequential disk file; returns a string of characters from the keyboard or from file number y.

INSTR Function

Syntax   instr($x,x\$,y\$$)

Description   Searches for the first occurrence of $y\$$ in $x\$$ and returns the position.

INT Function

Syntax   int(x)

Description   Returns the integer portion of an expression.

IOCTL Statement

Syntax   ioctl #*filenum, x$*

Description   Transmits a control string to a device driver.

IOCTL$ Function

Syntax   ioctl$(*#filenum*)

Description   Receives a control string from a device driver.

KEY Statements

Syntax   key *keynum,x$*
        key list
        key on
        key off

Description   Allows resetting of the soft keys at the bottom of the screen; turns them on or off.

KEY(*X*) Statements

Syntax   key(*x*) on
        key(*x*) off
        key(*x*) stop

Description   Activates or deactivates trapping of a specific key.

KILL Command

Syntax   kill *filename*

Description   Deletes a file from disk.

LEFT$ Function

Syntax   left$(*x$,y*)

Description   Returns the leftmost *y* characters of *x$*.

LEN Function

Syntax   len(x\$)

Description   Returns the number of characters in the string expression.

LET Statement

Syntax   let $x=y$

Description   Assign values to variables; the "LET" is optional.

LINE Statement

Syntax   line $(x,y) - (x1,y1), color, bf, style$

Description   Draws and removes straight-line objects; the b makes a box; the f means fill; the *style* is a bit pattern.

LINE INPUT Statements

Syntax   line input ; *"string"*;x\$
line input# *filenum,*x\$

Description   Allows entry of string variables up to 255 characters long; reads characters from a sequential file until it reaches a carriage return.

LIST Command

Syntax   list *line1-line2, file*

Description   Lists the program to the screen or other devices.

LLIST Command

Syntax   llist *line1-line2-line3*

Description   Lists the program to the line printer.

LOAD Command

Syntax   load *filename*[,r]

Description   Loads a program into memory; the optional **r** runs it.

LOC Function

Syntax   loc *filenum*

Description   In a random-access file, returns the record number within the file; in a sequential file, returns the current position divided by 128.

LOCATE Statement

Syntax   locate *row,col,cur,*start,stop

Description   Moves the cursor to a specified position on the screen.

LOF Function

Syntax   lof *filenum*

Description   Returns the number of bytes allocated to a file.

LOG Function

Syntax $\log(x)$

Description   Returns the natural logarithm of x.

LPOS Function

Syntax $\text{lpos}(x)$

Description   Returns the current position of the pointer in the printer buffer.

LPRINT and LPRINT USING Statements

Syntax   lprint *explist*
            lprint using *string;explist*

Description   Directs unformatted printing to a line printer; directs formatted printing to a line printer.

LSET Statement

Syntax   lset $x\$ = y\$$

Description   Moves and left-justifies data into a random-file buffer.

MERGE Command

Syntax   merge *filename*

Description   Merges a program from disk into one already in memory.

MID$ Function and Statement

Syntax   mid$ $(x\$,x,y)=y\$$
$x\$=mid\$(y\$,w,y)$

Description   Returns a portion of a string or replaces a portion of a string with another string.

MKD$, MKI$, MKS$ Functions

Syntax   mkd$$(x)$
mki$$(x)$
mks$$(x)$

Description   Converts numbers to strings in preparation for random-access file handling.

MKDIR Command

Syntax   mkdir *path name*

Description   Makes a new subdirectory.

NAME Command

Syntax   name *oldfilename* as *newfilename*

Description   Renames files.

NEW Command

Syntax   new

Description   Removes a program from memory.

OCT$ Function

Syntax oct$(*x*)

Description Returns the octal equivalent of an expression.

ON Statements

Syntax on com(*n*) gosub *line*
on error goto *line*
on exp gosub *linelist*
on exp goto *linelist*
on key(*x*) gosub *line*
on play(*x*) gosub *line*
on timer(*x*) gosub *line*

Description Enables branching in programs to selected subroutines by values.

OPEN Statements

The BASIC open statement is used to control access to sequential data files.

Syntax open *device,*
filename for *mode* as #*filenum*
len = *recl* open com
dev:speed,parity,data,stop,rs,cs,ds,cd,lf,pe,asc,bin as
#*filenum*

Description Opens a file on disk for access; opens a communications port for access.

OPTION BASE Statement

Syntax option base *x*

Description   Declares the minimum value for subscripted arrays; x is 0 or 1.

OUT Statement

Syntax   out x,y

Description   Sends a byte of information to the selected output port; both must be in the range of 0 to 65535.

PAINT Statement

Syntax   paint $(x1,y1),paint,border$

Description   Fills an area on the screen with the selected color.

PEEK Statement

Syntax   peek x

Description   Allows viewing of a particular byte in memory.

PLAY Statements and Functions

Syntax   play x\$
             play(x)
             play on
             play off
             play stop

Description   Plays music as specified by the string expression.

PMAP Function

Syntax   pmap *exp,func*

Description   Maps world coordinates to physical locations or maps physical expressions to a world-coordinate location for graphics mode.

POINT Functions

Syntax   point (*x,y*)
point (*func*)

Description   Allows reading of the pixel color from the screen.

POKE Statement

Syntax   poke *x,y*

Description   Allows changing of a particular byte in memory.

POS Function

Syntax   pos(*x*)

Description   Returns the current cursor position.

PRESET Statements

Syntax   preset (*x,y*),*attrib*
preset step (*x,y*),*attrib*

Description   Turns one pixel on or off on the screen.

PRINT and PRINT USING Statements

Syntax   print *explist*
print using *strexp,explist*
print# *filenum explist*
print# *filenum* using *strexp,explist*

Description   Directs unformatted printing to a line printer; directs formatted printing to a line printer; directs unformatted printing to a file; directs formatted printing to a file.

PSET Statements

Syntax   pset *(x,y),attrib*
pset step *(x,y),attrib*

Description   Turns one pixel on or off on the screen.

PUT Statements

Syntax   put #*filenum,recordnum*
put #*filenum,numbytes*
put *x1,y1,array,action*

Description   Writes a record into the random-access buffer from a random-access file; allows fixed-length I/O for COM; writes pixels to an area on the screen.

RANDOMIZE Statements

Syntax   randomize *x*

Description   Seeds the random-number generator.

READ Statement

Syntax   read *varlist*

Description   Reads information stored in the DATA lines.

REM Statement

Syntax   rem *remark*

Description   Allows the user to include remarks or notes within the program.

RENUM Command

Syntax   renum *newnum,oldnum,increment*

Description   Renumbers the lines of code.

RESET Command

Syntax   reset

Description   Closes all currently open files.

RESTORE Statement

Syntax   restore *line*

Description   Restores DATA items.

RESUME Statements

Syntax   resume
              resume 0
              resume next
              resume *line*

Description   Resumes execution of a program.

RETURN Statement

Syntax   return *line*

Description   Returns control to the main program following a GOSUB statement.

RIGHT$ Function

Syntax   right$(*x$,y*)

Description   Returns the rightmost *y* characters of *x$*.

RMDIR Command

Syntax   rmdir *path name*

Description   Removes a subdirectory.

RND Function

Syntax   rnd(*x*)

Description   Generates a random number.

RSET Statement

Syntax   rset *x$=y$*

Description   Moves and right-justifies data into a random-file buffer.

RUN Command

Syntax   run *line*
run *filename,*[r]

Description   Runs a program; the **r** keeps all data files open.

SAVE Command

Syntax   save *filename,*[a],[p]

Description   Saves a program to a disk file; the **a** keeps it in ASCII format; the **p** puts it in binary protected format.

SCREEN Statement and Function

Syntax   screen *mode,burst,apage,vpage*
x = screen (*x,y,oper*)

Description   Used to set the screen format; 0 is alpha mode; 1 and 2 are graphics modes.

SGN Function

Syntax   sgn(*x*)

Description   Indicates the sign (positive or negative) of a number in relation to 0.

SHELL Statement

Syntax   shell *commandstring*

Description   Runs DOS commands.

SIN Function

Syntax   sin(*x*)

Description   Returns the sine of *x*, where *x* is in radians.

SOUND Statement

Syntax   sound *freq,dur*

Description   Generates a sound from the speaker; the frequency (*freq*) is 37 to 32767; the duration (*dur*) is the number of clock ticks (18.2 = 1 second).

SPACE$ Function

Syntax   space$(*x*)

Description   Returns a blank string *x* blanks long.

SPC Function

Syntax   spc(*x*)

Description   Allows spacing on print lines.

SQR Function

Syntax   sqr(x)

Description   Returns the square of x.

STOP Statement

Syntax   stop

Description   Stops program execution; CONT will continue it.

STR$ Function

Syntax   str$($x$)

Description   Returns a string representation of x.

STRING$ Functions

Syntax   string$($x,y$)
            string$($x,y$$)

Description   Returns a string x characters long of ASCII character y, returns a string x characters long of the first character of $y$$.

SWAP Statement

Syntax   swap $x,x1$

Description   Swaps one variable for another.

SYSTEM Command

Syntax   system

Description   Returns to DOS.

TAB Function

Syntax   tab(x)

Description   Moves the cursor x number of spaces on the current print line.

TAN Function

Syntax   tan(x)

Description   Returns the tangent of x, where x is in radians.

TIME$ Statement and Function

Syntax   time$ = $x$$
             $x$$ = time$

Description   Displays and resets the clock.

TIMER Statements

Syntax   timer on
             timer off
             timer stop

Description   Enables and disables real-time clock trapping.

TRON-TROFF Commands

Syntax   tron
troff

Description   Turns trace mode on or off.

USR Function

Syntax   usr *digit(arg)*

Description   Calls an assembly language subroutine.

VAL Function

Syntax   val(*x$*)

Description   Returns the numeric value of *x$*.

VARPTR Functions

Syntax x = varptr(*z*)
y = varptr(*#filenum*)

Description   Returns the location of variables in memory; returns the first byte of the file control block for the opened file.

VARPTR$ Function

Syntax   varptr$ (*x$*)

Description   Returns a string expression of the variable's memory address.

VIEW Statements

Syntax   view (*vx1,vy1*) –(*vx2,vy2*),*color,border*
view screen (*vx1,vy1*) –(*vx2,vy2*),*color,border*
view print *topline* to *bottomline*

Description   Defines the screen limits for graphics activity; defines the screen limits for graphics activity; defines the screen limits for text activity.

WAIT Statement

Syntax   wait *port,andbyte,xorbyte*

Description   Waits while monitoring the status of a machine port; port number is between 0 and 65535; *andbyte* and *xorbyte* are between 0 and 255.

WHILE-WEND Statements

Syntax   while *exp* wend

Description   Executes a series of statements until a given condition is true.

WIDTH Statements

Syntax   width *size*
width *filenum,size*
width *dev,size*

Description   Sets the printed-line width.

WINDOW Statements

Syntax   window (w*x1*,w*y1*) −(w*x2*,w*y2*)
window screen (w*x1*,w*y1*) −(w*x2*,w*y2*)

Description   Defines the size of a viewport.

WRITE Statements

Syntax   write *explist*
write# *filenum,explist*

Description   Writes information to a file.

CHAPTER FIFTEEN

Inside Your Computer

For most of you, looking inside your PC feels a little like peering into the cockpit of a 747. It may look overwhelmingly intricate, but considering what your PC can do, its inner parts aren't that complicated. You're probably hesitant to do any fiddling around in there—but take heart. You don't need electronic testing equipment to know what you're doing; you just need a basic familiarity with the components. This chapter will acquaint you with what you'll find "under the hood" of your PC.

The inside of your PC clearly reflects its makers' design aims in terms of electrical engineering, computer logic, and marketing. But the number of options for building something as complex as a PC are nearly unlimited, so the PC's design also reflects the *philosophy* of its designers. We'll take a look at that concept later.

Most of all, though, as you read through this chapter—preferably with your system's cover off, or at least with your computer's manual nearby—you'll get acquainted with the hardware modules of your machine.

THE SYSTEM'S ARCHITECTURE: THE DESIGNERS' INTENT

The PC is a prime example of what's called *open architecture* in the computer industry. That means the necessary technical information is readily available, and the design philosophy allows anyone to build add-on products or write their own software. PC owners are free to use a wealth of add-on products with their computers.

Since 1981 there has been some debate about IBM's approach to open architecture. Was it one of the most forward-thinking, intelligent decisions a major corporation has ever made? Or was it just an uncharacteristic over-sight, or even a happy accident? Some say the original IBM PC was thrown together in a serendipitous sort of way and then tossed into a free-for-all market to see who, if anyone, would buy it. Others point out that the PC's open design, combined with IBM's marketing clout, created a world stan-dard within a few short months.

In any case, IBM's timing was superb. Products then current could not even share files, much less programs. Businesspeople falling in love with VisiCalc were evidence of a ready market. As hardware producers jockeyed for position, potential developers hung back, waiting. When IBM finally jumped in, the whole picture changed. Everyone had faith (blind faith, some critics grouse) that Big Blue would succeed; doubting developers now jumped at the chance to make expansion products for an IBM product. If IBM's open architecture idea was a splendid marketing ploy, it worked brilliantly.

The Clone Industry

The IBM PC's open architecture helped to spawn a spirited *clone* industry—whole systems (not just add-on cards) compatible with IBM PCs but not made by IBM. You might expect some patent-related legal squab-bles, and IBM did sue a few early clone makers. The unique software in the PC's ROM BIOS (basic input/output system) could be copyrighted, just like a novel, and the cloners were ordered to stop copying IBM's BIOS software without permission.

The outcome of the early suits was never really in doubt. The main question, according to some reports, was just how far IBM would be willing to let clone makers go. IBM provided a clear answer: they protected their original BIOS program code. Since then, IBM has remained somewhat philosophical about the clone industry, which quickly learned to make functional copies of the IBM BIOS that perform identically but don't violate IBM's copyright.

In terms of hardware, the PC's off-the-shelf parts made it a generic sort of machine from the start. To put that in perspective, consider the automobile. All passenger cars have four rubber tires, an engine, a steering wheel, a transmission, a cooling system, and so on. But today's cars are certainly not copies of one another—even if they are functionally the same.

The same holds true of today's PCs. There are functional similarities that allow you to be confident about what you'll find inside your system unit, even without knowing the brand name. For the most part, all MS-DOS PCs can use the same software, the same add-on cards, and the same attachments. That doesn't make them direct copies of one another or of IBM's machine—they all have different chips and different internal circuits. But their parts interact in standard ways and do standard tasks. A CPU processes data, RAM stores it, power supplies provide stable voltages, and so forth.

READ.ME

Closed Designs, Open Designs, and the Apple Mac ROMs

High-technology pioneers dating back to the turn of the century, such as the maker of Victrola record players, have tried to restrict the use of alien equipment. When a product is hot in the market, the original vendor is easily tempted to force buyers to get all their parts, supplies, and materials from a source the vendor can control.

This strategy has sometimes worked. The Bell Telephone System did it for years. Until recently, you couldn't legally add so much as a rubber cup to the mouthpiece of your phone, and all phones were leased, not purchased, from Bell. Holders of other airtight patent rights, such as Xerox, have used similar marketing strategies. Many believe the public gets important benefits from these controlled technologies, because of the scientific research that these "protected" corporations can afford to do.

Closed Designs, Open Designs, and the Apple Mac ROMs (*continued*)

The strategy also has its failures, however. Texas Instruments reportedly lost more than $600 million on a home computer it marketed in the early 1980s, after the firm tried to control all the machine's hardware and software.

IBM certainly flirted with closed architecture on its mainframes, pressuring users to buy even their punched cards from Big Blue. But when the IBM PC was introduced in 1981, it was not your standard IBM announcement. The PC was basically an experiment, and the marketing clout IBM routinely committed to big-ticket mainframes was absent. Certainly, IBM didn't foresee the PC's popularity, nor attempt at first to tap all of its potential. For instance, the PC's original display was a simple "glass teletype" emulation — no graphics at all. Third parties rushed to supply true graphics boards that could be plugged into the PC, and an important industry was born.

The Macintosh Comparison

Like the IBM PC, the Apple Macintosh has a healthy number of third-party developers with successful add-on products, but there are no Macintosh clones. This is because the Macintosh equivalent of the IBM BIOS (the Mac ROMs) contain software routines more complex than those of the IBM BIOS. In fact, most functions performed by Macintosh applications programs take advantage of the software routines built right into the Mac ROMs.

Apple has vigorously protected its copyright of the complex code stored in Mac ROM chips. Because the code is so intricate, no one has been able to clone what the Mac does. As a result, Apple seems to own the Macintosh market. Its ROM-based software includes Quickdraw, a complete set of windows, icons, scroll bars, and a programmer toolbox — and none of it takes up valuable RAM operating space. The machine is justly famed for ease of use, and Apple's innovative, high-tech approach has won many admirers. Apple is now developing a strategy to license their Macintosh technology to clone makers.

Macintosh has attracted many software authors, but not the multitude of MS-DOS programmers who dream about vast numbers of paying users. Although Macintosh commands an impressive 15 percent of the market, more than IBM alone, MS-DOS-compatible systems together account for most of the remaining 85 percent.

GETTING COMFORTABLE WITH YOUR HARDWARE

If you're not technically minded, don't worry—you don't have to be a computer technician to read this chapter. You probably drive a car, yet chances are you're not a trained mechanic. On the other hand, some basic understanding of what goes on inside your car's engine can give you the ability to perform simple preventive maintenance and emergency repairs.

The same is true for your computer. Sooner or later you may need to install an add-on board, change a chip, diagnose a problem, or find out why your space game makes your PC clone machine act like HAL in *2001: A Space Odyssey*. Understanding what's "under the hood" will also help you use your computer with more confidence. For really specific information about what the electrons are doing inside your computer, you'll need a more technical source than this guide. But the following material covers the basics.

External PC Anatomy

Your system is housed in a box—maybe a large box, maybe small. It may lie flat or stand on end. It has disk drives, a reset button, and several indicator lights on the front, plus various connector plugs in back. Each of these major components has been described in earlier chapters, but another quick look at the outside will now give you your first hint of what you'll find inside.

On the back panel (Figure 15-1) you will see a plug receptacle for the power cord, and an inverted jack for the recessed power plugs used by some monitors. The monitor data jack and a round jack for the keyboard cable are also here on the back panel. Look for a row of long, vertical slots, each about a half-inch wide, closed by metal plates from inside the box. These are the access holes for expansion slots used by add-on boards, video cards, internal modems, and the like.

You may notice some additional receptacles. An internal modem, for example, may replace one of the blanks with a plate that has a telephone jack. There will likely be parallel ports for printers, and serial ports for modems and other devices. These ports may protrude from one of the vertical slot covers, or (if the ports were built into the machine) may be placed anywhere on the back panel. If built in by the manufacturer, they will usually be labeled on the back.

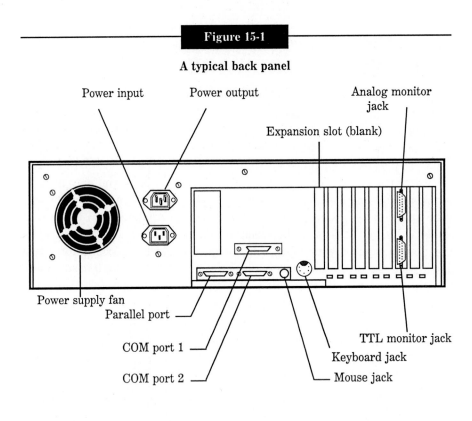

Figure 15-1

A typical back panel

Power input

Power output

Analog monitor jack

Expansion slot (blank)

Power supply fan

Parallel port

COM port 1

COM port 2

TTL monitor jack

Keyboard jack

Mouse jack

Special-purpose expansion cards, such as a scanner interface, may have special connectors that are accessible from the back panel. Usually you will also see a ventilation cover with fan blades visible behind it. You may notice a sticker with FCC regulations on radio frequency interference.

THE PC'S INTERNAL COMPONENTS

This chapter isn't about troubleshooting or maintenance, so you won't read a lot of details about working inside the system unit. Still, you may want to open your system unit now and refer to its contents as you read. Here are

READ.ME

Jacks, Plugs, and Other Connectors

Computers use a large and impressive array of cables and connectors, many of them standardized for particular purposes. If you look at the back of your computer, you'll see that only identical connectors have the same function. This helps you avoid accidentally plugging in components incorrectly.

There are plugs, jacks, ports, ribbons, shielded cables, 9- and 25-pin shielded or unshielded cables, phone wires, power wires, and more. (You won't need to memorize all these.) You do need to know a little more than how to turn on the digital ignition switch and put it in gear, but you won't have to get too technical. Here's a short course in Wires and Connectors in Your Desktop Computer.

- A *plug* is the male half of an electrical connection; it inserts into the female connector to make a circuit. Think of the modular plug on the end of your telephone cord—you plug that into the phone jack.

- A *jack* is the female counterpart of a plug, the connector or outlet into which you insert the plug.

- *Ports* are accesses by which data moves into and out of the system. Ports come in two basic types, serial and parallel, based on how many of the wires at a time are transferring data bits.

- The *RS232C* is a 25-pin connector used with serial ports to connect a computer to a modem.

- The *DG-9* is a 9-pin connector used for AT-class serial ports.

some things you should always do *before* you open the box:

1. Turn the power off and unplug the computer.

2. Clean off the table around the computer—you'll probably need some elbow room.

3. Disconnect the monitor and keyboard and move them safely out of the way.

4. Unfasten the screws or bolts that hold the cover in place, and slide the cover gently back. (See Chapter 18 for more details on procedures for removing parts from your computer.) Don't be surprised if the cover doesn't slide easily, especially if this is the first time you've opened it. You may have to nudge it a bit to get it moving, but do this gently.

Once the cover is off, look inside for loose screws, paper clips, and any other objects that may have fallen into the case. Short circuits caused by foreign objects can fry entire boards, including the motherboard (explained later). If you ever drop a metal part into the box, be sure to retrieve it before you close the box and turn the power on.

Looking Inside the Box

At this point, looking down into the case that holds your computer's parts, what you see will resemble Figure 15-2; the exact arrangement will vary. At the front on the right are the disk drive bays, containing one or perhaps more disk drives. At the right rear is the power supply, and at the left rear are the expansion slots. Lean forward and look straight down into the bottom of the case, and you'll see the motherboard underlying most of the left side (kind of an electronic floorboard). The motherboard contains the microprocessor and the rest of the basic circuitry.

Power Supply

If raw current from an AC line—the kind of power that comes out of a wall outlet—hits any of the chips in your computer, they can explode like tiny firecrackers. A computer's power supply therefore converts 115-volt line AC into DC, removes minor variations in the current, and feeds milder 5- and 12-volt DC to the system. The power supply module is the box in the right rear of the case.

If you bought your computer in North America, you can assume it will use 115-volt, 60-Hz power. Or you may have an optional European setting for 230 volts at 50 Hertz. Do not change this switch setting without a good reason; you can do serious damage by using the wrong setting.

Figure 15-2

Inside the system box

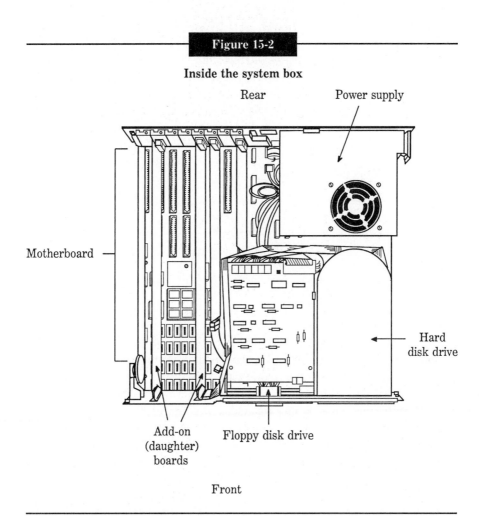

Power supplies, like light bulbs, are rated in watts. The original PC had a 40-watt power supply. As people added hard disks, more memory, and fancier circuitry, PCs needed more power. Today it's common to see power supplies rated at 180 watts, 220 watts, or even more.

The Motherboard

The motherboard (or system board) is the heart of the PC. It contains the PC's essential circuitry on a large printed circuit board made from a flat sheet of glass epoxy, usually tinted green. Power and signals travel through circuits formed by copper traces etched into two or more layers of the epoxy. The components—tiny resistors, capacitors, diodes, chip sockets, and so on—are soldered onto the surface. In almost all cases, chips are gently pressed into sockets, as illustrated here, rather than being soldered directly to the board.

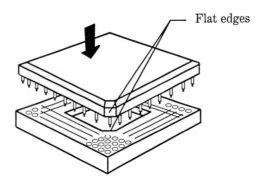

Flat edges

The design of the board itself is either 8-, 16-, or 32-bit. That means data is sent from one place to another on the board in groups of 8, 16, or 32 bits. The motherboard is the major transmission route for data within the machine; it takes data from add-on boards to disks to memory banks and so forth. For that reason it is often called a *bus*—an electrician's term for a central distribution point, like a house's breaker box, that distributes electricity as needed. In a computer, the electricity is a series of digital signals that make up data bits of information. *Bus mastery* means getting data signals from a source to the right destination.

Important circuitry on the motherboard includes the microprocessor or CPU, the math coprocessor (or its empty socket), the ROM chips, the RAM chips, the DIP switches, and some other items, all described in the paragraphs that follow.

The Microprocessor

The *microprocessor* or *CPU* (central processing unit)—a square chip about the size of your thumb—is the brain of the computer. Actually, it *is* the computer, since it does all the computing. Everything else in the box is there simply for the care and feeding of this one chip. The CPU can be an

Intel 8088, 8086, 80286, 80386, or 80486. Portables and laptops may use an 80186 or special CMOS chips labeled 80C88 or 80C86 (discussed in a later section).

The original PC used an 8088 chip, a 16-bit 8086 processor variant that used an 8-bit bus, making the circuitry cheaper to build. (The 6 at the end of 8086 refers to the 16-bit bus it uses; the 8 at the end of 8088 refers to its 8-bit bus.) The 8086 was developed from its immediate ancestors, the Zilog Z80 and the Intel 8080, which could address only 64K of memory. The 8086 and 8088 chips, both still in use, can address a full megabyte of memory, and have other technical advantages over their predecessors.

The 80286 marked the birth of the second generation of PCs: the PC AT. The 80386 and 80486 were major advancements in faster speed and added computing capacity, within both the AT-class of PC and IBM's newer PS/2 computers.

The Apple Macintosh family uses CPU chips from the Motorola 68000 family, and the original Apple II used a Motorola 6502. Because these machines use different microprocessors, they cannot run each other's software, nor can they run PC software directly. Instead, they must use special emulation software, which can be painfully slow, or install a faster but more expensive coprocessor expansion card. Neither approach guarantees 100-percent compatibility.

Intel chips, by contrast, can run software written for earlier-generation 8088 and 8086 chips, although the reverse is not always true. Software written for the later chips may require more RAM, use additional features, or depend on special protected-mode features not available in 8088 and 8086 chips.

Clock Speed

A PC's computing speed is set by a single crystal that vibrates at an extremely high and constant rate, sends out a signal, and drives an oscillator. The oscillator output frequency is used to time, control, and synchronize all of the computer's operations; it sets the machine's clock speed. The original PC ran at 4.77 megahertz (MHz), or millions of cycles per second. The PC designers picked that speed because it was compatible with a subfrequency used by color television sets.

This is not to say the original PC could perform 4.77 million operations per second; it takes several cycles to do even simple tasks. The clock did, however, set the maximum speed. Some later systems, such as the 6-MHz AT, allowed changing to a higher frequency (8 MHz) crystal, a delicate job affecting many other circuits. Changing crystal speeds affects how the machine's components interact, and is not a good way to upgrade an older machine. Turbo add-on boards have higher clock speeds, usually 8, 10, or 12 MHz. Adding a turbo board works much better than changing the main crystal speed because the add-on boards are carefully designed to interface correctly with the older, slower host system.

PC AT machines originally ran at 6 MHz and performed about three times faster than the original PC. Their clock wasn't three times faster, but speed depends on more than clock rates. The new 80286 chip used a 16-bit bus, was more efficient, and performed the same tasks with fewer operations. Before long, 6 MHz seemed slow, and the clone makers began working on speed improvement. Today you rarely see new ATs with a speed below 10 MHz. A 386 or 486 machine can operate at 33 MHz or faster. Slower 386 machines operate at 16 or 20 MHz, which is still about four times faster than a 6-MHz, 286 PC AT.

There is no easy way, looking under the hood, to determine the clock speed of your machine. There may be a number stamped on the CPU itself that identifies the maximum clock speed. Also, most diagnostic utility programs can accurately identify the speed and type of processor (see Norton Utilities' System Summary in Figure 15-3). If you really need to know, the clock speed is always reported in a machine's individual documentation.

Numeric (Math) Coprocessor

Next to the microprocessor, you'll probably find an empty chip socket for the numeric (or math) coprocessor. Not all coprocessors are the same; some are designed for specific purposes. Intel's numeric coprocessors are more generic, and are designed to do numeric calculations (number crunching) quickly. They excel in applications such as higher math, statistics, computer-aided design and drafting (CADD), graphics, and engineering (all discussed in Chapter 7).

A coprocessor is driven by the CPU, and does nothing until an applications program activates it. When an application knows how to do that, the CPU doesn't have to do any heavy number-crunching; it just hands these calculations over to the coprocessor and gets on with other tasks. Later, the CPU retrieves the answer. Even with a fast AT, adding a coprocessor can feel as if you're advancing to a 386.

Intel coprocessors are named after the CPU for which they are designed, but the coprocessor number ends in a 7. An 8087 works with an

---

Figure 15-3

Norton Utilities' SYSINFO reports a 25-MHz machine

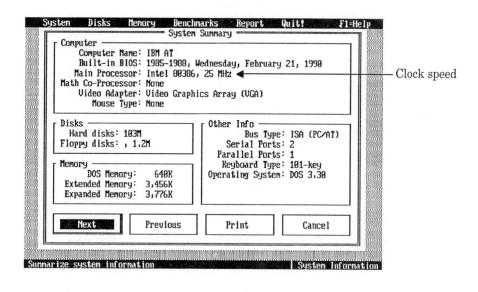

8088, an 80287 works with an 80286, and an 80387 with an 80386. The 80486 has a built-in numeric coprocessor, among other high-performance features.

ROM Chips

On IBM-compatible systems, ROM (read-only memory) chips contain the basic hard-wired programming a computer needs to "wake up" when you turn on the power. ROM programming routines are used by the operating system and other higher-level software packages to do common data-handling chores. These ROM BIOS routines include the handling of keyboard input and disk files. The original IBM PC's ROM BIOS also contained BASIC. You could boot up and use the machine as a computer, even if you hadn't purchased an optional floppy disk drive.

Since RAM (described next) is faster than ROM, some newer machines copy the BIOS into a special block of RAM after bootup, and run the BIOS from this *shadow RAM*.

RAM Chips

RAM (random access memory) is a primary factor in your computer's capacity, and the more of it you have, the better. RAM is organized to let any particular location be immediately addressed (used) by the CPU. By contrast, data kept nonrandomly, for example on magnetic tape, can be addressed only in the same sequence it was recorded. Random access is faster by several orders of magnitude.

The 8088 chip addresses (uses directly) one megabyte of RAM. The 80286 and above can address 16 megabytes of RAM. That means software written to take advantage of RAM can address the extra memory directly, without having to "page" data in and out of the lower 640K of RAM the way expanded memory does. See Chapter 17 for more on the different types of memory.

The motherboard of any machine has only a specific number of RAM chip sockets; any additional chips must be mounted on an expansion board. The amount of RAM you can stack onto the motherboard and any expansion boards depends on the computer model, but it's most commonly 1 or 4 megabytes on the motherboard, and the balance on an expansion card.

RAM Chip Arrangement, Size, and Speed

Memory chips often come in banks of nine, as shown at the front and to the left of the board in Figure 15-4. This allows one chip for each parallel bit in the bytes stored in that bank of chips. The ninth chip is for *parity checking*, which is a test that detects when an individual bit in any byte has gone bad and issues an error warning. One bad bit can distort your data and even crash the computer.

RAM chips vary in size and speed. Size indicates the number of bits (not bytes) they hold, as well as physical size. Each generation of RAM chip has held four times more data bits than the last. An older machine may use 64K chips, newer ones use 256K chips, and the newest machines have 1MB chips. Chips with 4MB and 16MB capacities are already on the drawing board.

As for speed, RAM chips are rated in *nanoseconds* (ns), or billionths of a second. The range is a high of 200 ns down to 60 ns, with 150 ns and higher considered slow and 80 or lower considered fast.

Static Versus Dynamic RAM

On the technical side, some RAM chips are static and some are dynamic. This refers to the electrical engineering approach used in their design. Both

Figure 15-4

Memory chips, in banks of nine, on the motherboard

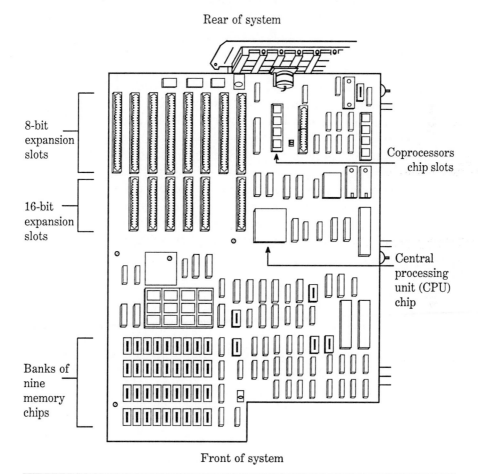

Rear of system

8-bit expansion slots

16-bit expansion slots

Coprocessors chip slots

Central processing unit (CPU) chip

Banks of nine memory chips

Front of system

types of chip work the same in terms of computer logic, and both types lose their contents when the machine is turned off, but static RAM is generally faster. It's also more expensive, so static RAM is used mostly for disk caching and other specialized, high-speed uses. (A *disk cache* is intermediate RAM storage of recent disk reads and writes, and is covered in more detail in Chapter 17.)

Most RAM is the less-expensive dynamic RAM. When you go shopping for RAM, you'll usually be looking for dynamic RAM chips, often listed as DRAMs (pronounced "D-RAMs").

CMOS Chips

AT-class computers are fitted with CMOS (complementary metal oxide semiconductor) chips. These chips consume very little power, so it is practical to use a small battery to save the data contents of a CMOS chip after the system has been turned off. On AT-class machines, CMOS chips do nothing but maintain data about system settings between bootups, so you don't have to reset the time and calendar every time you restart the machine, as you must on an XT. CMOS settings automatically include the date, time, and information about your hardware. Entries can include types of disks, amount of memory, whether special features are enabled, and the like.

CMOS chips cost more than standard designs and so are used mostly for maintaining settings on a desktop machine. On laptops, it's a different story. Designed to be run with batteries, laptops must use as little power as possible. Since you can design a CMOS chip to do anything a regular chip can do, laptops often contain CMOS chips as their CPU. You can tell if your machine has a CMOS processor because the CPU will have a *C* in its name (80C88, 80C86, and so forth).

Expansion Slots

You have read how the PC's successful open architecture design turned it into a commodity that has since sold in the tens of millions of units. With a PC, you don't really have a "complete" system until you plug in one or more add-on expansion boards. Figure 15-5 shows how boards are typically plugged into the system unit. As you look down at your system's motherboard, you'll probably notice at least two expansion boards, usually plugged in on the far right and far left. The card on the left controls the monitor; the one on the right, the disk drives.

Note: The terms *card* and *board* are used interchangeably when referring to add-on items. Add-ons are also sometimes called *daughter boards*.

Laptops, many portables, and even some desktop models come with their monitor and drive-control circuits built into the motherboard. Some machines do not provide for any expansion boards at all. The PS/2 comes with built-in controller circuits, but also includes expansion slots.

Empty expansion slots make the PC a tool of enormous flexibility. There are add-on cards for just about any use you can conceive. You can get a board to connect your machine directly to a mainframe, a phone line, laboratory equipment, or scanning devices. You can add fax capabilities,

Figure 15-5

Typical daughter boards (full- and half-sized)

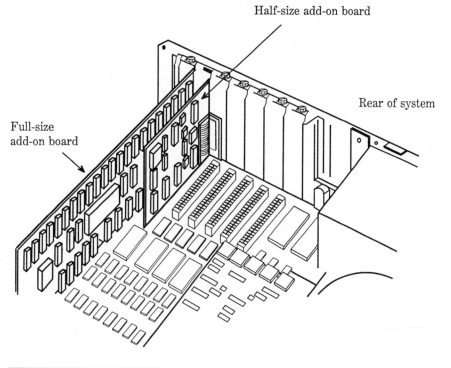

Half-size add-on board

Rear of system

Full-size
add-on board

voice recognition, text-to-speech translators, or extra memory. If enough
users wanted a kitchen sink inside the system box, no doubt someone would
design and market a board for that, too.

Video Cards

One important type of expansion card is the video card. When third-party
firms rushed to provide the graphics capability IBM offered only as expensive options or not at all, each company used their own approach. After the
dust settled, the following varieties of video display terminals (VDTs) remained:

- *MDA*   Monochrome display adapter with no graphics.

- *Hercules*   A monochrome graphics adapter that produces true black-
  and-white graphics on an ordinary monochrome monitor. The Her-

cules board is widely cloned and, like the PC, has become an informal but widely recognized hardware standard.

- *CGA*   Color graphics adapter, IBM's first stab at graphics for the PC.

- *EGA*   Enhanced graphics adapter, a digital display system with higher resolution.

- *VGA and Super VGA*   Video graphics array, an analog system that permits more color changes than the digital EGA can manage.

- *MCGA*   Graphics circuitry built into the PS/2 Model 30; compatible with the CGA.

- *Others*   High-density graphics designed for large monitors, used in engineering, design, and graphic arts settings.

There are other types of displays, many of which can be driven from a good-quality video card. You may see connectors for three other display technologies:

Liquid crystal display (LCD)
Gas-plasma display
Electro-luminescent (EL) display

Other display technologies, such as the vacuum fluorescent display (VFD), electro-phoretic displays, and light-emitting diode (LED) displays, are seldom used.

As computers run at faster clock speeds, the bus speed becomes more critical for video displays. Video cards of 16 bits are faster than 8-bit cards, and so can handle a wider bandwidth, meaning they can process and display more visual information in a given unit of time. Also, some manufacturers put the display circuitry on the motherboard itself. This is faster than on an expansion card, but hard-wired circuits cannot be disabled, making later upgrading difficult or impossible.

Not all software supports every video display, but many PC software packages have multiple video drivers.

Other Motherboard Items

Several other chips on the motherboard are either ROM or RAM chips. The ROM chips are usually wider, with printed adhesive labels on top noting the revision level of the software they contain. The Ergo Brick portable system unit mentioned early in this book uses erasable, reprogrammable ROM chips that let you access new ROM upgrades by modem, and then incorporate any debugs or improvements into your own machine. If your machine can be updated by modem (a feature that is not yet common), remember to check in with the manufacturer from time to time to get any ROM upgrades.

DIP Switches

Also on the motherboard you'll see DIP (dual inline pin) switches, sometimes called "bugs" because their two rows of mounting pins along the bottom make them resemble caterpillars. DIP mountings are used for both memory chips and switches. DIP switches configure various options within the computer—for example, how much RAM is addressed in a PC or XT, or the operation of the display circuitry you can use. The two most common types of DIP switches are sliders and rockers; you set them using the tip of a ball point pen, *never* a pencil, which can cause graphite-induced short circuits.

The roles of various switches depend on the machine, so pay attention to your hardware documentation, or you'll play a frustrating game of trial and error when they need resetting. DIP switches are preset at the factory, so you shouldn't have to deal with them unless you add or remove memory.

Other types of packages are described briefly in "DIPs, SIPs, ZIPs, and SIMMs."

Jumpers and Other Connectors

Jumpers are small, square fittings that slip over two or three adjacent, upright pins, as shown here:

Setting is off   Setting is on

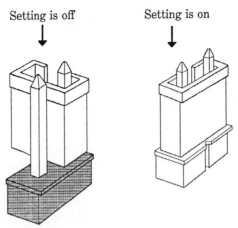

When there are two pins, a jumper that has been slipped over both pins is set to ON; it's the same as closing a switch. If a jumper is slipped over one pin but not the other, the setting is OFF, as in an open switch. If there are three or more prongs on a connector, the jumper straddles any prongs it connects.

On the motherboard you'll also see connectors for the keyboard, the speaker, the power supply, and (if you own an antique, first-generation PC) a cassette player for data tapes. Tape player interfaces were provided with the earliest PCs—just in case PCs found a low-end market where data handling speed didn't matter. This technology was quickly bypassed because users preferred faster floppy disks.

Data Bus (Expansion Slot) Architecture

The data-carrying circuits on the motherboard are in the PC data bus. Since the expansion slots make add-on cards logical extensions of the motherboard, the slots themselves are sometimes considered the bus. There are several varieties of expansion slots, and they have some important physical differences.

IBM has three main types of expansion board connector tabs. They fit the 8- and 16-bit ISA bus, the 32-bit EISA bus, and the 32-bit MCA buses. Each connector tab design is unique, but only the MCA is not downwardly compatible with the earlier ISA design. The three types of expansion boards (and slots) are discussed next.

ISA: Industry Standard Architecture
The bus structure used by the original IBM PC, PC XT, and PC AT didn't have a name at first. Then IBM released the Micro Channel Architecture,

READ.ME

DIPs, SIPs, ZIPs, and SIMMs

These little black epoxy "bugs" hold memory chips and switches. They come in different designs, and computer documents are sometimes heavily salted with their acronyms. Here's what they mean.

- *DIP* Dual inline pin package, the traditional bug, has parallel rows of 8, 14, 24, or 40 or more metal prongs, evenly divided right and left, like a millipede. Pin number 1 is always indicated by a notch in the housing. A DIP bug looks like this:

Notch
indicates
pin number 1

- *SIP* Single inline pin package, used with chips. The logic prongs are lined up in a straight line on the bottom, like a comb's teeth. They can be single or multiple chips on a small card, and often use a proprietary SIP connection map.

- *ZIP* Zig-zag inline pin package; similar to a DIP. The pins are in two parallel rows, but they're offset so the pins on one side line up with the spaces between pins on the other side.

- *SIMM* Single inline memory module. A tiny circuit board that has individual logic devices, often DIP or SIP memory chips. This is a component module that you can plug into a larger device, making installation and replacement easier than with other designs. A SIMM looks like this:

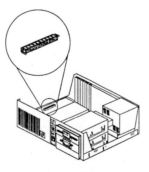

Memory is also available in surface-mounted, half-inch square epoxy blocks designed for soldering directly onto a motherboard surface.

or MCA, and a label for the original design became necessary. Engineers quickly settled on ISA, for Industry Standard Architecture.

When you plug in an ISA card, a narrow connector tab along the bottom of the card, lined with metallic "fingers," is pressed into an expansion slot on the motherboard. The first generation of PCs and XTs used 8-bit expansion slots that accepted boards with a single-edge connector. The PC AT introduced 16-bit architecture that required more connections, so a second slot was added to accomodate them. The 16-bit cards that fit these ISA buses have two connectors at the bottom of the board, one for each slot. A single-connector, 8-bit card works fine with a 16-bit bus; it simply leaves empty the shorter, 16-bit slot.

Original IBM PCs had five 8-bit ISA expansion slots, and XTs had eight. Today's standard AT has six 16-bit ISA slots and two 8-bit ISA slots. Most PCs today use that or a similar arrangement. The 8-bit slots are for modem cards and other simple devices; the 16-bit slots hold memory expansion boards and more complex devices. Some clones provide special, 32-bit slots for proprietary memory expansion boards built only for that machine.

Disk bays often limit room in the expansion slot area, so full-length boards sometimes won't fit on one side. Most new boards, though, are only half-length anyway, and there are always at least a few 16-bit slots available for full-length boards.

MCA: Micro Channel Architecture

The PS/2 and its clones are available with a new type of expansion slot called Micro Channel Architecture interface. The MCA-edge connectors have been entirely redesigned, with old ISA functions relocated, and new functions added. An MCA board fits two slots, as does a 16-bit ISA board, but an MCA board's long and short connectors are of different lengths. This keeps the MCA board from fitting into an ISA slot and getting fried.

MCA architecture lets intelligent expansion cards (cards with their own onboard processing chips) share the host computer's main circuitry. The fast, 32-bit MCA bus has two independent I/O processors and multidevice hardware bus control, or bus mastery, that elevates PCs to the functional level of minicomputers. A single MCA machine can manage full multitasking, several workstations, and all the rest of a minicomputer's bag of tricks. The bus master acts as a data traffic controller, letting all the independent tasks proceed simultaneously.

EISA: Enhanced Industry Standard Architecture

With MCA, IBM adopted a less open policy. Cloners can license the MCA design for use, but it's expensive. Many manufacturers have purchased the license, and MCA has strong supporters. However, one group of nine clone makers has, in response to MCA, created an Enhanced ISA (EISA) bus design with two outstanding characteristics. First, it's freely available to cloners, with no royalties expected—that's good for manufacturers. Second, it's compatible with existing 16-bit ISA boards, and that's great for users.

The EISA design pulls this off by making its 32-bit connector tabs longer, so they insert more deeply into the slots, rather than by changing the relative positions of the tabs. That leaves the 8-bit and 16-bit ISA connectors in their normal locations, so there's no conflict. EISA connector tabs have alternating thick and thin metallic fingers, with one deep gap, and then several regularly spaced, shallow gaps between fingers. That lets the board fit into the slot as a key does into a keyhole.

This key-like design also keeps an EISA board from fitting into an ISA bus, producing strange voltages and short circuits that would give the term "smoke test" more literal truth than humor. On the other hand, an ISA board, with its shorter, shallower connector tabs, will fit into the top part of an EISA bus and run perfectly well.

The MCA-EISA Bus Wars

The competition between MCA and EISA has been dubbed the "Bus Wars." Different victors are announced periodically, with great conviction, by various parties with an interest in the outcome. At this writing, though, it is too soon to say which new bus (if either) will eventually dominate the industry.

Performance tests do not show a great difference between MCA and EISA boards, but users who upgrade to EISA designs can keep using their older ISA boards. That means they keep their investment in boards that drive mice, scanners, digitizers, specialized graphics devices, modems, and thousands of other products.

Consider, too, that MCA has IBM behind it. Some say MCA could have major faults and still win anyway—and since it's actually of sound design, it's an odds-on favorite. Others think that IBM goofed when it dropped the IBM standard and let it be renamed the ISA standard, arguing that IBM thereby lost a huge existing customer base. In any other industry, a natural upgrade path (ISA to EISA) might guarantee the design's eventual acceptance as the industry standard. In the world of IBM-compatible computing, however, the outcome is far from certain.

Disk Bays

Disk bays may be side by side or stacked, and some larger machines have one set for 5 1/4-inch and another for 3 1/2-inch form factor drives.

Unless you have a "diskless workstation" (in which case you'll have a network interface card in one of the expansion slots), you'll find at least one disk drive in the bays. More likely, you have a hard disk and either one or two floppy disk drives. One bundle of wires connects them to the power supply (rear right). A separate ribbon cable connects them to the disk controller board or to a connector on the motherboard. The connectors' plugs are designed so that you cannot plug them in backwards.

Most drives sold today are *half-height* or *low-profile* (roughly one-fourth-height), meaning you can stack more of them in a full-height disk bay. Remember, though—it's always a good idea to keep some distance between disk drives so their generated heat can dissipate.

Closing the Case

When you put the case back on, make sure nothing pinches the disk controller's ribbon cable. The cable is made long enough to accommodate various designs, and may bend out and rub against the case if the cable is not tucked neatly away. There will probably be pins in the front of the cover that fit into holes in the body, so jiggle the cover slightly until they slide together. The cover should go on snugly; if it doesn't, remove it and try again. Never force it. Only when the cover is on correctly should you reconnect the keyboard, monitor, and power cable.

SUMMARY

This chapter has presented an overview of the components inside your system unit. If you were looking inside your system case while you read this chapter, you now have a good idea of what it looks like normally. If damage occurs later, you may save much time by being able to recognize damaged components by changes in their appearance.

In the next chapter, you'll read about hard disks—how they work, and (in basic terms) how to install and replace them. If you don't have a hard disk, you may wish to skip to Chapter 17. There you can read about how to fine-tune your PC into a truly personal instrument, tailored to your specific tastes and needs.

CHAPTER SIXTEEN

Understanding Your Hard Disk

In the early days of microcomputers, a hard disk was considered a luxury. Now it's standard equipment. In overall storage capacity, efficiency, and speed, hard disks are superior to floppy drives.

A hard disk is a mass storage device that can hold the equivalent of many floppies—with current hard drive sizes, the number gets into many hundreds. Floppy disks tend to get scattered from box to box, drawer to drawer, or office to office. Also, you need a separate floppy (or set of floppies) for each application you wish to run, so running several applications requires constantly switching these disks back and forth. By storing all your programs and data in one central area, a hard disk avoids this inconvenience, at the same time increasing speed and efficiency.

Certainly it is possible to run a hard disk without having a clue as to how it works, but you'll get the most out of your investment if you start with a general understanding of the technology. You will also be less likely to make costly mistakes.

It's estimated that over 75 percent of all PCs now in use have a hard disk; it has become an essential part of today's personal computer system. This chapter explains how a hard disk works, what to look for when buying

509

one, how to install the new disk, and how to format it. If you're an experienced hard disk user, you may want to skip the basics and go directly to "What To Look for When Buying," although we recommend reading straight through.

HOW A HARD DISK WORKS

Hard disk technology is a complex intertwining of electronics, mechanics, and magic, but to understand how it works, you only need a basic tour of the system.

In many ways, hard disks are similar to floppy drives. Both have recording media spinning around a hub. Across this medium moves an arm, with read/write heads that pick up or lay down magnetic signals. A crude analogy is a phonograph, with its record turning at 33-1/3 RPM and the tonearm moving across the surface, picking up signals that let the phonograph play a song.

Just as they are a world apart from phonographs, however, hard disks differ in major ways from floppy drives. A floppy disk rotates at 360 RPM, but a hard disk turns at 3600 RPM, ten times faster. The heads in a floppy drive ride directly on the recording surface. Hard disk heads, on the other hand, float above the recording surface on a cushion of air.

Another difference is in the *data encoding* schemes used (the magnetic coding method used to record data on the surface of the disk). Hard disks use smaller, more compact signals than floppies, which means the read/write heads must be more accurate. It also means the read/write heads don't have to travel as far to read the same amount of data.

Inside the Hard Disk

When working with your hard disk, you would be wise to be familiar with its operating and design characteristics. Here's a breakdown of some of the components that make up a typical hard disk (see Figure 16-1).

Electronics

The drive's electronic components control the mechanical parts of the disk, turning and regulating the spindle motor and moving the heads across the recording surface.

Figure 16-1

Inside a hard disk

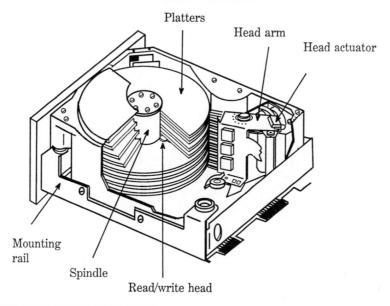

Platters

Head arm

Head actuator

Mounting
rail

Spindle

Read/write head

Platters

The physical disk itself contains several *platters*. This is where your data is stored. A platter is an aluminum disk with a magnetic coating on both sides. Platters are stacked one above the other inside the drive, spaced far enough apart so as not to touch. The more platters in a drive, the larger its storage capacity.

Tracks, Cylinders, and Sectors

A disk, whether floppy or hard, normally comes from the factory blank. Before any information can be saved to the disk, it must be prepared. This is called *formatting* a disk.

Formatting lays down the physical addresses on the disk surface by creating *tracks* and *sectors*, as shown in Figure 16-2. Data is written on a *track*—a ring around the disk or platter. The tracks form a series of concentric circles across the recording surface. A 5 1/4-inch 360K floppy has 40 tracks per side; hard disks may contain thousands of tracks per drive.

Figure 16-2

Tracks and sectors on a disk

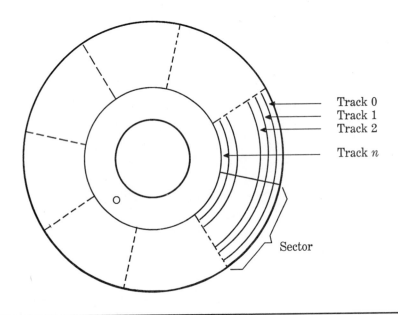

Track 0
Track 1
Track 2

Track n

Sector

Tracks are laid down on the platters, one above the other, so if you view the tracks in your imagination as stacked one on top of the other, they look like cylinders. Each platter has its own read/write heads, and the heads of the various platters are linked together so that they all move at the same time. As a result, the heads always line up on the same tracks regardless of which platter they are for. Because the tracks are stacked like cylinders, the head position is referred to by cylinder number. For example, consider a hard disk with five platters. The disk will have ten track zeros, two on each platter. In a sense, then, track zero runs through the entire drive as an imaginary cylinder. The number of cylinders in a hard disk varies with the model. They commonly run between 614 and 1024, although larger ones are now available.

Each track on a platter is further divided into a consistent number of *sectors*. The number of sectors per track depends upon the encoding scheme; typical examples are 17, 26, and 34. Sectors are like wedges of pizza, each one individual and isolated from its neighbors, yet part of a whole. Sectors on the outside tracks cover more physical area than sectors on the inside. Each sector stores the same amount of data (usually 512 bytes). Data is saved in groups of sectors.

The Actuator and the Read/Write Heads

The *actuator,* or head assembly, is similar to the tonearm of a phonograph. Like the tonearm, the actuator moves out across the platters to a precise *address* — a unique position on the disk — and reads the data there. However, where a phonograph tonearm has but a single, "read-only" stylus, the hard disk actuator has multiple read/write heads. Usually there is 1 head for each side of each platter, totalling 4 to 16 heads in most drives.

Stepper Motors and Voice-Coil Actuators

There are two basic types of head actuators in use today. One has a stepper motor, and the other uses voice-coil technology.

A *stepper motor* works by turning in tiny steps, each step moving the heads a certain distance across the disk surface. Technically, a stepper motor works by transferring the stepped, rotating energy into linear movement through back and forth linear motion. Steppers are widely used because they get the job done adequately and are cost effective. However, stepper motors are slow. Worse, they are limited to the minimum distance they can move for each step.

The future is in *voice-coil* actuators like the one shown in Figure 16-3. As magnetic recording technology improves, providing more condensed storage, it allows the spacing between tracks to narrow, thereby increasing capacity. Stepper motors are proving unable to read these new, more condensed storage systems reliably.

Voice-coil actuators have no motors. The heads are sent back and forth across the platters magnetically, by changes in electric current through coils of wire. With no physical motor to set limits, the actuator is capable of very precise movements. This makes voice-coil actuators more accurate than stepper motors, but they are also more expensive.

Floating Heads

A major difference between hard disks and floppy drives is in their read/write heads. The heads of a floppy drive are in direct physical contact with the *medium* (the magnetic material where information is recorded), riding the disk just as video and audio heads do when rubbing against tape in

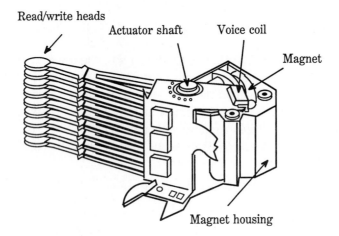

Figure 16-3

Hard disk head assembly (voice-coil actuator)

cassettes. When a hard disk is spinning, the heads never touch the disk surface, but rather float on a cushion of air only four microns away from the spinning platters. (By comparison, a human hair is a whopping 80 microns thick.) This is why you never want to bump or jar a PC while it's running. If you bounce a head into the platter at 3600 RPM, nasty things are likely to result. At minimum, you may produce what technicians call divots, which are small nicks in the magnetic recording surface. Your only remedy then may be to have the hard disk overhauled and the media replaced. This touchy procedure requires a clean room, and can be done only by a hard disk manufacturer or repair specialist.

How a File Gets Read

When the actuator moves, all the heads move across all the platters—they have to, because they're fixed in place. So how does the computer know where to position the heads and, once positioned, which head to read? How does data get read?

Every file has a unique address on the disk, expressed in clusters. A *cluster* is a group of sectors, usually four or eight, that represents the smallest area on a disk that the heads can read or write to in one action. All files, therefore, take up at least one full cluster, even if their actual size is smaller. The unique file address tells the file's exact location, including cylinder, head, and sector.

Let's say you want to edit a document called WALDO.TXT. As you issue the retrieve command from your word processing software, DOS routes the request to the hard disk controller, which interprets it and sends signals down the drive cables. The head actuator goes to the directory of files you specified in the retrieve command and finds WALDO.TXT listed there.

Among the information DOS finds in the file directory is the starting cluster location code of the file. DOS then goes to that location in the file allocation table (FAT), which tells where to find the rest of the file by physical location on the disk. Suppose a file starts at cylinder 230, head 5, sector 10. The actuator moves out to cylinder 230. Once there, head 5 is selected to do the reading. Head 5 waits for sector 10 of the cylinder 230 track to pass under it; as the sector spins by, head 5 reads it (and any other sectors in that cluster). That done, the actuator moves on to the next cluster number in the sequence supplied by the FAT, and so on until the heads reach the end of the file.

As the file is read, electrical impulses travel from the selected head, up the controller cables, and into memory. From there, DOS routes the information to its final destination—the display, an I/O port, or, after your editing, back to disk storage.

The Controller Card

The hard disk can't do all this alone. It needs a controller card to tell it what to do. Usually mounted in an expansion slot, the *controller card* processes all signals going into or coming out of the hard disk. It tells the disk what to do and interacts with the CPU.

The controller determines the data encoding scheme—an important task. Once the drive has been formatted by a specific controller, only another drive with the same encoding method will be able to read it—you cannot arbitrarily mix controllers. If a controller with different data encoding is put into the system as a replacement, the hard disk must then be reformatted with that card. The good news is that a new controller, with perhaps a denser encoding scheme, can increase your total storage capacity. The bad news is that you may be taking a chance with your data if the recording surface isn't rated for the denser encoding.

At this writing, there are four principal controller types in use:

ST-506/412 (original encoding standard)
ESDI (enhanced small device interface)
SCSI (small computer systems interface)
IDE (integrated drive electronics)

A detailed technical study of these is beyond the scope of this guide, but here is a brief overview to help when you go shopping for a new hard disk.

ST-506/412

The ST-506/412 was the original standard controller system used in the first IBM PCs. It used MFM encoding, later enhanced by RLL and ARLL encoding that took advantage of improved material technology. Here are explanations of these encoding types:

- *MFM* Modified frequency modulation is still used today, although it is quickly losing favor to more advanced methods that allow greater speed and larger drive sizes.

- *RLL* Run length limited encoding stores data in a series of polarity-reversing bits that represent zeros and ones. The reversed polarity eliminates some encoding (nondata) bits, so RLL takes fewer bits than MFM does to store the same data. The result for you is better performance and higher storage capacity.

- *ARLL* Advanced run length limited encoding changes the RLL encoding method to make it more tolerant of older disks. In the process, it improves achievable densities.

One noticeable technical difference between MFM and RLL is in sectoring. MFM drives use 17 sectors per track, and RLL drives commonly use 26. An RLL version of the same drive will pick up a 30 percent or better increase in capacity, as compared with an equivalent MFM. One popular 30MB drive, for example, is basically an RLL version of a classic 20MB MFM drive.

ESDI

ESDI is a step up from the ST-506 standard, offering larger capacity drives and enhanced speed. ESDI drives of 300 or 600 megabytes are not uncommon.

The ESDI system was designed to take full advantage of features such as clock speed in 80286 and 80386 microprocessors. The DTR, or *data transfer rate* (the speed at which information can be read from the disk), is four or more times faster for ESDI than for ST-506 disks, which are timed for the slower 8088 microprocessor. As with the ST-506, an ESDI controller card allows up to two physical hard disks to be attached to the system at once.

SCSI

The SCSI (pronounced "scuzzy") interface has many fans and is growing in popularity. SCSI is not just a controller card but an "intelligent" bus interface, meaning it has its own processor that allows it to become an extension of the motherboard. SCSI's drive sizes and data transfer rates compare to ESDI.

One of the benefits of SCSI is its ability to control peripherals other than hard disks. Modems, CD ROMs, optical scanners, and printers all can be run off a single SCSI adapter. This greatly improves a system's flexibility. SCSI supports up to eight separate devices, but the computer counts as one of the eight. Thus you can drive up to seven additional hardware items in the combination you choose.

Note: Under DOS, a SCSI adapter recognizes only two physical hard disks (because of BIOS addressing). If you want to attach up to another five drives or any other SCSI device, such as a tape unit or CD-ROM to the system, you'll need a third-party device driver such as Ontrack's Disk Manager to tell SCSI that the other devices exist.

IDE

The controller for an IDE drive is part of the drive itself. IDE is a new type of interface that compares favorably to ESDI and SCSI in capabilities, but at a lower price—as long as you are buying both a controller and a drive anyway. IDE controllers mainly come as installed equipment on new systems, where the manufacturer mounts a disk connector right on the motherboard. This saves the cost of a controller card, and makes an extra expansion slot available.

An older system can use an IDE drive, but it requires a low-cost interface card that will use up one of your expansion slots, leaving you with one fewer slot for other uses.

WHAT TO LOOK FOR WHEN BUYING

Buying a hard disk can be easy, if you give it a little forethought. Remember, you're not just purchasing a drive. You'll also need a controller, cables, brackets or other mounting hardware, and possibly installation software. Although you can buy the hard disk from one vendor, a controller from another, and the rest of the parts from a third, you may wind up with compatibility problems. You're better off buying all your hardware from one source.

Even if you usually shop by mail, consider going to a local retail dealer for your hard disk and controller. The extra support from a dealer can be quite helpful. Tell the dealer what make and model computer you have, and then ask for recommendations. If you have your eye on a particular hard disk, find out if it's compatible with your system. Look for drives and controllers that can be purchased together, as matched—and guaranteed compatible—sets.

Controller Compatibility

As a general rule, it's wise to get a controller that is matched to the hard disk. Compatibility problems in the disk storage area lead to unreliable data, and that's something no one wants.

Users have had uneven success mixing and matching drive and controller types. For example, MFM and RLL drives are both members of the ST-506 standard. They look the same, both will work in an XT-type system, and you can often get away with running an MFM drive on an RLL controller. It's tempting, since a certified RLL drive costs a little more, but formatting an MFM drive with an RLL controller is courting disaster. There are differences in the media thickness, plating, and quality control of these two items. RLL electronics are designed for faster data transfer rates. Moreover, you can void warranties on new disks by using mismatched equipment. If you get into trouble, you'll have to pay your own way.

To be fair, many users have tried experimenting and have had no compatibility problems. Others were not so lucky—their drives worked for a while, and then quit. Rather than risk a lot of aggravation for a marginal saving, buy matched equipment. Get an RLL drive with an RLL controller. Use an ESDI drive with an ESDI controller.

Other Compatibility Questions

The compatibility issue goes beyond disk and controller. When you purchase a hard disk kit, make sure your computer will support it. (Once again, ask your dealer.) You may get a fabulous price on a 100MB ESDI drive and controller, but it won't do you much good in your XT. ESDI was created to take advantage of the 80286 microprocessor and its 16-bit bus, but XTs use the 8088 or 8086 chip and an 8-bit bus. Other obvious problems aside, you just can't fit a 16-bit card into an 8-bit slot.

On the other hand, you *can* put an 8-bit card into a 16-bit slot, which is one way to scrimp on a controller. There's nothing inherently bad about this, although hard disk performance will suffer. But if all that's needed is storage capacity, not speed, who cares? Still, most users chafe at unnecessary waiting, and prefer the faster speed of a 16-bit controller.

Data Transfer Rate (DTR) and Seek Times

You've learned that the data transfer rate (DTR) is the rate at which information can be read from the disk. Speaking more technically, it is the top speed at which data bits can flow from the disk surface to the controller. DTR is rated in millions of bits per second (Mb/s), and is directly related to speed. In general, the higher the DTR rating, the faster the card.

ST-506 controllers are designed to work in the slower clock speed environment of the IBM XT, so they're rated at 5 Mb/s. ESDI, SCSI, and IDE have DTRs at or above 20 Mb/s. Obviously, they're much faster than the ST-506 standard.

Seek times measure how long it takes to move the heads of a disk from one location to another and to find a specific piece of information or a specific track. Seek times can vary from 110 milliseconds (ms) on very old hard disks to under 15 ms on some of the newer "screamer machines." While these speed increases have been impressive, they are not as practically important as the DTR. You should be most concerned about how fast you can *access* the data, not how fast you can find it.

Storage Capacity

Today's disk drives range in capacity from 20MB to a gigabyte and beyond. The business standard has currently settled at 40MB, although as the technology improves, 100MB machines are taking over. Experience has long shown that, however much disk storage capacity "real estate" you may have, your program and data files will increase to fill it. If you have a choice, don't buy a new disk with storage capacity smaller than 40MB. Although 20MB and 30MB drives are available, you'll probably have a hard time limiting your hard disk needs to these smaller storage sizes—even if that looks like a lot of space to you now. If the direct expense is not an issue and you have an AT-type machine, consider a 100MB disk in one of the 16-byte controller varieties such as ESDI or SCSI.

Choosing the Right Combination

Don't worry too much about all the technical questions relating to choosing the right combination of controller and disk—remember, the important thing is to get a controller matched to the disk. Unless you're a glutton for technical information, you won't need to bother with it when you go shopping for a hard disk. A good dealer will help you make choices, if there are any, and will do (or help you do) the formatting.

The main concerns in picking a controller are

- Compatibility with the drive and your system
- Performance in terms of speed and versatility
- Storage capacity

INSTALLING THE DISK

The idea of opening your computer to install a hard disk may be daunting, but it's a relatively painless process. It can even be easy. Naturally, individual situations will vary, and the ease of installation depends upon any number of factors. Some of the newer, larger disks may present some difficulties, so if you're uneasy about it, you can have a professional do it.

That said, let's look at the basic procedure for installing a single hard disk as the only hard disk in a PC-compatible system.

Before You Start

Preparation is important. Before you touch a screw, check these items:

- The drive and controller must be compatible. Are they a matched set?

- Are both the drive and controller compatible with your PC's existing parts? You cannot put a 16-bit card in an 8-bit slot.

- Do you have all the connectors, cables, brackets, and screws necessary for the job?

- What about special software? If you aren't using special drive formatting software, you'll need a bootable DOS floppy disk that contains the DEBUG command.

Finally, before you proceed any further, write on a piece of paper all information you can find on the outside of the drive. This may include model and/or serial numbers; bad sector locations; number of cylinders, heads, and tracks; storage capacity; and anything else technical about the drive. Keep this information with the manufacturer's instructions, or in a special file of technical information about your system. You will need this data later, and it is hard to read the outside of a disk drive that's already mounted in its bay.

Tools
Here is a partial list of tools you will be likely to need:

- A standard and a Phillips screwdriver

- A set of precision screwdrivers (the type with rotating heads), available for under $10 in hardware stores

- A 3/16-inch and 1/4-inch socket wrench or nut driver

- A pair of tweezers, or a mechanic's dropped-parts retriever, for handling and retrieving small screws and parts

Hardware Procedure
Read the following sections carefully before doing the installation.

Open the Case and Check the Arrangements
First, turn the computer off and unplug it. Then turn off and unplug all attached peripheral equipment such as printers. Better safe than sorry.

READ.ME

Save Money—Heed These Warnings

Follow these cautions when you install a hard disk. They can save you from failed controllers, disks, and even motherboards.

- Never plug a component into a computer while it is running. Always turn off your PC.

- Keep track of everything you disconnect. Before you unplug it, remember or write down where it went and how it fit into place. Not all connectors are keyed for installation in only one direction, so to be safe, label connectors with tape or Post-its.

- Keep small parts and fasteners in a cup or other small container, so they won't roll off the table and get lost.

- Keep your work area clean. Make sure your hands are free of dirt and grease.

- Avoid static electricity—it can damage electronic equipment. Rid yourself of static by touching either the metal chassis on a plugged-in PC or some other object you know to be grounded. You can also buy a wrist grounding strap at Radio Shack.

- Handle circuit boards carefully. Avoid touching the gold edge connectors with your hands; skin oils can tarnish the connectors and hamper electrical connections.

Next, remove the case. Most XT/AT-type boxes have three to five screws in the back. Remove these and slide the top case gently forward, away from the power supply. (Chapter 18 has some illustrations of typical cases being opened.)

Finally, with the case open, look inside and survey the entire layout. Look at where the drive and controller will go. If you bought a full-height drive, but you see only half-height spaces, or if you bought a 5 1/4-inch form factor drive and discover you only have a 3 1/2-inch drive bay available, this is a good time to stop. You need to talk to your vendor about trading drives.

Note: Portables and designs that do not follow the IBM PC convention may pose problems during installation of a hard drive. Screws may be hidden or require special tools. On some PCs, figuring out how to get the case open is the toughest part of the installation. If you have problems, try calling your computer dealer, or friends, or check the newspaper for a local PC user group for your type of system.

Remove Old Cards, Cables, and Components

When you're sure you have the right equipment, take a second look around the inside to memorize or record how everything goes in. Draw a diagram, and attach labels to components and connectors (include their orientation). You won't be sorry you took the extra time. Once everything is identified and correctly labeled, remove whatever cards and cables are in the way.

Install a Power Supply If Needed

This section may not apply to your situation—but make sure it doesn't before you skip it.

You may need to upgrade your power supply in order to add a hard disk. The power supply is the square box attached with bolts at the back of the system unit; it probably has a label that says DANGER, or some other such warning, because of the high-voltage capacitors inside the box. *Do not open up the power supply itself.*

The original IBM PC came with first 40-watt, then 63-watt power supplies. These were meant to power the internal electronics and one or two floppy drives. When the XT came along, the power supply was boosted; some XT clones go as high as 130 watts. The extra watts are for the hard disk. To tell if you need a new power supply, look at the power box sticker. If it rates below 100 watts, you should replace it. If you don't, your system may suffer from sluggish performance, hardware problems, overheating, and possibly drive failure.

To replace the power supply, remove the power connectors to the motherboard and floppy drives. Then remove the four screws at the back of the case that secure the power supply assembly to the chassis. Slide the power box forward and up, as shown in Figure 16-4, to disengage it from the bracket underneath. Then install the new power supply. Refastening the power cable connectors is usually fairly uncomplicated; most PCs use keyed connectors that fit only one way.

Check the Drive Select

Before mounting the hard disk into the computer, make sure the drive select jumpers or switches are properly set. These are usually located at the back or bottom of the disk assembly.

Figure 16-4

Removing the power supply box

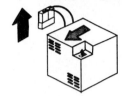

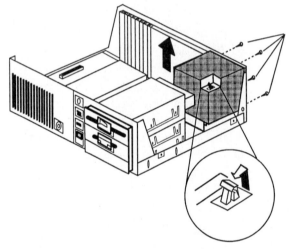

Secured
by two to
four screws

Link to power
switch—disengage
if present

Hard disk drives normally come preset from the factory as drive 0, the first physical drive in the system. (The tech sheet that comes with the disk explains this.) If you will only use one hard disk in the PC, leave the drive select unchanged. Check the drive select, however, just in case it's set wrong. If it is, the computer will not recognize the drive and you'll get an error message at startup.

If the new disk is the second one in the system, move the drive select to the drive 1 position. You will also have to change the terminating resistors, as described in the tech sheet supplied with the disk, if the new disk is the second one in the system.

Install the Disk

Your hard disk comes with installation instructions. Follow them. The first step is almost always to install a mounting kit, which includes various rails onto which you will slide the drive assembly. If the kit is missing, go to a dealer for advice; he or she can probably find the right mounting kit. For problems that are less severe, like missing screws or small hardware, your dealer may have the items stocked in the back of the store.

If some unexpected difficulty arises, you may have to improvise. One common problem is a drive mount that doesn't quite fit the arrangement of your system unit drive bays. You may have to (carefully!) bend the mounting's rails to get a smooth fit; these items are not precision engineered. If you bought a 3 1/2-inch form factor hard disk drive, but have only a 5 1/4-inch bay available, you probably need an adapter kit. Most smaller-sized hard disks come with a 5 1/4-inch bay adapter; if yours does not, your dealer can get you one.

When all is ready, the drive assembly simply slides into its rail mountings, and you can connect the controller, data, and power cables to their respective connectors. Figure 16-5 shows a half-height drive fitting into its bay.

Figure 16-5

Half-height disk drive sliding into bay

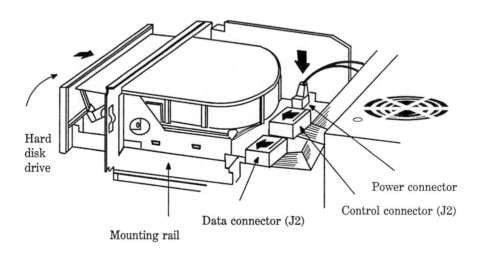

Hard
disk
drive

Mounting rail

Data connector (J2)

Power connector

Control connector (J2)

A final note—if you are installing a second hard disk, it's best not to mount it directly above the first one. Install a floppy drive between them, or, better yet, mount them side by side, if you have a choice. Hard drives generate quite a bit of heat, and extra air space will help avoid heat buildup.

Install the Controller Card

The controller card plugs into the expansion bus on the motherboard. Place it as close to the drive as possible, in the first or second slot near the power supply. Route the cables neatly to the hard disk. Avoid placing them where they can get pinched by the top of the case when you slide it back on.

A standard XT/AT-type controller comes with two hard disk cables, one with a 34-pin connector, and one with a 20-pin connector. A stripe on the edge of the cable indicates which wire goes to pin number one. There will usually be a number 1 silk-screened on the circuit board near the appropriate controller connector pin.

On XT cards that are hard disk controllers only, the 34-pin controller ribbon connector is labeled J1. The 20-pin data ribbon connector is labeled J2 or J3. Use J2 if you're installing a single hard drive.

If an adapter controls more than one device, it's called a *multifunction card*. Most AT-type controllers fit this qualification. Not only do AT-type controllers manage a hard disk controller, they also govern the floppy drives and sometimes the parallel/serial ports as well. The numbering system for AT-type hard disk controllers is different, since they can control two floppy drives. J1, the first connector, is reserved for the floppies. J2 is usually missing, J3 and J4 are for the 20-pin data cables, and J5 is for the 34-pin controller ribbon.

Preliminary Testing

The hardware is now in place, so reconnect the AC power cord. Do not replace the cover yet—only in a perfect world does everything go right the first time, and you're probably too optimistic if you reassemble the PC at this stage. Do a "smoke test" first.

Insert a DOS boot disk in the floppy drive, and turn on power to the system. Does the hard disk sound like it's spinning? Does the LED indicator light blink and go off? If so, good. If not, you've got a problem. If your monitor shows a disk-related error message, shut off the PC and check your connections. Reseat any boards you installed or replaced; they may not have been put in properly.

When you can boot from the floppy drive and get the DOS time and date display, you're ready for the software portion of hard disk installation.

FORMATTING THE DISK

If your new disk was preformatted by the dealer or manufacturer, you've saved a bit of trouble. But chances are, if you installed the disk yourself, you'll have to format it yourself. Most hard disks do not come preformatted from the manufacturer. To find out if your disk was preformatted,

- Ask your vendor.

- Open the floppy drive door and try booting directly from the hard disk. If you get the C prompt, the disk was preformatted.

- Boot from the floppy drive, and then list the hard disk directory by typing **DIR C:**. If you don't get an error message, the disk is preformatted.

- Run FDISK. If you can't create a DOS partition, the disk needs to be low-level formatted. If it gives you an option to create a DOS partition, the disk was preformatted; press ESC to return to DOS.

If the disk was preformatted, you need to determine if it's a low-level or high-level format. Try copying a file to the disk. If you succeed, the disk has been high-level formatted. If you fail, but FDISK says you can create partitions, the disk has been low-level formatted but needs a high-level format.

Doing a Low-Level Format

If FDISK can't create a partition, you'll have to do a low-level format. The *low-level format* creates a data encoding pattern that lays out tracks and sectors on the surface. In essence, it prepares the disk for the DOS (high-level) format. There are several ways to low-level format a hard disk. Two of the most common are with ROM-based programs and third-party software.

Using ROM-Based Controller Programs

The DOS DEBUG program is often used to low-level initialize a hard disk, as described in this section. Technicians use it all the time. But DEBUG is a dangerous program; if you don't know what you're doing, you can really foul things up. Moreover, not all controllers use the ROM-based programming described here. If you feel at all unsure of your ability to use DEBUG correctly, don't hesitate to call in a technician. Or use a friendlier, third-party formatting program.

A ROM-based controller program is software embedded in a controller's ROM chip. You access it by booting from a DOS floppy and entering the DEBUG command. A dash will appear onscreen, acting as a prompt. *For most controllers*, type the following address at the dash:

```
g=c800:5
```

Note: The address for your controller may be different. Some ROMs may prompt you to enter the right address when booting up on the unformatted disk; others do not. The tech sheet or booklet that came with the controller should tell you what values to enter.

In many systems an initialization menu now appears, requiring you to answer specific questions about the disk, such as total number of cylinders, number of heads, precomp cylinder, interleave factor, and so on. The answers to these technical questions should be available in table format in the documentation that came with your disk. If you don't see these questions, reboot the machine to cancel the address. Then locate the correct address in your controller documentation and try again.

On the initialization menu, most items will have a default value, which you should select. Others, though, need a specific piece of information and you must supply it. The necessary parameters may not be listed on the hard disk itself, but may be in the tech sheet. If you cannot find the answers, call the dealer, or call the controller card manufacturer's tech support line. Don't try to guess these values.

Note: Some controllers that do have the DEBUG option may not have it active from the factory, and you may need to change a jumper setting in order to activate it. Consult the tech sheet.

Using Third-Party Formatting Software

As you can see, DEBUG has its drawbacks. Another, often easier, option is to use a third-party formatting program. Three of the best are Ontrack's Disk Manager, Golden Bow Systems' V-Feature Deluxe, and Storage Dimensions' SpeedStor programs. Addresses and telephone numbers for these manufacturers are listed next.

Disk Manager
Ontrack Computer Systems, Inc.
6321 Bury Drive, Suites 16-19
Eden Prairie, MN 55436
(800) 753-1333

V-Feature Deluxe
Golden Bow Systems
P.O. Box 3039
San Diego, CA 92163
(800) 284-3269

SpeedStor
Storage Dimensions
2145 Hamilton Avenue
San Jose, CA 95125
(408) 879-0300

These packages are popular because they automate the hard disk installation process for you and let you customize your drive. You may even get a copy of one of these programs free when you purchase the hard disk. Many manufacturers include one in their package because they know it will make things easier for the user. If you get one with your disk, use it.

Defective Sectors

It's a fact of life: hard disks come with bad sectors. As mentioned earlier, they are listed on the label at the top or side of the drive. It is best to store such information where you can easily find it.

A third-party formatting utility will ask you if you want to enter the bad sectors. Answer "yes." You don't want to try to use a questionable sector. It will only come back to haunt you.

If you format with DEBUG, you may not be asked to enter defective sectors—this depends upon the controller. For example, ESDI keeps the defect list embedded on the disk, so it automatically flags bad sectors. The ST-506 interface does not.

It may seem that you have "too many" bad sectors, but don't assume this to be so. The unformatted capacity of the disk is always larger than the formatted capacity. For instance, a 30MB disk actually contains around 32MB. After you conclude high-level formatting, a directory will display how much usable space you have.

Partitioning the Disk

After completing the low-level format, the hard disk should be partitioned. Partitioning a disk accomplishes several things. First, it lets you better organize the system by dividing a large physical disk into separate logical drives—C, D, and E, for example. You can put all your accounting software on drive C, all word processing on D, and everything else on E. Or your binary programs can go to C while data files go to D and E.

Another reason for partitioning is that your hard disk will operate faster and you'll use disk space more efficently. Finally, you must partition if you plan to have more than one operating system on the same disk, for example, a DOS partition on drive C and a Xenix partition on D. Because operating systems have unique structures and require their own boot files, they must be kept isolated from one another.

On AT-class machines, after partitioning you'll have to reboot in order to change the CMOS entry for the drive type, described next.

The CMOS Chip and Drive Type

AT-class computers and above have a special chip called a complimentary metal oxide semiconductor, or *CMOS*. This is a low-power chip that can remember the system configuration for long periods of time using only the power supplied by a tiny, built-in system battery. The CMOS keeps information on memory size, monitor type, and a few other things, including some hard disk parameters.

In some systems you access CMOS using a program named SETUP, AT-SETUP, or something similar. Other machines let you do it from the keyboard alone, by pressing a combination of keys, such as CTRL-ALT-ESC, CTRL-ALT-=, or CTRL-ALT-S.

The most common CMOS setups offer you 47 different drive types from which you select to tell your system what kind of drive you have. Other manufacturers have started including a type 48, for which you enter all the settings yourself. Third-party partitioning software often will use a device driver that takes over the CMOS type 1 setting. Such device drivers will override the CMOS values for type 1 drives when needed.

If you have a disk larger than 1024 cylinders (which is about 140MB), such as a 1224-cylinder 180MB drive, DOS versions below 3.3 may still treat it as a 1024-cylinder disk. You'll lose megabytes of storage—about 40, in the case of the 180MB drive. If you think you might have this problem, run FDISK to see how many cylinders DOS thinks you have. If this number is different from the CMOS setting you entered, you may want to upgrade to DOS 3.3 or higher, or use one of the solutions suggested in the next section.

When 47 Drive Types Aren't Enough For later-model disk drives, none of the standard 47 drive types may be an exact match, so if there is no "customizable" type 48, you must choose the type that comes the closest to your disk. Unfortunately, the closest drive type may be a hundred or more cylinders shy of what you actually have, so you lose a few dozen megabytes of usable disk space. After paying good money for a large capacity drive, you'd like to use every bit of space you can; here are three work-around solutions.

You can use one of the third-party formatting programs mentioned earlier. For example, Ontrack's Disk Manager and Golden Bow's V-Feature Deluxe let you work around the CMOS setting by setting device driver parameters for "Non-Standard Drives." On drives with more than 1024 cylinders, such device drivers perform a translation that makes DOS think it's dealing with only 1024 cylinders, thus letting you use every bit of your storage investment.

Another solution is to install a set of auxiliary ROMs with additional drive settings that provide for your drive's parameters. Fortunately, a number of computer manufacturers have extended the BIOS drive settings in their machines, which may help you avoid the problem.

If you are planning to change operating systems or install a local area network, you could add a board such as Golden Bow Systems' DUB-14. This will correct inaccurate drive tables as part of readying a system for the new operating environment.

XT-type PCs don't generate much excitement these days; compared to the features available in 286, 386, and 486 machines, XTs seem antiquated. But they share a great virtue with many other older technologies: they're simple by comparison. In the case of a hard disk, they don't put you on the hook to provide a drive type.

Setting DOS Partitions

Until DOS 4.0 became available, the largest DOS partition you could have on a disk was 32 megabytes. This was fine if your drive was 30MB or smaller, or if you could make do with two 32MB partitions on a 60MB drive. If you needed a really large partition (say, for a huge database), or if you had a 40MB disk and wanted to use it as a single, large C drive, you were out of luck. You had to create one 32MB partition, or two 20MB partitions, and another at 8MB.

This limitation in DOS 3.*x* occurs because of limits to the size of the file allocation table. DOS 4.0 quadrupled this limit to allow one 28MB partition.

DOS 3.3 offers a partial work-around for this limit. It allows the physical disk to have a 32MB-maximum bootable C partition, and an unlimited extended DOS partition, so a 100MB disk can be divided as a 32MB DOS partition and a 68MB extended DOS partition. Unfortunately, the 68 megabytes cannot be used as is; they must be subdivided into partitions no larger than 32MB. Logically, you're stuck with three 32MB partitions and one small partition for the leftover 5 to 10 megabytes. Apart from using DOS 4.0 or a special version of DOS like COMPAQ 3.3*x*, the only way around the 32MB limit is to use third-party formatters like Disk Manager, V-Feature Deluxe, or SpeedStor to break the 32MB DOS barrier.

Device Drivers and CONFIG.SYS

Some third-party hard disk partitioning programs and certain versions of DOS create their own device drivers in the root directory. Such a device driver tells DOS how to interface with the hard disk. Without it, you won't be able to get into the other partitions.

After the disk installation, partitioning, and formatting are completed, use the TYPE command to inspect the contents of your CONFIG.SYS file. Enter the command **TYPE CONFIG.SYS**. If your partitions require a device driver, you'll see a line that looks something like this:

```
DEVICE=DRIVER.SYS
```

Always keep a copy of the CONFIG.SYS file and the drivers on a floppy disk. If you ever have trouble getting into the other partitions, check the CONFIG.SYS file on your hard disk. If it's been altered or corrupted, it's much easier to copy the file from your backup floppy than to reformat the disk.

Tip: Some programs, such as Norton Utilities and PC Tools, have ways to make a "rescue disk" that will deal with this situation automatically.

Using FDISK to Partition

Use the DOS utility FDISK only if you are *not* using a third-party program to prepare your drive. Type **FDISK** to bring up the FDISK menu. Option 1 asks if you want to create a DOS partition; select it. It will prompt you for the partition size, which depends on how many partitions you plan to make. It will ask you to enter the number of cylinders, from 0 to 614.

For best storage efficiency, make your partitions larger than 16MB and smaller than 33MB, when possible. The reason for this has to do with the way DOS manipulates file allocations and cluster size. For partitions under 16MB, DOS creates 4K clusters; for those from 16MB to 33MB, it makes 2K clusters. Above 33MB clusters may be 4, 8, or 16K. (This is for hard disks with cluster sizes set at 512 bytes, the most common setting.) Since the smallest unit that can be written to the disk is a cluster, a partition of under 16MB will waste space if you have lots of small files. For example, a file containing one name and address is allocated a full cluster on the drive, which is just as much space as another file with 500 names and addresses. If, as most power users do, you use many short batch files, the amount of waste can be surprising.

After creating the disk partitions, go back to the FDISK menu and select option 2 to make the first partition active, or bootable. (Some partitioning programs will do this step for you automatically.) Now you're ready to move on. Reboot the system from the floppy disk and wait for the DOS prompt.

Doing a High-Level Format

A high-level format is accomplished by the standard DOS FORMAT command that all floppy disk users come to know and love. To use the command on a hard disk, insert a floppy disk containing the DOS FORMAT program into drive A or B and type **FORMAT C: /s**. This tells DOS to format the C partition and place the hidden system files on it. The /s option automatically copies the two hidden boot files and COMMAND.COM to the hard disk, making it bootable.

When formatting is complete, you will see a display of the number of bytes in the partition, along with other information. Reenter the FORMAT command, without the /s option this time, for the next logical drive: **FORMAT D:**. Continue until all your logical drives are formatted.

Volume Label Option
If you want to give your partitions distinctive names, use the /v option with FORMAT to attach a volume label. On newer versions of DOS, the FORMAT command will prompt you for a volume label automatically. The label

can be up to 11 characters. For example, the command FORMAT C: /s /v formats a bootable drive C with a label, and FORMAT D: /v formats drive D with a label. Alternatively, you can use the DOS LABEL utility.

Completing the Installation

If all has gone well, you should now be able to boot from drive C and access other partitions with no difficulty. Try it. If all goes well, you are finished. Shut off the PC and replace the top cover. Be careful not to pinch the cables or knock loose any connectors. If all does not go well, you may need to call the drive manufacturer or contact a qualified technician for further guidance.

Your hard disk installation is now done and you can load your software. See Chapter 10, "DOS and the Hard Disk," for tips on loading and organizing the software to be stored on your new hard disk.

MAINTENANCE

Some important things you can do to keep your hard disk running smoothly are listed here. Many of these are discussed more thoroughly elsewhere in this book, but if you've just installed a hard disk, it won't hurt to review them.

- Don't shut off the computer while the hard disk is accessing data unless your system is frozen. Most machines have a red indicator light on the front panel to tell you when disk access is taking place.

- Hard disks *are* fallible. Your data is important, so back it up regularly to floppies or some other backup medium.

- Today's newer, larger hard disk drives have automatic head-parking mechanisms that safely move the heads and lock them away from the platters when power is lost. Smaller drives don't have this feature. For these smaller drives it's an excellent idea to use a third-party head-parking utility as part of your powering-down routine. However, be sure the utility you use is compatible with your hard disk. Generic head-parking utilities that use BIOS calls are safe to use on most drives, but if you make a mistake you can do exactly what you're trying to avoid—damage your hard disk. So be cautious.

- Every so often, run one of the many available diagnostics programs on your hard disk. Some of the third-party formatters such as Disk Manager or V-Feature Deluxe provide scanning capabilities, as do the larger utility packages, such as Norton Utilities, Mace Utilities, and PC Tools. Scan for defects, and if your disk is ailing, you will discover it early enough to save much grief down the line.

- Run a disk optimizer regularly (see Chapter 8, "Utilities—Computer Housekeepers"). It will improve performance and reduce wear. When you first copy files onto a new hard disk, they go on contiguously, one cluster after another. Over time, though, as you delete and create new data, files get fragmented, or scattered across the disk surface. And when you save a file, DOS looks for the first available space on the disk; it doesn't care if it has to store your file in five or ten widely separate spaces. An optimizer makes your files contiguous again.

SUMMARY

This chapter has given you the basics about how a hard disk works, and an outline of the tasks involved in installing or replacing a hard disk drive. When you begin your installation process, be sure you have the manufacturer's instructions at hand, and use them along with the general guidance of this chapter to do a worry-free installation. If you don't have these specific installation instructions, you may want to consult a technician or call the manufacturer for more detailed help.

In the next chapter, you will learn some ways to fine-tune your computer system, to get it working faster, better, and more in tune with your exact needs.

CHAPTER SEVENTEEN

Getting the Most from Your System

Tweaking is electronics slang for fine-tuning a piece of equipment to enhance its performance. In the computer world, that means making a functioning system work faster, easier, better, or more to its user's personal preference. This chapter is about ways to take your system that extra distance. It describes an assortment of software and hardware for you to consider.

There are six major ways to enhance your system:

- Use RAM more effectively

- Tune the DOS environment

- Build a better command-line toolbox

- Make your hard disk work better

- Eliminate system power robbers

- Enhance other major components

USING RAM EFFECTIVELY

System RAM can be used to significantly speed up system operations. Data put into RAM gets erased when the power is turned off, but RAM is the fastest storage and working area your machine has. It's where a PC can access and process information at top speed. Taking full advantage of available RAM increases the number of operations performed in a given amount of time, so processing goes much faster. The result is better performance. Here are some ways to use RAM more effectively.

DOS Buffers

Buffers are a simple form of disk cache. A single DOS buffer is set automatically at exactly the same size as one disk sector, usually 512 bytes. (Hard disks that use special device drivers may have larger sector and buffer sizes.) Buffers store copies of the most recent disk sectors read by your current program; you establish the exact number of buffers for your system in the CONFIG.SYS file.

Here's how it works. Programs often have DOS refer to data or overlays that have already been read, so these reads are repeats of sector reads already done. When a data request is "remembered" in a system RAM buffer, DOS supplies the data from the buffer instead of from the disk. This bypasses the hardware, so everything speeds up. Buffers thus speed up disk access and reduce disk drive wear.

There are limits to what a DOS buffer can do. Buffers are only effective on short, sequential tasks. A utility program like DISKCOPY, for example, takes maximum advantage of buffers, because it scoops up several contiguous sectors at a time. Other programs do not always read sectors sequentially—especially on fragmented disks. Also, buffers aren't sophisticated enough to suppress unnecessary disk writes, so their speed improvements are marginal. An intelligent disk cache (discussed later in this chapter) produces much better results, and so it is a vital upgrade item for hard disk users.

Even though DOS buffers aren't as advanced as disk caching programs (see "Disk Caches" in Chapter 8), setting the right buffer size can make a big difference in your system's performance. Moreover, if your system doesn't have an intelligent disk cache, correct buffer use becomes critical.

The Right BUFFERS= Statement

How many buffers to set depends upon several things, but mostly the best number depends on whether you have a disk cache. To find out, look at your

AUTOEXEC.BAT file for any command containing the word *cache*. (Use the command FIND "CACHE" < AUTOEXEC.BAT if you have no file searching utility.) If no cache is installed, try looking in CONFIG.SYS. No indication of a cache in either of these boot files probably means you have no cache installed.

If you do have a disk cache program, check its manual to see if it supports both floppy disks and hard disk drives. If it does, you can probably set your DOS buffers quite low—to 2 or 3—without sacrificing performance. When a disk cache does not support floppies, too small a buffer setting will slow down any operation involving reading or writing of floppies. You may want to keep at least ten buffers just to handle floppy disk transfers. If you have no hard disk or have a large capacity hard disk, set buffers to 15 or so.

For systems without a disk cache, the right number of buffers will depend on the applications you use, and on whether you have a hard disk. For most applications, 15 to 25 buffers works best. Start at 15 and work up, because each additional buffer takes a sector's worth of memory, plus some overhead—usually a total of 528 bytes. Look in your applications program manuals for specific advice on the number of buffers they need, and use the highest recommended number to determine your BUFFERS= value. Although this means you'll be dedicating a little more RAM to buffers, at least you won't have to reboot with a different CONFIG.SYS file, specifying more buffers, when you want to use the application that requires a higher BUFFERS setting. Weigh the benefits of enhanced performance against the conventional memory you're giving up. If you don't have enough memory to run a critical application, you may have to sacrifice some performance by reducing the number of buffers and using that memory for your applications program instead.

If you have a DOS version or a utility program that lets you use upper memory blocks (UMBs) instead of main memory for buffers, you can be less conservative and just set your buffers to 25 without having to do all the research. Don't worry about conserving available DOS conventional memory, but don't set your buffers much higher than 25. DOS looks into each buffer before it reads the disk, and that takes time. Too many buffers can degrade system speed.

You can find the optimal DOS buffer size for larger applications programs if you're willing to take the time to experiment. Some word processors, spreadsheets, and database managers work faster when you fine-tune the DOS buffers. Start with 10 buffers and work your way up, rebooting each time you change the number of buffers in your CONFIG.SYS file. The alternative preferred by most users is to set the number of buffers at 15, 20, or 25, depending upon what their largest application requires. If you really want to optimize performance, you're better off with an intelligent disk cache anyway.

Read-Ahead Buffers

Starting with DOS 4.0, DOS supports secondary buffers, and the BUF-FERS command has two options. Instead of BUFFERS = [*value*], the syntax is BUFFERS = [*value*][,*value*] where the *value*s are the number of primary buffers and the maximum number of sectors they can read ahead.

Let's look at the second BUFFERS value, the one that sets the read-ahead information for reading file data. This option is useful if you're moving through a file sequentially. When you read the first sector, DOS will also read as many sectors ahead of that one as you have specified in the second BUFFERS value. The recommended setting for this value is the size of a cluster, in sectors—because that's the size DOS has to read anyway. If DOS later must come back to read other data in that cluster, it's already in a buffer.

To determine the cluster size, use a utility such as the Norton Utilities 5.0 SYSINFO program, or PC Tools PC-SHELL. Figure 17-1 shows SYS-INFO reporting four sectors per cluster; so BUFFERS = 16,4 would set 16 buffers, with disk reads that are 4 sectors (that is, 2K) long. This setting will greatly increase the illustrated system's efficiency at repeated, sequential disk reads.

The Right FILES= Statement

The FILES= statement in CONFIG.SYS determines the number of *file handles* DOS can use at one time. Don't confuse file handles with files—20 files in a directory doesn't mean you have 20 file handles available in that directory. Rather, a *file handle* is a number that tells DOS the names and locations of active files and devices. Each open file (that is, each file currently in use by DOS, including all active overlays and TSR programs) requires one or more file handles.

DOS uses five file handles just by booting up, so the default value of FILES=8 is seldom enough. Since each file handle takes relatively few bytes of memory, many users have settled on a standard of FILES=20. Twenty was the highest number you could set, anyway, until DOS 3.0 raised the maximum to FILES=255, and 20 works well for almost all applications.

Figure 17-1

SYSINFO disk report

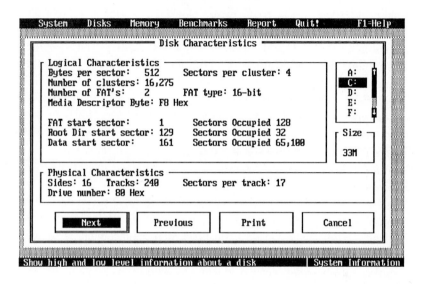

```
 System    Disks    Memory    Benchmarks    Report    Quit!        F1=Help
┌─────────────────────────── Disk Characteristics ───────────────────────────┐
│ ┌ Logical Characteristics ─────────────────────────────────┐    ┌────┐      │
│ │ Bytes per sector:   512      Sectors per cluster: 4       │    │ A: │▲     │
│ │ Number of clusters: 16,275                               │    │ C: │      │
│ │ Number of FAT's:    2        FAT type: 16-bit            │    │ D: │      │
│ │ Media Descriptor Byte: F8 Hex                           │    │ E: │      │
│ │                                                          │    │ F: │▼     │
│ │ FAT start sector:      1     Sectors Occupied 128       │    └────┘      │
│ │ Root Dir start sector: 129   Sectors Occupied 32        │    ┌ Size ┐    │
│ │ Data start sector:     161   Sectors Occupied 65,100    │    │      │    │
│ │                                                          │    │ 33M  │    │
│ └──────────────────────────────────────────────────────────┘    └──────┘    │
│ ┌ Physical Characteristics ────────────────────────────────┐                │
│ │ Sides: 16   Tracks: 240    Sectors per track: 17         │                │
│ │ Drive number: 80 Hex                                     │                │
│ └──────────────────────────────────────────────────────────┘                │
│      ┌──────────┐   ┌──────────┐   ┌──────────┐   ┌──────────┐              │
│      │   Next   │   │ Previous │   │  Print   │   │  Cancel  │              │
│      └──────────┘   └──────────┘   └──────────┘   └──────────┘              │
└─────────────────────────────────────────────────────────────────────────────┘
 Show high and low level information about a disk       │ System Information
```

You can afford to be more generous if you're using a utility program or DOS version (DR DOS, and some proprietary DOS versions) that takes advantage of upper memory blocks. On systems that multitask or operate in a multiuser or network environment, set the number of DOS files higher, if you can. The documentation for these types of applications will provide a recommended setting, which may range from 40 to as high as 99. Specifying too many files won't slow your system down, but it will waste some memory—62 bytes for each file handle. That's not much, but it can add up, and there's no point in reserving room for dozens of file handles that will never be used in a single-tasking environment.

Using a RAM Disk

A RAM disk simulates a disk in memory, using high-speed RAM arranged logically into mock tracks and sectors. The original RAM disk program for

PC-DOS was called VDISK (virtual disk). In MS-DOS, the equivalent device driver is RAMDRIVE.SYS.

DOS treats a RAM disk exactly as though it were a physical disk drive. The main difference is the RAM disk's speed compared to a physical disk. With a RAM disk there's no need to move any read/write heads, no disk drive motor to wait for, and no delay while the right physical disk sector rotates under the heads. Rather, it's all done electronically, at the speed of the computer's CPU.

RAM disks have only three major limitations. First, they are not always as big as you want them to be. A hard disk may have 20MB or more of storage, while a RAM disk is often only 360K or so. Some RAM disks do have 5 or 6MB, but even a 1MB RAM disk is considered enormous.

Another limitation arises if power is interrupted—everything on a RAM disk disappears as memory is wiped clean.

Finally, once a file is copied to a RAM disk, it stays there until you take the trouble to erase it. By contrast, disk caches revise their contents dynamically in an earliest-used, first-discarded replacement scheme. Data only goes to a cache the first time it's actually needed, and only stays there if it continues to be referenced from time to time. A cache is a very efficient use of memory.

If you have a disk cache, you may want to try setting up a small RAM disk for COMMAND.COM and temporary program files, as outlined in the following section, and use the disk cache to handle other programs.

RAM Disk Benefits   The main use of a RAM disk is to hold small or frequently used files, temporary files, and the COMSPEC copy of COMMAND.COM. The ability to keep COMMAND.COM on a RAM disk is a real bonus on a floppy-based system, where users chafe under the need to switch floppies to provide DOS with a copy of its command processor. A RAM disk does away with that annoyance. Even hard disk system performance can improve markedly when DOS reloads COMMAND.COM from a RAM disk instead of waiting for a physical disk read.

Programmers like RAM disks for doing source code compilations, which is a time-consuming, disk-intensive process. Anything that takes many disk read/writes will go faster on a RAM disk. Spell-checking, sorting, indexing, and other disk-intensive operations all speed up with a RAM disk. Programs that create temporary files as they process also run much faster when they can use a RAM disk for that purpose.

When a DOS batch file copies work files to a RAM disk before processing begins, performance will sometimes improve markedly. The improve-

---

READ.ME

Saving Work Automatically from a RAM Disk

You can lose the work you do on a RAM disk if you forget to save it before you turn off the computer. To reduce this danger, use a batch file modeled after this example:

```
echo off
: rem edit.bat uses ed.exe program to edit %1 file on ram disk
copy %1 e:\           (Copy work file to RAM disk)
ed e:\%1              (Edit work file in RAM disk)
copy e:\%1            (Copy work file back to physical disk)
```

Even with this batch file in place, a power failure or other traumatic event will destroy any work done on the RAM disk. In normal practice, though, the batch file will save your final version to a physical disk as soon as you leave the editor program.

---

ment is especially dramatic on a floppy-based system. Batch files also run much faster on a RAM disk, especially if you have no disk cache.

Installing the RAM Disk

The DEVICE = statement syntax for a VDISK RAM disk in DOS 3.x is

DEVICE = VDISK.SYS [*size*] [*sector size*] [*directory size*] [/e or /a]
or
DEVICE = RAMDISK.SYS [*size*] [*sector size*] [*directory size*] [/e or /a]

Here are definitions of the DEVICE = variables.

- *Size* RAM disks default to 64K in size. If that is wrong for your needs, specify the size you want in kilobytes. On a PC or XT with no extended memory, you may want to set the minimum size of 4K (VDISK.SYS) or 16K (RAMDRIVE.SYS), and use it only for small batch or utility files. On systems with 1024K installed, a larger-size RAM disk in upper memory (up to a maximum of 384K) will be more useful for temporary files created by programs. On still larger systems with expanded or extended memory, you can set a size as large as the space required for all the files you expect to use on the RAM drive. For example, if you frequently search a 1MB database, you may want to copy it to a large RAM disk and search it there. Bear in mind that, for most purposes, a large disk cache makes better use of memory than a large RAM disk.

Note: If you locate a RAM disk in lower memory, DOS requires at least 64K of lower memory left over from the RAM disk for normal use by DOS. If you try to make the RAM disk too large, DOS will adjust the size downward automatically, as needed.

- *Sector size*   If your goal is to speed up batch files and small utilities, the default sector size of 128 bytes will do nicely. For a single, large database or overlay file, a larger sector size of 256K or 512K (VDISK.SYS), or even 1024K (RAMDRIVE.SYS) will produce extra storage space for the same size RAM disk. If you're going to increase the sector size, be sure also to specify the RAM disk capacity—even if you're keeping it at the 64K default—because DOS always interprets the first number it sees as the RAM drive capacity.

- *Directory size*   Acceptable range is 2 to 512 filenames (VDISK.SYS) or 2 to 1024 filenames (RAMDRIVE.SYS). The default is 64 filenames, which is fine for most purposes. To hold many small batch or utility files, however, increase the maximum directory size to 96 or 128 (few users need more). Increasing the number of directory entries may use additional memory. If you're going to change the directory size, be sure to specify a drive capacity and sector size first, even if you are using their default values.

- *Memory type*   On an AT-class machine with 384K of extended memory available, specify /e to locate the RAM disk in the upper memory blocks. If you have expanded memory, specify /a to locate the drive above the bottom 1024K of RAM. If you specify neither /e nor /a, DOS will carve the RAM disk out of conventional memory. In conventional memory, DOS will adjust the size of your RAM disk downward if the specified size doesn't leave you at least 64K of free memory for DOS.

To show how this all works together, here's an example. Assume you are using MS-DOS 3.2. To create a 384K RAM disk in upper memory, with a sector size of 128 bytes and a directory that can hold 96 files, add the following line to your CONFIG.SYS file:

```
device=ramdisk.sys 384 128 96 /e
```

The appropriate disk size, sector size, and directory size will all depend upon how many files you expect to copy to the RAM disk, and how big they are. A low maximum number of files may be just right to hold a swap-out file for a major environment, such as HomeBase, Windows, Carousel, Back and Forth, or the like. Increasing sector size also can buy a little extra space.

Note: MS-DOS RAMDRIVE.SYS versions 3.2 and higher permit the /e and /a options. PC-DOS VDISK.SYS didn't allow that choice until version 4.0. Several third-party RAM disk drivers are available that use upper memory with earlier DOS versions.

READ.ME

Changing the COMSPEC

A principal RAM disk benefit is to let you move COMMAND.COM there and never have to wait for DOS to read COMMAND.COM from a physical disk upon leaving a program. To speed up your system by placing a copy of COMMAND.COM on a RAM disk, follow this procedure:

1. Set up the RAM disk in your CONFIG.SYS file. In DOS, you'll use either VDISK.SYS or RAMDISK.SYS. You can also use any of the numerous third-party RAM disks; some of them are faster, more efficient, or more fully featured than the DOS versions.

2. Copy COMMAND.COM to the RAM disk. You can make this step automatic each time you start your system, by adding the following command to your AUTOEXEC.BAT file. (Assume the RAM disk uses the logical drive letter E.)

   ```
   copy c:\command.com e:\
   ```

3. Finally, instruct DOS to look on the RAM disk instead of the floppy or hard drive when it needs to read COMMAND.COM. This step also can be placed in your AUTOEXEC.BAT file, as follows:

   ```
   set comspec=e:\command.com
   ```

Placing the RAM Disk First in PATH Always specify RAM disks first in your PATH statement. Searching a RAM disk for a file takes very little time anyway, since it happens in memory. Placing the RAM disk first in the path simply removes unnecessary waits for mechanical disk operations.

Using a Disk Cache

When disk caches first became available, they were hard to get, expensive, and didn't always work well. Today they're so popular that a disk cache is often built into a hard disk or its controller card. (Cards with built-in caches are called *smart* controllers.) Motherboards sometimes come equipped with caches. There are even high-speed caches for data already held in standard memory, called *memory caches*.

Many software-based disk caches are available commercially and through user-supported software. Starting with DOS 4.0, MS-DOS also supplies a disk cache, called SMARTDRV.SYS. The SMARTDRV.SYS cache isn't very fast compared to other disk caches, but it is an improvement over DOS's buffers and is guaranteed to be DOS compatible. Only the later versions of SMARTDRIVE.SYS are compatible with Windows 3.

Third-party disk caches offer the most options and best performance, and they continue to improve. A number of these caches are bundled with other software (PC Tools, Norton Utilities, and Mace Utilities). Other leading caches include Multisoft's PC Kwik, Golden Bow System's VCACHE, the Aldridge Company's Cache86, and Future Computer Systems' FAST!

With any cache program, it is important to check the documentation for compatibility warnings. Disk cache incompatibilities can cause major problems. For example, some formatting systems change the number of bytes per sector in order to "fool" DOS into handling larger partitions, while the disk cache may assume you have the standard 512 bytes per sector. With your drive and your cache marching to different drummers, the results are completely unpredictable. Disk optimizers, too, warn against using incompatible caches, for the same reason. If you ignore such warnings, you can thoroughly trash your files.

Memory Management

Effective memory management is essential to maximize your system's performance. System memory is a primary computer resource, and gets used up quickly. On newer machines, attempts to manage additional memory using the device drivers that come with DOS can cause strange results. Device drivers use up conventional memory. You will save memory by moving them to the upper memory blocks. Third-party memory managers offer this alternative—they stretch available memory by effectively adding memory to your main DOS working area.

You may be planning to spend your first system-enhancement funds on a larger hard disk, but the chances are good that you'll run out of RAM long before you run out of disk storage. If you manage your memory correctly, however, you'll be able to use a healthy number of files, buffers, print buffers, and so forth, without ever having to invest in new hardware. That makes a good memory manager, such as QEMM, 386-MAX, or HeadRoom, a true cost-effective bargain.

Memory managers for 386-class machines perform three critical tasks. They make expanded memory available for applications that can take advantage of it. They reserve as much directly extended memory as you specify. And they can be used to load device drivers, TSRs, and DOS files and buffers into upper memory.

TSR memory managers load and unload memory resident programs from conventional memory (below 640K) without fuss and bother. You don't need extra memory in your system to benefit from TSR memory management. TSR management utilities that map, manage, and release occupied memory on demand are covered in more detail a bit later in this chapter. See Chapter 8 for more about upper memory managers.

Extended, Expanded, and Upper Memory

High RAM, or *upper memory*, is the 384K area of memory between 640K and 1024K that DOS cannot use, but that an 8088 chip can directly control. This memory originally was intended for part of the DOS working area, but during the original IBM PC design process a debate started about how much RAM was really needed. A large group of engineers wanted to use the entire 1024K, but another group lobbied for a 640K limit, and won. The 640K allocation was ten times the then normal 64K memory capacity, and lowering the addressable memory size made it easier to manage memory in some highly technical ways. It was a reasonable, if disputed, decision.

The 640K limit now hinders programmers and users alike. Upper memory can be made usable by various special programs, and is becoming increasingly important. It's wise to take full advantage of upper memory by loading drivers and TSRs there; everything you put in upper memory leaves more room below 640K for programs.

There are different types of high memory located above the 640K DOS limit.

- *Upper memory*   AT-class systems come with 384K of upper memory, which is sometimes loosely considered part of extended memory, or sometimes part of expanded memory, depending upon how it is used. It's simpler just to call this area upper memory, because it lies between the DOS-addressable, 640K limit and the 8088-addressable, CPU 1024K limit. With a 386 or 486 processor, you can use upper memory to "load high," in the blocks between 640K and 1024K. On 286-, 386-, and 486-based systems, the 384K of upper memory, if used as extended memory, is faster than either conventional or expanded memory. It can be used as extended memory by only a limited number of programs designed specifically for extended memory, such as RAM disks and cache programs.

- *Expanded memory*   This memory above 1MB is managed by a standard known as the Lotus-Intel-Microsoft (LIM) standard, designed by a multicompany team. Under LIM, the top 64K of regular memory is reserved as a "page" that holds up to four 16K increments of program code, or data, on an as-needed basis. When a program needs information from this page, the existing data is removed (paged out) to a remote high-memory address, and the new data is installed (paged in). This lets a program operate as though a great deal more than the 640K conventional memory were available—up to 32 extra megabytes.

    Expanded memory is slower than extended memory and requires an expanded memory manager (EMM) like QEMM or 386-MAX. Some programs, such as PCED, take advantage of the large 16K minimum increment by adjusting their operating size to fit. More often, the 16K minimum increment just leads to wasted memory space. Still, the paging technique has made large chunks of additional memory available to programmers, and many programs now run best in expanded memory.

- *Extended Memory*   This is memory located above 640K that can be directly addressed on 286- and 386-based systems when the CPUs operate in what is called *protected mode*. On 286-based systems, the upper memory (between 640 and 1024K) can be used by device drivers. However, once you enter protected mode to access memory above 1024K, you cannot get back to normal DOS without rebooting. On

386-based machines you can switch back and forth, but it takes time. As a result, extended memory is used more often in multitasking operating systems, such as OS/2 and UNIX. It is most often tapped by DOS in unprotected mode using EMM paging programs like QEMM and 386-MAX.

Shadow RAM and Memory Cache

Shadow RAM, employed by some 386 systems and by the NEAT ChipSet from Chips & Technologies, is a technique using high-speed memory to duplicate the slower memory of the BIOS ROM chip. In normal operation, a computer makes frequent reference to the ROM BIOS I/O information (in programming, these references are named *BIOS calls*). By storing the BIOS information in fast RAM instead of slow ROM, program operation (and everything else involving I/O) proceeds much more quickly.

Shadow RAM is usually put into upper memory, so computers with this feature will have less high memory for device drivers. Most systems that use shadow RAM have settings to enable and disable it. Disabling shadow RAM lets you use that memory for other purposes, such as a RAM disk or additional expanded memory. You'll need to experiment to see if shadow RAM is the most effective way to use your system's upper memory blocks (UMBs).

Controlling Memory Resident (TSR) Programs

Software giant Borland International didn't invent terminate-and-stay-resident programs, but the Borland TSR notebook program, Sidekick, launched the TSR as a significant way to extend a PC's power. Back in 1981, there was little information for programmers who wanted to use the DOS quirk that makes TSRs possible. Borland changed that. Today there are hundreds of useful TSR programs, including little "tool kits" that turn ordinary programs into resident ones. The TSR has become an important item in most users' bags of tricks.

Here are some common terms used by TSRs and by programs that mangage TSRs in lower memory.

- *Mark* This operation marks the memory location where a TSR program has been loaded.

- *Release* The act of removing the TSR from the memory it occupies, making the memory available to other programs.

- *Unload* The more sophisticated TSR programs can unload, or release themselves from memory, without help from a TSR manager.

- *Disable* This operation deactivates a TSR program, usually one that is conflicting with another TSR, without unloading it from memory.

- *Enable* This reactivates a disabled TSR program.

Managing TSRs is a problem for systems that lack memory managers to load TSRs "high." The only realistic alternative to loading a TSR high is to release it when you need the space for another program. In order to do this, it must be the last program loaded. If your TSR program does not have the ability to unload itself, then without a TSR manager you either run out of memory or have to reboot to reclaim the memory.

Loading TSRs into Conventional, Expanded, or Extended Memory
The memory area you use for your TSRs will depend on your system. The best rule of thumb when loading a TSR or device driver is to leave yourself as much available conventional memory as you can. Here are the common configurations for different types of machines:

- *PC or XT* A system with an 8088/8086 processor is probably limited to conventional memory. Add-on boards give access to expanded memory.

- *286-Based Systems* These AT-class systems can handle both conventional and extended memory. Add-on expanded memory also is available.

- *386- and 486-Based Systems* These systems come supplied with conventional, extended, and expanded memory, and are equally at home with any of them.

Managing the DOS Environment

The DOS environment (Chapter 11) is an area of RAM set aside to hold variables such as PATH, PROMPT, COMSPEC, and applications program information. If you run short of memory, and have enlarged your environment using the SHELL command, you may be able to trim your environment without losing performance or features. Here are some ways to do it.

Reduce Size Directly You may have used the SHELL command to enlarge your environment, as described in Chapter 11, more than is really necessary, to leave room for temporary environment variables and the like. Half a meg—512 bytes—is a common size, but you rarely need more than 256 or 320 bytes. Because the entire environment size is added to the size of every TSR when it's loaded, the extra environment bytes get subtracted from available environment space accumulatively, once each time a TSR is loaded. Try an environment size of 256 bytes (or any amount lower than your current size) to see if you gain enough memory to solve your problem.

Make Room "On the Fly" If you maintain a small DOS environment size, you may run out of space when you try to set a new variable. You could enlarge the environment size, but if conventional memory is already at a premium, that creates new problems. Instead, try using a batch file to set an existing variable to zero, "borrow" its space, and then reset the original variable when you're finished. For example, suppose you normally use the variable LIST=D:\BIN\WP, and you need to set EDIT=C:\ED +A. The following batch file steals from LIST to supply room for EDIT:

```
: rem Steal from LIST to make room for EDIT
set list=              (Cancels LIST variable)
set edit=c:\ed +a      (Sets new variable)
edit %1 %2 %3          (Runs EDIT with parameters)
set edit=              (Cancels EDIT variable)
set list=b:\bin\wp     (Resets LIST variable)
```

Use SUBST to Shorten the PATH Statement If you have a path full of long directory specifications, you can trim a lot of space by using the DOS SUBST command. If you enter the commands SUBST G: D:\WORDPROC \WORDSTAR and SUBST H: C:\BIN\UTIL\MOUSE, you can represent these two directory paths in your PATH command as G:\;H:\ instead of with the longer names. The SUBST drive letters are not as descriptive as the original directory names, so the strategy works best for subdirectories you rarely visit but do need to have in the path.

Start Programs Using Batch Files To use this path-shortening trick, create batch files to start your major applications and utility programs. For example, the following batch file might start a database program:

```
echo off
: rem Starts PC-FILE on specified database
c:
cd \pcfile\data
..\pcf %1 %2 %3
```

Store all such batch files in a single directory (say, C:\BATCH). Then you can set PATH=C:\BATCH and leave out all the individual directories that hold your application programs. A path shortened this way can save a lot of DOS environment space.

Use a Shorter Prompt   Fancy prompts of the sort described in Chapter 11 are fun, but they do take up environment space.

IMPROVING YOUR COMMAND LINE TOOLBOX

DOS's COMMAND.COM supports a series of internal commands, such as DIR, COPY, DEL, and so on. These are called *resident* because they are part of the DOS command set kept in memory at all times. Alternative COMMAND programs offer the ability to place additional commands— including ones you invent yourself—into memory residence. That keeps them available at all times, the way the COMMAND.COM resident commands are. This greatly enhances your command line flexibility.

Both DOS and some third parties supply a variety of external utility programs (*external commands*, as Microsoft calls them). With batch files (covered in Chapter 11) you can construct your own command line utilities, again tailored to your specific needs.

Command line tools—resident and nonresident—save time and keystrokes. Saving time increases productivity; saving keystrokes reduces typing errors. Here are some command line tools you can try.

Command Line Editors

Command line editors work through *synonyms*, sometimes called *aliases* or *command macros*. These operate like small batch files held in memory;

thus, a synonym D might stand for DIR %1 /p, and another synonym DW might stand for DIR %1 /w. When you enter the single letter D at the command line, it processes the command just as if you had typed DIR /p. You save both time and potential typing errors.

For more complicated synonyms that represent multiple DOS commands, each command is separated by a special character. For example, the popular synonym program PCED uses the caret (ˆ) to separate individual DOS commands. A line such as

```
syn  gl   'c:^cd \ref\glossary^gl.exe'
```

thus creates a memory-resident equivalent to a small batch file with these lines:

```
c:                      (Change to drive C)
cd \ref\glossary        (Change to GLOSSARY subdirectory)
gl.exe %1 %2 %3 [...]   (Run the program GL.EXE)
```

Synonyms are not quite as flexible as batch files in some ways—for example, they can't branch very well. Any batch file done without branching, however, can be made into a synonym. On the other hand, synonyms are much more flexible than stand-alone DOS commands, because (like batch files) they let you specify parameters as part of the synonym you type on the command line. You don't have to memorize the options or type them accurately every time you use the command.

If you work at the DOS prompt (and if you're tweaking your system, you probably do), try a synonym/alias program like PCED, ALIAS, or ANARKEY. You'll wonder how you ever got by without it.

Batch Files as Command Line Tools

Batch files are another powerful command line tool, and they're more flexible and powerful even than command synonyms—but there are penalties for this power. Short batch files, for their size (typically 50 to 200 bytes), take a lot of disk space (typically 2K minimum). They also are slow to run from a disk, since DOS must read them one line at a time. Without a disk cache, especially if you're working from floppies, it gets truly annoying.

The read/write heads grind back and forth as the machine reads one slow line at a time. It can wear *you* down faster than it wears out a disk drive! But there are solutions:

- A disk cache is an excellent answer to head-grind, for it allows the batch file to be read in a single pass. The cache passes the batch file commands to DOS one at a time, and the days of listening to heads grind back and forth are gone forever.

- Another solution is to create a RAM disk large enough to hold your small batch files, and copy them to the RAM disk at bootup. Held in a RAM disk, your small batch files are almost as fast as synonyms, since DOS never has to wait for physical disk operations. In a floppy-based system the improvement is truly dramatic. The result will be a quiet, fast operation with a minimum of fuss.

- A third solution to head-grind is to use one of several utilities that compile batch files into executable binary files, which are read all at once, instead of a line at a time. Douglas Boling's program, BAT2EXEC, is one example. It is available free on many BBSs.

Compressing Batch Files to Save Disk Space   A side benefit of loading batch files onto a RAM disk is that you can use the floppy disk default sector size of 128 bytes (the default for both PC-DOS' VDISK.SYS and MS-DOS' RAMDRIVE.SYS). Small batch files will be stored efficiently, without a lot of wasted space. Since most hard disks have a 512-byte sector size, you can pass this benefit on to your overcrowded hard or floppy disk. Just archive your smaller batch files into a single compressed file, using any good file compression utility. Both authors prefer PKZIP, but the slower LHA, (NoGate Consulting's highly configurable PAK program), and ARC are also good choices. All are available through shareware sources. What these programs do is fold all your small batch files into one larger file that does not waste valuable disk space.

When your batch files are compressed, you won't be able to use them directly; you'll first need to uncompress them on your RAM disk at bootup.

READ.ME

Fast, Quiet RAM Drive Bootups

As you tailor your system more and more to your own liking, you'll notice your AUTOEXEC.BAT growing longer. You may even want to keep several different AUTOEXEC.BAT files for your various applications programs. For example, one program may be compatible with an enhanced TSR ANSI graphics program. Another may require a startup with no TSRs, and yet a third may need extended memory at boot time.

To speed the bootup procedure, you can create a tiny, universal AUTOEXEC.BAT like this:

```
echo off
copy c:\command.com e:\
if exist e:\command.com set comspec=e:\command.com
copy finish.bat e:\
e:
finish
```

This batch file transfers control to FINISH.BAT on the RAM disk instead of grinding away on a physical disk. The IF EXIST test allows for the possibility that a RAM disk didn't get created for some reason, so that COMMAND .COM did not get copied. (If that happens and you SET COMSPEC=E: \COMMAND.COM, you'll freeze at bootup.) With the IF EXIST test, the transfer of control is conditional on whether a copy of COMMAND.COM exists on your RAM drive. If the copy command doesn't succeed, things may go haywire, but at least your computer won't hang and you'll be able to determine what happened.

Now you can make FINISH.BAT as complex as you like. Since you have several different boot routines, you only need to decide which one will become FINISH.BAT for this particular startup. To give yourself the option, you can keep three different versions of FINISH.BAT under three different names, for example:

ANSIDRIV.FIL   (Fancy ANSI graphics bootup)
VANILLA.FIL   (No TSRs bootup)
EMMBOOT.FIL   (Special memory setup)

Each of these is actually a batch file—FINISH.BAT—in disguise.

READ.ME

Fast, Quiet RAM Drive Bootups (*continued*)

To change startup procedures, you simply copy the appropriate file to FINISH.BAT. For example, to reboot for the fancy ANSI graphics program, you could first enter this command

```
c:\>copy ansidriv.fil finish.bat
```

and then reboot. A short batch file (on the RAM drive, of course) similar to the following would make it even easier:

```
echo off
: rem CHOOSE.BAT sets different FINISH.BAT versions for bootup

: rem Allow upper- or lowercase parameters, and select direct file
for %%v in (ansi vanilla emm ANSI VANILLA EMM) do if %1. == %%v. goto %%v

: rem If %1 doesn't fit the "%%v" set, show syntax
echo Syntax: CHOOSE  [ANSI]  [VANILLA]  [EMM]
goto EXIT

:ANSI
: rem ANSI graphics bootup routine
copy c:\ansidriv.fil c:\finish.bat
goto EXIT

:VANILLA
: rem Plain vanilla bootup routine
copy c:\vanilla.fil c:\finish.bat
goto EXIT

:EMM
: rem Special expanded memory setup
copy c:\emmboot.fil c:\finish.bat

:EXIT
echo Ready to reboot.
```

The result will be a smooth, flexible, quiet boot routine that takes maximum advantage of your RAM disk.

For example, if your RAM disk is drive E and you used PKZIP to create a file named MYBATS.ZIP, insert the following line into your AUTOEXEC .BAT:

```
pkunzip mybats e:\
```

This command will uncompress your batch files automatically onto the RAM disk whenever you start the machine. If you've placed your RAM disk first in your PATH statement, as recommended earlier, your batch files will run quickly and quietly. You'll also save wear and tear on your disk drive.

Enhancements and Replacements for DOS Utilities

Here's a final mention about non-DOS (external) utility programs. These were discussed in Chapter 8, and the main point made there still holds true: DOS was designed as a powerful, flexible program, but ease of use was not first on the manufacturer's spec sheet. The following paragraphs describe some DOS areas where enhancements are helpful. You can get some of them in the alternative programs 4DOS and DR DOS, or as small utilities available through user-supported software channels. There are thousands of available third-party utility programs.

- A file delete command should tell you exactly which files it is deleting. There should also be an option for the user to confirm deletions. The next illustration shows how 4DOS reports progress when deleting a wildcard file group, with user confirmation. Note how deletion confirmation can save you from unintentionally deleting files.

```
m:\ » del *.fst /p
Delete m:\sysinfo2.fst ? (Y/N) : N
Delete m:\sysinfo.fst ? (Y/N) : Y
Delete m:\pct-info.fst ? (Y/N) : Y

m:\ »
```

- A file copy command should warn you when you're about to copy over another file with an identical name. This is one of the most common ways to lose data, and it is easy to avoid.

- A directory maintenance utility should let you see and mark a list of files before taking action, so you can tell what the results will be in context.

- There should be a move command to reassign a file to a different directory by changing its path name, rather than by copying it to a different directory and then deleting the original. Move commands work much faster than copy commands, and they avoid copy errors.

- The delete and format commands should warn you specifically of what you are about to do.

4DOS, DR DOS, and every major DOS shell program take care of many of these DOS shortcomings. Even so, every power user who ever tweaked a system has a personal collection of third-party utilities that fit his or her own needs and tastes.

ENHANCING HARD DISK OPERATION

Although most people purchase a hard disk because of its speed, most of those same users don't take advantage of their disk's top speed potential. Getting the absolute most out of a hard disk is a specialty in its own right, some of it involving technical craft beyond the scope of this book.

For the most part, however, you can improve hard disk performance in areas of both hardware and software, using some of the suggestions in the paragraphs that follow.

Working with a hard disk was discussed in both Chapter 10, "DOS and the Hard Disk" and Chapter 16, "Understanding Your Hard Disk." You may wish to review these chapters before continuing.

Upgrading the Controller

If you already have an MFM (modified frequency modulation) hard disk and controller, and are in need of more storage space, you might consider upgrading to an RLL (run length limited) or ARLL (advanced run length limited) controller, as explained in Chapter 16. Remember, though, that using RLL encoding on a disk not rated for it is risky, and your MFM hard disk may or may not be capable of using RLL or ARLL encoding. The only way to find out is to try it. Not all MFM-rated drives have a recording medium fine enough and dense enough to store data reliably at the higher RLL densities. If your disk can handle RLL, you'll effectively increase your storage capacity by at least 50 to 100 percent. You will also notice a marked improvement in your data access speed. One upgrade controller, the Perstor, is specifically designed for this kind of upgrade.

As stated, tweaking a disk beyond its rated capacity in this way is a risk. If you try it, *keep frequent backups* for several months, until you have complete confidence in the disk's reliability under the RLL encoding system. If bad sectors start cropping up on a regular basis, it means your disk is having trouble with the higher-density data storage. In this case you may be better off going back to MFM formatting on your original drive, and installing a second, RLL-rated drive using the new controller. See Chapter 16 for more details.

Caution: MFM-rated drives may perform well when reformatted to RLL, but the conversion may affect the warranty.

Making Other Hardware Improvements

Other hardware adjustments you can make to tweak your hard disk performance include the following:

Buy a Second Drive   Daisy chain your second hard disk to the first one. Almost all hard disk controllers are designed to handle two physical hard disks at once, and the second disk can be bigger and faster than the first one. Note, though, that faster seek times—the time it takes the heads to find a specific piece of data—are not as important to operating speed as the data transfer rate (DTR)—the rate at which data, once found, can be moved around. DTR is affected by the controller as well as the disk. A second disk may have a faster data seek speed and will certainly increase your storage capacity, but it may not have much effect on how fast you can access information.

Change to a New Type of Disk   This approach, while expensive, truly lets you set your own performance standard. Remember, though, that the newer, faster ESDI and SCSI drives are not compatible with PC and XT systems.

Buy a Hardware Data Compressor   An add-in board called the Stacker compresses your data before recording it on the disk. In effect, this lets you put more data into the same space. Several TSR programs are available that do the same job, but may slow your data transfer rate.

Making Formatting Changes

You learned in Chapter 16 how low-level formatting lays down a disk's tracks and sectors. In the process, you pick a disk's partition size. DOS also sets a default value for the *interleave,* which is the number of times a disk must rotate before the next sequential sector comes under the read/write heads. You can repartition your disk, or reset the interleave value, and perhaps see some impressive performance improvements.

Partition Size

If you have any logical drives with capacity smaller than 16MB or larger than 33MB, consider repartitioning your hard disk. You can do this using the DOS FDISK utility, or third-party disk formatting software, such as Ontrack Systems' Disk Manager, Golden Bow Systems' V-Feature Deluxe, or Storage Dimensions' SpeedStor.

Setting new partitions lets you optimize the cluster size. Partitions of 16 to 33MB have 2K clusters. Outside that range, they have 4K or 8K clusters. Since a cluster is the smallest area a drive can read in one pass, a smaller cluster size reduces the minimum data read per disk access—and thus improves disk speed.

Interleave

The interleave of your hard disk greatly affects disk access speed; the wrong setting can exact a surprisingly large speed penalty and your hard disk's default values may be far from optimum. If you haven't done so already, consider testing your drive's interleave.

Several inexpensive programs can adjust interleave. Three well regarded examples are Norton Utilities 5.0, SpinRite II, and OPTune. Choose carefully; it is important to use a program that is compatible with your equipment. If you have a nonstandard controller, special partitioning software, BIOS extensions, or formatting that uses a device driver, you can run into trouble. When in doubt, check with a qualified technician before using any program that affects low-level formatting.

Choosing a Backup Device

There is one rule that everyone using a hard disk should follow: *Back up your hard disk frequently!* The original and still standard method for backing up a hard disk is to run a software program that copies your files from the hard disk to floppies. Though dependable, this method takes a good deal of time and is also annoying, since you must sit and wait and change the disk each time one fills up. When the machine beeps, you remove the full disk, replace it with an empty one, and sit, and wait until the machine beeps again. This continues until your hard disk has been completely backed up.

Several hard disk backup devices have been created to speed up this process or at least make it more convenient. These peripheral devices relieve you of the floppy-disk backup shuffle by automatically backing up the entire disk to one data tape cartridge (or some other storage unit, such as digital audio tape). Anyone with a hard disk larger than 40MB will benefit greatly from using a dedicated hardware device to make backups.

There are three types of hardware backup devices: tape, magnetic disk, and optical storage. The price of each system varies, as do the advantages and disadvantages of each. Consult your dealer about the best backup hardware for your system and environment.

Software Tools

There are many software tools that speed up a hard disk, make it more reliable, save wear, and make its data more reliable. Some of these are

- Defragmenters and disk optimizers
- Directory sorters and relocators
- Directory squeezers that eliminate empty file entries
- File finders, to speed up locating a needed file
- Shells and menus, to reduce keystrokes
- Task switchers that swap programs out to expanded memory and let you jump back and forth between tasks almost instantly

Using Disk Organizers

In Chapter 10 you read about organizing your drive into a logical subdirectory tree. Another form of disk organization controls how files and subdirectories are stored on the recording medium. This is not something a casual user thinks about, and floppy disk users pretty much ignore the subject entirely. But on a hard disk it can make a big difference.

One simple and reliable way to achieve faster hard disk operation is to make sure files and subdirectories are laid down efficiently. Various third-party utilities are specifically designed to help you with that, such as the disk organizers discussed in Chapter 8, and are well worth their minor expense.

Periodically running a disk organizer does take some time, especially on a large, highly fragmented disk. But it is time well spent. The better organizers use tricks such as these:

- They locate all subdirectory names at the outside of the disk, where they can be read with almost no head travel. The effect can be a significant speedup.

- They put .EXE, .COM, and .OVL files immediately after the directory entries. These are the program files that you use frequently but rarely change, and having them on the outside of the disk accelerates access.

- They place fragmented files on the inside of the disk. These are usually your working files, and they get fragmented as you work on them. If they're kept at the inside of the disk, you won't have to move as many files to get the entire disk defragmented.

Managing Floppy Directory Limits

Most floppy disks (360K and 720K) are limited to 112 separate entries, counting one for the volume name, one for each of the hidden files on a bootable floppy, and one for each subdirectory. High-density floppy disks allow 224 files in the root directory. Hard disks normally allow 512. In any case, if you store too many small data or utility files in the root directory, you'll run out of directory room long before you run out of disk storage space.

For DOS accounting purposes, a subdirectory off the root is counted the same as a single file. At lower levels, adding a file does not add to the root directory "load." The net effect is, if you run out of directory space on a floppy, you need only make room for one more entry. You can do this by temporarily deleting a file, and then using that directory entry to create a subdirectory. You can then copy files into the subdirectory until you run out of disk space.

ELIMINATING TIME STEALERS

On computers, everything happens in cycles. That's why a faster clock generally leads to faster processing. Chips are refreshed more often, the CPU does more additions, subtractions, and compares every second, and the video display can handle more data without wavering or flickering. To get the fastest possible performance from your machine, you need to take advantage of every clock cycle, wasting as few as possible.

Some users accomplish this by removing every device driver and background program that doesn't absolutely have to be resident in memory. For example, instead of loading ANSI.SYS or one of its faster alternatives, they'll keep ANSI.SYS out of the CONFIG.SYS file entirely. Then, when they need an ANSI driver, they just invoke Michael J. Mefford's fast, small, removable TSR program, ANSI.COM.

Most users don't need to go to that extreme. Still, some types of programs truly degrade perceived performance, by robbing cycles from one program to run another, or to do something the user doesn't realize exacts a time penalty.

Using Background Processors

Background programs operate in memory (the "background") but leave the system available for use by other programs. Instead of taking all your computer's time, a background program makes use of the extra time available to the CPU while your human-slow fingers type at your word processor, database, or spreadsheet. Background programs also can dramatically improve efficiency by accomplishing long, slow operations like printing in the background while you go about your next task. The computer uses dead time to get the background task done without demanding your time.

Any background program must share the computer's processing time. While it's working, whatever you do in the foreground (tasks that are visible on the monitor) will be processed more slowly, because they don't get to use all the processing cycles. As to whether a foreground slowdown is better than waiting or going out for coffee during a task like a long print job—that is up to you. If the slowdown is preferable, then a background processor is an enhancement. Otherwise, removing the background processor to gain speed is the enhancement.

A few typical background processors are described here.

Printer Spoolers

A printer may be the slowest device you ever attach to your computer. Sometimes it seems to take forever to print a long document. To keep printers from tying up a mainframe computer's processing time, IBM invented a method called simultaneous peripheral operation online or SPOOL. Spooling allows a printer to run while the computer continues doing other things. A program or device that works this magic is called a *spooler*. Microcomputers don't have the raw power of a mainframe, and their time is usually not so expensive to waste, but they do have the same problem with printers that a mainframe has: a printer without a spooler makes you sit and wait while it grinds out the pages, one at a time.

If you have never before used a printer spooler, you are in for a pleasant surprise. There are many commercial and shareware printer spoolers. DOS, too, offers one—PRINT.COM—that acts as a background copying utility for copying disk files to the printer port. PRINT.COM is slow, but it's a good way to get acquainted with the idea. If you quickly find it indispensable, as many users do, consider moving up to one of the faster third-party spooling programs.

Hardware printer spoolers are also available. They provide their own storage and processing capabilities, so when you print a file, the hardware spooler takes over printer operation. Hardware spoolers do not cost any CPU cycles, which makes them preferred for heavy-duty printing or for multiuser, networked systems. For single-user systems, a software spooler usually does the job.

One trick to using a printer spooler is to let your applications program do all the formatting required for the document, and then print the results to disk. (Most large applications can do that.) You then copy the formatted file to the spooler, which handles the printing.

Background Communications

Communications programs that run in the background let you work on other projects while you upload or download (send or receive) large files. While your computer works away for an hour or more sending files over the telephone, you can continue working at something else instead of waiting.

Programs Tied to the Clock or to DOS Interrupts

Most background programs don't interrupt critical operations such as file copying, but instead stay in memory and use up available cycles by checking periodically to see if they (the programs) have been called into action. Not all of them will significantly degrade your system's performance by making these checks. An enhancement like a pop-up help system, for example, might make your system run 2 percent slower by breaking in from time to time to see if you're calling for help. But if that help lets you work 15 percent faster on balance, you're coming out well ahead.

Other background programs take more processing time. For instance, there are programs that put a clock in the upper right-hand corner of the screen. These clocks may be useful to some people, but they can cost up to a 20 percent system speed penalty because they are continually updated. Updating a time calculation and then updating the display takes more cycles than simply checking now and again to see if the user has pressed a hot key. If you want to use a constantly updated clock, but don't want the delay inside your application, you may be able to disable the display portion temporarily and use those CPU cycles for other purposes.

Unnecessary and Duplicate Files

Every file in your directory, including zero-byte marker files and erased temporary files, exacts a time toll while DOS is passing through a directory looking for a program. DOS even stops at erased filenames, to determine whether they have been erased. You can increase your computer's efficiency by eliminating temporary files, unnecessary files, and duplicates. After erasing them, use a directory-squeezing utility (see Chapter 8) to eliminate the erased filenames from your directory area.

CPU, SYSTEM UNIT, AND OTHER HARDWARE ENHANCEMENTS

If you find you are not satisfied with the speed or capabilities of your present system, there may be other answers besides buying a new computer. Especially in recent years, users have been able to get affordable add-ons and upgrades to enhance system performance on a budget. Here are some suggestions and cautions.

Upgrading the Motherboard

If you use a PC or XT system, you might want to consider upgrading to an AT-style motherboard. These "baby-AT" motherboards can be found for less than $150 and are reasonably easy to install. Most of them let you simply reconnect your peripherals. In some cases, you may need a new power supply or memory chips, which will add another couple of hundred dollars to the tab. If you are wary of installing a new motherboard yourself, you can have it done by a qualified technician for a small fee.

Recently, motherboards have come on the market that can boost 286-based machines to 386 and even 486 performance levels. They are more expensive than a "baby-AT" board, but they still cost less than buying a complete new system.

Installing Turbo Cards

Another popular hardware enhancement—the *turbo card*—is not quite as effective as replacing an entire motherboard. Yet turbo cards can increase your system's overall speed and performance, and offer an upgrade alternative for PC users who cannot justify the cost of a new motherboard. The improvement in system performance is close to that of a new CPU, at a fraction of the cost.

Turbo cards have a long and honorable history. Back in the days of the original Apple II, CP/M cards with Z80 chips let Apple users run WordStar and other power programs designed for Intel and Zilog processors. More recently, 286-based turbo cards have transformed XTs into fast ATs on 8-bit buses. Now a host of 386-powered turbo cards are offered for both XT- and AT-type PCs, giving them 32-bit processing power and multitasking abilities on either 8-bit or 16-bit buses.

The most recent arrivals are 80486-based turbo cards, designed to be plugged into 286- and 386-based machines. Some of these come from the original equipment manufacturers, not aftermarket sellers. For example, IBM offers a 486 turbo card for its PS/2 Model 70; it combines in a single chip the original machine's 25-MHz processor, the 82385 cache controller and static RA cache, and 80387 math coprocessor.

Reducing CPU Wait States

The *wait state* on your computer is a number that represents a special delay introduced to the CPU while it reads data from memory chips. This is necessary because today's high-speed CPUs often make requests for data faster than the memory chips can respond. You've probably heard the term "1 wait state." This means that a system's processor stops for one clock cycle each time the memory chips need to catch up. Most machines have a wait state of 1 or 0. A wait state of 0 means the system is running as fast as possible, with no delay for memory.

If you use an AT or PS/2 Model 50 or 60 at wait state 1, you may be able to reduce the wait state to 0 without losing reliability. Your machine may be set with 1 wait state because of a device that needs the extra time. Instead of letting the device slow down your entire system, you can replace it with one that's faster, or hook it up to a spooling device. (Some users who have an old, standby PC have set it up precisely as that—a general-purpose spooler that does nothing but drive printers, modems, and so on, independently of the main 286 or 386 system.)

Adjusting the RAM Refresh Rate

In order for your chips to hold memory, they must be *refreshed* every few clock cycles. The refresh rate is configurable, and most manufacturers set it high just to avoid problems with the occasional fluke system that can't handle a lower rate. The philosophy is to overbuild most of the machines rather than sell some that don't come up to specification.

If you lower the refresh rate, you can often speed up the operation of your entire system by 10 percent or more (unless you have one of the fluke problem machines). To quickly and easily test and reset your system's refresh rate, use one of the special utility programs (such as REFRESH or CBOOT) that are available as user-supported software.

Replacing BIOS Chips

Every computer contains BIOS chips. These chips contain the set of basic system programs that software designers use and build upon to create their own programs. BIOS programs handle low-level operations like screen control, disk reads and writes, and so on.

The date and version number of your BIOS chips have a bearing on your PC's performance; two users who purchase the same machine with slightly different BIOS versions may notice performance differences. By changing your BIOS chips, you can rid your system of previous BIOS bugs and add useful utilities, such as built-in CMOS setups or internal hard disk support. Contact the manufacturer for information on available BIOS upgrades.

Upgrading Memory Chips/Increasing Memory

Upgrading memory chips accomplishes two things: it adds faster memory to your system (to reduce wait states); and it adds more memory to your system (to increase capacity).

Early PCs had slower memory chips than are available today. If you have one of these slower memory chips, you should seriously consider upgrading. To check the speed of your memory chips, ask your local computer store for a diagnostic program designed to test chip speed. Or you can open your case and examine the printed number on each chip. Chip speed is measured in nanoseconds (ns), or billionths of a second. The lower the number on a chip, the faster the chip. If you see the number −20 on a chip, it stands for 200 ns. Today you can find XT chips as fast as 150 ns (−15) and AT chips as fast as 60 ns (−6).

Getting faster memory chips won't speed up your system unless they reduce your system's wait state. A system will operate no faster than its clock speed, even if your memory chips are much faster. On the other hand, your memory chips must be at least fast enough for your system's clock speed. Memory chips rated too slow for the clock will be unreliable and can cause parity errors, checksum errors, and other problems. Faster chips on an older machine, although more reliable, may be an unnecessary extravagance unless you plan also to install a faster clock.

Buying New RAM Chips

If you've got a system with 128K or 256K of conventional memory, you'll definitely want to upgrade to a full 640K. Most users nowadays have at least that much memory, and some programs now require that much just to load and run. If you have a full 640K and find you still need more memory, you are not out of luck. Although 640K is the DOS limit, you can add extended memory (on AT systems) or expanded memory to your system.

Adding memory can make programs run faster and increase your system's overall capability. This is especially true in the newer 386-based systems, where 1 to 4MB more memory can make the difference between a so-so and a super system. The additional memory lets programs run in the background. You can use it to perform several tasks at once and do other tricks that would boggle the mind of a 1981 PC user. Indeed, adding memory to your system may be an upgrade second in importance only to installing a hard disk and disk cache.

Before purchasing chips, find out whether your motherboard requires SIMMs (single in-line memory modules) or SIPPs (single in-line pin packages). If single chips are required, order them in groups of nine to fill one bank of chips at a time. Make sure that each bank of memory chips comes from the same manufacturer—if possible, from the same lot. Performance varies from one lot to the next, and mixed batches can cause parity errors. You can get the batch number by checking the date code printed on each chip.

Upgrading Your Microprocessor

Some processors have more efficient alternative processors, such as the NEC V20 in place of the Intel 8088. Check with your dealer or technician before changing processors, since hardware compatibility problems can occur.

Adding a Coprocessor

If you use a math-intensive program, you can lessen your processor's workload (and so speed up your entire system) by installing a *math coprocessor*. A coprocessor works in tandem with the main processor, supporting much of the mathematical workload.

Math coprocessors excel at multiplying and dividing large numbers, doing floating point arithmetic, handling statistics and scientific notation, and calculating pure graphics. Coprocessors can speed up calculation of standard deviations and statistical functions as much as 80 percent. On the other hand, word processing and database programs will probably be unaffected. Spreadsheet calculations will go faster only if your formulas are more complex than standard arithmetic and use floating point math. The reason is that simple arithmetic and alphanumeric operations are handled by the primary processor.

Programs that benefit from coprocessors include statistical analysis packages, other scientific or higher-math applications, and any programs that display or manipulate graphics using floating point calculations. If you have an 8088 processor, you'll want an 8087 math coprocessor. With 80286 or 80386 CPUs, you'll want 80287 or 80387 coprocessors. Intel 80486 CPUs have math coprocessors built in.

Note: A math coprocessor chip does not need to be the same speed as your system. If it is faster, your system will use it at the fastest speed your system chips can handle. Make sure the coprocessor is not slower than your system clock, however.

Adding Disk Drives

If you don't have a hard disk, you don't know what you're missing. Hard disks read and write data much faster than floppy drives, and greatly improve your system's overall efficiency—a computer without one is like a car running on half its cylinders. If you already have a hard drive, you might even want to add a second one; you can on most systems. (See Chapter 16 for more information about hard disks.)

If you are unsatisfied with your system's 360K floppy drives, you can upgrade to a faster floppy drive, or to disks with larger storage capacities. You can get a 1.2MB, 5 1/4-inch drive, or choose between 720K and 1.2MB 3 1/2-inch drives. These higher capacity drives are becoming standard, and commercial programs are often distributed on both 5 1/4-inch and 3 1/2-inch disks.

Note: An upgrade to a better floppy drive often requires a new controller. Also, upgraded floppy drives may not be compatible with older systems. Check with a computer technician if you're not sure.

Multi-I/O Cards

If you're running out of expansion slots, consider getting a multifunction card to consolidate several other cards. For example, multifunction boards can combine a clock, serial ports, parallel ports, a floppy drive controller, and game ports all on a single card.

Adding a Modem

If you'd like to telecommunicate—that is, connect your computer to other computers over a standard telephone line—you need a modem. With a modem, you can send and receive electronic mail, documents, and program files. If you find yourself shipping disks or documents to your friends and colleagues more than once a month, and if they have modems, consider getting your own. It will pay for itself in a year. Modems are cheap—you can get a high-speed, 2400-bps modem for as low as $100. There are many good communications programs available. Learning to communicate by modem can be a pleasure, as well as a productivity tool.

When purchasing a modem, you must choose between internal and external models. Also, speed (or baud) rates differ. Internal modems take an entire expansion slot, but are cheaper. The more-expensive external modems can hook into a serial port on a multifunction board, and have visible indicator lights to tell you what the modem is doing.

At one time, the speed you chose for your modem was determined by the amount of money you could spend. Today, this really isn't the case. You can purchase a 2400-baud modem (the top speed needed by most users) for the same price as a 300- or 1200-baud modem. If you're really interested in speed, you may want to spend the extra cash on a 9600-baud modem, which may be priced from $400 to $1200.

Using a Mouse

A mouse (or other pointing device) is a fine extra, especially if you're using primarily computer graphics, Windows-based applications, or desktop publishing programs. You can use the keyboard to accomplish everything a mouse does, so in that sense the mouse adds no new capability. But it is a simple addition—most of these devices plug into a serial port and can be used immediately.

Once you have your basic system up, or if you find yourself with a spare $100 to spend on enhancements, a mouse can make some programs much easier to use. More and more software provides mouse support, and it really is easier to move the cursor long distances down or across the screen with a mouse. In a Windows 3.0 environment, and in many graphics and desktop publishing programs, a mouse or trackball is a virtual necessity.

There are two types of computer mice: bus and serial. To use either, you'll have to give up a serial port or an expansion slot; select the one that best fits the options available on your system.

Upgrading Your Printer

Many users start out with a 24-pin or even a 9-pin dot-matrix printer, and then discover they really need faster or higher-quality output. Higher speed is generally available for any type of printer; check at your supplier.

High-resolution output is available in various formats, but the fast, quiet, 300 dots-per-inch (dpi) laser printer has become a business standard. Laser printers are sophisticated devices, often having as much memory and computing capacity as the computers that drive them. Probably the most widely used model is the Hewlett Packard LaserJet Series II. Other laser printers, such as the Panasonic Laser Partner series, and "house" brands like Packard- Bell's personal laser printers, also are highly regarded. Most laser printers can emulate HP LaserJet printers, so compatibility is rarely a problem.

PostScript is another popular laser printer format, especially for desktop publishing. PostScript printers are more expensive and slower than LaserJet compatible printers, but their output is very fine. PostScript compatibility is possible on LaserJet printers using an add-on board.

Bear in mind that 512K of internal printer memory is a standard configuration, especially for LaserJet II-compatible printers. That's enough to handle built-in fonts of various sizes, but for full-page graphics at 300 dpi, you'll need at least 1MB of memory. Additional memory for the printer is available as an extra-cost option, as well as various type fonts in cartridges that plug into special ports provided on the printers.

At this writing, not many nonbusiness users can justify the expense of a high-resolution laser printer, although this is changing as prices drop. However, regular laser printers (and near-laser-quality, ink-jet printers) are currently available for under $1000 — and prices are still dropping.

Getting an Uninterruptible Power Supply (UPS)

In case of flickers in your line AC power, the computer's power supply capacitors can give you a few milliseconds grace period so that you'll never notice them. An uninterruptible power supply (UPS) will provide power from a constantly recharging battery whenever the line power is interrupted. A cheaper alternative is to get a stand-by power supply, which filters the power and switches you to battery power the moment the line flickers. (Laptop computers that run on a recharging battery have a UPS built in.)

SUMMARY

In this chapter you've read about different ways to get maximum performance from your system.

The next chapter offers troubleshooting help, for times when something goes wrong. It also gives you some maintenance tips, to help you avoid trouble in the first place.

Troubleshooting, Service, and Repair

There's an old saying that prevention is the best medicine, and it's as true of computers as of anything else — regular maintenance and reasonable care can stop trouble before it happens. But it's also true that nothing lasts forever, so when problems occur, it's time to troubleshoot (or find someone to do it for you).

Sometimes a problem is laughably simple, and no one likes to call in a $50-an-hour technician only to find the power cord unplugged. Doing your own troubleshooting can avoid that kind of embarrassment. Moreover, when you can diagnose your machine's illness yourself, you may also be able to cure it yourself. Other times you'll discover you do need to call in a technician, or take the machine to a computer store for repair. There's nothing wrong with having someone else do the repair work, but it never hurts to have a good idea first of what's wrong.

This chapter describes the kind of troubleshooting you can do without a voltmeter or oscilloscope. When you haul out that diagnostic hardware, you're getting past the scope of a user's guide, and it makes sense to consult a technician or get a hardware repair manual.

The very first troubleshooting step is to prevent or head off problems before they get serious. Chips are quite reliable, and you normally won't need to do much to stay out of trouble with the hardware. If you install the hardware correctly (see Chapters 3 and 4), you'll avoid a lot of headaches. Computer software is more trouble-prone, but there, too, you can head off a crisis before it occurs.

Preventing or avoiding problems is covered first in this chapter, since it is the first phase of troubleshooting. After problem prevention, you'll find a brief discussion of how to find competent service, which is as close as many users want to get to troubleshooting electronic equipment. Finally, there are sections on software and hardware problems.

AVOIDING PROBLEMS

Preventing trouble in the first place is without a doubt the easiest way to deal with it. The first principle to follow is simple: It pays to be careful. Taking reasonable precautions won't always keep you out of trouble, but being careless is sure to bring on misfortune. Here are some general areas where a little time spent before the fact can save a lot of grief later.

DOS Commands to Use With Care

Knowing DOS is no guarantee you'll never run into difficulty—far from it. But many common problems are easy to avoid. For one thing, here are some DOS commands to handle with care.

ASSIGN, JOIN, and SUBST ASSIGN lets one drive masquerade as another, JOIN lets a drive pose as a subdirectory on a different drive, and SUBST lets a subdirectory pose as a separate drive with its own drive letter. Each of these "surrogate" commands has its uses (see Chapter 11), but can also lead to trouble. Of the three, SUBST in particular is useful for shortening path statements and shrinking the DOS environment. To keep from making mistakes with these commands, use them from a batch file that cancels them automatically when you are finished.

COPY, XCOPY, and REPLACE These commands carry out necessary functions, and XCOPY in particular is a fine program. However, they also

Figure 18-1

Tagging your files before taking action

```
Directory of C:\DOS

4201       CPI    17089    9-13-88   12:00p A
5202       CPI      459    9-13-88   12:00p A
ANSI       SYS     1647    9-13-88   12:00p A
APPEND     EXE     5794    9-13-88   12:00p A
ASSIGN     COM     1530    9-13-88   12:00p A
ATIVIDEO   SYS      566    9-13-88   12:00p A
ATTRIB     EXE    10656    9-13-88   12:00p A
BACKUP     COM    30200    9-13-88   12:00p A
→BASIC     COM     1612    9-13-88   12:00p A
→BASICA    COM     1612    9-13-88   12:00p A
 BIOSDATE COM      398    9-13-88   12:00p A
CHKDSK     COM     9819    9-13-88   12:00p A
CHMOD      COM     6528    9-13-88   12:00p A
CLKDVR     SYS      735    9-13-88   12:00p A
CLR        COM      167    9-13-88   12:00p A
COLOR      COM      155    9-13-88   12:00p A
COMP       COM     4183    9-13-88   12:00p A
COUNTRY    SYS    11254    9-13-88   12:00p A
D          SYS       41    9-13-88   12:00p A
D2SETUP    COM    10030   12-15-88    1:37p A
DEBUG      COM    15866    9-13-88   12:00p A

    74 File(s)    6348800 bytes free
```

```
    PC COMPUTING — DIRMAGIC
(C) 1988 ZD ■ Michael J. Mefford

F1   Copy          F2   Delete
F3   Rename        F4   Move
F5   Clear marks   F6   Mark all
F7   Sort Name     F8   Sort Ext.
F9   Sort Size     F10  Sort daTe



═When combined with Alt key═
F1 Copy/V   ON   F2 Confirm  ON
F3 Protect  ON   F4 Sort   ↑ (A)
F5 Highbit OFF   F6 Attributes
F7 File search   F8 New path

↵ View file, or CHDIR ← exit
String commands: F=Find L=Next
Ctrl ↵ Run file, or Load Dir
Shift Ctrl ↵ Run then pause
+/-  Mark/Unmark   Esc to Exit
```

cause more data loss than any other DOS commands, because they let you copy files over identically named files on other disks or directories—without giving you any kind of warning. Third-party utilities are available that are safer to use; you can find them on BBSs or in shareware program libraries. Figure 18-1 shows one such utility, Michael J. Mefford's DIRMAGIC program with two files tagged for copying. The program will warn you if you try copy over a file with the same name. All major shell programs and file managers issue such warnings.

The easiest way to avoid trouble when copying a file is to call up a directory in the target location first, so you can make sure no file with an identical name exists there. This is particularly important when you use wildcards (* and ?) in copy commands.

DEBUG This helpful program can write directly to your hard disk, .COM and .EXE files, board-mounted memory, and your CMOS. Using DEBUG well is an art, and you can easily get into trouble if you haven't studied it.

DEL and ERASE These are the classic troublemakers, especially when used with wildcards. When you tell DOS to delete everything (*.*) in a directory or disk, the only warning you'll ever get in most DOS versions is "Are you sure? (Y/N)." There are dozens of third-party file-management utilities (see Chapter 8) that let you tag files one at a time before deleting them—such programs are a much safer alternative than the DOS commands.

FORMAT To store files on a disk, you must format the disk. Unfortunately, in the process you wipe out any files that are already stored there. Worst of all, if you forget to enter a target drive and just enter the command, FORMAT, you can wipe out your current disk—even if it's the hard disk. To prevent this disaster, use the FORMAT.BAT strategy described in Chapter 11.

RECOVER This dangerous DOS utility is best avoided; it can truly cause a crisis. It attempts to retrieve a file that has been written to a bad sector, or to retrieve some of your files if a disk file allocation table (or FAT) becomes scrambled. *Always* reboot your machine before using programs such as RECOVER that change or rearrange basic disk-storage information; rebooting often fixes apparent FAT problems. And *always* follow the RECOVER command with a specific filename, unless the FAT is completely unreadable.

If you forget to enter a specific target filename, RECOVER will devastate a hard disk. It only handles the first 512 files on a disk, moving them into the root directory and giving them sequential FILE000.REC filenames. The rest of your files are consigned to limbo. Some of the .REC files will be your old directory tree entries, which compounds the problem. Moreover, it's all done in memory, so there are no blinking drive lights to alert you that something drastic is going on. When RECOVER is finished, all your files are in chaos, and you may never get them back.

Unfortunately, RECOVER and RESTORE (the DOS backup/restore utility) are so closely named that it's easy to confuse them. Many users simply delete RECOVER.COM from their DOS disk, or rename it to something they can't enter by accident (for example, !RECOVER.COM). Then they use a third-party file recovery program instead. Good ones—with good documentation—are available in Paul Mace Utilities, Norton Utilities, and PC Tools, among others.

Third-party utility programs also offer a partial solution if you have already fallen into the RECOVER trap. For example, Norton Utilities includes a DISKTOOL option that tries to restore files subjected to RE-COVER. Still, it's better not to depend on third-party utilities to pull you out of DOS-level trouble. So if you must use DOS RECOVER, be careful; better yet, don't use it.

Redirection and Piping These symbols ($<$, $>$, $<<$, $>>$, and $|$) can trash existing files, create files that exist only in the subdirectory area (0-byte files), and leave you hanging with no prompt as you ponder what to do next. Too many users find out about redirection symbols only when an accidental $>$ sign writes a 22-byte error message over a 97K data file. Use reasonable care with these symbols.

Avoiding Incompatibility

Installing new hardware and software can cause unexpected compatibility problems, although programmers and hardware designers try hard to avoid them. Solving such conflicts is part of tweaking your system to get maximum performance. Here are some things you can do to reduce compatibility problems.

- *Stay current with DOS* Programmers write to current versions of DOS because current versions are more powerful. If you're using an ancient version of DOS, like 2.0 or even 1.1, you may solve most of your problems just by updating to the most recent version of DOS.

- *Upgrade your ROM BIOS* Hundreds of bugs in BIOS firmware have been corrected since the early days, but some of the early BIOS chips are still around and can cause problems. These chips are usually replaceable by new, plug-in chips. If you've got an old machine, consider replacing the BIOS.

- *Don't mix and match your DOS versions* A given version of DOS often refuses to run DOS utilities written for a different version. A program called VERSION, by Mark Perko of *Computer Time* magazine, fixes this in some cases, but it's best to avoid mixing DOS versions in the first place.

- *Watch for mouse-driver conflicts* Generally programs with built-in mouse support are trouble free, but programs that add mouse support later (often as a TSR) can cause difficulty. If you're using a mouse when a problem develops, try the program without using a mouse.

- *Change keyboards* Extended, regular, and special keyboards all return different key codes, which can confuse programs. Keyboard remapping and macro programs can make things even worse. If pressing a key doesn't accomplish what you know it should, try rebooting without any TSRs or keyboard mappers. If that solves your problem, you'll need to modify your TSR or program loading sequence.

- *Specify monochrome on laptops* The LCD screens used in laptop computers need to run in monochrome. If you copy a program with color screens to your laptop, the screens may not be readable. Sometimes you can fix this by issuing the MODE BW80 command, but don't count on it. Most programs now come with monochrome, or even LCD, display options.

- *Use an autoswitching video card* With nonautomatic EGA or VGA cards, a program that tries to force a different display mode will sometimes display garbage on the screen. You may need to manually change the display mode whenever you use one of these programs. A better solution is to buy an "autoswitch" video card, or to use only programs that let you select the desired mode on the command line or during installation.

- *Follow compatibility recommendations for multitaskers and windows* Multitasking or other window programs have strict hardware and software compatibility requirements. If you're going to try these most sophisticated of PC tools, read the documentation first, and follow it carefully.

Preventing Hardware Problems

Try to make these simple rules part of your everyday operation:

- Read and follow any maintenance instructions that come with your computer.

- Follow the suggestions in Chapter 3 for choosing a site for your computer. They'll help you avoid situations that invite hardware failures.

- Keep your work area clean. Don't eat or keep cups of liquids next to the keyboard. Keep magnetic objects away from the system unit and from your floppy disks. Use commonsense housekeeping around the machine.

- If you smoke, don't smoke around your computer. Hard disk vent filters can keep out most smoke particles, but tar and other particles are murder on floppies. Combustion gases do get through to hard disk platters and condense there as tar, coating everything inside the computer, changing electrical resistances and attracting dirt and dust.

- Be careful about changing interleave. Hard-disk interleave changing programs are wonderful—but only if they're designed for your type of hard disk and controller. If you don't understand interleave, or RLL, ESDI, and SCSI disk formats, you're better off relying on your computer dealer or a consultant to know about these technical issues. At the very least, read Chapters 15 and 16 first. It's easy to get into trouble by getting too technical, too soon.

- Make connections carefully. Keeping a "spaghetti factory" of wires, plugs, and power strips under your desk is asking for trouble.

- Keep a "clean" power supply. Replace outlets if they seem loose when you plug something into them. Keep power cords out of the way of foot traffic and cleaning crews. If you see sparks or hear buzzing when you plug in a power cord, replace the outlet.

Bimetallic Expansion

One of the most serious enemies of hard disks and solid-state electronic components is *bimetallic expansion* caused by fluctuating temperatures. When two metals, such as a hard disk platter and its recording medium, are bonded or mixed, the object can become distorted when it heats up because the two metals expand at different rates. Hard disk platters lose their shape, semiconductors develop hairline cracks, and soldered connections crack or work loose. Data transmission becomes garbled and unreliable.

Turning off power has the reverse effect: two metals cool and contract at different rates. A hard disk platter no longer returns to its original shape but, instead, over a period of time can become slightly but permanently distorted. The recording medium then may peel away from the platter, and the read/write heads can gouge their way into the disk recording surface, like a phonograph needle into a vinyl record.

The only way to deal with bimetallic expansion is to minimize it. Since keeping the power off all the time or on all the time obviously isn't a practical solution for most people, you have to compromise. The best plan is to turn a computer on only once a day, leave it on (even during breaks), and turn it off again only when you are really finished working for the night. Systems that are turned on and off any more often during a 24-hour period always have lower reliability than systems that are kept turned on.

Preventing Software Problems

For software, the best preventive maintenance of all is simple: Get to know your programs. Here are some additional easy ways to keep out of trouble.

- Never use your master (original) disks to run a program. Always make a working copy and use it instead. On a hard disk system the working copy can be on the hard disk, but even so, the master floppies can still suffer accidents. Careful users make second floppy-disk copies of their master disks even on hard disk systems.

- Read the manuals for all your programs, and keep the manuals handy for future reference. They will have important information on compatibility, minimum memory requirements, DOS version needed, and other important tips and traps.

- Save your work often. You'll be furious at yourself when you realize, if your system freezes, that you haven't saved your work for hours. If your program has an option to save work automatically, perhaps on a timed schedule or after so many keystrokes, take advantage of it. Then you won't have to worry about it. If you use a program without this feature, figure out a way to remind yourself to save your work at regular intervals.

- Run new programs from the DOS command line first, by themselves, to eliminate bugs. Only after you get them running the way you like should you try them in a multitasking or task-switching environment.

- Don't press keys at random if something goes wrong. You'll only add to the problem and make it harder to identify.

OBTAINING COMPETENT SERVICE

For many users, the main repair problem they face is where to find a good repair shop. When you have to turn service and repair over to someone else, it's a bit like choosing an automobile mechanic. There are questions of trust, competence, and turn-around time. People sometimes think if they knew enough to be able to pick a good technician (or auto mechanic), they wouldn't need one—they'd do the work themselves. Even so, most of us occasionally need a good repair service.

The best approach is to ask for help from others in your area who have MS-DOS machines. Computer users are usually happy to share their service and repair experiences, good or bad. If you don't know another computer user, it might be worthwhile to join a user group (see Chapter 7 for tips on finding one).

With help from cohorts or without it, here are some things to consider when picking a repair shop:

- *Off-site or local repair* Many dealers send all their repair work elsewhere. This can mean longer turn-around times and more expense.

- *On-site staff* Repair facilities often are staffed by employees who have passed a basic course on computer repairs, and that's a step in the right direction. Some larger, well-established dealers do even better—they employ staff engineers with some years of experience in hardware maintenance.

- *Loaner policy* When repairs will take more than a day or two, some dealers will loan you a computer (perhaps a demo model) so you can keep working in the meantime. (If you keep an older machine as a spare, a loaner may not be important.)

- *Dealer software support* Your repair shop, if it is also your dealer, should be willing to help you get out of trouble with those $500 programs you buy. There are many programs and new arrivals every day. A strong dealership will probably either help you with any problems or maintain a list of outside technical resources available to consult on problems.

- *Business support* The largest dealers will offer service calls to your facility. They have field sales representatives, consultants to help design hardware and software solutions for specific problems, and even programmers who can customize programs to your needs. You may have to purchase a service agreement to be eligible for such extended support. Sometimes classes and seminars are available for businesses that have a large staff that will be using the newly purchased equipment.

TROUBLESHOOTING WITHOUT METERS

Sooner or later, something in your setup will cause problems—despite your reasonable care to avoid them. There's no need to throw up your hands when that happens. Even without an engineering degree and a van full of meters, you can do a lot. In fact, you're likely to come upon a simple solution long before you need to invest in meters and scopes. Solid-state circuits are very reliable, so by the time you need a meter, you might be better off just replacing the board.

Before taking such drastic action, though, try a little common-sense *fault isolation*. That's the process of starting at the simplest, easiest problem and working from there into more complex possible causes. It's how experts simplify their repair work. The first step is to make some immediate decisions about what strategy to take, depending on what sort of problem occurred.

Check for the Most Obvious Problem

Of the many things that can go wrong, probably the most frustrating is when a working machine suddenly stops. When you push the power switch, instead of hearing beeps and grinds and seeing flashing disk drive lights, all you get is silence. Ominous thoughts like "Blown power supply!" usually leap to mind, but fortunately, the solution is often much simpler. True, some sort of acute hardware failure might be at fault, but a pulled power plug is more likely the cause.

The section headed "Power from the Outlet" later in this chapter gives some easy steps to check power, component by component, from the wall outlet to the inside of the machine. If power isn't the problem, you'll have to look elsewhere for the cause.

Making Early Assessments

First you'll need to decide how serious the problem is. Although you can't always tell right away, there are some dependable ways to assess the situation, so let's examine them.

Troubleshoot or Service Call?

Immediately referring the problem to a qualified technician might make life simpler, but there are risks. It's like deciding whether to turn your car over to a mechanic before you have a general idea of what needs to be done. So try to do some troubleshooting *before* you turn over the keys and credit card.

If your computer is still under warranty, and the problem is clearly a hardware failure—like a crashed disk or blown monitor tube—you're in a different ball park. Without delay, copy your files to floppy disks (if you can), shut off the power, and send the unit in for service. Refer to your computer's warranty information for whom to call and where to send the equipment.

Many manufacturers require you to call them and get a return authorization number before shipping anything back to them. Place this number prominently on the outside of the carton, so your machine does not get lost on the receiving dock. UPS is often the most economical shipping method. Use your original packaging, which you should still have if you followed the recommendation in Chapter 3. To collect on a damage claim, you may need to ship the equipment back in its original carton; if you pack it up in the box your punch bowl came in, the unit may come right back to you with your damage claim refused.

Note: Physical repair of a hard disk will almost always result in loss of all data. However, sending a failed hard disk out for data recovery probably will result in an unusable hard disk. The next section, "Estimating the Risk to Data," offers some guidance on deciding whether to opt for data retrieval or hard disk repair.

Estimating the Hardware Risk

The following are some danger signals and events, ranging from the truly serious to the mere nuisance. A good rule of thumb is to err on the side of caution. If you think it's really serious, turn off the machine; if you're not sure, here are some signs to look for.

High-Pitched Shriek or Smoke   If you hear a high-pitched, tortured shriek or a series of loud beeps, or if there's smoke pouring out the back of the machine, or if you spilled liquid into the case—*turn off the power.* You may be able to retrieve data or even get the machine running again later, but for now, don't take any chances. Turn it off, and then refer to the section "Inside the Case" later in this chapter for what to do next.

Continuous Tone or Frozen Keyboard   This is probably a software problem. Software glitches, though annoying, won't fry the motherboard. They may produce a warning tone, so if you hear a continuous tone, or if your keyboard freezes up, *reboot the machine immediately.* The tone may be a symptom of damaging feedback or other software conflicts; if you let the machine keep running, smoke pouring out the back may be the next stage. (See "Look for Software Conflicts" later in this chapter for tips on isolating this kind of problem.)

Repetitive, Grinding Noise   A repeated grinding noise, especially when the hard-disk light stays on, can indicate your hard disk has been or is being gouged by the read/write heads. Especially with older disks, the grinding sound comes from the read/write heads, stuck like a phonograph needle in a scratch, trying to work themselves loose. *Don't turn off the power yet.* See "Hard Disk Problems" later in this chapter for tactics in this case.

Other Erratic Behavior   When you get trouble reports displayed to the screen and there's no immediate warning shriek or fire danger, *don't* turn off the power right away. At this point you're still up and running, and booting up successfully later may not be a sure thing. So stop and think before doing anything rash.

Liquid Spills and Accidents   If you have accidentally dropped your system unit, spilled coffee or other liquids into it, or suffered some other accident, the machine probably sustained hardware damage. Turn off the power and go straight to the hardware troubleshooting procedures given later in this chapter.

Estimating the Risk to Data
Before taking steps, take stock. If your data is at risk, do something to save it—especially if you suspect a failing hard disk. If the data is hard to replace, you may want to risk a worsened hardware failure and take the time to copy every file you can to a floppy before you turn off the power. Whether to take such a chance can be a tough decision, especially when you

hear those dramatic grinding noises. Unfortunately, there's no way around it; you're the one on the spot and you must decide. So take a moment to assess what you're up against.

In your decision, consider how recently you performed the last backup. If it was indeed recent, you may not be in that much trouble, datawise. Then again, if it's been a year, you may be about to learn the bitter lesson that makes every expert urge other users to make frequent backups. When you have lost data to a hard disk failure at an awkward time even once, it's salt in the wound when a backup you didn't take time to do could have saved irreplaceable data.

See the later section "Hard Disk Problems" for ways to save your files when your hard disk is failing.

Getting Down to Causes

Now it's time to isolate the cause of whatever has gone wrong. The first step is to back away for a moment and take a look at the most likely villains. Don't assume that troubleshooting is difficult. Much of the time, you never even have to open the case. The philosophy in this chapter is to avoid using any kind of meter, and you may be surprised at how much you can do without them.

The trick is to do the easy stuff first, and work toward the more complex. Once you find a problem, stop and fix it, and then try the computer. Fixing that single problem often gets things back to normal. Sometimes one breakdown will create a chain of others, like a failed hard disk controller leading to a burned-out power supply. If you win one skirmish and the computer still doesn't run, go back to troubleshooting at the point where you fought the first battle, and look for another enemy.

If you need help, get it. As we've already affirmed several times, you're not honor bound to do your own repair work. Call your dealer or get a qualified computer technician. Paying a $100 repair bill is a lot easier than having to replace an $800 piece of equipment you accidentally destroyed.

Here are some ways to isolate problems.

Running System Diagnostics

Some computers are shipped with a floppy disk containing a diagnostics program. Other machines have diagnostics built in, and a few come without any diagnostics at all. Many users purchase separate diagnostic programs, or download them as utilities from bulletin boards. These programs can help you discover which component has malfunctioned, or at least will report a failing motherboard or peripheral device. If your computer has such a program, and the computer still works, start by trying to use this program to isolate the problem.

Resetting the CMOS—"Press Key to Reconfigure"
One of the first, and simplest, failures to look for is a dead battery in an AT-class or later machine, or on an XT add-in clock board. The symptoms include a clock that won't keep time and, on an AT, an error message telling you to reconfigure the CMOS when you boot up (Figure 18-2).

The CMOS keeps track of system settings such as time, date, hard and floppy disk drive types, video adapter type, and the amount of memory in

---

Figure 18-2

CMOS error report at bootup

```
Errors have been found during the power on self test in your computer.  The
errors were:



Incorrect configuration data in CMOS
Memory size in CMOS invalid









SETUP will attempt to correct these errors through auto-configuration.
Hit any key to continue:
```

your machine. When the system boots up, it looks at each CMOS entry and uses that information to set up the system to run. If these settings get lost, your machine may go automatically to the CMOS setup program when you turn on the power or it may request that you run a setup program.

To run the CMOS setup program, follow the onscreen prompts to get to the setup screen (Figure 18-3). The setup screen will explain how to set the date, time, and the other variables. Normally, as shown in the figure, you will use the arrow keys to select and change the stored information.

Determining Drive Type   The main CMOS variable that may have you at a loss is the hard disk type number. This one- or two-digit number tells DOS where to look in the built-in drive type table for information such as disk sector size, number of cylinders, head parking locations, and storage capacity. Without this information, DOS can't boot from the hard drive, and will display hard-disk error messages.

Figure 18-3

CMOS setup screen

```
┌─────────────────────────────────────────────────────────────────┐
│                  Phoenix Technologies Ltd,   Version              │
│                  System Configuration Setup  4.03 00              │
│ Time:  14:36:11                                                   │
│ Date:  Mon Sep 24, 1990                                           │
│                                                                   │
│ Diskette A:          5.25 Inch, 1.2 MB                            │
│ Diskette B:          3.5 Inch, 1.44 MB    Cyl  Hd  Pre  LZ  Sec Size│
│ Hard Disk 1:         Type 49             1024  9  512 1024  30  135│
│ Hard Disk 2:         Not Installed                                │
│ Base Memory:         640 KB                                       │
│ Extended Memory:     320 KB                                       │
│ Display:             VGA/EGA                                      │
│ Keyboard:            Installed                                    │
│ CPU Speed:           Fast                                         │
│                                                                   │
│ Coprocessor:         Not Installed                               │
│                                                                   │
│ PgUp for options, Up/Down Arrow to select, Left/Right Arrow to change,│
│ F1 for help, F10 to Exit, Esc to reboot,                         │
│                                                                   │
│                                                                   │
└─────────────────────────────────────────────────────────────────┘
```

Recent models of AT-class computers can recognize 47 or more drive types, and may include a wildcard drive type number, for which you supply your own number based on the drive documentation. Your setup program probably provides a way to access a list of conventional numbers stored in the drive type table; pressing F1 is a common way to view the list. Figure 18-4 shows part of such a list displayed by a 386 machine. Once you have the list of drive types onscreen, press SHIFT-PRINT SCREEN to print out the table.

Next, look in your drive documentation for information on the number of cylinders, heads, sectors, a parking (or "landing zone") sector number, and the drive capacity. Match that information against the drive type table you just printed out to find the correct two-digit number for your machine.

If you don't have drive documentation, Appendix C lists the required information for many common models of hard disks. Look for your own disk in the table, and match it against the table of drive type numbers that you

Figure 18-4

Drive type number table from a 386 machine

Drive Type	Cylinders	Heads	Write Precomp	Landing Zone	Sectors	Megabytes
1	306	4	128	305	17	10
2	615	4	300	615	17	20
3	615	6	300	615	17	30
4	940	8	512	940	17	62
5	940	6	512	940	17	46
6	615	4	-1	615	17	20
7	462	8	256	511	17	30
8	733	5	-1	733	17	30
9	900	15	-1	901	17	112
10	820	3	-1	820	17	20
11	855	5	-1	855	17	35
12	855	7	-1	855	17	49
13	306	8	128	319	17	20
14	733	7	-1	733	17	42
16	612	4	0	663	17	20
17	977	5	300	977	17	40
18	977	7	-1	977	17	56
19	1024	7	512	1023	17	59
20	733	5	300	732	17	30
21	733	7	300	732	17	42

Hit any key to continue:

printed out. If the number of cylinders and heads matches the entries for a two-digit drive type number, and the sector size is the same, you have a match. Use that two-digit number in your setup.

If these approaches don't work, you may have to open the hard disk case and perhaps remove the hard disk. You will then find a drive type number on a sticker attached to the hard disk itself. If there is none, but you know the drive brand and model number, call the manufacturer and ask for the required information on cylinder numbers, heads, sector size, and capacities.

Note: Some nonstandard hard disk drives, such as RLL drives, may require software device drivers. Any such disk should have either a "smart" controller that makes the disk recognizable to DOS, or a separate small partition that DOS sees as a normal, bootable hard drive. Check your system or hard disk documentation, or consult your dealer, if you cannot find a two-digit drive number that lets your computer recognize your hard disk.

Replacing the Battery   To replace the battery, you'll need to locate it inside the case. (The section "Inside the Case" later in the chapter gives instructions for opening the case.)

On an XT clock board, look for a round, 25-cent-sized, watch-type battery. To remove it, first take the board out of the case. Then check which side of the battery faces up; you'll need to know this when you replace it. Often the battery has a + or − on the topside. Usually it is flat on top, but has a mushroom-like ring separating positive from negative on the bottom. Often the top is silvered.

Next, use a flat-bladed screwdriver to gently pry up the battery's retaining clip. Turn the board upside down, and the battery will fall right out. Take it to an electronics shop or large drug store and buy a replacement; place it in the battery housing with the correct side up, and replace the board in the case.

On an AT-type machine, if you don't see a battery pack, check your documentation to see if the motherboard uses NiCad or lithium batteries. An AT battery is usually located toward the rear of the motherboard, close to the keyboard connector. If you see any corrosion or "bleeding," the battery is bad. Replace it yourself or have a shop replace it.

What Happened Last?

Many times a problem occurs right after you've done something new to or with your computer. Thus knowing what you did last can often lead directly to the trouble—which doesn't give you an automatic solution, but is always a step in the right direction. Diagnosis can be 90 percent of the repair job. The following are events that are particularly likely to be followed by irregularities.

You Moved the Machine   Did you just move the machine? If you did, did you remember to park your hard disk? That's an oversight anyone can make . . . once. After that, most people remember.

If you parked the heads, did you leave the machine exposed to the sun? Extreme temperature changes are damaging to electronic equipment. In some climates, 20 minutes of sunlight streaming in the car window can raise your vehicle interior to 115°F or more. If your system unit happens to be in that sunlight, perhaps resting on the passenger seat while you run an errand, it can climb to 150°F inside the case. The section on bimetallic expansion at the beginning of this chapter explains how such extreme temperature changes can damage hard disks and other components.

You Installed Something New   Did you just install new hardware? If so, look there first for trouble. New software? Same advice: anything new in your system may be the culprit.

Was it the Software or Hardware?

All computer problems fall into one of two categories—software glitches and hardware failures. If you're just getting a machine up and running, you may have a problem telling which is responsible for your problem; but after you've run your computer successfully for a while, you'll probably know the difference.

New Machines   For a new machine, most dealers and vendors will provide technical support while you're getting started. Unless you got an extreme discount, you have a right to expect some help, since the money you spent was probably not insignificant. Some "special" deals, such as machines assembled from parts in someone's garage, may have limited support or none at all, but hopefully that's not your fate. Even mass merchandisers stock computers whose manufacturers generally supply a support telephone number.

If you have a support number, don't hesitate to use it. The best help often comes from the people who made the unit. If you bought your machine from a computer store or a large mail-order firm, generally they too will provide help setting up your system.

Working Machines If you've used your computer for a while when the problem crops up, you've got an experience base to start with; that will help in locating the source of problems. In addition to the diagnosis suggestions you've read so far in this section, here are some other ways to pinpoint software versus hardware difficulties.

- *Is it program-specific?* If the problem always occurs when you're using a single program, the program is probably your culprit.

- *Is it activity-specific?* If the trouble repeatedly happens when you are doing a specific type of task, focus your troubleshooting efforts there. In communications, for example, take a good look at your modem. If you're having difficulty entering data successfully, it might be the keyboard, or you could have a mouse driver conflict or a broken mouse signal cable. Use your most recent activity to isolate the most likely areas at fault.

- *Is it obviously the hardware?* Sometimes you just can't miss the problem area—such as when your monitor goes blank. When you're positive about the trouble area, go directly to this chapter's hardware troubleshooting section.

- *Is it a nonspecific or general problem?* Some problems keep happening no matter what program you're using. In this case there's a good chance something is wrong "under the hood." Check the hardware troubleshooting procedures described later in this chapter.

SOLVING SOFTWARE PROBLEMS

It happens. You're running a familiar program, maybe Flight Simulator or a hard disk backup program. You've used the software a thousand times before, but this time you press the wrong key. It's like missing a freeway exit when your attention wanders—a nuisance but nothing to panic over. But maybe it appears to be more serious. You may have transferred a program to a different machine and found that everything has gone haywire. Nothing obvious has changed—you've even created the same subdirectory for your program files—but you're getting strange error messages or, worse, nothing at all on your screen. (Appendix D contains a list of DOS error messages and their definitions.)

Programmers know such problems are common, and they do their best to make programs fail-safe. This means if something does go wrong, it usually goes wrong in ways that won't hurt your data. But nothing's perfect, and there are many ways to get nailed when you're using a system as flexible as DOS and the programs that run under it. Programs differ so vastly that there's no foolproof troubleshooting procedure for software problems.

However, there are some general techniques for helping to pinpoint the obstacle most of the time. These are discussed next.

Reboot Before Using CHKDSK /f, RECOVER, or Disk Medic Programs

If you get data errors or other indications of a problem with disk file storage, don't assume that CHKDSK /f (or RECOVER, or any other *disk medic* type of program) can provide accurate diagnosis and repair. Often, the real problem is simply that something—perhaps a magnet—garbled part of your machine's internal memory-based file tables. When this happens, data suddenly disappears from storage and diagnostic programs report errors.

The solution, however, may be simpler than it looks. *Always* reboot before using disk medic programs like CHKDSK, DISKFIX, POWER DISK, or Norton DISK DOCTOR. These powerful programs manipulate files, clusters, and lost chains to repair file damage. If low-level format actions are based on garbled memory tables, your once orderly files can get permanently hashed. Simply rebooting may clear everything up.

Always boot from a DOS floppy disk or a backup boot disk, containing the correct device drivers, before using disk medic programs. Unload any disk caches or other disk-oriented TSRs. The closer you are to a pure DOS environment when using disk repair programs, the less likely you are to get strange results.

Quit the Current Program

Sometimes a complex program like an outliner or word processor may seem "stuck"—keys no longer do what you expect. Don't start hitting keys at random; that's a prescription for trouble. Try quitting the program by using the "return to DOS" or exit command, if you can. See if CTRL-C or CTRL-BREAK will exit the program. Or try turning on the printer. (Some programs hang if you accidentally tell them to print something and there's no printer in the system.) If nothing works, you might have to reboot.

If this error happens often, think about what you are doing when it crops up. You may be able to locate the cause and even recreate the problem. If so, you're two steps ahead, because:

- Since you know what creates the error, you know how to avoid it. Find another way to accomplish this procedure and put the problem-causing keystrokes on your mental "avoid" list.

- You may have located a bug in the program—a pattern of keystrokes that causes trouble the programmers didn't catch. Report the problem to the publisher, and you may receive a free upgrade when they fix the bug.

Look for Software Conflicts

Malfunctions specific to particular programs occur only when using that program, either by itself or in combination with other specific programs. Finding such conflicts involves trying various programs in different combinations until you can reproduce the problem. Then you can simply avoid that combination or situation.

Conflicting Interrupts

A software conflict happens when one program interferes with another—for example, when a program tries to dominate the DOS functions or interrupt requests (IRQs) that another program is using. The results, especially when hardware conflicts also are involved, can be bizarre and complicated. Such clashes are common when you're using TSR programs, task switchers, and multitaskers. These sophisticated programs make DOS seem like it's doing more than one thing at a time. Conflicts also can develop between device drivers, utilities, programs that call each other into memory, and even new hardware. Modems, for example, are notorious for causing interrupt conflicts.

TSR Loading Order TSRs are among the most prominent DOS-level problem children. They're touchy about what order you use in loading them. They interfere with other programs. They can repeatedly hang your machine until you finally isolate the one causing the problems. Although most users consider TSRs worth the trouble, because of all the additional capabilities and flexibility they put at your fingertips, integrated programs and other high-power software are making stand-alone TSRs less commonly used than in the past.

If you have a conflict with TSRs, reboot your machine with no TSRs installed by your AUTOEXEC.BAT file and then load one TSR program at a time until you see your problem and know which TSR (or combination of TSRs) is the culprit. If you can't isolate the problem, or if it's too complex for your experience level, call in a technician. These situations can become very troublesome.

Memory Limits

Many of today's programs assume you have a full 640K of available memory. If you're using a machine with 512K (or less) memory, one of these programs may stall or display some strange behavior. All you can do is add more memory, or substitute an earlier version of the program or a different program.

File Handles (FILES=) Set Too Low

The FILES= statement in CONFIG.SYS designates how many file handles DOS can keep open when running a program. A *file handle* is an entry in an internal DOS table that tells DOS the name and location of any files to which it needs to read or write. The default is eight handles, of which DOS automatically uses five. That leaves only three file handles for your applications programs—or fewer, if (like most users) you install a TSR (memory resident or background) program or two.

The answer is to use a FILES=*nnn* statement in CONFIG.SYS. In DOS 2.*x*, 20 is the maximum value for *nnn*; in DOS 3.*x*, the maximum is 255. FILES=20 is enough for most applications programs; when it's not, your applications program manual will tell you so.

Extended Memory Problems

Older programs designed to use the 384K extended memory area of AT-class machines may not work correctly with 386-class machines that have shadow RAM. The problem is that shadow RAM may not let such programs "load high" (load into upper memory) correctly. You may have to refrain from using such outdated programs.

Expanded Memory Problems

Expanded memory (see Chapter 17) requires management, and expanded memory managers differ. Your EMM may not be compatible with a new program, and there's not much you can do short of changing EMMs. EMM usage causes fewer problems than it used to, but incompatibilities do still happen.

Disk Cache Problems

Problems like hashed files and data read/write errors may result from misuse of a disk cache. Caches can be dangerous, especially if you forget to unload or disable them before optimizing (reorganizing) a hard disk. Disk optimizers do extensive disk rewriting, but disk caches sometimes bypass the normal DOS calls in order to speed up operation. The result can be chaotic, because when the cache next writes to the disk, the data goes to the wrong sector.

The solution is simple. Disable or remove any disk cache before you optimize your disk. To be safer yet, many users reboot after optimizing, to eliminate possible confusion about a file's proper storage location.

Note: Some disk caches are designed to work with specific disk optimizers. PC Tools, Norton Utilities, and Golden Bow Systems offer such combinations, and they can indeed speed up the optimizing process. But unless you are certain your optimizer and your cache can work together, it is best to unload a disk cache before optimizing your disk.

SOLVING HARDWARE PROBLEMS

More than half of all hardware troubles involve loose connectors of one kind or another. For example, new cables won't fit, and you discover you need a gender changer because both connectors are male (or female). Installed cables come loose and need reseating. Connectors age or oxidize, becoming discolored. Any aged, loose, or intermittent connection can interfere with the smooth flow of data. Luckily, you don't need any special training to fix a loose connection, although finding it can sometimes be tricky. User-fixable problems like these are described in the next sections.

Important Tools and Supplies

To deal with hardware problems, especially inside the case, having the proper supplies and tools helps. You won't need anything fancy; here are some suggestions.

Keep a bootable floppy disk handy (a disk that was formatted using the FORMAT /s command) in the event your hard disk doesn't boot successfully, or should any number of other things happen. Make your bootable floppy using the same DOS version as is installed on the computer's hard disk, to avoid incompatibilities. Be sure it contains any device drivers or other programs that your system requires for startup.

Perhaps the most often forgotten supply item is tape or adhesive-backed note paper for labeling parts, noting which side of connectors face up, and so forth. It's not a sure thing that you'll remember exactly how a part was installed, and you'll save hours of trial and error by attaching a piece of tape or a Post-it with a jotted reminder or two.

Another important item is a small container or plastic bag for the screws and tiny pieces that can roll off the table or migrate deep into cracks and crevices. Many technicians keep a separate container for the small parts from each major component; that way they can label the containers and save time later.

Tools that will help inside the case include

- A flat-bladed screwdriver, preferably nonmagnetic (you'll use it for gentle prying, as well as for removing slotted screws)

- A Phillips screwdriver (medium-sized)

- A 1/4-inch nut driver

In the category of nice-but-not-necessary equipment, electric screwdrivers are a fine convenience. Also, many stores carry small computer tool kits that contain such items as graspers, tweezers, and chip-pullers. Finally, since you're dealing with 5- to 12-volt power supplies, an automotive 12-volt continuity tester with a small light is great for testing whether you have electrical power to internal components.

Error Reports: Parity and Beeps

With early IBM PCs and compatibles, the most common error reports were parity errors, caused by faulty timing chips or defective chips on the motherboard. (See the later section "Chip Problems" for help in this area.) Another method your computer has of reporting problems at boot time is using a pattern of beeps during the initial power on self test (POST) hardware check. One beep is normal; it means everything checked out OK. Other standard patterns are described in Table 18-1.

Major Component Checks

The following paragraphs describe things to look for when troubleshooting the computer's main components.

Power from the Outlet

Most computers have power indicator and disk activity lights on the front of the system case. If none of these is lit, power may have been interrupted.

Table 18-1

Startup Troubleshooting Beeps

Pattern	Most Likely Problem Area
No beep	Power supply
Continuous tone	Power supply
Repeating short beeps	Power supply
1 long, 1 short	Motherboard
1 long, 2 short	Video adapter card
1 short with no display	Video card, cable, or display
1 short, no boot	Disk drive, cable, or adapter

To check for power supply problems between the outlet and your computer, start at the wall and work toward the machine, checking items as follows:

1. *Power cord connection*   Make sure the computer is still plugged in. The cleaning crew or a passerby may have unplugged the power cord at the outlet or at the surge protector.

2. *Power at outlet*   Plug something else like a small fan or light into the outlet to see if it works. If it doesn't, something has cut off power to the outlet. Check your breaker box.

3. *Power at surge protector*   If you have power at the outlet, check the surge protector or power strip next. If your fan (or whatever) does work at the outlet but not at the surge protector, you've found your problem.

4. *Surge protector switch*   Many surge protectors have an ON/OFF switch that controls power to anything plugged into it. Some protectors also have a light to show when the power is on. Make sure the power switch at the surge protector is in the ON position.

5. *Surge protector breaker*   If the power switch is turned on, look for a small, built-in breaker; this is what cuts power and protects your equipment if there is a voltage spike. Rocker switches and push buttons are common breaker types; the illustration here shows a push button. Reset the breaker and check for power again. If you still can't get power from the surge protector, replace it.

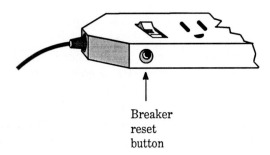

Breaker
reset
button

6. *Power cord*   If you have power at the surge protector, check the power cord to the system unit. If it seems firmly seated, try substituting a different cord; the connectors are fairly standard for computers. You may have to borrow a cord from another piece of equipment (for example, the printer). If that solves the problem, replace the power cord.

If none of these steps identifies or solves the problem, you will have to check for faults elsewhere.

The Monitor

If your monitor doesn't display colors correctly, or remains blank, something may have changed your color settings. Using the adjustable dials or knobs on your monitor, change settings a little at a time to see if the display improves. If it does, fiddle with the settings until the display is to your liking. A loose monitor cable is another common problem. Reseat your monitor cable and see if the screen returns to normal.

Your monitor has controls for scrolling and for adjusting the image area that are often recessed in the back of the monitor. If you've experienced a shivering image, horizontal or vertical scrolling problems, or an image "bleeding" out of the picture, try moving the controls a little at a time to see how they affect your display.

Manufacturers often make these controls hard to reach to keep users away from them. If you are hesitant to adjust these controls, or if changing their settings does not help, try plugging in another monitor if you have one. If a monitor that you *know* works won't work with your machine, the problem is in the video adapter of the system unit, not in your monitor. Take the system unit, monitor, or both to a shop for repairs.

The Keyboard

If your keyboard doesn't respond correctly or the unit doesn't recognize that a keyboard is present, check for a loose keyboard cable or connector. If that's not the problem, check to see if it's any of the following keyboard-related situations.

Keyboard Lock   Make sure the keyboard lock on the front of your unit (AT-level or higher) is unlocked.

XT/AT Keyboard Switch   Keyboards often have a switch at the back or underneath that toggles between XT and AT key codes. This switch makes it possible for one keyboard to fit all systems, but the switch must be set right or your computer can't tell that a keyboard is present. Changing this switch setting can't hurt your computer, but it may solve your keyboard glitch. If it doesn't, switch it back to its original position and keep looking.

Dirt Between Keys   Debris can accumulate between the keys to the point where they won't operate correctly, or perhaps interfere with one another. Try turning your keyboard upside down and spraying between the keys with canned air. You may be surprised at how much debris falls out. If this doesn't help, many keyboards come apart fairly easily. Try taking apart the keyboard and cleaning all contacts thoroughly; use electronic contact cleaner that leaves no residue, available at most electronics stores. *Don't use soap, water, or spray-on cleaners.*

Key Stops Working   When a single key simply stops working, the switch under the key may be disconnected. This can happen if wear and vibration crack the original solder. If you are comfortable with a soldering iron, take apart the keyboard and check the key switch action while watching underneath; resolder the connection if it appears loose or you see cracked solder.

   If none of these steps pinpoints the keyboard malfunction, you may need to replace the keyboard or have it repaired by a shop.

Inside the Case

Some computer cases open easily from the top; others require you to remove several mounting screws on the back. Be careful not to remove the power-supply mounting screws located near the ventilation fan exhaust on the back of the machine. The case mounting screws that you *do* want to remove are usually of a different size from the power supply screws and are located along the top or in the corners of the case, not around the exhaust vent. Today's IBM machines have a case lock and thumbscrews on the back. Figure 18-5 shows how some typical desktop and upright cases are removed.

   Figure 18-6 shows the usual components inside the case of an AT-class machine. The arrangement inside your own computer may differ, but the basic components will be similar. The following paragraphs discuss some basic procedures and common problems.

Figure 18-5

Desktop and upright case removal

Lock

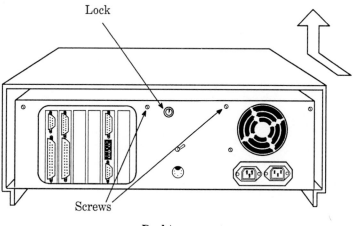

Screws

Desktop

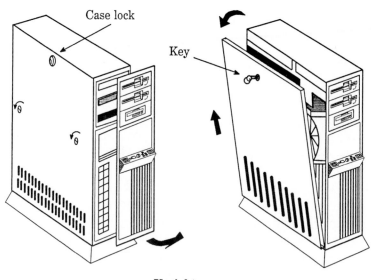

Case lock

Key

Upright

Figure 18-6

AT-class system unit components

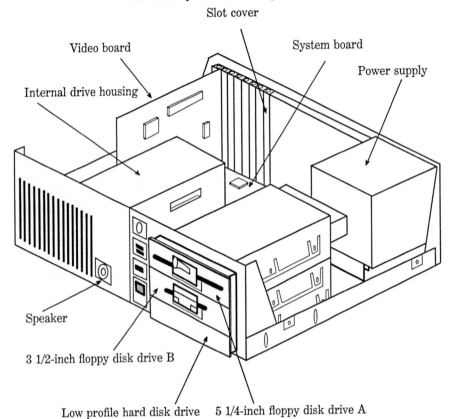

Slot cover

Video board

System board

Power supply

Internal drive housing

Speaker

3 1/2-inch floppy disk drive B

Low profile hard disk drive   5 1/4-inch floppy disk drive A

Troubleshooting Internal Components

After you open the case, examine the boards and components for scorch marks or other evidence of damage. On older ATs, there is an 8.1 microfarad capacitor beside each memory chip; it's a small, round component mounted to the board by two wires. If one is missing or burned—and they do blow out—you can get a replacement at any electronics store and solder it into place. If you see other evidence of physical damage, take the unit to the repair shop.

When you are working inside the system unit case, follow these guide-lines:

- You won't hurt a computer by carefully unplugging internal cables and connectors—as long as the power is turned off (to avoid sparking) when you do it. Unplugging things merely removes them from the system; no harm is ever done by that.

- Don't open the power supply's housing—that's the box with cables running to disks and boards, probably labeled "Do Not Open," "Hazardous," or some such warning. Inside are capacitors that can hold charges of up to 50,000 volts, so *never* fool around in there. It's the only part of the system unit that can be hazardous.

- Stay grounded. That's not just for your safety, but to keep static electricity away from tiny microcircuits. Technicians who know what they're doing sometimes ground a system by leaving it plugged in with the power supply switch turned off, and touch the power supply housing (or some other grounded surface) with a hand before handling any components. A safer approach is to unplug the machine and touch some other grounded object (such as a lamp) before handling the internal electronics.

- When you open the case, take a moment to look for foreign objects like screws, paper clips, or other things that may have fallen inside. If there are any, remove them.

- Get rid of any dust, hairs, and so on inside the case. Most electronics stores have canned, pressurized air for that purpose. A small vacuum cleaner also works, as does a large, soft paintbrush (but try not to leave any brush hairs behind).

- If you use canned air, blow it into the ventilation fan exhaust on the back of the case. It will reverse the normal air flow, and you may be surprised at how much dust and debris get dislodged. Vacuum, blow, or sweep the debris out of the case.

Reseat Cables and Boards

When one of your add-on boards—video board, disk controller, and so on—goes bad, it can cause serious difficulties. More often, however, the problems are caused by loose connectors or boards, or damaged ribbon cables. The following steps will take you from the simple to the complex, as you test out one component after another until the fault is isolated.

Clean Edge Connectors with an Eraser   When you pull out one of your add-on boards, you can rub a pencil eraser lightly across the bottom gold-colored edge connections to clean them. Don't touch the connectors with your hands. You can also use a cotton swab saturated with electronic contact cleaning solution. These connectors are usually gold-plated to resist corrosion, but they can be adversely affected if exposed to any tobacco smoke, smog, and other pollutants. Use a soft cloth to clean the eraser crumbs or excess cleaning solution from the contacts before you reinstall the board.

Pull P8 or P9 Connectors   If you're not sure your motherboard is working at all, find out by removing all power from the add-on boards. This isolates the motherboard from other influences. To disconnect add-on board power, look for cables that attach with plug-in connectors to places on the board labeled P8 and P9. The other end of these cables will run to the main power supply.

Disconnect the cable from the rearmost of the P8 or P9 connectors. That will remove all power from add-on boards. The connector may be latched; if so, you'll have to carefully release the latch, using your thumbnail or a small, flat-bladed screwdriver, while pulling on the connector. Be careful when rocking the connector to loosen it, and don't expect it to just slide off—it will take a bit of heft. Don't pull on the wires, just on the connector; it will probably be seated quite firmly.

Once the add-on power connector is loose, turn the power back on. If the trouble is with an add-on board, your motherboard should now power up OK; the speaker will beep once (see Table 18-1 for power on self test beep patterns). You may hear other normal drive-test startup noises. An automobile voltage tester (one of the nice-but-not-necessary tools mentioned earlier) can confirm whether power is getting to the board, by testing for voltage at the P8 or P9 cable connector.

If you do hear the single beep or get other evidence that your motherboard is trying to work, reconnect P8 or P9 and look elsewhere for the problem. You may have a short circuit on one of your add-on boards, for example. If the motherboard isn't booting, you may have an open or a short circuit, or the power supply may have blown. Consult a technician if this is the case.

Check Other Power Leads   Sometimes power connectors simply pull free or work loose on their own. Check each connector, making sure they all appear uniform and firmly seated. If one is higher or looks different from the others, try pushing the wire or the connector itself farther into the housing. Also inspect each board's power connectors, pulling them loose and reseating them with the heel of your hand. (The drive controller may be the only one separately powered.)

Disconnect All Boards and Reconnect Them One at a Time If reseating the connectors doesn't solve your problem, you've worked up to the ultimate no-meter test. Pull each board from its slot, labeling each one so you know which board is which. The graphics adapter connects to the monitor signal cable; the disk controller has several internal cables running to the disk drives. Other common boards include internal modems with telephone cord jacks, input/output boards with a joystick, and serial and parallel ports. (Various connector types are described and illustrated in Chapter 4.)

When every board is unplugged, turn the power back on and listen to the beeps. If you hear a single beep, turn the power back off. If you hear no beep, a continuous tone, or more than one beep, the problem is not with any of your add-on boards. Check for loose chips (see "Chip Problems" later in this chapter) or send the machine out for repair. In the next part of this procedure, you will reinstall one at a time the boards you removed.

Not all cases are precision engineered. Sometimes, to get a board to seat correctly, you may have to slightly bend the L-shaped lip on the back of the board to fit it to the back of the machine, or you might even have to leave off the screw. If you can't get one slot to work correctly, try another. When pressing a board into a slot, use the heel of your hand and press firmly, but don't pound on it. Seating a board takes about 35 pounds of pressure.

Now plug in the graphics adapter (the one to which the monitor was connected) *without* hooking up the monitor, turn the power back on, and listen again. If you hear the single beep, turn the power off, connect the monitor signal cable to the board, power up, and listen again. If it boots OK, you will now see screen reports and will no longer have to rely on the beep patterns.

Once you have the monitor working, try the disk controller and, after that, any other add-on boards you had in the system. When the problem occurs again, you've pinpointed the bad board or cable.

Many glitches arise because of loose connectors, loose boards, or damaged ribbon cables. (Ribbon cables are particularly notorious for failing in ways that are hard to notice.) Don't be surprised if simply unplugging and reseating the boards and cables dissolves your trouble. Contacts get oxidized or coated with tobacco tars, vibration works connectors free, all sorts of things can happen. Then you do something in passing, and it fixes the problem, and you never do figure out exactly how you did it.

Chip Problems

While the case is open, look for loose chips, ROMs, and other removable small parts. These plug-in components on the motherboard or on other major boards, like the disk controller, do work loose sometimes. Other possible problems are described in the following sections.

Parity Errors

Parity checks are a primitive way for your computer to keep a constant check on data integrity. When a parity error occurs, it means something has changed the sequence of 1's and 0's that make up the bytes from which data is composed. Rather than compound the error, your computer simply reports the parity error and shuts down. Anything in RAM becomes inaccessible at that point; you lose your work and are left simply with the error message. It can be very frustrating.

Parity errors are of two types:

- *Parity check 1*   Reported more cryptically only as "110" on PS/2 machines, this error message indicates a broken chip or other memory error on the motherboard.

- *Parity check 2*   Reported as "111" on PS/2 machines, this error message means there is a broken chip or memory error on an add-on board.

Locating Faulty Memory Chips

Figure 18-7 shows the typical location for memory chips on a motherboard; they are usually arranged in banks of chips, or caterpillar-like single inline memory modules (SIMMs).

There are two approaches to locating failing memory chips, short of using testing equipment. The easiest approach is based on the fact that memory chips with hairline cracks get warm. Right after an error shuts you down, or after several hours of operation, turn off the power and feel the memory chips with back of your finger. If one feels hotter than the others, try cooling it down with a cooling spray (available in many electronics stores). These sprays, consisting of Freon or CO_2, will take the chip temperature down to near freezing. Then reboot to see if the error has gone away. If it's gone, replace the faulty chip or SIMM.

Figure 18-7

Location of motherboard memory chips

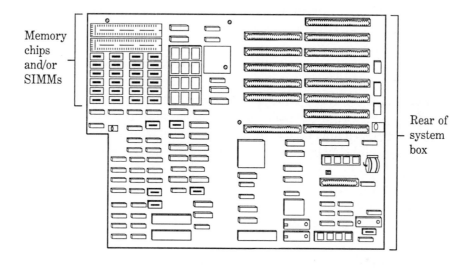

Memory chips and/or SIMMs

Rear of system box

If you cannot locate a hot chip, the other approach is to painstakingly change the physical chip locations on the motherboard, and see if that removes the difficulty. This works because you rarely operate with all 640K of lower memory in use. Rotate SIMMs from inside the edge of the board toward the outside. Cycle the chips in bank 0 so that they move one at a time to the last bank of the board, the second chip becomes the first, and so on. Run the computer for several sessions each time you move a chip and watch for the error to occur. Eventually you may find that a frequent error becomes an infrequent one. When that happens, replace the last chip you moved to the back.

Replacing Damaged Chips and SIMMs

Motherboard memory chips are often simple to change, needing only to be pulled from a socket. Older chips may need to be unsoldered; be careful not to apply too much heat. If you're not at home with a soldering gun, leave this chore to a trained technician.

Memory chips arranged in banks can be replaced one chip at a time. Manufacturers usually silkscreen labels onto their boards such as "bank 0," "bank 1," and so forth. Single inline memory modules (SIMMs) are more reliable and easier to replace than single chips, and have become standard on newer machines. When changing SIMMs, remove the inner ones first. SIMMs come in several physical sizes, so if you replace one, be sure to use the right part number when ordering the new one.

If the problem is in a ROM or CPU chip, you should at least consult a computer technician about alternative replacements rather than automatically replacing the original. It may pay to upgrade. See Chapter 15 for more information on the major chips and chip sets on the motherboard.

Hard Disk Problems

Dirt, dust, and smoke particles only rarely get inside a hard disk and are not a common cause of hard disk failure, despite common belief. Hard disks are assembled in clean rooms, and the filters on hard disk vents are very efficient. Some other things that can, and do, go wrong with hard disks are described here.

Note: Do not try to service a hard disk internally; leave that to qualified technicians working in clean rooms.

Hard Disk Not Recognized
If your CMOS settings are lost, DOS will not be able to find the information it needs in order to use your hard drive. Boot up using a bootable floppy disk, and consult your system documentation for how to access your setup program. See "Resetting the CMOS" earlier in this chapter for information on CMOS drive type settings.

Hard Disk Connector Problems
Problems with the following cables and connectors can interfere with smooth hard disk operation:

- *J1 twisted ribbon cable 34-pin (floppy drives)* A twisted ribbon cable, shown here:

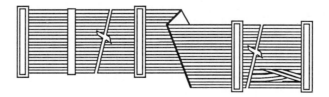

that's been incorrectly installed won't hurt anything, but the hard disk just won't work right. These cables have one edge that is a different color from the rest; typically, the colored side faces up as you look down at the board. Toward the middle of the board you can usually see two 34-pin connectors, labeled J1 and J5. The J1 pins serve a cable to the floppy drives. Be sure that pin 1 on the board is connected to pin 1 on the drive; the colored wire is handy for checking that. On a single-floppy system, connect the drive to the *end* (not middle) connector, on the cable with multiple twisted pairs of wires to the floppy drive. For dual floppy drives, the center connector goes to drive B and the end connector goes to drive A.

- *J3 and J4 20-pin connectors*   These are used with controllers that can operate any combination of up to two floppy and two hard drives—the standard drive capacity for ATs. J4 goes to the first hard drive (usually C); J3 goes to the second hard drive. The drive end of the cables has an edge connector that only fits one way.

- *J5 twisted cable 34-pin (hard drives)*   The ribbon cable from the connector labeled J5 (34 pins) goes to the hard drives. If you have only one hard disk, connect it to the end connector. If you have more than one, determining which one is drive C depends on the disk drive; see your hard disk documentation. Drive C always goes to the end connector.

- *J6 system drive activity light*   This two-wire cable goes to the activity light on the front of the machine. On some machines, if you reverse this connector it will drain the CMOS battery. If the board is marked POS and NEG, and the battery is marked also, you're OK. Just connect positive to positive, and negative to negative. If nothing is marked, use (or ask a technician to use) an ammeter to check for current when the switch is off. If you find a current drain, reverse the polarity (and mark the destination of each lead, for next time).

- *Power supply cable*   The hard-disk power supply cable runs from the square power supply box at the back of the system unit to the hard disk itself. Remove the connectors from the hard disk, and then press them on again to reseat them.

- *Failed controller card*   Controllers do fail, and this can really play havoc with your system, but it is not a terribly common occurrence. Always suspect loose connectors before you go out and buy expensive new components. In the case of a controller card, clean the card's contacts with an eraser as described earlier, and reseat the card and cables before you assume a failure is irreversible.

Buzzing or Vibrating Disk Mount

A buzzing disk mount is annoying, and stresses a disk's metal parts. Don't overtighten the mounting bolts to try to correct the noise, however, since a disk must have room to expand when it warms up. The best solution is to slide a piece of bubble pack (with small, not large, bubbles) under the weight-bearing mounting surface. This makes a fine shock absorber and lessens the vibration.

Freeing Stuck Hard Disk Heads

If you hear disk heads grinding as described earlier, your hard disk read/ write heads are probably stuck. It is sometimes possible to free them and save many of the endangered files. Your best chance to do this is when the problem first occurs, *before* you turn off the power. Once you turn off the power, your chances of freeing the heads are much slimmer.

Freeing a stuck hard disk head isn't that difficult, but it takes judgment to know what to do, when to do it, and when to stop trying. Although it is best to call in a qualified technician, sometimes that's not an option. To do it yourself, you must break the heads free, as you would the needle from a phonograph record. That means jarring the desk or table that supports the system unit, using your arm or knee, until the heads come free. It may take several tries. When the grinding stops, the heads are free.

Next, think of the most important file on your disk, and copy it to a floppy. Then think of the second most important file, and so forth. Continue until either the disk fails or you're done copying files. Then turn off the power.

An alternative is to turn off the power at once to minimize further disk damage, remove the disk from the system unit, and send it out for data recovery or repair.

Saving Your Files or Your Hard Disk

Whether you saved your files or not, don't try to service a hard disk yourself. Instead, unplug all cables and power leads and remove the disk from the system unit. Send the disk out for repair or for data recovery, depending upon the circumstances. Which approach to take depends upon you, your data, and the date of your most recent backup. See "Estimating the Hardware Risk" and "Estimating the Risk to Data" earlier in this chapter.

- *Disk Repair* Most hard disk manufacturers can rebuild disks to like-new condition for much less than it would cost to buy a new one. Bear in mind, however, that manufacturers treat any data currently on the disk as disposable—in fact, they'll probably simply replace the platter, among other parts.

- *Data Recovery* Many hard-disk data recovery services exist; ask your dealer for a reference, or look for ads in the back of any computer magazine. One good service was started by Paul Mace, author of the original Paul Mace Utilities, in Ashland, Oregon. Another excellent one is run by OnTrack Systems, Inc., publisher of the Disk Manager hard disk formatting programs that come with Seagate hard drives. Both these services are fully bonded, should data security be an issue. A disadvantage of data recovery services is that they make no attempt to save or rebuild your disk; the hardware is secondary to recovering your data.

Closing the Case

Take a moment before you close the case to reseat all add-on boards by pressing them firmly into their slots using the heel of your hand. Sometimes you have to undo the screw, pull the board entirely out to break the connection, and then press the board back in. Also reseat any cable connectors and unsoldered chips.

SUMMARY

In this chapter you have read about troubleshooting your computer. It began with information on how to avoid trouble in the first place and how to find help when needed. The chapter then described various problem-solving steps for both software and hardware that you can carry out without using meters or other electronic test equipment. Procedures requiring test equipment or procedures specific to certain machines are beyond the scope of this book. These questions should be brought to the attention of a qualified technician.

Glossary

Actuator   The drive assembly that moves the read/write heads across the surface of a hard disk platter.

Address   A unique location on the hard disk where an application or operating system can find a specific file or other information.

Alias   A type of command macro or synonym.

ANSI codes   American National Standards Institute ("an-see") codes, which are used to control the appearance of the screen. Each sequence of characters (the code) begins with an escape character followed by a left bracket ([).

ANSI driver   A program that lets DOS interpret ANSI codes.

Applications   Programs designed to carry out specific tasks, such as creating, editing, and printing documents.

Architecture   In computing, a PC's design philosophy; for example, modular architecture allows replacement of selected parts.

ARLL   Advanced RLL (run length limited) encoding that is more tolerant of older disks and improves data density.

ASCII characters   American Standard Code for Information Interchange ("az-key") seven-bit characters plus a parity bit; used to exchange data among computers. Standard ASCII characters include the punctuation marks, letters, and numbers found on the keyboard, as well as other characters not found on the keyboard.

ASCII file   Any file containing bytes that represent readable characters. *See also* Binary file.

AUTOEXEC.BAT   A special batch file executed by DOS as soon as COMMAND.COM is read into memory at startup.

Batch file   A file that has the filename extension .BAT, in which each line consists of a single DOS command line. DOS reads and executes one batch file line at a time, just as if you had typed the commands from your keyboard.

Bimetallic expansion   The expansion and contraction of metals at different rates. When two metals are bonded, as with the magnetic coatings on hard disks, the difference in expansion can peel the medium off the platter.

Binary digits (bits)   The two digits (1 and 0) used in the base 2 number system. Any number can be expressed as a combination of 1's and 0's, translated in a computer to high and low, or on and off voltages.

Binary file   Any file that contains only 1's and 0's in machine-readable form. Used for programs, compressed data, and other nonalphanumeric files.

BIOS   Basic input/output system; a tiny program located on a hardware chip that governs the flow of data into and out of the system.

BIOS calls   References to the I/O information contained in the ROM BIOS.

Bitmapped A method of storing graphics in memory in which each pixel on the screen is represented by a single bit turned on or off. It is an alternative to the character-based display method.

Boot disk The hard disk or floppy disk that contains the operating system and that is used to start the computer.

Bootstrap programs Programs that are loaded one after another when the computer is turned on, until the system is ready to accept commands.

Bridge programs Programs that let two different computer systems copy files to each other by direct-connect cables.

Buffers Sector-sized memory areas used to hold data from recent disk reads.

Bulletin board system (BBS) An electronic service where users post information, contact other users, and share programs and advice via modems.

Bus The circuit that carries data between the CPU and the rest of a computer's hardware (disk drive, serial port, modem, and so on).

Byte The basic unit used by a computer to store and manipulate data; usually 8 bits—enough to represent each of the 256 standard characters in an IBM code page.

Character-based A display method in which only the 256 standard characters are available for onscreen display. Each character is represented by a single byte. Since the characters do not have to be drawn graphically, this method is faster than bitmapping.

Clock speed Speed (in MHz) on which a PC bases its operations; determined by a clock crystal on the motherboard.

Cluster The smallest number of sectors that can be read or written to at once on a disk.

CMOS Complementary metal oxide semiconductor ("see-moss") — a special, low-power chip used to store AT system settings between sessions; maintained by a battery.

Code page A table of 256 characters, comparable to the 256 standard ASCII values in the U.S., that defines a specific set of characters for a particular country. Used to configure a keyboard, monitor, and printer to deliver appropriate language and currency characters. For example, the £ currency character appears in the character set for Great Britain, instead of the U.S. $.

Command A short series of keystrokes, entered at the DOS prompt, that tells DOS to carry out a certain task.

Command interpreter Software that translates your commands into machine language that the hardware can understand. In MS-DOS, this task is carried out by the file named COMMAND.COM.

Command line interface A system of communicating or interacting with a computer by entering commands at the DOS prompt.

Command macro or synonym A user-definable command that acts like an internal DOS command, or like a small batch file held in memory for instant use.

Command-driven A term used to describe an application or operating system in which you type in commands at the DOS or other operating system prompt. Menus and graphic displays are not used.

COMSPEC The DOS environment variable that specifies the name and location of the command interpreter for a given session.

CON The system name for the console, under DOS, OS/2, and UNIX.

CONFIG.SYS A special file in the startup disk root directory. Read by DOS at startup, this file configures the machine and installs device drivers.

Console Generally, the part of any computer system that allows communication between the user and the CPU. In DOS, the console consists of the keyboard and screen used as standard input and output devices—the normal setup.

Controller card The hardware that tells a hard disk what to do, and interacts with the CPU.

Coprocessor The special purpose processor that works with the CPU to speed up time-consuming floating point math and graphics operations.

CPU Central processing unit; the microprocessor that does a PC's actual computing.

Cylinder A term that refers to all tracks with the same number on all platters of a hard disk; describes how they would appear if taken off the platters and stacked one on top of the other.

Data transfer rate The speed at which information can be read from a disk; sometimes abbreviated DTR.

Database A collection of related information.

Default drive Also called the current drive, this is the floppy or hard drive where DOS automatically looks first for files.

Default value Any value DOS assumes to be true unless you tell it otherwise.

Desktop publishing (DTP) programs Programs that combine text and artwork to enable the user to design newsletters, brochures, fancy letterheads, reports, or graphs for presentation purposes. Graphical in nature.

Device drivers Programs installed by CONFIG.SYS that let DOS recognize devices that are not part of the computer, such as nonstandard disk drives, a mouse, a modem, and so forth.

Devices Specific computer parts or equipment used for specific purposes, such as a monitor/video display, keyboard, or printer.

DIP Dual inline package (sometimes called dual inline pin); an epoxy housing for switches, memory chips, and other components. Two rows of mounting pins along the bottom resemble legs; thus DIPs are sometimes called bugs.

Directory   The table of contents for a disk or subdirectory; a list showing filenames, sizes, and the date that files were created or last modified.

Directory tree   A system of subdirectories, much like a family tree, that branches out from a root directory; used to organize file storage.

Disk cache   Software that retains the most recently read hard disk data; smarter and faster than buffers.

DOS environment   An area of memory (the default is 160 bytes), set aside by DOS to hold COMSPEC, PATH, and other operating variables used by programs or batch files. The CONFIG.SYS file can include commands to increase the environment's size.

DOS prompt   *See* Prompt.

DRAM   Dynamic RAM; used for most working memory.

Edge connector   A long tab along the bottom of an add-on circuit board, with gold or copper "fingers" that connect with circuits in a PC's expansion slots.

EISA   Enhanced industry standard architecture; the clone industry's answer to MCA. It shares most of MCA's 32-bit bus benefits, but also is compatible with ISA boards.

Encoding scheme   The method used to magnetically record information on a disk surface and make it retrievable later.

End of file (EOF) marker   ASCII character (number 026) used to indicate where a nonbinary file ends.

Escape codes   Any sequence of characters beginning with ASCII character 27 and ending with a terminating code that indicates the function of the sequence. Used by console drivers, such as ANSI.SYS, to let you control screen appearance and color, cursor location, and keyboard key assign-ments. Also used by printer drivers to control print appearance, such as bold or italic type.

Executable file Any file with a filename extension of .COM, .EXE, or .BAT that DOS can run as a program.

Expanded memory Up to 32MB of memory above 640K that can be addressed using the LIM paging memory-management standard; usable by 8088, 8086, and 80286 machines with special hardware. 80386 and 80486 machines require appropriate memory management software.

Expansion slots Slots provided on the motherboard for connecting add-on circuit boards.

Extended characters The characters in the Appendix E table with ASCII numbers 128 or higher; for instance, box, graphics, foreign, math, and other special characters.

Extended memory Memory above 1024K; in AT systems, sometimes in-cludes the upper memory blocks between 640K and 1024K.

External commands The name used by Microsoft to describe small DOS utility programs like CHKDSK or DISKCOPY. An external command is really just the filename of any executable file provided with DOS. Also called *transient commands.*

Fault isolation The process of moving logically along the path of what might have gone wrong, from the simplest cause to the increasingly com-plex, when troubleshooting a hardware/software malfunction.

File Similar to a file in a filing cabinet, a disk file is a collection of information in one subject area, such as a letter, collection of phone num-bers, or last year's tax return.

File handle A number kept in an internal DOS table that tells DOS the name and location of active files and devices.

Filename   The name you assign to a file. Up to eight characters long, it can be followed by a period and an optional filename extension of up to three characters.

Filename extension   This consists of one to three characters at the end of a filename, preceded by a period, to help identify the type of file. For example, an extension of .LET might signify a file that contains a letter. The extension is optional. Extensions of .COM, .EXE, and .BAT indicate executable files.

Filespec   Short for file specification, this is a file's name and extension, as in FILENAME.EXT.

Filters   In DOS, three programs (MORE.COM, SORT.EXE, and FIND .EXE) that let you control standard input and output; they read input, transform it in some way, and then output it (usually to the screen or to a file).

Fixed disk   *See* Hard disk.

Flat-file database   A simple, matrixed system that stores information and records in any easy-to-access rows-and-columns format.

Floppy disk   A flexible data storage device; comes in a variety of storage capacities. *See also* Hard disk.

Form factor   The outer measurements of a hardware assembly.

Freeware   *See* Shareware.

Graphics   A display mode that shows information on the screen using dot-by-dot (pixel) representation rather than text-based characters.

GUI   Graphical user interface; pronounced "gooey." A bitmapped user environment, typically operated by using a mouse or other pointing device.

Hard disk   A rigid, nonvolatile, high density data storage device; called a *fixed disk* by IBM.

Heat sink A device that pipes extra warmth away from the heat-producing components of an electronic device.

Hidden files Files whose names do not show up on a directory listing; they are hidden from DOS commands and most programs.

High RAM The 384K of memory between 640K and 1024K on AT class computers.

Icon A picture or symbol of a command choice. You use a mouse or the keyboard arrow keys to make the selection.

Instruction set Operations a chip can carry out.

Integrated programs Multiple major applications included in a single program with a unified user interface. Most integrated programs combine the Big Four applications: word processors, databases, spreadsheets, and telecommunications.

Internal commands Commands contained in COMMAND.COM, the DOS command interpreter. These commands respond immediately when you enter them because they are already in memory; DOS recognizes the command and does not search on a disk for an executable file of that name.

Interrupt vectors Pieces of program code that point to where specific programs begin and end in memory. Used to place a process on hold temporarily while the CPU carries out another task.

Interrupts Certain machine-level binary sequences that make DOS interrupt an action to do something that has a higher priority.

I/O Input/output.

ISA Industry standard architecture; the 8- and 16-bit expansion-slot bus designs used on original PCs, XTs, and ATs.

Key return code Binary signal sent to the BIOS when you press a key; determines what character appears on the display or what action the computer takes next.

LAN Local area network; this software allows several PCs to hook into a central computer so that all systems have access to the same files and other resources.

Language In computing, systematic signs, words, and symbols that program the computer.

LIM standard The Lotus-Intel-Microsoft standard for managing expanded memory.

Logical drive A disk area treated by DOS as an independent disk drive. DOS assigns a letter to each logical drive. A hard disk can include several logical drives on a single drive unit.

Low-level format A format which prepares a hard disk to be laid out in tracks and sectors.

Macro A program used to shortcut a series of commonly used keystrokes; activated or run by a specially assigned key or icon.

Matrix storage A system of access to data that requires two or more coordinates, such as the rows and columns of a spreadsheet program.

MCA Micro channel architecture; a high-capacity, 32-bit, hardware-controlled expansion slot introduced by IBM for its PS/2 computers. *See also* EISA and ISA.

Medium A layer of magnetic material, on the surface of a nonmagnetic platter, where magnetic information is recorded.

Megabyte (MB, Mbyte, meg) 1,048,576 bytes, or 1024 kilobytes.

Megahertz (MHz) Electrical voltage, AC frequency, of one million cycles per second.

Memory The storage area that holds the data to be processed by the CPU.

Memory-resident program *See* TSR.

Menu-driven   A term used to describe a command system that lists choices on a screen; a mouse or keyboard arrows are used to make selections.

Metacharacter   One of several combinations of the $ character and a second character in the DOS prompt command line that make the prompt display special values.

MFM   Modified frequency modulation; a standard ST-506 hard disk data encoding scheme.

Modem   A device that sends digital data over analog telephone circuits, enabling two computers to trade data.

Motherboard   The main printed circuit board of a PC, where the chips and other major components are mounted.

Multitasking   Ability of a computer to do more than one task at a time without putting one of them "on hold."

Nanosecond   Billionth of a second; abbreviated ns.

Null parameter   A symbol that does not show on the screen. It takes up a space and tells DOS that the empty space is intentional—that there is no accidentally missing information.

Operating system   Software that controls a computer's hardware components. Frequently abbreviated OS.

Outliner program   An applications program that creates complex text outlines, reorganizes written material, and organizes thoughts; such programs feature complex text manipulation.

Page frame   Space reserved (usually 64K) at the top of DOS memory so that data held in expanded memory can be "paged" into conventional memory, then "paged" back out, on demand.

Parallel port   Output connector that sends eight parallel bits—a full byte—to a peripheral device, typically a printer. *See also* Serial port.

Parameters Options or any other operating variables, such as filenames, that you specify when running a program.

Parent directory The directory from which the current directory is branched; for example, if the current directory is C:\UTIL\BIN, the parent directory is C:\UTIL.

Parity bit An extra 1 or 0 added to each byte for a parity check of data integrity.

Parity checking A process that detects if a bit has been changed, thus corrupting a data byte, in memory.

Partition The physical area of a hard disk reserved for use as one or more logical drives. Partitions may be *primary* (bootable) or *extended* (nonbootable).

PATH command A command that tells DOS where to look for executable programs.

Path name The full route through a disk's directory structure to a file, starting at the root directory and ending with the filespec. An example of a path name is C:\SUBDIR\FILENAME.EXT.

Peripheral device Any device that is external to the system unit box, that works in conjunction with the system unit and is connected to it by cables (printer, modem, scanner, and so on).

Piping A command format that uses the vertical bar symbol (¦) to tell DOS to route the output of one program into the input of another program.

Pixel The smallest dot a graphics adapter can make on the screen; stands for *picture element*.

Platter A physical disk, coated with magnetic material, on which information is recorded. A single hard drive has multiple platters.

Plotter A graphing and drawing tool, similar to a printer, but designed for engineering and other high-precision uses.

Plotting program A program that graphs information on a two-dimensional area and drives the plotter.

PRN In DOS, the designation for output to a printer, typically via the LPT1 parallel port.

Program The specific computer instructions for doing a certain task or set of related tasks.

Prompt A symbol, or set of symbols, determined by the user, that tells you DOS is ready to accept a command and may convey additional information.

Protected mode A special 80286 and 80386 operating mode that allows multitasking; used more by OS/2 than by DOS.

RAM Random access memory (as opposed to disk storage, or read-only memory storage).

RAM disk An area set aside in memory that mimics a physical disk storage device; useful for temporary files, for providing fast access to data, for program overlays, and so on. Sometimes called a *virtual disk*.

Read (files) The process of retrieving information from storage, such as from a file in a hard disk directory or from a floppy disk.

Read/write heads The part of an actuator that moves across the platter, picking up or laying down data as a series of magnetic signals.

Reboot To restart the computer by turning off the power (cold reboot) or by pressing CTRL-ALT-DEL (warm reboot), which wipes the memory clean.

Redirection A command format using three symbols (>, <, and >>) to redirect input or output normally intended for one device (such as the monitor) to another device (such as the printer).

Relational database An organizational system that lets you access several data files at once (for example, a mailing list and a phone book).

Replaceable parameters   A set of special batch file symbols, %1 through %9, for which DOS substitutes values specified by the user at the time the batch file is run.

RLL encoding   A higher-density data encoding scheme compatible with many standard MFM hard disks. Stands for run length limited.

ROM   Read-only memory.

ROM BIOS   Read-only memory, basic input/output system; hard-wired programming that controls bootup, data transfer, and other system-level functions.

Root directory   The directory that DOS creates when a disk is formatted; it is identified by a single backslash (\). On floppy disks it is generally the only directory used. On a hard disk it is the most senior parent directory.

Script   When designated with DOS' input redirection symbol (<), a file which automatically gives DEBUG, or some other DOS command, its input. Serves as an alternative to direct keyboard input.

Sector   Divisions of a platter that split each track into a set number of areas, typically 17, 26, or 34 per track.

Seek time   Time required for the read/write heads to find a specific piece of data or a specific disk track.

Serial port   Output connector designated COM1 through COM*n* that sends bits one after another to a peripheral device, typically a modem. *See also* Parallel port.

Shadow RAM   High-speed RAM chips used to store the slower ROM BIOS information in order to speed operation.

Shareware   Programs that are available for a small registration fee, often including updates for little or no extra charge.

SIMM   Single inline memory module; a caterpillar-like assembly of memory chips used in place of individual banks of memory chips.

Software The procedures, routines, languages, and programs used in a computer system; also includes assemblers, compilers, subroutines, and operating systems.

Spreadsheet programs Applications programs that provide an electronic financial grid, similar to the old-fashioned paper grids. These supercalculator programs automatically recalculate affected values when you insert new values. Often spreadsheet programs are capable of graphing the results.

Stepper motor The type of actuator control used with most hard disks.

Storage Any place data is kept outside of the main operating RAM; typically a floppy disk or hard disk.

String Any sequence of characters, including letters, numbers, and spaces; for example, any individual word or group of words can be considered a single string.

Subdirectories Logical storage areas branched off the current directory. For example, if the current directory is C:\UTIL, one of its subdirectories might be C:\UTIL\BIN.

Swap-out file A file read into conventional memory, used, then read back out to disk or to extended memory to make room in main memory for another file.

System call A procedure which allows a program to interact directly with the operating system by giving it an assignment (such as file saving) without the user's direct intervention.

Target The parameter of a DOS command representing what results or is acted upon; for example, in the command, TYPE THISFILE, THISFILE is the target file.

Telecommunications programs Programs that allow one computer to call another. They coordinate activity between the computer, modem, telephone line, and remote computer.

Text editor programs Simple word processors. They usually generate text with no special formatting characters.

Text-based *See* Character-based.

Timeslice Period of time during which a program takes control of the CPU in a multitasking environment.

Timetick Basic CPU time-counting unit; there are 18.2 timeticks per second.

Track The circular area of a spinning floppy disk that lies under a read/write head.

TSR Terminate-and-stay-resident program; a program that waits in memory, then pops up on the screen when you press a hot key.

Turbo card An add-in board that plugs into a lower performance motherboard and provides enhanced performance; for example, a 386-based card that plugs into a 286 motherboard and provides 386 processing power.

Upper memory blocks Also called UMBs; RAM higher than 640K, used as extended memory, video memory, and so forth.

User environment The way a user interacts with the computer system; it can use menus, icons, or typed commands.

User interface What the user sees and uses to give the computer instructions; the user's onscreen environment.

Utilities Small programs that accomplish specific tasks, such as system housekeeping chores.

Voice coil New actuator control technology that provides finer control than a stepper motor does.

Wait state Intentional processing delay to accommodate slow memory chips.

Wildcards Special characters (* and ?) that can stand for unspecified characters or patterns in filenames, just as the joker in a deck of cards can stand for any other card.

Word processors Complex editing programs that usually include formatting, a spelling checker, a thesaurus, multiple-column output, indexing, comprehensive printer support, and other features.

Write (files) The process of transferring information (data) to a storage area, usually a disk or tape.

WYSIWYG What you see is what you get (pronounced "wizzy-wig"). A display mode in which the monitor shows what will be printed, including various type styles such as italic and boldface. WYSIWYG requires graphics-based, not character-based, display hardware.

Using the Keyboard

PC keyboards have evolved along with the PC itself. PCs that predated the IBM, such as the original Apple II, were fairly primitive—to get lowercase letters in the original Apple II, you had to install a chip, attach an alligator clip, and run a wire between two contacts inside the box. A kit for this purpose was first offered by Dan Palomar, an early entrepreneur remembered fondly by Apple enthusiasts. You'll still hear references to the "Palomar kit" at Apple user group meetings.

The original IBM PC keyboard, introduced in 1981, was different. It had 83 snappy keys and a tactile feel that many think has never been topped. Since then hundreds of variations on the original PC keyboard theme have appeared. Some differences are as small as a change in location for one or two keys or the addition of rear fold-out legs that adjust the keyboard tilt. Other, more major enhancements include entire new keyboard sections, such as those on the 101-key extended keyboard.

Compare Figure B-1 with your own keyboard; most of your keyboard's keys will be in the same place as those in one of the two keyboards in the figure, although you may find some minor differences. On older or special-

Figure B-1

Two common keyboard styles

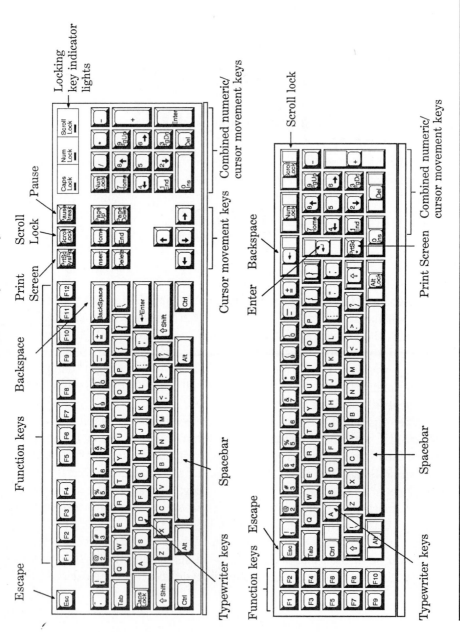

design keyboards, the differences will be greater. Original PC and XT keyboards have ten function keys to the left of the typewriter keys. Key placement may also be different for the ESC (Escape) key, the CTRL (Control) key, and others. However, if the key is there on your keyboard, its purpose remains the same no matter what its position.

THE TYPEWRITER KEYS

If you know how to use a typewriter, you know how to use these keys. These letter and number keys work just as they do on an electric typewriter—when you press a key, the selected letter or number appears on the screen at the cursor position. To use capital letters or the punctuation marks and other symbols above the top-row numbers, hold down the SHIFT key while you press the letter or number key, just as you would on a typewriter. If you hold down one of these keys without releasing it, after a short pause it will start to repeat automatically. This is handy for drawing lines, making dot leaders, and for other repetitive chores.

Number Keys

The top row of keys includes the number keys. Note that on a computer, the key for the digit 1 is not the same as for the letter l, although on typewriters they are often treated as the same. Also, the CAPS LOCK key has no effect on the number keys.

The BACKSPACE Key

If you make a mistake while typing, you can use the BACKSPACE key to erase it. BACKSPACE moves the cursor back one space. This key may be indicated with the word *Backspace,* or by a left-pointing arrow, as shown here:

Don't confuse the BACKSPACE key with the LEFT ARROW key, which doesn't erase the character as it moves the cursor to the left one character at a time.

The SHIFT Key

The SHIFT key reverses the current letter case of a typewriter key—that is, if the CAPS LOCK key is toggled off, pressing SHIFT will result in capital letters. Unlike on a typewriter, if the CAPS LOCK key is toggled on, pressing the SHIFT key will result in lowercase letters. Regardless of whether the CAPS LOCK key is turned on or off, the SHIFT key always results in numbers from the numeric keypad to the right of the typewriter keys, symbols from the top row of keys, and the upper characters on the keyboard's other punctuation keys.

The SHIFT key is often symbolized by an open up-arrow, as illustrated here:

The TAB Key

The TAB key is often marked with two arrows, one pointing right and the other left, as illustrated here:

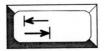

It moves the cursor to the next tab stop to the right, or to the left if you press TAB with the SHIFT key.

SPECIAL KEYS

Unlike a typewriter, your PC keyboard has a variety of special keys. Since your PC performs functions other than just preparing written documents, the keyboard is designed to work with programs that have many additional key options. The following sections describe how these special keys work at the DOS level.

The ENTER Key

The ENTER key is sometimes called the carriage return, or CR, because of the way electric typewriters worked in the days when the platen (or carriage) moved back and forth as you typed. ENTER is often indicated by the same symbol used for electric typewriter carriage return keys: an arrow hooked to the left. Here are several styles of ENTER keys:

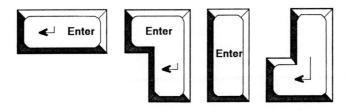

On a computer, the ENTER key has two purposes. The first is to mark the end of a line or paragraph in a word processing document, by placing a carriage return and line feed character at the end of a line in a document. (Most word processors have a word-wrap feature that does this automatically.) Pressing ENTER moves the cursor down and to the left (as indicated by the hooked arrow on the key), at the beginning of the next line.

The second purpose for ENTER, at the DOS level and in some applications programs, is to indicate when you have finished entering a command or a data field. Used this way, ENTER tells the computer to stop waiting for more keystrokes and to start processing the input.

If you press ENTER after a typing error, DOS will announce that you've made a mistake, like this:

```
A>dur
Bad command or file name
A>
```

Simply retype the DIR command correctly and press ENTER.

Note: When your typing error happens to result in the legitimate name of a program or batch file, DOS won't know you made a mistake, so if you see some unexpected results, try pressing CTRL-C or CTRL-BREAK to stop the operation. If that doesn't work and you are sure you need to stop the operation, press CTRL-ALT-DEL to reboot. Rebooting can damage files, so use it only in extreme circumstances.

The ESC Key

Like the function keys (explained later), ESC (Escape) doesn't do anything of its own accord—but most programs take advantage of this key. With some exceptions, pressing ESC cancels what you are doing in a program and opens the way to do something else. In many cases, ESC also brings a menu to the screen, from which you can pick another action for the current program to take.

At the DOS command line, pressing ESC cancels the entire contents of the current line. This is handy if you make a typing mistake in a command and want to change it without having to press a long series of backspaces. When you press ESC, DOS displays a backslash (\), discards the command you just entered, and moves the cursor down a line, where it waits for more instructions.

The PAUSE Key

On an extended keyboard, the PAUSE key stops the display in its current position until you press another key. This can be used, for example, to pause a long directory display. Some special utility programs such as FANSI-CONSOLE have options to make the PAUSE key act as a toggle that first stops, then restarts the scrolling display. In PAUSE's default state, you must press some other key, such as the spacebar, to restart the screen after you press PAUSE.

The PRINT SCREEN Key

This key sends a copy of the contents of your current screen display to the printer. Often you must press SHIFT-PRINT SCREEN for this key to work. This key is handy for obtaining printed copies of screen reports that you cannot otherwise save to a file for later viewing. Another use is to get a printed copy of, for example, only one or two critical paragraphs of a long document.

Note: As described in the next section, pressing CTRL-PRINT SCREEN makes the computer print a continuous copy of the monitor display as it changes.

REPEATING KEYS VERSUS HOLD-AND-COMBINE KEYS

Most keys, except the hold-and-combine keys described next, are *repeating* keys. If you hold down a repeating key without releasing it, after a brief pause you will see a string of the chosen character march across the screen—like pressing the Underline key on an electric typewriter. However, on a computer, you can adjust the key's repeat rate using special utility software (see Chapter 8).

Several keys do nothing when used by themselves, but do affect what other keys do—similar to a typewriter's Shift key. To use one of these keys, you *hold* it down while you *combine* it with another key, by pressing and releasing the second key. For instance, to break out of a running program you can hold down the CTRL key while you type **C**. That keystroke combination is represented as

CTRL-C

These are the hold-and-combine keys:

SHIFT
CTRL (Control)
ALT (Alternate)

Some common hold-and-combine key combinations used from DOS follow.

- CTRL-BREAK (or CTRL-C) often stops an active command.

- CTRL-NUM LOCK pauses the screen.

- SHIFT-PRINT SCREEN prints the contents of the screen.
- CTRL-PRINT SCREEN gives you a *printer echo,* which sends all subsequent screen contents to the printer as they appear. This is useful for diagnosing problems in batch files or for deciphering error messages that flash to the screen, before they disappear.
- CTRL-ALT-DEL resets (or reboots) your computer, but will not save your work. Use it cautiously.

LOCKING (OR TOGGLE) KEYS

Most of today's keyboards have indicator lights to tell you whether the locking (toggle) keys are turned on or off. In Figure B-1, these lights are shown in the upper-right corner of the keyboard. Some keyboards, however, mount the lights on the toggle keys themselves. Pressing a toggle key releases its current state—that is, if it is off, pressing the key will turn it on and vice versa.

- CAPS LOCK   This key enables and disables capital letters. CAPS LOCK is similar to an electric typewriter Shift-Lock key, with two main differences. First, the CAPS LOCK key doesn't affect numbers and punctuation marks; only the letter keys are reversed to uppercase. Second, when you press the SHIFT key using SHIFT with CAPS LOCK on, all letters (not just lowercase) are reversed. Thus, if you type the following line using SHIFT with CAPS LOCK on,

Acme Machine Shop Company

you'll get this on your screen:

aCME mACHINE sHOP cOMPANY

This feature frustrated many touch typists when they first used a PC keyboard. The indicator lights brought a measure of relief; at least you could glance at the keyboard and see if CAPS LOCK was turned on. Programs such as FANSI-CONSOLE and various single-purpose utilities can change the way the CAPS LOCK key works, if you're so inclined. Most people eventually get accustomed to their keyboard's traits.

- NUM LOCK   This key changes the numeric keypad at the far right of the keyboard from cursor-control arrows to numbers arranged in a standard ten-key calculator square. This is a blessing for users who need to enter long strings of numbers by touch. On AT and higher machines, which have separate cursor-control arrows next to the keyboard, NUM LOCK is automatically on when you boot up.

- SCROLL LOCK   The function of this key varies from program to program. Often, however, SCROLL LOCK is used to lock the cursor on its current screen line, and make the text rather than the cursor scroll up and down when you press a cursor-control arrow key. This can be especially convenient in spreadsheet programs.

FUNCTION KEYS

DOS uses a few of the function keys, or F-keys (notably F1 and F3), for command line editing. Each applications program uses these keys to accomplish its own unique operation. Most popular programs do take advantage of the function keys, and their operations have become somewhat standardized. For example, the F1 key often calls up a help screen, and F10 often exits a program.

NUMERIC KEYPAD AND CURSOR-CONTROL KEYS

The numeric keypad and cursor-control keys, also called the *number pad* and the *combined numeric keypad and cursor-control pad*, serve double duty. When NUM LOCK is turned on or SHIFT is pressed, the numeric keypad becomes the familiar number pad used on calculators. In the unshifted state when NUM LOCK is also off, they act as cursor-control keys that duplicate the functions of the cursor-movement keypad.

Having two sets of cursor-movement keys may seem like overkill, but a separate cursor-control keypad was not available on the original PC and XT keyboards, and many users got accustomed to using the arrow keys on the unshifted numeric keypad. As mentioned earlier, ATs boot up with the NUM LOCK key turned on by default, giving the typist one cursor-control pad and one number pad. A variety of small utility programs are available that will turn off NUM LOCK at bootup if you prefer to use the arrow keys on the number pad.

BOXES AND OTHER SPECIAL
ALT-KEY CHARACTERS

From time to time you may need to enter a special character, one that is not on your keyboard. For example, you may want to draw a box or enter a foreign language character. Or you may need to enter the 027 ASCII escape character in a batch file in order to change screen colors. Using the ALT key with the numeric keypad, you can enter any nonstandard character in the ASCII character set shown in Appendix E.

To enter nonstandard characters, hold down the ALT key and use the numeric keypad to type the three-digit ASCII code for the character you want. Release the ALT key, and the desired character will appear on the screen. For example, to type the standard small square bullet character, follow these steps:

1. Press and hold down the ALT key.

2. Type the number **254** using the numeric keypad.

3. Release the ALT key.

Here are two tips to remember when using the ALT-ASCII combination:

- Always use the numeric keypad. The number keys in the top row of the typewriter key section won't work.

- NUM LOCK can be off. Once ALT is pressed, the computer interprets any typed number key as the number, not the cursor-control code.

Note: Not all programs or printers accept ALT-ASCII special characters. Some have their own character sets, or have been programmed in other ways to get the same characters. If the ALT-ASCII technique doesn't work for you, check your program manual for an alternative approach.

Hard Drives: Geometries for CMOS Settings

Any AT-class or higher computer uses one- or two-digit drive-type identifier codes in a built-in drive-type table. Sometimes these tables follow the semiofficial IBM list, but not always. You will need to determine which drive-type ID code to use when you reconfigure your CMOS, and since neither the computer manufacturers nor the drive makers have settled on a standard, it can be tricky. Sometimes you simply have to use trial and error based on what you know of your drive's geometries in terms of cylinders, heads, sectors, and capacity.

Chapter 18 suggests ways to access your machine's drive type table. The next task is to match that table to your hard disk. The tables in this appendix list drive geometries for many of the most popular hard drive makes and models. If yours is listed, simply match the listed data to the data in your machine's drive type table to get the correct drive type ID number.

If your hard drive is not listed, check your drive documentation for the appropriate information on capacity, sector size, number of heads, and number of cylinders. If you can't find it there, look for stickers on the drive itself. If all else fails, you can call the hard drive manufacturer and ask.

In some cases, such as when your drive or controller has an onboard ROM that takes over the disk read/write functions, the drive documentation tells you to set the hard drive type to None or 0. You then have the best of all possible worlds—you can just let the controller take care of it.

Table C-1

Drive Geometries for Leading Hard Drive Makes and Models

Model	Cylinders	Heads	Sectors	Capacity
ATASI				
3046	645 CYLINDERS	7 HEADS	17 SECS	39 MB
3051	704 CYLINDERS	7 HEADS	17 SECS	42 MB
3051+	733 CYLINDERS	7 HEADS	17 SECS	44 MB
3058	1024 CYLINDERS	8 HEADS	17 SECS	71 MB
BRAND TECHNOLOGY				
BT8085	1024 CYLINDERS	8 HEADS	17 SECS	71 MB
BT8128	1024 CYLINDERS	8 HEADS	26 SECS	109 MB
BT8170	1024 CYLINDERS	8 HEADS	34 SECS	142 MB
CMI				
CM-6626	640 CYLINDERS	4 HEADS	17 SECS	22 MB
CM-6640	640 CYLINDERS	6 HEADS	17 SECS	33 MB
CONNER PERIPHERALS				
CP-342	981 CYLINDERS	5 HEADS	17 SECS	42 MB
CP-3102-A	776 CYLINDERS	8 HEADS	33 SECS	104 MB
CP-3102-B	772 CYLINDERS	8 HEADS	33 SECS	104 MB
CP-3024	615 CYLINDERS	4 HEADS	17 SECS	21 MB
CP-3044	977 CYLINDERS	5 HEADS	17 SECS	42 MB
CP-3104	776 CYLINDERS	8 HEADS	33 SECS	104 MB
CONTROL DATA				
9415-519	697 CYLINDERS	3 HEADS	17 SECS	18 MB
9415-536	697 CYLINDERS	5 HEADS	17 SECS	30 MB
9415-538	733 CYLINDERS	5 HEADS	17 SECS	31 MB
94155-48	925 CYLINDERS	5 HEADS	17 SECS	40 MB
94155-57	925 CYLINDERS	6 HEADS	17 SECS	48 MB
94155-67	925 CYLINDERS	7 HEADS	17 SECS	56 MB
94155-77	925 CYLINDERS	8 HEADS	17 SECS	64 MB
94155-85	1024 CYLINDERS	8 HEADS	17 SECS	71 MB

Table C-1

Drive Geometries for Leading Hard Drive Makes and Models (*continued*)

Model	Cylinders	Heads	Sectors	Capacity
CONTROL DATA (*continued*)				
94155-85P	1024 CYLINDERS	8 HEADS	17 SECS	71 MB
94155-86	925 CYLINDERS	9 HEADS	17 SECS	72 MB
94155-96	1024 CYLINDERS	9 HEADS	17 SECS	80 MB
94155-96P	1024 CYLINDERS	9 HEADS	17 SECS	80 MB
94155-120	960 CYLINDERS	8 HEADS	26 SECS	102 MB
94155-120P	960 CYLINDERS	8 HEADS	26 SECS	102 MB
94155-135	960 CYLINDERS	9 HEADS	26 SECS	115 MB
94155-135P	960 CYLINDERS	9 HEADS	26 SECS	115 MB
94156-48	925 CYLINDERS	5 HEADS	17 SECS	40 MB
94156-67	925 CYLINDERS	7 HEADS	17 SECS	56 MB
94156-86	925 CYLINDERS	9 HEADS	17 SECS	72 MB
94166-101	969 CYLINDERS	5 HEADS	34 SECS	84 MB
94166-141	969 CYLINDERS	7 HEADS	34 SECS	118 MB
94166-182	969 CYLINDERS	9 HEADS	34 SECS	151 MB
94186-383	1412 CYLINDERS	13 HEADS	34 SECS	319 MB
94186-383H	1224 CYLINDERS	15 HEADS	34 SECS	319 MB
94186-442H	1412 CYLINDERS	15 HEADS	34 SECS	368 MB
94204-65	941 CYLINDERS	8 HEADS	17 SECS	65 MB
94204-71	1024 CYLINDERS	8 HEADS	17 SECS	71 MB
94205-51	989 CYLINDERS	5 HEADS	17 SECS	43 MB
94205-77	989 CYLINDERS	5 HEADS	26 SECS	65 MB
94216-106	1024 CYLINDERS	5 HEADS	34 SECS	89 MB
94205-77	1024 CYLINDERS	8 HEADS	17 SECS	71 MB
94216-106	989 CYLINDERS	5 HEADS	17 SECS	43 MB
CORE INTERNATIONAL				
HC150	1250 CYLINDERS	7 HEADS	35 SECS	150 MB
HC310	1747 CYLINDERS	7 HEADS	52 SECS	325 MB
HC650	1661 CYLINDERS	15 HEADS	53 SECS	658 MB
HC315	1447 CYLINDERS	8 HEADS	57 SECS	340 MB
HC655	1447 CYLINDERS	16 HEADS	57 SECS	680 MB

Table C-1

Drive Geometries for Leading Hard Drive Makes and Models (*continued*)

Model	Cylinders	Heads	Sectors	Capacity
CORE INTERNATIONAL (*continued*)				
HC1000	1787 CYLINDERS	15 HEADS	77 SECS	1056 MB
HC150S	969 CYLINDERS	9 HEADS	35 SECS	155 MB
HC310S	1447 CYLINDERS	8 HEADS	56 SECS	330 MB
HC650S	1447 CYLINDERS	16 HEADS	56 SECS	663 MB
HC1000S	1918 CYLINDERS	16 HEADS	64 SECS	1.5 GB
OPTIMA/40MB	963 CYLINDERS	5 HEADS	17 SECS	41.9MB(MFM) 64MB(RLL)
OPTIMA/70MB	918 CYLINDERS	9 HEADS	17 SECS	71.9MB(MFM) 109.9MB(RLL)
OPTIMA/40MB (3.5″)	733 CYLINDERS	7 HEADS	17 SECS	44.7MB(MFM) 68.4MB(RLL)
ATPlus/43MB	988 CYLINDERS	5 HEADS	17 SECS	42.9MB(MFM) 65.7MB(RLL)
ATPlus/44MB (3.5″)	733 CYLINDERS	7 HEADS	17 SECS	44.7MB(MFM) 68.4MB(RLL)
ATPlus/72MB	924 CYLINDERS	9 HEADS	17 SECS	72.3MB(MFM) 107MB(RLL)
OPTIMA/80MB	1024 CYLINDERS	9 HEADS	17 SECS	80.1MB(MFM) 132MB(RLL)
ATPlus/80MB	1024 CYLINDERS	9 HEADS	17 SECS	80.1MB(MFM)
DATA-TECH MEMORIES				
DTM-553	1024 CYLINDERS	5 HEADS	17 SECS	44 MB
DTM-853	640 CYLINDERS	8 HEADS	17 SECS	44 MB
DTM-885	1024 CYLINDERS	8 HEADS	17 SECS	71 MB
FUJITSU				
M2225D	615 CYLINDERS	4 HEADS	17 SECS	21 MB
M2227D	615 CYLINDERS	8 HEADS	17 SECS	42 MB
M2241AS	754 CYLINDERS	4 HEADS	17 SECS	26 MB

Table C-1

Drive Geometries for Leading Hard Drive Makes and Models (*continued*)

Model	Cylinders	Heads	Sectors	Capacity
FUJITSU (*continued*)				
M2242AS	754 CYLINDERS	7 HEADS	17 SECS	45 MB
M2243AS	754 CYLINDERS	11 HEADS	17 SECS	72 MB
M2247E	1243 CYLINDERS	7 HEADS	36 SECS	160 MB
M2248E	1243 CYLINDERS	11 HEADS	36 SECS	252 MB
M2249E	1243 CYLINDERS	15 HEADS	36 SECS	343 MB
HITACHI				
DK511-3	699 CYLINDERS	5 HEADS	17 SECS	30 MB
DK511-5	699 CYLINDERS	7 HEADS	17 SECS	42 MB
DK511-8	823 CYLINDERS	10 HEADS	17 SECS	71 MB
DK512-8	823 CYLINDERS	5 HEADS	17 SECS	35 MB
IMPRIMIS				
9415-519	697 CYLINDERS	3 HEADS	17 SECS	18 MB
9415-536	697 CYLINDERS	5 HEADS	17 SECS	30 MB
9415-538	733 CYLINDERS	5 HEADS	17 SECS	31 MB
94155-48	925 CYLINDERS	5 HEADS	17 SECS	40 MB
94155-56	925 CYLINDERS	9 HEADS	17 SECS	72 MB
94155-57	925 CYLINDERS	6 HEADS	17 SECS	48 MB
94155-67	925 CYLINDERS	7 HEADS	17 SECS	56 MB
94155-77	925 CYLINDERS	8 HEADS	17 SECS	64 MB
94155-85	1024 CYLINDERS	8 HEADS	17 SECS	71 MB
94155-85P	1024 CYLINDERS	8 HEADS	17 SECS	71 MB
94155-86	925 CYLINDERS	9 HEADS	17 SECS	72 MB
94155-96	1024 CYLINDERS	9 HEADS	17 SECS	80 MB
94155-96P	1024 CYLINDERS	9 HEADS	17 SECS	80 MB
94155-120	960 CYLINDERS	8 HEADS	26 SECS	102 MB
94155-120P	960 CYLINDERS	8 HEADS	26 SECS	102 MB
94155-135	960 CYLINDERS	9 HEADS	26 SECS	115 MB
94155-135P	960 CYLINDERS	9 HEADS	26 SECS	115 MB
94156-48	925 CYLINDERS	5 HEADS	17 SECS	40 MB

Table C-1

Drive Geometries for Leading Hard Drive Makes and Models (*continued*)

Model	Cylinders	Heads	Sectors	Capacity
IMPRIMIS (*continued*)				
94156-67	925 CYLINDERS	7 HEADS	17 SECS	56 MB
94156-86	925 CYLINDERS	9 HEADS	17 SECS	72 MB
94166-101	969 CYLINDERS	5 HEADS	34 SECS	84 MB
94166-141	969 CYLINDERS	7 HEADS	34 SECS	118 MB
94166-182	969 CYLINDERS	9 HEADS	34 SECS	151 MB
94186-383	1412 CYLINDERS	13 HEADS	34 SECS	319 MB
94186-383H	1224 CYLINDERS	15 HEADS	34 SECS	319 MB
94186-442H	1412 CYLINDERS	15 HEADS	34 SECS	368 MB
94196-766	1632 CYLINDERS	15 HEADS	53 SECS	664 MB
94204-65	941 CYLINDERS	8 HEADS	17 SECS	65 MB
94204-71	1024 CYLINDERS	8 HEADS	17 SECS	71 MB
94205-51	989 CYLINDERS	5 HEADS	17 SECS	43 MB
94205-77	989 CYLINDERS	5 HEADS	26 SECS	65 MB
94216-106	1024 CYLINDERS	5 HEADS	34 SECS	89 MB
94246-383	1747 CYLINDERS	7 HEADS	53 SECS	331 MB
94354-135	1072 CYLINDERS	9 HEADS	29 SECS	143 MB
94354-160	1072 CYLINDERS	9 HEADS	29 SECS	143 MB
94354-172	1072 CYLINDERS	9 HEADS	36 SECS	177 MB
94354-200	1072 CYLINDERS	9 HEADS	36 SECS	177 MB
94355-100	1072 CYLINDERS	9 HEADS	17 SECS	83 MB
94355-150	1072 CYLINDERS	9 HEADS	26 SECS	128 MB
94356-111	1072 CYLINDERS	5 HEADS	36 SECS	98 MB
94356-155	1072 CYLINDERS	7 HEADS	36 SECS	138 MB
94356-200	1072 CYLINDERS	9 HEADS	36 SECS	177 MB
KYOCERA				
KC20A	616 CYLINDERS	4 HEADS	17 SECS	21 MB
KC20B	615 CYLINDERS	4 HEADS	17 SECS	21 MB
KC30A	616 CYLINDERS	4 HEADS	26 SECS	32 MB
KC30B	615 CYLINDERS	4 HEADS	26 SECS	32 MB

Table C-1

Drive Geometries for Leading Hard Drive Makes and Models (*continued*)

Model	Cylinders	Heads	Sectors	Capacity
LAPINE				
TITAN20	615 CYLINDERS	4 HEADS	17 SECS	21 MB
MAXTOR				
XT1065	918 CYLINDERS	7 HEADS	17 SECS	55 MB
XT1085	1024 CYLINDERS	8 HEADS	17 SECS	71 MB
XT1105	918 CYLINDERS	11 HEADS	17 SECS	87 MB
XT1140	918 CYLINDERS	15 HEADS	17 SECS	119 MB
XT2085	1224 CYLINDERS	7 HEADS	17 SECS	74 MB
XT2190	1224 CYLINDERS	15 HEADS	17 SECS	159 MB
XT4380	1224 CYLINDERS	15 HEADS	34 SECS	319 MB
XT8760	1632 CYLINDERS	15 HEADS	51 SECS	639 MB
MICROPOLIS				
1323	1024 CYLINDERS	4 HEADS	17 SECS	35 MB
1323A	1024 CYLINDERS	5 HEADS	17 SECS	44 MB
1324	1024 CYLINDERS	6 HEADS	17 SECS	53 MB
1324A	1024 CYLINDERS	7 HEADS	17 SECS	62 MB
1325	1024 CYLINDERS	8 HEADS	17 SECS	71 MB
1333	1024 CYLINDERS	4 HEADS	17 SECS	35 MB
1333A	1024 CYLINDERS	5 HEADS	17 SECS	44 MB
1334	1024 CYLINDERS	6 HEADS	17 SECS	53 MB
1334A	1024 CYLINDERS	7 HEADS	17 SECS	62 MB
1335	1024 CYLINDERS	8 HEADS	17 SECS	71 MB
1353	1024 CYLINDERS	4 HEADS	34 SECS	71 MB
1353A	1024 CYLINDERS	5 HEADS	34 SECS	89 MB
1354	1024 CYLINDERS	6 HEADS	34 SECS	106 MB
1354A	1024 CYLINDERS	7 HEADS	34 SECS	124 MB
1355	1024 CYLINDERS	8 HEADS	34 SECS	142 MB
1551	1224 CYLINDERS	7 HEADS	34 SECS	149 MB
1554	1224 CYLINDERS	11 HEADS	34 SECS	234 MB
1555	1224 CYLINDERS	12 HEADS	34 SECS	255 MB

Table C-1

Drive Geometries for Leading Hard Drive Makes and Models (*continued*)

Model	Cylinders	Heads	Sectors	Capacity
MICROPOLIS (*continued*)				
1556	1224 CYLINDERS	13 HEADS	34 SECS	277 MB
1557	1224 CYLINDERS	14 HEADS	34 SECS	298 MB
1558	1224 CYLINDERS	15 HEADS	34 SECS	319 MB
MICROSCIENCE				
HH-325	615 CYLINDERS	4 HEADS	17 SECS	21 MB
HH-725	615 CYLINDERS	4 HEADS	17 SECS	21 MB
HH-1050	1024 CYLINDERS	5 HEADS	17 SECS	44 MB
HH-1060	1024 CYLINDERS	5 HEADS	26 SECS	68 MB
HH-1075	1024 CYLINDERS	7 HEADS	17 SECS	62 MB
HH-1090	1314 CYLINDERS	7 HEADS	17 SECS	80 MB
HH-1095	1024 CYLINDERS	7 HEADS	26 SECS	95 MB
HH-1120	1314 CYLINDERS	7 HEADS	26 SECS	122 MB
HH-2120	1024 CYLINDERS	7 HEADS	34 SECS	124 MB
HH-2160	1276 CYLINDERS	7 HEADS	34 SECS	155 MB
4050	1024 CYLINDERS	5 HEADS	17 SECS	44 MB
4060	1024 CYLINDERS	5 HEADS	26 SECS	68 MB
4070	1024 CYLINDERS	7 HEADS	17 SECS	62 MB
4090	1024 CYLINDERS	7 HEADS	26 SECS	95 MB
5100	855 CYLINDERS	7 HEADS	34 SECS	104 MB
7040	855 CYLINDERS	3 HEADS	26 SECS	34 MB
7100	855 CYLINDERS	7 HEADS	26 SECS	79 MB
MINISCRIBE				
3053	1024 CYLINDERS	5 HEADS	17 SECS	44 MB
3085	1170 CYLINDERS	7 HEADS	17 SECS	71 MB
3130	1250 CYLINDERS	5 HEADS	34 SECS	108 MB
3180	1250 CYLINDERS	7 HEADS	34 SECS	152 MB
3425	615 CYLINDERS	4 HEADS	17 SECS	21 MB
3438	615 CYLINDERS	4 HEADS	26 SECS	32 MB
3650	809 CYLINDERS	6 HEADS	17 SECS	42 MB

Table C-1

Drive Geometries for Leading Hard Drive Makes and Models (*continued*)

Model	Cylinders	Heads	Sectors	Capacity
MINISCRIBE (*continued*)				
3675	809 CYLINDERS	6 HEADS	26 SECS	64 MB
6032	1024 CYLINDERS	3 HEADS	17 SECS	26 MB
6053	1024 CYLINDERS	5 HEADS	17 SECS	44 MB
6053II	1024 CYLINDERS	5 HEADS	17 SECS	44 MB
6074	1024 CYLINDERS	7 HEADS	17 SECS	62 MB
6079	1024 CYLINDERS	5 HEADS	26 SECS	68 MB
6085	1024 CYLINDERS	8 HEADS	17 SECS	71 MB
6128	1024 CYLINDERS	8 HEADS	26 SECS	109 MB
8051A	981 CYLINDERS	5 HEADS	17 SECS	42 MB
8425	615 CYLINDERS	4 HEADS	17 SECS	21 MB
8438	615 CYLINDERS	4 HEADS	26 SECS	32 MB
8450	771 CYLINDERS	4 HEADS	26 SECS	41 MB
8450XT	805 CYLINDERS	4 HEADS	26 SECS	42 MB
9230E	1224 CYLINDERS	9 HEADS	34 SECS	191 MB
9380E	1224 CYLINDERS	15 HEADS	34 SECS	319 MB
9780E	1661 CYLINDERS	15 HEADS	53 SECS	676 MB
MITSUBISHI				
MR522	612 CYLINDERS	4 HEADS	17 SECS	21 MB
MR535	977 CYLINDERS	5 HEADS	17 SECS	42 MB
MR535RLL	977 CYLINDERS	5 HEADS	26 SECS	65 MB
MR5310E	977 CYLINDERS	5 HEADS	34 SECS	85 MB
NEC				
D3126	615 CYLINDERS	4 HEADS	17 SECS	21 MB
D3142	642 CYLINDERS	8 HEADS	17 SECS	44 MB
D3146H	615 CYLINDERS	8 HEADS	17 SECS	42 MB
D3661	915 CYLINDERS	7 HEADS	36 SECS	118 MB
D5126	615 CYLINDERS	4 HEADS	17 SECS	21 MB
D5126H	615 CYLINDERS	4 HEADS	17 SECS	21 MB
D5127H	615 CYLINDERS	4 HEADS	26 SECS	32 MB
D5146H	615 CYLINDERS	8 HEADS	17 SECS	42 MB

Table C-1

Drive Geometries for Leading Hard Drive Makes and Models (*continued*)

Model	Cylinders	Heads	Sectors	Capacity
NEC (*continued*)				
D5147H	615 CYLINDERS	8 HEADS	26 SECS	65 MB
D5452	823 CYLINDERS	10 HEADS	17 SECS	71 MB
D5652	823 CYLINDERS	10 HEADS	34 SECS	143 MB
D5655	1224 CYLINDERS	7 HEADS	34 SECS	149 MB
D5662	1224 CYLINDERS	15 HEADS	34 SECS	319 MB
D5682	1633 CYLINDERS	15 HEADS	53 SECS	664 MB
NEWBURY				
NDR320	615 CYLINDERS	4 HEADS	17 SECS	21 MB
NDR340	615 CYLINDERS	8 HEADS	17 SECS	42 MB
NDR360	615 CYLINDERS	8 HEADS	26 SECS	65 MB
NDR1065	918 CYLINDERS	7 HEADS	17 SECS	55 MB
NDR1085	1024 CYLINDERS	8 HEADS	17 SECS	71 MB
NDR1105	918 CYLINDERS	11 HEADS	17 SECS	87 MB
NDR1140	918 CYLINDERS	15 HEADS	17 SECS	119 MB
NDR2190	1224 CYLINDERS	15 HEADS	17 SECS	159 MB
NDR4170	1224 CYLINDERS	7 HEADS	34 SECS	149 MB
NDR4380	1224 CYLINDERS	15 HEADS	34 SECS	319 MB
PRIAM				
502	755 CYLINDERS	7 HEADS	17 SECS	46 MB
504	755 CYLINDERS	7 HEADS	17 SECS	46 MB
514	1224 CYLINDERS	11 HEADS	17 SECS	117 MB
519	1224 CYLINDERS	15 HEADS	17 SECS	159 MB
617	752 CYLINDERS	11 HEADS	34 SECS	144 MB
623	752 CYLINDERS	15 HEADS	34 SECS	196 MB
630	1224 CYLINDERS	15 HEADS	34 SECS	319 MB
V130	987 CYLINDERS	3 HEADS	17 SECS	25 MB
V150	987 CYLINDERS	5 HEADS	17 SECS	42 MB
V170	987 CYLINDERS	7 HEADS	17 SECS	60 MB
V185	1166 CYLINDERS	7 HEADS	17 SECS	71 MB

Table C-1

Drive Geometries for Leading Hard Drive Makes and Models (*continued*)

Model	Cylinders	Heads	Sectors	Capacity
PTI				
PT225	615 CYLINDERS	4 HEADS	17 SECS	21 MB
PT234	820 CYLINDERS	4 HEADS	17 SECS	28 MB
PT338	615 CYLINDERS	6 HEADS	17 SECS	32 MB
PT351	820 CYLINDERS	6 HEADS	17 SECS	42 MB
PT238R	615 CYLINDERS	4 HEADS	26 SECS	32 MB
PT251R	820 CYLINDERS	4 HEADS	26 SECS	43 MB
PT357R	615 CYLINDERS	6 HEADS	26 SECS	49 MB
PT376R	820 CYLINDERS	6 HEADS	26 SECS	65 MB
QUANTUM				
Q520	512 CYLINDERS	4 HEADS	17 SECS	17 MB
Q530	512 CYLINDERS	6 HEADS	17 SECS	26 MB
Q540	512 CYLINDERS	8 HEADS	17 SECS	35 MB
RODINE				
203	321 CYLINDERS	6 HEADS	17 SECS	16 MB
204	321 CYLINDERS	8 HEADS	17 SECS	22 MB
202E	640 CYLINDERS	4 HEADS	17 SECS	22 MB
203E	640 CYLINDERS	6 HEADS	17 SECS	33 MB
204E	640 CYLINDERS	8 HEADS	17 SECS	44 MB
RO3000A-NAT	625 CYLINDERS	5 HEADS	27 SECS	43 MB
RO3000A-XLAT	992 CYLINDERS	5 HEADS	17 SECS	43 MB
RO3060R	750 CYLINDERS	5 HEADS	26 SECS	49 MB
RO3075R	750 CYLINDERS	6 HEADS	26 SECS	59 MB
RO3085R	750 CYLINDERS	7 HEADS	26 SECS	69 MB
RO5040	1224 CYLINDERS	3 HEADS	17 SECS	31 MB
RO5065	1224 CYLINDERS	5 HEADS	17 SECS	53 MB
RO5090	1224 CYLINDERS	7 HEADS	17 SECS	74 MB
SEAGATE				
ST125	615 CYLINDERS	4 HEADS	17 SECS	21 MB
ST138	615 CYLINDERS	6 HEADS	17 SECS	32 MB

Table C-1

Drive Geometries for Leading Hard Drive Makes and Models (*continued*)

Model	Cylinders	Heads	Sectors	Capacity
SEAGATE (*continued*)				
ST138R	615 CYLINDERS	4 HEADS	26 SECS	32 MB
ST151	977 CYLINDERS	5 HEADS	17 SECS	42 MB
ST157R	615 CYLINDERS	6 HEADS	26 SECS	49 MB
ST213	615 CYLINDERS	2 HEADS	17 SECS	10 MB
ST225	615 CYLINDERS	4 HEADS	17 SECS	21 MB
ST225R	667 CYLINDERS	2 HEADS	31 SECS	21 MB
ST238R	615 CYLINDERS	4 HEADS	26 SECS	32 MB
ST251	820 CYLINDERS	6 HEADS	17 SECS	42 MB
ST250R	667 CYLINDERS	4 HEADS	31 SECS	42 MB
ST277R	820 CYLINDERS	6 HEADS	26 SECS	65 MB
ST412	306 CYLINDERS	4 HEADS	17 SECS	10 MB
ST4026	615 CYLINDERS	4 HEADS	17 SECS	21 MB
ST4038	733 CYLINDERS	5 HEADS	17 SECS	31 MB
ST4051	977 CYLINDERS	5 HEADS	17 SECS	42 MB
ST4053	1024 CYLINDERS	5 HEADS	17 SECS	44 MB
ST4096	1024 CYLINDERS	9 HEADS	17 SECS	80 MB
ST4144R	1024 CYLINDERS	9 HEADS	26 SECS	122 MB
SIEMENS				
MEGAFILE-1200	1216 CYLINDERS	8 HEADS	34 SECS	169 MB
MEGAFILE-1300	1216 CYLINDERS	12 HEADS	34 SECS	254 MB
SYQUEST				
SQ312RD	612 CYLINDERS	2 HEADS	17 SECS	10 MB
SQ315F	612 CYLINDERS	4 HEADS	17 SECS	21 MB
SQ338F	612 CYLINDERS	6 HEADS	17 SECS	31 MB

Table C-1

Drive Geometries for Leading Hard Drive Makes and Models (*continued*)

Model	Cylinders	Heads	Sectors	Capacity
TANDON				
TN262	615 CYLINDERS	4 HEADS	17 SECS	21 MB
TN362	615 CYLINDERS	4 HEADS	17 SECS	21 MB
TN703	578 CYLINDERS	5 HEADS	17 SECS	25 MB
TN703AT	733 CYLINDERS	5 HEADS	17 SECS	31 MB
TN705	962 CYLINDERS	5 HEADS	17 SECS	41 MB
TN755	981 CYLINDERS	5 HEADS	17 SECS	42 MB
TOSHIBA				
MK-53F	830 CYLINDERS	5 HEADS	17 SECS	36 MB
MK-53F-R	830 CYLINDERS	5 HEADS	26 SECS	55 MB
MK-54F	830 CYLINDERS	7 HEADS	17 SECS	50 MB
MK-54F-R	830 CYLINDERS	7 HEADS	26 SECS	77 MB
MK-56F	830 CYLINDERS	10 HEADS	17 SECS	72 MB
MK-56F-R	830 CYLINDERS	10 HEADS	26 SECS	110 MB
MK-134FA	733 CYLINDERS	7 HEADS	17 SECS	44 MB
MK-153FA	830 CYLINDERS	5 HEADS	34 SECS	72 MB
MK-154FA	830 CYLINDERS	7 HEADS	34 SECS	101 MB
MK-156FA	830 CYLINDERS	10 HEADS	34 SECS	144 MB
TULIN				
TL226	640 CYLINDERS	4 HEADS	17 SECS	22 MB
TL240	640 CYLINDERS	6 HEADS	17 SECS	33 MB

DOS Error Messages

This appendix consists of an alphabetical listing of DOS error messages and their definitions. Many DOS messages require you to answer yes or no (Y/N). Whenever you encounter this request in an informational or error message, *stop and think* before you type your answer. If there is any doubt, enter N. Exact wording of messages may vary depending on your version of DOS.

Abort, Ignore, Retry, Fail?

A disk or device error. You cannot read from or write to the device specified.

A terminates the command and returns control to DOS. This is the safest response.
I ignores the problem and tries to continue the program (the most dangerous response). This is appropriate if you are trying to retrieve corrupted data.
R retries the command; use it to continue an operation after correcting the error condition.

F causes the current DOS system operation to stop trying; control reverts to the current application. This is appropriate for breaking out of an empty disk drive error situation. (The F option appears only in later DOS versions.)

Access denied
You tried to delete, change, or replace a file that was write-protected, read-only, or locked. Use a new filename.

Active Code Page not available from CON device
The necessary code page for your system is not available from the console (screen) you are using. Install DISPLAY.SYS in your CONFIG.SYS file and issue a MODE CON CODEPAGE PREPARE command.

All files in directory will be deleted!
Are you sure (Y/N)?
You used a wildcard (*.*) symbol with the DEL or ERASE command to delete files in the current directory, or you specified a subdirectory name. Type Y if you wish to remove the files; type N if you don't. Remember—when in doubt, type N.

An error occurred while installing DOS
Press Enter to continue, or Esc to exit SELECT
You will be given choices at the command line to fix this error. Answer appropriately.

APPEND/ASSIGN conflict
APPEND cannot be used on an assigned drive. Cancel ASSIGN, and then reissue the APPEND command.

Are you sure (Y/N)?
Any time you see this inquiry at the command line, stop and think and then answer appropriately. Usually you will see it if you tried to delete a file, directory, or subdirectory. If you're not sure, type N.

Attempted write protect violation
The disk you want to format is write-protected. Either change disks or remove the write-protect tab to allow FORMAT to continue.

Backup file sequence error
RESTORE did not begin with the first backup disk in the sequence. Start over and insert disks in the right order.

Bad call format
or
Bad command
A device driver sent invalid or incompatible information to DOS. Return the software to the dealer or publisher if it is defective.

Bad command or file name
DOS does not recognize the command you entered. Make sure the spelling, the path you wish to use, and the drive names are all correct. If they are, something else is wrong; use the DIR command to double-check the file information.

Bad or missing *d:path* SMARTDRV.SYS
You don't have the SMARTDRV.SYS file in the SMARTDrive path specified in your CONFIG.SYS file. Edit your CONFIG.SYS file to enter the correct drive and path name.

Bad or missing command interpreter
DOS can't find COMMAND.COM on the disk because the file is either the wrong version, damaged, or missing from the root directory. Reboot the system with a disk that has the correct version of COMMAND.COM (or copy the COMMAND.COM file from your backup master disk).

Bad or missing filename
DOS bootup procedures can't find a device driver file specified in CONFIG .SYS, either because it is missing, or there was an error as the device driver was loaded into memory. Make sure all spellings are correct and that the filename is correct in the CONFIG.SYS file. If so, there is a programming error; consult your dealer or manufacturer.

Bad or missing keyboard definition file
DOS can't find the KEYBOARD.SYS file you entered with the KEYB command. Make sure the file you want exists on the disk and that the path you are in has this file. Then reenter the command. If you get this message again, your KEYB.COM file may be corrupted.

Bad partition table
There is no DOS partition on the hard disk, or the DOS partition has been damaged. Use FDISK or a third-party partitioning program to create a new DOS partition. You may need to low-level format before partitioning.

Bad Unit
Your device driver for the disk has found an invalid device reference, or there was a critical error during I/O. Use PRINT SCREEN to print out all the error messages, and call your dealer or the product's manufacturer for technical support.

Batch file missing
DOS cannot find the batch (.BAT) file it was running, in order to read the next line or exit. Check if the file has been renamed or deleted or the disk with the batch file has been changed.

Cannot CHDIR to root
Processing cannot continue
CHKDSK tried to set the current working directory to the root and failed. You may have a faulty disk; see Chapter 18.

Cannot CHKDSK a SUBSTed or ASSIGNed drive
The SUBST and ASSIGN commands hide information needed by CHKDSK. Remove the commands and again run CHKDSK. Certain nonstandard drives will also cause this error message; these may require a special edition of CHKDSK.

Cannot COPY from (or to) a reserved device
The COPY command does not recognize printers, asynchronous communications devices, or NULL. You must use a temporary file to make the copy.

Cannot compare a file to itself
The COMP command cannot compare a file to itself. Enter two different filenames.

Cannot create extended DOS partition while logical drives exist
FDISK will not create an extended partition while your disk has one or more logical drives assigned to it. Delete all logical drives using the FDISK command and then create the extended DOS partition.

Cannot create extended DOS partition
without primary DOS partition on disk 1

You're trying to create an extended DOS partition on a hard disk that lacks a primary DOS partition. First, make the primary DOS partition on your hard disk. Then, if there is space, create the extended DOS partition.

Cannot create a zero cylinder partition

FDISK will not make a partition without any cylinders. You must allow at least one cylinder for any partition you create on your hard disk.

Cannot create Subdirectory BACKUP
on drive n (or x)

BACKUP is unable to use the specified target disk. Make sure the root directory of the target disk is not full, that the disk is not write-protected, and that an identical directory does not already exist. The target disk may be defective.

Cannot DISKCOMP to or from
an ASSIGNed or SUBSTed drive

One of the drives you specified has been reassigned using ASSIGN or SUBST. Cancel the ASSIGN or SUBST command and reissue DISKCOMP.

Cannot DISKCOPY to or from
an ASSIGNED or SUBSTed drive

ASSIGN and SUBST interfere with DISKCOPY. Cancel ASSIGN or SUBST before running DISKCOPY.

Cannot do binary reads from a device

You can't use the COPY /b option in the command line when the source of COPY was a device name. COPY can't recognize the end-of-file mark (CTRL-Z) that ends the operation.

Cannot edit .BAK file --
rename file

EDLIN will not edit backup files. It assumes there are other, more up-to-date versions. Use COPY or RENAME to change the file extension if you must edit such a file with EDLIN.

Cannot execute FORMAT

SELECT is showing an error when running FORMAT. Make sure FORMAT is on the source disk and run SELECT again.

Cannot execute XCOPY
SELECT is showing an error when running the XCOPY command. Make sure XCOPY is on the source disk and run SELECT again.

Cannot find system files
Your system files are not on the current disk. Reissue the FORMAT or SYS command with a disk that has the proper system files on it.

Cannot FORMAT a SUBSTed or ASSIGNed drive
FORMAT will not format a substituted or assigned disk drive. Clear all assignments to return the drive to its original configuration, and rerun FORMAT.

Cannot FORMAT a nonremovable drive x
You cannot format a hard disk with the /f option of the BACKUP command. If you are sure you want to back up your files to a hard disk, use one that's already been formatted.

Cannot LABEL a SUBSTed or ASSIGNed drive
DOS can't change the volume label on an assigned or substituted drive because the path substitution hides necessary information. Remove the path substitution and try again.

Cannot load COMMAND, system halted
DOS can't reload the command processor after it was overwritten; or the COMSPEC environment variable was lost; or COMMAND.COM was not found in the drive and path specified by the COMSPEC statement in your CONFIG.SYS file. Reboot DOS.

Cannot perform a cyclic copy
You can't specify a target that is a subdirectory of the source directory if you are using the BACKUP /s option. You may have to use a temporary disk or file, depending on the directory tree structure.

Cannot recover .. entry,
Entry has a bad attribute (or link or size)
CHKDSK has discovered that the parent directory is defective and cannot be recovered. If you specify the /f option, CHKDSK automatically tries to correct the error.

Cannot start COMMAND, exiting

DOS tried to run a second copy of COMMAND.COM, and there wasn't enough memory. Remove excess memory-resident programs.

Cannot use FASTOPEN for drive *x*

FASTOPEN will operate only on hard disk drives, or you may be overextending the command's maximum four-disk limit. Determine the correct FASTOPEN command line and put that command into your AUTOEXEC .BAT routine.

Cannot XCOPY to or from a reserved device

XCOPY does not support a printer device. You must use a temporary file to perform the XCOPY command.

CHDIR .. failed, trying alternate method

CHKDSK cannot return to its current working directory after checking the tree structure. It will continue to return to that directory by starting over at the root and searching again, unless you reboot DOS.

Code page not prepared

MODE does not recognize the code page you have selected; or you do not have the correct font to support the current video mode. Use the MODE PREPARE command to prepare a code page for your system. If you have installed the DISPLAY.SYS device driver, be sure the device command line in CONFIG.SYS allows for additional subfonts.

Code page *xxx* not prepared for all devices

You have chosen a code page not currently supported by a device. First, be sure your device supports code page switching, and that it is currently online. If the device does support code page switching, use the MODE PREPARE command to prepare the device for the code page. Retry the CHCP command.

Code page *xxxx* not prepared for system

CHCP cannot select a code page for the system. Make sure that NSLFUNC is installed. Use the MODE command to prepare the code page for use. Retype CHCP and try again.

Code page operation not supported on this device
DOS does not recognize your chosen device and code page combination as valid. Make sure the device you chose exists, is operational, and has a supported code page.

Code page requested (*xxx*) is not valid for given keyboard code
or
Current keyboard does not support this code page
The keyboard template and the chosen code page are incompatible. Select either a different code page number or a different keyboard template.

Code page specified has not been designated (or prepared)
You have typed a message that the keyboard doesn't recognize. Use the MODE CODEPAGE PREPARE command to issue the specific code for your console screen device. Then retype the keyboard command.

Code page specified is inconsistent with invoked code page
This warns you that you have selected a KEYB option that does not coincide with your chosen code page for your console screen device (CON). Use the MODE SELECT command to change to the correct CON code page.

Code pages cannot be prepared
Either you have a duplicate code page, or more code pages than the device will support. Look in CONFIG.SYS to find out how many prepared code pages are allowed for the device. Then use the status option of the MODE command to find out what code pages have been prepared for the device.

COM port does not exist
MODE does not recognize the COM port you specified. Check the command format and reissue the command.

Configuration too large for memory
You have too much loaded into memory to hold anything else. Restart DOS and eliminate nonessential memory-resident programs.

Content of destination lost before copy
COPY overwrote your source file before the command was finished. If you were concatenating files, this message is usually not serious. Check to see if your data is still usable. If it is not, restore the source file from your backup disk and check your COPY syntax before reissuing the command.

Convert directory to file (Y/N)?

A subdirectory has become corrupted and is no longer usable.

Y converts the directory to a file so you can examine it with DEBUG or any similar software.
N leaves the directory alone.

Convert lost chains to file (Y/N)?

CHKDSK found information on the disk that was not correctly allocated in the disk's file allocation table. If you used the /f option,

Y lets CHKDSK recover the lost blocks it found when checking the disk. Then CHKDSK creates a file for each lost chain with a filename in the form file*xxxx*.chk.
N tells CHKDSK to free the lost blocks for re-allocation and not to recover any lost data.

Corrections will not be written to disk

CHKDSK found errors on the disk, but you must reissue the command and specify the /f option for the corrections to be recorded. Try rebooting before reissuing CHKDSK with the /f option.

Current drive is no longer valid

The DOS command interpreter tried to use the current drive or change to a specified drive and found it invalid. Set the current default drive to a valid drive.

Data error

DOS can't read or write the data correctly. Use CHKDSK to examine both the source and target disks. Make sure you correctly inserted a properly formatted disk.

Data (or disk) error reading (or writing) drive *x*

Your disk may be defective, may be inserted incorrectly, or may not be formatted; DOS cannot read the data properly. Type R (Retry) several times, or A (Abort) to end the program.

Delete current volume label (Y/N)?

LABEL gives this message when a command was issued for a disk drive that already has a valid volume label. Answer appropriately.

Device error during operation/prepare/select
status/write of font file to device
DOS found errors with the specified device, and MODE cannot access it. Check the device command in CONFIG.SYS for syntax errors.

Device or code page missing from font file
DOS did not find the specific code page for the device. Use the MODE command to choose another code page. Make sure the font file supports the correct code page.

DEVICE support not present
DISKCOMP or DISKCOPY does not recognize the specified disk drive. Retry the command with a different disk drive.

Device *xxxx* not prepared
The MODE CODEPAGE PREPARE command failed to issue a code page for the device. Make sure that there is a valid code page and device name in the command line, and that the proper device drivers are installed in CONFIG.SYS.

Directory is joined,
tree past this point not processed
CHKDSK will not process joined disks or directories. Enter JOIN *D*: /d to unjoin the directories; then reissue the CHKDSK command.

Directory is totally empty, no . or ..
No working or parent directories exist. Delete the specified directory and re-create it.

Diskette/Drive types not compatible
DISKCOMP/DISKCOPY require compatible disk types for source and target. To make these commands work, use compatible disks and reenter the command.

Disk error reading (or writing) drive *x*
See Data error.

Disk error reading (or writing) FAT
One of the two file allocation tables has a bad sector; DOS automatically uses the other FAT. Copy all files onto another disk. The CHKDSK /f

option will correct the error automatically. If both FATs are invalid, try rebooting to see if the problem corrects itself. FORMAT will make the disk usable if it is not defective, but all data will be lost.

Disk full. Edits lost

Target disk is full. The EDLIN E command exited during an editing session, without enough room on the disk to save the data. Always make sure there is enough room on the disk *before* beginning an editing session.

Disk not compatible (bad or incompatible)

You are trying to use an incorrectly formatted disk or the wrong disk type for the drive. You can't DISKCOPY from a single-sided disk to a double-sided one, or compare a high-density disk with a low-density one. Use FC or COMP if you want to compare files across different disk types. XCOPY or COPY will copy between different disk types. You can reformat the target disk so that it's the same capacity, or get a correct disk for the drive and reissue the FORMAT command.

Disk unsuitable for system disk

FORMAT found a bad track on the system disk sectors and can't create a bootable system disk. Get another disk for bootup and use this faulty disk for storage only.

Divide overflow

DOS resumes control of your system when a program tries to divide a number by 0, or an internal error causes DOS to invoke the divide-by-0 interrupt. Usually this is a software problem; consult the software publisher.

Do not specify filename(s)
Command format: DISKCOPY d: d: [/1]
(or Command format: DISKCOMP d: d:[1][8])

You issued an invalid parameter (either an incorrect option or a filename) in the DISKCOPY command line. Correct the command format and reissue the command.

Drive not ready error

DOS can't read from or write to the drive you specified. Make sure you have correctly inserted a compatible disk and that the drive door is closed.

Drive (x:) not ready
Make sure a disk is inserted into
the drive and the door is closed

You either forgot to put a disk into the drive, put it into the wrong drive bay, inserted a disk incorrectly, or forgot to close the door. Double-check, and reissue the command.

Duplicate file name or file not found

RENAME can't find the specified source file to rename, or a duplicate filename already exists on the target disk. Enter DIR to check for duplications.

Entry error

You entered an EDLIN syntax error. Check for correct syntax and reenter the command.

Entry has a bad attribute (or size or link)

CHKDSK found a directory error with an invalid size or bad cluster links. The message may be preceded by one or two dots that point to the bad subdirectory. To correct this problem automatically, specify the CHKDSK /f option. Always reboot before specifying /f.

EOF mark not found

COMP looks for a CTRL-Z marker in the last block when it examines two files. Not all files need the EOF marker. This error message is not usually serious.

Error in country command

Wrong syntax for the COUNTRY command in the CONFIG.SYS file. Check your syntax and reconfigure your system as needed.

Error found, F parameter not specified
Corrections will not be written to disk

The CHKDSK command was issued without the /f option. It found errors but did not correct them. Reboot to see if that fixes the problem. If it does not, reissue the CHKDSK command with the /f option to fix the disk error or use a third-party disk medic program.

Error in EXE file

The DOS command line interpreter does not recognize the relocation information stored at the beginning of the .EXE file and cannot run the program. Make sure you have the correct version of DOS. If that doesn't fix the problem, contact the software dealer.

Error in EXE or HEX file

DEBUG cannot read files with invalid records or data. Try to get an uncorrupted copy of the file, perhaps from a backup copy or from your dealer.

Error loading operating system

DOS was unable to load the operating system from the hard disk. Reboot the system; if that doesn't work, boot from drive A, and use a disk medic program. You may have to use the SYS command to recopy the hidden files to the hard disk.

Error opening log file

DOS is unable to open the backup log file. You must specify a filename for the log, or DOS will try to open and create BACKUP.LOG on the source disk. Make sure you are issuing the commands from the correct drive and path, and that the log file is not located on the target drive.

Error reading/writing fixed disk

After five unsuccessful tries to read or write the bootup record from the hard disk, FDISK shows this message. Reboot DOS, and retry FDISK. If it still won't work, consult a technician.

Error reading/writing partition table

FORMAT could not read or write a hard disk partition table. Run FDISK on the hard disk and reformat and repartition it.

Error writing to device

A DOS command failed to send information to a hardware device, usually because you tried to send too much. Check the failed command to make sure it is valid.

Errors on list device indicate that it may be off-line. Please check

PRINT cannot send data to your printer. Your printer or printer spooler may be turned off. Check your cables, and make sure the printer is online.

EXEC error

The program may be defective, or the CONFIG.SYS FILES= statement is set too low. Try increasing the FILES= number and rebooting.

Failure to access code page font file

The MODE command will not open the font file for a specific code page. Make sure the filename and path name are correct. Check CONFIG.SYS to see if the device driver is properly installed. If all is well, reboot DOS and then reenter the MODE command.

Failure to access COUNTRY.SYS

DOS can't open the COUNTRY.SYS file. Check spelling, paths, and commands; then try again.

Failure to access device:*xxx*

DOS cannot access the device for the code page you specified. Check spellings, and retype the command using a working device.

Failure to access KEYBOARD.SYS

DOS can't open the KEYBOARD.SYS file using SELECT. Make sure KEYBOARD.SYS is in the specified path.

FCB unavailable reading (or writing) drive *x*

A program bug probably exists, unless file sharing is installed. Enter **R** (Retry) or **A** (Abort). This error usually requires the attention of an experienced programmer.

fc: cannot open filename - No such file or directory

You specified a nonexistent file. Check your directory.

fc: incompatible switches

You selected options that were not compatible. Do not combine binary and ASCII comparison options (switches).

fc: out of memory

You ran out of RAM before FC could complete the comparison. Unload some TSRs to gain more memory or use the FC/LB *nnn* option to reduce memory (or memory required). Try LB=50 or less.

File allocation table bad, drive x
Abort Retry, or Ignore?
DOS can't read the FAT for the designated disk. Reboot, and run a disk medic program or CHKDSK with the /f option.

File cannot be copied onto itself
If the source and target filenames are identical, COPY, XCOPY, and RE-PLACE will not proceed. Change the filename or extension, or specify a different drive.

File creation error
You tried to create a new file with a duplicate name; to create a file when the directory was full; to write to a read-only, nonreplaceable file; or to access a hidden file. Check your spelling, and reenter the command.

File is Read Only
You cannot edit, delete, or change a read-only file.

File not found
or
File not in PRINT queue
For both these messages, the files you wanted were not found. Check your spelling against the directory listing. Make sure you have inserted the right disk. Reenter the command.

FIND: Access denied
or
File not found
You can't access the specified file. Check your spelling against the directory listing. Make sure the disk isn't write-protected or read-only.

First cluster number is invalid,
entry truncated
CHKDSK found an invalid cluster pointer in the specified filename's data area. The CHKDSK /f option will truncate data found at the bad cluster number to a zero-length file.

FIRST diskette bad or incompatible
DISKCOMP does not recognize the format on the source disk. Run CHKDSK to help identify the problem.

Font file contents invalid

DOS cannot read the specified font file as issued by the MODE command; your font file may be altered or corrupted. Check your spelling. Copy the original font file from your DOS disk. Reenter the command. (*Note*: This error may cause certain existing code pages to be undefined; refresh them with the CODEPAGE PREPARE command.)

FOR cannot be nested

The DOS batch command interpreter cannot execute two FOR commands on a single line. Edit the .BAT file so that only one FOR is in each command line.

Format failure

Specified disk is unusable. DOS will often add a message telling why. Make sure the disk is inserted correctly or use the FORMAT command to format a different one.

FORMAT not supported on drive x

The FORMAT command does not recognize this disk (usually a virtual disk drive). If it is not a virtual disk drive, and your device parameters are correct, reboot DOS and reissue the FORMAT command. If there's still a problem, check that you don't have an alternate disk device driver in CONFIG.SYS. If you do, remove it and reboot.

General failure

or

General failure reading drive n

DOS shows this error message when a hard disk is not properly installed, cables are loose, the controller has failed, or there has been another type of system failure. With floppy drives, the disk may not be properly formatted, the disk and drive types are not compatible, or a readable disk is not inserted correctly. Find the problem, correct it, and reissue the command.

Has invalid cluster, file truncated

CHKDSK found a bad cluster. The /f option will truncate the damaged file.

Illegal device name

You specified a device name not recognized by your computer. Use LPT1, LPT2, LPT3, COM1, or COM2. Reenter the MODE command with the correct device name.

Incompatible system size

The system files on the source disk occupy more space than is available on the target disk. SYS cannot put the new files into a smaller disk space. FORMAT a new disk using the /s option; then use XCOPY to copy all files from the original disk.

Incorrect DOS version

Many DOS commands won't run on older DOS versions, and some require the exact version they were written for. To use the command, install the correct version and reenter the command. It may be simpler to get a third-party utility program (see Chapter 8) that does the same job.

Incorrect parameter(s) (or number of parameters)

You typed an incorrect value in the command line. Make sure your spelling, syntax, and names and number of parameters are correct; then reenter the command.

Insufficient disk space
or
Insufficient space on disk

You don't have enough room on the target disk to sort or copy the specified files. Clear out (move or delete) older files, or use a different target disk.

Insufficient memory

You don't have enough system memory to run the specified command or program. Remove unnecessary TSR programs, device drivers, disk buffers, or shells and try again. You may have to edit the CONFIG.SYS file.

Insufficient room in root directory
Erase files in root and repeat CHKDSK

The CHKDSK command automatically moves lost clusters into the root directory. In this case, it cannot because the root directory is full. Delete or move some files to make room, and run CHKDSK again.

Intermediate file error during pipe

DOS tried to create temporary files during the piping process, but failed because of insufficient disk space. Be sure the disk has enough room for the temporary file and that the disk is not write-protected, and try the command again.

Internal stack failure, system halted

DOS exceeded the special interim storage area (stack limit), which has a default stack value of 9. Reboot from a floppy disk, add STACKS=32,256 to CONFIG.SYS, and try again. If this message occurred while you were loading an application, check the manual to see if it recommends a different stack size.

Internal stack overflow
System Halted

DOS attempted to use too many stacks, causing the system to halt. Reboot. Edit your CONFIG.SYS file, allowing for more stack resources.

Invalid argument

DOS did not recognize the parameters. Check your command line for proper usage.

Invalid baud rate specified

You entered an invalid baud rate with MODE. Check your device's rate, and enter at least the first two digits, as follows: 110 (11), 150 (15), 300 (30), 600 (60), 1200 (12), 2400 (24), 4800 (48), or 9600 (96). Reissue the MODE command.

Invalid characters in volume label

You entered too many or incorrect symbols in the volume label when using LABEL or the FORMAT /v option. Reissue the command using allowable filename characters (see Chapter 9).

Invalid code page

You chose an invalid three-digit code page. Correct the code page values and reenter the KEYB command.

Invalid COMMAND.COM in drive n
(or Invalid COMMAND.COM)
Insert COMMAND.COM disk in default drive
and strike any key when ready

DOS did not find COMMAND.COM on the disk, or can't find the correct version. Insert a disk with a COMMAND.COM version that matches the DOS version you booted with.

Invalid current directory

CHKDSK found an invalid directory while trying to read the current directory. Reboot DOS, and reenter the CHKDSK command. If the problem persists, you may be able to COPY the files to another disk; otherwise, format the disk for reuse, or replace it.

Invalid Date/Time

BACKUP did not recognize the specified DATE or TIME option. Check the command line syntax and try again.

Invalid device

You used an invalid device name with the CTTY command. Use CTTY only with AUX, CON, COM*x*, NUL, or PRN. Check your spelling and syntax. Reenter the command.

Invalid device parameters from device driver

FORMAT shows that the hard disk partition does not start on a track boundary (it may have been previously formatted with an older version of DOS). Or you may have set a third-party partitioning parameter incorrectly. Use FDISK or a third-party disk medic program to correct the hard disk partition, and then reenter FORMAT.

Invalid directory

You have specified a directory that is either invalid or does not exist. Check your spelling and directory listing for the correct name; then reenter the command.

Invalid disk change
or
Invalid disk change reading (or writing) drive *x*

You changed the disk in a current drive while DOS had open files on the disk. Reinsert the correct disk, and press **R** (Retry).

Invalid drive in search path

The drive you specified is wrong or nonexistent. Use DOS PATH or SET PATH= commands to fix the error, and reenter the command.

Invalid drive or file name (or file not found)
(or Invalid drive specification)
Specified drive does not exist,
or is non-removable

The file or drive you entered is not recognized by DOS, is nonexistent, or you have specified the same drive destination for both the source and target drives. Check your spelling and syntax, and make sure the drive identification is correct. If working with a floppy disk, make sure the disk is inserted correctly.

Invalid environment size specified

You entered COMMAND.COM environment values with the /e option that were not alphanumeric characters between 160 and 32,768 (bytes). Reset the environment with the correct information.

Invalid keyboard code specified

You selected an incorrect two-digit KEYB country code. Reenter the correct code using the KEYB command.

Invalid media or track 0 bad --
disk unusable

DOS can't use a disk if track 0 is bad (this is where the DOS boot record is stored). Replace the bad disk.

Invalid parameter
or
Invalid number of parameters

You entered incorrect (too many, too few, or nonexistent) options or strings in your command line. Double-check the syntax of the desired command, and reenter it correctly.

Invalid path, not directory, or directory not empty

You can't remove the directory with RMDIR (reasons will be listed). Make sure the directory to be removed is empty or that the specified path name is correct; or change your default directory to a different directory from the one you wish to remove.

Invalid path or file name (or file not found)
You have typed an incorrect path name or filename. Check your spelling; correct and reenter the command.

Invalid subdirectory entry
You typed an incorrect (or nonexistent) subdirectory name. Check the directory, make sure you are in the correct drive (or have inserted the disk with that subdirectory on it), and reenter the command. Use CHKDSK /f to fix the invalid directory or subdirectory.

Invalid syntax
You typed the incorrect syntax for a command. Correct it and reenter the command.

Invalid volume ID (or label)
FORMAT can't run unless the volume label you specify on a hard disk matches the one on the destination disk. Use the VOL command to find the correct name, and reissue the FORMAT command.

Invalid working directory
process cannot continue
CHKDSK found errors that render the disk damaged and unusable. Reboot, and try CHKDSK again. If the same error is reported, a third-party disk medic program may be able to repair the damage.

KEYB has not been installed
There is no alternative keyboard code installed in your system. If you want a keyboard code other than the standard, default U.S. (QWERTY) one, enter the KEYB command to install it.

Keyboard routine not found
DOS did not find your keyboard routine in the current directory of the disk. Modify the disk as needed, and reenter the command.

Label not found
Your batch file contains a GOTO command referencing a label that does not exist, so the batch file quit early. If ECHO is off, enter the command ECHO ON. Then edit the .BAT file and correct the error.

Last backup disk not inserted
Insert last backup disk in drive *x*
Strike any key when ready
You did not insert the final backup disk. Put a disk into the specified drive, and reenter the BACKUP command.

Last file not backed up
BACKUP was unable to complete the command, because the target disk was full, or because BACKUP found an error in the source file or on the target disk. Back up this last file on a separate disk.

Line too long
An EDLIN R (Replace) command string exceeded the 253-character limit. Divide the long line into two lines, and retry the R command.

List output is not assigned to a device
PRINT does not recognize the specified device. Check your DOS PRINT command for syntax accuracy, and reissue the command.

Make sure a disk is inserted into
the drive and the door is closed
DISKCOPY or DISKCOMP thinks you failed to insert a disk properly or close the drive door completely. Double-check the floppy, close the drive door, and retry the command.

Memory allocation error.
Cannot load DOS (or COMMAND), system halted
DOS's memory allocation table has become corrupted. Reboot the system.

Missing from the file is either the device ID
or the code page
The code page is not supported in the code page information (.CPI file), or the .CPI file does not support the printer specified. Check for valid values in the MODE command, and try again.

Must specify COM1, COM2, COM3, or COM4
The MODE command line is missing a serial port specification. Review the MODE command and try again.

Must specify destination line number

The EDLIN C (Copy) or M (Move) command did not specify the necessary destination line number. Reissue the command with the number included.

No Append

The data file search path is not being used. To append a path for data files, use the APPEND command.

No DOS partition to delete
or
No primary DOS partition to delete

You selected the Delete DOS Partition option from the FDISK main menu, but no DOS partition exists. Examine the partitions available, using the Display Partition Data option on the FDISK main menu.

No fixed disk present

FDISK thinks you don't have a hard disk installed, or that it is not installed correctly. On an internal hard drive, make sure the cable connections between the rear of the drive and the controller are correct. Also check your CMOS settings (see "Determining Drive Type" in Chapter 18.) If you have an external hard disk drive, make sure the power is on, the cable is firmly seated, and any required device drivers are present in your CON-FIG.SYS file. If DOS still fails to recognize the drive, contact your dealer or the disk manufacturer for further assistance.

No free file handles
Cannot start COMMAND, exiting

You tried to load a secondary command processor or other program, but could not because of insufficient file handles (the default is 8, which is often not enough). File handles determine the number of files DOS can keep open when running a program. Reboot the system. If the message reappears, increase the file handles value to 20 or higher in the CONFIG.SYS FILES= command line.

No paper error writing device *dev*

The printer is out of paper or not turned on. Check your printer, and retry the command.

No partitions to make active

You tried to use the FDISK Set Active Partition option before a partition has been created. Use the Create DOS Partition option before setting an active partition.

No path

You haven't set a command search path. If APPEND was used, no path was specified in the APPEND command line. Check the command syntax and reissue the command.

No retry on parallel printer time-out

Check the MODE command syntax for specific printer time-out retry operations, type them, and reissue the command.

No room for system on destination disk

SYS can't transfer the DOS system files to the target disk. Make room on the disk, or format a blank disk with the FORMAT /s option. Use XCOPY to copy the files to the new bootable disk.

No room in directory for file
or
No room in root directory

Your root directory is limited in size and unable to hold any more files; EDLIN could not save the new information. Free up space in the directory, or use a different disk or directory to edit the file. Use CHKDSK if the directory listing shows room on the disk; if there is memory available, use MKDIR to create a subdirectory (which is not size-limited).

No source (target) drive specified

BACKUP requires you to specify a source or target drive (usually A: or B:).

No space for *nnnn* cylinder partition

You selected a partition size too large for the number of available disk cylinders. Run FDISK using its default value, or choose a smaller cylinder number.

No space to create a DOS partition

FDISK was unable to make a new partition on the hard disk. Modify existing partitions by removing or reducing them, and run FDISK again to create the new partition.

No space to create logical drive
There is no room on the disk for FDISK to make an additional logical drive.

No system on default drive
You tried to transfer system files to a target disk without SYS files on the source disk. Use a source disk with the necessary system files on it and try again.

Non-DOS disk
or
Non-DOS disk error reading (or writing) drive x
DOS does not recognize the disk format, the format contains a different operating system, or the disk was inserted incorrectly. Try running CHKDSK to correct the problem. If the message reappears, use FORMAT to make the disk usable (all information will be lost, however).

Non-System disk or disk error
Replace and strike any key when ready
DOS cannot continue its startup process because it cannot find the necessary system files in the root directory. Place a disk that has the DOS system files already on it in drive A, or open the drive door so DOS can boot from the hard drive, and press any key.

Not able to backup (or restore) file
DOS found an error in the source file or target drive. Use CHKDSK or a disk medic program to determine the cause.

Not enough room to merge the entire file
EDLIN cannot complete its file transfer (option T) because of insufficient memory. Remove excess files to another location (or delete them entirely), or break the merging file into smaller files for easier manipulation.

Not found
EDLIN cannot find a source string for a Search (S) or Replace (R) operation. (*Note*: EDLIN differentiates between upper- and lowercase.)

Not ready
or
Not ready error reading (or writing) drive x
DOS does not recognize the specified device. Check drive doors, power cables, paper feeders, or other possible sources of trouble with the particular device (usually a drive or PRN printer) you are using. Type R (Retry) to try again.

O.K.?
The EDLIN S (Search) or R (Replace) operation needs to know whether to continue processing. To continue without replacing, press any key but Y or ENTER.

One or more CON code pages invalid
for given keyboard code
You entered an invalid three-digit code page in the KEYB command line. Correct the code and reenter the command.

Out of environment space
The DOS environment is full. Either remove some existing variables (with the SET command) or increase the enviroment size in the CONFIG.SYS file by specifying a larger shell.

Parameters not compatible
or
Parameter not compatible with fixed disk
or
Parameters not supported
or
Parameters not supported by drive
You have selected parameters or options that won't work with one another or with the specified drive, or that DOS doesn't recognize. Make sure the command syntax and DOS versions are correct and compatible, and reenter the command.

Path not found
You specified a parameter, command file, or path that does not exist. Reenter the command with the correct information.

Path (pathname) too long
You entered a path or path name with more than 63 characters. You may have to change directories to access files stored in lower-level (deeper) subdirectories.

Primary DOS partition already exists
You can create only one primary partition per hard drive. Use the FDISK option to create an extended partition instead.

Print queue is full
No more files can be added to the maximum (10) in the printer waiting area. Use the PRINT /q option to increase the queue limit to 32 files.

Printer error
MODE cannot complete the PRINT command because the power is off; the printer is out of paper, offline, or timed out; or an I/O error has occurred. Find and correct the error, and reenter the command.

Probable non-DOS disk
Continue (Y/N)?
DOS doesn't recognize the disk as usable. Make sure the disk format, your DOS version, and the drives are compatible. Reboot and try CHKDSK again. Check to see if the disk was inserted correctly. If necessary, use FORMAT to make the disk usable.

Processing cannot continue
CHKDSK can't continue processing because of insufficient memory on your system. Remove nonessential programs to make room in memory for CHKDSK. Then reenter the command.

Program too big to fit in memory
There is not enough free space in memory for DOS to load the program. If you are shelled-out of another program, exit the shell and quit the program to gain more memory. Or remove some memory-resident programs and retry the command.

Read error in drive (or \path or \filename)

DOS cannot read the entire program file. Check spelling and syntax for errors. If necessary, use COPY or XCOPY to make a new file on a different disk. Then reenter the command.

Read error, KEYBOARD.SYS

DOS is unable to read KEYBOARD.SYS. Reenter the command. If the same error message occurs, the COUNTRY.SYS file may be corrupted. Use RESTORE with your backup disks to fix the bad files.

Read fault
or
Read fault error reading drive x

DOS can't read the specified device (usually a disk drive). Make sure all connections are secure and the device has power, the doors are closed, the disks are correctly inserted, and the drive name is correct. Retry (R) the command.

Restore file sequence error

You did not load the backup disks in the correct order. RESTORE will not reload them out of sequence. Correct the error.

Second disk bad or incompatible

DISKCOMP can't compare the source and target disks. Make sure the disks are formatted the same and are of equal density. Run CHKDSK to verify that the target disk has no bad sectors.

Sector not found
or
Sector not found error reading (or writing) drive x

DOS can't find the data sector on the specified disk. If you are using a floppy disk, reboot, and run CHKDSK to determine the problem. If the same message occurs, copy all files from the disk to another newly format- ted disk. Then discard the disk or use FORMAT to make the bad disk usable. On hard disks, this message often begins to appear right before a drive failure. Reboot immediately, back up your files (don't overwrite your most recent backup), and run a disk medic program.

Sector size too large in file *filename*

CONFIG.SYS tried to load a device driver that required a sector size larger than other device drivers in the system, and DOS cannot run this device. Return the program to the dealer or publisher.

Seek
or
Seek error reading (or writing) drive *x*

DOS cannot locate the specified track or disk information. Make sure the disk is the correct type and properly seated in the drive. Reboot; if the message continues, run CHKDSK to determine the problem.

Source and target drives are the same

BACKUP and RESTORE cannot operate on the same drive. Change the drive identifier and reenter the command.

Source disk bad or incompatible

DISKCOPY found an error. Reboot and, if necessary, run CHKDSK to find the problem.

Source does not contain backup files

You can't RESTORE files from a disk that isn't backed up. Use DIR to list the contents of the source disk.

Source path required

The REPLACE command needs at least one source path name. Check your syntax, correct the error, and repeat the command.

Specified command search directory bad
or
Specified DOS search directory bad

You typed an invalid path name or command shell. Check the CONFIG.SYS file for errors, make sure that COMMAND.COM exists where DOS can find it, and reenter the command with the correct path name.

Specified drive does not exist, or is non-removable

DISKCOMP and DISKCOPY do not operate from a hard disk drive. Specify a floppy drive.

Syntax error

You entered an invalid command request. Make sure all spelling and names are correct and that the syntax and options are right for the command specified.

System files restored
The target disk may not be bootable

RESTORE is telling you the target disk may contain system files from an earlier DOS version, which may not be bootable. Boot a valid DOS system disk and use SYS to make the target disk bootable.

Target cannot be used for backup

BACKUP cannot use the target disk. Try to back up again with a newly formatted disk. Then, after a backup is made, reboot and run CHKDSK or a disk medic program on the original target disk to determine the problem.

Target is write protected
or
Target disk write protected
Correct, then strike any key

The target disk has a write-protect tab, and you can't write to it. If you want to write over any data on the disk, remove the protective tab and reenter the command.

Target disk may be unusable

DISKCOPY determined the target disk to have too many errors. Try using XCOPY, which will skip over bad sectors on the target disk, or use a different target disk.

Target is full

The target disk can't hold any more restored files. Delete unwanted files from the target, and reenter the RESTORE command.

The last file was not restored
You ended the RESTORE operation, or the target file ran out of space. Remove unwanted files and repeat the command.

Too many drive entries
FASTOPEN opens a maximum of four hard drives, and you tried to open more. Retry the command with the correct number of drive entries.

Too many files open
DOS can't open .BAK files or write the volume label, because it lacks sufficient file handles for the operation. Increase the number of file handles with the FILES= entry in your CONFIG.SYS file. Reboot and try again.

Too many name entries
You exceeded the maximum number of files (999) that FASTOPEN can keep track of at once. Retry, using an allowable number.

Too many open files
DOS lacks available system file handles to compare or copy the specified files. Increase the value of FILES= in CONFIG.SYS.

Track 0 bad - disk unusable
FORMAT can work around bad sectors, except when the bad sectors are near the beginning of the disk (the space reserved for DOS). Make sure the disk is properly seated. If it is, use another disk.

Top level process aborted, cannot continue
A fatal error occurred during the bootup procedure, or you tried to call a secondary command processor while selecting the Abort (A) option. Reboot. Use a different DOS disk if necessary.

Transfer size adjusted
You specified an invalid transfer size for VDISK.SYS in the CONFIG.SYS file. See Chapter 11.

Tree past this point not processed
CHKDSK can't continue past this error message. Reboot, and reenter CHKDSK or use a disk medic program.

Unable to copy keyboard routine
DOS can't open a KEYBXX.COM file. Have CHKDSK or a disk medic program examine the disk.

Unable to create directory
DOS can't create the specified directory (with MKDIR or XCOPY) because an identical directory already exists; or a path entry cannot be found; or the root directory cannot hold any more directories; or the new directory has the same name as an existing file or directory; or the chosen directory name is invalid. Make sure there is no name conflict, use a new disk, or reboot; then reissue the command.

Unable to create KEYB table in resident memory
KEYB loads memory-resident, country-specific codes along with other software. This message indicates there was not enough available memory. Check available memory to be sure there is enough for this table; also, load KEYB before loading other memory-resident software.

Unable to erase
BACKUP was unable to erase the files on the target disk. Make sure those files are not read-only, and that the disk is not write protected.

Unable to write BOOT
The FORMAT /s option was in the command line, and the first track or cylinder in the partition could not be written to. Use a new disk, or reboot and reenter the command.

Unrecognized command in CONFIG.SYS
DOS detected an invalid command in CONFIG.SYS. Edit your CONFIG .SYS file to correct the error, and then reboot. In DOS versions earlier than 3.3, lines beginning with a period or REM statement produced this message. It does not affect the boot procedure, and you can ignore it.

Unrecognized printer
You are using the program GRAPHICS with a non-IBM printer or an IBM printer that GRAPHICS does not support. Make sure you have entered your command correctly, and that you have specified a printer that GRAPHICS supports.

Unrecognized printer port

You have selected an invalid printer device name. Set the printer port correctly with the MODE command.

Unrecoverable error in directory
Convert directory to file (Y/N)?

CHKDSK cannot correct an error in a directory. Answer Y, and you can fix the bad directory or delete it after it has been converted to another file. An N response may disallow you from either reading from or writing to the bad directory. You may be able to reboot and reissue the command, using RECOVER to fix the problem. Better still, answer N and then run a disk medic program.

Unrecoverable read (or write) error on drive x
Track xx, side x

The DOS commands DISKCOPY and DISKCOMP are unable to read or write successfully after several repeated attempts (Retry). At this point you can Abort (A) the program. Your disk is either damaged or copy-protected. Copy undamaged files to a new disk, and use FORMAT or a disk medic program to correct the errors on the corrupted disk.

Warning! All data on non-removable
disk drive x will be lost
Proceed with FORMAT (Y/N)?

You are using the FORMAT command to format a hard (or fixed) disk. All data on that disk will be wiped out. (Consider copying all files to a floppy disk before proceeding.) Remember to stop and think, and then answer the question appropriately. Some DOS versions give even less information in the warning.

Warning! Data in the primary (or extended) DOS partition
could be destroyed.
Do you wish to continue...?[n]

This FDISK warning tells you that the Delete DOS Partition option will wipe out all information on the partition specified. Answer either Y or N (the default is N), and press ENTER.

Warning - directory full
nnn **file(s) recovered**
Your specified directory was full, so RECOVER did not continue processing. Remove some files from the root directory to free up space for the recovered files. Then reenter the command.

Warning! Diskette is out of sequence
Replace the disk or continue
Strike any key when ready
You are not restoring your backed up disks in order. If this is OK, proceed. If not, insert the correct disk and continue.

Warning! File *filename*
is a hidden (or read-only) file
Replace the file (Y/N)?
Using the /p option in the RESTORE command line gets this request. Do you want to copy over a file marked as read-only? Answer appropriately.

Warning! File *filename*
was changed after it was backed up
Replace the file (Y/N)?
The /p option of the RESTORE command is asking if you want to copy over a file on your target disk that has been changed since you last backed up your files. Answer appropriately.

Warning! Files in the target drive
Drive: \BACKUP (*root*) directory will be erased
Strike any key when ready
This is a reminder to back up files found on your target directories; you did not specify the /a option to append changed files. All files on your target (or root) directory will be erased with the BACKUP command. Press any key to continue; or press CTRL-BREAK to discontinue the command.

Warning! No files were found to back up (or restore)

BACKUP (or RESTORE) did not find any files that matched the ones you specified. Check your spelling against the directory listing. Change to the root directory on the source or target drive and try again. (It's a good idea to run RESTORE only from the root directory of the target drive.)

Warning! Target is full

BACKUP or RESTORE found the destination device full. Remove files to make space available, or change disks, and reenter the command.

Write fault
or
Write fault error writing drive x

DOS can't write to the specified device. Make sure the disk is properly inserted. Type R (Retry); if the problem recurs, type A (Abort). Use CHKDSK to examine the disk.

Write protect
or
Write protect error writing drive x

DOS can't enter data on a write-protected disk. Remove the write-protect tab if you really must write to that disk, or get another disk and proceed with your command.

x is not a choice, Please enter y-z

The FDISK command does not recognize option x. Choose a valid option from those shown (y or z).

x is not a choice. Enter Y or N

FDISK expects a yes or no answer.

x(xxx) lost cluster(s) found in *y(yyy)* chains
Convert lost chains to files (Y/N)

CHKDSK found information on the disk that is not properly allocated in the disk's FAT. If the CHKDSK /f option was used, a Y response lets CHKDSK recover the lost blocks, and creates a proper directory entry and a file for each lost chain with the filename file*xxxx*.CHK. If you used CHKDSK without the /f option, DOS displays "*x* bytes would be freed." Type N, and CHKDSK frees the lost blocks for reallocation and does not recover any lost data. If you didn't specify the /f option, CHKDSK does nothing. Before specifying /f, reboot to see if the problem persists. If it does, enter Y or run a disk medic program.

xxxx error on file *filename*

PRINT found a fatal error when trying to read the designated file. Check the directory to make sure the file is still available.

xxxx version of Graphic Character Set Table is already loaded

You tried to load the Graphic Character Set Table into memory with GRAFTABL, which automatically reloads memory-resident software when called. Run GRAFTABL just once per user session.

ASCII Codes

Decimal Value	Hexadecimal Value	Control Character	Character
0	00	NUL	Null
1	01	SOH	☺
2	02	STX	☻
3	03	ETX	♥
4	04	EOT	♦
5	05	ENQ	♣
6	06	ACK	♠
7	07	BEL	Beep
8	08	BS	◘
9	09	HT	Tab
10	0A	LF	Line-feed
11	0B	VT	Cursor home
12	0C	FF	Form-feed
13	0D	CR	Enter
14	0E	SO	♫
15	0F	SI	☼
16	10	DLE	►
17	11	DC1	◄
18	12	DC2	↕
19	13	DC3	‼
20	14	DC4	¶
21	15	NAK	§

Decimal Value	Hexadecimal Value	Control Character	Character
22	16	SYN	▬
23	17	ETB	↕
24	18	CAN	↑
25	19	EM	↓
26	1A	SUB	→
27	1B	ESC	←
28	1C	FS	Cursor right
29	1D	GS	Cursor left
30	1E	RS	Cursor up
31	1F	US	Cursor down
32	20	SP	Space
33	21		!
34	22		"
35	23		#
36	24		$
37	25		%
38	26		&
39	27		'
40	28		(
41	29		)
42	2A		*
43	2B		+
44	2C		,
45	2D		-
46	2E		.
47	2F		/
48	30		0
49	31		1
50	32		2

Decimal Value	Hexadecimal Value	Control Character	Character
51	33		3
52	34		4
53	35		5
54	36		6
55	37		7
56	38		8
57	39		9
58	3A		:
59	3B		;
60	3C		<
61	3D		=
62	3E		>
63	3F		?
64	40		@
65	41		A
66	42		B
67	43		C
68	44		D
69	45		E
70	46		F
71	47		G
72	48		H
73	49		I
74	4A		J
75	4B		K
76	4C		L
77	4D		M
78	4E		N
79	4F		O

Decimal Value	Hexadecimal Value	Control Character	Character
80	50		P
81	51		Q
82	52		R
83	53		S
84	54		T
85	55		U
86	56		V
87	57		W
88	58		X
89	59		Y
90	5A		Z
91	5B		[
92	5C		\
93	5D		]
94	5E		^
95	5F		—
96	60		`
97	61		a
98	62		b
99	63		c
100	64		d
101	65		e
102	66		f
103	67		g
104	68		h
105	69		i
106	6A		j
107	6B		k
108	6C		l

Decimal Value	Hexadecimal Value	Control Character	Character
109	6D		m
110	6E		n
111	6F		o
112	70		p
113	71		q
114	72		r
115	73		s
116	74		t
117	75		u
118	76		v
119	77		w
120	78		x
121	79		y
122	7A		z
123	7B		{
124	7C		¦
125	7D		}
126	7E		~
127	7F	DEL	⌂
128	80		Ç
129	81		ü
130	82		é
131	83		â
132	84		ä
133	85		à
134	86		å
135	87		ç
136	88		ê
137	89		ë

Decimal Value	Hexadecimal Value	Control Character	Character
138	8A		è
139	8B		ï
140	8C		î
141	8D		ì
142	8E		Ä
143	8F		Å
144	90		É
145	91		æ
146	92		Æ
147	93		ô
148	94		ö
149	95		ò
150	96		û
151	97		ù
152	98		ÿ
153	99		Ö
154	9A		Ü
155	9B		¢
156	9C		£
157	9D		¥
158	9E		Pt
159	9F		ƒ
160	A0		á
161	A1		í
162	A2		ó
163	A3		ú
164	A4		ñ
165	A5		Ñ
166	A6		ª

Decimal Value	Hexadecimal Value	Control Character	Character
			o̲
167	A7		
168	A8		¿
169	A9		⌐
170	AA		¬
171	AB		½
172	AC		¼
173	AD		¡
174	AE		«
175	AF		»
176	B0		░
177	B1		▒
178	B2		▓
179	B3		│
180	B4		┤
181	B5		╡
182	B6		╢
183	B7		╖
184	B8		╕
185	B9		╣
186	BA		║
187	BB		╗
188	BC		╝
189	BD		╜
190	BE		╛
191	BF		┐
192	C0		└
193	C1		┴
194	C2		┬
195	C3		├

Decimal Value	Hexadecimal Value	Control Character	Character
196	C4		—
197	C5		+
198	C6		╞
199	C7		╟
200	C8		╚
201	C9		╔
202	CA		╩
203	CB		╦
204	CC		╠
205	CD		═
206	CE		╬
207	CF		╧
208	D0		╨
209	D1		╤
210	D2		╥
211	D3		╙
212	D4		╘
213	D5		╒
214	D6		╓
215	D7		╫
216	D8		╪
217	D9		┘
218	DA		┌
219	DB		█
220	DC		▄
221	DD		▌
222	DE		▐
223	DF		▀
224	E0		α
225	E1		β

Decimal Value	Hexadecimal Value	Control Character	Character
226	E2		Γ
227	E3		π
228	E4		Σ
229	E5		σ
230	E6		μ
231	E7		τ
232	E8		ϕ
233	E9		Θ
234	EA		Ω
235	EB		δ
236	EC		∞
237	ED		$\varnothing$
238	EE		ϵ
239	EF		$\cap$
240	F0		$\equiv$
241	F1		$\pm$
242	F2		$\geq$
243	F3		$\leq$
244	F4		$\lceil$
245	F5		$\rfloor$
246	F6		$\div$
247	F7		$\approx$
248	F8		$\circ$
249	F9		$\cdot$
250	FA		$\cdot$
251	FB		$\sqrt{}$
252	FC		η
253	FD		^{2}
254	FE		$\blacksquare$
255	FF		(blank)

How and Where to Buy a Computer

This appendix offers some tips on how and where to buy a personal computer system. A computer is a significant investment. You should use as many resources as you can to help you make the right decision.

DO SOME RESEARCH

Chapter 2 includes significant help on picking out a system based on design, version, performance, compatibility, and other hardware characteristics. In addition, however, you'll want to talk to people who already own a system, and do some reading.

Ask Your Friends

Almost everyone who works with PCs will be happy to share their experiences—you usually have only to ask. If a friend has a system that meets your needs, consider getting a similar setup. That way you'll already have a knowledgeable contact and ally if you run into problems. At the very least, a friend may know the name of a good store—or can warn you away from a bad one. As a general rule, given a choice, it's a safe decision to buy the hardware or software that a friend or colleague already knows how to use. It will give you a head start, and you'll have an experienced teacher as near as the phone or the next desk over.

Read the Reviews

Go to your library and look at a few issues of computer magazines. All such magazines review computers and related equipment, sometimes offering comprehensive comparison tests between brands. *PC Magazine,* for example, says its staff performs more hands-on hardware testing in a year than the organization Consumer's Union. *Byte Magazine* also tests equipment. If you want a less technical, more user-oriented approach, look at *PC World, PC/Computing, Compute! PC,* or *Home Office Computing.* The comparisons and reviews from such publications can help you get a handle on what to look for in both hardware and software—as well as what to guard against.

Join a User Group

Chapter 7 describes how to find a local PC user group. These organizations are fountains of information about the who, what, where, why, and when of acquiring and using computers and other hardware and software. Computer user networks are friendly, accessible, valuable sources of expert opinion, experience, and information. Consider joining one even before you've set up a system.

CHECK AT LOCAL STORES

Computer stores are there to sell computers, and they are staffed by people who are paid to know about computers. It's the staff's job to help customers learn, so don't ever feel shy about letting them do so.

Like new cars on a showroom floor, computers exhibited by a dealer are likely to have every available option attached. The proprietor will show each model in its best configuration, and you'll be able to gain a sense of what's available within your price range. Here are some computer window-shopping hints.

- *Pay attention to the shop's specialty*   Not all salespersons know about all computer brands. If you're interested in an MS-DOS machine, don't go to an Apple expert. If you're determined to do desktop publishing on an Apple Macintosh, don't go to an IBM enthusiast. A master of computer games can't tell you much about accounting programs, nor can a numbers expert help you wipe out a Romulan starbase. Find someone with expertise in your field.

- *Go to more than one store*   Even if you liked the first one very much, visiting several stores will give you perspective.

- *Take notes as you go*   Notes let you debrief yourself later. As you go from store to store, you'll get hazy about the people, places, and computer models you've seen. The notes will help you recall reliable information, even if you don't go back until weeks later.

- *Collect business cards*   When you meet a staff member who is polite and knowledgeable, ask for a business card. After just a short time of wandering from store to store, you'll begin to treasure the informed salesperson who really wants to help. Don't let that source slip away.

- *Try some machines using real-world tasks*   The litmus test of a machine's usefulness is to try out the kind of task you intend to do once you get it home. (For this kind of test driving, there's no substitute for a good computer store.) If you'll be doing word processing, for example, take along a book, and try typing a page or two. Do you like the way the keyboard feels? Can you read the screen clearly? Is the machine faster or slower than other machines?

- *Try out some software*   A test drive is even more important with software. Ask a salesperson to show you different packages, and try to get a sense of what may work best for you. Magazine reviews can help.

- *Try programs on several machines*   This will help isolate the hardware's influence. Programs that feel wonderful at 25 MHz may feel intolerably slow on a 10 MHz machine. The flip side is that a fast machine may be overkill for smaller programs written for slower machines. Try your chosen programs on a machine that costs less to see if performance degrades significantly.

- *Consider cost effectiveness*　If a program you like runs well on a less costly machine, consider using the money you save for other purposes—such as buying a better monitor, a larger hard disk, or more memory.

- *Ask about technical specifications*　Compare prices on different systems. Sometimes, for a little more money, you can move up to a significantly better machine. For example, a low-end 286 machine does not cost much more than a high-end XT-type 8088 machine, but for the difference you get a 16-bit bus instead of an 8-bit bus. (Chapter 15 goes into more detail about the importance of this technical difference.)

Don't Let Buzzwords and Jargon Bother You

If you ask a question, and the answer only faintly resembles English, don't assume you're out of your league, and don't be nervous about asking for further explanation. "Computerese," like any jargon, is helpful because it compresses a lot of meaning into a short word or phrase—but it's still jargon. Sometimes people who are neck-deep in buzzwords forget that not everyone speaks the language, and that normal people may need the few extra words it takes to uncompress the jargon into standard English.

If a staffer won't (or can't) respond clearly to your questions, look for someone who can communicate better. It's reasonable for you to expect an explanation of any unfamiliar terms a staff member uses when speaking to you. Don't let them flimflam you into buying something you don't want or need, and don't be afraid to insist on a salesperson with whom you can communicate effectively.

THE TRADE-OFFS OF DISCOUNT PRICES

If cost is more significant to you than service and local accessibility, or if other financial factors come into play, you can save quite a bit of money by buying through channels other than computer stores. Such sources, however, do present some trade-offs. For example, if you buy through local, state, or federal government channels, you can often get up to 50 percent off list price. The trade-off is that, typically, there will be no post-sale support unless you contract for it separately. Here are a few significant discount channels that you should consider.

Warehouse Stores

High-volume discount stores such as buying clubs and catalog warehouse operations typically offer up to a 35 percent discount. They usually charge cost plus 5 to 10 percent. Aside from warehouse operations, which are a new phenomenon, no company has ever stayed in business for long with mark-ups of less than 15 percent.

Be aware that these organizations do not (in general) provide any post-sale service. Also, computer models offered through mass market outlets may lack some features, such as extra memory, that are standard in models marketed through dealers.

Mail-Order Sales

As with retail dealers, there are good mail-order firms and there are poor ones. Computer magazines have occasionally ordered secretly from mail-order companies and then rated the various firms. Ratings are based on pre-sale disclosure, timely delivery, quality of merchandise, post-sale support, and so forth. Such research is worth a trip to the library to read. Also, most of the major magazines have an ombudsman to mediate any disputes with companies that advertise in the magazine's pages.

In case you have problems with a mail-order firm, if you paid with a credit card you can cancel payment or ask the credit card company to mediate. Be aware, though, that some mail-order houses levy a 1 1/2 to 5 percent surcharge on credit card transactions. Also, although you can often order using a toll-free 800 number, the phone numbers for technical support are likely to be long-distance calls.

If you do call for support, don't be surprised if the company uses a voice-mail system. On the positive side, most companies that use voice mail will call you back at their own expense rather than put you on hold for extended periods.

Software-Only Stores

These stores are the software equivalent of high-volume discount stores, and they do offer some heavy discounts. Stores such as Software Etc. and

Egghead Software can save you hundreds of dollars when you buy major applications programs. Because of the heavy merchandise turnover, however, don't expect post-sale support. Before buying, you may want to make sure adequate support is available from the software publisher. Also, remember the general rule quoted earlier: Other things being equal, buy the program used by a friend or colleague.

THE USED COMPUTER MARKET

The supply of used computers available to you can cut your initial outlay in half or more. There are hundreds of levels of computer systems, especially when you count the many different peripherals you can get as part of the setup. The chances are good that the system just right for you is one that someone else has outgrown.

Buying used electronic equipment, including computers, has both rewards and risks. The primary reward is cost—computers evolve so quickly that last year's state-of-the-art computer is this year's standard equipment. Like driving a new car off the lot, just opening the brand new computer's box and plugging it in can reduce a computer's resale value by 40 percent. A user who paid a premium for new, advanced equipment last year must expect to get back only a fraction of the cost when selling this year. For many sellers, that's an acceptable part of the cost of doing business.

The risk for the buyer is that used solid state electronics, although quite reliable, probably have no warranty if something goes wrong. As with used cars, lemons do exist. What you bought is what you got, and returns are often not accepted—although that has been changing of late. The good news is that the market for used equipment has matured, and a set of trading conventions useful to both sellers and buyers has evolved.

Partly because of the leadership of Dr. Alex Randall of the Boston Computer Exchange, buyers of used equipment are no longer alone in the water with sharks. The BCE has established policies that have been adopted by many user groups across the country. One of BCE's primary contributions is a policy of third-party escrow: When you get a used machine through BCE listings, BCE holds your payment to the seller until you've proven to yourself that the equipment works properly. BCE acts as a disinterested mediator to such purchases, with advantages to both buyer and seller. (The benefit to sellers is that they know your check is good before they ship the equipment.)

Getting in Touch with Sellers

If you want to consider a used system, you can telephone the BCE in Boston at (617) 542-4414. Your local user groups may also keep buy-and-sell listings. Many electronic BBSs have a trading post area, where callers can post notes about equipment they're selling. And store owners will sometimes sell returned or showroom demo equipment for discount prices. You can expect to pay a bit of a premium at a computer store, even for used equipment, to get the additional support and guarantee they will probably provide.

In general, it's safest to buy used equipment through a user group, a store, or an exchange organization. Riskier, but also possibly cheaper, is buying from individuals who advertise in newspapers or on bulletin boards. In all cases, it's wise to research the field first, know what you want to buy, and test the equipment before you buy it.

PICKING A COMPUTER STORE

There are many ways to judge a computer store, if that's how you decide to go. In addition to comparative pricing, pay close attention to sales and service policy. Here are some tips.

Sales

Look for a wide variety of products. You don't want a dealer who recommends a certain machine because it's the only one they have in stock. Some other areas to examine are

- *Demo models* Ask to try out any machine offered, so you'll know how each special feature works.

- *Hours* If the store is never open when you can visit, you'll have a hard time talking to anyone after the purchase. Can you make an appointment after hours? Sometimes it may be worth a little extra to buy from a dealer who stays open past your working hours.

- *Prices* Most dealers offer a 15 to 20 percent discount off suggested list price; the discounted amount is what magazines call the "street price," and you shouldn't pay too much more than that unless you also get significant service extras.

- *Refund policy*   Will the store cheerfully refund your money if a machine doesn't meet your needs? If so, for how long? How about letting you trade in the machine if you want to upgrade later?

- *Warranty options*   Does the store offer any extended service plans? Sometimes these can be a kind of insurance policy, and may be well worth their price. Does your credit card offer an extended warranty on electronics? Some stores will double the warranty period as part of their service if you have such a card. You might as well take advantage of it.

- *Advertisements*   A dealer will sell to anyone, but often has a "business slant" toward a special clientele, such as government agencies or large companies. If you're paying dealer prices for extra service, make sure you are in the favored customer group; it's easy enough to determine. Many stores advertise in newspapers, magazines, and the Yellow Pages. Are the ads consistent? Does the store still carry the merchandise advertised in long-term sources like the Yellow Pages?

- *Premises*   A store size of 1200 to 3500 square feet is average. Less than 1200 square feet often means limited facilities and resources. Is the store well kept, neat, and orderly? If there is a service area on the premises, try to get a look at it. Is it neat and clean? Would you trust your machine to its keeping? Look at the signs outside—are they permanent, or would a fly-by-night outfit find them easy to move?

Service

If you plan to buy from a store, make sure you clearly understand their service policies. Profit margins are not high enough to sustain indefinite post-sale support, and the store should make this clear to you. If a dealer says, "Don't worry, if anything ever breaks we'll just fix or replace it," take a hard second look. Either they're unrealistic and may go out of business, or (let's be generous to the store) maybe you misunderstood. Ask about

- *Established policy*   Do they have a written policy or service agreement you can read?

- *Repair practices*   What repairs can the store make on the premises? What work do they send out? What is their repair turn-around time?

- *Delivery and setup* Does the computer's price include delivery and setup? Will they train you or your employees?

- *Time limits* What if the machine operates well for a month or two, and then fails—what are the time limits for warranty service?

- *Housecalls* What happens if a chip vibrates loose—will they send someone to your house or business to service it, if that is what you want and are willing to pay for?

- *Loaner machines* Will the store loan you a machine if you must bring yours in for service?

Training Policy

Training is part of the service at some dealers, and that can be an important benefit if you're a beginner. If you're going to spend a thousand dollars or more in their store, you have a right to some training. They should spare you at least a couple of hours to teach you how to use your machine. Find out how much training is included. Asking if it is "included in the purchase contract" is more polite than asking if they'll put it in writing.

Now we come to the final area of concern to many new users: becoming reasonably competent in the shortest time possible. The next few paragraphs discuss getting "up to speed" on your new computer.

LEARNING TO USE YOUR COMPUTER

Children aren't afraid of computers. Most adults don't need to be, either, but some are unwilling to go through the reasonable steps necessary to learn any new technology. They may take a single three-hour class and expect everything to operate magically and automatically from there. But that's not how it works when you learn any new activity.

When it comes down to it, most people who hesitate to touch a keyboard only suffer from lack of information, not from unreasonable fear. And lack of information is an easy problem to solve; here are some well-traveled avenues to computer fluency.

Store Training

When you buy a computer at a retail store, expect more than just a smile and a handshake. Insist on some training, at least to the point where you know how to turn on the machine and load a program. Look for stores where training is free or provided at low cost. Highly advertised stores that rely on training as a primary source of revenue may spend more time selling you classes than they do actually training you or tailoring a system to meet your needs. Some training centers charge as much as $75 an hour, and a few dollars off the retail price for your system probably will not offset that extra training cost.

Formal, in-store training generally costs $25 to $100 for sessions that last from 45 minutes to 3 hours. Since you bought your system at the store, the employees there know the equipment and are probably well qualified to teach you how to use it.

Other Training Sources

One of the first places to look for help is always the manual that came with the program or hardware component. At minimum, keep a DOS manual and reference on your desk. Treat it as you would a dictionary—when you need it, you need it, so keep it handy. Other possibilities include

- *Community colleges and university classes* Many local institutions of higher learning offer classes for $5, $10, or $15 an hour. The total for a semester course averages $20 to $75, not including books. College-level classes may also be good for 3 to 12 academic credits. Instruction is quite detailed, and may offer more training than many people need or want.

- *Adult education classes* These are often subsidized by state and federal funding, but there may be a small charge to you. The courses typically last three to seven weeks, with a single three-hour session each week; they often are aimed at people reentering the job market who are seeking new skills. Training is usually on a fairly basic level, often oriented toward learning a specific program, such as Word-Perfect or Microsoft Works.

- *Company training* Many companies conduct in-house training programs, or contract with outside organizations for on-site classes or individual tutoring. Such training answers specific company needs, often covering specific word processors, spreadsheets, project management software, and the like.

- *Friends and neighbors* You can get terrific help from friends and neighbors who already have a computer. Most of the questions beginners ask are very specific. If you're a beginner and know someone who has been using a computer for a while, try giving him or her a call. It's likely you'll get a quick, easy solution for a seemingly baffling problem.

- *Teaching yourself by computer* There are many computer training products, including plastic keyboard templates that fit over the function keys to tell you what the keys do in a particular program. There are interactive tutorials that walk you through different operations of DOS, word processors, and other major programs. There are very effective typing tutors that keep track of your progress and automatically increase difficulty as you proceed. There are pop-up general help screens, and even help systems that change the entire user interface for specific programs. If you're having trouble with a specific program, or with DOS itself, consider purchasing one of these programs. They have helped many a user through the early hurdles and have become part of their permanent bag of computing tricks.

SUMMARY

When all is said and done, if you set aside a reasonable budget for your system and don't just go for the lowest price, you'll come out OK. Post-sale service is worth a little extra; so is a reasonable training period, and having someone available when you need to call for help. The best approach to learning about your computer may be to tap several of the aforementioned training sources.

The time you spend researching your purchase before you buy is part of your investment. It will pay off handsomely in the long run.

80286 (286) machines, 26-27, 44
80386 (386) machines, 27-28, 44
80486 (486) machines, 28-29
8088 machines, 25-26, 35-36, 44

A

Accounting packages, 223-225
Actuator (hard disks), 513-515
Add-on boards, 101-102, 500-501
Aliases (command macros), 552
ALT-key characters, 640
ANSI codes, 338-341
ANSI macros, 369-373
ANSI screen control functions,
   339-340
ANSI.SYS device driver, 317
Antirogue programs, 263-264
Antivirus programs, 263-264
APPEND command, 376-377
Apple DOS, 159
Apple Macintosh design, 488
Applications programs, 4, 171-233
      and the PC revolution, 173-174
      traditional Big Four, 180, 183
      See also Programs; Software
Architecture, PC systems, 486-488
Archiving utilities, 259-261
ASCII codes table, 691-699
ASCII format, 193
Assembling the PC system, 75-84
Assembly language, 19
ASSIGN command, 367-368, 378, 574
Asterisk character (in DOS com-
   mands), 282-283
AT systems, 26-27, 36, 53

Atasi disk drive geometries, 642
ATTRIB command, 378-379
AutoCAD, 221
AUTOEXEC.BAT, 96, 139-142,
   326-327
      for RAM disk bootup, 555-556

B

Background processors, 563-565
Background programs, 563
Backing up files, 328-332
BACKIT.BAT batch file example,
   363-365
BACKSPACE key, 633-634
BACKUP command, 328-329, 379-380
Backup device, choosing, 560-561
Backup files, 278
Backup programs, 254-255
Basic DOS commands, 124-137
BASIC language, 20, 95, 439
      constants and variables, 440-443
      expressions and operators,
         443-444
      functions, 440
      introduction to, 437-451
      keywords, 439
      lines and programs, 446-447
      loading, 444-446
      modes of operation, 445-446
      screen editor, 448-450
      statements, 440
      versions of, 438
BASIC language command reference,
   453-483
      See also BASIC language

Basic PC, 8-17
Batch file commands/utilities, 246, 434-435
Batch files, 139-140, 142, 277, 311, 343-367
    aborting, 345
    breaking out of, 141-142
    CLS command in, 347
    as command line tools, 553-554, 557
    creating and using, 344-345
    ECHO command in, 345-346
    FOR command in, 353-356
    fundamental operations, 345-347
    GOTO command in, 360-362
    IF command in, 356-360
    PAUSE command in, 347
    REM command in, 346-347
    SHIFT command in, 362-363
    SYS-A.BAT example, 347-349
    three examples of, 363-367
    using decision commands, 353-363
    using dummy parameters, 349-352
Battery (computer), replacing, 589
Battery packs, 73-74
Big Four applications, 180, 183
Bimetallic expansion, 579-580
Binary system, 5-6
BIOS, 156
BIOS calls, 549
BIOS chips, replacing, 567
Bits (binary digits), 6-7
Boot disk, 136, 154
Booting up, 95
Bootstrap loader, 96
Bootstrap procedure, 96
Bootstrapping, 95
Bootup errors, 115-116
Brand Technology disk drive geometries, 642
BREAK command, 380-381
Breaking out of batch files, 141-142
Breaking out of a program, 138-139
Bricklin, Dan, 174
Bridge programs, 209-210
Brightness control (monitor), 86
Budget programs, 231-232

Buffers (DOS), 538-539
    read-ahead, 540
Bugs, 89
Bulletin board systems (BBSs), 182
Bundled software, 178
Bus, 17, 27, 494, 505-507
Bus mastery, 494
Bus Wars, 507
Button, Jim, 181
Buying a PC system, 701-711
Bytes, 6-7

C

Cable connections, 77-84
Cables, 491
Caches, disk. *See* Disk caches
Cascade Virus, 263-264
Cataloging utilities, 261
Catalogs, 179
CD-ROM, 16
Cell (spreadsheet), 196
Centronics port, 17
CGA monitors, 12-13, 49
CHCP command, 381-382
CHDIR or CD command, 291, 297, 299, 382-383
Child directory, 290
CHKDSK command, 136-137, 383-384, 592
Choosing a computer, 21-56
Cleaning the computer, 150-151
Clock (system), 116-118
    setting, 140-141
Clock speed (microprocessor), 495-496
Clone industry, 486-487
Clones, 10
CLS command, 347, 384
Clusters (hard disks), 260, 514
CMI disk drive geometries, 644
CMOS, 95
    chips, 500, 530-531
    error report, 586
    resetting, 586-589
    settings, 641-653
    setup screen, 100, 587
Cold boot, 120
COM ports, 17

COMMAND.COM, 96, 154, 271
    placing, on a RAM disk, 545
COMMAND command, 384-385
Command-driven interfaces, 164
Command files, 277
Command line interface. *See* DOS
    command line
Command macros, 552
Command reference (DOS),
    375-435
Commands (DOS). *See* DOS com-
    mands
Communications, 18
    background, 564
COMP command, 133-134, 385-386
Comparing files, 133-134
Compatibility issues, 29, 577-578
Compilers, language, 437-438
Compiling a program, 20
Compressed archives, 259
CompuServe, 182
Computer aided drafting and design
    (CADD), 220-221
Computer furniture, 65-67
Computer Shopper, 179, 181
Computer unit. *See* System unit
Computers. *See* PC systems
CONFIG.SYS, 96, 312-326, 532, 538-
    541, 594
    BREAK command, 314
    buffers and files, 315
    BUFFERS command, 315-316
    command summary, 315
    commands, 435
    COUNTRY command, 316
    device driver files, 316-323
    DRIVPARM command, 323
    FCBS command, 323
    FILES command, 316
    INSTALL command, 323
    LASTDRIVE command, 323-324
    REM command, 324
    SHELL command, 324-325
    STACKS command, 326
Connecting cables, 77-84
Conner Peripherals disk drive
    geometries, 643
Contrast control (monitor), 87

Control Data disk drive geometries,
    643-644
Controller cards (hard disks), 515-519
    installing, 526
    smart controllers, 546
    upgrading, 558-559
COPY command, 131-133, 386-387,
    574-575
Copy protection, 144-145
Copying files and disks, 132-133
Core International disk drive
    geometries, 642-643
CP/M, 159
CPUs, 4-5, 9-10, 25-29, 44, 494-496
    upgrading, 569-570
    wait states, 566-567
Cross-fertile applications, 205
Cross-linked files, 250
CTTY command, 387-388
Current date, 116-117
Current directory, 288
Current path, 290
Current time, 117-118
Cursor, 114
Cursor-control keys, 639-640
Customizing your system, 332-343
Cylinders (hard disks), 511-512

D

Daisy wheel printers, 54
Dak catalog, 179
Data bus, 17, 27
    architecture, 505-507
Data encoding (hard disks), 510
Data encryption, 262
Data processing, 2
Data security utilities, 262-264
Data-Tech Memories disk drive
    geometries, 644
Data transfer rate (DTR), 517, 519
Databases, 200-204
    reports, 203
    searches and sorts, 202-203
    summary of popular programs,
    204
DATE command, 388-389
Date and time display, 116-118

Daughter boards, 8, 500-501
DB-9 connector, 81
DBMS (database management system), 201
DEBUG program, 389, 527-528, 575
Default directory, 288, 303-304
Default drive, 130, 304
Defragmenting a disk, 255-258
DEL command, 134-135, 389-390, 576
Deleting files, 134-135
Delimiters in DOS commands, 129
DeskMate, 169
Desktop accessories, 246-247
Desktop computers, 39
Desktop publishing (DTP), 214-217
DesqView, 170
Device drivers, 316-323, 532
Diagnostics, system, 585-586
Digital audio tape (DAT), 16
DIN connector, 77-78
DIP switches, 73, 503-504
DIR command, 125, 127-130, 308-309, 390-391
Directories, 273, 288
    capacity limits (floppy disks), 274, 562
    dot and double-dot, 305-306
    setting a default, 303-304
    and subdirectories, 290
Directory listings. *See* DIR command
Directory maintenance utilities, 250-254, 258-259
Directory names, 294
Directory squeezing, 258-259
Directory trees, 241, 288-290
    creating and using, 297-308
    designing, 291-296
DIREDIT utility, 251, 254
DIRSORT utility, 251, 253
Disk bays, 507-508
Disk caches, 248-249, 322-323, 499, 538-540, 546, 595
Disk defragmenters and optimizers, 255-258
Disk drives, 10, 46-47, 107-111, 114, 509-535
    adding, 570

Disk drives, *continued*
    changing the default, 130, 304
    compatibility, 275
    half-height, 508
    removing the shipping inserts, 90
Disk maintenance utilities, 250-251, 254-258
Disk management commands (DOS), 290-291
Disk medic utilities, 249-250, 592
Disk organizers, 561-562
Disk storage, 274, 286-287
DISKCOMP utility, 144, 391-392
DISKCOPY utility, 131-132, 143-144, 392
DISKEDIT utility, 258
Disks. *See* Floppy disks; Hard disks
DISPLAY.SYS device driver, 317
Documentation, PC system, 84
DOS
    evolution of, 160
    hardware control, 267
    types of, 159-161
    versions of, 160
    working with, 265-283
    See also DOS command line; DOS commands; Filenames (DOS); Files (DOS)
DOS buffers, 538-540
DOS command line, 121-123, 267-268
    commands, 376-434
    condensing keystrokes, 302-305
    correcting mistakes, 137-139
    editing, 139
    editors, 245-246, 552-553
    toolbox, 552-558
    using the FOR command on, 355-356
    See also DOS; DOS commands
DOS commands, 123-137, 268, 270-272
    basic, 124-137
    breaking out of, 138-139
    changing drives, 271
    command reference, 126-127, 375-435
    delimiters in, 129
    for disk management, 290-291

DOS commands, *continued*
    internal and external, 271-272
    parameters to, 269, 280
    pausing, 138
    and punctuation, 281
    specifying the path, 269-270
    structure of, 269-270
    to use with care, 574-577
    See also DOS; DOS command line
DOS environment. *See* Environments
DOS error messages, 655-690
DOS prompt. *See* System prompt
DOS shells, 237-244
DOS utilities, 557-558
DOSSHELL command, 392-393
Dot and double-dot directories, 305-306
Dot matrix printers, 54
DRIVER.SYS device driver, 317-321
Drives. *See* Disk drives
Dummy (replaceable) parameters, 349-352
Dynamic RAM (DRAM), 498-499

E

ECHO command (in batch files), 345-346
Editing on the command line, 139
EDLIN command, 393-394
Educational programs, 230-231
EGA monitors, 13, 49
Electronic spreadsheets, 196
Encryption, data, 262
Engineering programs, 221-223
Enhanced Industry Standard Architecture (EISA), 28, 506-507
ENTER key, 635-636
Environments, 153-154, 162-170
    changing the size of, 325
    customizing, 332-334
    explained, 332
    and integrated programs, 211
    managing, 550-552
    variables in, 324, 332-334
ERASE command, 394, 576
Ergo 386-based Brick computer, 23-25
Error messages, 98-99, 655-690

Errorlevel (exit code), 246
ESC key, 636
ESDI controller card, 516-517
Excel spreadsheet, 197
EXE2BIN command, 394
Executable file, 278
EXIT command, 395
Expanded memory, 198, 547-548
Expansion slots (system unit), 500
Extended characters, 338
Extended memory, 26, 547-549
    problems with, 594-595
External DOS commands, 123-124, 156, 271-272, 552
External modems, 15, 81

F

Family tree directory model, 289
FASTOPEN command, 395-396
Fault isolation, 582
FC command, 396-397
FCC ratings and approvals, 38
FDISK utility, 397-398, 532-533
Fields (database), 201
File allocation table (FAT), 515
File compression, 260-261
File-finders (utilities), 239
File handles, 540, 594
File management utilities, 241-244
File recovery utilities, 135, 249-250
File tagging (utilities), 240
File transfer (bridge) programs, 209-210
File transfer protocols (telecommunications), 205-206
Filenames (DOS), 273-280
    reserved characters, 279-280
    reserved extensions, 277-279
    reserved names, 277
    rules for naming, 125, 127
Files (DOS), 11, 272-283
    backing up, 328-332
    comparing, 133-134
    copying, 132-133
    deleting, 134-135
    renaming, 134
Filters, 334, 336-338

Finance programs, 231-232
FIND command, 398-399
Finder program, 169
First Publisher, 188
Fixed disks. *See* Hard disks
Flat file databases, 203
Floating heads (hard disks), 513-514
Floor stands, 66-67
Floppy disks, 10-11
    backing up, 328
    booting from, 119
    capacities, 46, 562
    copying, 132-133
    formatting, 135-136
    handling, 111-112
    inserting, 109
    organizing, 148-149
    organizing files on, 287
    write-protection, 110-111, 113-114
    See also Disk drives
Floppy shuffle, 285
Fluegelman, Andrew, 181
Footprints, 23
FOR command (in batch files), 353-356
Forecasting programs, 222-223
FORMAT.BAT batch file example,
   365-366
FORMAT command, 135-136, 399-400,
   576
Formatting changes (hard disk), 560
Formatting a disk, 511
    floppy disk, 135-136
    hard disk, 527-534
Fragmentation, disk, 257
Frankston, Bob, 174
Freeware, 181
Fujitsu disk drive geometries, 644-645
Function keys, 639

G

Games, 228-230
GEM/Desktop, 168
Gender mender, 83
Gigabytes, 7
Glossary of terms in this book, 613-629
GOTO command (in batch files),
   360-362

GRAFTABL command, 400-401
Grammar checkers, 184-185
Graphical user interfaces (GUIs),
   165-169
GRAPHICS command, 401
Graphics programs, 225-228
Ground wire, 62-63
Grounding, 60-63

H

Half-height drives, 508
Hard copies, 13
Hard disks, 10, 45-47, 285-309
    actuator and read/write heads,
      513-515
    choosing, 518-520
    electronics, 510
    formatting, 527-534
    head assembly, 514
    installing, 520-526
    maintenance, 534-535
    organization, 286-291
    partitioning, 530-533
    platters, 511
    speeding up, 558-565
    storage capacity, 519-520
    tracks, cylinders, and sectors,
      511-513
    troubleshooting, 608-611
    See also Disk drives
Hardware. *See* PC systems hardware
Help programs, 247
Hewlett-Packard NewWave, 169
High-level format (hard disks),
   533-534
Hitachi disk drive geometries, 645
Home applications, 231-232
Horizontal/vertical holds (monitor), 87
Hot key, 246
Household inventory programs, 231
Housekeeping, 235-264
HyperPad, 170
Hyphenation, automatic, 189

I

IBM-compatible computers, 21-29

IBM PC ATs, 26-27, 36, 53
IBM PC XTs, 25-26, 35-36
IBM PCs, 25, 35
IBM PS/2 systems, 28
Icon-driven interfaces, 165
IDE controller card, 517
IF command (in batch files), 356-360
Imprimis disk drive geometries, 645-646
Incremental compilers, 438
Industry Standard Architecture (ISA), 28, 505-506
Information managers, 217-218
Information services, 182
Ink jet printers, 54-55
Input, redirecting, 336
Input devices, 14
Installed user base, 183
Installing
    a hard disk, 520-526
    a PC system, 75-103
    programs, 142-147
Instructional programs, 230-231
Integrated circuits, 2-3
Integrated programs, 210-213
Intel chips
    80286, 26-27
    80386, 27-28
    80486, 28-29
    8088, 25-26
Interfaces, 162-170
Interleave (hard disk), changing, 560
Internal DOS commands, 123-124, 271-272
Internal expansion slots, 17
Internal modem, 15
Interpreter programs, 437-438
Interrupts, conflicting, 593

J

Jacks, 491
JOIN command, 367-369, 401-402, 574
Jumpers, 503, 505

K

Kapor, Mitch, 174, 199

Key-code values for special keys, 370
KEYB command, 402-404
Keyboard locks, 86, 92
Keyboards, 9
    connecting, 77-79
    controls for, 87
    function keys, 639
    introduction to, 114
    layout styles, 632
    special keys, 635-637
    toggle keys, 638-639
    troubleshooting, 599-600
    types of, 50-53
    typewriter keys, 633-634
    using, 631-640
KEYB*xx* command, 404
Keyed DIN connector, 77
Keywords (programming language), 439
Kilobits, 7
Kilobytes, 7
Kyocera disk drive geometries, 646

L

LABEL command, 405
Lapine disk drive geometries, 647
Laptop computers, 41-42
Large directories, listing, 127-129
Laser printers, 55
Learning to use your computer, 709-711
Library utilities, 261
Life cycle of PCs, 33-36
Light pen, connecting, 82-83
Linking applications, 211
Listing large directories, 127-129
Lost clusters, and file recovery, 250
Lotus 1-2-3, history of, 174
Lotus empire, history of, 199
Low-level format (hard disk), 527-529
Low profile drives, 508
Luggable computers, 40-41

M

Machine code, 19
Macintosh design, 488

Macros (DOS), 369-373
Magnetic medium (hard disks), 513
Mainframes, 3
Maintaining a hard disk, 534
Manuals (documentation) for your PC
    system, 84
Math coprocessor, 496-497, 569
Mathematical toolbox programs, 223
Maxtor disk drive geometries, 647
MCA (micro channel architecture),
    506-507
Megabytes, 7
MEM command, 405-406
Memory, 10
    configurations, 45
    limits, 594-595
    managing, 546-550
    size, 45
    versus storage, 11-12
Memory caches, 546, 549
Memory chips
    problems with, 606-608
    upgrading, 568
Memory managers, 247-248
Menu-driven interfaces, 165
Menu programs, 244-245
Merge 386 environment, 170
Metacharacters, 341
Micro channel architecture (MCA),
    28
Micropolis disk drive geometries,
    647-648
Microprocessors, 4, 9-10, 25-29, 44,
    494-496
    upgrading, 569-570
    wait states, 566-567
Microscience disk drive geometries,
    648
Microsoft Windows, 168
Microsoft Works, 188, 190, 198,
    211-212
Minicomputers, 3
Miniscribe disk drive geometries,
    648-649
Mitsubishi disk drive geometries,
    649
MKDIR or MD command, 291,
    298-300, 406-407
MODE command, 407-414

Modems, 15, 18, 55
    adding, 570-571
    connecting external, 81
    unpacking, 71
Monitors
    connecting, 79-80
    controls, 86-87
    introduction to, 114
    power plugs, 81
    troubleshooting, 599
    types of, 47-50
    unpacking, 70
Monochrome (MDA) monitors, 12,
    48-49
MORE command, 414
Motherboard, 8, 493-494
    location of memory chips on, 607
    memory chips on, 499
    switches and connectors, 503-505
    upgrading, 565-566
Motif graphics interface, 169
Mouse
    connecting, 82-83
    using, 571
MS-DOS, 159-161. *See also* DOS
MS-DOS standard computers, 21
    history of, 25-29
Multifunction controller cards, 526
Multimeter, 60
Multitasking, 28, 158

N

Naming directories, 294
Naming files. *See* Filenames (DOS)
Nanoseconds (ns), 498
NEC disk drive geometries, 649-650
Nesting IF tests in batch files, 360
Newbury disk drive geometries, 650
NLSFUNC command, 415
Nondocument mode, 193
Notebook computers, 42-44
Number keys (keyboard), 633
Numeric (math) coprocessor, 496-497
Numeric keypad (number pad), 639-640

O

Ohmmeter, 60-61